FREDERICK HOUK BORSCH

THE SON OF MAN
IN MYTH AND HISTORY

new
test
ament
lib
rary

FREDERICK HOUK BORSCH

Seabury-Western Theological Seminary, Evanston, Illinois

THE SON OF MAN IN MYTH AND HISTORY

SCM PRESS LTD

BLOOMSBURY STREET LONDON

To Reuben and Pearl

FIRST PUBLISHED 1967
© SCM PRESS LTD 1967
PRINTED IN GREAT BRITAIN BY
W. & J. MACKAY & CO LTD, CHATHAM

CONTENTS

PREFACE

IT REMAINS AS my duty and pleasure to thank the many who have so kindly assisted me in the formation of this study. One must begin with his teachers and colleagues, as well as the library and other staff members, at Princeton University, the University of Oxford and New College, the General Theological Seminary and Seabury-Western Theological Seminary. Thanks are due to the Faculty and Senate of the University of Birmingham (where an earlier form of this work was accepted as a doctoral dissertation in 1966) for the several courtesies extended. In particular I want to indicate my gratitude to the Department of Theology in the University of Birmingham and to the faculty of the Queen's Theological College, as well as to other staff members of these institutions. I wish to express my thanks to the many students whose interest and insights have continually helped me along the way.

Among all of these the following must be singled out: John Eaton, Sebastian Brock, John Hinnells and Lester Singleton; the Rev. John Alford; Canon Arthur Gribble; Dr Raymond Hammer and Dr Jack Van Hooser; the Rev. Professors Reginald Fuller, J. Gordon Davies and Christopher Evans (to whom I now present an *expanded* version of a tutorial essay first submitted in October of 1957). My thanks are also due to my diligent and careful typists, Mrs Mary Matthewman and Mrs Julie Stahl, and to the staff of SCM Press, especially Miss Jean Cunningham. The Rev. John Bowden has given of his friendship and numerous talents ever since the inception of these ideas.

Nor can I let pass an added expression of admiration for the many scholars to whose work the references in this study bear but a small testimony. Whether in agreement with them or not, I here gladly and gratefully salute their accomplishments.

The book itself is witness to the patience, love and understanding of Barbara.

Seabury-Western Theological Seminary
6 June 1967

ABBREVIATIONS

AJSLL	*American Journal of Semitic Languages and Literatures*, Chicago
ANCL	Ante-Nicene Christian Library, Edinburgh
ANET	J. B. Pritchard, *Ancient Near Eastern Texts relating to the Old Testament*[2], Princeton and London, 1955
AO	Acta Orientalia, (Leiden) Havniae-Copenhagen
AThANT	Abhandlungen zur Theologie des Alten und Neuen Testaments, Zürich
BASOR	*Bulletin of the American Schools of Oriental Research*, New Haven
BJRL	*Bulletin of the John Rylands Library*, Manchester
BNTC	Black's New Testament Commentaries, London (Harper's New Testament Commentaries in the USA)
BO	Bibliotheca Orientalis, Leiden
BWANT	Beiträge zur Wissenschaft vom Alten und Neuen Testament, Stuttgart
BZNW	Beihefte zur *Zeitschrift für die neutestamentliche Wissenschaft und die Kunde der älteren Kirche*, Berlin
CBQ	*The Catholic Biblical Quarterly*, Washington
CH	*Corpus Hermeticum*
Charles II	R. H. Charles, *The Apocrypha and Pseudepigrapha of the Old Testament*, Vol. II, Oxford, 1913
CJT	*Canadian Journal of Theology*, Toronto
ET	English translation
EvTh	*Evangelische Theologie*, München
ExpT	*Expository Times*, Edinburgh
FRLANT	Forschungen zur Religion und Literatur des Alten und Neuen Testaments, Göttingen
GCS	Die griechischen christlichen Schriftsteller der ersten (drei) Jahrhunderte, (Leipzig) Berlin
HTC	S. Mowinckel, *He That Cometh*, Oxford, 1956
HTR	*Harvard Theological Review*, Cambridge, Mass.
JBL	*Journal of Biblical Literature*, Philadelphia
JEH	*Journal of Ecclesiastical History*, London

JHS	*Journal of Hellenic Studies*, London
JNES	*Journal of Near Eastern Studies*, Chicago
JR	*Journal of Religion*, Chicago
JTS	*Journal of Theological Studies*, Oxford
K-EKNT	Kritische-exegetischer Kommentar über das Neue Testament, Göttingen
LCL	Loeb Classical Library, (New York) Cambridge, Mass., and London
NEB	The New English Bible
nf	Neue Folge
ns	New series
NT	*Novum Testamentum*, Leiden
NTA	E. Hennecke, *New Testament Apocrypha* (ed. W. Schneemelcher; English editor, R. McL. Wilson), London, 1963–5
NTS	*New Testament Studies*, Cambridge
parr.	Parallels
PEQ	*Palestine Exploration Quarterly*, London
Qumran	Abbreviations for these texts as in D. Barthélemy and J. T. Milik, *Discoveries in the Judaean Desert*, I, Oxford, 1955, pp. 46ff.
RB	*Revue Biblique*, Paris
RGG	*Die Religion in Geschichte und Gegenwart*, Tübingen
RHPR	*Revue d'Histoire et de Philosophie Religieuse*, Paris
RSV	The Holy Bible: Revised Standard Version
S-B	H. L. Strack and P. Billerbeck, *Kommentar zum Neuen Testament aus Talmud und Midrasch*, München, 1922–8
SBT	Studies in Biblical Theology, London
SEA	*Svensk Exegetisk Årsbok*, Lund
SHAW	Sitzungsberichte der Heidelberger Akademie der Wissenschaften, Heidelberg
SJT	*Scottish Journal of Theology*, Edinburgh
SPAW	Sitzungsberichte der Preussischen Akademie der Wissenschaften zu Berlin, Berlin
ST	*Studia Theologica*, Lund
TLZ	*Theologische Literaturzeitung*, Leipzig and Berlin
TR	*Theologische Rundschau*, Tübingen
TU	Texte und Untersuchungen zur Geschichte der altchristlichen Literatur, Berlin

TWNT	*Theologisches Wörterbuch zum Neuen Testament* (eds. G. Kittel and G. Friedrich), Stuttgart, 1933ff. Now being translated by G. W. Bromiley as *Theological Dictionary of the New Testament*, Grand Rapids and London, 1964ff.
TZ	*Theologische Zeitschrift*, Basel
UUA	Uppsala Universitets Årsskrift, Uppsala
VT	*Vetus Testamentum*, Leiden
ZNW	*Zeitschrift für die neutestamentliche Wissenschaft und die Kunde der älteren Kirche*, Berlin
ZRGG	*Zeitschrift fur Religions- und Geistesgeschichte*, Köln
ZTK	*Zeitschrift für Theologie und Kirche*, Tübingen

OTHER JOURNALS

Le Muséon	Revue d'Études Orientales, Louvain
Mnemosyne	(Bibliotheca Classica Batava) Lugduni Batavorum (Leiden)
Numen	International Review for the Study of Religions, Leiden

Bible quotations are from the Revised Standard Version except where it has been felt necessary to indicate a special nuance or emphasis.

Who is this Son of Man?

John 12.34

I

THE PROBLEM

Who do men say that the Son of Man is? (Matt. 16.13)

'EMBARRASSING' MIGHT BE the kindest word for it. The insistent problem of the meaning of the designation Son of Man has plagued and vexed New Testament scholars ever since higher criticism began. One critic, who has devoted much time to the issue, is stating nothing but the obvious when he writes, 'The Son of Man problem in the Gospels is one of the most perplexing and challenging in the whole field of Biblical theology.'[1]

Not, of course, that there has been any lack of interest or energy. Indeed, there has been so much written on the subject, so many diverse and conflicting points of view presented, that one senses a certain weariness with the whole matter. 'The Son of Man Again' is the title of a recent contribution,[2] and an echo of that 'again' has probably resounded in a number of theological faculties. The pained ennui resulting from repeated attempts to force this seeming brick wall has led several scholars to a counsel of despair and many others to circumvent or avoid the problem in a manner which is hardly faithful to the evidence of the Gospels.

Yet the article quoted first above continues, 'It might well seem a fruitless task to continue trying to solve the insoluble, but . . .'[3] The heart of the conundrum is summed up in that word 'but', for it is impossible to maintain that this is a peripheral matter. The Son of

---

[1] M. Black, 'The Son of Man Problem in Recent Research and Debate', *BJRL* 45, 1963, p. 305. J. Knox, *The Death of Christ*, New York, 1958, p. 87, describes it as a jigsaw puzzle in which some of the pieces are missing and others have been altered in the course of transmission. J. M. Robinson, in *A New Quest of the Historical Jesus* (SBT 25), 1959, pp. 100ff., uses the Son of Man problem to illustrate what he calls 'the methodological impasse'.

[2] E. Schweizer, *NTS* 9, 1962/3, pp. 256ff.

[3] *Op. cit.*, p. 305.

Man problem cannot justifiably be set aside, because the Son of Man is at the very centre of the Gospel record and, as presented to us, is undeniably more essential to Jesus' teaching about his own mission than any other single factor.

Past attempts to minimize this issue or to treat it as just another difficult problem need to be severely questioned. It ought even to be recognized that the many books which have dealt with the Son of Man as but one of the several 'names of Jesus' are not presenting an adequate picture. The Gospels do not offer it to us as one title among many; they clearly state that this is the designation of which Jesus spoke, and spoke consistently, as most revelatory of his work.

These are strong words, but it is far from difficult to substantiate them. Even a student beginning his study of the Gospels quickly becomes aware of the centrality of the Son of Man designation. In addition to the fact that it occurs some sixty-eight times in the synoptic Gospels and is there practically the only title which Jesus himself mentions, at several of the most crucial points in his ministry Jesus is said to have taught explicitly that his mission could not be comprehended apart from some understanding of the Son of Man. The whole transfiguration scene is made to point to the death and *resurrection* of the Son of Man.[1] At the so-called confession at Caesarea Philippi[2] and during his trial before the Sanhedrin[3] Jesus redirects seeming efforts to understand his work in terms of messiahship by again pointing to the Son of Man. Both when he predicts his betrayal[4] and when this occurs,[5] Jesus speaks with reference to the Son of Man.

The use of the term is also basic to the Fourth Gospel, where it occurs twelve times. Almost every essential theme of John's Gospel is associated with the enigmatic designation. Since, however, the title is employed somewhat differently in this Gospel and there provides several distinct problems of its own, it is generally found helpful to deal with it apart from the synoptic usage.[6] At the same time it must constantly be remembered that all four Gospels are concerned with

[1] Mark 9.9f.; Matt. 17.9. Luke slightly delays the message until 9.44.
[2] This comes out most clearly in Mark 8.30f. See Luke 9.21f.; Matt. 16.21.
[3] Mark 14.62 and parr. On the importance of this feature cf. W. Manson, *Jesus, the Messiah*, London, 1943, p. 114.
[4] Mark 14.21 and parr.
[5] Mark 14.41 = Matt. 26.45; see Luke 22.48; John 12.23; 13.31.
[6] See esp. ch. VII below. One aim of this study is to show how the Synoptic and Johannine Son of Man logia may be related to similar background materials. In this writer's view, this has been a failure, sometimes conspicuous, of earlier research.

the fundamental traditions, and no effort to understand the Son of Man can afford to categorize and isolate too strictly.

The substantial features of the Son of Man problem in the first three Gospels along with the several ramifications and contingent difficulties are by now quite familiar. None the less it is important in a study of this kind that we begin by reviewing them in order that they may be sharply in mind.

As we have said, the designation occurs some sixty-eight times in the synoptic Gospels.[1] Thirteen of these occurrences are in Mark, twenty-nine in Matthew and twenty-six in Luke. Within Matthew and Luke there seem to be at least eight instances of the Son of Man from the so-called Q source.[2] Omitting all the obvious or seeming parallels (and here employing the customary theory that Matthew and Luke used Mark),[3] there remain thirty-nine instances of the term, as follows: thirteen in Mark, eight in Q, ten in Matthew and eight in Luke. Especially when the relative sparsity and status of other titles are used as comparison,[4] this must be recognized as a considerable and consistent frequency.

[1] These figures can only be approximate, for reasons which will become obvious as we proceed.

[2] This writer has grave doubts about the viability of Q as a written source; on which see below at various points and cf. S. Petrie, ' "Q" Is Only What You Make It', *NT* 3, 1959, pp. 28ff., and T. R. Rosché, 'The Words of Jesus and the Future of the "Q" Hypothesis', *JBL* 79, 1960, pp. 210ff. Since, however, it is a familiar and useful means of classification, we shall employ the designation while questioning arguments which seem dependent upon the Q theory.

[3] We also have many reservations about this hypothesis and welcome, without accepting his conclusion, the overdue challenges of W. R. Farmer, *The Synoptic Problem*, New York, 1964. It is our view that, despite all their attractions, the simpler solutions to the source problem are manifestly insufficient. The complexity of the evidence suggests a need to reconsider theories which respect the capacities of oral tradition or, at the least, possibilities concerning different recensions of Mark or a source common to the three Gospels. (See, e.g., R. L. Lindsey, 'A Modified Two-Document Theory of the Synoptic Dependence and Interdependence', *NT* 6, 1963, pp. 239ff.) None the less, in order to communicate more readily with the majority of scholars, and so as not to make our study more controversial than necessary, we shall generally assume that Mark was used by Matthew and Luke. From time to time, however, we shall note other possibilities while striving not to make our theories dependent on them.

[4] On the manifest ascendancy of the Son of Man designation over all others and esp. that of the Christ, see E. Stauffer, 'Messias oder Menschensohn', *NT* 1, 1956, pp. 81ff. On the importance of this, see A. Richardson, *An Introduction to the Theology of the New Testament*, London, 1958, pp. 125ff. A. J. B. Higgins, 'The Old Testament and Some Aspects of New Testament Christology' in *Promise and Fulfilment* (ed. F. F. Bruce), Edinburgh, 1963, pp. 128ff., remarks on the manner in which the Son of Man keeps *intruding* upon other Christological terms.

At first glance the testimony of form-criticism seems less convincing. Although the designation does find occasional use in several of the recognized forms[1] and there are strong hints that it may once have held a greater place in the parabolic materials,[2] it is mainly instanced in a variety of different *sayings* which are often but loosely attached to their contexts. On the other hand, it is just this category which many would regard as the least susceptible to alteration and the most likely to retain authentic data.[3] The very fact that the title is rarely situated in materials which were apparently used more flexibly by the Church may be instructive.[4]

An important and often noted characteristic of the Son of Man sayings is the rule that only Jesus speaks about the Son of Man. With the minor deviation of Luke 24.7, where, in fact, the angel is quoting Jesus' own words, the tradition presents this feature to us with amazing fixity. (The same is true of the Fourth Gospel, except where the crowd is once made to take the term from Jesus' lips and ask him about it, in John 12.34.) This and the generally private nature of the teaching seem confirmed by Jesus' reported lack of exposition on the

---

[1] In a miracle story, Mark 2.10 and parr. In a kind of paradigm story, Mark 2.28 and parr. In the interpretation of a parable, Matt. 13.37, 41.

[2] E.g. Luke 12.40 = Matt. 24.44.

[3] See T. W. Manson, *The Sayings of Jesus*, London, 1949, pp. 11ff.; E. Stauffer, *Theology of the New Testament*, ET, London, 1955, pp. 25ff.; M. Dibelius, *From Tradition to Gospel*, ET, London, 1934. Compare even R. Bultmann's treatment of 'The Tradition of the Sayings of Jesus' with 'The Tradition of the Narrative Material' in *The History of the Synoptic Tradition*, ET, Oxford, 1963. Such a broad category, of course, contains much material that would be disputed. We mean only to contend, however, that the words reported to have been spoken by Jesus, esp. in the form of pithy, easily memorizable sayings (and the majority of the Son of Man logia have this quality—as though they may have been condensed from more lengthy materials), would soon have gained a measure of inviolability. Here, we believe, lies the real value of many of B. Gerhardsson's insights in *Memory and Manuscript. Oral Tradition and Written Transmission in Rabbinic Judaism and Early Christianity*, Lund, 1961. Cf. his *Tradition and Transmission in Early Christianity* (Coniectanea Neotestamentica 20), Lund and Copenhagen, 1964, and the balanced remarks of G. Widengren, 'Tradition and Literature in Early Judaism and in the Early Church', *Numen* 10, 1963, pp. 42ff. To us it is wellnigh inconceivable that men who believed Jesus to have risen from the dead would not, from the first, have made every effort to remember and pass on his words, however much they were also interested in preaching him as the risen Christ. These sayings may well have been preserved in a different manner and with more care than narrative and parabolic materials. Often noted in this connection is Paul's habit of distinguishing a 'word of the Lord' from his own teaching.

[4] So Stauffer (*Theology*, pp. 25f.) contends, 'The most reliable sayings of Jesus that we have, and also those which are most distinctive of him, are those about the Son of Man.'

subject other than (and then not at any length) to his disciples.[1] Where any note of conflict is at all present (Mark 2.10; 2.28; 14.62), the challenge is not taken up in such a way as to debate the meaning of the title. This at least tends to suggest that it was not a current title in Church usage.

Further corroboration of the fact that the term Son of Man was thought to have come only from Jesus is found in the way it is confined to the Gospels. Not only does the title itself practically disappear from the rest of the New Testament,[2] but the Church (as opposed to some gnostics) from that point on uses the designation quite infrequently and rarely, if ever, with the force and meaning Jesus gave to it. When employed,[3] it is used to convey teaching about the Lord's humanity, which, as we shall see, hardly does justice to the Gospel presentation.

Yet another strange but obvious factor: the overall record is quite ambiguous as to the exact relation of the Son of Man figure to Jesus. There are times when it seems perfectly clear that Jesus is speaking of another. This is especially so when he talks of the Son of Man as a future, eschatological figure. Yet, at other times, the tradition has Jesus speak of the Son of Man as though he were already at work on earth (for example, forgiving sins, Mark 2.10; without a place to lay his head, Matt. 8.20 = Luke 9.58). It is difficult to avoid the impression that sayings such as these, in some way, lay claim to the role of

[1] Jesus speaks to the crowd or to other individuals six times about the Son of Man (once in Mark, three times in Q and twice in Luke). Four times Jesus says something about the Son of Man to Jewish officials (three in Mark, once in Q). But twenty-nine times teaching about the Son of Man is imparted only to the disciples (nine times in Mark, four in Q, ten in Matthew and six in Luke).

[2] See ch. VI. It is interesting that in his article 'The Influence of Circumstances on the Use of Christological Terms', *JTS*, ns 10, 1959, pp. 247ff., C. F. D. Moule finds it very difficult to provide any circumstances in which the later Church would have used the Son of Man designation. He stresses the mystery of these sayings and doubts if they were understood even by the evangelists. R. P. Casey, 'The Earliest Christologies', *JTS*, ns 9, 1958, pp. 253ff., is forced by these factors to treat the title rather quixotically, an attitude which, if we may say so, is shared by many commentators.

[3] See Ignatius, *To the Ephesians* 20.2; Irenaeus, *Against Heresies* V, 21.3; *Epistle of Barnabas* 12.10; and in the *Gospel Acc. to the Hebrews* (so Jerome, *De vir.ill.* 2). A use more in keeping with that of the Gospels is found in Eusebius, *Eccl. History* II, 23.13; Justin, *Apology* I, 51.9; yet these are likely derived from the Gospels and indicate no further understanding or common use of the term. J. M. Robinson (*New Quest of the Historical Jesus*, p. 102 n. 2) is quite wrong to attempt to minimize the significance of this factor. When compared with the use of other titles in the apostolic, sub-apostolic and patristic literature, this reticence is astounding. On the *gnostic* usage see in ch. II.

Son of Man for Jesus himself. This is yet more apparent in the sayings which relate to the death and resurrection of the Son of Man.

It is probably fair to say that this feature of almost studied ambiguity has led to most difficulties in efforts to understand the Son of Man. Once it is decided that Jesus spoke only of a future figure or, contrariwise, only of himself as the Son of Man on earth, reasonably understandable results might be achieved. If, however, some synthesis is sought, all the embarrassment and frustration return.

However this matter is decided, Jesus certainly is presented as believing that he is intimately associated with the work of the Son of Man. If the Son of Man were to be an earthly figure, such is abundantly clear, even if Jesus is not to be equated with him in any direct and simple fashion. If, however, the Son of Man is thought to be only a future figure, still Jesus would seem to be his *messenger* or advocate, one who can closely relate his own mission to that of the Son of Man. 'Everyone who acknowledges me before men, the Son of Man also will acknowledge before the angels of God' (Luke 12.8). 'In the new world, when the Son of Man shall sit on his glorious throne, you who have followed me will also sit on twelve thrones . . .' (Matt. 19.28).

The above analysis certainly suggests one further way of viewing the material which has been adopted by almost every scholar who has dealt with the problem. Three sets of circumstances seem to be predicated of the Son of Man: some manner of earthly ministry, suffering and death (sometimes resurrection as well) and a future appearance or *parousia* (primarily as a kind of heavenly judge).[1] To an extent these categories are academic, and there are several sayings which seem to bridge the classifications or do not easily fit into any category at all. None the less they can be a useful shorthand and will aid us in our study. Again omitting parallels and remembering that such figures are only approximate, there are ten sayings which appear to apply to an earthly ministry (three each in Mark and Q, two each in Matthew and Luke), eleven which predicate suffering or are set in the context of references to the passion (seven, or eight, in Mark, none in Q and probably two each for Matthew and Luke),[2] and eighteen which posit a future appearance (three in Mark, five in Q, six in Matthew and four times in Luke).

[1] From one point of view, of course, the first two of these classes belong together, as both conceive of a Son of Man who has appeared on earth.

[2] There might, however, be others in Luke if one sees an independent tradition behind several of his sayings only partly paralleled in Mark.

There is one more element in all this upon which there is rarely sufficient comment. Especially in connection with the predictions of suffering, we find a note of *mustness* or *oughtness*. Nor does Jesus claim that this is just a result of his own sense of mission. '. . . how is it written of the Son of Man, that he should suffer many things and be treated with contempt?' (Mark 9.12). '. . . and he began to teach them that the Son of Man must suffer many things . . .' (Mark 8.31). 'For the Son of Man goes as it is written of him' (Mark 14.21). '. . . so must the Son of Man be lifted up . . .' (John 3.14). Where might Jesus have found such *predictions*, and who is this extraordinary Son of Man?

And yet these are just the outlines of the problem. Further difficulties will only become clear as we deal with some of the many efforts which have been made to solve the puzzle and as we go over the evidence again and again. For such continuing and persistent research the Gospels themselves are, however, our clear mandate.

2. PROPOSED SOLUTIONS

It will not be our purpose to attempt to survey all the answers which have been proffered.[1] What we shall try to do is to set forth and discuss the most representative of these and to cover the range of ideas which have been put forward, while also demonstrating, as best we can, why they are felt to be erroneous or inadequate. For these purposes it will be convenient to present the variety of solutions under three main headings.

A. *Dissociation of Jesus from the use of Son of Man as a title*

In this first category we will discuss theories which seek, in one way or another, to dissociate Jesus from the use of this expression as a title. *The Son of Man*, in such circumstances, would cease to be a problem with regard to the historical Jesus and be of interest only for our study of developing Christology in the early Church.

---

[1] In addition to discussions to be found in works mentioned below, special attention may be paid to surveys by C. C. McCown, 'Jesus, Son of Man: a Survey of recent discussion', *JR* 28, 1948, pp. 1ff.; Higgins, 'Son of Man-*Forschung* since the *Teaching of Jesus*' in *New Testament Essays* (ed. Higgins), Manchester, 1959, pp. 119ff., and his *Jesus and the Son of Man*, London, 1964, pp. 21ff.; H. E. Tödt, *The Son of Man in the Synoptic Tradition*, ET, London, 1965, pp. 284ff., 297ff.; G. Haufe, 'Das Menschensohn-Problem in der gegenwärtigen wissenschaftlichen Diskussion', *EvTh* 26, 1966, pp. 130ff.; and I. H. Marshall, 'The Synoptic Son of Man Sayings in Recent Discussion', *NTS* 12, 1965/6, pp. 327ff.

The most radical of all solutions is also, in its effects, the simplest, and, as is the fashion with methods both radical and simplifying, was once found to be very attractive. Shortly before the turn of the century linguistic research caused scholars to realize that the expression 'the Son of Man' was in Greek (ὁ υἱὸς τοῦ ἀνθρώπου) a rather inelegant barbarism.[1] The phrase seemed only to have a meaningful status as a Semitic expression and as such might better have been translated as ὁ ἄνθρωπος, which could then have been translated into English as 'the Man'. In this sense the expression had a certain kinship with the well-known phrase 'the children (or sons) of Israel' which obviously refers to Israelites.

One could, however, go much further, for there was evidence from the post-Christian period which indicated that the possibly equivalent Aramaic expressions like bar (ᵉ)nāšā and especially bar (ᵉ)nāš were sometimes little more than idioms which could be used to indicate a man, any man. It then seemed natural enough to read back over the usages of the Hebrew ben 'ādām expression in the Old Testament and see there also a rather uncomplicated reference to a human being, a synecdochical image for humanity. In almost every Old Testament usage[2] the phrase is found in parallelism with words for man ('îš or 'enōš) and all of these references (both to man and son of man) are in turn sometimes rather indiscriminately translated by bar nāšā or bar nāš in the Targums.[3] Perhaps similarly the Palestinian Pentateuch Targums are even prepared to use both bar nāšā and bar nāš to translate hā'ādām at Gen. 9.5f.[4]

[1] The initial stages of the debate as to the proper interpretation of the expression were carried on over a period of about ten years by scholars like H. Lietzmann, J. Wellhausen, A. Meyer, N. Schmidt, N. Messel, R. H. Charles, G. Dalman and P. Fiebig. We may avoid again recording the long list of theses, replies and counter-replies by referring to E. Sjöberg's Der Menschensohn im äthiopischen Henochbuch, Lund, 1946, pp. 40ff., and his 'Ben 'ādām and bar 'enāš im Hebräischen und Aramäischen', AO 21, 1950, pp. 57ff., 91ff. See also S. Mowinckel, HTC, pp. 346ff.; J. Bowman, 'The Background of the Term "Son of Man"', ExpT 59, 1947/8, pp. 283ff.; J. Y. Campbell, 'Son of Man' in A. Richardson's A Theological Wordbook of the Bible, London, 1950, pp. 230f.; M. Black, 'The "Son of Man" in the Teaching of Jesus', ExpT 60, 1948–9, pp. 32ff.; and G. Vermes, 'The Use of Bar Nash/Bar Nasha in Jewish Aramaic' in M. Black's 3rd ed., to be published shortly, of An Aramaic Approach to the Gospels and Acts, Oxford, pp. 310–330.

[2] E.g. Pss. 8.4; 80.17; Num. 23.19; Job 25.6. Further and for a different interpretation see below in ch. III. On what is perhaps similar language in the Dead Sea Scrolls, see in ch. V. The references to Old Testament verses are always given in the numbering of the English versions unless otherwise indicated.

[3] So in Ps. 8.4 both 'enōš and ben 'ādām are translated by bar nāš while bar nāš is used in Ps. 80.17 for ben 'ādām.

[4] See Bowman, op. cit., p. 286.

The use of the appellative *ben 'ādām*, so frequently employed by God in addressing Ezekiel, is no problem in such an analysis, since it is interpreted to refer to Ezekiel in his human status.[1] Even in the celebrated Dan. 7.13 the actual expression itself, 'as a *bar 'enāš*', need mean no more than that the figure looked human.[2]

When one comes to Aramaic writings such as the Palestinian Talmud and the *Genesis Rabba*, which are particularly important[3] since they reflect Aramaic usage of a Palestinian and Galilean provenance that in parts goes back to the early second century AD, such expressions are used in an apparently idiomatic fashion. The precise relevance and weight of this evidence is still much disputed, but it does seem reasonably clear that these expressions (especially *bar nāš*) were sometimes used as indefinite pronouns meaning *any man* and possibly also (but only possibly), in a manner familiar to several languages, as a first-person circumlocution.[4]

Thus, with a whiff of grammatical grapeshot, the barricades seemed to have been cleared. The whole problem was but a gigantic mistake occasioned by the evangelists' failure to recognize a Semitic idiom. The apparent interchange between the use of the first person and *the son of man* in a few instances in the Gospels (e.g. Luke 6.22 with Matt. 5.11 and Luke 12.8 with Matt. 10.32) was held to be illustrative of the manner in which the mistake may have occurred. In other passages it was thought not difficult to believe that Jesus had actually been speaking of himself in an idiomatic way with no intention of conferring upon himself some special dignity or title (e.g. Mark 2.10).

One could now proceed to go through the Gospels making this emendation, and, if this did not everywhere produce an intelligible

[1] See esp. P. Parker, 'The Meaning of the "Son of Man"', *JBL* 60, 1941, pp. 151ff., further below and in ch. IV.

[2] On the Danielic usage see in ch. IV.

[3] See Sjöberg, *AO* 21, 1950, p. 92.

[4] In this the expression may be somewhat equivalent to the more frequent Aramaic idiom *hāhū gabrā*, which can be both a first- and second-person circumlocution. (II Cor. 12.2ff. is often suggested as an illustration of the idiom transposed into Greek.) For discussions of the possible use of these expressions as first-person circumlocutions, see Sjöberg, *op. cit.*, pp. 91ff., and esp. Vermes, *op. cit.* Despite Vermes's convictions, however, it does not appear to us that any of his examples provide unambiguous illustrations. The references may still be just to *any man*. Though the speaker may occasionally include himself under this reference, this does not make it into a genuine circumlocution any more than would a comparable usage in English. E.g. 'A man can't work miracles. What do you expect of me?'

translation, the alternative was ready to hand: Jesus was simply using the term to refer to mankind in general (e.g. Mark 2.28). Since the idiom could itself be flexible, there was no need to decide between these alternatives outside of the context; whichever gave the best sense could be adopted in individual texts.

Yet, from the first, there was something disquieting about all this. Even granting the difficulty of understanding the idioms of ancient languages, it was hard to *hear* Jesus so frequently speaking in such a roundabout way, harder still to imagine that all four of the evangelists could have completely misunderstood the idiom when there must still have been a few *ear*-witnesses who could have corrected the error, or at least several persons who knew both Greek and Aramaic. Nor, even so, does the emendation everywhere make good sense, especially in the sayings about a future appearance, yet more so in the Fourth Gospel. And why is the idiom used so inconsistently? Why is it missing from passages where it would seem so appropriate? And why not 'Everyone who acknowledges *the son of man* (me) before men, the son of man also will acknowledge before the angels of God' instead of 'Everyone who acknowledges me before men, the son of man also will acknowledge . . .' (Luke 12.8)? Or must we suppose the whole saying to be the result of a long process in which first the idiom was misunderstood and then the first half of it, but not the second, was somehow correctly interpreted?

In an attempt to account for the Gospel evidence Dalman argued that *bar* (*'e*)*nāš* and especially the more determinative *bar* (*'e*)*nāšā* held certain poetic nuances which hearkened back to the Old Testament and distinguished them from the simple words for *a man*.[1] Further study, however, has not given much support to his particular arguments. *Bar* (*'e*)*nāšā* and *bar* (*'e*)*nāš* appear to have been used somewhat indiscriminately, and Dalman's failure to confine and extend his scrutiny in the writings particularly relevant to Palestinian Aramaic usage was a weakness in his theory. Still, Sjöberg, while recognizing the more extensive use of the idiom in Palestinian Aramaic, contends that it remains quite possible that such forms could have conveyed a distinctive sense.[2] Writes Mowinckel, 'The result of this discussion is that there is no valid linguistic ground for denying either that the expression was a definite Messianic designa-

[1] G. Dalman, *The Words of Jesus*, ET, Edinburgh, 1902, pp. 234ff., 256.
[2] See *AO* 21, 1950, pp. 100ff., and *Der verborgene Menschensohn in den Evangelien*, Lund, 1955, p. 239.

tion within certain circles, or that Jesus could not have used it of himself.'[1] None the less, it also cannot be denied both that the idiomatic usage of a *bar nāšā*-like expression was known to Palestinian Aramaic, quite possibly in the time of Jesus, and that (outside of Daniel, the New Testament and lacking a Semitic original for the crucial sections of I Enoch) the evidence for such an Aramaic expression being used in a messianic fashion is scanty and late, stemming mainly from interpretations of Dan. 7.13.[2]

Perhaps, however, an overconcentration on the use of a *bar nāšā*-like expression as an idiom could cause us to miss the real point at issue. It has recently been emphasized that particular attention must be paid to the style of the discourse and to the context in which the phrase is found.[3] When these criteria are applied to the Gospels, it becomes clear, probably beyond any dispute, that *sometimes* some such expression was employed in a very special way. The possibility that those logia which speak of a heavenly champion are built around idiomatic references (e.g. Jesus referring to himself in some deferential manner) appears too minuscule for credibility. Nor does it seem at all probable, as we shall see, that these kinds of sayings were formed last and can be explained as a devolution from the earlier misunderstanding.

How it came to be that some such expression could be employed with a special and distinctive force is one of the questions which this study will try to answer, but the fact that it did, and that even by themselves the Gospels are evidence for this is of crucial significance. Thus there is hardly a scholar who would today contend that the expression was never used in a titular sense either by Jesus or at some very early point in the life of the Church.[4]

If, in fact, the Gospel traditions did use for *the Son of Man* some Aramaic expression, which without any alteration could also be utilized to mean *any man* and/or as a circumlocution for *I*, then it is necessary to realize that the argument from idiomatic usage can probably be turned right around. In given contexts, within certain

[1] *HTC*, p. 347.

[2] For these references see Bowman, *op. cit.*, pp. 285f.

[3] So Vermes (*op. cit.*) in arguing that the idiomatic circumlocution is found in contexts where the speaker so refers to himself out of humility or deference. The point we are making is, however, equally valid, for one must notice how little there is in common between the examples brought forth by Vermes and at least the vast majority of Son of Man logia in the Gospels.

[4] See the views cited below, but, e.g., Higgins, *Son of Man*, pp. 16f.; F. Hahn, *Christologische Hoheitstitel* (FRLANT 83), 1963, pp. 13ff., esp. 24f.

frames of reference, some such expression evidently gained or was found to have particular nuances.[1] Indeed, as we shall come to see, some such method of referring to the *leader* of the society may once have been a widespread phenomenon. In other words, even if it is held that *bar nāšā* was a phrase which could have meant *I* or *any man*, this is no guarantee that in certain circles it could not have been given a special meaning. The linguistic argument cannot be based solely on the evidence from the slightly later rabbinic usage and thus conducted in a kind of vacuum. The Christian usage is evidence in its own right and to its witness must very probably be added the manner in which rather similar designations (e.g. *the Man*) came into prominence in the second century AD and the background upon which that development probably rests. 'The contribution of the history of religions', writes Ethelbert Stauffer, 'has taught us better ... *Son of Man is just about the most pretentious piece of self-description that any man in the ancient East could possibly have used.*'[2] Proof of this statement must await us in the next few chapters, by which time, however, it should not be difficult to see why a complete solution of the Son of Man problem in terms of a misunderstood idiom has largely passed out of vogue.

It needs also to be said that many have perhaps far too easily assumed that Jesus used an expression identical with one which was also capable of the idiomatic connotations in other circumstances. We regard this as at all times debatable. It is still remarkable that the Gospels use such an awkward phrase to translate whatever they found in their traditions. (This apparent endeavour to offer a distinctive and demonstrative expression is similarly reflected in the Ethiopic of I Enoch and the Gospels and in the Syriac of the Gospels.)[3] It is equally remarkable that the Gospels give not the slightest hint at other times of having any difficulties with references to 'this man', 'that man', 'a certain man'. A number of other possibilities

[1] By way of a possible illustration, it is said that the officials who work in the White House in Washington are prone to speak of *the man*, by which they mean not just anyone, but rather *the Man*, that is their boss, the President.

[2] *Theology*, p. 108. A wide range of scholars would concur; e.g. Mowinckel, *HTC*, pp. 347ff., 364ff.; Sjöberg, *Henochbuch*, p. 59; Richardson, *Theology*, pp. 128f.

[3] On the three Ethiopic expressions employed see pp. 146ff. The Syriac normally uses *brē d'nāšā* for the title and is evidently striving to give a more definite and demonstrative force. Otherwise forms equivalent to the Aramaic *bar ᵉnāšā*, *bar nāšā* and *bar nāš* are used in verses like Matt. 12.12; Mark 2.27; Acts 10.26; Rom. 1.23; 6.6; 12.18; Rev. 21.17. Christian Palestinian Aramaic also chooses forms which could not be confused with the idiom.

remain open[1] (including the possibility exemplified in other literature of the period, that Jesus may have employed Hebrew for some of the important words in his message, especially if these were derived from scriptures).[2]

It may then be wondered why we have here expended effort in producing and then refuting the argument. The answer lies in the word *complete* used above. Such a solution, as we shall soon see, is far from having been banished as a partial answer, a way of dealing with sayings which cannot otherwise be accounted for by a particular theory, and it keeps slipping in again through the back door. Thus armed we may be prepared to meet it at a future date.

One positive factor which has, however, resulted from this discussion is the realization that the expression *the Son of Man* might, in some ways, be better translated as *the Man*. Obviously, to avoid confusion, we had best not do so here, though it is well to keep the alternative rendering in mind. Nevertheless, it may also be wise to remember that particular expressions (even idioms) are usually created and employed for some purpose. We may yet find significant nuances which give value to the whole of the expression.

A very different method has been essayed which, while it usually holds that *the Son of Man* is a genuine title and a highly honorific designation throughout, does yet achieve the result of withdrawing it from any direct relationship to Jesus himself. First by H. B. Sharman[3] and now most trenchantly by Phillipp Vielhauer[4] it has been argued

---

[1] The composite expression *bar 'ādām* is found in the Targum of Ezekiel and at Dan. 8.17. On this cf. G. S. Duncan, *Jesus, Son of Man*, London, 1947, p. 135 n.4. Bowman (*op. cit.*, p. 284) points out that such would better be translated 'Son of Adam', but the peculiar nuance could well have been lost in translation. Some have suggested that *hāhū bar nāšā* might have been used, though the precise form is unknown. See Dalman, *op. cit.*, pp. 249ff.; Sjöberg, *Henochbuch*, pp. 42ff. In any case some account ought to be taken of the definite articles in the Greek, for the Greek phrase, in a strict sense, could probably only be translated back into Aramaic as something like the Syriac expression above.

[2] Cf. Widengren, *Numen* 10, 1963, p. 65.

[3] *Son of Man and Kingdom of God*, New York, 1943, pp. 89ff.

[4] 'Gottesreich und Menschensohn in der Verkündigung Jesu', in *Festschrift für Günther Dehn* (ed. W. Schneemelcher), Neukirchen, 1957, pp. 51ff., and 'Jesus und der Menschensohn: zur Diskussion mit Heinz Eduard Tödt und Eduard Schweizer', *ZTK* 60, 1963, pp. 133ff. Rather similar are the views of E. Käsemann, 'Sätze heiligen Rechtes im Neuen Testament', NTS 1, 1954/5, pp. 256f., and *Essays on New Testament Themes*, ET (SBT 41), 1964, pp. 38f., 43f.; H. Conzelmann, 'Gegenwart und Zukunft in der Synoptischen Tradition', *ZTK* 54, 1957, pp. 281ff., and 'Jesus Christus' in RGG³, III, 1959, cols. 630f. H. M. Teeple, 'The Origin of the Son of Man Christology', *JBL* 84, 1965, pp. 213ff., also rejects the authenticity of all the Son of Man logia. However, he departs rather radically

that the whole of the Gospels' Son of Man tradition is a post-resurrection phenomenon and development. Even the sayings about the coming eschatological hero are an outgrowth of the period in which Jesus was looked for as the champion who would return from heaven. The vital insight, on this view, involves the apparent lack of integration between Jesus' teaching about the Kingdom of God and his reported statements about the Son of Man.[1] According to Vielhauer this is not in the least surprising, since the two conceptions are based on very different premises and issue from diverse *milieux* of ideas. Among other things, it is important to realize that the Son of Man (who in essential respects is a Messiah-like figure) belongs to a rather apocalyptic, interim kingdom, while the far less apocalyptic Kingdom of God belongs to the end of the ages. In such significant respects the two conceptions are incompatible; they are not found to have been linked in the Judaism of the time[2] and could not both have been preached by Jesus. Only the post-resurrection faith that Jesus was the Son of Man and that as the Son of Man he would return to rule (which belief, in fact, tended to oust Jesus' preaching about the Kingdom of God)[3] permitted the two themes to be brought into the same traditions, though even so they do not mix easily and are thus quite visibly striated in the Gospels.

(and in our opinion becomes even less convincing) from Vielhauer's position by suggesting that the sayings are a relatively late product of Hellenistic Jewish-Christianity seeking a substitute for the Messiah Christology. Some of the *unanswerable* questions asked by Teeple (*op. cit.*, pp. 220f.) we shall attempt to answer in this study.

To this list should now be added the important study of N. Perrin. *Rediscovering the Teaching of Jesus*, London, 1967. See, for instance, his revised view on Matt. 10.23b, pp. 201f.

[1] In *F. Dehn*, pp. 53, 76. In a well-known remark Sharman wrote: '. . . they create the impression of two foci that do not belong to the same ellipse . . . the Son of Man has no kingdom and the Kingdom of God has no Son of Man' (*op. cit.*, p. 89).

[2] Of course, Dan. 7.13ff. is sometimes brought forward as evidence to the contrary (so Higgins in *New Testament Essays*, p. 130, and both L. Dequeker and J. Coppens in their *Le Fils de l'Homme et les Saints du Très-Haut en Daniel VII, dans les Apocryphes et dans le Nouveau Testament*[2] [Analecta Lovaniensia Biblica et Orientalia, III/23], Bruges-Paris, 1961), but one can ask whether the kingdom there should be equated with the Kingdom of God as preached by Jesus. In any case, Vielhauer holds that this vision is not admissible as evidence, since the Son of Man there is not an individual but rather a symbol for the heavenly kingdom (*op cit.*, p. 73).

[3] *Op. cit.*, p. 79.

Several scholars have found cause to reject Vielhauer's theory,[1] the most thorough refutation having been undertaken by H. E. Tödt.[2] He maintains that there is not enough information available to establish criteria which would demonstrate that the Kingdom of God and the Son of Man were so fully incompatible. Vielhauer assumes too readily that the Son of Man can be equated with types of the Messiah,[3] while our data regarding precise eschatological beliefs held about the Son of Man is very limited. Similarly we really have little basis on which to assess Jewish beliefs about the kind of eschatological Kingdom of God that Jesus preached.[4]

In Tödt's view the all-important Q source shows that, although the two ideas may never have been fully wedded (can we hold that because two ideas are not formally joined they were separately transmitted?), they still belong together. While arguing that the sayings about the future Son of Man found in Q are reasonably authentic, he tries to demonstrate that they correspond with Jesus' teaching about the Kingdom of God in important essentials: both are related to Jesus' person in the same manner, and both present a similar *crisis* theology along with a tendency to tone down apocalyptic motifs and details.

Tödt particularly faults Vielhauer for contending that several crucial sayings which tell of a future heavenly champion are Christological. In his opinion it is important to realize that they are soteriological and very likely authentic precisely because they do not identify Jesus with the Son of Man. In the vital logion Luke 12.8f. (partially echoed by Mark 8.38) this distinction is clearly to be seen.

---

[1] Higgins, *Son of Man*, pp. 22f.; Black, *BJRL* 45, 1963, p. 310; R. H. Fuller, *The Foundations of New Testament Christology*, London, 1965, pp. 122f.; Schweizer, 'Der Menschensohn', *ZNW* 50, 1959, p. 186, and *Lordship and Discipleship*, ET (SBT 28), 1960, p. 40. Hahn (*Hoheitstitel*, pp. 27ff., esp. p. 30) maintains that in the Judaism of the time one can glimpse the manner in which the conception of the new age, to which the Son of Man rightfully belonged, and the idea of the Kingdom of God were growing together.

[2] *Son of Man*, pp. 329ff.

[3] So Tödt (*op. cit.*, p. 331) objects to Vielhauer's use of K. G. Kuhn's analysis (in art. βασιλεύς, etc., *TWNT* I, 570ff.) showing that the Messiah and Kingdom of God are heterogeneous. The Messiah of whom Kuhn was writing was a nationalistic leader, while the Son of Man is a universalistic figure more in keeping with the terms of reference of the Kingdom of God.

[4] Tödt, *op. cit.*, p. 332. Vielhauer (*ZTK* 60, 1963, pp. 136f.) still maintains that there is a sufficient basis. None the less it is true that the eschatological Son of Man, as such, is far from widely represented and that in S-B I, p. 179, the Kingdom of God is instanced only a few times in Jewish apocalyptic literature.

Haufe also questions Vielhauer's attempt to explain Luke 12.8f. on the basis that the Church was distinguishing between two statuses of Jesus (for is not Vielhauer contending that the Church was eager to see the earthly Jesus as the Son of Man?), and makes the yet more damaging criticism that Vielhauer is unable to bring forward any early logia which reveal the Church picturing Jesus being exalted to heaven as the Son of Man.[1]

Vielhauer, however, sticks adamantly to his guns. Even if there is not available all the information that might be desired, what material there is does not suggest any link between the Kingdom and the Son of Man.[2] Tödt assumes far too much about the character and order of a Q source and, in any case, fails to show that the ideas were there integrated.[3] Tödt's contention that certain of the Son of Man sayings are not Christological is a dubious matter of opinion. While some logia may not explicitly identify Jesus with the Son of Man, they nevertheless, upon scrutiny, reveal themselves to be sayings created by the community[4] and, as such, undoubtedly assume that identity. In fact, Tödt is found to be eclectic and inconsistent in choosing some sayings of this type to be authentic and others not. They do not differ in form; several future Son of Man logia which Tödt rejects also do not explicitly identify Jesus and the Son of Man.[5]

If one is willing to accept a number of Vielhauer's preliminary arguments, his case is clearly forceful and difficult to deal with. There is a certain irremediable dichotomy between the Kingdom of God and Son of Man sayings, as they are now found, which cannot be lightly set aside. We would, for instance, go so far as to agree with him in believing that the often noted, apparent link between the two at Mark 8.31–9.1 is artificial (though our method of explaining this is radically different from his).

Yet can his method of accounting for this dichotomy be justified? In due time we shall come to question the theory that statements which imply or state a degree of *Christology* can always be relegated to Church activity. Nor do we believe that Vielhauer has sufficiently explained the fact (whatever is implicated or has been assumed) that logia about the future Son of Man do not make clear the identity with

[1] Haufe, *EvTh* 26, 1966, pp. 135f.
[2] *ZTK*, 60, 1963, pp. 136f.
[3] *Op. cit.*, pp. 137f.
[4] Only Luke 17.26f. is set aside as not demonstrably a post-resurrection saying. But in the face of all else this saying, too, must be a late formulation.
[5] *ZTK* 60, 1963, pp. 145, 173.

Jesus. Equally his theory does not adequately account for the restriction of the title to Jesus' lips.

Our most serious reservations, however, arise out of Vielhauer's assumption that Jesus would not have preached somewhat anomalous or even contradictory ideas. We would also agree with those who wonder if sharp and firm distinctions can be made between the terms of reference of the Kingdom of God and the Son of Man eschatologies (and we think that Vielhauer has oversimplified Jesus' teaching about the Kingdom, which can itself often be seemingly ambiguous and contradictory).[1] If the Church could have proffered both themes despite their anomalies, so also could have Jesus. Indubitably the post-resurrection faith of the Christian community was a catalyst making possible new syntheses, but there are also solid grounds for believing that Jesus' own preaching was catalytic in its own ways.

And it is necessary to reckon with the fact that Jesus was living in a rather syncretistic time even so far as *orthodox* Judaism was concerned. Especially in works of an eschatological bent, uniformity of viewpoint is not an outstanding feature. How much less must it have been so in the course of preaching which was likely to have been offered spontaneously and more for its effects than its logic? If teaching about the advent of the Kingdom and the belief that the Son of Man would soon appear could both make men aware of the present crisis, why not preach both?

And could it not be that it was the early Church, on the one hand carrying on Jesus' preaching about the nearing Kingdom and on the other passing on (but not preaching) the Son of Man sayings, which has rather caused the two themes to gravitate toward different levels of traditions? On the grounds that the Church has fully used, reshaped and reformulated much of the material it received, is it not as logical to contend that they are the ones who have tended to striate the two conceptions (which might have been much better synthesized in the more comprehensive mind of their leader) as it is to hold that that they have wholly created the one or the other?[2]

[1] It is a virtue of G. E. Ladd's *Jesus and the Kingdom*, New York, 1964, that it brings out the many facets of the teaching about the Kingdom.

[2] If it comes to that, we would be so bold as to wonder if the Kingdom of God teaching ought to be preferred to that about the Son of Man. (See E. Bammel, 'Erwägungen zur Eschatologie Jesu' in *Studia Evangelica*, III [ed. F. L. Cross, TU 88], 1964, pp. 3ff.) Once parallels and the many obvious editorial usages and repetitions are taken into account, the two ideas are mentioned about an equal number of times (while the Kingdom has practically no status in John's material). We know that the idea of the Kingdom was popular in Church preaching and

It is our claim that the Son of Man sayings have a most legitimate claim on authenticity and that Vielhauer's analysis of the logia is based far more on his theory than on any problems intrinsic to the sayings themselves. We shall come in our own turn to set out a theory and to examine the sayings, but, in the meantime (and this will also apply to some of the theories discussed below) our final criticism is this: if Vielhauer were right, we must suppose, between the time of Jesus' death and the *hardening* of the earliest strands of tradition,[1] an intervening group of disciples so captivated by the Son of Man idea and so persuasive in their own preaching and teaching that they managed deeply and permanently to affect all four (five if we count a Q) channels of transmission. Instead, however, of plainly identifying Jesus with the figure which was all-important to them, they managed rather to leave the situation in an ambiguous state. Daring so to alter the whole basis of the tradition, they yet failed to make crystal clear what must have been their essential motive. Then we must further suppose that the early Church (and presumably its leaders and the disciples of Jesus themselves, if they were not the ones directly responsible), having been wholly convinced by them, yet allowed this same influential group to pass out of sight without a verifiable trace.[2] Almost immediately thereafter the Church must have ceased to speak of the Son of Man, so quickly that the synoptic evangelists seem themselves to have no certain understanding of the designation.[3]

One cannot claim that such an eventuality is impossible: stranger things have happened in history. But is it at all likely? Is there any real evidence for such a group?[4]

---

teaching (and we must remember that the Church still has a strong bias in favour of preaching about the Kingdom as opposed to the Son of Man as he is depicted in the Gospels). On the distinct possibility that teaching about the Kingdom may sometimes have replaced that about the Son of Man, see our views in ch. VIII and esp. on Mark 9.1 with Matt. 16.28 and Luke 22.29f. with Matt. 19.28.

[1] Tödt also (*op. cit.*, p. 346) has rather pointedly asked Vielhauer why the communities chose to call Jesus the Son of Man if there were no references at all to the figure in Jesus' message. Is it enough to suggest some parallel with the exaltation of Enoch to the Son of Man (Vielhauer, *F.-Dehn*, p. 79) when the Gospel logia do not reveal any direct relationship with the materials of I Enoch otherwise?

[2] On theories about a continuing Son of Man group of some kind, see in ch. VI.

[3] On this see Knox, *Death of Christ*, p. 95 n. 8, and further below.

[4] Knox (*op. cit.*, p. 57) speaks of 'the absence of evidence that the primitive Church, or any part of it, was accustomed to use the term in expressing its own faith'. Haufe also points to the lack of evidence that there were any 'prophets' making statements about the Son of Man which were then included in collections of Jesus' authentic words. *EvTh* 26, 1966, p. 135. See below, p. 316 n. 3.

B. *Deletion of one or more of the classifications of sayings*

A second category of solutions to the Son of Man problem involves some process of deleting one or more of the classifications of sayings. Either Jesus spoke of a Son of Man on earth (and perhaps also of one who had a destiny which included suffering) and with whom he tended to identify, or else he spoke of a future eschatological hero who was other than himself. Indeed, it would seem to be suggested from a number of quarters that the Son of Man as now presented by the Gospels is so contradictory and so baffling that Jesus simply could not have spoken in such a fashion. Only the Church could have created such *confusion*. What connection could there be between an earthly Son of Man like this and one who is yet to appear at a future time in heaven? Perhaps there is none, and the most sensible way to escape the conundrum is to cut the Gordian knot which the Church's faith in Jesus as the Son of Man has tied.

Behind certain types of these analyses there seems at times to rest a belief with which we are not in accord, a kind of assumption which has long played a part in New Testament scholarship. Far too often, and however many the protestations to the contrary, there can be discerned the attempt to cut through the complications and contradictions and get back to the simple prophet of Galilee.[1] There is apparently some law which decrees that religion must develop from the simple to the complex. *High* Christology, ambiguities and difficulties must be *late*. The heart, at least, of Jesus' message must have been simple and direct.[2]

---

[1] We do not intend to imply that G. Bornkamm in *Jesus of Nazareth*, ET, London, 1960, is more guilty of this attitude than others; in several ways he is less so. Nevertheless, in his treatment of the Son of Man it is implicit. On p. 229 he speaks of a search for a 'simpler' solution; on p. 230 he objects to the solutions which view the several-sided conception as coming from Jesus, because they present us 'most decidedly with problems that are difficult to solve'. But can we assume that such were not indigenous to Jesus' ministry?

[2] E.g. a classic statement from the older school of scholarship: '. . . the message of Jesus, so far as it consisted of teaching, was of the greatest simplicity possible' (A. Loisy, *The Origins of the New Testament*, ET, London, 1950, p. 33). Even if the message can be reduced to some kind of a minimum, is it rather not fraught with mystery and *hardness*? But beliefs like this do not just influence the earlier generations of scholars. In *A New Quest of the Historical Jesus*, p. 121, J. M. Robinson writes, 'The essential content of Jesus' message was: "Repent, for the Kingdom of God is near." ' This was probably essential to Jesus' message, but this is not the same thing as 'the essential content'. (In a similar category falls the rigid canon of certain scholars, often based on Matt. 11.2–6 = Luke 7.18–23, that, since only the Church could have turned the proclaimer into the proclaimed,

In fact, one might legitimately claim that religions develop in a reverse fashion. In the first revelations, in the genius of the founder's message, are inherent a host of seeming contradictions and ambiguities. (How can high religion avoid them?) It is left to succeeding generations to begin working these out and to try to simplify them. This simplifying process is one of the functions of popularization. No doubt details of narrative and various embellishments are added to increase interest, but the main drive is toward the ironing out of difficulties in the traditions.

We must refrain, however, from decreeing a law of our own. Probably there are no such rules. Yet this is to say that we cannot know, from the start, whether Jesus' teaching was simple or ambiguous and difficult. This is what we are trying to find out, if possible, not what we begin by assuming.

The Gospel presentation of the Son of Man may contradict our modes of understanding; it may be a continuous embarrassment to the thoroughness and neatness of our scholarly views; some may even find it, as it stands, an apparent cause for questioning the intelligence or sanity of Jesus.[1] Yet none of these feelings, in themselves, can provide sufficient grounds for either circumventing or radically recasting the nature of the continuing problem.

Still, it would also be a gross mistake on our part to hold that attempts to solve our problem by deleting one or more classes of saying are wrong in principle. Indeed, any possible solution to the complex issue is worth hearing, and some of these approaches have been set forth skilfully and persuasively.

Let us first attempt to see the Son of Man solely as a figure who has appeared on earth, who is, above all, a man, a human figure. As a man he may have a high calling, a prophetic message to utter, a destiny to fulfil, but, in so far as the Son of Man designation goes, he is a human, though a unique one. He is *the* man among men, the

---

Jesus would never even have speculated about any role or office for the proclaimer.) Such emphases on simplicity can only lead to distortions of history. Nor do such theories, as they sometimes purport, really do away with assumptions based on the self-consciousness of Jesus. In fact, they assume a great deal about Jesus' basic simplicity of method and intention. Hegel's dead hand is not missing here.

[1] For the former see the implications of J. Y. Campbell's 'The Origin and Meaning of the Term Son of Man', *JTS* 48, 1947, pp. 145ff. For the latter, Knox, *op. cit.*, pp. 58ff., 64; Higgins, *Son of Man*, p. 19. They, of course, do not intend any irreverence, but rather work out answers by deleting or emending the *contradictory* texts.

ideal man, *the Man*. Indeed, it should be remembered that this has been the Church's primary understanding of the term from at least the end of the first century until nearly the end of the nineteenth. 'Son of Man and Son of God' was employed as a way of stating the Chalcedonian definition.[1]

It was once popular to make this association in a rather *spiritual* fashion; little attention was paid to a close analysis of the texts. The picture of an eschatological Son of Man appearing in heaven was either ignored or interpreted as the later glorification of the earthly Jesus.

More scholarly efforts to establish this view of the Son of Man have fastened on the use of the term in Ezekiel. This is certainly legitimate, and, at first glance, there is much to be said for such an association. After all, the term there appears as a form of address used of the prophet nearly one hundred times. G. S. Duncan writes, 'The very frequency of this use of the term is in itself an argument for tracing its use by Jesus back to Ezekiel rather than to the one phrase in Dan. 7.13.'[2] With Ezekiel as his example, and with the description of the humble and yet exalted status of *man* (as set forth in Ps. 8 and Gen. 1f.) in mind, Jesus understands his mission as one which will fulfil God's high hopes for humanity.[3] In the end Jesus must suffer and die like all the prophets, but he is then to be redeemed in glory.

As we shall see, this view has some merits. Nevertheless, as a complete explanation of the term, it has most serious deficiencies. Duncan's attempts to explain away or drastically to curtail the strong futuristic and supranatural features associated with the Son of Man are wholly inadequate. To contend, as he does, that modern criticism has been too absorbed with the eschatological and apocalyptic and that such ideas are not helpful in the understanding of Jesus' conception of his redeeming mission[4] only begs the very questions we are trying to answer.

Nor can we easily dismiss the efforts to understand the Son of Man in relation to somewhat similar figures from myth and eschatological

---

[1] Thus see the view of O. Moe, 'Der Menschensohn und der Urmensch', ST 14, 1960, pp. 119ff.

[2] *Jesus, Son of Man*, p. 145 n. 3.

[3] Duncan, *op. cit.*, pp. 142ff. Among others: W. A. Curtis, *Jesus Christ, the Teacher*, London, 1943, pp. 127ff. Parker, *JBL* 60, 1941, pp. 151ff.; Campbell, *JTS* 48, 1947, pp. 145ff., and in *Theological Word Book of the Bible*, pp. 230f. For this applied to the Fourth Gospel, see E. M. Sidebottom, *The Christ of the Fourth Gospel*, London, 1961, and our comments thereon in ch. VII.

[4] Duncan, *op. cit.*, pp. 138ff.

lore (both before and after Jesus' time) by means of a footnote.[1]
Actually we may well find that Ezekiel's own use of the term could
imply some awareness of this background and that it is even there to
be seen as something more than a simple prophetic designation.[2]

In addition, we cannot ignore the lack of any direct association
between the Son of Man of the Gospels and Ezekiel and the absence
of the distinguishing features of this prophet's work. Only infrequent
reference is made to Jesus as a prophet. In fact, the whole tenor of the
Gospel message argues that Jesus saw both himself and certainly the
Son of Man as much more than a prophet, a difference hardly to be
explained by degree, but rather by kind.[3] Nowhere does this appear
more true than in the presentation of the Son of Man who will suffer
as the scriptures say he must and who will one day appear in heaven
like lightning (Matt. 24.27=Luke 17.24) and with the holy angels
(Mark 8.38, etc.).

A different attempt to establish the primacy of the earthly Son of
Man sayings has been presented by Eduard Schweizer. 'The *parousia*
passages do not seem to be genuine.' What instead has happened is
that simple remarks by Jesus, referring to his exaltation and vindication, have been greatly augmented by the Church.[4] On the other hand,
'The sayings which describe Jesus as walking on earth in humility,
rejected by an unbelieving people, can be traced back to Jesus himself
with the greatest degree of certainty.'[5] Schweizer reports these as
'astonishing facts'.

They are, however, the results of an interpretation which over-
stresses the applicability of a rather generalized pattern of humble
suffering followed by exaltation,[6] and which adapts the sayings (or

[1] Duncan, *op. cit.*, p. 145 n. 2. See also, among a number of others, Knox, *op. cit.*,
p. 62 n. 13.

[2] See in ch. IV.

[3] This, of course, is yet to be demonstrated. In the meantime reference may be
made even to those texts which Duncan uses in his argument: Mark 2.10; 2.28;
10.45. Are these authorities and functions those of Ezekiel?

[4] 'Son of Man', *JBL* 79, 1960, p. 121. The original sayings referred only to his
coming day or to his appearance as the vindicated one, not to his *coming*. (The
strong future references may, in part at least, be misunderstandings of what the
Aramaic intended by a Church anxiously expecting the end. See J. A. T. Robinson,
Jesus and His Coming, London, 1957, and below in chs. IV and VIII.)

[5] *Lordship*, p. 39. Also see *ZNW* 50, 1959, pp. 185ff., and NTS 9, 1962/3,
pp. 256ff. He is less certain about the suffering sayings, but tends to see an original
form behind the stylized Marcan versions.

[6] *Erniedrigung und Erhöhung bei Jesus und seinen Nachfolgern* was the title of the
work from which *Lordship and Discipleship* was somewhat condensed. (The German

omits certain of them) to fit this view. Schweizer sees this pattern as important to the Jewish understanding of life.[1] Many undoubted references to the value of humility and chastisement are cited. The Qumran *Teacher of Righteousness* might seem an outstanding example. The exaltation or assumption of the righteous man to heaven is also a well-known theme, beginning with Enoch and Elijah.[2] Especially important to Schweizer are Wisd. 2–5. There we find a righteous man (ὁ δίκαιος) who is oppressed, who suffers, but who yet is found to be immortal and is vindicated by God. This same design is clear in the rest of the New Testament. In Acts the term 'the righteous one' (again ὁ δίκαιος) is expressly used, and Schweizer refers to passages such as Phil. 2.6ff.; I Tim. 3.16; Col. 1.15ff.; I Peter 3.18ff., and the central argument of the Epistle to the Hebrews.[3] As the representative of the true Israel, Jesus fulfils this pattern.[4]

Schweizer thus has no difficulty in demonstrating the existence of a pattern of lowliness followed by some manner of vindication and its later manifestations in the New Testament. One may also agree with him on its importance in John's Gospel. Unfortunately the pattern, as such and as an integrated design pertaining to the Son of Man, is not so immediately apparent in the synoptic Gospels, and Schweizer is taken to task by Tödt on this crucial point.[5] Nevertheless, something like this pattern can hardly be said to be totally absent, although we believe that a basis and approach different from Schweizer's is needed in order to trace its fragmentary outline.

There are, however, more fundamental criticisms of Schweizer's thesis, which, while they may not completely undermine it, none the

---

work is now in a rev. ed. [AThANT 28, 1962], with later bibliography and comment. See esp. pp. 33ff., 65ff.) Schweizer finds the pattern to be especially visible in the Fourth Gospel. *Lordship*, pp. 39f.; *ZNW* 50, 1959, pp. 203ff.

[1] *Lordship*, pp. 22ff.
[2] And figures like Adam, Moses, Isaiah and Baruch in the later literature. See below in chs. IV and V.
[3] *Lordship*, pp. 61ff., 68ff.
[4] *Op. cit.*, pp. 42ff.
[5] *Son of Man*, p. 287. If to be found at all, only then as Lucan additions, 9.51; 22.69; 24.46. Yet Tödt's contention that the heavenly *appearance* of the Son of Man does not imply his vindication is based on his own dismissal of the earthly sayings. There was no earthly Son of Man to be vindicated. Otherwise the implications, at least, would seem inescapable, *if* the different sayings refer to the *same* Son of Man. But these are the *complications* which we must strive to penetrate.
For a critique of Schweizer, see also Vielhauer, *ZTK* 60, 1963, esp. pp. 155, 167ff., on the humility-exaltation pattern.

less do question its adequacy. Schweizer claims that his pattern includes atoning suffering.[1] It would be wrong to deny the idea of redeeming suffering to late Judaism, but what is not clear is that this idea was widespread, and the individuals employed by Schweizer to illustrate the theme of exaltation are very often ones which have little or no redeeming significance.[2] Where atonement, on the other hand, is present in normative Judaism of the period, we rarely hear of exaltation.[3]

This suggests the final criticism, for what Schweizer has, in fact, failed to do is to connect his conception of the pattern with the Son of Man designation. In the last analysis he is unable to tell us why it was that Jesus chose this designation (and why it is that, as the humility-exaltation pattern becomes more clear in the teaching of the Church, the title drops from view). The Son of Man of Jesus as presented by Schweizer has little to do with any known or even hypothetical background for the term.[4] There is perhaps some partial parallel in the exaltation of Enoch as the Son of Man in I Enoch 70f.; but Schweizer does not really tell us how this is applicable, and he omits from the authentic words of Jesus precisely those sayings which are like most I Enoch's with the contention that it was Jesus himself who selected a rather amorphous designation. He then filled it out with the idea of the lowly-exalted righteous man and gave to *the Son of Man* a unique significance and value.

We may now turn to the other means of solving the problem by excision: this time all the earthly sayings are cut out, and it is the eschatological figure who comes to the fore. There are a number of variations on this theme; but the majority involve similar methods, and we may conveniently begin by employing the theories of Rudolf Bultmann as illustration.[5]

Bultmann is certain that Jesus spoke only of the advent of a future Son of Man, an eschatological figure with whom Jesus never identified himself. The earthly Son of Man sayings are largely misunder-

---

[1] *Lordship*, p. 26.

[2] Enoch, Elijah, Moses, the righteous man in Wisd. 2–5, etc.

[3] II Macc. 7.37f.; IV Macc. 1.11; 6.28f. Both atonement and exaltation, however, could be found in IV Macc. 17.20ff.

[4] Although denying that *the Son of Man* as a title results simply from a mistaken interpretation of an idiom, Schweizer believes that Jesus employed it in logia like Luke 6.22; 7.34; 9.58; 11.30; 12.10 as a kind of circumlocution for his own person.

[5] A very similar view was first presented in *The Beginnings of Christianity*, London, 1920–33 by F. Jackson and K. Lake, art. 'Christology', I, pp. 368ff. See Knox, *Death of Christ*, pp. 87ff.

standings of *bar nāšā*. Jesus was either referring to himself or to *man* as mankind.[1] The sayings which predicate suffering of the Son of Man are all creations of the Hellenistic Church which came to believe that Jesus was himself the Son of Man.[2] Although Bultmann holds that the myth of a First or Primal Man has influenced the Gospel of John, he believes that its only impress on the synoptic sayings was mediated through Jewish eschatology and apocalyptic. Jesus, then, spoke simply enough about a coming eschatological deliverer, a Messiah-like figure found in Daniel, I Enoch, II (4) Esdras and II Baruch. Jesus saw himself as a messenger, proclaiming the imminence of the approaching day and the Son of Man's appearance.

In large measure the arguments against Bultmann's thesis must be postponed to chapter VIII where we may discuss the passion predictions at some length. Here, however, two difficulties with his theory must be noticed.

Any attractiveness in the theory of a misunderstood idiom begins to lose much of its force when we are asked to believe that it was a *part-time* misunderstanding. It is perhaps just conceivable that Jesus regularly used an expression which, in some circles at least, was freighted with overtones, while yet he himself employed it merely as an idiomatic substitute for *I* while intending none of these overtones. It is, however, very hard to believe that he used it in both ways and that neither he nor his immediate followers passed on any means of distinguishing between the two usages.[3]

Secondly, on Bultmann's view, we are required to suppose that the later Church (and he does refer to it as the *Hellenistic* Church),[4] a Church which Bultmann believes did not even understand the original expression,[5] nevertheless made use of this same term for the process of reading Jesus' passion predictions back into the tradition. Why would they do this so indirectly? And, if there was some reason for being so indirect and mysterious, why would they choose a

---

[1] The first explanation is usually given preference. *The Theology of the New Testament*, ET, London, 1952–5, I, p. 30.

[2] So called by Bultmann *vaticinia ex eventu*. *Theology* I, pp. 26ff. Individual texts are discussed in his *History of the Synoptic Tradition*. In fact, however, Bultmann rejects the suffering sayings without much real argument. They all stem directly from the Marcan tradition. *Theology* I, pp. 29f.; *Synoptic Tradition*, p. 52 n. 1.

[3] And so, among others, Tödt, *Son of Man*, pp. 124, 127, 138; Teeple, *JBL* 84, 1965, pp. 231ff., and Higgins, *Son of Man*, pp. 26, 123 n. 1, wholly reject this method and see that the expression must everywhere be a title of special meaning.

[4] *Theology* I, p. 30.

[5] *Ibid.*

Semitic designation otherwise no longer in use as a Christological title?[1]

The force of both of these criticisms is seen and accepted in the closely argued study of Heinz Tödt.[2] The bulk of the Son of Man sayings cannot be creations of the later Church, but must instead belong to the early Palestinian traditions where the designation was still valued and used. We cannot presume at this early stage accidents due to a misunderstood idiom. None the less, in so far as texts authentic with Jesus are concerned, Tödt's actual results are just as drastic.

His procedures follow in detailed fashion along the lines of source and form-criticism. The three classes of sayings are so analysed in three separate chapters. Each text is studied in the light of the pre-dilections and editorial tendencies of each synoptic evangelist. The results are as follows: the sayings in Q can be shown to be the earliest. These never tell of the suffering of the Son of Man. Such mainly stem from Mark's source and are later insertions into the tradition. In Q only the eschatological appearance of the Son of Man (with little apocalyptic detail)[3] and several sayings about his earthly presence are found. These latter can be accounted for by the eagerness of the very early Church to identify Jesus with the Son of Man. This Church, however, attributed to the earthly Jesus only the *authority* ($\dot{\epsilon}\xi o\upsilon\sigma\dot{\iota}\alpha$) of the Son of Man. They carefully refrained from giving to him the end-of-the-ages *power* ($\delta\acute{\upsilon}\nu\alpha\mu\iota\varsigma$) of the heavenly figure.[4]

Slightly later the communities continued this process by creating for Jesus, their leader, in the name of the Son of Man, sayings such as Mark 2.10 and 2.28. The suffering predictions were also now fashioned, and the Son of Man title was used for these because of the grandeur and *mystique* associated with it, and because the Church now unquestionably assumed that Jesus was the Son of Man. This usage would give a certain verisimilitude to the traditions. Also, at about this time, and afterwards under the pressures of apocalyptic fervour,

---

[1] So Bultmann himself argues, *op. cit.*, pp. 79f. And see Stauffer, *Theology*, p. 328 n. 838 and, again, Knox, *op. cit.*, p. 57.

[2] 'Why should the Hellenistic community have been interested in transferring an Aramaic name to Jesus? We learn from the New Testament texts that the name Son of Man was not current within the Hellenistic community . . .' (Tödt, *op. cit.*, p. 117). See also Higgins, *op. cit.*, p. 33.

[3] For the rejection of these details see *op. cit.*, pp. 34f., 65f. Much of this has been added by the Matthean tradition, pp. 68ff.

[4] *Op. cit.*, p. 295.

features from Dan. 7.13 and elsewhere were read into Jesus' less highly imaginative words about the future Son of Man.

Jesus' own teaching about the Son of Man can thus be traced back to a few sayings: Matt. 24.27 (Luke 17.24); Matt. 24.37, 39 (Luke 17.26, and also 17.30); Matt. 24.44 (Luke 12.40); Luke 11.30 (more original than Matt. 12.40), and the saying at the heart of Luke 12.8f. and Mark 8.38. These all are characterized by soteriological interests and the absence of Christological overtones, for Jesus did not think of himself as the Son of Man.[1] At the same time, Jesus did believe that his own mission was integrally involved with the approaching appearance of the Son of Man. Thus, inherent in his message, is a promise of reward by the Son of Man for those who follow Jesus and punishment for those who do not. The basic theme is, however, so simple that it is almost synonymous with 'Repent, for the Kingdom of God is at hand'.[2] This can be regarded as further proof of the authenticity of these sayings. Tödt also believes that because these texts lack any reference to scripture for authentication (a habit which developed in the early Church), we can place even more reliance on them as Jesus' own words. Jesus' authentic preaching was delivered on the basis of his own sense of authority and mission.

The simplicity of the Son of Man figure which thus emerges can further be demonstrated by the absence of any attribution of pre-existence or stress on themes of humility (or suffering) and consequent exaltation. These are the product of the Church in the aftermath of the Easter experience.[3] Clearly, then, there is no need to resort to any other materials for the explanation of such features; nor need we exercise ourselves in seeking to find a more developed conception of the Son of Man which might have influenced Jesus in his lifetime.[4]

Tödt's careful answer to the Son of Man problem has much value in that he has striven to find a genuine historical setting for all the

---

[1] Op. cit., pp. 42, 67, etc.

[2] Simplicity is an important criterion in assessing the content of Jesus' message. 'In Jesus' teaching all importance is attached to the fact that God's reign stands at the door, that the Son of Man will come.' Op. cit., p. 66. Tödt cannot believe that Jesus would have spoken in a contradictory manner about the Son of Man. Op. cit., p. 124, etc. One wonders, however, what might have happened had Tödt heeded strictures he lays upon Vielhauer (op. cit., p. 336): even though ideas from the same source may contain certain differences and not be wholly integrated, this does not prove that one or the other is unauthentic.

[3] Op. cit., pp. 284ff. Emphasis on such texts as Phil. 2.6ff. has led commentators into the error of reading such ideas back into the authentic Gospel traditions.

[4] So his very summary treatment of the background, op. cit., 22ff., esp. p. 24 n. 1.

sayings.[1] While the great majority of these logia are seen to be the work of the disciples, still each has its place as part of a possible historical development and in a life-situation. The word *possible*, however, must be emphasized: it *might* have happened this way, but is it really as likely as Tödt believes?

As was the case with Vielhauer's argument, we are again left with the need to imagine a group of disciples, otherwise wholly unknown and lost without other trace,[2] who advanced a great deal of new teaching about Jesus—the Son of Man. Granted that Tödt has supplied us with an original core of sayings out of which such a tradition could have grown, and he has been careful, for the most part, to confine the activity which caused these sayings to be formulated to the early Palestinian Church, where such disciples might more feasibly have flourished and disappeared; but it is still a remarkable set of circumstances.

Not only this, but how careful must they have been in their treatment of the traditions. Only Jesus uses the title; there is not a slip in any of the sources by the disciples who worshipped him by this name above all others.[3] Though Tödt maintains that this was in adherence to the fact that the basic traditions showed only Jesus using the title, Tödt himself has narrowed this basis so drastically that one wonders how it could so have imbued and guided all else.

Actually our credulity about the care which these disciples exercised must be stretched a good deal further, for the distinction that Jesus always spoke of the heavenly Son of Man as though of another was retained by disciples who believed he was this figure even as new sayings of the type were formulated. Yet more: even those logia (of the earthly-working and suffering types) which seem to assume an identification between Jesus and the Son of Man were not so constructed as to do this with absolute clarity. Despite their own beliefs,

[1] For praise of Tödt and also Schweizer in their efforts to establish a genuine historical context for the sayings, see P. C. Hodgson, 'The Son of Man Problem and Historical Knowledge', *JR* 41, 1961, pp. 91ff.

[2] Tödt agrees. There is not another sign outside of the Gospels!

[3] As G. Kittel once rightly asked, Why then did not Peter confess, 'Thou art the Son of Man' instead of 'Thou art the Christ' at Caesarea Philippi? Cf. art. 'Menschensohn', *RGG*[2] (1929) III, col. 2119. (See our interpretation of this passage in ch. VIII). The attempt by R. E. C. Formesyn ('Was There a Pronominal Connection for the "Bar Nasha" Selfdesignation?' *NT* 8, 1966, pp. 1ff.) to answer this question finds no support whatsoever in Dan. 7.13 and I Enoch. Though he professes to be bolstering the views of Tödt and Hahn, his suggestion could only play havoc with their belief that the authentic sayings show Jesus speaking of another figure.

these hypothetical disciples somehow managed to leave the association in a rather vague condition and, even if unintentionally, satu-
rated with a kind of mystery.

And from where did Jesus get this great sense of authority? Would
he have offered no justification for his words and acts other than his
own sense of mission? Might he not have seen himself in some role or
office which permitted him to speak and act in the way that he did?

And is authority always, as Tödt suggests, the key to an understanding of the Son of Man sayings? Is not an excess of interpretation
required in order to read this issue into vital sayings like Matt. 11.19
= Luke 7.34 and Matt. 8.20 = Luke 9.58? If so, if these sayings are
not to be so accounted for, can it be that the Church would have
formulated them and attributed them to their Lord? Were it not for
the insistence that Jesus could not have spoken as the Son of Man on
earth, do not these logia have as much or more a claim on authenticity as any others?

Is it legitimate to label the capacity to rise from the dead as
authority? Is it not rather a genuine supranatural *power* attributed to
the Son of Man on earth? If so (and regardless of the authenticity of
such sayings) what happens to the fine distinctions which Tödt has
tried to establish?

Our major criticisms, however, involve methodology. Tödt's
analyses are almost exclusively of a literary character. We ourselves
are sympathetic with the desire to set other matters aside and confine
oneself to such an approach, but we wonder if it can really be pro-
ductive of anything but an abstraction. Can one hope, for instance,
to solve the Son of Man problem in the synoptic texts while making
hardly a reference to both parallel and divergent sayings in John's
Gospel?

By closely restricting his research into the background of the term
Tödt has made it abundantly clear from the start that he does not
believe Jesus could have conceived of any Son of Man figure who
would have been on earth. Such an idea would not have been feasible
until the faith of Christians made it so. Therefore logia which tell of
an earthly Son of Man are fully suspect before their examination
begins. Yet Tödt himself has criticized Vielhauer for assuming too
much knowledge about the Son of Man on the basis of so scanty a
known background as Daniel, I Enoch and II (4) Esdras. And if
Tödt is right, as he may well be, to maintain that Jesus was not
directly influenced by any of these, how can it be assumed with such

certainty that the only Son of Man Jesus knew about was a distant heavenly figure? Does not research which finds so little that directly bears upon the Gospels' way of speaking about the Son of Man suggest that the field of study might need to be broadened or even that the immediate background for Jesus' conception of the Son of Man is unknown to us?

It may be countered that it is the examination of the Gospel sayings themselves which indicates that only logia telling of the heavenly Son of Man can be authentic. Yet, unless great care is exercised, one may find that he has been indulging a circular argument. The merits of Q, for instance, as a viable source[1] and as very nearly the sole deposit of anything which might go back to Jesus, are far from obvious to all. And is it very meaningful to use (as is frequently done) an argument like this?

The manner in which the Son of Man is used in Mark 2.10, which contrasts with the authentic parousia sayings, supports our assumption that the saying was formed by the community.[2]

[1] According to Tödt (*op. cit.*, pp. 247ff.), Q derives from a group of very early Christians primarily interested in carrying on the teaching of Jesus. Yet even if this were so (and it involves not only a highly interpretative view of the Q material but also a number of assumptions about the forms of earliest Christianity), how can we be sure that the document is not itself selective and *biased* in its interpretation of Jesus' teaching? What, for instance, if it came from a circle akin to that represented by the Epistle of James? Is it not quite conceivable that such a group may have been less *Christological* than Jesus himself?

There are many other questions which would need to be asked about the possibilities that Mark, Matthew or Luke have recorded some Q material left out by the others or that all three have incorporated portions of Q so that these passages now seem *Marcan* to our eyes. With regard to the Q theory and the Son of Man passion sayings, see our discussion in ch. VIII regarding these logia. In the meantime, one must ask about the nature of any document or group which was not strongly affected by the passion and resurrection events. If enough time had passed so that Jesus, on Tödt's view, could now be identified with the Son of Man and so that sayings about him as the Son of Man on earth had been fashioned, surely also there was time for some development with regard to the passion materials. If, then, the group which collected and composed Q was at all representative of early Christianity, Q can hardly be representative of all their thought. Otherwise, again, Q must have been the product of so anomalous a Christian group that we certainly must wonder what they did represent.

[2] *Op. cit.*, p. 130. Luke 17.25 and 22.48 are examples of sayings which receive a very similar treatment. Elsewhere Tödt employs the argument from singularity: a particular saying could not have come from Jesus, since it has no parallels in the tradition. Another tool used is that which seeks to discover some trace of an evangelist's or of the later Church's language in certain logia. Rarely is it asked whether the evangelist or his tradition might have adapted an authentic saying. See our discussion of these matters in ch. VIII.

We can hardly claim some novel methodology of our own which escapes the difficulties of all circular argumentation, but we do dispute Tödt's frequent use of the word *proved* in conjunction with his discussions. Once his arguments are reduced to their essentials, they seem to us to be caught in the grooves of syllogisms whose major premise is always that Jesus could have spoken only of the heavenly Son of Man.[1] It is our intention to give grounds for severely questioning this major premise, after which we think that many of the logia may appear in a quite different light.

Since our criticisms of Tödt were first formed there has appeared not only an English translation of his original German study (which was published in 1959) but also, in what appears to be the *new wave* of thinking on the subject, works by Hahn,[2] Higgins[3] and Fuller[4] which either are very appreciative of Tödt's approach or come to rather similar independent conclusions. We have found this all very useful and stimulating, as it has forced us to sharpen our own thinking on these matters, and we shall, of course, want to pay special attention to their ideas as we continue.

[1] Cf. M. D. Hooker, *The Son of Man in Mark: A Study of the Background of the Term Son of Man and its Use in St Mark's Gospel*, London, 1967. By omitting this premise she finds all the Marcan Son of Man sayings to have a claim on authenticity. We are grateful to Miss Hooker for permitting us to see this study before its publication, for certainly we agree with many of its insights. Cf. also Marshall *NTS* 12, 1965/6, pp. 327ff.

[2] In *Christologische Hoheitstitel*, pp. 13ff., Hahn accepts most of Tödt's findings and argues that they fit in with his understanding of the development of the Son of Man logia in the Fourth Gospel and with the whole development of the Christological pattern. For views which were already in advance of Bultmann's position in the direction of that of Tödt and Hahn (but which, in fact, probably stand closer to Higgins's present position), see the summary by G. Iber in *TLZ* 80, 1955, cols. 115f. Cf. also Bornkamm, *Jesus of Nazareth*, pp. 228ff.; W. Marxsen, *Anfangsproblem der Christologie*[2], Gütersloh, 1964, pp. 20ff.

[3] *Jesus and the Son of Man*. Although Higgins has clearly gone ahead on independent lines, we feel that Tödt (*op. cit.*, pp. 348ff.) is fully justified in accepting him as far more a friend than a foe. Higgins's attitudes toward the Servant and Son Christologies (in which areas he is far less critical than he is with the Son of Man) differ from Tödt's, and he makes many points of his own on particular sayings; but his basic approach and results, in so far as the Son of Man is concerned, are similar. With regard to Higgin's views on the Fourth Gospel, see below in ch. VII.

[4] In *The Foundations of New Testament Christology*, Fuller finds himself won over by what might be called the Tödt-Hahn line. With minor deviations he accepts their understanding of the Son of Man development which he calls 'the most primitive Christology of all'. He must, however, have a few mental reservations, for he is commendably candid about his awareness that sayings are sometimes being fitted to a theory rather than *vice versa* (*op. cit.*, p. 124) and feels sufficiently doubtful about Tödt's approach to several of the sayings to suggest a return to the mistaken idiom theory in certain cases (*op. cit.*, p. 125).

C. *More comprehensive answers*

The third and last category is that of solutions which seek a more comprehensive answer by regarding as authentic many both of the earthly suffering and of the heavenly Son of Man sayings. Since in this study we also shall be attempting a solution which will result in a comprehensive view and thus will be dealing with some of the following ideas at a later stage, it is best that we here treat them somewhat summarily.

In the main, these more inclusive theories reveal one of two tendencies: either they emphasize the role of Jesus' self-consciousness as the vital constructive and integrating factor in the Gospels' conception of the Son of Man, or else they contend that the figure of the suffering and yet glorious Son of Man was already known in Jesus' time and was adopted and adapted by him. This is not to say, of course, that the two approaches are mutually exclusive; they can be combined in various ways. But the stress generally falls on one or the other.

The theories which focus upon Jesus' self-consciousness are difficult to criticize. There is little basis for objectivity, and we are forced to walk, more than ever, upon the quicksands of subjective reasoning. On the other hand, Jesus did have a self-consciousness, and to ignore this would not only be to empty the incarnation of all meaning, but it would, as a principle, totally dehumanize history. Obviously, in the last analysis, some room has got to be left for his personality and sense of mission.

And yet there is another side to the incarnation, for Jesus entered history as an historical person. To maintain that Christianity is an historical religion while yet minimizing the effects of history upon its formation is, at the very least, to indulge an acute distortion. If Jesus did teach about the Son of Man, it is likely that he based his teaching upon ideas and conceptions which were part of his environment. Indeed, it is hard to believe that he would have wished to do otherwise. The needs of communication demand this, and we shall assume that preaching and teaching are evidence of a desire to communicate.

Few scholars, however, go quite so far as to contend that Jesus, through his own religious genius and imagination alone, fabricated the figure of the Son of Man virtually out of thin air. Yet there are theories which would seem to provide very little air. It is sometimes suggested that on the basis of one Old Testament text (Dan. 7.13)

Jesus formulated the whole conception. Here, after all, it is maintained, can be found the single scriptural reference to the Son of Man which is explicitly used in the Gospels.[1] And, however uncertain the exegesis of the Danielic scene may be, we have there an exalted figure, the features of which correspond in several ways to the eschatological judge and champion of the Gospels. The earthly ministry and the suffering of the Son of Man can then best be explained as the result of Jesus' own sense of mission. Jesus knew that he was the Son of Man or else that he was destined to become the Son of Man after his resurrection. In the latter case he was a kind of Son of Man designate.[2] In his own life he found the calling to an earthly ministry, the necessity of suffering and a belief in an exaltation or vindication yet to come.

Occasionally this interpretation is defended on the grounds that Jesus might have deliberately chosen a title which was little known and vaguely understood.[3] It served him as a form of protection against undesired attributions of messiahship by those who could not understand his true mission. Yet this thesis hardly does justice to the compelling manner in which suffering and glory are predicated of the Son of Man. It seems far more a motivation of great and powerful concern than a *device* with little content or meaning in its own right.

Often this theory of Danielic derivation is expanded by reference to the Suffering Servant from II Isaiah. From Daniel came the picture of exalted glory; from Isaiah was derived the idea of a suffering and atoning figure. From these two Old Testament conceptions

[1] See W. Manson, *Jesus, the Messiah*, p. 117; C. F. D. Moule, *The Phenomenon of the New Testament* (SBT, Second Series 1), 1967, pp. 34f. For a classic presentation of this interpretation see V. Taylor, *The Names of Jesus*, London, 1953, pp. 25ff. '. . . there is good reason, I believe, to think that Jesus's use of the title was independently derived from reflection upon the basic Old Testament passage, Dan. 7.13.' The popularity of this view, esp. among English scholars, is indicated by Taylor's own footnote to the statement just quoted. See Mowinckel's critical comments on this attitude in *HTC*, pp. 348ff.; and cf. C. L. J. Proudman, 'Remarks on the "Son of Man" ', *CJT* 12, 1966, pp. 128ff.

[2] On Jesus as the Son of Man *designatus*, see R. Otto, *The Kingdom of God and the Son of Man*, London, 1938, p. 219, and T. Preiss, *Life in Christ*, ET (SBT 13), 1954, p. 48. The view approximates that of A. Schweitzer in *The Quest of the Historical Jesus*[2], ET, London, 1911, pp. 363, 393. See also R. H. Fuller in *The Mission and Achievement of Jesus* (SBT 12), 1954, pp. 95ff., who formerly understood Jesus to be speaking proleptically of the Son of Man in the same way that he speaks proleptically of the Kingdom of God as already present on earth.

[3] So, among others, Fuller, *Mission and Achievement*, pp. 106ff.; E. Percy, *Die Botschaft Jesu* (Lunds Universitets Årsskrift, nf. Avd. 1, Bd. 49/5), Lund, 1953, p. 259; Coppens in *Le Fils de l'Homme*, pp. 85ff.

Jesus fashioned his own understanding of a suffering Son of Man.[1]
There are several telling criticisms which have been levelled against this proposed form of synthesis. It is, in the first place, problematical as to whether direct influences from the Isaianic Servant played much part at all in Jesus' teaching;[2] any direct relationship with the Son of Man logia is even more questionable. In addition, there has been given (at least in the usual forms in which the theory is stated) no clear evidence that the Son of Man and the Suffering Servant were previously combined in Judaism or that they had much, if anything, to do with one another.[3] It may well be necessary, therefore, if we are to adopt this kind of a Son of Man-Suffering Servant synthesis, to stake our credence upon what is an almost wholly unique and novel creation by Jesus.[4]

Also damaging to this theory is the understanding of Jesus' self-consciousness upon which it is based. To say that this turns him into a kind of Bible concordance is perhaps an exaggeration, but he does, in this view, seem more like a scholar studying and conflating texts than a leader of men and a preacher of repentance and eschatological salvation. To contend that Jesus, or anyone, built so dynamic and many-sided a figure on the basis of texts from two points in the Old Testament is, to this writer, incredible. It would appear to suggest that Jesus fashioned his private conception in total independence of the historical and environmental forces which surrounded him, arriving at this hybrid figure by means of solitary inspiration.[5]

This same thesis has, however, been given a variation in the dis-

---

[1] See again Fuller, *op. cit.*, p. 107; T. W. Manson, *The Servant-Messiah*, Cambridge, 1953, esp. pp. 72f.; C. H. Dodd, *According to the Scriptures*, London, 1952, p. 119; W. Manson, *op. cit.*, p. 131; Richardson, *Theology*, pp. 135f.; O. Cullmann, *The Christology of the New Testament*, ET, London, 1959, pp. 81, 175, 183f.

[2] See esp. M. Hooker, *Jesus and the Servant*, London, 1959, pp. 62ff.; also the title essay in H. H. Rowley's *The Servant of the Lord and Other Essays on the Old Testament*, London, 1952. It is, chiefly according to Acts, a belief of the Church, and this should put us doubly on guard against the dangers of its having been read back into the Gospels. See F. W. Beare's severe rejection of the authentic place of the Servant in the Gospels in *The Earliest Records of Jesus*, Oxford, 1962, p. 229, and also that of W. G. Kümmel, *Promise and Fulfilment*, ET (SBT 23), 1957, p. 73.

[3] This, of course, is debated. See esp. in ch. IV. J. Jeremias is the scholar who has most consistently argued for the importance of the suffering motif and the place of the Servant of God idea both in late Judaism and in the New Testament. See W. Zimmerli and J. Jeremias, *The Servant of God*[2], ET (SBT 20), 1965, pp. 45ff.

[4] For examples of this stress on a unique synthesis, see the views of Fuller, Dodd, etc., cited above.

[5] Mowinckel, *HTC*, p. 347 n. 3: 'It is a question, not of literary influences, but of traditions and ideas which were in circulation.'

cussions of T. W. Manson, who has emphasized the *corporate* nature of the Son of Man figure.[1] Primary support for this is found in Dan. 7, where it might appear (vv. 22ff.) that the 'saints of the Most High' are used synonymously with the earlier expression 'one like a son of man'. Manson argued that the same corporate features can be found in the Suffering Servant as well as in messianic conceptions. A similar oscillation between the individual and the corporate is said to be characteristic of the Son of Man of the Gospels. Emphasis is placed upon the possibility that Jesus might once have imagined that some of his disciples would die with him.[2] The Son of Man actually became a single personification only in the mind of Jesus and only after circumstances had forced him to realize that he alone could carry out the mission of the saints of the Most High as *the* Son of Man.

In order to defend his thesis Manson felt constrained to discover a pattern of development in the Gospels.[3] Jesus spoke little, if at all, of the Son of Man until the decisive turning-point in his ministry (Peter's confession at Caesarea Philippi and the transfiguration). From that time on the conviction grew that he alone must do the work of the Son of Man and finally that he would be vindicated by God and exalted in this role. In the end, he alone was the remnant from which the new Israel would be formed.[4]

Manson's views have been found wanting by a number of scholars.[5] The difficulty of establishing his understandings in the crucial arena of the Gospel sayings themselves has been often pointed out. In addition, not only is his theory of a development in the Son of Man logia undemonstrable,[6] but, even if there were the semblance of such

[1] *The Teaching of Jesus*, Cambridge, 1931, pp. 211ff.; 'The Son of Man in Daniel, Enoch and the Gospels', *BJRL* 32, 1950, pp. 171ff.; *The Servant-Messiah*, pp. 72ff.

[2] See 'The New Testament Basis of the Doctrine of the Church', *JEH* 1, 1950, p. 6. Here Manson suggests that it was because the disciples understood the Son of Man as a collective term that they misunderstood the passion predictions. In 'Realized Eschatology and the Messianic Secret' in *Studies in the Gospels: Essays in Memory of R. H. Lightfoot* (ed. D. E. Nineham), Oxford, 1955, pp. 209ff., Manson also finds that this collective conception was at the basis of the so-called messianic secret.

[3] *Teaching of Jesus*, pp. 213ff.

[4] *Op. cit.*, pp. 227ff.

[5] Sjöberg, *verborgene Menschensohn*, p. 241 n. 1. (Sjöberg believes that the Son of Man is already an individual figure in I Enoch. Manson earlier rejected this, *op. cit.*, p. 229, and, in any case, continued to question the relevance or decisiveness of the views in I Enoch for those of Jesus.) Cf. Percy, *Botschaft Jesu*, p. 239 n. 1; Schweizer, *Lordship*, p. 44; McCown, *JR* 28, 1948, p. 9; Higgins, *Son of Man*, p. 20.

[6] While it is true that Mark has only two Son of Man sayings before Caesarea

a progression, it is the very order in which the events, stories and sayings of Jesus' ministry are presented which has the least claim to a firm basis in the tradition. Were we, for the sake of argument, yet to grant Manson this development, and while it might be agreed that several texts could admit of a corporate sense, still no provision has been made for a truly adequate background which would have made the figure of the Son of Man meaningful to others in Jesus' lifetime.

Some scholars have thought themselves to find the missing background in the 'Similitudes of Enoch' (I Enoch 37–71), where the designation appears with some frequency.[1] Rudolf Otto, for one, has argued that in this figure, derived in part from Daniel, of an eschatological champion and judge who is pre-existent and hidden with God before the creation of the world we have the forerunner of Jesus' Son of Man. Since it would seem, at the end of the 'Similitudes', that the earthly Enoch is somehow exalted to become this Son of Man, the possibility becomes more intriguing. There may even have been a circle of disciples, themselves speculating about the Son of Man, out of whose faith the 'Similitudes' were written and with which group Jesus could have had some direct or indirect contact.[2]

Because the themes of mystery, concealment and revelation play roles in I Enoch and may be found in the Gospels, Erik Sjöberg has also contended that I Enoch provides the vital background.[3] The Enochian Son of Man is a divergent and specialized form of the messianic ideal[4] which was popular in certain restricted circles at about the time of Jesus.[5] It was against this background that Jesus

---

Philippi and Luke only four and none of these are eschatological, Matthew has ten and several of these are eschatological. Q, if there be a Q, cannot be reconstructed with any confidence whatsoever. In fact, in order to conform the Gospels to his thesis, Manson treated the various sayings with a radicality otherwise surprising in him. He also found it necessary to deal with several of the early, more *individualistic* Son of Man logia by use of the mistaken idiom theory.

[1] Also often adduced at this point are the references in II(4) Esd. 13 and possible allusions to the figure at other points in the late Jewish literature. These texts will all be discussed in ch. IV.

[2] Otto, *The Kingdom of God and the Son of Man*, pp. 177, 189ff., 212ff.

[3] Sjöberg, *verborgene Menschensohn*. In I Enoch, pp. 44ff., in the Gospels, pp. 99ff. Many of the themes are seen to be general in late Jewish apocalyptic, *op. cit.*, pp. 41ff.

[4] See *Henochbuch*, pp. 140ff., and further on Sjöberg's views on I Enoch in our ch. IV. Otto (*op. cit.*, pp. 193f., 389ff.) felt that the Son of Man was a syncretistic figure, fused now with messianic ideas, but perhaps ultimately derived from the *fravashi* conception of Iran. See below in ch. II.

[5] *Henochbuch*, pp. 59f.

preached the mystery of his own mission, and this, in fact, provides the clue for an understanding of the so-called *messianic secret* in the Gospels.[1] Jesus was the pre-existent, end-of-the-ages Son of Man on earth, but his identity and true nature had to be hidden (except from chosen disciples) until the final revelation.[2]

Sjöberg, however, has in some ways not gone nearly so far in his claims as did Otto. While Otto believed that a kind of direct literary influence between I Enoch and the Gospels could be established,[3] Sjöberg is more content to show that the figure in I Enoch was a part of the *milieu* in which Jesus lived.[4] There is no question of one delimiting source, for Jesus leaves out features found in I Enoch and develops others which are not a part of the earlier work. Both Sjöberg and Otto, for example, are convinced that no genuine suffering is to be found in connection with the Son of Man in I Enoch.[5]

This admission, however, is a serious weakness if the Son of Man in I Enoch is to be regarded as anything more than a minor reflection of an idea used by Jesus. In the Gospels suffering is at the centre of the teaching; this was the Son of Man's destiny. Just here I Enoch fails us.

It is, in fact, for the reason that there are so many disparate features between I Enoch and the Gospels that a number of scholars have minimized I Enoch's influence or even rejected it outright.[6] Tödt argues that the whole mood and the eschatology are different. He feels as well that Sjöberg has greatly exaggerated or even manufactured any possible hints of pre-existence or concealment regarding the Son of Man in the Gospels.[7] (And, it must be said, any theme of concealment really only pertains to the Messiah, and the two titles

---

[1] See *Henochbuch*, p. 102; *verborgene Menschensohn*, pp. 1, 40, and also Otto, *op. cit.*, pp. 192, 233f.

[2] *Op. cit.*, pp. 219ff. On this point see also T. Preiss, *Le Fils de l'Homme*, Montpellier, 1951, pp. 44f.

[3] Otto, *op. cit.*, pp. 189ff., 382ff.

[4] There is no doubt but that Jesus found himself in this *milieu*, *verborgene Menschensohn*, p. 242. Sjöberg here also quotes Mowinckel with approval: these ideas about the Son of Man were 'in the air'. See *HTC*, p. 417.

[5] Otto, *op. cit.*, p. 255; Sjöberg, *Henochbuch*, pp. 116ff.; *verborgene Menschensohn*, pp. 225ff. See also Mowinckel, *HTC*, pp. 410ff.

[6] Forcefully by J. Y. Campbell, *JTS* 48, 1947, pp. 145ff. The challenge to the integrity of the Son of Man passages in I Enoch and their dating will be taken up in ch. IV.

[7] Tödt, *Son of Man*, pp. 300ff. Cf. T. A. Burkill, 'The Hidden Son of Man in St Mark's Gospel', *ZNW* 52, 1961, pp. 189ff. Enoch's Son of Man is hidden in heaven, not on earth.

cannot be so easily equated in the Gospels; nor is it at all clear that the two designations belong to the same levels of tradition.) While Enoch might be seen to become the Son of Man in heaven by a kind of exaltation, Jesus could only be the pre-existent Son of Man on earth by some incarnation, of which the Gospels say nothing. In any event, Jewish apocalyptic does not suggest any manner of a Son of Man at work on earth.[1] In addition, the pre-existent, heavenly Son of Man in I Enoch is a passive figure, while Jesus is reported to have been a Son of Man acting with full authority on earth.

Probably we have said enough to indicate the inadequacy of I Enoch as the explanation for the Son of Man in the Gospels.[2] I Enoch may have a place in the story, but, even coupled with the short references in Daniel and II (4) Esdras, it is very doubtful if such can tell the whole story. None of these, separately or together, would provide a sufficient background for a Son of Man who walks the earth, suffers and later appears in heaven.

Attempts have therefore been made to derive the Son of Man from the well-known hypostatization of Wisdom, perhaps also in some connection with *Logos* speculation.[3] Jewish writings speak of a heavenly role for Wisdom, of the manner in which mankind mistreats Wisdom. In addition, a wise man might be said to represent Wisdom on earth. Yet the figures of the Son of Man and of Wisdom are so different (eschatological *versus* cosmological; Wisdom is almost always a rather less personal hypostatization and often seen as female) that such hypotheses are difficult to square with the facts. Undoubtedly the Son of Man has wisdom, but this, as we shall see, is to be explained otherwise than by understanding him as Wisdom or a Wisdom figure. Also, as we again shall see, the sense in which Wisdom

---

[1] This point is admitted by Sjöberg. It was a new feature in Jesus' teaching; *verborgene Menschensohn*, pp. 245f.

[2] H. H. Rowley, among others, has asked the always pertinent question: Why, if I Enoch is so important to an understanding of the Gospels, is the figure of Enoch himself never even mentioned? *The Relevance of Apocalyptic*, London, 1944, p. 56 n. 1.

[3] See A. Feuillet, 'Le Fils de l'Homme de Daniel et la tradition Biblique', *RB* 60, 1953, pp. 170ff., 321ff., who believes that the Wisdom conception has mixed with features of the prophetic Messiah and Ezekiel's Son of Man. Emphasizing the role of both Wisdom and the Adam figure is G. Quispel, 'Der gnostische Anthropos und die jüdische Tradition', *Eranos Jahrbuch* 32, 1953, pp. 195ff. For a discussion and, in the main, a rejection of such theories, see J. Coppens, 'Le messianisme sapiental et les origines littéraires du Fils de l'homme daniélique' in *Wisdom in Israel and in the Ancient Near East* (*VT* Suppl. III, ed. M. Noth and D. W. Thomas), 1955, pp. 33ff.

came down from heaven to be or to indwell a unique man does not become a feature of the Son of Man story until after Jesus' lifetime.

More promising, perhaps, are the efforts to see a relationship between the Son of Man and ideas which are ultimately derived from once-popular myths and rituals of the Near East. In the figure of the Primal Man and/or the sacral king a few scholars have thought themselves to have uncovered the soil from which the Son of Man, as both a suffering and an exalted hero, could have grown. For a number of reasons, however, these theories have not yet won much success. Some of the difficulty is involved with the ambiguities of the evidence from Israel and other cultures. And then, even if such sub-soil can be uncovered, there has yet been a lack of organic connection between it and the New Testament growth. In addition, most of this research has been carried on by Old Testament and Near Eastern scholars who so far have not convinced many students of the New Testament that their findings should be carefully applied to the Gospel traditions. The efforts which have been made are, as a result, sporadic or episodic in character; the sweep of the ideas and their possible interrelationship have not been followed through from beginning to end, and, therefore, no convincing historical picture has yet emerged. Since, however, these are problems which will be deliberated in the ensuing chapters, we shall, with one exception, await further discussion of these theories until the relevant evidence has been examined.

The one exception is Oscar Cullmann, who more than any other New Testament scholar has adopted a form (though a rather truncated one) of this line of approach to the Gospels. In his *The Christology of the New Testament*[1] he argues for the authenticity of the Son of Man sayings[2] and believes that there was some connection between this term and the nexus of ideas involving First Man speculations, primarily as these are found in the rejuvenated concern with Adam.[3]

Unfortunately, however, Cullmann's thesis seems to fall down precisely at the points where it needs to have the most strength. The connection between Jesus and these ideas is not demonstrated. (If, as he suggests, the *Hellenists* are the group most responsible for preserving

---

[1] Pp. 137ff.

[2] *Op. cit.*, pp. 152ff. (although he sees at least two sayings as the likely result of a misunderstood idiom). Tödt, of course, hotly disputes Cullmann on this and other points in *Son of Man*, pp. 319ff.

[3] He stresses the possible link with later speculations about Adam in the Pseudo-Clementine literature (*op. cit.*, pp. 145ff.). See below in our chs. II and V.

and developing the Son of Man theology,[1] how much of it can
with any certainty then be traced back to Jesus?) 'We can only
conjecture about the connection Jesus drew between himself and the
first man.'[2] Furthermore, we are left with no better understanding of
a Son of Man who could suffer. This was again 'something completely new'[3] with Jesus, a combination on his part of the Son of Man
and the Suffering Servant. Clearly, if the suggested link with First
Man ideas is at all valid, some of these deficiencies must be made up,
and for this a thorough study of the materials will be necessary.

[1] *Op. cit.*, pp. 165ff. On the *Hellenists* see below in ch. VI.
[2] *Op. cit.*, p. 164.
[3] *Op. cit.*, p. 161.

II

THE FIRST MAN

O Man of a greatly exalted name.
(Hippolytus *Refutation* V, 6.5)

I. THE MAN HERO IN THE CENTURIES SURROUNDING
CHRISTIAN ORIGINS

WE ARE GOING to begin our own research into the background of the Son of Man figure not chronologically but by reviewing some of the evidence which has often been brought forward to show that the figure known to Jesus as the Son of Man was related to a rather widespread, roughly contemporary phenomenon. Many of the materials used to demonstrate this possibility are of a slightly later period (at least so far as their composition is concerned) and stem from various circles espousing a *gnostic*-type religion. This has been the starting-point for several earlier scholars, and it will be helpful and meaningful to begin here and then strive to trace some of the more basic ideas backward before adopting a more chronological procedure in the ensuing chapters.

Again and again in the Fifth Book as well as elsewhere in his *Refutation of All Heresies*,[1] Hippolytus found it necessary to report a variety of beliefs concerning some *Man* figure. During this period it is clear that over a wide area and in many versions or distortions some myth (or myths) concerning a *Manly* figure of heroic dimensions was making its influence felt. Usually he was given a title or description which played upon the word *man* in one of several languages. Thus we find *the Man* (ὁ ἄνθρωπος), *Protoanthropos, Archanthropos, Pre-existent Man, the Great Man, the Perfect Man, the Upper Man, the Inner Man, the Son of Man, the great and beautiful Man, Adam, Anush, Adamas, Adakas, the Heavenly Man, the True Man, the Man according to the Image* and other such designations.

---

[1] References are to the edition of P. Wendland (GCS XXVI), 1916, but translations, in part, from the ANCL ed., VI, 1868.

It is notoriously not true, however, that the many representations of this figure are all alike. Any acquaintance with the literature of this period would lead one to suspect a great deal of syncretism and outright confusion with regard to such a hero type, and this is certainly the case.[1]

(i) *According to Hippolytus*

Hippolytus in his *Refutation* gives us the most information outside the extant gnostic texts. Much of this data is clearly second- or third-hand, and a good deal of it is said to be derived from a group who called themselves the *Naassenes*, a second-century, Egyptian, gnostic sect heavily influenced by Judaism and Christianity, though they may very well have begun as a pagan or Jewish pagan movement in Syria.[2] In one of the more significant passages we read:

> In order, therefore, that finally the Great Man from above may be overpowered, 'from whom', as they say, 'the whole family named on earth and in the heavens' has been formed, to him was given a soul, that through the soul he might suffer; and the enslaved image may be punished of the Great and most glorious and Perfect Man, for even so they call him.[3]

There is magnified 'a Man and a Son of Man. And this Man is a hermaphrodite, and is denominated among them Adamas; and hymns many and various are made to him . . . "O denizen of heaven, O Man of a greatly exalted name".'[4]

This *Son of Man*, which is seemingly an ancillary title elsewhere

---

[1] There is no claim here to be comprehensive. We shall single out those descriptions in which *the Man* appears to play an important role. Some scholars also find the influence of the Man figure in other writings. References to a part of the vast literature on the subject will be found below and a useful bibliography in H.-M. Schenke's *Der Gott 'Mensch' in der Gnosis*, Göttingen, 1962.

[2] The name is probably derived from the Hebrew *nāḥāš* meaning snake. Many would relate this to the serpent in the garden of Eden story, though such may only be a secondary influence. They are to be linked with the Ophites (ὄφις = snake) and related groups of this same locale. See R. P. Casey, 'Naassenes and Ophites', *JTS* 27, 1926, pp. 374ff.; Schenke, *op. cit.*, pp. 57ff. R. Reitzenstein (*Poimandres. Studien zur griechisch-ägyptischen und frühchristlichen Literatur*, Leipzig, 1904, pp. 81ff., and with H. H. Schaeder, *Studien zum antiken Synkretismus, aus Iran und Griechenland*, Leipzig-Berlin, 1926, pp. 161ff.) was convinced that the influence of Christianity was a result of later syncretism. J. M. Creed, 'The Heavenly Man', *JTS* 26, 1925, pp. 113ff., thought this possible. Schenke believes the Jewish influence to have been integral. Cf. also H. Schlier, 'Der Mensch im Gnostizismus' in *Anthropologie religieuse* (*Numen* Suppl. II, ed. C. J. Bleeker), 1955, pp. 60ff.

[3] *Refutation* V, 7.7.

[4] *Refutation* V, 6.4f.

used explicitly of Jesus, may well be one of the signs of secondary Christian influence. We are told, moreover, that the Naassenes trace their belief through Mariamme to James, the Lord's brother, though Hippolytus wishes to argue that it actually derives from barbarian and Greek mystery rites, and in any case, much of the detail is almost certainly extra-Christian in origin.

There is added speculation, as a commentary on a Phrygian hymn to Attis,[1] concerning First Man figures such as the Boeotian Alalcomenes who sprang up from a lake, about Oannes of the Assyrians and several others. The Chaldeans spoke of an earthly Adam made according to the Image of the celebrated Man, Adam, who is above, and concerning whom there is said to be much discussion.[2] There follows the passage regarding the soul of the Adam above which fell into the Adam below.[3] Further information is given concerning this Adam, 'the blessed Man from above', from whom have come the souls of other men and who is present in all men.[4] The Samothracians worship Adam as the Primal Man (or *Archanthropos*) and are said to have in their temple two naked statues, one symbolizing the Primal Man, the other the spiritual Man who is born again to be in every respect like the Primal Man.[5]

From 'many waters' the one below cries out to the Man above to be saved. He is the one who, though lowly on earth, has been exalted to heaven, several Old Testament psalms being applied to him in this regard.[6] After adding further such bits of esoteric information concerning the Man, Hippolytus passes on to other forms of heresy.

Yet, as he proceeds, Hippolytus finds it necessary to make further allusions to this figure in other settings. The *Anthropos* had some part to play in the system of Valentinus, another Egyptian gnostic who

---

[1] On Attis, and Attis as seen by the Naassenes, see Creed, *op. cit.*, pp. 113ff.

[2] *Refutation* V, 7.3ff.

[3] The motif of *descent* has an important place in a number of gnostic works. We find not only descents from heaven but also the theme of going down into the *chaos*, the unformed, *watery* area, the darkness or the underworld, where are dangerous beasts, powers and dragons. From out of this the hero must be *born*, saved or rise by his own power. So, for example, in the *Pistis Sophia*, the heroine descends into chaos and is saved through her acts of repentance. See further below.

[4] *Refutation* V, 8.2ff.

[5] *Refutation* V, 8.9f. Epiphanius in *Panarion* (ed. K. Holl, GCS XXV, XXXI, XXXVII, 1915–33) XXVI, 3.1, quotes a fragment of the *Gospel of Eve* which tells of a 'tall man and another of shorter stature'. H.-C. Puech, 'Gnostic Gospels and Related Documents', *NTA* I, pp. 241f., conjectures that this may refer to the *Anthropos* and his earthly likeness or to the Man and the Son of Man.

[6] *Refutation* V, 8.15ff.

later went to Cyprus.[1] One Marcus, who at some point was in Gaul, styled Jesus as the Son of Man and the Man.[2] The *Anthropos* descended in Jesus. Satornilus, a second-century Syrian gnostic of Antioch, asserted that men were made from a copy of a brilliant image which appeared in heaven.[3] Monoïmus, an Arabian, is said to have spoken of *that Man* who can be equated with the universe. There is then a *son* of this Man who is begotten and subject to passion. 'Man was and his son was generated.'[4] The Son of Man is the image of the perfect, invisible Man. The Man is the father of the Son of Man. All things are produced from the Son of Man. Rays flow down from heaven from him.

The Elkasaites, a baptizing sect known from the beginning of the second century, held the figure of Adam in high repute and contended that Christ had appeared before in other men.[5] This conception of *reappearance* is frequently to be found in conjunction with Man speculations.

Hippolytus' report of Simon Magus's teaching concerning one standing below in a stream of water could well be a relic of an aspect of the Man mythology. This figure is begotten below in the image, but will one day stand above with the Infinite Power when his image is perfected.[6]

(ii) *According to Irenaeus*

Irenaeus in his *Against Heresies* supplements our sources of information. Indeed, the *Anthropos* did play a role in Valentinian thought.[7] Followers of Ptolemaeus and Colorbasus are said to have believed in a saviour, the Son of Man, who is a descendant of the *Anthropos*.[8] The

---

[1] *Refutation* VI, 30.3.

[2] *Refutation* VI, 11. For an earlier report on Marcus, on which Hippolytus' account is based, see Irenaeus, *Against Heresies* (*Libros quinque adversus Haereses*, ed. W. W. Harvey, Cambridge, 1857, but references in accord with ANCL ed., V, IX, 1910–11) I, 13ff. Marcus is thought to have been active in the second part of the second century.

[3] *Refutation* VI, 28.2. On his thought with regard to the ideal, heavenly man, see R. McL. Wilson, *The Gnostic Problem*, London, 1958, pp. 210, 251f.

[4] *Refutation* VIII, 12f.

[5] See *Refutation* IX, 13ff. Further on the Elkasaites see below in ch. V.

[6] *Refutation* VI, 17.1. Cf. H. Jonas, *The Gnostic Religion*[2], Boston, 1963, p. 105 and Wilson, *op. cit.*, p. 103.

[7] *Against Heresies* I, 1.1; I, 8.5. Clement of Alexandria tells of a myth used by Valentinus concerning a celestial Anthropos who can be thought to have an existence in the earthly Adam. (*Stromateis* II, 36.2–4.)

[8] *Against Heresies* I, 12.3. On Ptolemaeus cf. R. M. Grant, *Gnosticism, an Anthology*, London, 1961, p. 163.

Barbelo-gnostics spoke of a 'perfect and true Man whom they also call *Adamas*'. From *Anthropos*, the tree of gnosis, he was produced.[1]

Speculation on the First Man was central to the faith of an un-designated group which can now be recognized as the Ophites or Sethians, who are related to the Naassenes. He is a certain 'primary light' and is named 'the Father of All'. From him there was produced a son, and 'this is the Son of Man—a second Man'. From these two and a feminine spirit was born the Christ.[2] Seemingly it is he who becomes entrapped in the waters and must free himself.[3] There appears on the scene one Ialdabaoth who is said to have above him 'the Father of all, the First *Anthropos*, and also *Anthropos*, the Son of *Anthropos*'.[4] Ialdabaoth, acting as the creator-god, then makes man 'after our image', a man of immense breadth and length. There follows an interpretation of the history of Israel with Ialdabaoth playing the role of Yahweh. Men are reminded of the incorruptible light, the *Anthropos* above them, and of the descent of Christ.[5] It is Jesus who comes as the Son of the First Man, or rather it is the Man or Christ above who descends into the Jesus born below.[6]

(iii) *Poimandres*

An important source for teaching about the Man is the first treatise of the Hermetic Corpus called the *Poimandres*.[7] In the main this is a kind of allegory based on the Genesis account of creation although there is a strong admixture of extra-biblical elements which some-times run counter to the Jewish story.[8] C. H. Dodd is among those

---

[1] *Against Heresies* I, 29.3. These Barbelo-gnostics also spoke of a *Proto-Anthropos*. It is apparently their apocryphal Coptic *Gospel of Mary* in which we find the sayings, 'For the Son of Man is within you', and 'Put on the Perfect Man'. See in *NTA* I, pp. 340ff.

[2] *Against Heresies* I, 30.1. See Grant, *op. cit.*, p. 89, on an Ophite diagram de-scribed by Celsus which may relate to this teaching.

[3] *Against Heresies* I, 30.3.

[4] *Against Heresies* I, 30.5f. Ialdabaoth's name some would, significantly, derive from words meaning 'son of chaos', others from a combination of *Yah, Adonai, El, Sabaoth*.

[5] *Against Heresies* I, 30.11.

[6] *Against Heresies* I, 30.12.

[7] See Reitzenstein, *Poimandres*; Dodd, *The Bible and the Greeks*, London, 1935, pp. 99ff., and *The Interpretation of the Fourth Gospel*, Cambridge, 1953, pp. 10ff.; Schenke, *op. cit.*, pp. 44ff. The work emanates from Egypt probably during the second century, though it has been dated considerably earlier and somewhat later. The standard text of the *Corpus Hermeticum* is that of A. D. Nock, with a French translation by A. J. Festugière; see Vol. I, Paris, 1945.

[8] Schenke and Dodd stress the Jewish background. Reitzenstein concentrated

who find in this clear evidence of a 'form of a widely spread myth of the *Urmensch* or primeval man'. 'That there was a widespread myth of the *Urmensch* is certain.'[1]

Mind, the Father of all, 'gave birth to a man like himself . . . the Man was very beautiful, bearing the image of his Father'.[2] The Man desires to create; he bends to earth, sees his form reflected in the water and unites with Nature. He thus becomes a being of two natures, 'mortal because of the body, immortal because of the essential Man'. Man, originally bisexual, later has descendants who are male and female. Though he be immortal and set over all things, he nevertheless is made to suffer the condition of mortals, being subject to Destiny. Though descended from the unsleeping one and himself sleepless, he is now overcome by mortal sleepiness. It is then suggested that the task of salvation for each man consists in waking from mortal slumber, recognizing the essential divine nature, and ascending by freeing himself from the body.

Elsewhere in this work the role of the Man, so-named, is small. In IV, 2 we hear that God sent the Man down to be an ornament of the divine body. At X, 25 we read, 'Man on earth is a mortal God; God in heaven is an immortal Man.' As in the Naassene philosophy, there seems little doubt that we are dealing with a story concerning one who was sent from heaven to earth. Yet at the core of the legend is this theme of the rebirth and ascent of the Man. It is as though there was a Man both in heaven and on earth whose stories have somehow been combined.[3]

---

on the pagan features (on which see also Dodd, *Bible and Greeks*, p. 151). Schenke (*op. cit.*, p. 46) rightly insists on the absence of any definite signs of Christian influence.

[1] *Op. cit.*, p. 146 n. 1.

[2] The following is from *Poimandres, CH* I, 12ff. Often noted in connection with the Primal Man of the *Poimandres* is the figure mentioned by Zosimus in his 'Authentic Memorandum concerning the Letter Omega' which also points to the blending of Egyptian-Hellenistic speculation on the Man with Jewish and Near Eastern ideas very similar to that found in the *Corpus Hermeticum*. '. . . the Primal Man is called by us (Greeks and Egyptians) Thoth, and by them (Chaldaeans, Parthians, Medes and Jews) Adam . . . in relation to his body. Thus the embodied Adam is called Thoth in relation to his outward appearance, but his inner Man, his spiritual Man, possesses an authentic (name) and an appellative (name).' The authentic name is unknown; the appellative name is *Light*. Here is the by now traditional distinction between the earthly and heavenly Man. The heavenly Man clothes himself with Adam to bring the earthly Man into being. See Reitzenstein, *Poimandres*, pp. 105ff., 192ff.; Schenke, *op. cit.*, pp. 52ff.; J. Doresse, *The Secret Books of the Egyptian Gnostics*, ET, London, 1960, pp. 100f.

[3] *CH* X, 25 stresses the distinction between divinity which does not come down

(iv) *The Apocryphon of John*

This probably Sethian work, now extant in three versions of varying length thanks to the two copies in the Nag-Hamadi discoveries, also shows the influence of the myth.[1] In fact, it may be doubly influenced, as it seems to offer two stories of the Man's creation. Clearly it is a highly syncretistic work, having contacts with other forms of gnosticism and, like other gnostic writings, priding itself on its knowledge of Zoroastrianism.[2]

We hear of 'the First Man, the image of the invisible spirit' who is androgynous.[3] This is the Perfect Man who is called Adamas.[4] 'Man exists and the Son of Man.' Ialdabaoth was the creator of all, and he is the image of the Father, 'the First Man, for in the shape of Man his image was revealed'.[5] A being is then made in the likeness of the First Perfect Man, whose image is seen in the water, and is called *Adam*.[6]

Further information is given, not all of which can be readily summarized here. The First Man has a great body made by many angels; light is hidden in him. We hear of the serpent, the woman and the eating of the fruit.[7] Adam, knowing the image in him, brings forth the Son of Man and calls him Seth.[8] There is a kind of series

---

to the earth and Man below. Yet Man may mount up to the heaven; he may ascend to measure heaven even while not quitting the earth below.

[1] See esp. S. Giversen, *Apocryphon Johannis*, Copenhagen, 1963, with bibliography. The work shows knowledge of both Judaism and Christianity. It can be dated not later than about 180 AD as it was known to Irenaeus (*Against Heresies* I, 29). Giversen believes it to have been composed by the Sethians, whom he regards as having come from Syria and Palestine to Egypt (*op. cit.*, p. 330). Puech (*NTA* I, p. 317) thinks it may have once existed in a pre-Christian form. See the attempt of K. Rudolph to see in the *Apocryphon*, in relationship to Jewish and esp. heterodox Jewish speculation, a kind of prototype of Primal Man beliefs. 'Ein Grundtyp gnostischer Urmensch-Adam-Spekulation', *ZRGG* 9, 1957, pp. 1ff.

[2] In Giversen, *op. cit.*, pp. 83, 152f., 253. On this point more generally, cf. Doresse, *op. cit.*, pp. 100, 279ff.; Widengren, 'Der iranische Hintergrund der Gnosis', *ZRGG* 4, 1951, pp. 97ff.

[3] *Op. cit.*, p. 57, lines 3ff.

[4] *Op. cit.*, p. 61, lines 32ff. The name is Adam in the Berlin Codex version, ed. W. Till, *Die gnostischen Schriften des koptischen Papyrus Berolinensis 8502* (TU 60), 1955. This Adamas, who figures in a number of gnostic works, becomes Adamas, the Tyrant who persecutes the heroine throughout the *Pistis Sophia*.

[5] *Op. cit.*, p. 73, lines 14ff.

[6] *Op. cit.*, p. 75, lines 9ff.

[7] *Op. cit.*, pp. 75ff.

[8] *Op. cit.*, p. 93, lines 35f.; p. 95, line 1.

of rebirths of this image in men, a struggle of light versus darkness for the soul of Man, and a description of a fall and recovery.[1]

(v) *Nag-Hamadi*

The discovery of additional copies of the *Apocryphon of John* at Nag-Hamadi (more accurately at Chenoboskion) represents only a part of what is actually a sensational find of a whole library of gnostic works written in dialects of Coptic. Here we have over forty writings, some of which are Christian-gnostic or influenced by Christianity, while others seem wholly independent of Christianity in content and outlook. Although these texts are probably to be dated from the third and fourth centuries, it is clear in many cases that they are translations and/or revisions of works composed in Greek at a somewhat earlier time.[2] Not only do they tend to corroborate much of the information given to us by Hippolytus, Irenaeus and others and to supply us with books to which these Fathers referred, but they, of course, give us much new information and better grounds upon which to assess the whole gnostic movement. It is becoming more and more apparent, for instance, that men who venerated Seth were of great importance in the spread of gnostic teachings and also that these *Sethians* were very closely allied (if not to be seen as nearly identical or regarded as a kind of subdivision) with the Ophites, Naassenes and the Peratae.[3] It is significant for our purposes to recognize that Seth (or *Setheus*) is himself sometimes regarded as a Man figure, being, of course, the Son of Adam (or Son of Man), through whom the whole lineage of mankind was often traced.[4]

Teachings about the Man found at Nag-Hamadi were in a sense foreshadowed by another Coptic gnostic treatise known earlier from the Bruce Codex. In her commentary on this text the editor noticed

[1] *Op. cit.*, pp. 95ff.
[2] For an introduction to the works, see Doresse, *The Secret Books of the Egyptian Gnostics*, and the useful discussion and bibliography by S. Schulz, 'Die Bedeutung neuer Gnosisfunde für die Neutestamentliche Wissenschaft', *TR*, nf 26, 1960, pp. 237ff.
[3] Doresse, *op. cit.*, pp. 50, 249ff.
[4] Gen. 4.25f.; 5.3ff. The lineage through Cain (Gen. 4.17) was often ignored due to his crime. Kenan represents Cain in the Sethian list. The importance of Seth for a gnostic was due to the fact that it was to him first that the knowledge of the First Man, his father, was passed on. (There is little doubt that Seth in Egyptian gnosticism has been in some measure confused with his homonym, the ancient god Seth, but clearly much of the teaching concerning him comes from Jewish lore. This is, however, a reminder that the precise forms which gnosticism took in different locales were much influenced by older, indigenous religions.)

the similarity of the Man there presented with the figure described to us by the Naassenes of Hippolytus.[1] He is to be praised[2] and is seen as a cosmic figure, made in many sections, so that he might even be designated as a *city*, or perhaps a prototype of human society.[3] *He* is androgynous and wise.[4] He is the creator, both father and son, the primal source of all things.[5] He wears the *aeons* like a crown and rays dart forth from him.[6] He is the image of the father who brings him into being from out of the worlds which are his members.[7] He is called Adam, 'who is of the light'.[8] He is given various other names, and the several conceptions presented to us are split into different aspects and blended in a typically confusing manner. The creator father is Setheus, who is also the only begotten. He is the *Word* and saviour, the king wearing his crown.[9] The son is hidden within him; he sends forth a spark which is then portrayed as 'a Man of light and truth'.[10] All his followers wear crowns.[11] The twelve who surround him wear crowns and are robed in glory as they bless the king.[12] Elsewhere we find that the stones of their crown are derived from 'Adamas, the Man of light'.[13] Amid several clear references to the New Testament it is claimed that this Man is the image of the invisible.[14] This is the Man whom all desire to see and know.[15]

In one of the Nag-Hamadi treatises we hear of *Adamas-light* who is born of the Primordial Man and also of the seed of the great Seth who is the Son of Adamas. We find the cry, repeated in other gnostic works, 'Man exists and so does the Son of Man.' The image of the celestial Man is reflected in the waters and the Man below is formed.[16]

[1] C. A. Baynes, *A Coptic Gnostic Treatise contained in the Codex Brucianus* [Bruce MS 96], Cambridge, 1933, p. 16.
[2] *Op. cit.*, p. 12.
[3] *Op. cit.*, p. 26.
[4] *Op. cit.*, p. 26.
[5] *Op. cit.*, p. 42.
[6] *Op. cit.*, pp. 42, 56.
[7] *Op. cit.*, p. 54.
[8] *Op. cit.*, p. 58.
[9] *Op. cit.*, pp. 87, 91.
[10] *Op. cit.*, p. 94.
[11] *Op. cit.*, pp. 102, 127.
[12] *Op. cit.*, p. 108.
[13] *Op. cit.*, p. 141.
[14] *Op. cit.*, p. 160.
[15] *Op. cit.*, pp. 168f.
[16] From a synopsis of the *Sacred Book of the Invisible Great Spirit* or the *Gospel of the Egyptians* described by Doresse, *op. cit.*, pp. 177ff. This is found in two Nag-Hamadi copies designated by Doresse as 2 and 7.

The Revelation of Adam to his Son Seth tells of secret books whose contents Adam was able to pass on to his son, offering him primordial knowledge.[1] The theme and matter of this work, Jean Doresse argues, is related not only to earlier Jewish speculation, but also to Zoroastrian forms.[2]

In a text described as an *Epistle of Eugnostos the Blessed* an androgynous Man is produced. The first, celestial, immortal Man unites with *Sophia* and produces a hermaphrodite son, called the first father, who begets the Son of Man who is entitled the Adam of the Light.[3] In a copy of the *Sophia of Jesus*, known earlier but also found at Nag-Hamadi, the Adam-Light is called the Christ and the Son of God. The Son of Man joins with Sophia to produce a lustrous saviour who comes to awaken Adam.[4]

The *Gospel of Philip* speaks of Christ, the Perfect Man, who visits Adam in the garden, bringing with him the bread of heaven.[5] This Man of heaven is contrasted with the Man of the earth. Others may receive the Perfect Man through the communion sacrament, and by going down into the water they may put on the Living Man. Christians are of the race of the True Man and the Son of Man.[6] 'There is the Son of Man, and there is the son of the Son of Man. The Lord is the Son of Man, and the son of the Son of Man is he who is created through the Son of Man.'[7] Various baptisms and anointings are of special importance in this work, which by its teaching and glosses upon Aramaic and Hebrew names reveals a likely Jewish-Christian provenance.[8]

The Jewish-gnostic *Hypostasis of the Archons* relates the story of Adam-Man's creation in the image of God. Once more we find that this image was first seen reflected in the waters below.[9] In a text which bears no title Ialdabaoth, while boasting of his greatness, is told that an immortal Man, a Man of light, existed before he himself did.[10]

---

[1] Designated by Doresse as text 12, *op. cit.*, pp. 182f.

[2] *Op. cit.*, pp. 185ff.

[3] *Op. cit.*, pp. 192ff. Texts 3 and 8.

[4] *Op. cit.*, pp. 198f. Text 4.

[5] See R. McL. Wilson, *The Gospel of Philip*, London, 1962, logion 15.

[6] *Op. cit.*, logion 102.

[7] *Op. cit.*, logion 120.

[8] Cf. Doresse, *op. cit.*, pp. 224f.

[9] See Doresse, *op. cit.*, pp. 159f. Text 39. See Schenke, ' "Das Wesen der Archonten", eine gnostische Originalschrift aus dem Funde von Nag-Hamadi', *TLZ* 83, 1958, cols. 661ff.; *Gott 'Mensch'*, pp. 61ff.

[10] Doresse, *op. cit.*, pp. 166ff. Text 40. See Schenke, 'Vom Ursprung der Welt, eine titellose gnostische Abhandlung aus dem Funde von Nag-Hamadi', *TLZ* 84,

Later we hear of a Man seen in the heavens descending in a shining light. There is an Adam-Light and we are told of the creation of the earthly Adam. But Adam is wickedly opposed by the Archons and sent out of paradise.

Obviously the above remarks offer only an eclectic glance at an important series of documents, many of which are still in the process of being edited and translated and which will require many years of interpretation. For our purposes, however, such a glance is sufficient to show that the Man figure, in varying guises, had a quite legitimate place in works which were given their final form in Egyptian gnostic settings. Yet we would not wish to leave the impression that he was the central character in these writings. Though Adam or the Man or Jesus as the Man is several times given important consideration and at least mentioned in a number of other passages,[1] it is not difficult to come to the opinion that for these gnostic authors the significance of the Man speculation is waning rather than waxing, and that they are remembering a conception which seems to have many of its roots in earlier Jewish-Christian, Jewish and pagan beliefs.

Another by-product of the Nag-Hamadi discoveries has been a strengthening in the realization that there must have been points of contact between these forms of western gnosticism and later Manichaeanism and Mandaeanism. Recent commentators have noted a number of common ideas, names, titles, etc., which are in many cases best explained by thinking in terms of earlier conceptions and patterns of belief which could have exercised a general influence.[2]

1959, cols. 243ff.; *Gott 'Mensch'*, pp. 49ff., but for the full text, A. Böhlig and P. Labib, *Die koptisch-gnostische Schrift ohne Titel aus Codex II von Nag Hammadi* (Deutsche Akademie der Wissenschaften zu Berlin, Institut für Orientforschung 58) Berlin, 1962.

[1] In the Christian-gnostic *Pistis Sophia* (see the 2nd ed. of G. R. S. Mead, London, 1921), though Christ is never called the Man, *Jeu* is twice named the First Man. III, cxi; IV, cxxx. Doresse (*op. cit.*, 107f.) notes that the Man conception may have affected certain formularies of Greek magical papyri. See esp. the work 'Prescription for Immortality' in A. J. Festugière's *La révélation d'Hermès Trismégiste*, Vol. I, Paris, 1944, pp. 303ff. In *Die Psalmen des Thomas und das Perlenlied als Zeugnisse vorchristlicher Gnosis* (BZNW 24), Berlin, 1959, pp. 48ff., A. Adam finds a version of the Man legend to be contained in the 'Hymn of the Pearl' and holds that it is pre-Christian at the core. Although we recognize that features such as the dragon and the shining, glorious garment can be explained on the basis of older materials (see below in ch. III), we believe that several post-Christian ideas are of the essence of the 'Hymn'. Cf. Jonas, *Gnostic Religion*, pp. 116ff.

[2] See, for instance, Doresse, *op. cit.*, passim; Rudolph, *ZRGG* 9, 1957, p. 17, and further below.

(vi) *Manichaeanism*

In the various forms which Manichaeanism took the Primal Man (*nāšā qadmāyā*) was often of central importance.[1] Begotten by the King of the Paradise of Lights and pictured as a young man, he was forced to do battle with Satan or the King of the Dark. He initially loses his fight and is seen lying deep in the abyss of matter, in a ditch surrounded by wild beasts and demons.[2] Yet he is rescued by God and summoned forth, himself to become divine. This legend is then made into a kind of story of *everyman*, or better of every soul. Each soul must do battle against darkness and evil matter and be rescued in order to ascend to the spiritual realm of light. In this struggle he will be aided by the Primal Man (thus often referred to by scholars as the *Saved Saviour* or the *Redeemed Redeemer*), who is now said to dwell in the sun, though he has periodically made visits to earth in the form of messengers as diverse as the Buddha, Zarathushtra, Adam, Seth, Noah, Jesus and Mani.[3]

Since all men's souls have been originally formed from out of this First Man, they are like him and their ultimate hope of salvation also lies in him. Thus, as C. H. Kraeling noted, 'the Primal Man dwells in the world, macrocosmically as the *world soul* and microcosmically as the individual soul'. His true home is heaven, yet 'to think of the Primal Man as dwelling simultaneously in heaven and on earth did not involve a contradiction for Mani'.[4]

[1] Reference may be made to F. C. Burkitt, *The Religion of the Manichees*, Cambridge, 1925 ('The tale [of the Primal Man] is indeed fundamental to Manichaeism', p. 21); H. H. Schaeder in *Studien zum antiken Synkretismus*, pp. 240ff.; W. Manson, *Jesus, the Messiah*, pp. 174ff.; Puech, *Le Manichéisme, son fondateur, sa doctrine*, Paris, 1949, pp. 76ff.; Schenke, *op. cit.*, pp. 108ff.; Schulz, *TR*, nf 26, 1960, pp. 209ff. Controversial use of these materials was made by Reitzenstein (see esp. *Das iranische Erlösungsmysterium*, Bonn, 1921), and by W. Bousset, *Hauptprobleme der Gnosis* (FRLANT 10), 1907, pp. 175. Cf. the strictures laid on attempts to delineate pre-Manichaean forms and on Reitzenstein's use of the Turfan fragments by C. Colpe, *Die religionsgeschichtliche Schule. Darstellung und Kritik ihres Bildes vom gnostisschen Erlösermythus* (FRLANT 78, nf 60) Göttingen, 1961, pp. 29ff., and also see M. Boyce, *Manichaean Hymn-Cycles in Parthian*, London, 1954, who, however, attests to the fact that the myth of the Man is to be found in both Coptic and Iranian sources. *Op. cit.*, pp. 16ff.; examples on pp. 102f. and Coptic Manichaean Psalm 246, *op. cit.*, p. 13.

[2] On the battle and defeat, see Jonas, *op. cit.*, pp. 218ff., and Widengren, *Mani and Manichaeism*, London, 1965, pp. 43ff.

[3] C. H. Kraeling in *Anthropos and Son of Man*, New York, 1927, p. 33: 'It should then be evident that Manichaean soteriology regards the divine messengers as manifestations of the Primal Man.'

[4] *Op. cit.*, p. 23. See Augustine, *To Faustus* II, 4f., on a Manichaean view of Christ: 'You represent your fabulous Christ, the son of your fabulous Primal Man,

(vii) *The Mandaeans*

When we return in our chapter V to a discussion of gnostic teach-ings, we shall want to look more closely at the Mandaean religion, a still extant sect with records which go back to the seventh century AD, but which may have roots reaching back much further. Two impor-tant figures in their thought are of interest: *Anush* (or *Enosh, man*) a kind of angel who appeared on earth, but especially Adam as a hero glorified in several ways, as an archetype and as one now hidden in each man. Several scholars are convinced that this figure of the exalted Adam, Adakas, etc., played a crucial part in the earliest forms of Mandaeanism.[1]

(viii) *Jewish and Jewish-Christian sects*

Also in chapter V we shall want to examine the place of the Man in the teachings of several Jewish and Jewish-Christian sects of the first, second and third centuries. One of these, for example, is the group whose records are left in the so-called Pseudo-Clementine literature.[2] Here First Man, Adam, is once more glorified. His initial sin is even denied, and Adam and Jesus, the Son of Man, are closely related in thought. The true prophet first manifested in Adam and later in others was finally known in Jesus Christ.[3]

---

as bound up in all the stars . . . (yet) conjoined and compounded with the earth and all its products.'

We shall in this study, however, treat the evidence from Manichaeism with such extreme care that we shall, in fact, make little use of it. Its witness to the importance of the Man legend is late and not essential to our major thesis. Yet it is possible that before we are through we shall have been able to shed some light on the relationship between the Manichaean form of the myth and earlier ideas.

[1] See Lady E. S. Drower, *The Secret Adam. A Study of Nasoraean Gnosis*, London, 1960; Kraeling, *op. cit.*, p. 62: 'The Great Adam who here and there appears in our texts was at one time the most important person in the Mandean pleroma.'

[2] The literature was given its final form in the early third century. Cf. O. Cull-mann, *Le problème littéraire et historique du roman pseudoclémentin*, Paris, 1930, and 'Die neuendeckten Qumrantexte und das Judenchristentum der Pseudo-Klementinen' in *Neutestamentliche Studien für R. Bultmann* (BZNW 21, ed. W. Eltester), 1954, pp. 35ff. He sees the group as more Jewish than Christian in basic orientation and under the influence of gnosticism. More recently see J. Irmscher, 'The Pseudo-Clementines' in *NTA* II, pp. 532ff.

[3] *Recognitions* I, 45: Jesus Christ was anointed from the tree of life. I 47: Adam was also so anointed. On the glorification of Adam, see *Homilies* III, 17f., 42, and VIII, 10. In III, 20 Christ, the true prophet, has appeared in many forms and names, firstly in Adam. In III, 22 Adam is also seen as a type of the Son of Man who prophesies better than those born of woman (i.e. John the Baptist, see Matt. 11.11 = Luke 7.28), because he is the son of the male, Adam.

(ix) *Rabbinic evidence*

Several of these ideas are paralleled and given different expression in rabbinic and allied teachings of this period. In chapter IV we shall discuss the tendency to overlook or reinterpret Adam's sin, to glorify him as the First Man, and even to see him in quasi-messianic terms. In addition we shall want to take into consideration the writings of Philo, the Alexandrian Jewish philosopher, who found cause for praising both a Heavenly Man and also the First Man of the earth.

(x) *Late Jewish literature*

Lastly, of course, we shall not overlook the better-known Jewish sources such as Daniel, I Enoch and II (4) Esdras. There we meet the eschatological Man figure appearing in glory at the end of history. The importance and meaning of this data will be judged in chapter IV, but, in the meantime, it may be regarded as further evidence of a tendency to venerate some type of a Man conception.

2. IMPRESSIONS AND PROPOSED ANSWERS

From this brief survey we may certainly gain the impression of a widespread phenomenon, for it is very difficult to believe that there is not *some* relationship between many of these conceptions despite all their diversity. When, however, we seek to define this relationship or to search out a source for this mode of thought, we find that we have opened a veritable Pandora's box from which there issues forth a vast amount of literature and a host of conflicting opinions. Endeavouring to find the source of the Man mythology is in many ways like trying to identify *the* source of gnosticism. Indeed, it is probably wrong to speak in terms of a source. Rather should we think of sources, and, if we are to presuppose anything, it is probably best to reckon with a variety of ideas and cultural backgrounds intermingling, complicating and affecting one another as versions of a legendary Man story were told in different *milieux*. In addition it should be pointed out that figures bearing at least some resemblance to the Man of the early Christian centuries have been located in other ages and places as distant as China or Scandinavia.[1] There may be something almost archetypal about the basic conceptions involved.

[1] See A. Christensen, *Les types du premier homme et du premier roi dans l'histoire légendaire des Iraniens*, Stockholm and Leiden, 1917–34, I, p. 34.

Nevertheless the complexities of the problem should not be allowed to obscure the fact that over a period of four or five centuries surrounding the beginning of the Christian era a peculiarly powerful interest in Man ideas was making its influence felt. There ought to be some cause or causes for this as well as a way of explaining the repetition of certain features which do not always seem natural to the particular thought environments in which the idea is given expression. In spite of all the hazards involved we think that it may be possible to chart the course of what might be called a kind of impulse, a potent core of ideas, which, while not traceable to a single locality and date, can be seen to have a more generalized background in certain primitive conceptions.

Are there, then, earlier forms of mythology and religious practice which can help us to understand a syncretistic figure who seemingly could be on earth or in heaven, or even, somehow, in both places at once? The Man was the image or archetype from which First Man on earth was made, or again he was both the image above and the actual First Man below. Or he was the protoplast from which other men (or even the rest of creation) were fashioned. Though appearing at the time of creation, some also thought that he had manifested himself on earth at other times or that he was even present in all men. Some pictured him as a salvation hero at the end of time; and/or salvation might consist in discovering the essential Man within oneself. Aid in this process would come through secrets revealed by divine messengers who were often regarded as representatives of the Man in heaven.

A number of these mythical descriptions are equally strong in the conviction that the Man or his copy had to fight a great battle (often as the result of some grave sin which he had committed) in which he was overwhelmed by the powers of evil and darkness, death and chaos (frequently represented by waves or waters). He then himself had to be rescued. Though this last sequence of events is not always emphasized or developed during the gnostic period, fragments of the idea do keep reappearing, and it would appear sufficiently strong to have a genuine place in the story. Even in versions of the tale which concentrate on the praise and honour due to the Man, explicit or latent echoes of his time of suffering are to be heard. 'Throughout our sources we thus find a twofold interpretation of the heroic Anthropos. He is both a victorious and a defeated champion.'[1]

[1] Kraeling, *Anthropos*, pp. 99f.

But before we can begin our search for this background in earnest, two preliminary matters must be dealt with. Several scholars have recently argued and others have suggested that we can only do our research properly if we are willing to recognize the presence of at least two separate and distinct myths. Writes Sigmund Mowinckel, '. . . an essential distinction must be made between the idea of the Primordial Man and that of the first created man.'[1] There is a heavenly cosmological figure from which the First Man and then others were made; this is to be contrasted with stories about the First Man on earth. H.-M. Schenke would divide the material into three classes of myths with subdivisions. The basic two are roughly equivalent with Mowinckel's distinctions: there is an *All-god* or first giant and a First Man often seen as the king of paradise. Thirdly, there is the gnostic Man, a figure of more speculative and allegorical concern.[2]

Now one can readily agree that it is often possible and useful to make these distinctions; yet the employment of such categories could well cause us to overlook and misunderstand some of the very close relationships between these figures. In the ancient materials, as we read them, there are not really two sets of distinct myths, one about Primordial Man and the other about First Man; nor are the gnosticized versions easily regarded as a separate category, even though they are later and new and transforming emphases are to be found. In fact, Primordial Man and First Man are so often presented as types of each other that the stories and attributes of the one can readily become those of the other, while in later gnostic writings it is, in part, the blending or confusion of the two which furthers the transformation of the ancient myths.

Schenke himself as much as admits this when he goes on to speak of the manner in which his different classifications are sometimes combined. Mowinckel also is forced into the same admission:

. . . the two conceptions have many points of contact, and, on the whole are akin to each other . . . That is why we often find, in the numerous variants of the oriental myth of the Primordial Man or Anthropos, many elements borrowed from myths and legends about the first man . . . the Primordial Man sometimes appears as king of paradise . . . Conversely, we note that ideas about the Primordial Man influence and transform the conception of the first man.[3]

[1] *HTC*, pp. 422f. Cf. also Colpe, *religionsgeschichtliche Schule*, pp. 162f.
[2] Schenke, *Gott 'Mensch'*, pp. 17, 153.
[3] *HTC*, p. 424. Here Ezek. 28 and Job 15.7f. are said to be references to the

Obviously, then, if the people who once told these stories were so little concerned to preserve nice distinctions, it would be more than academic of us to try to make any rigid demarcations for them. Moreover, as one of the by-products of this study, we hope later to show why the relationship between these two figures was often so intimate that they could act in the role of the other.

Secondly, though we here even further anticipate ourselves, it is advisable at this stage to make a few remarks about the so-called *soul myth* and the *Saved Saviour*.[1] These much-debated conceptions, as we shall see, are found in their developed forms only in later and more gnosticized versions of the myth. Some would even regard them as direct outgrowths from heterodox presentations of Christianity.[2] Although such a single-source hypothesis is itself questionable, we shall in any case not find these ideas flourishing in comparable forms in the more primitive materials.

On the other hand, it is quite possible that we shall be able to recover from ideas of relative antiquity the incipient patterns of thought out of which the later teachings grew. This is especially true of the conception of the *Saved Saviour*, but even this belief, and yet more so that regarding the *soul myth*, seem to have required a less Semitic view of man and a more speculative atmosphere in order to reach their full forms.[3]

We may now take up our search for the background of this *impulse* to glorify and venerate the Man. Four basic theories have been put

---

'first Man, and not to the Primordial Man'. Yet on p. 426 these are cited as instances of Judaism's later familiarity 'with conceptions of the Primordial Man'. Kraeling (*op. cit.*, p. 61) speaks of the Manichaean 'confusion of the heavenly man and the protoplast on earth'. This seeming confusion is found in many of the sources. On this point and against Mowinckel see also A. Bentzen, *King and Messiah*, London, 1955, pp. 96f. n. 11; I. Engnell, 'Die Urmenschvorstellung und das Alte Testament', SEA 22–23, 1957–8, p. 268; and our discussion in ch. III.

[1] These ideas as pre-Christian teachings were vigorously set out by Reitzenstein. See esp. *iranische Erlösungsmysterium*, pp. 55ff. Cf. also W. Staerk, *Die Erlösererwartung in den östlichen Religionen* (Soter II), Stuttgart-Berlin, 1938, pp. 231ff. See discussion and criticisms in Colpe, *op. cit.*, esp. pp. 171ff.; Wilson, *Gnostic Problem*, pp. 98, 226ff.; Black, 'The Pauline Doctrine of the Second Adam', *SJT* 7, 1954, pp. 177ff.; Quispel in *Eranos Jahrbuch* 22, 1953, pp. 201f., 224.

[2] See E. Bevan, *Hellenism and Christianity*, London, 1930, pp. 89ff. Quispel, 'The Jung Codex and Its Significance' in *The Jung Codex* (ed. F. L. Cross), London, 1955, p. 78, would agree with regard to the *Saved Saviour*. Kraeling (*op. cit.*, p. 172) sees the soteriological element as clearly post-Christian. Schenke (*op. cit.*, pp. 144ff.) finds the whole conception to be post-Christian. See also Fuller, *Foundations*, pp. 93ff.

[3] See esp. p. 277 n. 1, and in ch. VI on our interpretation of Phil. 2.6ff., pp. 250ff.

forward, but those which suggest that this tendency was the result of a corruption and mystical orientation of Greek philosophical ideas[1] and/or that Christianity itself was the dominant influence[2] rightly find very little support today. Far more cogent is the contention that Judaism was the predominant source for the Man beliefs.[3] This is especially true if we allow for the penetration of a degree of Hellenistic thought into Judaism before the first century AD and a pursuant interaction of Hellenistic, Jewish and Christian ideas. It will have been noticed that in almost every example of the myth cited above the Genesis story or Adam or both had some part to play. It is even possible to read many of these versions as forms of anthropological allegory verging on myth rather than as true myths.[4] Frequently is

[1] To be sure in Hellenistic areas and spheres of influence beliefs about the Man have been affected by Greek metaphysics and esp. by the doctrines of Stoicism. Yet the myth is found in other areas and in forms in which there is little evidence of Greek thought. Even in Hellenistic *milieux* features are often associated with the Man which cannot be readily understood as developments from philosophical speculation. We shall hold that this is true of Philo as well. See Schenke, *op. cit.*, pp. 16ff.; Doresse, *Secret Books*, p. 263. If it is correct to argue that there is a kind of progression from dramatic practices and myths to more speculative literary forms (see T. H. Gaster, *Thespis. Ritual, Myth and Drama in the Ancient Near East*, New York, 1950, and H. Jonas, *Gnosis und spätantiker Geist*, II/1. *Von der Mythologie zur mystischen Philosophie* (FRLANT 63, nf 45), 1954,) it may support our belief that the Man beliefs often entered western gnostic religions in fragmentary forms which do not appear to have been indigenous.
  Of course, there are stories of the descent, death and new life of heroes in early Greek materials, but these do not relate to the later beliefs nearly as well as other primitive ideas which we shall study. Even if one follows C. H. Gordon (*Before the Bible*, New York, 1962) in his argument for a measure of parallel development between Greece and Israel, resort must still be made to earlier cultures. In Gordon's view, significantly, one looks to Ugarit.
[2] So Burkitt (*Religion of the Manichees*, pp. 75f.) wanted to see the Manichaean saviour Man almost exclusively as a type of Jesus. Cf. also his *Church and Gnosis*, Cambridge, 1932. Many scholars wished to view the whole of the gnostic movement as a Hellenization of Christianity, but, and most certainly in the case of the Man legend, this is impossible. There are gnostic forms of the myth in which Christianity, if at all present, is of quite secondary importance. A variety of features attributed to the Man, both in Christianized and pagan versions, are hardly explicable as the result of speculation based on Christianity. Forms of the legend, as we have seen or shall see, are contemporary with or pre-date Christian beginnings. (On this point see Kraeling, *op. cit.*, p. 190.) Even the later presentations, many of which show signs of having been often reworked, must be backdated to some degree. In addition, 'The ubiquity of the conception in the middle and further East from the second century AD onwards in so many forms is difficult to explain as due entirely to Christian influence'. Black, *SJT* 7, 1954, p. 177.
[3] See Dodd, *Bible and Greeks*, esp. p. 147; Quispel in *Eranos Jahrbuch* 22, 1953, pp. 95ff.; Schenke, *op. cit.*
[4] Schenke would stress this allegorical interpretation of Jewish thought (*op. cit.*, pp. 72ff.).

this so in certain western gnostic presentations where the Man appears at the beginning of time but does not always reappear as a later salvation figure.

Yet there still remain features for which no legitimate accounting can be offered on this basis. Why is Man or Adam occasionally seen as a huge, cosmological giant? Why is he worshipped as a glorified hero and often reckoned as sinless? Why is he sometimes a hermaphrodite, sometimes seen as though a kind of sun divinity? How can the Adam of Genesis be regarded as one who has since been represented on earth in others? Why is he born from water?

If it then be countered that many of these attributes were already showing themselves in Jewish thought and that they can be understood as constituent elements of heterodox Jewish speculation,[1] we yet must ask what other influences helped to fashion various forms of Jewish heterodoxy during this era. And what accounts for the desire to become involved with Adamite speculation in the first place? Why does Adam or First Man become so important both within and without Judaism?

The answer to this last question will be a major concern in the next several chapters. While it looks to us very much as though Judaism was both a catalyst and breeding-ground for the development of these ideas during this period, Judaism had no exclusive right to many of these beliefs, and it is imperative that we cast our net yet more widely. We shall find legends which may even pre-date those of Genesis and which may also have helped to give new life to the conception of Adam as the Man at a later date.

We come then to the fourth of the theories regarding the sources of beliefs about the Man. We should prefer to call this, however, not so much an answer to our problem as the direction of an answer, the way we must look, a pointer passing through and beyond Judaism to yet more ancient and fundamental conceptions of the Near East. There is hardly anything new about this approach in general, and it would now appear, in one version or another, to be accepted by a great many, perhaps by the majority of scholars who have dealt directly with the materials involved.[2] Mowinckel comments in this fashion:

---

[1] So esp. Quispel, *op. cit.*, pp. 195ff.

[2] Kraeling (*Anthropos*, p. 126) saw 'an unbroken line of tradition running from the littoral Orient via Jewish-Gnostic and Pagan Mesopotamia' onward to Iran. See Staerk, *Soter* II, pp. 421ff.; Creed, *JTS* 26, 1925, p. 122; A. von Gall, βασιλεία τοῦ θεοῦ, Heidelberg, 1926, pp. 409ff.; W. Manson, *Jesus, the Messiah*, pp. 174ff.; E. R. Goodenough, *By Light, Light*, New Haven, 1935, p. 361; Otto, *Kingdom of God and*

The Oriental, Hellenistic 'god Anthropos' is of mixed Iranian and 'Chaldean' origin . . . In Iranian, Chaldean and Indian religio-philosophical speculation, and in many of the Gnostic systems (both pre-Christian Jewish and Christian Gnostic) an important part was played by the Primordial Man, the divine Anthropos. This is also true of Mandaism and Manicheism.[1]

In several of his books G. Widengren has attempted to trace the Man myth and other related ideas back to more primitive forms. 'Behind Manicheanism, Mandeanism and Christian gnosis we find a common religious language based on old Babylonian myths.'[2] From this source issues the picture of the defeated saviour who yet becomes the victor over the powers of evil.[3]

Different scholars have pointed to a variety of figures whom they believe to be the source or an important source for the later Man myths. Kraeling[4] and Schmithals[5] have, for instance, looked to Marduk, the king-god of Babylon. Ludin Jansen singled out Ea-Oannes, the wise high-god of the same city.[6] In due course we shall try to ascertain the place and influence of these and other hero figures, but at this point it is most fitting that we should turn to that

---

Son of Man; L. Jansen, *Die Henochgestalt. Eine vergleichende religionsgeschichtliche Untersuchung*, Oslo, 1939, pp. 86ff.; H. Gressmann, *Der Messias* (FRLANT 43, nf 26), 1929; Doresse, *Secret Books*, p. 263. On the east to west passage of ideas in general, cf. E. O. James, *The Ancient Gods*, London, 1960; Widengren, *ZRGG* 4, 1952, pp. 97ff. Jonas in *Gnostic Religion*, pp. 23ff., speaks of an explosion in the east, a wave of symbols of ancient oriental thought moving from east to west. See also R. C. Zaehner, *The Dawn and Twilight of Zoroastrianism*, London, 1961, p. 144.

This theory also, of course, begs the whole question of the sources of the gnostic movement in general and the difficult problem of when gnosticism might be said to have begun. We shall have more to say on this later, but cf. the judicious remarks by R. McL. Wilson, 'Some Recent Studies in Gnosticism', *NTS* 6, 1959/60, pp. 32ff., and J. Munck, 'The New Testament and Gnosticism', *ST* 15, 1961, pp. 181ff.

[1] *HTC*, pp. 424f.
[2] *Mesopotamian Elements in Manichaeism* (UUA), Uppsala, 1946/III, p. 177. For a stress on the importance of the Iranian background, cf. his 'Stand und Aufgaben der iranischen Religionsgeschichte', *Numen* 1–2, 1954–5, pp. 16ff., 47ff.
[3] *Mesopotamian Elements*, pp. 42ff., 52ff.
[4] *Anthropos*, pp. 264, 187.
[5] *Die Gnosis in Korinth* (FRLANT 66, nf 48), 1956, pp. 91ff. See the survey involving many such figures by W. Staerk, *Soter. Die biblische Erlösererwartung als religionsgeschichtliches Problem* (Soter I), Gütersloh, 1933, and *Soter* II, and the literature cited by Mowinckel, *HTC*, p. 422 n.1.
[6] *Henochgestalt*, pp. 105ff.

area of research which occupied the attention of several of the pioneering scholars in this field.

3. IRANIAN SOURCES

We thus enter upon one of the most curious and difficult chapters in the whole history of comparative religions study. Probably the most influential and well-known scholar of what has come to be known as the *history-of-religions school* was Richard Reitzenstein. His ideas were anticipated or supplemented and in some cases turned into new channels by men like Wilhelm Bousset and Hugo Gressmann.[1] Reitzenstein believed himself to see in the religions of the Near or Middle East the vital background for the Man myth and many related ideas. Mandaeanism and Manichaeanism could both be traced back to more primitive and largely Iranian forms. The original conception of the Man was primarily to be found in the Zoroastrian and pre-Zoroastrian First Man, Gayomart. In Iranian folk-religion lay the seed bed and developing-ground for the *Saved Saviour*, the *soul myth* and attendant rites and mysteries. Christianity had been directly influenced by this background.

Like all pioneering scholars, Reitzenstein made a number of mistakes and tended to brush aside some of the complicating objections to this thesis. His ideas have recently been put to the test again by Carsten Colpe and found wanting in a number of important areas.[2] There was admittedly a tendency to treat centuries as though they were decades and to leap thousands of miles in the middle of a paragraph. The coincidental interest in Mandaeanism and the discovery of new Manichaean materials somewhat unsteadied his balance. Nevertheless continuing study, while revealing errors and misjudgments in Reitzenstein's approach, has done little to suggest that his basic orientation was wholly errant. Mandaeanism, Manichaeanism and several forms of gnostic religion are related to one

[1] The best bibliography is now given by Colpe, *religionsgeschichtliche Schule*. As Schenke (*Gott 'Mensch'*, p. 3) has pointed out, Reitzenstein can still stir up much discussion in Germany and the Scandinavian countries, while he has been virtually ignored elsewhere. Where he is mentioned at all in English language books, it is often by means of a passing footnote as though he were some manner of charlatan, though the few scholars who treated him seriously (cf. Kraeling, *Anthropos*; W. Manson, *Jesus, the Messiah*; Creed, *JTS* 26, 1925, pp. 113ff.), were by no means wholly critical.

[2] Colpe, *op. cit.* See the interesting criticisms by R. N. Frye, 'Reitzenstein and Qumran Revisited by an Iranian', *HTR* 55, 1962, pp. 261ff.

another and do have some roots which in one way or another reach back into common conceptions and beliefs. It is only right, therefore, that we include some discussion of the figure of Gayomart and then see where this might lead us.

Gayomart, who is essentially a hero found only in the later Pahlavi texts, seems to have a history which extends back to one *Gaya maretan* (or *mortal life*)[1] and a still more primitive conception called *Gaya*. The precise dating of the earlier texts is, of course, debated, but in hymns which belong to an early or intermediate stratum of Zoroastrianism we hear of Gaya maretan who first listened to the teaching of the great God and from whom Ahura 'formed the race of the Aryan nations'.[2] Here and elsewhere the praise and worship of Gaya maretan or Gaya (or his *fravashi*, a kind of counterpart in heaven) is inculcated.[3] He is *holy* and presented as the prime example of human virility and strength.[4] As *Saoshyant* (quite likely a version of Gaya maretan's fravashi) he will reappear at the end of time.[5]

These scattered references obviously do not supply a very strong foundation for speculation about the importance of a Primal or Heavenly Man figure in Zoroastrian thought, and it is not until we come to the much later Pahlavi *Bundahis* that a fuller myth about Gayomart becomes evident. Here we find a true primeval champion. Ahuru Mazda made him (sometimes as a bisexual being), and he was 'the first of the human species. Gayomart was produced brilliant and white.'[6] Elsewhere he is also presented as though a kind of

---

[1] The name is variously interpreted. Some would translate as 'mortal man' or even more abstractly as 'human life'. Zaehner (*Dawn and Twilight*, p. 72) takes it as 'dying life'. On the importance of Gayomart to Zoroastrianism and later thought, perhaps overstressed, see also von Gall, *op. cit.*, pp. 409ff.

[2] *Yast* XIII, 85ff. Most of the texts here given concerning Gayomart and Yima are to be found in the series *Sacred Books of the East* (gen. ed. F. Max Muller), Oxford. See esp. Vols. V, XXXVII (tr. F. W. West) on the Pahlavi texts and for the *Zend-Avesta* (tr. J. Darmesteter and L. H. Mills) IV², XXIII, XXXI (1880–95).

[3] *Yasna* XIII, 7; *Visparad* XXI, 2. In *Yasna* LXVIII, 22, praise to Gaya is listed just before that to the *fravashi* of or to Zarathushtra himself. The exact nature of a *fravashi* is difficult to ascertain. Zaehner (*The Teaching of the Magi. A Compendium of Zoroastrian Beliefs*, London, 1956, p. 17) writes, 'Man is, by origin, a spiritual being, and his soul, in the shape of what the Zoroastrians call his Fravashi or Fravahr, pre-exists his body.' There are times, however, when the *fravashi* seems to have a yet more independent existence than this.

[4] *Yast* VIII, 44. See VIII, 14. Another important reference to the First Man, though he is not named, is in *Yasna* XIX, 3.

[5] *Yasna* XXVI, 10. See *Yast* XIII, 145.

[6] *Bundahis* XXIV, 1.

glorious shining sun-god figure.[1] Due to his position in time he is, of course, set at the head of a number of genealogies. He is the first of personages like *Siyamak*, *Hosang* and *Taxmoruw*, all apparently early king-heroes, and is himself quite obviously portrayed as a regal First Man.[2]

A number of times Gayomart is referred to as *the righteous man*, and, when he suffered, he apparently did so as an innocent victim, for Gayomart and his ox companion became subject to the designs of evil spirits. Thirty years of tribulation followed, but just before Gayomart died he was able to say, 'Although the destroyer has come, mankind will all be of my race.'[3] And so it was, because in another work we read that 'mankind and all the guardian spirits of the producers of the renovation were produced from his body'.[4]

It is said that religion first arose in this righteous thinker Gayomart.[5] And then, at the end of the ages, during the activity of his *eschatological* counterpart Saoshyant (a figure who is reported to have been *born* rising from water), we hear of the First Man again: 'First the bones of Gayomart are raised up.'[6] It shall be that 'of the light accompanying the sun, one half will be for Gayomart, and one half will give enlightenment among the rest of men'.[7] His important place is underlined by this remark: 'The religion of Zarathustra is the nature of Gayomart, and the nature of Gayomart is the religion of Zarathustra.'[8]

Kraeling, while noting the absence of anything like a *Saved Saviour* conception here (which he felt to have been added later), argued that the information given accurately reflected the earlier existence of a belief in Gayomart as a primeval hero. 'The similarity between the Iranian Gayomard and the Anthropos as defeated champion, as we have already outlined it, cannot be either secondary or fortuitous

---

[1] See A. J. Carnoy, 'Iran's Primeval Heroes and the Myth of the First Man' in *Indo-Iranian Studies* (ed. A. V. W. Jackson), London-Leipzig, 1925, pp. 203ff., who cites him as 'on his throne like a sun or a full moon over a lofty cypress'. He was born on a high mountain, like many another First Man, where the sun would first shine.

[2] On Gayomart as the first king, see Christensen, *types du premier homme*, I, pp. 66ff.

[3] *Bundahis* III, 23.

[4] *Dina-i Mainog-i Khirad* XXVII, 17.

[5] From a fragment translated in *Sacred Books of the East* XXXVII, p. 360.

[6] *Bundahis* XXX, 7.

[7] *Bundahis* XXX, 9.

[8] *Bundahis* XXXV, 1.

. . . the two figures must be fundamentally identical.'[1] Mowinckel is in general agreement and is among those who would stress the eschatological aspects of the figure. 'When the new world comes, it is the Primordial Man who returns; and the eschatological saviour Saoshyant is regarded as an incarnation both of Zarathushtra, the founder of the religion, and of Gayomart, the Primordial Man.'[2]

Yet, valuable as the interpretations of such scholars may be, it cannot be gainsaid that much guesswork is involved and that there are numerous problems which are not easily brushed aside. The *Bundahis* (or *The Original Creation*), from which much of the vital information derives, can be dated no earlier than the Mohammedan conquest of Persia. Although it is rightly maintained that the work is ultimately a translation or an epitome of one of the books into which the basic Zoroastrian scriptures were divided,[3] we still do not know how much new material or reinterpretation has crept in. Doubtless Gayomart does go back to Gaya maretan and Gaya, but the fact of the matter is that these earlier figures are not well developed, at least as we see them now. The Pahlavi description of Gayomart could be as much or more the result of a parallel and related development to the gnostic *Anthropos* as a precursor and/or source.[4]

[1] *Anthropos*, p. 102. It is doubtful if even at the time Kraeling would have stressed the *identity* of the figures. It would be enough to say that they are definitely related.

[2] *HTC*, p. 423. In *The Western Response to Zoroaster*, Oxford, 1958, p. 89, J. Duchesne-Guillemin writes, 'The notion of an eschatological saviour appears to be connected, both in Iran and in Judaism, with that of Primal Man.' Gayomart, however, does not become such a figure until the Pahlavi texts and there in relation to Saoshyant. In 'Some Aspects of Anthropomorphism' in *The Saviour God* (ed. S. G. F. Brandon), Manchester, 1963, p. 93, Duchesne-Guillemin objects to any simple identification of Gayomart and Saoshyant. On the two cf. also S. Hartman, *Gayōmart. Étude sur le syncrétisme dans l'ancien Iran*, Uppsala, 1953, pp. 27ff. *Yast* XIII, 145 tells of the worship of *fravashis* 'from Gaya maretan down to the victorious Saoshyant'. The meaning may well be from First Man to last, without, however, telling us how closely the two figures are to be related.

[3] See E. W. West, *Sacred Books of the East* V, p. xli.

[4] In his study *Gayōmart*, Sven Hartman wishes to argue that the genuine evolution of this conception only took place in Zurvanite times. He is a later presentation in some ways to be compared with the development of the Mithra figure. While Zurvanite thought or at least Zurvanite tendencies can be seen to reach back into the centuries before Christ, this was not their real period of ascendancy. Hartman's argument is complicated in that he sees two strands of ideas being combined, one concerning a religious figure, a First Man or prototype, and the other a more nationalistic conception, a first king of the world. This is perhaps overly schematic and might merely recognize two aspects of the same general idea, yet it may well indicate that Gayomart himself was a figure who was being developed and, as such, was not a conception of great antiquity. Cf. Duchesne-Guillemin, 'L'homme

There is, however, another hero of proven antiquity in Iranian lore who, in many ways, is far more interesting than Gayomart. Both Gressmann and Bousset pointed to the *Yima*, who has a genuine place in the early literature and an equally ancient counterpart in the Yama of the Indian *Rig-Veda*.[1] Indeed, it is quite possible that Gayomart is a kind of later substitute figure for Yima, and also possible that the later interpretations of Mithra have been influenced by this same figure.[2]

Yima is described as the First Man and the first king who once dwelt in an earthly paradise, where he ruled for one thousand years. He, like Yama, is the son of the sun-god *Vivahvant*, and as a royal king is said to shine forth like the sun. As the First Man he was often regarded as the progenitor of the human race.

At some point he committed a sin (a fact emphasized in the time of Zoroaster) and so lost his glory, forfeiting his immortality and that of all his seed.[3] Yet it is said that he will re-emerge from a subterranean place at the end of time. And despite Zoroaster's apparent attempts to denigrate Yima, as a semi-divine figure he went on being worshipped into Mohammedan times.[4]

---

dans la religion iranienne' in *Anthropologie religieuse* (*Numen* Suppl. II, ed. C. J. Bleeker), 1955, pp. 93ff.; Quispel in *Eranos Jahrbuch* 22, 1953, pp. 229f.; Zaehner, *Dawn and Twilight*, pp. 181ff., 217. Colpe, *op. cit.*, pp. 140ff., stresses the caution with which information about Gayomart must be used.

[1] Zaehner, *op. cit.*, p. 135. The teaching about Yima belongs 'to a very old stratum of Iranian folklore', certainly previous to the time of Zoroaster. On Yama see the *Rig-Veda* X. (In the *Rig-Veda* one *Manu* (= man) appears as a kind of brother and counterpart to Yama and is also pictured as a first of men.) S. G. F. Brandon, *Creation Legends of the Ancient Near East*, London, 1963, pp. 200f., speaks of 'the probability that Yima was in ancient Iranian tradition a kind of Primal Man, who lived in a golden age and was a benefactor and saviour of man and beast. Now this Yima was undoubtedly a counterpart of a somewhat similar figure, named Yama in Vedic mythology, and the two are probably to be traced to some common prototype in Aryan or Indo-European mythology.'

[2] See Zaehner, *op. cit.*, pp. 136f., on Gayomart as a substitute for Yima. Gaya maretan may have been adapted to replace Zoroaster's version of Yima. See also Christensen, *types du premier homme* II, p. 78. Zaehner suggests that Yima and Mithra may once have been regarded as twins and that they originally had to do with the equinoxes. Mithra later took over many of Yima's life-giving attributes and his royal heritage.

[3] Zoroaster would seem to have emphasized that the crime lay in the killing of the sacred ox. See Brandon, *op. cit.*, p. 201. It may also have had to do with giving men meat to eat.

[4] For this summary see Zaehner, *op. cit.*, pp. 132ff. We may also refer to the following texts: *Yasna* IX, 4. Yima is the son of the First Man, 'called the brilliant . . . the most glorious of those yet born, the sun-like one of men'. He reigns and

Christensen, in his study of First Man and first king figures in Iranian legends, stressed the realization that Yima is really but the outstanding type of the First Man-king or royal First Man.[1] There were similar types localized in other areas. Apparently there were later attempts to fuse these traditions, and this resulted in different orders in various lists of the ancient kings. Though Yima is often first, sometimes he becomes the son of a Siyamak, Hosang or Taxmoruw. Gaya is occasionally worked into this order, and the resulting confusion is such that Vivahvant himself is reduced to becoming the son of one of these ancient first kings. Christensen delineates this tendency for the son of the First Man to become the First Man, or for the father of the First Man to come to be regarded as the First Man.[2] Not only may this result from the later blending of different traditions, but it would seem that kings, as they succeeded to the throne, were anxious to trace their lineage back to the *eponym* or first hero of their own tribe and so caused the records to be rewritten in their own times. They wanted to regard themselves as types or representatives of the first king of the paradisaical era, and there seems to have been a recurrent myth regarding the *return* of the glorious primal king at the commencement of each new age or reign.

---

has control over plants and animals. *Yasna* IX, 6, infers that he himself was the First Man. In *Yast* XIII, 130 he again is pictured as ruling over the natural forces. (See *Sacred Books of the East* XXIII, p. 60, where we hear of 'shining Yima'. The translator sees him as an original solar hero who like the Vedic Yama became an earthly king before he sinned and was overthrown.) *Yast* XV, 15: 'Unto him did the bright Yima, the good shepherd, sacrifice from the height Hukairya, the all-shining and golden, on a golden throne, under golden beams and a golden canopy.' This clearly involves further sun imagery and shows Yima as a priest-king sacrificing on a holy mountain. In *Yast* XV, 16, Yima asks a boon of his sun-god father that he may become 'the most glorious of the men born to behold the sun'. He rules over all creatures and the paradisaical nature of his rule is then described. *Yast* XIX, 7 begins with praise of bright Yima's rule and shepherding. He is, however, attracted to falsehood and loses his glory. He trembles and is in sorrow before his foes. In the *Vendidad* fargard II, 1ff., he is first king and ruler in paradisaical circumstances. He is said to enlarge the earth and is described like the sun as he does so. See further *Yasna* IX, 1, 10; *Yast* IX, 8ff. A number of other references affirming these same qualities are collected by Christensen, *op. cit.* II, pp. 11ff. Several lists of kings headed by Yima are given. The later *Denkard* III, 179.2 praises all kings who resemble Yima. Later we hear that Yima's disobedience was caused by demons, but that he becomes victorious over them. He is represented also as the great law-giver, the revealer of religion. As with Yama, there is a later tendency to see him as a ruler over the land of the dead, even to regard him as a god of death.

[1] *Op. cit.* I, pp. 134ff.
[2] *Op. cit.* II, pp. 36ff.

In addition, and this is a feature we shall also meet with in other sources, there appears to have been some mythical tendency to regard the earthly king as the living representative of the king-god in heaven. They tend to become equivalent figures, sharing common attributes, and this is apparently one of the reasons why the king-god above *becomes* the Man on earth, while the earthly ruler can be glorified as though he were the god. This introduces what seems like an added measure of confusion into these lists, though it may not have been all that confusing to the men who first used them.

Thus, although it may now seem that Yima was always venerated as a kind of god, the impetus of the story suggests that he was also once a mortal as well, a man, the Man who became divinized and to whom sacral qualities and godly attributes were given. Although he is the First Man, it is as the first royal Man, the first semi-divine king ruling over his paradisaical kingdom that he is really venerated.

Widengren has several times emphasized the importance of this theme and the part which it has to play in the ideology of Iranian sacral kingship.[1] He finds that there was a definite tendency to think of succeeding kings in a similar fashion right on into Sassanian times. They were regarded as types of the cosmic ruler, a kind of divine sun-god, the son of the sun-god. The essence of their kingship is thought to be related to that of Yima. Their essential royalty derives from this figure now conceived of as a heavenly god, though he was once the first king of the earth. Each king will introduce 'again, the golden days of the mythical ruler Yima, the ideal Iranian king'.[2] This Yima, because of his antiquity, is far more likely to be a source or part of the earlier background of Primal Man thought than Gayomart.

We have noticed a relationship between the Iranian deity Mithra and Yima. Since Mithra is himself a figure of antiquity (worshipped as early as the fourteenth century BC), and since in this case we also know him as a deity whose veneration definitely moved into the Mediterranean world, it may be of some interest to glance at his place in this general background.

He shares a number of attributes in common with Yima. Though

---

[1] On Yima as a first king and Man, on his persecution, suffering, loss of glory and death and on traces of his place in New Year rites, see Widengren, *Die Religionen Irans*, Stuttgart, 1965, pp. 52ff. For a summary of his views cf. 'The Sacral Kingship of Iran' in *La Regalità Sacra/The Sacral Kingship* (*Numen* Suppl. IV), 1959, pp. 242ff.

[2] Widengren in *La Regalità Sacra*, p. 249.

often conceived of in human form, he, too, is strongly associated with solar imagery. The traditional picture shows him accompanied by two figures, one with a torch pointing up and the other down, representing the two equinoxes. From information given by a number of classical travellers and writers it would appear that the worship of this Mithra and the kingship cult in Persia and areas under its influence were closely allied over a period of centuries.[1] Widengren believes that, remembering that he was a dynasty god whose name was used by many kings of city-states from Asia Minor to Mesopotamia, one can glimpse evidence of his place in New Year rituals and of the idea of the king as a reincarnation or representative of Mithra with a birth like his birth.[2]

In the *Mithra Yast*[3] we hear of the veneration of the king-god Mithra who triumphantly progresses on his chariot from east to west, preceding the sun. He defeats his enemies and a home above the earth is built for him. (Zaehner surmises that a counterpart of this house- or temple-building was taking place on earth.[4] This, then, could possibly be likened to the ritual hut found in other kingship cults. Like many another sun-god type, Mithra is thought to have a palace or temple on a high mountain. There he can be said to have been born.)[5] He is next, however, pictured as complaining to his *Wise Lord* that he is not being properly worshipped. This is set right and even the Wise Lord is said to worship him. Mithra is acclaimed as the universal provider through whom the waters flow (he is often represented as offering life-giving water to his followers), through whom plants grow and flocks and herds are given. He is praised as the light who illumines the whole world.

Due to the expansion and development of Mithraic worship in Roman times it is often difficult to be sure which features belonged to the earlier Mithra. His slaying of the bull (the bull figure is, of course,

[1] See A. S. Geden, *Select Passages Illustrating Mithraism* (Translations of Early Documents), London, 1925, pp. 25f.; F. Cumont, *The Origins of Mithraism*, ET, Chicago, 1903, pp. 8f.; W. J. Phythian-Adams, *Mithraism*, London, 1915, pp. 16ff.

[2] See *Die Religionen Irans*, pp. 222ff., 238ff. He points esp. to Mithridates Eupator of Pontus. Like all priest-kings of this type, Mithridates must undergo persecutions and privations before assuming this kingship. For traces of these themes in older Iranian materials, cf. *op. cit.*, pp. 41ff.

[3] See I. Gershevitch, *The Avestan Hymn to Mithra*, Cambridge, 1959. Cf. Zaehner, *Dawn and Twilight*, pp. 107f.; M. J. Vermaseren, *Mithras, The Secret God*, ET, London, 1963, pp. 16f.

[4] Zaehner, *op. cit.*, p. 113.

[5] See Vermaseren, *op. cit.*, p. 16.

also associated with Yima and later with Gayomart) came to be of central interest. Originally this may have been related to myths found elsewhere which tell of the defeat of the primal monster by the king-Man or king-god at the time of creation. As in the stories of the *Anthropos* and the Primal Man, it is also often not clear whether Mithra is primarily a heavenly hero or one who does his heroic acts on earth. Probably of old he was thought to have been on the earth, but then to have ascended to heaven, where he is now to be worshipped.[1] It is said that he 'shared in the divinity of that star (i.e. the sun) and was its representative on earth'.[2] Certainly there grew up a belief that he would soon reappear,[3] even to be known again on earth,[4] which, as with Gayomart, probably reflects a growing emphasis on eschatological aspects of the stories of heroic figures in a number of places.[5]

There are records which depict a battle said to have taken place between Mithra and the sun-god. The sun, as it were, is uncrowned and stripped of his glittering raiment. Sometimes he is represented as kneeling before Mithra. After this harmony is restored (so Mithra is often presented with *Sol* at his side or eating together with him), and they both ascend in a chariot out of the waters from which Mithra is sometimes said to be born.[6] (Usually he is pictured emerging from a cave or out of a rock.)

Water plays an important part in the later Mithraic cult. In the initiatory rites there are sufferings and ordeals,[7] a baptism, ritual death and a rising out of the waters.[8] The vernal equinox was an especially favoured time for these rites, and this, along with the resemblance of the pattern to Mithra's own battle and triumph,

[1] See Zaehner, *op. cit.*, pp. 123f.

[2] See in Cumont, *op. cit.*, p. 102.

[3] Like many another such deity, Mithra was often pictured as a stern judge, esp. as the guardian of truth and contracts.

[4] Cf. *Mithra Yast*, 74.

[5] Mowinckel would stress the eschatological factor: 'But in most of these varying forms it is an essential feature that the Primordial Man (Anthropos) is an eschatological figure, as well as belonging to primordial time. Even in those spiritualized Gnostic systems which have a strongly individualistic tendency, something of the eschatological role of the Primordial Man is still apparent.' *HTC*, p. 425. See above p. 78, n. 2. Christensen (*op. cit.* II, p. 58) believed that eschatology had a long tradition in popular forms of Iranian religion. These myths seemed always to look forward, in one way or another, to the *new day*. See below in chs. III and IV.

[6] Cf. Phythian-Adams, *Mithraism*, pp. 59ff.

[7] Vermaseren, *op. cit.*, pp. 131ff.

[8] Phythian-Adams, *op. cit.*, pp. 59ff.

certainly suggests that these initiations were intended to emulate Mithra's story.

The obvious parallels between this Mithraic practice and Christian rites of baptism, taken together with the sacred meal of Mithraism, once prompted some to try to see Mithraism as a direct influence upon Christian derivations. The differences, however, as many have pointed out, are far greater than the similarities, and there is little if any reason to believe that Mithraic ideas affected Jesus' thinking or the earliest stories about him.[1] (The same may also be said with respect to the possible influence upon the earliest Christian forms by Greek mystery religions generally. As such they are not proximate forces.)[2]

Yet Mithra's worship holds some points of interest for us, and, due to his kinship with Yima and certain of the features associated with him, he is probably to be regarded as a variant type of the Primal Man (or at least a figure influenced by such beliefs) as well as a king-god figure.[3] But more than this would be difficult to demonstrate. We prefer the far safer course of viewing Mithra as but another parallel sign, much transformed in later circles, of the influence of some myth or myths concerning a Man-king and/or a royal Man-God of primitive times. The resurgence of interest in him may in some ways be analogous to the development of the gnostic *Anthropos* and the interest which came to be shown in Gayomart.

4. ANTHROPOS – IRAN – SON OF MAN?

That there is some relationship between the early Iranian conception of a kind of royal First Man, seen better in Yima than in Gayomart or Mithra, and the later types of the *Anthropos* would be hard to deny. There are distinct parallels in the patterns of their stories and in their attributes which would be difficult to explain

[1] Probably the outstanding parallels would be the star said to have heralded Jesus' birth and the attendant shepherds, but these appear to have a place only in later accounts.

[2] See A. D. Nock, 'Hellenistic Mysteries and Christian Sacraments', *Mnemosyne* 4,v, 1952, pp. 177ff. (also in *Early Gentile Christianity and Its Hellenistic Backgrounds*, New York, 1964). We cannot agree with all his points, but the discussion about differences in language is esp. useful. Certain features of figures like Attis and Osiris are not unrelated to a complete understanding of stories about the royal Man, but, and esp. in their Hellenistic dress, they are outside the scope of this study. Cf. G. Wagner, *Das religionsgeschichtliche Problem von Römer 6, 1–11* (ATHANT 39), 1962.

[3] He was even represented as making himself garments and naked in a garden cutting something from a tree (see Cumont, *op. cit.*, p. 132), but these could be due to later cross-influences.

were one to insist that there was no relationship at all. Since the older Iranian conceptions continued to be employed and venerated in one form or another up to and beyond the age of the *Anthropos*, they are to this extent contemporary with one another. Despite the geographical distance between them, in such a fluid and syncretistic era one can well imagine how two figures seen as resplendent cosmic heroes and yet also as first men and primal ancestors of an earlier golden age might have had a genuine degree of influence upon one another. While there was some flaw in their character or some manner of suffering and/or loss of immortality found in their story, they shared in common the consideration that they might reappear or come in a new form in the new age.

Yet it is no easy matter to go on from this point and to take the much larger step of asserting that the earlier Iranian primal hero and the gnostic *Anthropos* are so directly related that the latter has been fashioned from the former. And even while we might agree that there is some definite axis of ideas between Iranian and gnostic forms, and that we might speak in very general terms of a Primordial Man-*Anthropos* myth, it is not necessarily true that we are any closer to the solution of our major problem and that we have found in Iran the source of the Jewish and Christian Son of Man beliefs. Again there is almost surely *some* relationship. Mowinckel, after making lengthy lists of the similar attributes of the *Anthropos* and the Son of Man, concludes, 'A comparison of these two figures puts it beyond doubt that they are akin to each other', and he then goes on to hold that they have 'common roots' and that 'Anthropos and the Son of Man both go back to the myth about the Primordial Man'.[1] But how and why does this kinship exist? Have Judaism and Christianity, along with gnostic-type religions, simply borrowed an idea from the lore of Iran? What are the more precise interstices and connections in this story? Can we not provide a more viable historical context in which such borrowing might have taken place?

There have been attempts to answer this last question in the affirmative by pointing out the important contacts between Judaism and Iran from the time of Cyrus right up into the third century AD.[2]

[1] *HTC*, p. 431.
[2] Cf. Widengren, 'Juifs et Iraniens à l'époque des Parthes' in *VT* Suppl. IV, 1957, pp. 197ff.; and his *Iranisch-semitische Kulturbewegung in partischer Zeit*, Koln-Opladen, 1960. Probably of chief importance would be the Parthian defeat of the Romans and invasion of Palestine in 40 BC, which made them heroes in the eyes of many Jews.

In addition, the Dead Sea Scrolls have only served to underline the well-known fact that Judaism was in the process of being influenced by and developing thoughts parallel to Iranian beliefs over a long period of time.[1] It is certainly worth pointing out that this is nowhere more evident than in the books of Daniel and I Enoch where the Son of Man also makes his appearance.

Still the link must remain tenuous, and we would have only the vaguest of contexts into which we might set this process of borrowing and transforming an Iranian figure. The issue is only made more difficult by our uncertain knowledge concerning Iranian practices and beliefs during the crucial period from the Achaemenid dynasty to the Sassanian. While it is quite proper for scholars like Reitzenstein and Widengren to argue forward and then backward by demonstrating the influence of Iranian religion on Manichaeanism and Mandaeanism,[2] or to point to the manner in which Babylonian forms may have served as intermediaries,[3] and thus to speculate and make informed guesses about Iranian folk-religion during this era,[4] and, while it would be remiss of us totally to neglect such possibilities simply because it is a period of which we know comparatively little, such would not leave us with very firm grounds on which to proceed. Others have walked this way before us, and whole generations of scholars have been suspect of their efforts. J. H. Moulton once amusingly overstated this attitude when he castigated those 'previously ingenious people who write as if there was a complete set of the Sacred Books of the East in Aramaic on the shelves of a public library in Nazareth or Capernaum'.[5] This is an overstatement, because there is obviously no need to think in terms of direct literary

---

[1] See how much is granted even in the cautious statement by W. F. Albright, *From the Stone Age to Christianity²*, Baltimore, 1957, pp. 361ff. Cf. Zaehner, *Dawn and Twilight*, pp. 51ff. Evidence of strong Iranian influence is recognized in areas from Nabataea northwards. See the conflation of Jewish and Iranian ideas in Adiabene indicated by Josephus, *Jewish Antiquities* (LCL, ed. 1930–65) XX, 17ff.

[2] See Widengren, *The Great Vohu Manah and the Apostle of God. Studies in Iranian and Manichaean Religion* (UUA), Uppsala, 1945/V. Kraeling emphasized its role in syncretistic religions generally. 'The Influence of Iranian Religion upon Hellenistic Syncretism' in *Oriental Studies in Honour of C. E. Pavry* (ed. J. D. C. Pavry), London, 1933, pp. 223ff. See above, p. 73 n. 2.

[3] See Widengren, *Mesopotamian Elements in Manichaeism*; W. Bousset with H. Gressmann in *Religion des Judentums im späthellenistischen Zeitalter³* (Handbuch zum NT 21), Tübingen, 1926, and below in ch. III.

[4] Widengren, *op. cit.*, p. 9. Cf. Zaehner, *Dawn and Twilight*, pp. 167ff.

[5] *Early Zoroastrianism*, London, 1913, p. 296.

influence. Rather are we very likely in this instance dealing with a powerful and persistent idea which seemed capable of manifesting itself in various ways and strongly affecting the hopes and beliefs of men in different cultures at different times.

Before, however, we should even begin to make ourselves dependent upon so slender a theory, it is prudent and vital that we also consider other possibilities. If we are correct in understanding the Man myth as a pervasive conception, it should have made its presence felt at an early date in other faiths than those of Iran. Perhaps by seeing the idea against a yet larger background we shall be better able to account for certain variant emphases and aspects of the story as they are found at a later time. Perhaps, in addition, we may find that it is not simply a legendary conception which has been imported into the locale of our particular concern, Palestine, at a comparatively late date, but one which, though affected by other cultures, has a much more indigenous place in Palestinian understandings. Obviously, if this were so, we could hope to recover a far more reliable historical context for its relationship to late Jewish and then Christian beliefs.

No one is more conscious than this author of the rather superficial manner in which we have here covered a great sweep of history and the relevant aspects of a number of religions. Fortunately we will be able to return to many of these matters as we continue, but in the meantime, despite the sketchiness of the outline, it is our contention that we have good cause for suspecting that there was a mythical conception of relative antiquity concerning a primal hero, conceived of as a Man who was once on earth, whose story contains some reference to defeat or death. Yet somehow he was also regarded as one who was or who was very closely allied with a glorious, cosmic Man figure of the heavens. While such legendary beliefs are never found in exactly the same guise and often appear only in fragmentary forms, and while we do not necessarily postulate some one original myth, there is reason to conclude that the variant descriptions are related. And thus it will be worth while now to hold in mind some of the more distinctive strands of ideas which we have so far surveyed as we make analysis and comparison with other Man figures. In particular we would here recall the frequent association of the Man with solar imagery, the way in which he is often pictured as a radiant semi-divine Man. Somewhat less prominent, but frequent enough to arouse our interest, is his association with water as the element from which he is born, where he must struggle or into which he is said to descend or out of which he arises. Yet, above all, the aspect which must by now have commanded our attention is the tendency to present the Man as a royal hero, a kind of ideal king. It is this feature which very properly provides our next point of departure.

IIII

THE ROYAL MAN

But let thy hand be upon the man of thy right hand,
the Son of Man whom thou hast made strong for thyself.
(Ps. 80.17)

I. FIRST MAN AND KING

AAGE BENTZEN IN his book *King and Messiah* held that the anointed king was, above all, the First Man. 'The king, then, is Primeval Man.'[1] Indeed, he would go further, for behind the conceptions of the ideal king, the ideal prophet and the ideal priest can be found the ideal eponym, the great and perfect patriarch, the first of men. This belief was fundamental not only in Israel but in many of the ancient religions of the Near East.

Ivan Engnell in his *Studies in Divine Kingship in the Ancient Near East*[2] lays the stress somewhat the other way around. Behind the conception of ideal Man there is to be seen the figure of the great and perfect king of primordial time. He is the royal god-Man, son of the high-god, manifested in all succeeding kings.

It is the argument of this chapter that, although differences in these understandings do exist, both Bentzen and Engnell are substantially correct, while there is no need for us to decide which conception is more fundamental. We wish only to establish that the two figures were, in many crucial respects and over a long period of time, intimately related, and that, just as we have tended to discover that the First Man was often seen as first king, so men were able to regard the first king as the First Man, one who was believed to be represented in later royal personages (especially in their role as the king of paradise in creation festivals) and also in the conception of an ideal king during subsequent generations.[3] In the course of this discussion

[1] *King and Messiah*, p. 17.
[2] Uppsala, 1943.
[3] We and others find it surprising that Mowinckel should be the one to set himself against this understanding. (See his 'Urmensch und Königsideologie', *ST* 2, 1948/9, pp. 71ff. In reply cf. Bentzen, *op. cit.*, 39ff., and 'King Ideology—–

we hope to show that these ideas are basic to an understanding of the background for both the Son of Man and the Jewish Messiah. Also we wish to demonstrate how and why the First Man-king of the earth and the royal, Primordial God-Man cannot be regarded as wholly distinct figures.[1] The influence of each upon the other has been profound, and, in ritual and mythical terms, for good reasons.

2. THE ROYAL RITES

The attempts to recover patterns of events and ideas which were central to Near Eastern rites of kingship cannot be said to have met with universal acceptance, and it would be foolish to think that we could in one chapter adequately sum up the whole matter and answer the many doubts and questions which have been raised.[2] We hope that we are conscious of the very real dangers of pattern-ism[3] and recognize that, due to complexities and ambiguities in-

---

"Urmensch"—"Troonsbestijgingsfeest" ', *ST* 3, 1949/50, pp. 151ff.) He is con-strained to admit that First Man beliefs have influenced Babylonian and Israelite ideas of kingship. (See *HTC*, pp. 37 n. 6, 47 n. 2, 55, 81.) Well realizing the central role of the king in the creation festival, that the king's enthronement often occurred at this time, that the royal figure rules over the *waters* and is influenced by the conception of the first gardener in paradise, while the beasts which assault him are analogous with the dragon(s) of the creation myth (cf. his *The Psalms in Israel's Worship*, Oxford, 1962, I, pp. 196ff., 152ff., and *HTC*, pp. 80f.), Mowinckel would yet try to dismiss these factors with the argument that such events were mythopoeic, idealized and thought to be contemporary rather than belonging to the time of creation. (See *HTC*, pp. 36f.; in reply, Bentzen, *King and Messiah*, p. 89 n. 19.). This sounds odd coming from one who has taught us so much about cultic *reality* and who can maintain, 'In Babylon, as elsewhere in the East, the chief annual festival was regarded as an actual recreation of the world' (*HTC*, p. 40).

[1] Mowinckel admits that the Son of Man was viewed as a type of the first king of paradise (*HTC*, pp. 382f.), but since he wants to insist on a distinction between earthly First Man and the divinized Primordial Man (see above, p. 70 n. 3) and holds that the Son of Man is derived only from the latter, he would deny that this conception of the Son of Man has any significance for royal ideology.

[2] See K.-H. Bernhardt, *Das Problem der altorientalischen Königsidelogie im Alten Testament* (*VT* Suppl. VIII), 1959, and J.-H. Kraus, *Worship in Israel*, ET, Oxford, 1966, both of whom, however, schematize and simplify the views with which they disagree. Nothing said below questions the historical basis of kingship in Israel and elsewhere. (Cf. M. Noth, 'Gott, König, Volk im Alten Testament. Eine methodologische Auseinandersetzung mit einer gegenwärtigen Forschungsrichtung', *ZTK* 47, 1950, pp. 157ff.) Historical and myth-ritual attitudes are not mutually exclusive.

[3] See H. Frankfort's *The Problem of Similarity in Ancient Near Eastern Religions*, Oxford, 1951, and his frequent critical remarks in *Kingship and the Gods*, Chicago, 1948. In reply to Frankfort's own imbalance, cf. S. H. Hooke's introductory essay in *Myth, Ritual and Kingship* (ed. Hooke) Oxford, 1958, pp. 1ff.

herent in our research into such matters, the critic who maintains this or that theory not to be *proven* is but stating the obvious.

Nevertheless, we find ourselves increasingly appreciative of the work of a number of scholars who have sought to find certain degrees of commensuration between the kingship ideologies of several Near Eastern cultures over a period of many centuries. Although these scholars are never in perfect agreement with one another, they do tend to point to many of the same themes and practices, and, in many cases, even to the same patterns for these beliefs and rites. Their theories have the virtue of helping to account for much evidence and information which would otherwise remain inexplicable. It is our intention to offer an outline of some of the salient features of these kingship ideologies as we see them, especially singling out the aspects which are of special relevance for this study. This will be followed by an attempt to give the outline more body by mentioning the important pieces of evidence out of which the outline itself has emerged. Unavoidably we shall be selective,[1] and—this must be stressed—the outline which follows is not in its totality demonstrably that of any single culture at a point in time. It can probably be regarded as relatively synthetic, containing features both from more agriculturally oriented practices and from those of the more urbanized peoples dedicated to the worship of their city's king-god as a kind of solar deity. Yet, at the same time, it must be remembered that these ancient practices were themselves synthetic. Though we shall find ourselves to be more interested in the advanced and usually later types of belief,[2] we realize that they have often incorporated (or themselves are but new interpretations of) the older agricultural patterns of worship.

[1] We shall largely leave aside Egyptian beliefs with their more obvious stress upon the king's divinity. Although Egyptian thought can hardly be divorced from kingship ideologies found in Mesopotamia and elsewhere, it is clear both that the differences were rather more far-reaching and also, importantly, that it was not the Egyptian pattern as such which had direct effects upon beliefs in Palestine (though, even so, it is worth noting the Egyptian names in the Davidic court). On Egyptian kingship with emphases on the differences, see Frankfort, *Kingship and the Gods*, pp. 15ff.; and cf. H. W. Fairman, 'The Kingship Rituals of Egypt' in *Myth, Ritual and Kingship* (ed. S. H. Hooke), Oxford, 1958, pp. 74ff.

[2] Thus we shall not express much interest in the dying and rising god as a pure vegetation deity of the Tammuz (who as Dumuzi reaches well back into Sumerian lore) type. With regard to the realization that the solar and fertility myths were by no means mutually exclusive, see Engnell, *Divine Kingship*, pp. 19f. More generally, see in Frankfort, *Kingship and the Gods*, pp. 286ff., who notes how king-gods like Marduk and Ashur were affected by variants of the Tammuz myth.

Nor shall we want to argue that the conception in its entirety or in a particular pattern passed on unaltered from locale to locale and era to era. We shall, however, hope to show that a number of the constituent ideas as well as the attendant attributes possessed a vital longevity and that they left their imprint on the ideologies of several societies, and also that, despite the alterations and different stresses, these ideas continued to reform themselves and to affect the later beliefs and hopes of men.

(*1*) The all-important cultic period for the king and his society came at the time of the chief annual festival. Usually taking place at one of the equinoxes[1] (apparently regulated both by the position of the sun and with regard for the times of the fructifying rains), this festival was concerned with establishing good omens, giving promise of beneficial agricultural conditions, and with providing a social and cosmological harmony between the people and their ruler and between the ruler, representative of all the people, and the god or gods.

The festival was seen as a re-creation of the world. The powers of nature had been decaying, relapsing again toward chaos over the course of the year. The cycle had run its limit, and, if the natural order were to go on, the forces of chaos and death had to be defeated anew. During the days of the festival the creation story was therefore either ritually enacted or, at the least, ceremonially read. For these reasons the festival can be described, as it often was, as the festival of the New Year or the feast of the end or turning of the year.

The central figure was the king;[2] he was both chief actor and priest.[3] Not only did he function as the representative of the people

---

[1] Whether the stress fell on the spring or autumn equinox seems to have had much to do with local agricultural and seasonal patterns. Choosing the correct *day* was obviously of great importance (see below on the orientation of sun and temple), and it is probable that astral calculations (and mythology) played a more significant role than we now realize. See S. Smith 'The Practice of Kingship in Early Semitic Kingdoms' in *Myth, Ritual and Kingship* (ed. S. H. Hooke), Oxford, 1958, pp. 37ff. Both the heavenly royal Man and his frequent bull (or animal) companion (or enemy) could be seen among the stars. This might be one of the contributions to the several links which exist between Mesopotamian astral imagery and that of later gnostic-type religions.

[2] See Gaster, *Thespis*, pp. 32f. It would appear, however, that in some locales the *royal* characteristics of the festival and the place of the king in it may only have received particular emphasis in connection with the beginning of new reigns or at times of crisis.

[3] On important aspects of the pattern discussed below, see E. O. James, *The Nature and Function of Priesthood*, London, 1955, pp. 105ff.

and their intermediary with the divine, but he could assume for certain designated parts of the drama the role of the king-god. 'What happens to the king symbolizes what has happened to the god.'[1] The stage was cosmic; distinctions between earth and heaven were temporarily suspended. The king and the king-god could, representationally, be one, their attributes *confused*.[2] The human king, if not strictly regarded as a divinity for these purposes (and this doubtless varied from culture to culture so that there is properly much debate here),[3] became a sacred personage. 'In certain respects a union of divine and human takes place in his representative person.'[4] Bentzen has nicely employed the anachronistic adjective *Nestorian* to convey something of this dual status and its complexity.[5] Possibly this could be viewed as a kind of *incarnation* of the god, but this seems neither the intent nor the interest of the rites and myths. It is not so much that the divine has come to earth to be represented by a mortal man, as that the king-man has *become* a *divine* being and can represent the king-god to his people.

Nevertheless it is, we believe, just this cultic tendency to fuse roles which enabled the king-gods in mythical legends to share many of the characteristics of the earthly king, the king who is a figure of the First Man. The king-god can thus be described as a king or First Man now in heaven, though he often still plays a part in the lists of earthly kings of primordial times. So also to the earthly king, who is the son of the king-god, there are attributed qualities of the one who reigns in heaven.

(*2*) As the chief actor and in the role of the king-god the king must fight the creation battle against the primeval forces of darkness, evil and chaos. These powers are often represented as beasts or a chaos monster. In historified forms the enemies can be seen as foreign kings or peoples intent on overthrowing the society. It may be that versions of the myth which were agriculturally oriented have supplied the picture of chaos in terms of water and flood, while those

---

[1] Mowinckel, *HTC*, p. 42.

[2] Engnell speaks of a purposeful confusion of the high-god and the king (*Divine Kingship*, p. 24).

[3] Mowinckel stresses the *representative* character of the king's role, though he realizes that at times the god might have been thought to manifest himself in the king (*HTC*, p. 49). A. R. Johnson, *Sacral Kingship in Ancient Israel*, Cardiff, 1955. prefers to speak of the king in extant Israelite materials as *sacral* rather than *divine*. See further below.

[4] Mowinckel, *HTC*, p. 49.

[5] *King and Messiah*, p. 19.

which centred upon the conception of the king-god as a solar deity conceived of evil as the power of darkness. None the less, if this distinction be accurate, the variants have a common point in that the sun was often believed to set into the sea from out of which it must rise the next day.

In this struggle the king is at first defeated. He is near to drowning (in the subterranean waters or river which threaten to engulf and return the earth to chaos), and/or he goes down into the earth to a place of darkness and death. He suffers and is totally humiliated; he becomes a figure of contempt, even of ridicule. His royal regalia has been stripped away. He may actually have been struck and beaten, even immersed or put into a pit. Often this suffering was interpreted as a result of his sin, though at times he is seen to suffer as an innocent victim.[1] If he is a sinner, his great crime consisted in a lack of humility. Odd though it at first seems, he was accused of trying to make himself into a deity. Yet he is subject to all the pangs of mortality, and the gods are punishing him. He, of course, is deposed and ceases to be a king. In his woe and tribulation the king makes confession of sin and/or pleas of innocence. He performs acts of humility. He calls out for help to the god and cries for salvation.[2] Probably various sacrifices were made at this juncture.

[1] It is sometimes held that clear distinctions must be kept between various kinds of suffering undergone by royal figures: (1) a suffering in ritual or mythical battle; (2) suffering which comes upon an innocent figure; (3) a suffering which is penitential (often imposed by God) and accepted as the result of sin. Though the emphases are various and some sort of categorization is always possible, it is our belief that these forms of suffering, in so far as they do relate to the leader of the society, represent three ways of viewing the same ancient theme. Description and imagery often reveal that the suffering (at the hands of demons, beasts, evil forces or *foreigners*, in water, at the creation, that is horribly disfiguring, etc.) derives from stories about the suffering of the first king. Whether he is an innocent or a penitent depends on the particular standpoint and the version of the story which is being employed, though it is not uncommon to find the two ideas side by side in stories about both kings and first men. So, e.g., Ps. 69.4f. (and note that, whereas in v. 4 the suffering is caused by others, in v. 26 it is said to come from God). Cf. 1QH, ix. There seems a sense in which by confession of wrongs and humble submission (or through a very great deal of suffering) the figure becomes a kind of *acquitted* or innocent sufferer.

[2] Since the king was often regarded as one playing the part of the king-god in the drama up to this point, it is not always easy to understand which is the god to whom he now calls out for help. Sometimes it appears that it is to the high-god, the father of the king-god (and thus the father of the king acting the part of the king-god), but at other times it is the king-god himself whose help he requests. Partially to understand this we need to comprehend how the gods could sometimes exchange roles, solar deities often being seen in two guises. (See p. 104 n. 4.) It may be, too, that myth, and perhaps ritual as well, was in this matter willing to

(*3*) His cries are heard. He is saved and is raised up, or, in some forms, the stress falls on the idea that he himself is empowered to rise. Through the partaking of the sacred water and/or food his powers revive in him. He may now be given some of the appurtenances of his kingship. Thus armed, he overcomes the powers of evil and chaos, a victory in which both king and people share. Out of the body of the slain chaos monster the new creation is made.[1] It was probably at this moment that divine oracles were interpreted; the destinies for the new year were set.

An oracle was read proclaiming the favour of the god toward the king. He is seen as absolved, cleansed. He is born, arises and is pronounced the divine son, the rightful claimant to the throne. He becomes the adopted son or representative of the god, the true king. The defeated enemies are led in triumphal procession. The king ascends to a high *mountain*, symbolically to heaven.

(*4*) There follows the enthronement of the king, emulating the enthronement of the king-god in heaven. (Usually this was, of course, performed in the temple of the city-state either built like or actually set upon a mountain or hill. It would appear, however, that at times the enthronement might have taken place in a ritual hut,[2] a hut which was constructed both as a symbol of the order of the new creation and as a replica of the god's heavenly temple. This has affected later interpretations of the function of the temple.) The king is anointed. The holy garment is put on him together with the crown and other royal regalia. He is said to be radiant, to shine like the sun just as does the king-god. He is initiated into heavenly secrets and

---

recognize the distinction between the king-god whose victory had been won in the past and the king who was now near to death in the re-enactment of that *event*. It does appear that there was a version of the legend in which the king only *became* the king-god or his son or representative (depending on the prevailing conception of the king-god, whether he was himself the high-god) at the time of his enthronement. The suffering and *dying* were then no longer associated with the god himself. This may well have been a theological advance on the more original forms of the story.

[1] In a few presentations it would seem that the world was made from the body of the primordial king-god who had been killed in the battle. He was the dead ruler, while now the *new* king was raised up to rule in his stead. Behind this understanding there lies a myth of the battle of the seasons.

[2] Gaster, *Thespis*, p. 39, is among those who believe that the hut was once used for the king's consecration. This practice must stem from the time when there was heavy emphasis on the agricultural nature of the festival. This *temple* would have been mythically built in the first garden. See below on the hut.

given wisdom. He is permitted to sit upon the throne, often regarded as the very throne of the god. He rules and judges; all enemies are subservient. All do him obeisance.

(5) The final stage is one of great rejoicing. In several cultures the king now consummated the sacred marriage with a woman who was herself regarded as a representative of the goddess, wife of the king-god. This union not only demonstrated who the king was, but it was a mimetic act, intended to signal and encourage the reproductive processes of the world of nature.

All would be well with the society. Once more the people share in the drama of their king, now in its happy conclusion. Feasting ensues. The king fulfils his role as the great provider, giving to his people gifts of food and drink like those of which he had partaken. Mythically it is the food of paradise,[1] for now he rules in paradise next to the tree of life and beside the river of life which is peaceful and ordered again and over which he exercises control. All nature is his dominion. It is the beginning of creation all over again, and the king is the First Man and ruler restored, the father of his people. The cycle is ready to repeat itself.

3. NEAR EASTERN SOURCES

One of the most valued of our sources with regard to these beliefs and rites is material having to do with the festival of the New Year which took place at Babylon and almost certainly in other Mesopotamian city-states.[2] There the king was assuredly the central actor.[3] Were he not present, the festival could not take place. During the course of these rites the *Enuma elish*, the creation story, was twice recited. The role of the god Marduk was played by the king; '. . . at the annual festival their courses converged, and during the holy days of the festival the king and Marduk were identified.'[4] Like

---

[1] Sometimes the *meal* was regarded as a feasting upon the flesh of the dead monster. This may have been part of the original significance of the Iranian bull companion of the First Man.

[2] On literature regarding this whole festival, cf. Engnell, *Divine Kingship*, pp. 201f.; Bernhardt, *Königsideologie*, pp. 307ff. For suggestions regarding similar practices in Iran, see above pp. 79ff.

[3] See e.g., S. A. Pallis, *The Babylonian* Akîtu *Festival*, Copenhagen, 1926, pp. 139ff., 215f., 264ff.; Gaster, *Thespis*, pp. 35ff.

[4] Pallis, *The Antiquity of Iraq: A Handbook of Assyriology*, Copenhagen, 1956, p. 691. See Akîtu *Festival*, pp. 140f., where he notes the same point as well as the king's identification with the god Ashur in Ashur.

Marduk, the king had to do battle with the demons of the water; he must experience wounding, imprisonment and death before he vanquished them, rises to the top of the holy mountain and consummated the sacred marriage. The heavenly temple was then built.

Marduk was clearly regarded as a kind of year-god with a cycle representing his birth, youth, decline and *resurrection*.[1] Both Marduk and the king are at various times said to be serving under high gods like Ea (the god of wisdom who arises from the sea each morning) or the sun-god Shamash. It would seem that Marduk along with his high-god were often conceived of as a pair, the older god and the young, virile god-king who sometimes replaces him by himself ascending to become the high sun-god.[2] Obviously the symbolism had reference to the changing of the seasons.

In the *Enuma elish* we first hear that Apsu, another primeval chaos monster, was put to sleep, fettered and slain.[3] The cultic reed hut is built, and from the watery Apsu's heart Marduk is created, begotten of his father Ea. His huge, glorious and perfect body is praised; he possesses a double portion of eyes and ears. Ea addresses him: 'My little son, my little son: My son, the Sun: Sun of the heavens.' In due course, however, Marduk is yielded the supreme lordship, and we are told of the slaughter of the monster Tiamat and Marduk's enthronement.

In the 'Temple Program for the New Year's Festivals at Babylon' the 'bright, light' Marduk is acclaimed as the one who 'measures the water of the sea and cultivates the fields'. It is he 'who turns over the pure scepter to the king who reveres him'.[4] Amid directions to the priest we hear how the king is to be dealt with. From him the priest shall 'take away the scepter, the circle and the sword . . . and strike the king's cheek'. In the presence of the god Bel (i.e. Bel-Marduk) shall he drag the king 'by the ears and make him bow down to the ground'. The king shall say, 'I did not sin, lord of the countries . . .' After words engendering confidence, 'the king shall regain his composure . . . The scepter, circle and sword shall be restored to the king. He (the priest) shall strike the king's cheek. If,

[1] See S. Smith in *Myth, Ritual and Kingship*, pp. 39ff.

[2] Engnell, *op. cit.*, pp. 18f. On Marduk as a high-god see the opinion of Mowinckel, *HTC*, p. 453. Jansen (*Henochgestalt*, pp. 105ff.) regarded Ea-Oannes as one of the primary types of the Primordial Man, but Marduk, we believe, much more readily fits this role, while Ea-Oannes only shares in some of his attributes.

[3] See in *ANET*, pp. 60ff.

[4] Vv. 228ff.; *ANET*, p. 332.

when he strikes the king's cheek, the tears flow, the god Bel is friendly.'[1]

In such a rite as this the king is not only acting out his own loss of glory and kingship followed by re-enthronement, but there is an important sense in which he is playing the role of Marduk as well. 'By means of the rites of penance and lamentation, king and people share in the experience of Marduk's imprisonment and humiliation, which are the occasion of these rites.'[2] 'Through him they all experience the fate of the god become the "archetype" of the people.'[3] Engnell is another scholar who wishes to stress the atoning character of these practices and the realization that such suffering is necessary before victory can be granted.[4]

G. Widengren has further aided our understanding of the conception of the king, not only in Mesopotamia but elsewhere in the Near East, by piecing together the picture of the ruler representing the god in the garden of paradise. It is clear, for instance, that several Near Eastern temples had in their precincts a *garden* (the garden of the gods)[5] in which there were located the tree and waters of life.[6] This idea is carried right on into the Book of Revelation and has influenced earlier Israelite beliefs.[7] The king is the gardener, possessor of the *plant* and water of life.[8] Many times the king is pictured holding a twig or plant in one hand, while in the other he grasps a cup or vase of water. Occasionally we see him watering his tree of life.[9] He is so closely associated with these that he can even be *identified* with them and himself be seen as the tree under which his people find protection and as the source of the life-giving water.[10]

The sceptre of the king, the sceptre which is often said to bud, is

[1] Vv. 415ff.; *ANET*, p. 334.

[2] Mowinckel, *HTC*, p. 41.

[3] *HTC*, p. 236.

[4] *Op. cit.*, p. 35. See Pallis (Akîtu *Festival*, pp. 200ff.) on these dramatic themes of death and lamentation, resurrection and rejoicing.

[5] *The King and the Tree of Life in Ancient Near Eastern Religion* (UUA), 1951/IV, p. 45. It is hardly surprising that the garden in Mesopotamia is sometimes called *Apsu*, for it has been made from the slain monster's body.

[6] *Op. cit.*, pp. 9f., 17.

[7] *Op. cit.*, p. 36. See Rev. 22.2 and a number of texts as interpreted by Widengren: Ps. 46.5; Num. 5.17; I Kings 1.9, 38; Isa. 8.6; Ezek. 47.1f.; Zech. 13.1; I Enoch 13.7; etc.

[8] *Op. cit.*, p. 35. Note King Sargon as gardener in 'The Legend of Sargon', *ANET*, p. 119.

[9] Widengren, *op. cit.*, pp. 20ff.

[10] *Op. cit.*, pp. 56ff. Note esp. Ezek. 31.2–9 with regard to Pharaoh, and see further below on Lam. 4.20; etc. Note Dan. 4.20ff. regarding Nebuchadnezzar.

derived from the tree of life ideogram.[1] Widengren holds that this is behind the tradition of Moses' rod and points to Israelite legend in which it is maintained that this rod has been passed on from Adam to Seth and through his descendants to Moses (Moses, a figure later coloured by attributes pertaining to the ideal Man-priest-king-prophet).[2] So, too, in Israel as elsewhere, the description of the ruler as a *shoot* or *branch* ultimately depends upon this symbolism.[3] And it is from the tree of life that kings are said to be anointed, from which their garland crown is made, and from its branches the ritual hut is constructed.[4] Many of these ideas can be shown going back through Israelite to Canaanite beliefs, which in turn may have been borrowed from known Mesopotamian practices.[5]

The food of the tree of life and the libation from the water of life are considered to have a revivifying power. Not only do they revive the king, but he is also represented as feeding them to his people.[6] The same results are accomplished with an act of sprinkling the waters of life upon the king which is also regarded as a purificatory act. Widengren quotes from two texts in which a Mesopotamian royal figure is so besprinkled, and, as this is done, he is called in each text the *Man*.[7] As Widengren notes, the word *amēlu* used in the second of these texts in the expression 'the Man, the son of his god' is elsewhere interchangeable with the phrase 'the king, the son of his god'. Indeed, it could hardly be otherwise, as the king is obviously, in this whole portrayal, being considered as the First Man. Thus there are other Mesopotamian royal texts which tell of the king or the god being washed by that which is evidently regarded as the water of life.[8] In another essay Widengren sums up the conception:

[1] *Op. cit.*, p. 37.
[2] *Op. cit.*, pp. 38f., 60.
[3] *Op. cit.*, pp. 48ff. Widengren mentions a number of well-known texts: Isa. 4.2; 11.1; 53.2; Jer. 23.5; 33.15; Zech. 3.8; 6.12.
[4] *Op. cit.*, p. 39.
[5] *Op. cit.*, p. 52.
[6] *Op. cit.*, pp. 32f., 35f.
[7] *Op. cit.*, pp. 45f. In the first of these texts the water sprinkled on the *LUGAL* (the great Man) comes from Apsu (i.e. paradise) and is also sprinkled on the tree of life. Bentzen believed that particular attention ought to be paid to this older Sumerian word *LUGAL* as it is applied to both kings and primal men. 'This "First Man" is the origin of the functions of king, prophet and priest' (*King and Messiah*, p. 44).
[8] See *op. cit.*, p. 47, and Widengren's *The Ascension of the Apostle and the Heavenly Book* (UUA), 1950/VII, p. 8 n. 3. Cf. J. Laessøe, *Studies in the Assyrian Ritual and Series* bît rimki, Copenhagen, 1955, p. 14 n. 14 ('typically, bathing is followed by

Primordial Man as the Gardener is a widespread mythic-ritual conception in the ancient Near East, especially associated with royal ideology.
The king in Mesopotamia, for example, is the living representative of the
mythical Gardener in paradise. The Tyrian ruler, as the incarnation of
the Primordial Man in paradise, carries on this mythical tradition and, in
the Israelite combination of Primordial Man and ruler, the idea is still
living . . .[1]

Other heroes who emerge out of Sumerian and Akkadian lore
bear traces of a number of these motifs. If not genuine types of the
royal First Man, they have at least been imbued by the same nexus of
ideas. Gilgamesh, who is both a type of mankind and a semi-divinized
royal personage, like all such figures, is praised for his wisdom.
Several of the gods have fashioned him as a giant of superhuman size.
He is described as 'the joyful *man*' (LÚ = *amēlu*).[2] With his friend
Enkidu (a primitive who gains near-divinity through sexual knowledge)[3] Gilgamesh goes on a search for immortality.[4] Together they
slay a great bull beast and offer him to the sun-god Shamash.

In 'The Sumerian King List' we find that the king Ur-nugal was
known as the son of Gilgamesh. 'The divine Gilgamesh' is included
in the list as an historical priest-king.[5] In this same list we interestingly find one 'Meskiaggasher, the son of the (sun) god Utu', who
becomes high priest and king and who 'went (daily) into the (Western) Sea and came forth (again) toward the (Sunrise) Mountains'.[6]

More intriguing is Adapa, whose very name, like Adam's, could
signify man.[7] (In a seventh-century letter sent to the king Ashurbani-

---

anointing'); p. 16 n. 20 (on the ritual bathing of a statue of Ashur at the end of the
old year); pp. 65ff., 83ff.

   [1] 'Early Hebrew Myths and their Interpretation' in *Myth, Ritual and Kingship*
(ed. S. H. Hooke), Oxford, 1958, pp. 168f. Cf. Engnell, *Divine Kingship*, pp. 25ff.
   [2] 'The Epic of Gilgamesh' I, v, 14 (*ANET*, p. 75). On Gilgamesh see also *ANET*,
pp. 44ff. F. M. Th. Böhl, 'Das Menschenbild in babylonischer Schau' in *Anthropologie religieuse* (ed. C. J. Bleeker, *Numen*, Suppl. II), 1955, pp. 28ff., points to a
variety of royal features found in figures like Gilgamesh and Adapa and finds them
frequently described as the Man or the Great Man.
   [3] On Enkidu as another type of the First Man, see Brandon, *Creation Legends*,
p. 126.
   [4] In 'The Epic of Gilgamesh' XI, 226ff. (*ANET*, p. 96), Gilgamesh, while
bathing in the water, loses his opportunity to gain immortality from the plant of
life.
   [5] *ANET*, p. 265.
   [6] *ANET*, p. 266.
   [7] See 'Adapa', *ANET*, pp. 101ff. Albright (*From the Stone Age to Christianity*, pp.
379f.) has suggested a possible source for the Man designation in the late Assyrian

pal we hear that his grandfather, Sennacherib, was considered to be the offspring of Adapa, that is, a kind of son of Adapa, or, if you will, a son of Man.)[1] He is addressed both as Adapa and *man* (*eṭlu*). His story, like that of Gilgamesh, is built around the motif of man's lost opportunity of gaining immortality. Though he, too, is a figure of great wisdom and honour, this gift also eludes his grasp. He is created as the *model* of men, the 'seed of mankind'. He is a priest, the son of the god Ea. After an accidental drowning he mounts to heaven, clad in mourning garments; but there he is tricked into not eating the life-giving bread and water, thinking them to be vehicles of death. He is, however, allowed to anoint himself and put on a different garment (presumably a kind of royal robe). Yet, because he has lost his chance for immortality, he is mocked. He is called *perverse* or *corrupt* mankind and is returned to earth. He has brought ill upon all mankind.

This little story would seem to be a form of aetiological legend built up from kingship materials. We find variants in other locales (including the early chapters of Genesis) as well as mockeries of other kings who thought themselves able to arise to heaven and become divine, only to be doomed to die like other mortals.[2]

In the texts from Ugarit a number of scholars have found traces of similar ideologies and themes.[3] There is the complex of the chaos battle, creation, the sacred marriage and the building of the hut which strongly suggests that a New Year festival was once vital to this culture.[4] Primeval figures like Danel and Keret are kings; they are first kings in myths which may very well have devolved from

---

epic concerning Atrahasis in which Atrahasis is both a first of men and a royal figure, the son of the god Ea. (See 'Atrahasis', *ANET*, pp. 104ff., and the introduction there. The epic, beginning with the creation, of which our fragments are parts, once had the opening, 'When God, *Man* [*awēlum*] . . .') An important appellation, for the figure is *man* (*amēlu*). He is the Man, Atrahasis, whose name means 'exceeding wise', which in turn was given as a title to Adapa and other primal figures. Albright, in fact, inclines toward the view that Adapa may be a more recent name for Atrahasis, whose older name, going back at least another thousand years, was Atramhasis.

[1] 'A Letter to Ashurbanipal', *ANET*, p. 450.
[2] E.g. the taunt against the King of Babylon in Isa. 14.4ff., esp. vv. 12ff. Here, too, is the often-repeated idea that the great sin of both kings and first men was to try to make themselves like God.
[3] Cf. J. Gray, *The Legacy of Canaan* (*VT* Suppl. V), 1957, and Engnell, *Divine Kingship*, pp. 97ff., 143ff.
[4] Cf. L. R. Fisher, 'Creation at Ugarit and in the Old Testament', *VT* 15, 1965, pp. 313ff.

ritual practices. They are sacral king-priests who corporately represent the people and whom the gods regard as men, while to the people they are demi-gods, sons of the high-god.[1] The high-god is a sun-god and is styled ' "father of Man" and father of the king, implying the usual identity between king and mankind'.[2] Thus 'the divine king is also evidently bound up with the "primordial-man theology" '.[3] The commentary of Mowinckel, though he criticizes Engnell for going too far in his interpretation, is no less useful for our purposes. Keret is

a legendary king and the founder of a dynasty, who appears as a demi-god, but is at the same time, in relation to the gods, a human being . . . But Karit is no ordinary historical king. The theme of the epic is the securing of posterity to perpetuate the dynasty . . . Karit (is) a hero claimed as ancestor by a dynasty which was still reigning at the time when the epic was composed. The poem treats of Karit, the ancestor of the royal house, who lives on in later kings. . . . 'The Keret text presents the life of the king as the bearer of society, by describing the wedding festival of the ancestor king, birth of the family, the fertilization of the fields through the cult.' The same thought underlies the Dan'il-Aqhat legend. 'Behind the accounts of Danel and Keret in these two royal texts lies the interplay between the souls of the god and the king.'[4]

Associations of very similar motifs and ideas are also found in the texts from Ugarit which deal with the well-known god Baal, a deity worshipped in several places in Canaan as well and whose myth celebrates a number of fertility themes.[5]

[1] Engnell (op. cit., p. 108) quotes from J. Pedersen: 'In the legend of Keret we see that the king is a son of El and receives revelations direct from him, and in the character of Danel we see how king and god are merged.'

[2] Engnell, op. cit., p. 169 n. 3.

[3] Engnell, ibid. In 'The Legend of King Keret' (KRT A, i.36ff.; ANET, p. 143) we read:

> And in his dream El descends,
> In his vision the Father of Man ('ādām).
> And he approaches asking Keret:
> 'What ails Keret that he weeps,
> The Beloved, Lad of El, that he cries?
> Is it a kingship like Bull his father's he desires,
> Or authority like the Father of Man's?'

('Beloved' and 'Lad of El' are terms of intimacy and favour which may be compared to the typical expression 'Servant of El'. See KRT A, iii.53, 55; ANET, p. 144.)

[4] HTC, pp. 52f. The single quotation marks indicate that Mowinckel is quoting Pedersen.

[5] There is indeed little which indicates specifically that Baal's role was ever played by the actual king or that he was thought of as a type of the Primal Man,

In texts from many lands and times we find a continual association of the king and the sun.[1] The language used parallels descriptions and imagery which we have seen employed with regard to First Man figures. The idea seems to be that the king on his accession to the throne becomes like a sun-god. If it is too much to say that the king becomes identified with the sun-god, it is nevertheless true that 'The King could be viewed, in Mesopotamia as elsewhere, as an image of the sun-god'.[2] In this respect, as in others, the king resembles his god; he is his son, made like him in his image.[3] So, too, is the First Man thus created, and one, of course, thinks immediately of Gen. 1.26.[4] The point is succinctly illustrated by the little poem which Engnell uses as a prologue to his *Studies in Divine Kingship*:

> The shadow of God is Man (*amēlu*)
> And men are the shadow of Man.
> Man, that is the King,
> (who is) like the image of God.[5]

We are therefore not surprised also to learn that 'there can be no doubt that in the imperial age and in the first millennium the sun-

---

but he is the son of the high-god and his story clearly parallels those of others which do contain these features. In the view of A. S. Kapelrud (*The Ras Shamra Discoveries and the Old Testament*, Oxford, 1965, p. 66), 'The texts about Baal were the liturgy of the festival. Baal's conflicts with Prince Sea and Mot, his descent under the earth and triumphant return, the building of the temple, the festival of its dedication, and the sacred marriage all took place in the cult in a realistic and vivid presentation which lasted throughout the days when the autumnal New Year festival was celebrated. The worshippers were active participants in the cult, weeping and lamenting when Baal descended under the earth and joining wholeheartedly in the joyful celebrations when he returned triumphantly after defeating his enemies. The climax came with his enthronement and the great sacrificial feast, at which there was boisterous junketing and the wine flowed free, the whole ending in unrestrained debauchery when the god's marriage was celebrated.'

[1] See H. P. l'Orange, 'Expressions of Cosmic Kingship in the Ancient World' in *La Regalità Sacra/The Sacral Kingship* (*Numen* Suppl. IV), 1959, pp. 481ff.; Mowinckel, *HTC*, pp. 45, 51; Engnell, *op. cit.*, pp. 56, 80f.; Frankfort, *Kingship and the Gods*, p. 338. Cf. the salutations in various Akkadian royal letters (*ANET*, pp. 482ff.) and the description of Hammurabi in the prologue to 'The Code of Hammurabi' (i, 39ff.; *ANET*, p. 164) which Bentzen (*King and Messiah*, p. 17) holds to reveal the belief that Hammurabi was elected king at the creation.
[2] Frankfort, *op. cit.*, p. 308.
[3] Cf. Mowinckel, *HTC*, p. 48; Bentzen, *op. cit.*, p. 17.
[4] So even Mowinckel, *ST* 2, 1948/9, pp. 71ff.; *HTC*, p. 48.
[5] For a different interpretation, see Frankfort, *op. cit.*, p. 406 n. 35, who takes *shadow* in the sense of protection, but this does not vitiate our main point here. Cf. Engnell, *SEA* 22–23, 1957–8, p. 271 n. 9.

god was in some sense identified with the Hittite king.' In one text we read, '. . . so let the soul and heart (i.e. the selves) of the sun-god and of Labarnas (the king) become one.'[1] Another factor is hardly unexpected: 'The belief that the reigning Hittite king impersonated the spirit of the royal ancestor Labarnas appears to date from the earliest times.'[2]

In an interesting study of the Tyrian kingship rites J. Morgenstern has argued for the vital role of the solar myth.[3] In his view the sun divinity was *divided* in two for the purposes of the festival. As the old sun-god declined, the young god ascended in new strength. In this alternation of Baal-Shamaim and Melqart, the king played the parts of both the declining and vigorously arising divinities in a ritual which Morgenstern believes to be a parallel to the one involving Marduk at Babylon.[4] He contends that in one form or another this activity persisted from the tenth century down to the time of Antiochus Epiphanes. Its influence can be seen again in the descriptions by Josephus[5] and in Acts 12 of the *epiphany* made by Herod Agrippa to the people of Tyre. Putting on his shining robes, the king is enthroned as a god as the first rays of dawn shine over the holy mountain.

Such a rite must be supplemented by another relic having to do with Tyrian kingship ideology found in Ezek. 28. We have here two related oracles intended to mock the king of Tyre.[6] In the first (vv. 2–10) his claim to be a divine being, to sit on the throne of the gods[7] and to possess great wisdom[8] is derided. He is but a mortal and

[1] O. R. Gurney, 'Hittite Kingship' in *Myth, Ritual and Kingship* (ed. S. H. Hooke) Oxford, 1958, p. 117.

[2] Gurney, *op. cit.*, p. 121.

[3] 'The King-God among the Western Semites and the Meaning of Epiphanes', *VT* 10, 1960, pp. 138ff.

[4] *Op. cit.*, p. 143. Engnell (*Divine Kingship*, p. 55) notes that in many pictures showing two gods one is often an old man and the other a vigorous youth. Cf. Gordon, *Before the Bible*, p. 91: 'It is characteristic of theogonies that younger gods eclipse their older predecessors.' This helps to explain some of the *confusions* in lists of early kings and why it is that king-gods and kings representing king-gods can *ascend* to claim attributes properly belonging to the high-god.

[5] *Antiquities* XIX, 8.2. The text is cited below, p. 384.

[6] Cf. H. G. May, 'The King in the Garden of Eden. A Study of Ezekiel 28.12–19' in *Israel's PropheticHeritage* (ed. B. H. Anderson and W. Harrelson), New York and London, 1962, pp. 166ff. J. L. McKenzie, 'Mythological Allusions in Ezek. 28.12–18, *JBL* 75, 1956, pp. 322ff., is right to stress the relationship with the Genesis story, but this alone is not a sufficient basis.

[7] The throne is said to be set in the midst of the seas, which seems an allusion to the solar myth in which the sun rises from out of the seas. So often does the king rise up from the waters.

[8] On this and the firm association of wisdom with royalty and First Man

shall be defeated and die like one. Yet, though his claims be satirized, they were considered important enough to receive this treatment.

In the second oracle (vv. 12–19) we read in part:

12 You were the signet of perfection,
     full of wisdom and perfect in beauty.
13 You were in Eden, the Garden of God;
     every precious stone was your covering,[1]
    . . . .
    On the day that you were created
     they were prepared.
14 With an anointed guardian cherub I placed you;[2]
     you were on the holy mountain of God;
     in the midst of the stones of fire you walked.[3]
15 You were blameless in your ways
     from the day you were created,
     till iniquity was found in you.
    . . . .
17 Your heart was proud because of your beauty;
     you corrupted your wisdom for the sake of your splendour.
    I cast you to the ground;
     I exposed you before kings,
     to feast their eyes on you.
    . . . .
19 All who know you among the peoples are appalled at you;
     you have come to a dreadful end
     and shall be no more for ever.

Whatever Ezekiel's opinion of this king, and however much we grant that this language is poetic in force, the associations are clear. Some, at least, in the ancient Near East spoke of the king as the quasi-divine First Man who dwelt in the garden on the sacred mountain. Even the language which is used to describe his doom

---

generally, see N. W. Porteous, 'Royal Wisdom' in *Wisdom in Israel and in the Ancient Near East* (*VT* Suppl. III, ed. M. Noth and D. W. Thomas), 1955, pp.247ff.

[1] On these precious stones and their probable relationship with both king and First Man, see p. 123 n. 1.

[2] Widengren attempts to find a clear reference to the divinity of the figure in v. 14: 'You were a cherub, oh, what an anointed . . . a god you were; in the midst of the stones of fire did you walk' (*Sakrales Königtum im Alten Testament und im Judentum*, Stuttgart, 1955, p. 27, and in *Myth, Ritual and Kingship*, pp. 165f.). In any event he is right to hold that the two oracles are about the same figure. The point is not that we hear about a god in one and a human in the other, but that it is the Man claiming divine attributes that is being mocked.

[3] The reference is very likely to the stars of heaven.

strongly echoes that found elsewhere in association with the king's suffering in the ritual.[1] We can be sure, however, that in Tyre itself, and seemingly in a number of other cultures, the story did not end on this note.

4. THE KING IN JERUSALEM

Morgenstern, in commenting on the Tyrian kingship ideology, recalls that it was Hiram, the king of Tyre, who is said to have helped Solomon build his temple. Would not Solomon, aspiring so obviously to copy much of the royal life of the Near East, borrow more than just timber and the craft of Hiram's artisans? Working on the premise that Solomon would have attempted to emulate Hiram's kingship rites, Morgenstern goes on to find evidence for the possible continuation of such practices by the later kings of Judah, and he argues that the imagery and thought patterns from these practices have affected certain scenes in Daniel, I Enoch and II (4) Esdras. Certainly such an understanding would help to explain references to matters like having a *sea* within the temple at Jerusalem.[2] Also it might supply reason for the ceremony in which kings were anointed and made covenant with Yahweh while standing beside one of the two great temple pillars.[3]

It is, however, not our intention to try to demonstrate that a full kingship ideology was ritually operative in Israel. Indeed, it is tempting to think that we might avoid the need to contend that such ideas were known at all to the Israelites and still establish our major thesis. While obviating debate with certain schools of Old Testament scholarship, we might argue that aspects of these themes and beliefs were known in the areas in which Jesus eventually came to live (either as the result of later outside influences or through surviving indigenous beliefs) though they never had been accepted into more

---

[1] In addition to vv. 17, 19 quoted above, see v. 8:
> They shall thrust you down into the Pit,
> and you shall die the death of the slain
> in the heart of the seas.

Notice also, once more, that the *sin* of the Man-king consists in his claiming to be a god and to have the wisdom of a deity.

[2] I Kings 7.23ff.; II Kings 25.13; II Chron. 4.2ff. Notice the place of this *yām* in the creation story and liturgies: Gen. 1; Pss. 74.13; 95.5; 96.11; etc. See R. E. Clements, *God and Temple*, Oxford, 1965, p. 65, and more generally (pp. 40ff.) on cultic aspects of the Jerusalem temple.

[3] II Kings 11.14; 23.3. Morgenstern would regard these two pillars as a gate for the sun.

orthodox Jewish thought. Yet, whatever other merits such an approach might have, it would be neither adequate nor accurate to neglect aspects of similar ideas which are to be found in the Old Testament. Nor on the face of it could we very well expect any other eventuality. While making full allowance for Israel's uniqueness and individuality, it is hardly likely that their kingship ideology should have arisen and evolved in a near vacuum. Not only is there the possibility that a king like Solomon would have wished to assume the titles and practices of other kings and that, before this, David's attitudes toward kingship would have been affected by the earlier Jebusite rites in Jerusalem[1] (which themselves appear to relate to those of Ugarit and Canaan generally), but there must have been other channels of influence, both direct and indirect, now largely hidden from our eyes. The presence of many *foreign* words, names and place-names in the ancient strata of Old Testament materials at least suggests the borrowing of thought patterns as well.[2] That these beliefs are now difficult to single out, assess and relate is not surprising. What is surprising is that there is as much evidence as there is when we consider that we are dealing with records which were either given written form or very much rewritten during a time when Judah no longer had a king and when even the institution of kingship itself tended to be discredited. Without doubt a great deal has been omitted and, consciously or unconsciously, alterations have been made in the interests of conforming earlier conceptions to later theology.[3]

Some scholars, while agreeing that ideas about kingship which can profitably be compared with those from other cultures were present in Israelite thought, would yet contend that their purpose was always *poetical* and understood as such. Israel had borrowed the language from other nations, but not necessarily the beliefs which went with this language nor the ritual practice in which they were once rooted. There is room for argument here, though we do wonder whether such fine distinctions can now be drawn between beliefs and much of the terminology used. We also wonder if such a primitive

---

[1] See Johnson, *Sacral Kingship*, p. 46.

[2] See Gray, *The Legacy of Canaan*, pp. 189ff.; J. H. Patton, *Canaanite Parallels in the Book of Psalms*, Baltimore, 1944.

[3] E.g. in Ps. 132.18 the Masoretic text may subtly have changed 'upon him shall *my* crown flourish' (perhaps implying that David would wear the very crown of God) to 'upon him shall *his* crown flourish'. Also it would appear that much may have been done to *democratize* language which once applied more or less exclusively to the king. This could be true in psalms of lamentation, suffering and joy whose original contexts were no longer comprehended or appreciated.

people could have avoided the compulsion found elsewhere to act out and dramatize their legendary language. Yet we wish to make it abundantly clear that this viewpoint, stressing the poetic nature of these ideas, is still a sufficient basis for the purposes of our later discussions. All we really wish to show at this point is that the ideas were present and known in Israel, however little they may have been placed into a context of *actual* belief and practice.

The distinctive emphases in Israel's religion have, however, clearly made transforming demands upon materials which Israel converted to its own use. We noted earlier that the conception of god was bound to have pervasive effects upon all aspects of belief and practice. Obviously in Jerusalem, where, out of a situation of great tension, Yahweh came to be understood as the God in whom attributes of the older tribal deity and of both the high-god and his son the king-god had to be fused, this was true. Soon, for instance, it must have become impossible to think of him as a dying and rising god. While yearly celebrations of his kingship continued, it seems that these were no longer preceded by his *death* and resurrection.

This view of Yahweh had perforce to alter the status of the king. He could no longer be *identified* with Yahweh even for dramatic purposes. This need not mean that he never represented Yahweh in the cultus, for they both continued to be presented as enthroned kings at the same yearly festival. Yet there was no question of a full confusion of attributes, and Yahweh had taken to himself many of the features of the king-god, son of the high-god. Thus, out of all the Near Eastern religions, that of Israel came most to stress the humanity of the king. (See II Sam. 5.1; Ps. 89.19.) Nevertheless it does appear that the Jersualem king was considered to be not only the personification of his people (cf. II Sam. 21.17 and the implications of II Sam. 5.1; 24.1ff.) but also he who *became* his primal ancestor, the glorious son of God, ruling at God's right hand.

Such features play a significant role in the several birth oracles to be found in the Old Testament.[1]

> But you, O Bethlehem Ephrathah,
>   who are little to be among the clans of Judah,
> from you shall come forth for me
>   one who is to be ruler in Israel,
> whose origin is from old,
>   from ancient days.   (Micah 5.2)

[1] Cf. Bentzen, *King and Messiah*, pp. 17, 39ff.; Staerk, *Soter* I, pp. 1ff.

The new ruler's coming forth and his *origins* (or, perhaps better, *arisings* [*mōṣā'ōtāw*][1] as in a sunrise) are from *qedem*. He is from *'ōlām*. Both of these last words are frequently employed to refer to primeval time.[2]

So in Isa. 9.2 is the coming of the new king described like a sunrise, after which we read,

> For unto us a child is born,
>   to us a son is given;
> and the government will be upon his shoulder,
>   and his name will be called
> Wonderful Counsellor,
> Mighty god, (or *divine great Man* = *'ēl gibbōr*)[3]
> Everlasting Father, (*'abî 'ad* or *Father from*
> Prince of Peace.   *eternity* or *antiquity*)[4]
>   (Isa. 9.6)

In Isa. 9.7 we hear of the peace, justice and righteousness which shall be known during his rule. This is elaborated upon in Isa. 11; the new king will return men to paradisaical conditions upon God's holy

---

[1] For this word see also, significantly, Ps. 19.6. Bentzen (*op. cit.*, p. 17) compares the ἀνατολή (dawning) of Luke 1.78. See also Zech. 3.8 and esp. 6.12, which in the LXX might well be translated 'Behold, the man (Hebrew, *'iš*) whose name is the Dawn (ἀνατολή): for he shall dawn forth (ἀνατελεῖ)'. Cf. Mowinckel, *HTC*, p. 63. See further below on Zech. 6.12, p. 123 n. 1, p. 172.

[2] Against Mowinckel's contention (*ST* 2, 1948/9, pp. 82f.) that these refer only to the origin of the dynasty and not to the particular king, Bentzen (*ST* 3, 1949/50, pp. 151f.) rightly replies that the terms of reference cannot be dissociated in this manner.

[3] The main connotation of *geber* seems to suggest the warrior status of a great or mighty man. The root means to be *strong* or *strengthen*. On a number of other occasions the word is used to describe the king; e.g. Pss. 45.3; 89.19. It is interesting that it may also be employed to describe Yahweh: Pss. 24.8; 78.65; Isa. 42.13; Jer. 20.11; and see Ps. 19.5, where the sun is so described. In Ps. 18.25 it seems to be used of *man* in a more ordinary sense and has this more ordinary meaning often in Aramaic (cf. Dan. 2.25; 5.11), though it may still at times have overtones suggesting an exceptional man. This usage could present us with the nearest Hebrew equivalent for the Sumerian *LUGAL*. We ought not to rule out the possibility that it, together with such a generic word as *'iš*, could have relevance for our discussion, though, of course, expressions using the word *'ādām* are at the centre of our interest. For an excellent discussion of the messianic significance of *'iš* and esp. *geber*, see G. Vermes, *Scripture and Tradition in Judaism*, Leiden, 1961, pp. 56ff. Cf. Zech. 6.12; 13.7; II Sam. 23.1 ('The oracle of David . . . the *geber* who was raised on high'), all found in messianic contexts. See pp. 222f. on a similar usage in the Dead Sea Scrolls, and cf. the LXX interpretations of Num. 24.7, 17.

[4] Bentzen wonders whether Mowinckel (*op. cit.*, p. 82) by translating of the phrase as 'Father *of* eternal time' really demands a different understanding of the basic conception.

mountain. In 11.2 great wisdom is a quality which is, as often in Israel and other kingdoms, predicated of the new ruler.

It is probable that Ps. 110.3 also contains a reference to the mythical *birth* (often realized in terms of an *adoption*) of the king.

> In holy array step forth from the womb of Dawn,
> as Day have I begotten thee.[1]

If this or a similar translation of an admittedly difficult text is correct, we have a picture of the king being *born* and arising like the new sun. The *day* of his birth would not only be that of the festival; it would also be the day of creation.

In this same Psalm we are told that the new king is to be a 'priest for ever after the order of Melchizedek'. Since Melchizedek was most likely an ancestral priest-king of Jebusite Jerusalem,[2] much of the Psalm can be regarded as of great antiquity. The ruler born on this day is, at the least, like unto his ancestor.[3] He is established at God's right hand; the enemies will become his footstool, and with his sceptre he will rule in the midst of them. (These enemies may well be the foes who attack the king before they are defeated in ritual battle.) Finally we read (Ps. 110.7):

> He will drink from the brook by the way;
> therefore will he lift up his head.

This is again a difficult verse, but a number of commentators see here a reference to a scene in which the king refreshes himself during his mythical battle. Perhaps he drinks from the spring Gihon where

---

[1] This is Widengren's translation. Bentzen translates, 'On holy mountains I have begotten thee, from the womb of woman (i.e. the divine goddess), before the morning star and the dew.' *King and Messiah*, p. 87, n. 6, p. 88, n. 16. Also see A. R. Johnson, 'The Role of the King in the Jerusalem Cultus' in *The Labyrinth* (ed. S. H. Hooke) London, 1935, p. 110, and H. Ringgren, *The Messiah in the Old Testament* (SBT 18), 1956, p. 13. Mowinckel (*HTC*, p. 62) translates, 'On the holy mountain have I begotten thee. . . .' See this with reference to Ps. 2 discussed below.

[2] On an *earlier* penetration of Melchizedek, 'King of Salem . . . priest of El Elyon', into the lore of Israel, see Gen. 14.18ff. Many later kings of Jerusalem incorporated *ṣedeq* into their names. See Mowinckel, *Psalms* I, p. 132.

Some would find a *partial* acrostic on Simon the Maccabee's name in the Psalm and wish to date its origin in this period. This is most unlikely, as it fails to account for the antiquity of the other ideas. It is possible, however, that the Hasmonaean priest-princes made use of the Psalm. See below.

[3] The Hebrew *'al dibrātī* generally translated as 'after the *order* (or *rank*) of Melchizedek', has a meaning which includes the ideas of manner or mode or condition, as does the Greek τάξις used to translate it.

others were proclaimed as king.[1] Noting these several possibilities and the fact that Gihon is a name for one of the rivers of paradise, Bentzen wrote, 'The communion, the drink of the Fountain of Life, is the mighty strengthening of the elect warrior, who will fight the divine battle against the devils of the Chaos and help to re-create the world.'[2]

Another psalm which many scholars believe to have formed part of the liturgy dealing with the enthronement rites of the king is Ps. 2. We hear of the coming battle of foreign kings against Yahweh's Anointed and the promise that they will be confounded. God has established his king upon his holy *hill* of Zion.[3]

> I will tell of the decree of the Lord:
> He said to me, 'You are my son,
>   today I have begotten you.' (v. 7)

The context again is feasibly that of both the *today* of the ritual and the *day* of creation. Bentzen has given good reason for taking the particle *'āz* in v. 5 as such in indication.[4]

The same word is used in Ps. 89.19:

> 19 *Of old* thou didst speak in a vision
>   to thy faithful one and say:
>   'I have set the crown[5] upon one who is mighty (*gibbōr*),
>   I have exalted one chosen from the people.
> 20 I have found David, my servant;
>   with my holy oil I have anointed him;
> 21 so that my hand shall ever abide with him,
>   my arm also shall strengthen him.'

---

[1] See below.

[2] *King and Messiah*, p. 25. On the interpretation of the whole Psalm with relation to kingship ideology, see J. Coppens 'Les apports du psaume CX (vulg. CIX) à l'idéologie royale Israélite' in *La Regalità Sacra/The Sacral Kingship* (*Numen* Suppl. IV), 1959, pp. 333ff.

[3] See p. 110, n. 1. A number of kings (and king-gods) and first men are said to rule or be born upon this holy mountain where paradise is also often located. Many kings were thought to have been begotten like 'the birth of a new sun-god on an unknown mountain in the east' (Mowinckel, *Psalms* I, p. 54). Sometimes the mountain can be understood to be in the north, should this be regarded as the direction of the ancestral home of the people. See Ps. 48.2, which could well be an item borrowed from some Canaanite group.

[4] *King and Messiah*, pp. 18f. See the use of this particle in Ps. 93.2 (in parallel with *'ōlām*), with regard to God's rule and throne, which renders untenable Mowinckel's criticism in *ST* 2, 1948/9, p. 86, though see also Bernhardt, *Königs-ideologie*, pp. 193f.

[5] Or *help* or possibly *youth*.

Thus it seems that even in Israel the king's birth occurs in primordial time. It can be described as like a sunrise and regarded as divine in origin. He is the 'Father from eternity'; he may even be called a god (and see Ps. 45.6 where he is either addressed as a god or else is said to sit on the throne of God). More usually, however, he is regarded as the Son of God. This is true in II Sam. 7.14, while in Ps. 89.26f. God is his Father and the king is God's *first-born*. This last title is also used of foreign kings and could presumably refer to the king as the very first of God's creatures.[1]

If, then, Israelite beliefs have been affected by the idea that the king is a type of the first king and so a first of men, it is very likely that we should find the obverse of this thinking: that the first of men is regarded as a royal figure. And when we turn to the two accounts of the creation of Man in Genesis,[2] we do indeed meet with language now familiar to us from the stories of other first men and kings. In Gen. 1.26 we hear that the prototype has been made according to the divine image and likeness.[3] He is clearly to be conceived of as part human and part divine and he rules over the new creation.

The name 'Ādām, though it need not have been original to this particular story, appears to have a history reaching back into Canaanite lore. A typical Semitic *pun* is involved: Adam is made from the *'ªdāmā*, the red clay of earth. His can be a name both for mankind and also for a deity of the earth.[4] As we have noted, at Ugarit the god El can be styled the 'Father of 'ādām' and, since a king like Keret can be called El's 'lad', 'servant' and 'first-born', the implications are obvious. Adam's name is also treated as generic in Gen. 1.26 when the switch to the plural is made: '. . . and let *them* have dominion . . .'[5] This is again evident in Gen. 5.1f. There, in addi-

----

[1] Cf. Widengren in *Myth, Ritual and Kingship*, p. 175.

[2] There is no need here to consider at length the history of these two tales. It is usually thought that the first entered into Israel's lore last, perhaps having been adapted from Babylonian materials during the exile or at an earlier time. The second has been more fully accommodated to a Jewish viewpoint and may have a considerable history in Hebraic thought.

[3] The plural involved in 'Let *us* make man in our image' (v. 26) has been the cause of much speculation, though it holds little immediate interest for us. It might be a reference to an already pre-existent image of God or of a Heavenly Man (as many later thought it to be), but it is more likely a relic from a polytheistic version or even a simple use of the divine *we*. V. 27 may, in part, be an attempt to correct the polytheistic impression left by v. 26.

[4] See Widengren in *Myth, Ritual and Kingship*, p. 174.

[5] So also in v. 27 '. . . male and female he created them.' But Mowinckel's argument (*ST* 2, 1948/9, pp. 83ff.) that in Gen. 1–3 and Ps. 8 it is only generic man

tion, we find Adam's grandson, Enosh, whose name is generic as well and who may have his origin in some other version of a First Man story.[1]

In the account of Gen. 2–3 it is yet more certain that we are dealing with a mythical royal First Man. Though made from the earth, he has the divine breath within him. He is given a consort and from their union issues the whole human race. He is thus father and ancestor to all men. This Adam rules over paradise. From this garden of Eden springs the river (the water of life) which is the source of all the rivers of the world. In Adam's garden there also grows the tree of life and another tree, that of the knowledge of good and evil, a probable variant of the tree of life. Adam, in the pattern of other first kings and first men, sins by aspiring to become a full divinity; he suffers in consequence and loses his immortality. To the end of his days he is doomed to wander the earth, separated from his home of paradise.

Of course, in cultic terms this could never be the end of the story. It would go on to tell of *resurrection* and restitution. But here we are manifestly dealing with material which has been much worked over to suit new moral and aetiological purposes.[2]

For the sake of completeness we may also here mention Job 15.7f. where some scholars would find a brief reference to the myth of First Man:

> Are you the First Man ('*ādām*) that was born?
> Or were you brought forth before the hills?
> Have you listened in the council of God?
> And do you limit wisdom to yourself?

The passage is so curt and rhetorical that we hesitate to conclude very much. Doubtless, however, the appearance of such features as sharing in the council of the gods (participating in divine secrets) and

---

and not the First Man ancestor that is being presented misses the whole point of such an aetiological legend. Cf. Engnell, *SEA* 23, 1957/8, p. 279.

[1] In Gen. 4.1. we learn that Adam was the father of the second man, Cain. In 5.9 we find that Enosh was the father of Kenan which is another name for Cain. It looks as though traditions have been combined, the suggestion being that Enosh stood first in one of them. Perhaps one was a Kenite version and/or one in which it was said that Enosh was the first to call on the name of Yahweh (see the LXX of Gen. 4.26f.).

[2] Engnell, ' "Knowledge" and "life" in the creation story' in *Wisdom in Israel and in the Ancient Near East* (*VT* Suppl. III, ed. M. Noth and D. W. Thomas), 1955, pp. 103ff., would find yet further features of the royal man in Gen. 1–3.

possessing an exclusive degree of wisdom could intimate an acquaintance with the general myth. The fact that the Man is born before the hills were made suggests that he may be thought of both as a type of the Primordial Man as well as the First Man to be on earth.

Ps. 8 offers a far more distinct presentation of the First Man:

> 4 What is Man (*'enōš*) that thou art mindful of him,
>   and the Son of Man (*ben 'ādām*) that thou dost care for him?
> 5 Yet thou hast made him little less than God,
>   and dost crown him with glory and honour.
> 6 Thou hast given him dominion over the works of thy hands;
>   thou hast put all things under his feet,
> 7 all sheep and oxen,
>   and also the beasts of the field . . .[1]

Here we see the First Man ruling in paradise and created as one just less than God himself.[2] He is no typical mortal, and to regard him simply in this light involves an excess of modern interpretation. This is not to say that the figure is not human nor that the Hebrews were incapable of regarding the humanity of the king as an ideal pattern for all men. Still the one described here is the Man in a very special sense.

We are, of course, attentive to the parallelism which tends to equate the expressions *Man* and *Son of Man*. At this stage in our study we can begin to see very real point in the second designation, for the reigning king was the representative of his ancestor the Man, the first king, in whose office he now serves, but he is also the *son* of that Man, his descendant and legitimate heir. Thus, though both terms can refer to the present ruler, it is perhaps not quite correct to say that they are exact equivalents. They can nicely be used in parallelism, but Son of Man conveys these nuances of sonship, of being the legitimate and designated heir to the throne. We have already

---

[1] Of course, in other stylizations based on the older mythical materials these beasts, etc., represent the defeated monsters or demons. For the king ruling with the defeated enemies under his feet, see Ps. 110.1 and many pictures of Near Eastern kings which have survived.

[2] One could translate 'a little less than a god', or 'a little less than divine', but this could be somewhat misleading. The ideogram in the background is that of Gen. 1.26, and the conception of the Man as one in the god's image, ruling in honour just below him, is common elsewhere. The interpretation (see the LXX) of *'elōhīm* as angels is a device of later theological understandings.

On late traces of a messianic interpretation of *ben 'ādām* here, see S-B III, p. 682, but it is reasonably clear that in *normative* Jewish circles the older values of the phrase were either lost or largely ignored.

noticed the strong implications of this idea elsewhere, and E. Herzfeld maintains that it was also to be found over a long period in Babylon and Iran and at the time when the Persian king Darius I had extended his rule to the Mesopotamian city.[1]

We do not contend, however, that *Son of Man* was necessarily an official royal title in Jerusalem. It is not impossible that this was so at some point in time, but the rarity of its usage in such contexts suggests that it was more a kind of description, a way of referring to the mythical status of the king who had assumed the office of his primal royal ancestor. Thus we do not deny that the Hebrew expression *son of man* could also be employed in a rather democratized fashion to signify a human being in his *wholly* mortal guise, for, of course, this was always the other aspect of the Son of Man's being in any case.

Yet we ought to exercise great care before assuming that in certain other passages there are no overtones of the idea of the man/son of man as the Man, the royal personage. It is remarkable that in all these other verses (except in Ezekiel, which will be discussed later, and Ps. 146.3, on which see below) we come across this combination *man/son of man* almost as though it were a formula.[2] The reader himself might discover through a perusal of these texts hints of a form of irony, to wit, 'no man, not even the Son of Man'. We do not press the issue, since we are as eager as any to affirm that the humanity of the Son of Man was often insisted upon in Israel, and it is easy to see how this could have led to a democratized and stock use of the phrase. Still, one must watch out for the overtones, and the democratized usage by no means precludes a specialized reference in other contexts.

The point may well be illustrated by Ps. 144, which may originally have been one of the royal psalms. Is it not the king who speaks in vv. 1f., craving the help of Yahweh, his rock, fortress and deliverer?[3]

[1] *Zoroaster and His World*, Princeton, 1947, II, p. 840. The Hebrew and Aramaic expression *Son of Man* is very like the phrase *mār-banū = ādāta* used by Darius 'to justify his claim to the succession. It does not mean "individual of mankind", son of nobody, but "youth of noble extraction", "successor, heir to the throne".' Cf. also *op. cit.*, pp. 833ff.: 'The giving of sovereignty to the Son of Man means his investiture as heir to the throne.' See further below in ch. IV.

[2] See Num. 23.19; Job. 16.21; 25.6; 35.8; Pss. 80.17; 144.3; Isa. 51.12; 56.2; Jer. 49.18; 49.33; 50.40: 51.43. The expressions are alternatively *'enōš, ben 'ādām* (once *'ādām, ben 'enōš*, once *geber, ben 'ādām*) or *'īš, ben 'ādām*. Quite similar in usage are Ecclus. 17.30; Jub. 8.16; Test. Joseph 2.5.

[3] Notice also in v. 2: '(The Lord) . . . who subdues my people (or possibly, the peoples) under *me*.' This was probably the original reading, while again we find a subtle theological alteration to 'under *him*'. Regard the blending of individual and communal interests in this Psalm.

Is it not the king who in v. 7 asks for rescue from the *many waters* and who speaks (in v. 10) of the God who rescues 'David, thy servant'? When therefore we read in vv. 3f.,

> O Lord what is man (*'ādām*) that thou dost regard him,
> the Son of Man (*ben 'enōš*) that thou dost think of him?
> Man (*'ādām*) is like a breath,
> his days are like a passing shadow,

may not the figure described be the special Man, the king, seen here in his lowly status, as one who is humble and as a suppliant on behalf of his people? This suggestion is probably given more weight by the parallelism and the similar thought found in Ps. 146.3f.:

> Put not your trust in princes,
> in a Son of Man (*ben 'ādām*) in whom there is no help.
> When his breath departs he returns to his earth (*'adāmā*);
> on that very day his plans perish.

Our interest naturally now turns to Ps. 80:

> 14 Turn again, O God of hosts.
>   Look down from heaven, and see;
>   have regard for this vine,
> 15   the stock which thy right hand planted
>   (and upon the Son whom thou hast reared for thyself).
> 16 They have burned it with fire, they have cut it down;
>   may they perish at the rebuke of thy countenance.
> 17 But let thy hand be upon the Man (*'īš*) of thy right hand,
>   upon the Son of Man (*ben 'ādām*) whom thou hast
>   made strong for thyself.

This passage occurs in a short recitation of Israel's history and its present sad plight. It is difficult to avoid the conclusion that the Man, the Son of Man singled out, is any one other than the king. Who else would be described as God's right-hand Man, the one who sits at his right hand? (See again Ps. 110.1.)[1] If the half-verse given in parentheses did stand in the original Hebrew, it would serve to underline this understanding.[2] The *Son* is the Son of God, the king.[3] This

---

[1] That this was the Messiah was the impression of interpreters at a later time in Judah. Cf. Mowinckel, *HTC*, pp. 357, 434.

[2] It is found only in the Hebrew and many would regard it as a dittography and corruption of v. 17b, believing that it intrudes into the structure of the stanza. (Accordingly a few texts have *Son of Man* for *Son*.) This, however, is by no means certain. Understandably later scribes interpreted the Son as the Messiah.

[3] Of course, Israel is also God's *Son* as in Hos. 11.1 (and also the *vine* as in Hos. 10.1 and elsewhere), but so also is the king representative of all of Israel. (See

would also make yet more apparent another factor which is true in any case: the vine, 'the stock which thy right hand planted', is closely associated with the Man/Son of Man upon whom God's right hand rests.[1] Two clear impressions result from this: the king-Man is the representative for the whole people, an image of the society just as is the vine; the use of the vine and stock symbols gives us final assurance in our identification of this figure as the king.

In this last connection we recall Widengren's study of the association of the king with the tree of life and with stock, vine, shoot and branch imagery both elsewhere and in Israel. Widengren is convinced that,

. . . there existed long ago and for a very long period in Israel a very concrete symbolic notion of the ruler as a mighty tree, growing in Paradise, the Garden of God, 'in the midst of the earth', and providing shadow and protection for all living beings.[2]

Rightly does he then draw our attention to Lam. 4.20.

> The breath of our nostrils,[3] the Lord's Anointed,
>   was taken into their pits,
> he of whom we said,
>   'Under his shadow we shall live among the nations.'

Very probably it is Jeconiah who is here in mind, and brief and poetic though the reference may be, it gives a glimpse revealing how strong a hold such ideas had on the minds of men.

The parallel motif which also seems to make its appearance in Israel is that of the king as a provider of food for the people. Thus when David finishes the ritual practice described in II Sam. 6, he 'distributed among all the people, the whole multitude of Israel, both men and women, to each a cake of bread, a portion of *meat* (Hebrew uncertain) and a cake of raisins'.[4]

---

again II Sam. 21.17.) These ideas are complementary, not exclusive of one another.

[1] The LXX tends to make this parallelism even more clear.
[2] *King and Tree of Life*, p. 58. See above p. 98.
[3] On this idea of the king as the breath of life of his people in Near Eastern ideology, see Mowinckel, *Psalms* I, p. 55.
[4] II Sam. 6.19. See in this connection Ps. 132.15, where, however, it is Yahweh who provides the bread. It may well be that the original point of view has here been altered, though it could have been that both Yahweh and the king acting for him were regarded as the providers. Cf. J. R. Porter, 'The Interpretation of 2 Samuel VI and Psalm CXXXII', *JTS*, ns 5, 1954, pp. 161ff. In Ezek. 44.3 the

We have, in addition, adumbrated our reasons for thinking the Israelite king to be associated with the waters or water of life.[1] When Ezekiel tells us that the head of all waters issued from the temple precincts he is alluding to this idea that the temple contained the garden of God.[2] Certainly in this connection it is not surprising to find that the king-designate must be washed with water before he can be proclaimed king. So in I Kings 1.33ff. Solomon rides upon the royal ass to the pool where he is to be anointed and proclaimed king. This pool bears the name Gihon, traditionally the name of one of the rivers flowing out of Eden.[3] In Mowinckel's opinion, 'It seems that even in later times the ceremonial at the installation of the kings of Jerusalem included a rite of purification at the spring and of drinking its holy water . . .'[4]

The king also has control over the waters of life (presumably because he once was believed to have won the battle over the watery chaos, though in Israel this role is normally reserved for Yahweh).[5] In this capacity he is the one who can help to ensure the rains for the coming season.[6] Thus it is fitting that in Ps. 89.25 God should say of the king, 'I will set his hand on the sea and his right hand on the rivers.'[7]

Taking all these factors into account, it seems reasonable to conclude that

The connection between Primordial Man and the actual ruler cannot be doubted and therefore the mythical conception of paradise and the Primeval Man had played a considerable role in royal ideology, the king being, as it were, the Son of God, just because he is the representative of Primordial Man.[8]

If we needed any further corroboration of this point, it could be

---

prince sitting outside the eastern (see below) gate eats bread before the Lord. This could be a relic of a type of *communion* which was once part of the royal enthronement ceremony.

[1] See also Johnson, *Sacral Kingship*, pp. 9, 53.
[2] Ezek. 47.1ff. See Ps. 46.4; Zech.14.8; and Clements, *God and Temple*, p. 72.
[3] Gen. 2.13.
[4] *HTC*, p. 63, the latter point in connection with Ps. 110.7. See also Ps. 68.26; Zech. 13.1. Johnson, *op. cit.*, writes (p. 110): 'One cannot but conjecture (although it is no more than conjecture) that something like a baptismal scene within the confines of the spring Gihon may have been the focal point of the dramatic ritual.'
[5] See below.
[6] Ps. 72.6; I Kings 8.36; Jer. 8.19f.
[7] See also Ps. 72.8; and perhaps Zech. 9.10.
[8] Widengren in *Myth, Ritual and Kingship*, p. 175.

found in the use of sun imagery applied to both the king and Yahweh, for we have previously found these images employed to describe other first men as kings and primordial men as king-gods. Already, too, we have seen the place of this theme in connection with the *birth* oracles of the new ruler in Jerusalem. In addition we are made aware that the temple in Jerusalem, as other temples of the Near East, was built facing eastwards[1] and very likely oriented with the Mount of Olives over which or upon which it is sometimes said that God will appear to Judah.[2] It is from the East that the Lord comes to his temple, causing the earth to shine with his glory. This glory then shines right into the temple itself.[3]

After informing us that the glory of the Lord has now once and for ever entered in through this eastward gate, Ezekiel announces that no man (*'iš*) will ever again enter by it. Only the *prince* will be left the privilege of sitting near to this gate and going in by way of its vestibule.[4] The inference seems reasonably clear: at one time this was the gate by which the royal figure entered into the temple. He, like God, *came* from the East. In II Sam. 23.4 the king who rules justly over men 'dawns on them like the morning light, like the sun shining forth upon a cloudless morning'. It also seems a near certainty that the Masoretic recension (at I Kings 8.12f.) has disguised the fact that Solomon (during the autumnal festival) was reported to have offered prayer to Yahweh in language suitable for a sun-god.[5] Despite the fact that worship of the sun itself is explicitly forbidden in the Old Testament,[6] this older association of Yahweh (or Yahweh as El Elyon) with solar imagery has not been completely disguised[7] and

---

[1] Ezek. 44.1; 46.1; 47.1. H. P. l'Orange (in *La Regalità Sacra*, pp. 48ff.) argues that not only thrones and temples but whole cities were oriented to the sun's movements in the Near East. On the sun and temple at Jerusalem, see F. J. Hollis, 'The Sun-Cult and the Temple at Jerusalem' in *Myth and Ritual* (ed. S. H. Hooke), London, 1933, pp. 87ff.

[2] Zech. 14.4. Notice that the mountain of Marduk is depicted as splitting open before he arises from his subterranean place. See in *The Ancient Near East in Pictures* (ed. Pritchard), Princeton and London, 1954, p. 220. See also Ezek. 11.23, and on this in later interpretation, S-B I, pp. 480f.

[3] Ezek. 43.1ff. Cf. Gaster, *Thespis*, p. 41. See above, p. 106 n. 3.

[4] Ezek. 44.1ff.; 46.2. It is before this gate that the people will worship Yahweh on the sabbaths and new moon festivals.

[5] See Gaster, *op. cit.*, p. 40.

[6] Ezek. 8.16ff. See II Kings 23.5.

[7] See Pss. 50.2; 84.11; 97.11; 118.27 (in connection with the autumnal feast); Isa. 60.1. On El Elyon in this regard, cf. Johnson in *The Labyrinth*, p. 83; Mowinckel, *Psalms* II, pp. 137f. It may be that Ps. 19.5 was once intended to apply to the god or king.

was certainly recognized, if not practised, during later periods.[1]

If solar imagery once was employed as an aid to men's worship of Yahweh, it is not unlikely that Israel entertained the common picture of the God ascending like the sun in victory to be enthroned in radiant glory in the highest heaven. This would give context to the many references to the *arising* or *going up* of Yahweh.[2] In a similar context should we probably set texts relevant to the king's being *raised up* or *lifted up* on high,[3] a notion which is to be compared rather than contrasted with that of the God or king ascending the holy mountain to be hailed as king. Mythically they represent much the same idea, and this is apparently why, as noted earlier, the king may be said to sit on God's throne,[4] and why we find several other references which seem to indicate that the king could be thought to have a throne in heaven.[5]

Again all this would appear to fit in admirably with the background of the whole festival. Writes Johnson, 'I have no doubt that the sun played an important part in the autumnal festival at Jerusalem.'[6] Mowinckel is among those who support this interpretation. Many elements of the festival are reminiscent 'of an ancient sun and light ceremony'.[7] All this in turn would help to explain why it is that salvation for both king and society appears to come with the dawn.[8]

It is not practicable nor is it requisite for our later arguments that we should here undertake a lengthy exposition of what may have taken place at the autumnal feast or cycle of feasts of the seventh month in ancient Jerusalem.[9] Suffice it to say that we do know that a

---

[1] See Mishnah tractate *Sukkah* 5.4. Cf. Morgenstern, 'A Chapter in the History of the High-Priesthood', *AJSLL* 55, 1938, pp. 1ff., 183ff., 36off.

[2] E.g. Pss. 3.7; 7.6; 47.5; 68.1; 82.8; 94.5; 102.13; 132.8. See below, pp. 285f.

[3] II Sam. 23.1; Pss. 18.48; 30.1; 89.19.

[4] Ps. 45.6.

[5] See Widengren, *Sakrales Königtum*, p. 54, and Ps. 89.36f.; Jer. 17.12.

[6] 'Hebrew Conceptions of Kingship' in *Myth, Ritual and Kingship* (ed. S. H. Hooke), Oxford, 1958, p. 214. See *Sacral Kingship*, pp. 92f.

[7] *Psalms* I, p. 131.

[8] See Johnson, *Sacral Kingship*, pp. 84f., 108, 119, 125f., and Pss. 30.5; 45.6, and also the material above on the king being *born* like or at the sunrise.

[9] Useful studies, with attention to the role of the king, are H. Ringgren, *Messiah in the Old Testament* (see his summary, pp. 63f.); Widengren, *Sakrales Königtum*; Johnson, *Sacral Kingship*, and in *Myth, Ritual and Kingship*, pp. 204ff.; Mowinckel, *Psalms* I and II (esp. I, pp. 120ff.); W. O. E. Oesterley, 'Hebrew Festival Rituals' in *Myth and Ritual* (ed. S. H. Hooke), London, 1933, pp. 111ff. In opposition see R. de Vaux, *Ancient Israel. Its Life and Institutions*, ET, London, 1961, pp. 495ff.; and N. H. Snaith, *The Jewish New Year Festival*, London, 1947 (and in reply to Snaith, Mowinckel, *Psalms* II, pp. 228ff.).

great feast took place at this time, that the king played a central role
in it, and that it was regarded as being of the utmost importance for
the well-being of the society.[1] One of its functions was to help bring
the beneficial rains.[2] And, while final proofs are probably for ever
beyond our reach, it is difficult not to believe that the psalms and
stories dealing with creation, victory over the chaos monster and
enthronement were not employed in this context.[3]

There is, however, one feature in particular which requires our
attention. Whether or not it belonged to the seventh-month festival
and whether or not it was ritually enacted, the language which
speaks of the suffering and humiliation of the royal personage is of
great significance. We have noted repeatedly that almost every other
Man and/or king figure whom we have studied has experienced some
fall from high status, often resulting in suffering of one kind or
another before there can be any hope of restoration. This apparently

---

[1] See I Kings 8.2ff.; 8.65ff.; II Chron. 7.7ff. Many point to the significance of
I Kings 12.26ff.: Jeroboam felt it necessary to establish a similar festival (during
the eighth month due either to variations in calendar or in the agricultural season)
in order to bind the people to his royal house. Note, too, how the later prince priest
Jonathan puts on a crown of gold and a *purple* robe and garments in the seventh
month at the Feast of Tabernacles (I Macc. 10.20f.).

[2] See Zech. 14.16ff. Some would point also to Isa. 12.3.

[3] See esp. the complexes of Pss. 46–48; 93–100, and Job 9.8, 13; 26.12; Pss.
74.14; 87.4; 89.10; Isa. 51.9 on the chaos monster. These themes appear to have
influenced II Isaiah's view generally, while holding the influence to be the other
way around is most improbable when one considers the great antiquity of these
ideas in other cultures. See Johnson, *Sacral Kingship*, p. 54. On the antiquity in
Israel of 'accounts of the fight against dragons and chaos, creation, the first man
and so on', see Mowinckel, *Psalms* I, p. 167. On the interconnection of themes of
creation, epiphany and enthronement, cf. *op. cit.*, pp. 106ff.

Despite all the changes under post-exilic conditions, the seventh month continued to be the great festival season during which all these themes were enunci-
ated. (See Lev. 23.24ff., and Num. 29.12ff.; Deut. 16.13ff.; Ezek. 45.25 on the
Feast of Tabernacles proper. Neh. 8–9 speaks of the same holy days in a somewhat
different pattern. In Ezra 31.ff. Tabernacles is the time for planning the new temple.
cf. Hag. 2.1ff.) *Rosh ha-Shanah* was regarded as *the* New Year day (cf. H. Danby,
The Mishnah, London, 1933, p. 188 n. 3, and Josephus, *Antiquities* VIII, 4.1), and
Yom Kippur, which may be a partially democratized version of the older humiliation of the king (see below), and *Sukkah* follow. The rich imagery involving the
blowing of horns, water, light-dark and the carrying of branches is reminiscent of
antique practices. See the Mishnah tractates *Sukkah* 4.9; 5.4f.; *Rosh ha-Shanah*, 1.2.
Also see II Macc. 10.1ff. and John 7.37f.; 8.12 (with 7.1). On the branches, cf.
Lev. 23.40; Neh. 8.15 and probably Ps. 118.27 (often regarded as a psalm of the
Tabernacles festival). The trumpet blown on the first day should be compared with
that sounded at Yahweh's enthroning (Ps. 47.5; 48.6), at the creation and enthronement (Ps. 98.6) and at the king's enthronement (II Sam. 15.10; I Kings 1.
34ff.; II Kings 9.13).

was no less true in Israel, of course of Adam, but more importantly also of the king. There are a number of psalms involving either suffering and lamentation or joy at the termination of these woes which are ascribed to or very likely pertained to the royal person.[1] Writes Ringgren, '. . . there has existed in Israel a pattern of (innocent) suffering, death and restoration, and . . . psalms built on this pattern on some occasions have been laid in the mouth of a king.'[2] Finding many such psalms to be ancient in basic content and form, Johnson concludes that, 'The Davidic King is the Servant of Jahweh; but . . . at the New Year Festival he is the Suffering Servant. He is the Messiah of Jahweh, but on this occasion he is the humiliated Messiah.'[3] In many of these contexts the king is tried sorely; he is surrounded by beasts (derived from creation monsters?) or opposed by foreign kings, forsaken and left in desperate physical and mental condition, despised by men. He has been cast into the pit and is drowning. He is brought very near to death, right to the very gates of Sheol. Sometimes it is said that this burden has been laid upon him by his God:

> I shall not die, but I shall live,
>   and recount the deeds of the Lord.
> The Lord has chastened me sorely,
>   but he has not given me over unto death.   (Ps. 118.17f.)[4]

The suffering is, however, in no sense meaningless. On this 'day which the Lord has made', the king enters through 'the gate of the Lord'. God 'has answered me and become my salvation'.[5] His cries and pleas have been heard by the Lord who has lifted him up, set him on high, exalted him and saved him.[6] Not only is he vindicated and reinstated, but both his suffering and vindication appear to have been known vicariously by the people:[7] '. . . let us rejoice and be glad . . .'[8]

[1] Esp. Pss. 16; 18 (see II Sam. 22); 21; 22; 69; 89; 116; 118.
[2] *Messiah in the Old Testament*, p. 64.
[3] In *The Labyrinth*, p. 106. See his *Sacral Kingship*, pp. 102ff., etc.
[4] See also Pss. 69.26; 89.38ff.; II Sam. 7.14. The latter should be regarded as more than just a poetic extension of the idea of God's fatherhood, esp. when compared with these other texts.
[5] Ps. 118.20f. Is this gate that eastern gate to which Ezekiel (see again 44.1ff.; etc.) refers?
[6] See Pss. 18.16, 33, 48; 69.29; 144.7; etc.
[7] See Mowinckel, *Psalms* I, p. 61, and further below.
[8] Ps. 118.24.

They, too, may rejoice, since they, too, are renewed and saved.[1] Johnson writes:

The whole ceremony is one which compels a certain admiration. The King has been made to suffer humiliation; he has been 'chastened sore' and brought close to the gates of the Underworld. Nevertheless through the SEDEK of Jahweh he has been delivered from the power of 'Death' . . . but *ipso facto* the people themselves, as forming a psychic whole with its focus in the king, have also been delivered from 'Death' and proved SADDIK or 'righteous'. Thus the well-being, the 'Life', of the social unit is assured through another year. In the renewed life of the king, the people live again; his 'Salvation' is also their 'Salvation'.[2]

Our interest fastens on an intriguing aspect of the royal humiliation (be it poetic or dramatic). We have seen earlier how kings and king-gods must do battle with the watery chaos or water monsters before they can gain the mastery over water and creation can ensue. That such is what is being described in our Psalter is not certain, but there is no doubt that the king is involved in a *struggle* with water, out

[1] Again we notice the seeming persistence of similar ideas. Does the later Day of Atonement come in the seventh month by accident? Why does it begin at cockcrow at the eastern gate (Mishnah, *Yoma* 1.3, 8)? 'The whole east is alight' (*Yoma* 3.1). What is the origin of the wellnigh cultic weeping that takes place (*Yoma* 1.5)? We know that the high-priest, now that there no longer was a king, was laved and anointed, invested and mitred (or crowned or given a turban) to a quasi-royal office (cf. Lev. 8.1ff.; Ex. 28.2ff.; 29.1ff.; 40.12ff.) esp. during the time of the Hasmonaean prince-priests who had many other royal attributes (see I Macc. 10.20f.; 14.41ff.). Widengren in *Sakrales Königtum*, p. 27, and in *Myth, Ritual and Kingship*, p. 167, shows that the high-priest wore a pectoral item remarkably similar to that associated with the Man-king. See Ex. 28.17ff. with Ezek. 28.13. He also discusses the possession of the ephod and 'tablets of destiny' (*urim* and *thummin*) by king-priests and the high-priest. Cf. as well Ringgren, *Messiah in the Old Testament*, p. 52, and below, pp. 162ff. Might not the ceremony in which the crowned, enthroned high-priest Joshua (pictured as a temple builder, together with Zerubbabel called a *branch* of the Lord and also a *branch* who will *grow up* or the *dawn* who will *dawn forth*) takes off filthy garments and puts on rich apparel and a turban before an angel of the Lord have something to tell us about related ceremonies (see Zech. 3; 6.10ff.)? Is there not a sense in which the royal priest is still being humiliated and then cleansed when he confesses sins and immerses himself several times before putting on white garments and precious vestments (see Lev. 8; *Yoma* 3; etc.)?

[2] In *The Labyrinth*, p. 106. See also *Sacral Kingship*, p. 116, etc. Here (p. 54 n. 1) Johnson wonders if at an early date this aspect of the festival had not become far less cyclically oriented and was now directed more toward the future on the plane of history. We agree with him that an eschatological element was probably present from the beginning (see in our ch. IV), but it seems to us that the festival held the cyclical and, as it were, linear-eschatological viewpoints in tension. The latter never did oust the former until the time when it was no longer possible for the old rituals to be celebrated.

of which he must be delivered, lifted up and saved. Marked emphasis is given to this idea in Israel.[1]

> For the waves of death encompassed me,
>   the torrents of perdition assailed me.
>   (II Sam. 22.5; see Ps. 18.4.)

> He reached from on high, he took me,
>   he drew me out of many waters (or, great floods).
>   (II Sam. 22.17; see Ps. 18.16.)

> Deep calls to deep at the thunder of thy cataracts;
>   all thy waves and thy billows have gone over me.
>   (Ps. 42.7.)

> Save me, O God:
>   For the waters have come up to my neck.
> I sink in deep mire,
>   where there is no foothold;
> I have come into deep waters,
>   and the flood sweeps over me.   (Ps. 69. 1f.)

> Let not the flood sweep over me,
>   or the deep swallow me up,
>   or the pit close its mouth over me.   (Ps.69.15.)

> They surround me like a flood all the day long;
>   they close in upon me together.   (Ps. 88.17.)

> Stretch forth thy hand from on high,
>   rescue me and deliver me from the many waters,
>   from the hand of aliens.   (Ps. 144.7.)

> They flung me alive into the pit
>   and cast stones upon me;
> Water closed over my head;
>   I said, 'I am lost.'   (Lam. 3.53f.)

It would be most helpful and fascinating to know more about the uses to which this language was originally put. Did it involve that *sea* which was located in the temple? And/or might it be that this took place at the pool Gihon and had some connection with the king's initiation?[2] In which case is it plausible that the *suffering* in the water and the *baptism* in preparation for enthronement were actually

---

[1] This language has also influenced Jonah 2. Note there the references to the temple.

[2] See again I Kings 1.33ff.

two aspects of the same event, the dangerous, death-dealing waters having been conquered and transformed into the waters of life? These are questions which we simply cannot answer, but the language itself and some of these inherent possibilities will come later to have great significance for us.

5. SECOND ISAIAH'S SERVANT AND ZECHARIAH

As a final comment to this chapter we should like briefly to discuss one of the ways by which the older ideas associated with the Man-king and his suffering continued to have influence in Israel. It is our intention to avoid as far as possible the vexed controversy concerning the identity of the Servant in Isa. 40–55. The debate over whether he was corporate or individual, a prophet or a king, historical or ideal we leave to others.[1] Obviously we are not blind to the fact that the title *Servant* is associated with kings generally and particularly with Jerusalem kings,[2] nor that the apparent oscillation between corporate and individual features in the description of this figure admirably suits one who is the representative of his people and who can be identified with the nation. We realize that the expressions like *chosen, elect, light*, etc., employed to describe the Servant's calling and mission, are also used elsewhere of kings.[3] We are aware that Isa. 43.1ff. contains language which could apply to the Man of the creation story[4] and that the whole myth of the creation seems to

[1] In addition to the studies mentioned below, see in particular C. R. North, *The Suffering Servant in Deutero-Isaiah*[2], London, 1956, and his commentary *The Second Isaiah*, Oxford, 1964; C. Lindhagen, *The Servant Motif in the Old Testament*, Uppsala, 1950.

[2] On Keret and Danel (among other foreign kings) as Servants of El, see Bentzen, *King and Messiah*, p. 47. Cf. Pss. 89.3, 20, 39; 144.10; II Sam. 7.5, 8, 20; etc. Also see Zimmerli and Jeremias, *Servant of God*, pp. 22, 51f.

[3] So Engnell, 'The 'Ebed Yahweh Songs and the Suffering Servant in "Deutero-Isaiah" ', *BJRL* 31, 1948, pp. 54ff. In addition to the pronouncement of God's pleasure (42.1) and the connection of the call with creation (42.5), there is the revealing of the name (49.1), the calling from the womb (49.15), the giving of the spirit and bringing forth of judgment (42.1), the releasing of prisoners (42.7; 49.9), the Servant as a covenant (42.6; 49.8), the plea of the Servant and his statement of confidence in God (49.4), the subservience of foreign kings (49.7; see 52.15), God's help on a day of salvation (49.8), universal dominion (42.4; 49.6), the Servant as law-giver (42.4). Cf. also Gressmann, *Der Messias*, pp. 324ff., and W. Manson, who offers a convenient list of comparisons, *Jesus, the Messiah*, pp. 173f.

[4] Cf. the passing through waters and fire and the use of *'ādām* in v. 4. See Engnell, *op. cit.*, p. 64. Note also that the honour (*hādār*) of the Man in Ps. 8.5 is precisely what the figure loses in Isa. 53.2.

have much affected the phraseology and imagery of these chapters.[1] On the other hand we do not undervalue the prophet-like characteristics of the Servant,[2] although we would join with others who find that prophetic and royal attributes are not mutually exclusive, remembering, too, that the king was once considered a type of the prophet as well as of the priest.[3]

All of this, however, we are willing to let pass in order to concentrate on the descriptions of the Servant's suffering in Isa. 49.7; 50.6–9 and 52.13–53.12. Yet again we wish to tread circumspectly. We have seen how Johnson is willing to speak of the king as the 'Suffering Servant' in the Jerusalem royal rites. We would here accept his allusion only in so far as it suggests that motifs and themes used of the suffering king have strongly influenced those used of II Isaiah's Servant. We would not go so far as Engnell, who wishes to *identify* this Servant with the Messiah or king.[4] Nor, while we cannot help but agree with Engnell in finding that cultic language has been made to do service in these passages, shall we argue that we have before us a prophetic imitation of a cult liturgy.[5]

What we do affirm is this: whoever composed these particular passages, and whatever his purpose, he (or they?) had recourse to a general conception which was neither new nor unique. Of course, one may well feel that he has brought it to new heights of expression and meaning, but the description of one who suffers in these terms and whose suffering has an atoning effect for others is not an isolated phenomenon. To treat it as such involves a distortion of the Old Testament which at once exaggerates the importance of II Isaiah's Servant and which may blind one to the significance of the far more

---

[1] Cf. Mowinckel, *Psalms* I, pp. 116ff.

[2] See Mowinckel, *HTC*, pp. 187ff.

[3] So Bentzen, *King and Messiah*. On Moses as a royal figure, see Widengren, *Ascension of the Apostle*, pp. 28, 41f. Note that Rowley (*Servant of the Lord*, p. 15 n. 1), though emphasizing differences between the king and the Servant, does admit the Servant's royal features and that 'both concepts may have some roots in the cult . . . '. Later (*op. cit.*, p. 87) he confirms this view and says that he agrees with A. R. Johnson.

[4] *Op. cit.*, pp. 57, 92. H. Riesenfeld (*Jésus transfiguré*, Copenhagen, 1947, pp. 81ff.) speaks of the Servant as one aspect of a disintegrating concept of the older royal ideology. Cf. Engnell, *op. cit.*, p. 91.

[5] He is right, however, to point out that many features belie a purely historical interpretation. A number of the verbs appear to have a future reference and the descriptions are often exaggerated in cultic terms. *Op. cit.*, p. 64. Notice, for instance, that the Servant appears to have suffered and been exalted in the presence of foreign kings. Compare Pss. 2.2; 18.43–45; Ezek. 28.17; etc.

ancient and widespread conception in the very near background. To illustrate this point we should like to set out several parallel passages, one from Babylon, but the others from the royal psalms themselves. We do not offer them with the intention of demonstrating some manner of literary dependency, for the *borrowing* did not proceed along these lines.[1]

Psalms	'Temple Program for the New Year's Festivals at Babylon'	Second Isaiah
Thou hast removed the sceptre from his hand, and cast his throne to the ground. (89.44)	Take away the sceptre, the circle and the sword.	
The Lord has chastened me sorely. (118.18; cf. 69.19; II Sam. 7.14)	. . . and strike the king's cheek . . . he shall drag him by the ear and make him bow down to the ground.	I gave my back to the smiters, and my cheek to those who plucked out the beard; I hid not my face from shame and spitting. (50.6)
The Lord lives . . . who delivered me from my enemies. (18.46, 48; cf. 16.5f.; 69.6ff.; 118.17)	Have no fear: the god Bel will listen to your prayer . . . He will magnify your lordship.	For the Lord God helps me; therefore have I not been confounded. (50.7)
The Lord reward me according to my righteousness . . . I was blameless before him, and I kept myself from guilt. (18.20, 23; cf. 16.1; 18.6; 22.8; 69.4f.; 116.1f.)	I did not sin, lord of the countries. I was not neglectful of your godship. (Vv. 115ff.; *ANET*, p. 334)	Who will contend with me? . . . Who is my adversary? . . . Behold, the Lord God helps me; who will declare me guilty? (50.8f.)

A lengthy comparison of Isa. 52.13ff. with the relevant passages in the Psalter is not feasible here. We note only a few of the more

[1] The parallels offered are representative rather than exhaustive.

evocative passages relating to 'a man of sorrows, and acquainted with grief'.[1]

> But I am a worm, and no man;
>> scorned by men, and despised by the people.
> All who see me mock at me,
>> they make mouths at me, they wag their heads;
> 'He committed his cause to the Lord; let him deliver him,
>> let him rescue him, for he delights in him.' (Ps. 22.6–8.)

> I am poured out like water,
>> and all my bones are out of joint;
> my heart is like wax,
>> it is melted within my breast;
> my strength is dried up like a potsherd,
>> and my tongue cleaves to my jaws;
>> thou dost lay me in the dust of death. (Ps. 22.14f.)

> For it is for thy sake that I have borne reproach,
>> that shame has covered my face.
> I have become a stranger to my brethren,
>> an alien to my mother's sons. (Ps. 69.7f.)

> When I humbled my soul with fasting,
>> it became my reproach.
> When I made sackcloth my clothing,
>> I became a byword to them. (Ps. 69.10f.)

> Hide not thy face from thy servant;
>> for I am in distress, make haste to answer me.
> Draw near to me, redeem me,
>> set me free because of my enemies.
> Thou knowest my reproach,
>> and my shame and my dishonour;
>> my foes are all known to thee.
> Insults have broken my heart,
>> so that I am in despair.
> I looked for pity, but there was none;
>> and for comforters, but I found none. (Ps. 69.17–20.)

> For they persecute him whom thou hast smitten,
>> and him whom thou hast wounded, they afflict still more.
>> (Ps. 69.26.)

> Thou hast cut short the days of his youth;
>> thou hast covered him with shame. (Ps. 89.45; see vv. 50f.)

[1] In addition to other portions of these psalms and Pss. 16; 18; 116; 118; see Pss. 88; 42.10. See also Ezek. 28.18f.; Lam. 3.

In Isa. 52.13 and then in 53.10–12 the pattern of the kingship rites is followed in that God's favour is proclaimed, and the Servant is rescued from death and exalted.[1]

> He brought me forth into a broad place;
> > he delivered me, because he delighted in me.
>
> . . . who delivered me from my enemies;
> > yea, thou didst exalt me above my adversaries;
> > thou didst deliver me from men of violence. (Ps. 18.19, 48.)
>
> For thou hast delivered my soul from death,
> > my eyes from tears,
> > my feet from stumbling;
> I walk before the Lord
> > in the land of the living.
> I kept my faith, even when I said,
> > 'I am greatly afflicted.' (Ps. 116.8–10.)

Admittedly it is more difficult to give obvious parallels from the Psalms to the themes of atonement and justification found in Isa. 53. It would appear that, in this instance, II Isaiah has tended to make explicit what is implicitly true in the royal psalms. Yet even if to the earlier peoples it was a belief which they experienced rather than expounded, it still can be realized and understood in those portions of the liturgy where the prayer of the king for his salvation becomes that of the people, and where his joy then becomes their joy.[2]

> May we shout for joy over your victory,
> > and in the name of our God set up our banners;
> May the Lord fulfil all your petitions.
> > > (Ps. 20.5; see 20.9.)
>
> Let not those who hope in thee be put to shame through me,
> > O Lord God of hosts;
> Let not those who seek thee be brought to dishonour through me.
> > > (Ps.69 .6.)
>
> Let the oppressed see it and be glad;
> > you who seek God, let your hearts revive.
> For the Lord hears the needy,
> > and does not despise his own that are in bonds. (Ps. 69.32f.)

---

[1] See also Pss. 16; 18.43ff.; 22.22ff.; 30; 116; 118.21ff.

[2] See also Pss. 22.26; 30.4f.; 69.34ff.; 80.17ff.; 118.22ff.; 144; Hab. 3.13. In a similar fashion might be read the whole of Ps. 72.

Not to be neglected in this same regard are several passages from the prophet Zechariah.

> And I will pour out on the house of David and the inhabitants of Jerusalem a spirit of compassion and supplication, so that, when they look on him[1] whom they have pierced, they shall mourn for him, as one mourns for an only child, and weeps bitterly over him, as one weeps over a first-born. On that day the mourning in Jerusalem will be as great as the mourning for Hadad-rimmon in the plain of Megiddo. (Zech. 12.10–12)

The reference to Hadad-rimmon is obscure,[2] but a comparison of the verse with II Kings 23.29f.[3] suggests that it could be king Josiah, shot by an arrow at Megiddo, who is here in mind. Significant is the mention of *piercing, looking upon* (for both see Ps. 22.16f.), *first-born* and *mourning* which might again derive from the general background of the king-as-sufferer. For this reason some are prone to see here a relationship with II Isaiah,[4] while our inclination is to say that the same fundamental conception is affecting them both. Perhaps there is some connection between this possibility and the suggestion by a number of scholars that the whole complex of Zech. 12–14 (or even 9–14) has made use of themes relevant to the New Year festival.[5]

Also worthy of our attention is the mention of the shepherd who will be stricken, causing the sheep to be scattered (Zech. 13.7). This shepherd is called the *mighty man* (*geber*) 'who stands next to me' (i.e. to the Lord). Thus, in this rather independent oracle which might relate back to 12.10ff., there are three terms which can be readily associated with kings.[6] If nothing else, it emphasizes once more the corporate life and destiny of king and people.

Finally there is the well-known verse Zech. 9.9 occurring in the midst of a passage predicting future glory and triumph for the nation.

> Rejoice greatly, O daughter of Zion.
> Shout aloud, O daughter of Jerusalem.

[1] If the Hebrew is correct to read *me* instead of *him*, the reference is probably to Yahweh: i.e. 'They shall look unto me on account of the one whom they have pierced . . .'

[2] Perhaps it is a reference to heathen rites of lamentation for this god or a king bearing the god's name.

[3] Also II Chron. 35.20ff.

[4] See esp. Isa. 53.2, 4.

[5] See D. R. Jones, *Haggai, Zechariah and Malachi* (Torch Commentary), London, 1962, pp. 157ff.

[6] So the Targum interprets *geber* here as *ruler*.

> Lo, your king comes to you;
>   *acquitted*[1] and victorious is he,
> humble and riding on an ass,
>   on a colt the foal of an ass.

Many would find here a picture of the future king conceived on the basis of a memory of the Davidic king riding into the city at a stage in the rituals of the New Year festival.[2] He rides the royal colt;[3] publicly he still displays the requisite humility, though in the rites he has been declared *innocent* and his victory over enemies and evil forces is assured. This is followed in 9.10 by a typical royal oracle promising world-wide dominion to the king.[4]

[1] This gives the better sense of *ṣaddīq* than either *triumphant* or *righteous*. He has been made righteous, declared innocent of his sins. On the king's righteousness, see Pss. 45.7; 72.1; etc.

[2] Mowinckel, *HTC*, pp. 176f., speaks of a 'conscious archaism in the prophet's reference to the saviour king'. The shout may well be the festal shout of the enthronement procession. See I Sam. 10.24; II Sam. 6.15; Pss. 47.1; 100.1; 118.25; 132.9, 16; also Ps. 20.5. Cf. Johnson in *The Labyrinth*, pp. 104f.

[3] See again I Kings 1.33ff.; also Gen. 49.10f.

[4] Compare Pss. 2.8; 72.8; Micah 5.4; and commonly of foreign kings.

IV

THE MAN IN LATER JUDAISM

For that Son of Man has appeared,
And has seated himself on the throne of his glory.
(*I Enoch 69.29*)

I. THE CONTINUITY OF IDEAS

WE HOPE THAT we have now given good reason for holding that the legends involving First Man and king and Primordial Man (as a version of the king-god) are all inextricably bound one with another. Though obvious and useful distinctions are to be made, the fact of the matter is that myth and dramatic ritual seem often to have *confused* the attributes of these figures. Primarily it is the king, *playing* the role of his royal ancestor, who ascends to *become* the cosmic ruler, that has been the cause of this confusion. We find it, then, no wonder that there are numerous legends, fragmentary oracles and liturgies which tell of a royal Primordial-like First Man or *vice versa*, or which present the royal person in the guise of either or both of these figures.

It is to this general mythical-ritual background, dominated though not completely comprehended by kingship ideology and practice, that we are going to ascribe the source of the *impulse* for the later Man speculation. It is still preferable, however, to speak in terms of sources rather than a source, for we have seen that, despite the many common features and very probable cross-influences, there are many variations in the conception.

It is with this background in mind that we cannot accept the views of scholars who wish to study conceptions like the Messiah, the Son of Man, the Suffering Servant and the First Man as though they were wholly disparate in origin. This is not to say that they can be simply equated in later thought or that each has not tended to develop along different lines, but we are at one with a student of these matters like Bentzen when he finds that 'the Son of Man, Primeval Man and

Messiah have common roots'.[1] In their own way we feel that objectors to this thesis such as Sjöberg and Mowinckel are yet forced into partial acknowledgment of its correctness when they admit that the late Jewish Son of Man is an adaptation of the Primal Man who also has many royal attributes.[2] Their attempts to retain in distinct categories the conceptions of an earthly, human Messiah[3] and an heavenly, pre-existent Son of Man simply do not hold up, and their efforts to explain the many similarities and congruencies entirely on the basis of a later cross-fertilization of ideas are not satisfactory.[4] If 'there is doubtless a conception of the Son of Man as king of paradise, king from primordial times',[5] and, if again, 'at one time the role of king of paradise belonged to the Son of Man',[6] then the Son of Man is not in origin an entirely heavenly figure, however he may later have been imagined. Alternatively we find it hard to believe that pictures of the Messiah as one in the heavens or as a ruler in paradise are completely the result of late influence by Son of Man ideas. Since Mowinckel himself can write that 'the Messiah had come to be endowed with mythical, superhuman features, derived from the myths about paradise and primordial times' as early as Isa. 9.1ff.,[7] it becomes difficult to know where and when any absolute distinctions are to be made.

Approaching the subject from another angle, but without delving into all the background we have studied, William Manson was in our opinion reaching towards the truth of the matter:

. . . the concepts of the Davidic Messiah, the Suffering Servant and the pre-existent Heavenly Man, *however disparate in origin they may have been*, have in the religious thought of Israel been conformed to the same type, and are to be recognized, therefore, as far as the religion of Israel is concerned, as successive phases of the Messianic idea.[8]

[1] *King and Messiah*, p. 76.
[2] See Sjöberg, *Henochbuch*, pp. 145f., 190ff., and above p. 70. Cf. Engnell, 'Besprechung von E. Sjöberg, Menschensohn', *BO* 8, 1951, pp. 187ff.
[3] Regarding this Messiah, see Mowinckel, *HTC*, pp. 290ff.; G. F. Moore, *Judaism in the First Centuries of the Christian Era*, Cambridge, Mass., 1927–30, II, pp. 323ff.; and, e.g., Pss. of Sol. 17–18.
[4] See Mowinckel, *HTC*, pp. 357, 360ff., 415.
[5] Mowinckel, *HTC*, p. 382. We realize that Mowinckel speaks of this paradise as one which is no longer here on earth, but this does not escape the fact that at one time it was often conceived of as being on the earth, as Mowinckel himself admits.
[6] *HTC*, p. 383.
[7] *HTC*, p. 433.
[8] *Jesus, the Messiah*, p. 174.

The clause which we have italicized is crucial, for what Manson so rightly recognized is not to be explained only in terms of later attempts at conformity. Indeed, we believe that the reason such conformity could take place was due to the fact that the various conceptions still retained their points of congruency which once they possessed within a larger reference of mythical-ritual thought.

Manson speaks of the 'successive phases of the Messianic idea'. We find this to be another way of expressing that which we should call the fragmentation or disintegration of the once comprehensive conception.[1] No doubt there were certain tensions at all times, but the mythical idea of one who was both present king and yet the representative of his primal ancestor and at the same time the actor in the cosmic drama which involved battle, suffering, creation and enthronement was sufficiently cohesive as long as it stood in relative propinquity to the *toleration* of ritual practice. But when the ritual, or even phases of that ritual, could no longer be performed, the various aspects or pieces, as it were, began to become unstuck. Then there appeared the more static ideograms of a Heavenly Man, an earthly Messiah, a Suffering Servant and a purely aetiological First Man, while yet we have shown and will endeavour yet to show that they all still retain very definite signs and attributes of their origination.

Yet supposing that we are approximately correct in our analysis to this point, where does this leave us? Judah ceased to have a king early in the sixth century BC. Granting that the crucial ideas were, in part, still influential on II Isaiah later in that century, granting even that certain oracles in Zechariah could have been written in the fifth or possibly the fourth century, it is still a long step to the birth of Jesus. Of course, one could point to numerous examples of antique conceptions and patterns of ideas which have lingered on and are operative in our own time despite the scientific and industrial revolutions and even in the most sophisticated of minds, not to speak of isolated and more primitive parts of society. On this analogy it is far from impossible that beliefs based on the once potent kingship ideologies continued to have their effects upon the minds of men. Still, and again, the gap is long and, while it could be that this just happened in ways which are no longer visible to us, one would think that there should be evidence of some vehicles of transmission.

We shall not claim in this study that we can fully bridge this gap

[1] Cf. Riesenfeld, *Jésus transfiguré*, pp. 187ff.; Engnell, *BO* 8, 1951, pp. 187ff.

in time (though it ought also to be remembered that lacunae in our knowledge are not necessarily equivalent with gaps in the historical continuity of ideas). We do contend, however, that we can see certain possibilities, certain vehicles which the older ideas may have used to carry on their influences. Several of these possibilities we have already hinted at and will take up again in chapter V, but there is one in particular which has been more or less obvious.

2. ESCHATOLOGY AND CREATION

The Son of Man as he appears in the late Jewish apocalyptic literature is predominantly an eschatological figure. Mowinckel would go so far as to hold that 'in spite of his pre-existence, the Son of Man is in Judaism a purely eschatological being with a purely eschatological task'.[1] In fact, as we have realized, the appearance of such an eschatological hero was a fairly common phenomenon during this period.[2] We need not look far for the cause of this development.

One can debate at length the question of the extent to which eschatology was always present in the myths and rituals of an earlier era. Partly this is a matter of defining terms. Always there was a sense in which the cultus was a *failure*. It, of course, could never do all that it promised, and it may well be that prophecies like Micah 5.2 and Isa. 9.6f., in their vision of a perfect king, had already begun to leave ritually based aspirations behind and to look for a totally new age in the future. It is reasonably clear, however, that a thoroughgoing eschatology only manifested itself after the genuine collapse of the normal, recurrent methods for ensuring the safety and well-being of the nation. Peoples who could no longer enjoy or put their faith in the traditional hope of a periodic renewal began to dream of a final, dramatic renewal at the *end* of time.

This process evolved in different nations at different times, and, understandably, it tended to affect the dispossessed more than those who still had a reasonable stake in the society. For Israel it might be thought to have begun with the fall of the Northern kingdom and was obviously greatly accelerated by the Babylonian conquest of Judah. Yet, by and large, the Jewish people appear still to have hoped for a salvation within history, a return from exile and a

---

[1] *HTC*, p. 435. See Kraeling, *Anthropos*, pp. 149ff.; Sjöberg, *Henochbuch*, pp. 197f.

[2] See again *HTC*, p. 423.

refounding of the nation. Even during this period, however, in the prophecies of Ezekiel, II Isaiah and Zechariah the note of a final and decisive intervention by God begins to sound.

As the dream developed it was elaborated. People wanted to describe this vision, to make it more real to their imaginations, and the materials for such description lay ready to hand. The old myths and rituals were recast and given new meaning. The new age would be a return to paradise; the great day of creation or re-creation which had been dramatically enacted or read out at the yearly festival became the pattern for the end of time. In a whole body of literature the many symbols, themes and stories of the time of creation now recur. There we find the garden, the tree, the waters, the temple, the mountain, the tablets of destiny, and the forces or being of evil. The tale of the battle with and victory over the chaos monster is recast, and the beast (or beasts) seen as the objectification of all evil and destructive powers. In a great and terrible struggle, in which the Messiah-like figure often leads, this power is defeated. A great new, paradisaical reign can begin.

Because this was a period of a vast intermingling of peoples, because the borders of nations and national religions were being broken down, and because eschatology by its very nature was not particularly tolerant of the old orthodoxies and limitations, this was also an era of borrowing and even of syncretism.[1] For Judaism especially, however, this was a process of grafting on to a plant already growing from its own roots. Foreign influences were adopted, but they only provided a part of the growth and could be grafted in just because the general development within Judaism was kindred to that occurring elsewhere. Necessarily, however, certain anomalies and inconsistencies were introduced. Men of vibrant imaginations spun these prophetic dreams and wrote these works; they were far more concerned with the power of their vision than with informing their dreams with our kind of logic or uniformity of viewpoint.[2]

This whole process of adapting the old myth and ritual materials

[1] 'It is certain that there were borrowings in this realm from external sources, but as so often happens, these borrowings would be largely unrecognized as such by the borrowers and would be naturally accepted as part of the traditional faith of their fathers.' D. S. Russell, *The Method and Message of Jewish Apocalyptic*, London, 1962, p. 62.

[2] We would certainly agree, however, with a slightly different point: that among the Jews their conception of God tended to exercise a certain control over their use of these materials and the presentation of them. See S. B. Frost, *Old Testament Apocalyptic*, London, 1952, pp. 39ff.

to the new visions of the end of time has been called 'the eschatologizing of the myth'.[1] Could it be illustrated diagrammatically we might draw a circle representing the annual (or frequent) pattern by which the lives and hopes of the people came round to the great day on which they renewed their corporate life and relation to the divine and the powers of nature. The forces of history had now cracked this circle open. A new view of history tended to fling men's sight into the linear perspective. The day of creation now lay at the beginning of time; the wondrous day of re-creation would be found at the end of time. The end would be the new beginning, dreamed of in terms borrowed from the picture of the first beginning.

We are thus not surprised that concurrent with this rebirth of imagery from antiquity there was a renewed interest in figures from that time. Men like Adam, Seth, Enoch, Noah and Daniel live again in the literature. Who, then, should become more important than the royal First Man, the king of the first paradise? What more natural than to believe that he, in one form or another, would return at the end of time?[2] In numerous of the eschatological works now extant (and many have been lost to us)[3] this conception made itself felt. Often the new Messiah-like one would be like the great mythical king of old. Even at the very heart of what we regard as more orthodox Judaism there began to creep in a flourishing new interest in Adam, a tendency to glorify him, if not to predict the return of one like him. And there is the Son of Man, an obvious type of the royal Man, seen in a special new light by the needs of eschatology.

3. EZEKIEL AND DANIEL

We have suggested that the vision in Zech. 9.9 (and possibly other earlier oracles as well) might be considered one of the first signs of this new eschatological hope built upon the old fund of beliefs. Another of the first hints of our figure in one of his later guises may be found in Ezek. 1.26. The prophet has a vision of the glory of God

[1] Bentzen, *King and Messiah*, pp. 73ff. See Gressmann, *Der Messias*, pp. 149ff.; Frost, *op. cit.*, pp. 32ff.; Russell, *op. cit.*, pp. 280ff.; and esp. S. H. Hooke, 'The Myth and Ritual Pattern in Jewish and Christian Apocalyptic' in *The Labyrinth* (ed. Hooke), London, 1935, pp. 211ff. On the continuation of this process in the Dead Sea Scrolls, see M. Black, *The Scrolls and Christian Origins*, London, 1961, pp. 135ff., and further below.

[2] 'The king of primordial time has also become the king of the end of time.' Mowinckel, *HTC*, p. 383.

[3] See Russell, *op. cit.*, pp. 66ff.

on the heavenly throne-chariot mounted upon the 'living creatures'.

And above the firmament over their heads there was the likeness of a throne, in appearance like lapis lazuli; and seated above the likeness of a throne was a likeness as the appearance of a man ('ādām) upon it.

The bright, fiery and glowing nature of this vision is then further described. Obviously imagery associated with solar deities is being employed.

What first arrests us here is the hesitant, doubly qualified suggestion that God is like an 'ādām in appearance.[1] (It is almost as though it were the reverse of Gen. 1.26.) Granted that the theology of the Old Testament can be quite anthropomorphic (see Ex. 33.23), it is usually so allusively or when speaking of an appearance of God (or his angel?) on earth. The direct suggestion that the heavenly Yahweh has a human-like appearance is unique. One wonders: has Ezekiel been induced to describe God in terms influenced by the Babylonian conception of the divine king-god (like Marduk)?[2] Or does this derive from more indigenous Jewish materials about which we know little?

By itself such a possibility might have small significance for us, but our interest must be more than compounded by the form of address in Ezek. 2.1 which immediately follows this vision:

And he said to me, 'Son of Man (ben 'ādām), stand upon your feet and I will speak with you.'

One must ask whether these adjacent references to God (as a king-god) being like an 'ādām (however qualified) and to a human as the son-of-adam are really as innocent as is often inferred. Usually the prophet's epithet is taken as an indication of his humble office and status before God, but Widengren is among those who severely question this interpretation.[3] Is Ezekiel's status really so lowly? Has he not been exalted, as it were, from among men to serve Yahweh in a very important manner? Does he himself represent his function as a humble office? Do not we elsewhere see kings falling down before

---

[1] The ascription of partial human features or capacities was also given to the beasts who appeared in visions of this type (see Ezek. 1.5, 10; Dan. 7.4), but it is evident, once again, that the one who is fully man-like is always the superior and ruler of the bestial ones and of a different order.

[2] Compare the illustration of Ashur given by A. Parrot, Babylon and the Old Testament (Studies in Biblical Archaeology, 8), ET, London, 1958, p. 136.

[3] The Ascension of the Apostle, pp. 32f.

their king-god and then being told to stand upon their feet? Is Ezekiel not given the task of reading the book of heavenly secrets as was the king of old? In addition we must recall again that from antiquity the Man was regarded as a type of the chief priest, prophet and wise man as well as of the ruler.

We hardly mean that Ezekiel is obsessed by some Man or king ideology. Yet it appears quite feasible that, in his vision of God, in the character of his high calling and in the form of address given to himself throughout the book, Ezekiel has been influenced by descriptions of the heavenly god-Man calling his *son* to his service.

It may well have been this (possibly through Ezekiel's example) which caused Daniel to have himself addressed in the same manner, as *ben 'ādām* in 8.17. We want to be understood correctly here: we do not infer that Daniel knows or intends a reference to all the background which we have delineated. He does not thus think of himself specifically as a royal First Man or some such. At the same time it may be quite superficial to think that Daniel is here merely making indication of his humanity. He, too, may be thinking of his humanity as it is being used in a very special way, an exalted way.[1]

A similar general background may play a part in Dan. 10.[2] First we have the appearance of one who is described in a fashion not unlike that of Ezek. 1.26ff. This supernatural man (*'īš*)[3] is not, however, named, and he probably is conceived of as an angel rather than as God, though, even so, angels are sometimes a *disguise* for God in the Old Testament. In the presence of this *brilliant* being Daniel himself seems to become radiant (reminiscent of the sun-king before the sun-god); he falls down and has to be raised up. (See 8.17 and again Ezek. 1.28–2.2.)[4] In 10.16 his lips are touched by one who is

---

[1] There is little consistency in the use of words for *man* in these chapters. In 8.15 we meet one in the appearance of a *gāber* who seems to be Gabriel (itself a significant name). The voice of an *'ādām* speaks to this Gabriel. (The word often translated as *man* in the last half of 8.16 is actually *hābēn* = *the son*??.) 9.21 speaks of the *'īš* Gabriel. And see also the different usages in ch. 10 noted below. Some of these variants may have been caused by editors or redactors, but it is fairly obvious that we are dealing with no technical vocabulary. God, his angel and Daniel are all described as *man*-like or addressed as a *man*. This, on the other hand, should be a warning against taking any of the references as simple indications of humanity.

[2] It is tempting to see the mention of the *first* month and 'the great river' here as allusions to the larger myth.

[3] Compare Rev. 1.13ff., which may be an interpretation of this or a very kindred figure as 'one like a Son of Man'.

[4] Both here and in 8.17 Daniel falls into a deep sleep, a state often brought on by a theophany.

'in the likeness of the sons of men' (*benē 'ādām*), or quite possibly 'in the likeness of a son of man' (*ben 'ādām*).[1] In verse 18 this becomes one having the appearance of an *'ādām*. Daniel is then addressed as a 'man' (*'īš*) and told the contents of the heavenly book.[2]

Doubtless there is little terminological consistency here, and others may well wish to see all the factors noticed as coincidence (and also coincidental with the vision of Dan. 7.13f., which thus stands in isolation) or too circumstantial to bear any weight. We wonder, however, if their collocation would have seemed quite so circumstantial to the original readers.

Yet it is, of course, when we turn to Dan. 7 that we come upon one of the most important and debated references to a figure like a son of man. First we have the appearance of four beasts from the great *sea*.[3] They are used as symbols for four earthly kingdoms; as such their defeat is either told or foretold. Many scholars, in one way or another, would see in this a symbolism borrowed from the myth of creation. They would recall the pictures of the First Man or his counterpart (as the king-god or the king) either being attacked by beasts or ruling over them, depending upon what phase of the ancient myths is being described.[4] As Daniel watched,

> thrones were placed
>   and one that was Ancient of Days took his seat;
> his raiment was white as snow,
>   and the hair of his head like pure wool;
> his throne was fiery flames,
>   its wheels were burning fire. (Dan. 7.9.)

Myriads of people are assembled.

> . . . the court sat in judgment,
>   and the books were opened. (Dan. 7.10.)

---

[1] *Ben* is given in some texts and other variant readings might suggest that this was original. One variant would tell us that Daniel's lips were touched by the likeness of the hand (or hands) of an *'ādām*.

[2] Dan. 10.18 and also 10.11.

[3] *Yammā*. See again Ps. 74.13; etc.

[4] A pioneering study was H. Gunkel's *Schöpfung und Chaos in Urzeit und Endzeit*[2], Göttingen, 1922, esp. pp. 323ff., referring to the Babylonian myth of creation. Cf. Bentzen, *King and Messiah*, pp. 74f., and his *Daniel*[2] (Handbuch zum AT), Tübingen, 1952, pp. 56ff.; E. G. H. Kraeling, 'Some Babylonian and Iranian Mythology in the Seventh Chapter of Daniel' in *Oriental Studies in Honour of C. E. Pavry* (ed. J. D. C. Pavry), London, 1933, pp. 228ff. J. A. Emerton, 'The Origin of the Son of Man Imagery', *JTS*, ns 9, 1958, pp. 225ff., would stress a Ugaritic and Canaanite background. Others would find more of a basis in Gen. 1–2 and Ps. 8.

One of the beasts is slain, the others defeated.

13 I saw in the night visions,
     and behold, *with*[1] the clouds of heaven
          there came one like a son of man (*k^{e}bar 'enāš*),
     and he came to the Ancient of Days
          and was presented before him.
14 And to him was given dominion and glory and kingdom,
          that all peoples, nations and languages should serve him;
     his dominion is an everlasting (*'ālam*)[2] dominion
          which shall not pass away,
     and his kingdom one
          that shall not be destroyed.

Bentzen interprets this scene as 'an eschatologizing of the enthronement festival' with special reference to Ps. 2.[3] Gressmann stressed the whole mythological background with attention given to the myth of the solar heavenly Man.[4] Herzfeld, as we have already noticed, thinks it to be patterned on something like the sixth-century Iranian rites of enthronement. This coincides with much other Iranian imagery used in Daniel. The Son of Man comes not so much for judgment, but rather to claim a throne. The description 'like a son of man' means that he is the legitimate heir. So the same powers given to the son-of-man-like one are given to the king in Dan. 2.37 and 5.18.[5] C. H. Kraeling is among those who would emphasize the Babylonian features, viewing this as an enthronement not unlike that of Marduk.[6]

Morgenstern finds the background to be that of an ancient solar ritual akin to the one acted out in Tyre.[7] The scene portrays the young god taking the place of the old. For this purpose the king played the role of the god, perhaps in both phases. 'The king was the god and the god was the king.'[8] This pattern, he believes, was well

[1] Or *upon*. See below.

[2] The word is used both with reference to unlimited time in the future and also to great antiquity. Here both senses may be intended. See again in Micah 5.2.

[3] *King and Messiah*, p. 75. See H. Riesenfeld, 'The Mythological Background of New Testament Christology', in *The Background of the New Testament and Its Eschatology* (ed. W. D. Davies and D. Daube), Cambridge, 1956, p. 86.

[4] *Der Messias*, pp. 343ff.

[5] *Zoroaster and His World* II, pp. 831ff.

[6] *Anthropos*, pp. 145ff.

[7] 'The "Son of Man" of Daniel 7.13f. A new interpretation', *JBL* 80, 1961, pp. 65ff.

[8] *Op. cit.*, p. 69. 'The description "like a man" means that he wasn't being regarded as a man but rather as a god.'

known to Israelite kings and is now making its influence felt again. 'Plainly in all this there are definite reminiscences of the old institution of the king-god.'[1]

In the view of J. A. Emerton the figure like a son of man is actually playing a role which once belonged to Yahweh in a rite patterned on those known elsewhere in Canaan (in which El was the high-god and Baal the dragon conqueror) and perhaps borrowed from ancient Jebusite beliefs. He, too, sees a royal enthronement festival as the source of the imagery.[2]

Of course, there are a great number of other interpretations of this chapter and its central scene,[3] but we would certainly agree with the common and essential point of the explanations given above. There are too many relics from such enthronement sagas which cannot be fitted into other backgrounds. The sun-god appears in heaven on his fiery chariot.[4] He is described in a manner similar to Canaanite portrayals of El, as an old solar deity with grey hair probably known as the 'Father of Years'. The earthly king was viewed as his son, as was also the king-god Baal.[5] The books are now opened; soon judgments will take place. (Both features have a long association with the crucial day of the New Year's feast.) But first there comes upon the traditional scene the *young god*, who is said to be like the Man figure from antiquity. He is *akin* to him, probably as his descendant or representative, or perhaps because he is the son of the high-god and in his image. Clearly this takes place in heaven itself;[6] there may be hints of an ascension to this realm,[7] but the emphasis is mainly on the appearance, the presentation in preparation for enthronement. Only

---

[1] *Op. cit.*, p. 76.

[2] *JTS*, ns 9, 1958, pp. 225ff.

[3] On earlier views see H. H. Rowley, *Darius the Mede and the Four World Empires in the Book of Daniel*, Cardiff, 1935. Cf. Bentzen, *Daniel*, pp. 56ff.; J. Muilenberg, 'The Son of Man in Daniel and the Ethiopic Apocalypse of Enoch', *JBL* 79, 1960, pp. 197ff.; M. Black, 'The "Son of Man" in the Old Biblical Literature', *ExpT* 60, 1948/9, pp. 11ff.; Feuillet, *RB* 60, 1953, pp. 170ff., 321ff.; Dequeker and Coppens in *Le Fils de l'Homme et les Saints du Très-Haut*, pp. 15ff., 55ff.

[4] R. B. Y. Scott, 'Behold He Cometh with Clouds', *NTS* 5, 1958/9, p. 129, rightly notices the similarities with Ezek. 1.

[5] Cf. Emerton, *op. cit.*, p. 229; Gray, *Legacy of Canaan*, pp. 116f.

[6] Part of the debate has centred around the word '*im*. Is it intended to mean *on* or *with* the clouds? Later translations give both views. For a discussion see R. B. Y. Scott, *op. cit.*, pp. 127ff., but whatever nuance this word is given the result is the same. Originally the whole intent was to suggest a theophany, an appearance. Clouds are the traditional means for suggesting the heavenly setting. Only later was the idea of the figure *coming* to earth read into the picture.

[7] On this see T. W. Manson, *BJRL* 32, 1950, p. 174.

then is the figure given his dominion, glory and kingdom.[1] The question which asks whether this is a king-god or an earthly king *taken up* to heaven cannot be answered. In the Near Eastern lore he could be either or both, and here we have not sufficient information to know which idea may have been dominant in the background. Quite possibly the author was concerned only with the conception in general terms, the picture of a divine or semi-divine king ready to inaugurate a new and glorious reign. To him is given an *eternal* and universal dominion in language which can be echoed in many another passage devolving from kingship ideology.[2]

Therefore, for our purposes, there is no great need to trace all this to any one source, be it Babylonian, Iranian, Israelite, Ugaritic, Tyrian or Canaanite. Daniel was probably influenced by one source more than others, but the reference is too brief to permit exactitude.[3] Our point is this: around the year 176 BC there was known to the author of Daniel (and very likely to many of his readers) a kind of ideogram of an idealized, semi-divine, royal figure who would rule in the great age to come. He could be described as being 'like a son of man'. This manner of speaking may well have had at least a quasi-technical background, but Daniel himself may only be thinking of the grand conception, of a Man-like hero, a heavenly king who would rule over all the earth.[4]

Is he the Messiah? The best answer is both yes and no. He is the messianic king in the sense that he is the royal figure, derived ultimately from kingship ideology, who will do all that was expected of the Messiah. There would be no room both for a Messiah and for one such as Daniel describes. Yet he is not the Messiah in so far as others would be thinking of an earthly hero who would establish his glorious reign on earth. Seen in this way, the two conceptions are mutually exclusive even though they spring from the same soil. Needless to say, however, the logic which would make the different conceptions exclusive of one another was not everywhere observed. The figures shared too much in common, both because of their

[1] See J. G. Davies, *He Ascended into Heaven*, London, 1958, pp. 36f.

[2] See Pss. 2.8; 72.8ff.; 110.2; Isa. 9.7, and also, with regard to Nebuchadnezzar, Dan. 2.44.

[3] So see, quite interestingly, A. Jeffery in *The Interpreter's Bible* VI, New York, 1956, pp. 460f.

[4] 'We must therefore conclude that the seer of Daniel VII (or the tradition which he represents) was already familiar with the conception of a "Man" such as this who would one day come with the clouds of heaven . . .' Mowinckel, *HTC*, pp. 351f.

common background and because they were now bound to influence each other.

We have said that the figure is an idealized presentation. Some believe that he is so idealized that he is not conceived of individually at all.[1] Rather is he but a symbol for 'the saints of the Most High' who are later said to possess the eternal kingdom (7.18), to be given judgment (7.22),[2] and to whom all dominions will be obedient (7.27). Others would attempt to obviate this problem by regarding 7.13f. as an independent oracle.[3] Yet, even if this be so, it is not treated as such in the final recension of the book, and this is what ultimately concerns us.

From our point of view, however, the question is not really vital. Daniel is, of course, using symbolism. He tells us as much in verse 16. The whole point of symbolism is that it is a useful synechdoche. Still today an Englishman employs such a form every time he prays for his ruler, and it would be pedantic to inquire whether he is praying for the actual royal person or the nation. Nor is this contemporary example without significance for the ancient practice from which it also ultimately issues. We need not suppose that Daniel knew all about royal rituals when he interpreted a single figure as representative of the holy people of God. The idea is too much a part of his heritage (both as a Semite and a Jew) to require any fuller explanation.[4] So also could future generations think and likewise interpret this chapter, though clearly it was the dramatic picture of the

[1] A view from the far end of the spectrum could be represented by J. Klausner (*The Messianic Idea in Israel*, London, 1956, p. 229), who argues that Dan. 7.13 is explained quite simply by v. 18. The plain meaning is that other nations are beast-like and Israel is like a human being.

[2] Note that it is not specifically said in Dan. 7 that the 'one like a son of man' will be the final judge. Some think that in the vision proper this role is reserved for the Ancient of Days. Yet the role of judge may well be implied in v. 14, and, in any case, according to our interpretation, the Ancient of Days is passing on his function to the man-like figure. Mowinckel believes that the *thrones* (implying judgment) in v. 9 are meant to indicate one for him, though this may only be part of the traditional imagery of a council of the gods. We think it unlikely that the *thrones* were originally intended for the *saints*.

[3] Morgenstern, *JBL* 80, 1961, p. 66. Dequeker sees at least two redactors of the chapter and is among those who believe that the *saints* originally referred to angels and not people. *Op. cit.*, pp. 13ff. On the many theories see Rowley in *Servant of the Lord*, pp. 237ff. Muilenberg (*JBL* 79, 1960, p. 199), while recognizing the *foreign* elements in ch. 7, argues along with Rowley for one author, as does N. W. Porteous, *Daniel*, London, 1965, p. 96.

[4] As Jeffery points out (*op. cit.*, pp. 46of.), we need look no further than Dan. 2.37ff., where Nebuchadnezzar is both king and kingdom. The beasts have the same function in ch. 7.

heavenly, eschatological hero which later tended to predominate.

We notice that no suffering is explicitly predicated of this figure. It would be dangerous to assert very much on the basis of so elliptical a reference, and some would hold that the suffering of the 'saints' (7.25) means that their leader and representative must suffer, too.[1] This could be so, for the contention which argues that the figure as such could never suffer, since the appearance of one 'like a son of man' heralds a victory already won, misses the point of this kind of language and demands more precision than the passage was intended to give. Nevertheless, and this is most important, Daniel lays no real stress on this theme. The attention is almost entirely on the heavenly, eschatological appearance in glory. We have, in other words, only the final scene in the story of the royal Man.

Nor would we say that the associations of this figure with the beginning of time are prominent, though the imagery used is not without its effects. It is hard to believe that its allusiveness was lost on Daniel's audience.[2] Yet it, too, does not seem to be emphasized as such to any great purpose.

4. I ENOCH

The so-called 'First Book of Enoch' is made up of different parts which all reflect a more developed eschatological and apocalyptic outlook. There is a good deal of material concerning battles with the monsters Behemoth and Leviathan, and return to paradise, etc., illustrating much of what was said earlier in this chapter.[3] This long work is known to have survived as a whole only in Ethiopic (with Greek and Latin fragments), though its original language, always thought to have been Semitic, is now seen through the discovery of Aramaic portions in the caves of Qumran.

In a section (chapters 37–71) often called the 'Parables' or 'Similitudes of Enoch' there are a number of references to the Son of Man, but there is a good deal of debate concerning the use to which these

---

[1] See M. Black, 'Servant of the Lord and Son of Man', *SJT* 6, 1953, p. 8.

[2] See Muilenberg, *op. cit.*, p. 202.

[3] In I Enoch 14 there is a vision of God very reminiscent of that in Ezek. 1 and Dan. 7. Here, too, a *man* (identified with Enoch) is called up to heaven. It is going too far, however, to claim that Daniel modelled his vision on I Enoch 14 (see T. F. Glasson, *The Second Advent*[2], London, 1947, pp. 14ff.), or that Daniel's one 'like a son of man' was Enoch. Even if we were more certain of dates, this general ideogram seems to have been too widespread to permit such conclusions with regard to derivation.

chapters should be put.[1] The challenges may be summarized: (*1*) There is some uncertainty about the date of the 'Similitudes'. The possibility that it is post-Christian in origin has seemingly been enhanced by the fact that fragments of these chapters have not been found among other portions of the book at Qumran. (*2*) On these and/or other grounds some would contend that the references to the Son of Man, at the least, are Christian interpolations. (*3*) Previously we noticed that three different Ethiopic expressions are used: we hear of the Son of Man, Son of a man, and even of 'Son of the offspring of the mother of the living'.[2] In addition, we almost invariably find a demonstrative adjective preceding one of the expressions, i.e. *this* or *that* Son of Man. The phrase might only refer us back to the first appearance. Perhaps then there is no intended use of a genuine designation at all.[3]

We would reply in the following manner. (*1*) In our opinion very good arguments have been presented leading to the conclusion that I Enoch had, in all essential respects, been assembled into a unity before the birth of Christ.[4] The apparent lack of the chapters at Qumran may tell us more about these sectarians than it does of I Enoch.[5] In any event their absence there need hardly mean anything more than that they were written in some other locale before Christ was born, even if their inclusion did not occur until later.

[1] See esp. J. Y. Campbell, *JTS* 48, 1947, pp. 145ff.

[2] Cf. Mowinckel, *HTC*, p. 362; Charles II, pp. 174f.

[3] Note also that Noah is addressed, 'Thou, Son of Man . . .' in I Enoch 60.10. This, however, occurs in the garden on the day when the monsters are being defeated. Certainly he is not thought of as just any mortal, though it may be a warning against taking the expression as a full title even in this work. Alternatively, if, as many think, ch. 60 was interpolated into the 'Similitudes' at a later time, there may have been some other body of tradition in which the expression was used. For Noah, too, was an important descendant of Adam. Otherwise the later interpolater could have been influenced by the usage in the earlier Enochian materials.

[4] See esp. Sjöberg, *Henochbuch*, pp. 1ff. (Possible secondary additions would be 39.1f.; 54.7; 55.2; 60; 65–69.25.) Sjöberg offers a full discussion of the views of earlier scholars like Messel, Beer and Charles. With regard to the 'Similitudes', Mowinckel (*HTC*, p. 355) writes, 'Sjöberg has decisively refuted all the objections to the authenticity of the passages and the integrity of the text.' On the date, '. . . there is no ground for coming down into the Christian period.' Cf. C. P. van Andel, *De Structuur van de Henoch-Traditie en het Nieuwe Testament*, Utrecht, 1955, who would agree with both of these points. (See pp. 114ff. for a summation in English.)

[5] See A. Dupont-Sommer, *The Essene Writings from Qumran*, Oxford, 1961, pp. 299f.; G. H. P. Thompson, 'The Son of Man: The Evidence of the Dead Sea Scrolls', *ExpT* 72, 1961, p. 125.

Nevertheless it is not vital to us that the work should be considered as pre-Christian. We see no cause for believing that Jesus was much if at all indebted directly to I Enoch. If not pre-Christian, the 'Similitudes' were certainly written in the first century AD, probably in northern Palestine or perhaps in Syria (which could be why they are not found at Qumran), and as such would then be evidence for a roughly contemporary interest in the Son of Man.

(2) Theories which seek Christian interpolations into a work which originally spoke only of 'the Elect One', etc., appear quite improbable. To suppose that references to the Son of Man would have been interpolated without any further Christian changes or additions involves suppositions for which neither reason[1] nor textual support can be given. The expression was hardly the exclusive property of Christians. If the Son of Man was added to the text by some Jewish hand (though again there is no good reason for believing this), it would still reveal to us the esteem in which the figure was held.

(3) The use of different expressions to refer to the Enochian figure as *Son of Man* is perhaps not so complex and puzzling a matter as first appears. However esoteric the phrase 'Son of the offspring of the mother of the living' may seem to us, it is regularly used in the Ethiopic to translate *the Son of Man* of the Gospels.[2] The difficulties regarding the demonstrative may lie primarily with the translator who was working from a Greek version. Ethiopic has no definite article and the demonstrative adjective may represent an attempt to render slavishly the Greek definite article. (Sjöberg, however, suspects that the Greek itself might have had a demonstrative which could in turn reflect the original.[3] Yet Sjöberg holds that this would have indicated emphasis and not been a mere reference to the figure mentioned earlier.)[4] If the demonstrative did stand in the original, the expression might, as Mowinckel suggests, have been used as

. . . a description and not as a name or title, and the accompanying 'this' refers back to Enoch's first vision of 'a being whose countenance had the

---

[1] If anything, it would be more reasonable to assume that it is evidence of an anti-Christian polemic (i.e. Jesus was not the Son of Man; Enoch was), but there is no support for this alternative either.

[2] So also at Ps. 80.17; Ezek. 2.1; Dan. 7.13; etc. This expression, we suggest, derives from Semitic phrases like 'one born of woman' and 'son of thy handmaid' (e.g. 1QS, xi, 16, 20). Here again, however, and by an associated process, it has become a title of quasi-divinity without losing all its former nuances.

[3] At 48.2 the demonstrative, contrary to Ethiopic practice, follows the noun.

[4] *Henochbuch*, pp. 45ff. So the demonstrative is also found with divine titles like 'Lord of Spirits' and 'Head of Days'.

appearance of a man' . . . In an eschatological, apocalyptic context, this description was entirely explicit and comprehensible to Enoch's hearers and readers. 'That Son of Man' (the Son of Man whom you know) refers not only to an earlier mention of him in a writing or in a message, but to a heavenly Son of Man who actually exists, and of whom the hearers know.[1]

First let us reckon with the person of Enoch himself. Why is he chosen as the central figure for this and several other works, and why, as well, does he make his presence felt in other writings of the late New Testament and gnostic periods?[2] Is it simply because he is another of the antediluvian heroes?

It may be of significance that in other cultures, among the men who lived before the flood and who were regarded as kings, the seventh was conceived of as the one to whom special wisdom and privilege had been given.[3] There are a number of hints in Jewish literature that Enoch was seen as a king,[4] and, being the seventh *son of Adam*, there was a not surprising tendency to see him as the perfect son of his ancestor, the true representative of his father.[5] And so we hear not only of Enoch's close association with God, that he 'walked with God', but also that 'God took him'.[6] This last was interpreted to mean that Enoch did not die normally. Thus he (along with Elijah)

[1] *HTC*, p. 364.

[2] See Jude 14ff.; Heb. 11.5; in the *Pistis Sophia* (II, xcix; IV, cxxxiv) we hear that the *Books of Jeu* were written by Enoch in the paradise of Adam. Both the *Pistis Sophia* and the *Books of Jeu* are dedicated to Enoch. See Doresse, *Secret Books*, p. 254. This is another of the many little links between Jewish sectarianism and later gnosticism.

[3] See Hooke in the new *Peake's Commentary on the Bible* (ed. M. Black and H. H. Rowley), London, 1962, p. 183; Davies, *He Ascended into Heaven*, p. 16. Does the fact that Enoch lived for 365 years preserve an association with the sun?

[4] See below and also the Talmud passage which speaks of Enoch as 'reigning' over the people. They are said to shout to him, 'Long live the king!' Jub. 4.17 makes Enoch the first to learn writing and wisdom like many another first king and Man. He is taken from the children of men to the Garden of Eden, to the mountain. (Obviously in later tradition Enoch becomes a very composite figure. In III Enoch esp. he has picked up traits from the conception of a wise and transcendant scribe, though see again Widengren, *Ascension of the Apostle*, p. 13, pointing out that many kings were regarded as wise scribes and seers.)

[5] Enoch is third in Gen. 4, but seventh in the account of Gen. 5. The fact that he is the seventh son of Adam is stressed in this and other works: I Enoch 60.8; 93.3; Jub. 7.39; Jude 14. On his Adamic attributes see in the references to Jub. 4.17, the *Pistis Sophia* and I Enoch 14 in the notes above. Kraeling writes: 'Enoch's elevation to the office of Bar Nasha is thus but another expression of the connection between Adam and Messiah. This time it is not merely that the Christ re-enacts the role of Adam. The Messiah is here in person an Adamite' (*Anthropos*, p. 163).

[6] Gen. 5.21ff.

became the prototype for a long tradition concerning figures (Adam among them)[1] who were taken up or who ascended into heaven.

We first meet the figure referred to by the term of our special interest in I Enoch 46.

1 And there I saw One who had a head of days,
   And His head was white like wool,
   And with Him was another being whose countenance had the
      appearance of a man,
   And his face was full of graciousness, like one of the holy angels.
2 And I asked the angel who was with me and showed me all the hidden things, concerning that Son of Man, who he was, and whence he was, and why he went with the Head of Days. 3 And he answered and said unto me:
   This is that Son of Man who hath righteousness,
   With whom righteousness dwelleth,
   And who revealeth all the treasures that are hidden,
   Because the Lord of Spirits hath chosen him,
   And whose lot hath the pre-eminence before the Lord of Spirits in
      uprightness for ever.
4 And this Son of Man whom thou hast seen
   Shall put down [or raise up] the kings and the mighty from their
      seats . . .

It is easy to assume that Enoch is basing his vision here on that of Dan. 7. The similarities are obvious. Yet there are also differences, and it is quite possible that Encoh is using language and imagery, a kind of ideogrammatic way of speaking, which is not to be traced to any one source, but which was rather generally known during this era.

Both kings and first men are figures of righteousness and possessors of wisdom and divine secrets. The king is often said to put down foreign kings (or perhaps to cause them to rise in fear and astonishment),[2] especially as part of the ritual. These references may now, however, be too *popular* to mean anything more than that a royal-like figure is being described.

Still, such associations are basic and continue throughout the 'Similitudes', being attributed either to this Son of Man or the Elect

---

[1] In addition to references below, see H. Odeberg, *The Fourth Gospel interpreted in its relation to contemporaneous religious currents in Palestine and the Hellenistic-Oriental World*, Uppsala, 1929, p. 94.
[2] See Pss. 2.8ff.; 72.11; Isa. 49.7 (and Isa. 52.15, where this may be the thought intended).

One with whom he is equated.[1] He is also a judge who sits on a throne,[2] and this throne is identified as the very throne of God himself.[3] This last idea is hard to account for unless, perhaps, we reach back to the ancient conception of the young *god* coming to the throne of the old god.

Next we may read in I Enoch 48.2ff.:

> 2 And at that hour that Son of Man was named
> In the presence of the Lord of Spirits,
> And his name before the Head of Days,
> 3 Yea, before the sun and the signs were created,
> Before the stars of heaven were made,
> His name was named before the Lord of Spirits.[4]
> 4 He shall be a staff to the righteous whereon to stay themselves and
> not fall,
> And he shall be the light of the Gentiles,
> And the hope of those who are troubled of heart.
> 5 All who dwell on earth shall fall down and worship before him,
> And will praise and bless and celebrate with song the Lord of
> Spirits.
> 6 And for this reason he has been chosen and hidden before Him,
> Before the creation of the world and for evermore.
> ....
> 8 In those days downcast in countenance shall the kings of the earth
> become...
> 10 For they have denied the Lord of Spirits and His Anointed.[5]

Does the passage mean that the Son of Man has a premundane existence, or only that his name and office have long been fore-ordained, waiting for the time at which someone from the earth should become that Son of Man? 62.7 might well seem to indicate the former.

> For from the beginning the Son of Man was hidden,
> And the Most High preserved him in the presence of His might,
> And revealed him to the elect.

[1] On wisdom and revealing secrets see I Enoch 49.2, 3; 51.3.

[2] I Enoch 45.3; 49.4; 61.8; 62.3, 10; 69.27. See 63.11, where the unrighteous are filled with 'shame before that Son of Man' and driven from his presence.

[3] I Enoch 51.3; 61.8; 62.2.

[4] Mowinckel thinks there is a reminiscence here of the Primordial Man whose genesis and that of creation are bound together (*HTC*, p. 372 n. 2).

[5] The term *Anointed* (Messiah) seems here to be employed in its late, technical sense to refer to the coming king. The author apparently finds no difficulty in accepting this as an equivalent to the other expressions used for the figure, although *Anointed* plays a minor part, occurring only once again (52.4).

The matter, however, is further complicated by chapters 70 and 71. There both Enoch and his name are elevated; '. . . his name during his lifetime was raised aloft to that Son of Man' (70.1). Enoch, who is said to have ascended from the garden (60.8) sees heaven itself described as a new paradise.[1] He falls down and is raised up by Michael, the Archangel; he is shown all secrets. The Head of Days appears, and before him, Enoch prostrates himself once more;[2] he feels his body relax, and his spirit undergoes a transformation.[3] He cries out blessings, and these are pleasing to God. And then (ch. 71.14ff.), wonder of wonders, the angel speaks the will of God to him:[4]

14 'You are the Son of Man[5] who art born unto righteousness,
   And righteousness abides upon you,
   And the righteousness of the Head of Days does not forsake you.'
15 And he said unto me:
   'He proclaims unto you peace in the name of the world to come,
   For from hence has proceeded peace since the creation of the world,
   And so shall it be unto you for ever and ever.
16 And all shall walk in your ways since righteousness never forsakes
       you;
   With you will be their dwelling-places, and with you their heritage,
   And they shall not be separated from you for ever and ever and
       ever.'

It is this passage which has caused untold anguish to the commentators.[6] As is well known, R. H. Charles was so astounded by the idea of Enoch being proclaimed as the one who already seemed to

---

[1] I Enoch 70.4. See also 61.12. We may also point outside the 'Similitudes' proper to 32.3, where the Garden of Righteousness and the tree of wisdom are described.

[2] Some see evidence for two sources here. This is quite unnecessary; there is a double prostration either due to ritual background or for dramatic effect.

[3] Compare the *sleep* of Dan. 10.9 before his appearance is transformed in the presence of a heavenly being.

[4] It could be God himself who is speaking. See Sjöberg, *Henochbuch*, p. 153.

[5] Compare another royal *naming* oracle delivered by God through his *prophet*: 'You are my son . . .' Ps. 2.7.

[6] The following is our answer to the question, 'Is Enoch the Son of Man?' See *HTC*, pp. 437ff. Mowinckel himself, however, finally suggests that *son of man* here refers to Enoch as a mortal and not as *the* Son of Man. If on no other account, on the basis of Mowinckel's own arguments alone, this is quite incredible, and so he also suggests that the real idea behind the elevation of Enoch is that he is to be *with* the Son of Man rather than to become him. We see nothing that would support this expedient.

have a definite existence that he amended to the third person.[1] Others have proposed theories about the later addition of all or parts of chapters 70–71.[2] How could two people become one? Or must we resort to some *mystical* solution?[3]

But we are not astounded. Rather are we reminded—of the king who is thought to ascend to the heavenly realms, falls down before his god, is raised up by the *priest*, calls out to the god and is proclaimed to be the counterpart and ancestor, that one who was before the creation, he who can be thought now to have an existence in heaven, the first of kings, the Man, or (emphasizing the idea of a counterpart) the Son of Man.[4] The earthly king mounts to the throne of his primeval (now heavenly) ancestor and *becomes* him, or, if you will, becomes his representative. The Son of Man has existed before the creation, yes. But that one who is *now* to be the Son of Man, who is to be the king-Man, is now named and enthroned.[5]

The author of these 'Similitudes' may not himself have understood this idea perfectly, and we do not necessarily insist that every problem having to do with Enoch and the Son of Man is automatically solved, for such a work as I Enoch is not of a genre from which perfect consistency can be expected. Yet we would unhesitatingly maintain that our understanding brings us right to the heart of what is taking place in I Enoch. Our answer, we believe, has merit not only because it

---

[1] He also proposes some missing verses to make the transition easier.

[2] Against such treatments is Sjöberg. For his full discussion and reasons for seeing Enoch as the Son of Man (though he is not sure how), see *op. cit.*, pp. 160ff. Jansen (*Henochgestalt*, pp. 124ff.) would make a distinction between the earthly and the heavenly Enoch, while the function of this distinction is not clear.

[3] Mowinckel objects to any such theory, but we would not see our answer to the problem as such, unless the ancient kingship rites are to be called *mystical*. Rather is the ultimate background one of dramatic enactment.

[4] Originally the idea seems to have been that the true heavenly one was the Man, his counterpart being his *son*. Yet, since the son would ascend to become the Man and thus be the Man as the Son of the Man, it is not hard to see, as we have pointed out earlier, how and why the true heavenly one could be called the Son of Man. *Logically*, then, the *new* Son of Man should be called the *Son of the Son of Man*, but few would bother with such a nicety in this context (though the later gnostics, as we have seen, appear to have taken up this aspect of the matter and to have spoken of a Man and a Son of Man and even a third in this sequence; see below in ch. V).

[5] Obviously there is no question here of an *incarnation* of the Son of Man. (Here Sjöberg, *op. cit.*, pp. 171f., is quite correct.) No doubt there is a way in which this process might later be understood as a kind of incarnation, but this view of the matter would be primarily that, a later interpretation. Here the whole emphasis falls on the reverse idea, that of one ascending to become the Man, not the divine descending to become man.

helps to solve a hitherto insoluble problem, but also, and primarily, because it fits Enoch's elevation into an historical background in which it makes sense and so that it no longer stands in puzzling isolation. When we come to the book of II Enoch, we shall find another and more detailed picture of Enoch's enthronement which complements and fills out some of the details in this scene.[1]

Useful in the same regard is the preceding scene from I Enoch 69.26ff. There, immediately after a description of the creation of the world (which may be meant to come in the seventh month following great calamities),[2] comes a revelation of the name of the one who is now that Son of Man. He appears and sits on his throne of glory, judging and destroying all evil. In reality it is this same picture which reoccurs throughout the 'Similitudes': the rightful *king* reigns.[3]

We would therefore conclude that in this conception of the Son of Man, whom Enoch becomes, aspects of the language and imagery from the ancient enthronement rites of the royal Man are given a new life. As with Daniel, however, the focus is eclectic, centred almost exclusively on the last scene of all, the glorious appearance.

And it is this question of emphasis which is important. We have noticed how attributes of the Primal Man still cling to the Son of Man in I Enoch. Yet they are not, *in this particular work*, stressed; they are not part of the author's direct interest. The same is true with regard to the idea of suffering.[4] Those who hold that I Enoch's Son of Man should be seen as one who is a sufferer give two essential reasons. (*1*) The figure here stands in a close relationship with the righteous, holy and elect ones who are said to shed their blood,[5] while the Son of Man must also fight a battle against the wicked, and this implies a degree of his own suffering. The whole point is, however, that although these matters are mentioned (and we believe that they, too, derive from the older conception), they are given no significant

[1] II Enoch 22.6ff.

[2] See I Enoch 60.1.

[3] See 45.3; 51.3; 61.8; 62.2. Herzfeld (*Zoroaster and His World* II, p. 833) again sees this, as in Daniel, as an enthroning, a proclamation of the rightful heir described against an Iranian background.

[4] See the discussions by Mowinckel (*HTC*, pp. 410ff.) and Sjöberg (*Henochbuch*, pp. 116ff.), both of whom thoroughly reject the idea. Engnell (*BO* 8, 1951, p. 191) says that the figure is the sacral king/Primeval Man with the eschatology very much exaggerated, but he also regards him as a sufferer.

[5] On this cf. Sjöberg, *op. cit.*, pp. 127ff. See I Enoch 47. In 47.4 it is quite clear that *righteous* is being used as a collective term and not to refer to 'the Righteous One'.

place in the story, especially in relationship to the eschatological hero. Either consciously or more likely unconsciously they are under-emphasized. Attention is on the Son of Man, who appears in glory and acts triumphantly.

(*2*) It is also maintained that this Son of Man must be seen as a sufferer, since the author has employed language which he borrowed from the description of the Isaianic Servant.[1] This is illustrated by pointing to the name Elect, the naming procedure, the giving of the spirit and powers of judgment, the mention of being a 'light to (or *of*) the Gentiles', the association with righteousness, the bringing of peace and rejoicing to the people, and the confounding, amazement and subservience of foreign kings.

While, however, these comparisons may be made, they also can involve us in a faulty procedure. We doubt very severely that the author is here working on the basis of a few chapters from the Old Testament. Our writer is thinking, on a much larger canvas, of the royal hero to whom the author of II Isaiah is also, at least in part, indebted. That which I Enoch's Son of Man and II Isaiah's Servant share in common can be much more satisfactorily explained on this background. Doubtless there is no reason why I Enoch could not have borrowed an expression or two from II Isaiah, but we need go no further than this. What is more, and what is more to our point, to the extent that this Son of Man is related to the figure in II Isaiah, he is so in terms which do not involve a *suffering* Servant.[2]

This discussion leads naturally into two other matters: is the Enochian figure collective, and is he the Messiah? Our answers follow the same guide-lines given in the interpretation of Dan. 7. The Son of Man can, of course, be seen in collective terms, and there may be some tendency to identify him with the 'elect ones' here.[3] Yet the tendency is not strong. Perhaps because the once 'historical' Enoch was more easily imagined as an individual rather than as a symbol, perhaps because this writer (and his group?) felt inclined to place his hope on one who really would appear in heaven, the Son of Man seems in I Enoch to be very much an individual.[4]

[1] See North, *Suffering Servant*, pp. 7f. and, among others, W. H. Brownlee, 'The Servant of the Lord in the Qumran Scrolls, I', *BASOR* 132, 1953, pp. 8ff.

[2] So North rightly (*op. cit.*, p. 8). See Rowley in *Servant of the Lord*, pp. 78ff.

[3] See I Enoch 49.3, where the spirit of those who have fallen asleep in righteousness is *in him* and the remarks above on this Son of Man as a sufferer.

[4] So Sjöberg, *Henochbuch*, pp. 96ff. This Son of Man is linked with the community, but he is not just a symbol for it.

Certainly there are effective hints that the Son of Man was being thought of as a messianic figure: this is indicated by a number of attributes, culminating in the word *Anointed*. But again our answer is both yes and no, depending mostly on how we define our terms.[1] He is the Messiah in the sense that he derives from the same royal ideology and has many regal characteristics. Yet he is not the Messiah if one should prefer (as many did) to think of a less transcendental, less apocalyptic monarch.

Another question: was there an Enochian circle some of whom, at least, reverenced Enoch in terms of this Son of Man language? We have no genuine means of answering this query, but common inference would suggest that it was so.[2] It is hardly likely that one man wrote these chapters solely for his own benefit. On the other hand, there is no particular reason for believing that such a group was either influential or long-lasting. Of course, the interest in Enoch during this period was widespread, but not, so far as we know, in Enoch as the Son of Man in so many words. Quite possibly such a group flourished for a comparatively brief time in some corner of Palestine and then died away, leaving us only this record.[3]

We might even wonder whether it is right to go so far as Mowinckel when he argues that the evidence of I Enoch 'means that the expression "the Son of Man" was a current and comprehensible designation of the eschatological, heavenly deliverer . . .'[4] We should prefer to say that the specific expression was current and comprehensible to a degree. It appears to have had some contemporary coinage with

[1] This is essentially Sjöberg's opinion (*op. cit.*, pp. 59f., 140ff.).

[2] See van Andel, *Henoch-Traditie*, pp. 115ff.; Otto, *Kingdom of God and Son of Man*, pp. 177, 189ff., 212ff.

[3] This opinion ties in well with our evaluation of the relationship between the Enochian and the Gospels' Son of Man. Interesting parallels or partial parallels can be adduced, such as eating together with the Son of Man as their leader in 62.14, families being divided in 56.7, *shame* before the Son of Man in 63.11, and 62.7, 69.26 with the so-called *Jubelruf* of Matt. 11.25ff./Luke 10.21f. (On this last idea cf. Sjöberg, *verborgene Menschensohn*, p. 181, etc., though it remains hard to see that the Gospels' Son of Man is much affected by themes of concealment and pre-existence.) But all of these are much more practicably explained by a larger background and context.

R. H. Charles offered a long list of passages for comparison, *The Book of Enoch*[2], Oxford, 1912, pp. xcvff.; and see Otto, *op. cit.* pp. 382ff. Yet many of these are strained, and the others can better be explained as indicated. Charles concluded that I Enoch's influence on the New Testament 'has been greater than all the other apocryphal and pseudepigraphal books put together'. (Compare some contemporary claims for the Qumran scrolls.)

[4] *HTC*, pp. 364f.

reference to this Man-like figure, though we have little means of assessing the representative quality of I Enoch's usage. Nevertheless there is a certain literary *ring* to this work; one has the feeling that the author may be extrapolating and putting older and perhaps more widespread traditions and patterns of belief to a literary purpose.[1]

5. II ESDRAS, II ENOCH, THE TESTAMENT OF LEVI, ETC.

Next we may consider several figures from various writings which, while they are not described as the Son of Man, appear to bear certain definite resemblances. Whatever titles they are given and whatever their immediate provenance, they may well be influenced by the same background of thought. We begin with the composite hero found in II (4) Esdras.

This work probably did not receive its final form until after the fall of Jerusalem in 70 AD. It even has several Christian interpolations,[2] although these do not seem to have affected the crucial vision in chapter 13 and much of the book is clearly dependent upon earlier materials.[3] Perhaps in part because of this dependence and later reworkings, the eschatology of II Esdras seems hybrid and unduly confused, even for a writing of this period.

An earlier portion of the book is concerned with a Messiah who will appear and then die before the world is returned to 'the primeval silence seven days, like at the first beginnings'.[4] Then will come the end of the world. Here the Messiah is called the *Servant* or the *Son* of God.[5] He is again the Son or Servant in chapter 14, and several times the figure in chapter 13 is also so named.[6] In a vision he is identified with the lion (as symbol for the ruler of the house of Judah);[7] he is called the Anointed and, by some texts, said to spring from the seed of David.[8] In the same passage he is the Messiah 'who the Most High

---

[1] See Mowinckel, *HTC*, p. 355.

[2] Esp. in the Latin version.

[3] The Syriac 'Apocalypse of Baruch' = II Baruch has a number of parallels and both are probably based in part upon an earlier work, perhaps an 'Apocalypse of Salathiel'; cf. II (4) Esd. 3.1. See W. O. E. Oesterley, *II Esdras* (Westminster Comm.), London, 1933.

[4] II (4) Esd. 7.26ff.

[5] The versions give a variety of readings. Perhaps the Greek had παῖς which could be interpreted either way. Probably then the Hebrew was *'ebed*.

[6] II (4) Esd. 14.9; 13.32, 37, 52.

[7] II (4) Esd. 12.31ff. See Gen. 49.9ff.; Rev. 5.5; etc.

[8] So the oriental versions.

has kept unto the end',[1] which might seem a reference to his pre-existence in heaven. Obviously we are dealing to some extent with the more traditional Davidic Messiah; yet, just as obviously, he bears traces of a supernatural and perhaps even primordial character. No doubt this can here be explained as due to insertions and the blending of traditions, but, if redactors are responsible, they apparently felt no sense of conflict in these views.

After a seeming reinterpretation (?) of the Danielic vision concerning the beasts arising from the sea (toward the end of which the Messiah appears), the seer dreams again (II [4] Esd. 13.1ff.):

After seven days[2] I dreamed a dream in the night; 2 and behold, a wind arose from the sea and stirred up all its waves.[3] 3 And I looked, and behold, (this wind made something like the figure of a man come up out of the heart of the sea. And I looked, and behold)[4] that Man flew with the clouds of heaven; and wherever he turned his face to look everything under his gaze trembled, 4 and whenever his voice issued from his mouth, all who heard his voice melted as wax melts when it feels the fire.[5]

5 After this I looked, and behold, an innumerable multitude of men were gathered together from the four winds of heaven to make war against the Man who came up out of the sea. 6 And I looked, and behold, he carved out for himself a great mountain, and flew up upon it.

After the defeat of this host:

13.12 . . . I saw the same Man come down from the mountain and call to him another multitude which was peaceable.

The vision is then interpreted for Ezra:[6]

25 . . . As for your seeing a Man come up from the heart of the sea, 26 this is he whom the Most High has been keeping for many ages,[7] who himself will deliver his creation; and he will direct those who are left.

32 And when these things come to pass and the signs occur which I

---

[1] II (4) Esd. 12.32.

[2] A reference to the time of creation?

[3] May not the allusion again be to the creation?

[4] The words in parentheses are from the Syriac, but, almost without question, were part of the original version.

[5] On the idealized king, conquering in a similar fashion and without other weapons or help, see Isa. 11.4.

[6] Some believe the interpretations to have been added at a later date.

[7] Is this again a reference to pre-existence or at least some form of primordial existence? See again 12.32.

showed you before, then my Son will be revealed, whom you saw as a Man rising up (from the sea).[1]

34 And an innumerable multitude shall be gathered together, as you saw, desiring to come and conquer him. 35 But he will stand on the top of Mount Zion.[2]

51 I said, 'O sovereign Lord, explain this to me: Why did I see the Man coming up from the heart of the sea?' 52 He said to me, 'Just as no one can explore or know what is in the depths of the sea, so no one on earth can see my Son or those who are with him, except in the time of his (or *the*) day.'

Oesterley, in attempting to account for much of the detail in this chapter (a good deal of which the author has clearly not understood, so especially in 13.52),[3] concluded that it must be based on ancient mythological material.[4] He pointed (following Gunkel) to the story of Marduk in the Babylonian epic of creation and the description of the battle found there. The references to rising up from the sea and to the mountain were, however, not thus explained (though Marduk is said to have been created from the watery chaos monster and is pictured as rising out of a mountain), and he therefore turned to Iran and the story of Saoshyant who rises from the sea and burns the world with fire. Oesterley also singled out Yima, dwelling upon the mountain as king in the garden of paradise.

It may be possible to trace individual features of this vision to particular sources, but we would again prefer to look to the larger background and to the realization that such materials had become more or less common property. The one who rises out of the cosmic sea (was he once seen as struggling with this sea and storm?) and ascends to the holy mountain, there to win the battle and establish his rule, strongly suggests to us the mythologies associated with many a royal Man. II Esdras, more than Daniel and I Enoch, has conflated these images with the conception of an idealized Messiah, though, since the great king and the heavenly Man were once firmly related figures, it is not easy (nor perhaps very useful) to try to determine which features belong to which.

---

[1] Some texts omit 'from the sea'.

[2] This and the surrounding passage help further to indicate an identification with the traditional Messiah of Judaism.

[3] Also with reference to the mountain: '. . . the real significance of many of the features in the original version was lost . . .'. Charles, II, p. 616.

[4] Cf. his *II Esdras*, pp. 158ff. See also Charles, *op. cit.*; Mowinckel, *HTC*, pp. 381ff., and Gressmann, *Der Messias*, pp. 379ff., who discusses these details and others such as 'the other land' (paradise?) and the subterranean river in 13.40ff.

Finally in connection with II Esdras we notice that suffering again receives no emphasis. It is true that the Messiah has to die before the new and final paradise can begin (7.29),[1] and that his great struggle lives on in the imagery, but the author is concerned mainly with his victory and glory.

It is quite likely that we may catch additional glimpses of the Man or at least of his influence in other contemporary descriptions of a royal hero. While some would hold that these are the result of the impress of the scenes in Daniel and I Enoch, we hope it now seems far more probable that the ideas which helped to occasion these scenes are not to be so limited in their scope and operation. The attribution to the Messiah of an *eternal* existence, association with paradise and a heavenly appearance in glory originates from much more fundamental and widespread materials. Thus in II Baruch the Servant Messiah appears at the same time as Behemoth and Leviathan, but now at the end of time.[2] The beasts shall be used for food in an era when all plants will grow luxuriously. The Messiah is said to be like the fountain and the vine.[3] He seems to *come* from heaven[4] and to be the judge at the end of the world.[5] The nations who gather together are described as turbulent waters. The Messiah shall appear in heaven like bright lightning to destroy some and save others.[6] He shall mount his throne and a kind of paradise will ensue.[7] The dead will be raised.[8]

In II Enoch[9] we find again a version of the creation story with

---

[1] Mowinckel feels this is only a reference to his mortality. *HTC*, pp. 325f. But why, then, is it mentioned here? Is it only because some scribe wished to make this rather unnecessary point? We suggest that the thought might hark back to the old pattern, i.e. the king must *die*; then comes the new creation.

[2] II Bar. 29.4. This work was composed shortly after the fall of Jerusalem, though dependent upon earlier materials. It is thoroughly Jewish, with perhaps a Pharisaic cast.

[3] II Bar. 39.7, but see the interpretation given to these in ch. 36.

[4] II Bar. 30.1.

[5] II Bar. 70.9; 40.1. Rabbis often rejected the idea that the Messiah would judge the world, but the idea need hardly have been extra-Jewish in origin, since the king of the Psalter is pictured with foreign kings and peoples in subservience before him.

[6] II Bar. 72; 74.4. On the lightning-like appearance, see Matt. 24.27 = Luke 17.24 with regard to the Son of Man. The description of the slaying of some and the saving of others here is somewhat reminiscent of Matt. 25.31ff.

[7] II Bar. 73.

[8] II Bar. 30.2.

[9] Otherwise known as 'Slavonic Enoch' or 'The Book of the Secrets of Enoch', it is composite and related in various ways to I Enoch. Written during the first

many of the now familiar details. Enoch is then drawn up into heaven and there seen as a glorious angelic being.[1] In the scene which we alluded to earlier he is presented before God.[2] He falls down before the Lord, but is offered encouragement and told to stand up. Michael raises him up to stand for ever before the Lord, and he is then told to take away Enoch's earthly garments, to anoint him and to put on him 'the garments of My glory'. This is done, and the oil of anointment 'shining like the sun's ray' causes Enoch to shine like 'one of his glorious ones'.[3] He is given the heavenly books and initiated into heavenly secrets.

Of interest also is III Enoch with its description of the Metatron who is enthroned next to God on a throne like that of God.[4] His enthroning is described, understandably, to be not unlike that of earlier kings.[5] He is God's Servant and true vice-regent, all other angelic rulers being subject to him.[6] Secrets of creation were revealed to him from the beginning of time,[7] and he is called a *copy* of God and even 'the lesser Yahweh'.[8] Mowinckel, in taking these factors into account, would seem to agree with others in regarding him as 'a variant of the Primordial Man'.[9] This would be in line with the interpretation of later Jewish writers and mystics who (amid a wealth of speculation on this and related subjects) found the Metatron to be the Primordial Man once incarnate in Adam.[10]

Previously we noted that later scribes and teachers sometimes gave

---

century AD, it has a Jewish, perhaps a Jewish-Egyptian (which may be of significance with regard to our remarks above on Enoch and the gnostics) origin. For recent bibliography, see O. Eissfeldt, *The Old Testament, an Introduction*, ET, Oxford, 1965, pp. 622ff.

[1] On Adam as a glorious being in II Enoch, see below.

[2] II Enoch 22.4ff. For an attempt to connect this Enoch more firmly with the heavenly Man, see Staerk, *Soter* II, p. 447.

[3] It may be interesting to compare a description given in a later Jewish midrash 'Chapters about the Messiah': after the Messiah's investiture, God will 'endue him with a majestic sheen of lustre and attire him in glorious garments and make him stand upon a high mountain . . .' (quoted from T. H. Gaster's *The Scriptures of the Dead Sea Sect*, London, 1957, p. 348).

[4] The work is post-Christian in date, but seemingly somewhat anti-Christian in outlook.

[5] III Enoch 4.5.

[6] III Enoch 10.3ff.

[7] III Enoch 11.1.

[8] III Enoch 12.5; 48c.7; 48d.1.

[9] *HTC*, p. 439.

[10] Cf. H. Odeberg, *3 Enoch or the Hebrew Book of Enoch*, Cambridge, 1928.

a Messianic interpretation to Pss. 8.4ff.; 80.15ff.; and Dan. 7.13f.[1] It is, however, impossible now to tell whether this results from their knowledge of the earlier relationships, their sound contextual exegesis and awareness of the nuances of the terms and descriptive language there given, or the influence of contemporary interest (emanating in part perhaps from foreign sources) in the Man-Son of Man figure. The second alternative appears the more probable to us, with possibly a trace of the others; for, especially after the fall of Jerusalem, the rabbis disapproved of all that was associated with apocalyptic and were also, of course, later governed by anti-Christian interests.

These rabbis had begun at least a degree of their own speculation concerning the pre-existence and supernatural character of the Messiah. As far as we can now tell, however, theological reserve often caused them to limit this interest to the *name* or the *idea* of the Messiah.[2] But such a refinement was not always observed, and sometimes (apparently in connection with Dan. 7.13) they thought of the Messiah as one who would be revealed on the clouds of heaven.[3] The name of Anani (a descendant of Zerubbabel and so of David in I Chron. 3.24) is interpreted to mean 'the Cloud Man' and referred to the Messiah.[4] Perhaps with this kind of thought in mind the Sibylline Oracles tell us that 'there has come from the plains of heaven a blessed Man with the sceptre in his hand which God has committed to his clasp'.[5] We also hear that 'from the sunrise (or, the sun) God shall send a king'.[6]

These last references are not without their intriguing aspects, but they are scattered and infrequent, and it is now virtually impossible to determine their true significance in their own time. It may be that the Man-Messiah figure was once of some important influence even in rabbinic circles. Perhaps in a later era this manner of language

---

[1] See again Bowman, *ExpT* 59, 1947/8, pp. 284ff., and Moore, *Judaism* II, pp. 334ff. Ps. 144.3 is occasionally interpreted in this fashion as well.

[2] See Moore, *op. cit.*, p. 344. For a source for this see Ps. 72.17.

[3] See *Babylonian Talmud, Sanhedrin*, 98a, and Moore, *op. cit.*, p. 335.

[4] *Sanhedrin*, 96b, and Moore, *op. cit.*, p. 336.

[5] Bk. V, line 414. Books III–V of this work are primarily of Jewish authorship, III being pre-Christian and IV–V post-Christian. See III, 46ff. See also V, 256ff.: 'Then there shall come from the sky a certain exalted Man, whose hands they nailed upon the fruitful tree, the noblest of the Hebrews, who shall one day cause the sun to stand still.' As it stands this is an obvious Christian interpolation, but some commentators believe that there may once have been an original passage referring to Joshua.

[6] III, 652. Possibly also of interest is V, 238: 'There was once among men the bright sun-ray . . .'

was de-emphasized in anti-Christian polemic. Still, on the whole, it would appear that the figure of the heavenly Messiah and/or Son of Man had little genuine place in what we may call, for lack of a better term, the mainstream of Judaism at about the beginning of the Christian era.

We fare much better when we come to some most interesting passages in the Testament of Levi.[1]

4.2 Therefore the Most High has heard your prayer,
　　To separate you from iniquity and that you should become to Him a son,
　　And a servant, and a minister of His presence.

3 The light of knowledge shall you light up in Jacob,
　　And as the sun shall you be to all the seed of Israel.

4 And there shall be given to you a blessing, and to all your seed,
　　Until the Lord shall visit all the Gentiles in his tender mercies for ever.

5 Therefore there have been given to you counsel and understanding.

Widengren has pointed out how much of this language (especially when seen together with that from chapter 8 quoted below) harks

---

[1] The Testaments of the Twelve Patriarchs is probably in essence a work of the late Maccabean period. We are highly sceptical of the many theories which see Christian interpolations in sections like Test. Levi 4; 8; 18. Nor do we find that M. de Jonge (*The Testaments of the Twelve Patriarchs*, Assen, 1953) has satisfactorily explained them by his theory that a Christian has composed much of the Testaments, basing himself on earlier Jewish materials attributed to Levi and Naphtali. (On Levi 8 see *op. cit.*, pp. 43f., where it is held that the discrepancies in the lists show the Christian hand; on Levi 18 see *op. cit.*, p. 90, where it is said that the scene is based on Jesus' baptism, though the quite significant differences are hardly thus accounted for.) The fragments of Levi found at Qumran (see D. Barthélemy and J. T. Milik, *Discoveries in the Judaean Desert*, Oxford, 1955, I, pp. 87ff., and on them Milik, 'Le Testament de Lévi en araméen', *RB* 62, 1955, pp. 398ff.), added to those known earlier from the Cairo Genizah manuscripts (see de Jonge, *op. cit.*, pp. 129ff.), along with the later varying manuscript traditions, suggest to us that several versions of Levi already existed before the Christian era and that theories of Christian interpolations into these chapters are unnecessary and insubstantial. (Many of the same arguments could be used to show that portions of Isa. 40–55 were Christian interpolations!) Too little provision is otherwise made for the materials out of which Christian forms grew and took shape (while, if they are held to be Christian, we would again still want to ask about the sources for these Christian ideas). Against de Jonge, see Dupont-Sommer, *Essene Writings*, pp. 301ff.; M. Philonenko, *Les interpolations chrétiennes des Testaments des Douze Patriarches et les Manuscrits de Qumran* (Cahiers de *RHPR*, 35), 1960, and the discussion and bibliography of Eissfeldt, *Old Testament*, pp. 631ff. De Jonge only slightly modifies his theory in 'Christian Influence in the Testaments of the Twelve Patriarchs', *NT* 4, 1960, pp. 182ff.; 'Once More: Christian Influence in the Testaments of the Twelve Patriarchs', *NT* 5, 1962, pp. 311ff.

back to phrases and expressions used in connection with the Davidic priest-king and also to possible associations with Melchizedek and the Feast of Tabernacles.[1] We have here an oracle from a commissioning ceremony of some kind, and Widengren along with Jansen[2] infers that it may well derive from actual ceremonies performed at the enthroning of the Hasmonaean prince-priests[3] in Jerusalem. Levi, of course, would be a fitting cryptic name for a Jewish royal priest, and this rite would presumably then relate to the materials having to do with the regal high priest which we discussed earlier.[4]

Unfortunately, however, we do not know very much about the actual practices of the Hasmonaean princes, though what little we do know is intriguing. For instance, Jonathan is said to have put on the royal robe and crown during the seventh month at the Feast of Tabernacles,[5] and Simon was made the leader and high priest *for ever*[6] and wore purple and gold.[7] One might understandably presume that there were other royal practices going on as well, and there is no denying that the descriptions of Levi and his royal priesthood would correspond admirably with what we do know of one like John Hyrcanus.[8] Yet it is also possible that this language was employed in other circles which may have been thinking of an ideal royal high priest (with perhaps some Hasmonaean as a model) and that it was never actually made use of in official rituals (though it could still have had a place in *unofficial* sectarian practices).

After Levi comes up to heaven and is sent back to earth to fight a

---

[1] 'Royal Ideology and the Testaments of the Twelve Patriarchs' in *Promise and Fulfilment* (ed. F. F. Bruce), Edinburgh, 1963, pp. 202ff.

[2] 'The Consecration of Levi in the Eighth Chapter of Testamentum Levi' in *La Regalità Sacra/The Sacral Kingship (Numen* Suppl. IV), 1959, pp. 356ff.

[3] After the death of John Hyrcanus the actual title of *king* was employed by his successors.

[4] P. 123 n. 1. In addition to references below, see in the Testaments, Reub. 6.7ff.; Dan. 5.10f.; Jos. 19.5ff.; Sim. 5.5.

[5] I Macc. 10.20f. Perhaps this is a reading back of the practice of some later Hasmonaean.

[6] See Ps. 110.4 and Levi 6.3. The word had cultic associations assuring the continuation of the royal line.

[7] I Macc. 14.41ff. A warning against going too far with such evidence is given by M. A. Beek, 'Hasidic Conceptions of Kingship in the Maccabean Period' in *La Regalità Sacra* (as above), pp. 349ff.

[8] In Levi 8.15 Levi's is called a *new* priesthood, and it was indeed a new order of priests which was founded by the Maccabees. In 8.12–15 Levi is assigned three offices, that of king, priest and prophet. In *Antiquities* XIII, 10.7 Josephus specifically mentions these as belonging to John Hyrcanus. Yet, as we have seen, in mythical terms these offices always belonged to the ideal king, and it might be such a one who is here in mind.

battle (against Shechem),[1] a mysterious mountain also being mentioned,[2] he has another vision.

8.2 And I saw seven men[3] in white raiment saying unto me:
          'Arise, put on the robe of priesthood,
          and the crown of righteousness, and the breastplate of under-
              standing,
          and the garment of truth, and the plate of faith,
          and the turban of the *head*,[4] and the ephod of prophecy.'
    3 Then each of them brought forward (one of these) things
          and put it on me and said unto me:
          'From henceforth become a priest of the Lord,
              you and your seed for ever.'
    4 And the first anointed me with holy oil
          and gave me a staff of judgment.
    5 And the second washed me with pure water,
          fed me with bread and holy wine,
          and clad me with a holy and glorious robe.
    6 The third clothed me with a linen vestment like an ephod.
    7 The fourth put around me a girdle like unto purple.
    8 The fifth gave me a branch of rich olive.
    9 The sixth placed a crown upon my head.
  10 The seventh placed on my head a priestly diadem
          and filled my hands with incense,
              that I might serve as a priest to the Lord God.

We see that the two lists of things given to Levi or put on him do
not correspond. The first list (v. 2) correlates fairly closely with the
description of the articles worn by the high priest in Ex. 28 (especially
in the LXX version). These in themselves illustrate the ancient connections between priesthood and kingship symbolized and epitomized
in the figure of Melchizedek. (David, for instance, wears the linen
ephod in II Sam. 6.14.)[5] Yet it is the second list (vv. 4–10) which is
the most striking, as a desire to indicate the royal character of Levi

---

[1] Levi 5.

[2] Levi 6.1.

[3] Widengren notes that Mesopotamian kings were given seven attributes
(corresponding to the planets?) by a corresponding number of deities (*Promise and
Fulfilment*, p. 206).

[4] Κεφαλῆς. Charles supposed a corruption, but there might have been a reference
to the turban or mitre worn from the *beginning* of time, esp. if the original reading
was r'ōš.

[5] See also Ex. 29.5ff.; 40.12ff. Note how Christ (as one like a Son of Man) is
dressed as a priest in the vision of Rev. 1.12ff.

becomes manifest. There is now a girdle of purple, the royal colour. Levi holds a staff as do kings.[1] He is given a branch from an olive tree, derivatively a symbol of his lordship over the garden.[2] The anointing, purification with water[3] and the sacred meal (in this case of bread and wine)[4] stand in long association with kings or priest-kings. Because of such details, their apparent intrusion and otherwise unnecessary and incongruous presence, both Widengren and Jansen believe that the author is basing himself upon a cult pattern and not merely upon literary sources. If they are right, the author is dealing with materials and ideas which are *alive* to him and is not just indulging a spirit of archaism. Certainly *some* explanation is called for, and this seems a reasonable one, though, of course, it cannot be conclusive. And in all this we ourselves cannot help but be reminded of the descriptions of the enthronement of that Son of Man-Enoch in I Enoch 70–71 and of the investiture of Enoch in II Enoch 22.

Jansen goes on to try to show how the content of the following oracle (Levi 8.11–17) owes much to the language of oracles used of kings in the Old Testament. This, however, is less clear,[5] and our own attention is drawn on to 18.2ff., which provides the main reason for our having introduced the material at this point.

2 Then shall the Lord raise up a new priest,
  And to him all the words of the Lord shall be revealed.
  And he shall execute a righteous judgment upon the earth for a
    multitude of days.
3 And his star shall arise in heaven as of a king,
  Lighting up the light of knowledge as the sun the day.
  And he shall be magnified in the world.

---

[1] E.g. Pss. 2.9; 110.2.

[2] Cf. Widengren in *Promise and Fulfilment*, pp. 205f., and *King and the Tree of Life*, pp. 20ff., 64f.

[3] From other such rituals we might have expected the anointing to follow the washing. Aaron and his sons, for instance, are washed before being anointed. It is interesting that this tradition of anointing before the washing became the practice of *eastern* Syrian Christianity while the *western* rite (and the Mandaean) has the reverse. Does this point to at least two strands of *Jewish* baptismal practice, each having affected different Christian traditions?

[4] In 8.5, we might translate, 'bread and wine, the most holy things'. There is no need to suppose a Christian interpolation, unless we wish also to postulate one in Gen. 14.18, in the legend of Adapa (where he is offered the bread and water of life at the time of his ascension), etc. Similarly with other sacred meals of this period, most obviously in the Dead Sea Scrolls, 1QS, vi, 4f.; 1QSa, ii, 17ff. Cf. Black, *Scrolls and Christian Origins*, pp. 102ff.

[5] None the less see p. 163 n. 8 above.

4 He shall shine forth as the sun on the earth,
  And shall remove all darkness from under heaven,
  And there shall be peace in all the earth.
. . . .
6 The heavens shall be opened,
  And from the temple of glory shall come upon him sanctification,
  With the Father's voice as from Abraham to Isaac.[1]
7 And the glory of the Most High shall be uttered over him,
  And the spirit of understanding and sanctification shall rest upon
      him in the water.[2]
8 For he shall give the majesty of the Lord to his sons for evermore,
  And there shall none succeed him for all generations for ever.
9 And in his priesthood the Gentiles shall be multiplied in knowledge
      upon the earth,
  And enlightened through the grace of the Lord.
  In his priesthood shall sin come to an end,
  And the lawless shall cease to do evil.
10 And he shall open the gates of paradise,
  And shall remove the threatening sword against Adam.
11 And he shall give to the saints to eat from the tree of life,
  And the spirit of holiness shall be upon them.
12 And Beliar shall be bound by him,
  and he shall give power to his children to tread upon the evil spirits.

We have here further phraseology connecting the ideal priest with messiahship, a conception found elsewhere in the Testaments and in the literature of this period, especially at Qumran.[3] He, like many kings of old, is described as the day-star, the very sun itself, since his rule shall give light to all men and bring peace on earth. Over him 'in the water' (the site of his commissioning?) shall be uttered the divine proclamation giving to him the spirit of understanding and the sanctification necessary to his office.[4] Thus shall his dynasty be

[1] I.e. as a father to a son.

[2] Charles bracketed the words 'in the water' as a Christian interpolation even though they are omitted by only one manuscript. Against the background of other royal rites for initiatory and purificatory purposes, it is special pleading to argue that such a detail must be Christian. In any case, the voice and spirit do not come upon Jesus while in the water according to the Gospels, and it may be that a later redactor recognized this.

[3] If the Dead Sea Scrolls do expect two Messiahs, it would seem that the priestly Messiah had precedence. See 1QSa, ii, 18ff. It must, however, be remembered that the Qumran literature reveals no love of the Hasmonaean rulers, and their priest-Messiah would come from Zadok and/or Aaron. Whatever the relationship between the Dead Sea Scrolls and the Testaments in this regard, it does not appear to have been simple.

[4] See, for instance, II Sam. 7.12ff.; Isa. 11.2; I Kings 8.20; Pss. 89.4ff.; 132.11.

secured for ever. All sin and evil shall be defeated. Without doubt this way of speaking closely echoes that found in many royal liturgies (or myths) throughout the Near East.

And, of great significance to us, as the new royal priest he will rule in paradise. He will return to undo the work of Adam, and himself will open paradise to men and give the saints to eat from the tree of life. He will conquer over that evil beast which once defeated the first king of men, and in his power and victory shall all his people share. By whatever means unknown to us, and for whatever reason or cause, we have here another description of the royal Man.[1]

6. THE RABBIS AND PHILO

Levi, as the idealized royal priest, comes to redo the work of Adam. In this sense he is the counterpart of First Man, much as was the king of antiquity. In gnostic and other later versions of this idea, however, it was the First Man himself who was glorified. It was not important that the work of Adam should be redone; rather was it important to recognize the Man who was the glorious one, the cosmic champion who had or would triumph. This, we believe, is another aspect or another way of understanding the fragmented but now renascent legends. Against the clear statements of Gen. 3 it would have seemed doubtful that this idea of a glorified Adam could have made much headway in Judaism, but such was not the case. Indeed, the very fact that so much of the later gnostic (and Jewish and Jewish-Christian) speculation about the *Anthropos* was cast in language relating to Adam and the first chapters of Genesis would lead us to suspect that some similar speculation had already developed within Judaism. Almost from such evidence alone Mowinckel concludes, 'Thus it is established that Judaism was familiar with many varying conceptions of the Primordial Man and the god Anthropos.'[2]

Compare also Test. Judah 24, where there may be two oracles, one for a Messiah of Levi, another for a Messiah of Judah having been added, perhaps after the Hasmonaean house failed.

[1] This is one of the points at which Mowinckel argues that 'the role of the king of paradise belonged to the Son of Man' (*HTC*, p. 383). Yet there is no cause for bringing in the Son of Man, as such, at this juncture. The language belongs to the whole conception of the Man-king, and Mowinckel's attribution of it specifically to the Son of Man is arbitrary, based on his position that these details do not belong naturally to types of the Messiah. See also Bousset and Gressmann, *Die Religion des Judentums*, p. 261.

[2] *HTC*, p. 426.

Among the records left by the rabbis and in the apocryphal and pseudepigraphical literature of the inter-testamental period and just beyond[1] there are a great number of passages which praise and glorify Adam.[2] At times this may be done solely with the dramatic intention of emphasizing his great fall,[3] but not always. Sometimes it is denied that he sinned at all;[4] he even continued to wage the battle against the devil and sin.[5] One might perhaps trace these thoughts to various causes, but it is hard to believe that one of them is not the desire to conceive of Adam as a hero and a figure of pristine glory.

Adam was created worthy of the worship of angels.[6] Some saw him as the cosmic Man whose body was of enormous size, stretching from heaven to earth or from one end of the world to the other.[7] The materials used to make him came from all over the world. In turn, men might be thought to derive from different parts of his body.[8] More common was the conception of him as the *father* of all men; they are his descendants and like him both in character and through lineal descent. The sense of the unity of mankind was thus reinforced, and the idea was used as a principle for moral action.[9] He is the ruler of all the earth, the monarch of all creation, even the source of the world.[10] 'I placed him on earth, a second angel, honourable, great and glorious, and I appointed him as a ruler to rule the earth and to

[1] The dating of some of the thoughts referred to below may be questioned, but there is little doubt that a generous measure of them had their origins in the beliefs of the first century AD or earlier.

[2] At least several books with Adam in their title have been lost to us. In the rabbinic literature of the next several centuries the speculations on Adam as high priest, a cosmic being, and one who is successively *reincarnated* in Shem, Melchizedek, Moses, Elijah, the Metatron, Michael, etc., are in evidence. See E. Käsemann, *Das wandernde Gottesvolk. Eine Untersuchung zum Hebräerbrief* (FRLANT 55, nf 37) 1939, pp. 125ff.

[3] See N. P. Williams, *The Ideas of the Fall and of Original Sin*, London, 1927, p. 56. E.g. II (4) Esd. 7.11ff.; 7.118: 'O Adam, what hast thou done?' (seemingly countered by II Bar. 54.19).

[4] II Enoch 31.6; Life of Adam and Eve 16.4. The blame seems to be shifted in Wisd. 10.1ff.; I Enoch 6; Jub. 5.

[5] See generally in the Life of Adam and Eve.

[6] E.g. Life of Adam and Eve 12.1.

[7] S-B IV, pp. 946f.; Moore, *Judaism* I, p. 453. See also Sib. Oracles III, 24f.; Apocalypse of Abraham xxiii; *Genesis Rabba* (using Soncino Press edn., ed. H. Freedman and M. Simon, London, 1939) 8.1; 12.6; 21.3.

[8] See W. D. Davies, *Paul and Rabbinic Judaism*[2], London, 1955, pp. 53ff., and II Enoch 30.13.

[9] Davies, *op. cit.*, p. 55.

[10] See S-B IV, pp. 946f., and II Enoch 31.3; Wisd. 9.2f.; II (4) Esd. 6.54.

have my wisdom.'[1] He can be described as though both a microcosm and a macrocosm of the world.[2] His purity, beauty and wisdom are praised.[3] 'Above every living thing in creation is Adam.'[4] His face is so bright that even the brightness of his foot darkens the sun.[5] At least by some later rabbis he could be regarded as bisexual.[6] To him was the law once given.[7] It is then sometimes true that the enormity of his sin is stressed; he fell from such great glory, and the consequences of this are emphasized. He loses his immortality, suffers under the sentence of God and is left to wander homeless on the earth until death.[8] Yet at the resurrection the Messiah will come to awaken Adam first;[9] and the spirits of Adam and the Messiah can sometimes be closely associated.[10]

According to the Apocalypse of Moses, Adam at his death is carried up into heaven on a golden chariot. Amid clouds of incense the holy angels plead with God to pardon Adam, 'for he is thy image'.[11] Even the sun and moon are said to plead for him.[12] In the new paradise of heaven Adam will be placed upon the throne formerly held by Satan.[13]

In the Testament of Abraham[14] we find Adam sitting at the gate of heaven watching the good enter therein and the evil go to hell, while he reacts to their fates with appropriate responses. He is seated on a golden throne and the 'appearance of the Man ($\dot{\eta}$ $\iota\delta\epsilon\alpha$ $\tau o\hat{v}$ $\dot{\alpha}\nu\theta\rho\dot{\omega}\pi o\nu$)

[1] II Enoch 30.11ff. He has *seven* natures (30.9) and attendant stars (30.14).

[2] II Enoch 30.10.

[3] See Kraeling, *Anthropos*, p. 156; Moore, *Judaism* I, p. 479; S-B I, p. 802, etc. E.g. Wisd. 9.2f.; 10.1f.

[4] Ecclus. 49.16. This follows after great praises of Enoch, Joseph and many others. See Odeberg, *Fourth Gospel*, p. 93.

[5] S-B IV, p. 887.

[6] S-B I, p. 802; Moore, *op. cit.*, p. 453.

[7] Moore, *op. cit.*, pp. 247, 462.

[8] Davies, *op. cit.*, p. 46. On the last feature see Life of Adam and Eve 3.1ff. and in the Slavonic version 30.1ff. (Charles II, p. 134). Also Life of Adam and Eve 29.1ff.

[9] S-B III, p. 10.

[10] Cf. Bowman, *Exp T* 59, 1947/8, p. 288.

[11] Apoc. Moses 33.1ff.; 35.2.

[12] Apoc. Moses 35f.

[13] Apoc. Moses 39.2 and so also the parallel in the Life of Adam and Eve 48.3.

[14] This, of course, is not one of the twelve Testaments. It is a thoroughly Jewish (probably Jewish-Hellenistic) work (cf. G. H. Box, *The Testament of Abraham* [Translations of Early Documents], London, 1927, pp. XVff.), probably composed in the first century AD and extant in a longer and shorter recension. For the Greek texts, cf. M. R. James, *The Testament of Abraham* (Texts and Studies, II/2), Cambridge, 1892.

was terrible, like unto that of the Lord'. He is called 'a marvellous being', 'that marvellous Man' (ἀνήρ), 'this all-marvellous Man' (οὗτος ὁ ἀνὴρ ὁ πανθαύμαστος), 'the protoplast Adam' (ὁ πρωτόπλαστος Ἀδάμ).[1]

Following this we see on a fiery crystal throne 'a wondrous Man (ἀνήρ), shining as the sun, like unto the (or a) Son of God' (ὅμοιος υἱῷ θεοῦ). He it is who judges the souls of men.[2] In the next chapter we find that this 'dread Man' is not Adam but rather Abel, 'the son of Adam, the protoplast' (υἱὸς Ἀδὰμ τοῦ πρωτοπλάστου), or, if you will, a kind of version of the Son of Man. He holds his father's authority. 'For every man has sprung from protoplast Adam, and therefore here first by his son all are judged.'[3] We do not maintain that in this last vision we are discovering an occurrence of *the Son of Man* in any technical sense. But it does appear as though a similar idea is present: this figure is all-important and has the right to be judge and ruler because he is the son of Adam. As we have seen and shall see, this understanding seems to lie behind gnostic interpretations of the significance of Seth and others of the sons of Adam. In other circles such ideas could take different forms, and their relevance to our discussion is obvious.

A further aspect and indications of speculation about the Man figure are to be found in the writings of the Jewish-Alexandrian Philo.[4] He makes a distinction between the *man* created by God in Gen. 1.26ff. and the *man* of Gen. 2.7ff., a distinction invited not only by the different character of the two stories but by the *ambiguous* language of Gen. 1.26.[5] '. . . there is a vast difference between the man[6] thus formed and the man that came into existence earlier after the image of God.'[7] Nevertheless,

---

[1] Long rec. XI; see short rec. VIII.

[2] Long rec. VIII.

[3] Long rec. XIII. In short rec. Xf. we meet Abel as the judge, a Man of exceeding great stature wearing three golden crowns.

[4] See the LCL eds. of *On the Creation* (Philo I, 1929), *Allegorical Interpretation* (Philo I, 1929); *On the Confusion of Tongues* (Philo IV, 1932).

[5] So also, if Adam was only after the image of God, others were bound to begin wondering whether the image could not be said to have a separate existence (which is a curious, somewhat distorted echo of the royal Man myths). But in Life of Adam and Eve, Apoc. Moses 33; 35 and elsewhere Adam is not just in the image of God; he is that image. On the various interpretations of Gen. 1.26, etc., cf. J. Jervell, *Imago Dei. Gen. 1.26f. im Spätjudentum, in der Gnosis und bei Paulus* (FRLANT 76, nf 58), 1960.

[6] Ἄνθρωπος, and so generally.

[7] *On the Creation*, 134. See *Allegorical Interpretation* I, 31.

That first man, earth-born, ancestor of our whole race was made, as it appears to me, most excellent in each part of his being, in both soul and body, and greatly excelling those who came after him in the transcendent qualities of both alike: for this man really was the one truly beautiful and good (i.e. the *perfect*). (*On the Creation*, 136.)

Additional praise of the first created man follows; he is made in likeness and imitation to God's reason or Word.[1] A little further on we read,

Quite excellently does Moses describe the bestowal of names also to the first man: for this is the business of wisdom and royalty, and the first man was wise with a wisdom learned from and taught by Wisdom's own lips, for he was made by divine hands; he was, moreover, a king, and it befits a ruler to bestow titles on his several subordinates. And we may guess that the sovereignty with which that first man was invested was a most lofty one, seeing that God has fashioned him with the utmost care and deemed him worthy of the second place, making him his own viceroy and lord of all others. (*On the Creation*, 148.)

In *Allegorical Interpretation* I, 53 God is seen to have put two men into the garden. The one is made after the image and archetype, the other earthly.[2] The latter man alone is Adam, and it was to him (and not the heavenly man who had no such need) that injunctions and commandments were given.[3] This heavenly man is God's man (ἄνθρωπον θεοῦ); he is immortal, the Word of the Eternal, the Father of all men.[4] He is 'God's Firstborn, the Word', ruler of angels. Many names are his: 'the Beginning, the Name of God, Word, the man after the image, "he who sees" and Israel'.[5] We are all sons of God's invisible born, eldest image, the Word.[6] And the likeness of this way of speaking to the later gnostic language becomes obvious.

Few would question that these passages from Philo reveal a measure of pseudo-Platonic influence.[7] Yet we cannot find it tenable that this realization supplies us with the full explanation for Philo's thoughts on the subject. It is perhaps just conceivable that, given the right mixture of Plato and Genesis, Philo might have come up with

---

[1] *On the Creation*, 139.
[2] See also *Allegorical Interpretation* I, 88.
[3] *Allegorical Interpretation* I, 92.
[4] *Confusion of Tongues*, 41.
[5] *Confusion of Tongues*, 146.
[6] *Confusion of Tongues*, 147.
[7] See, for instance, *Symposium*, 189, and cf. Davies, *Paul and Rabbinic Judaism*, p. 49.

the teachings which we have observed. Yet is this the most reasonable solution in the face of all the comparable evidence which we have gathered? Was Philo completely out of touch with similar though less philosophical beliefs which were being set forward in Palestine? Would one understand those Jewish forms as Platonic? Is it merely coincidence that we find Jewish works containing speculation about Adam to have originated in or emigrated to Egypt? Though Platonic thought might account for the glorification of a heavenly Man, can it explain the corresponding glorification of the first earthly Adam? And, even if one were to answer all the above questions in the affirmative, we would still need to come back to this question *why*. Why did Philo become concerned so highly to praise both heavenly Man and Adam? Neither Plato nor Genesis provides any kind of an adequate answer to this query.

That Philo was in touch with less speculative and more mythical versions of these beliefs is quite possibly shown by a piece of exegesis which he performs on Zech. 6.12.[1] There we recall that in the LXX we read, 'Behold, a man (ἀνήρ) whose name is *Rising Up*', or *Branch* (ἀνατολή).[2] The original reference was messianic, and Philo (taking ἀνατολή in both an *horticultural* and a solar sense, the latter as he sees it relating to Eden in the East) tells us that this is a very strange title if one should take it to refer to a being composed of soul and body (i.e. Adam).

> But if you suppose that it is that Incorporeal One,[3] who differs not a whit from the divine image, you will agree that the name of 'Rising Up' assigned to him quite truly describes him. For this one is the eldest son, whom the Father of all *raised up*, and elsewhere calls him his Firstborn.[4]

This exegesis, however fanciful, appears to depend on the older association of beliefs concerning kingship and the Man of glory. Here the heavenly Man is identified with the Messiah. We hold, therefore, that Philo has been affected by this *impulse* to become concerned with First Man and also with his counterpart, a heavenly Man figure.

---

[1] *Confusion of Tongues*, 61ff.

[2] See above, p. 109 n. 1.

[3] Whom Philo calls ἄνθρωπος and not ἀνήρ. Mowinckel (*HTC*, pp. 360f.) holds that Philo has been influenced by the Son of Man idea when he several times refers to the Messiah as an *anthropos*. This was otherwise unnecessary, as the Davidic Messiah was, of course, a human being. Again, however, we see no cause for bringing the Son of Man as such into the discussion here. Philo uses *anthropos* because he has been influenced by the old connection between the king and the Man.

[4] Ps. 89.27.

Significantly he sees them both as royal types. These ideas he has adopted, adapted, and fitted into his own philosophic understandings.

And indeed what we see happening in Philo's mind and writings may be a kind of parable for us: one of the stages, of which there must have been many, by which ancient legends in contemporary Jewish forms were on their way toward being transformed into gnostic allegories and aetiological and salvation myths. Of course, we do not here intend anything so audacious as an explanation of the sources of gnosticism; nor as indicated earlier, do we mean to confine the Man myth to this one means of transmission through Judaism. Nevertheless, when Dodd writes, 'Adam is probably more directly the ancestor of the Hellenistic $\mathscr{A}\nu\theta\rho\omega\pi\sigma\varsigma$ than Gayomard',[1] we would certainly give our assent. It is within and through Judaism itself, having become a natural conductor for the East-West movement of ideas, that much of the impulse or current from these ancient forms of thought passed. As it did so it generated a renewed interest, through eschatology and other means, in the figure of the heavenly, royal Man and in his counterpart, the First Man of the earth.

[1] *Bible and the Greeks*, p. 147; see Kraeling, *Anthropos*, p. 165.

THE MAN IN SECTARIAN LIFE

And according to His mercies He exalted me;
and according to His excellent beauty He set me up on high,
And brought me out of the depths of Sheol;
and from the mouth of death He drew me.

(Odes of Solomon 29.3f.)

I. BACK TO THE STARTING-POINT

WE COME BACK, then, to our starting-point, to a time roughly contemporaneous with the life of Jesus and the birth of the Christian faith. We have seen something of 'Those images that yet/Fresh images beget', for it was Yeats' point and it is ours that the new is born from the old; indeed, that it must be born from the old. Even the unique must be comprehended by men in the light of already established patterns and beliefs, if it is to mean anything at all.

Yet it might fairly be asked how far we have actually progressed toward our essential goal, that of finding the more immediate context out of which Jesus could have adapted the figure of the Son of Man. As things now stand we could only delineate this in ways which would have to be regarded as rather vague. In addition, the older ideograms and beliefs are in this period only presenting themselves in a fragmented or disintegrated manner. We hear of First Man and of Primordial Man, often confused into one, and we hear of last Man, as it were, the figure in his final glory; yet often there is a tendency to view first and last as independent conceptions. Although they still share many attributes in common, although it is sometimes realized that the Messiah/Man is a type of Adam and Adam of the Messiah/Man, in an important sense there is no real drama, no progression and integration in their story. Of course, we do not expect to find the old legends about royal Man fully intact and operative in all respects; we suppose a certain degree of fragmentation and reordering of the material in a new age. Yet, commensurate with our under-standing to this point, we could only guess at the way in which Jesus might have grasped the relationship between these ideas.

It is not really difficult to discover why the older materials have seemingly lost their fuller and more dramatic character. The linchpin from the ancient legends is missing. There was only one means by which the Man of old could come to his glory: through humiliation and suffering. This was fundamental, and it is of interest that, when we see this element *restored* in some later gnostic versions, the dramatic quality returns.

Yet such is not characteristic of the Man within normative Judaism. While we have found that the Jewish First Man and heavenly Man of this era still bear traces of their history as sufferers, this phase of their story is much undervalued, especially in so far as any soteriology might be concerned. Here we are in agreement with a number of scholars who rightly contend that the mainstream of Judaism at this time had no real place for a suffering messianic figure. Any evidence to the contrary is so minimal, uncertain or late in character as to be of little value.[1] A crucified Messiah was a scandal to most Jews, and there is no getting around this central fact. Attempts to circumvent it by establishing a direct relationship between Jesus and the Suffering Servant of II Isaiah are contradicted not only by the failure of contemporary Judaism to expostulate at any length upon this figure as a sufferer, but also by a close examination of the Gospels. Indeed, we admit to being almost totally nonplussed by efforts to underplay the significance of the Son of Man in the tradi-tions while yet asserting that the Servant was vital to Jesus' sense of mission.

[1] We do not feel it necessary to discuss this issue at length, partly because it is the analysis of many other scholars, but mostly because our understanding of it runs counter to our major argument. We concede the point, as it were, for we doubt whether such an idea could have had impact in the *normative* Judaism of the period. This is not to say that no one was interested in Isa. 53 during this era, but even when it was commented upon, the interest was not messianic or soteriological. Figures like the Messiah-ben-Ephraim, if they can legitimately be introduced into the discussion, show no signs of having influenced the Gospels and little if any upon Judaism generally. See Mowinckel, *HTC*, pp. 325ff., 410ff.; Sjöberg, *Henochbuch*, pp. 116ff.; *verborgene Menschensohn*, pp. 255ff.; Rowley, *Servant of the Lord*, pp. 61ff. (Opposed to this understanding are Riesenfeld, *Jésus transfiguré*, pp. 81ff., 314ff.; Staerk, *Soter* II, pp. 406ff., and Jeremias in *Servant of God*, pp. 57ff., 77f.) Cf. the useful statement by Knox, *Death of Christ*, pp. 104ff., and the presentation of or reference to many of the important sources in S-B II, pp. 274ff. See below on the Qumran materials.

Nor, again, is this lack of a suffering hero within *normative* Judaism hard to understand. Not only was there a tendency in the theology of many which precluded the thought of any genuine saviour other than God himself,[1] but, more importantly, outside of some kind of cultic and/or mythical context, the whole idea would not have had a great deal of meaning. This is hardly to say that all Jews were insensible to the value of atoning suffering, but a leader who *had* to suffer could never have been a popular idea during this particular era.

Yet, obviously, if (*a*) we believe that Jesus did offer some teaching relevant to this subject, and, if (*b*) we think that he must have presented it within a viable historical context, our quest must continue. We must still search for a setting, some set of circumstances perhaps more esoteric, or, if you will, more on the fringe of what may be called *normative* Judaism, where this teaching might have taken shape.

Obviously, too, it is hardly likely that this should be a well-known and well-documented context. If it were otherwise, we could have come to the heart of the matter much more directly than we have done. We must ask the reader, therefore, to bear with us as we go back over some of our evidence and search among our meagre records from this period, endeavouring to detect lines of development which might intersect and begin to form a series of points of confluence. Our justification for doing so again lies in the importance of the question we are striving to answer.

Briefly to review, we have studied or glanced at several means by which older ritual-mythical forms of thought might have been passed along from earlier ages to the time of Jesus. Important among them in terms of our knowledge is eschatology with its concentration upon the heavenly royal Man of the end of time and the inverse product of this in the allied interest in the Primal Man of the first age. In addition it may be that certain contemporary practices within Judaism were of help in conveying some sense of feeling for earlier ideas from which they, too, were derived. We would single out the seventh-month festivals of *Rosh ha-Shanah*, the Atonement and Tabernacles, together with some of the practices and attributes which still pertained to the high priest.[2] Nor should we overlook the fact

[1] Some figure might be appointed to act for God on the final day, but he could do little more than that. He could not be the one who actually wrought salvation, much less would he need to suffer, since at God's *right hand* there could be no question of anything but triumph and victory.

[2] See above p. 121 n. 3; p. 123 n. 6.

ELEVEN AREAS FOR STUDY 177

that many of the ideas which we have laboriously pieced together were still to be found in the Old Testament itself. Those who themselves might have had a context for similar beliefs could well have been able to look back and see these in the scriptures far more easily than we.

There may, too, have been a degree of influence from kingship rites of the era, such as those involving Antiochus Epiphanes, Herod Agrippa[1] or the Hasmonaeans.[2] Lastly there are indications that during these intervening centuries there were extant certain sects or forms of folk-religion which could have provided a more or less continuous setting for the *life* of some of these beliefs. Many have looked to foreign soil for the home of these groups which may then have made contact with other Jewish or semi-Jewish groups,[3] but it is not impossible, though our knowledge here is very limited, that there could have been indigenous (more or less) Jewish groups which persisted in this area of thought.[4]

Yet it is to be admitted that this question cannot be answered to our complete satisfaction. The gap which we spoke of earlier cannot be fully and visibly bridged *by us*. In a sense it is the argument of the rest of this study that the bridge was none the less fashioned by men in their own times and therefore that these beliefs did have a certain place in Palestine during the lifetime of Jesus. Of all the solutions, we are going to favour the last, probably with help from eschatology, as being the most likely to have provided the means for this bridge-work, though they may all have had a part to play in carrying aspects of these thought forms into the beginning of a new era.

2. ELEVEN AREAS FOR STUDY

For convenience and clarity we shall assemble our *clues* under eleven major headings. As we proceed, we watch for motifs having to do with kingship, the Man, water rites, *suffering*, passage from *death* to *life*, *ascension*, becoming like the god, and paradise.

(i) 'I Will Praise the Lord of Wisdom'

We begin, perhaps a bit oddly, with an ancient text often considered to be representative of the genre of Babylonian wisdom

---

[1] See pp. 102f. and Morgenstern, *JBL* 80, 1961, p. 74.
[2] See pp. 162f.
[3] See pp. 85ff.; Drower, *Secret Adam*, and further below.
[4] E.g. see below and p. 218 n. 1.

literature, and which we now entitle, from its first line, 'I Will Praise the Lord of Wisdom' (i.e. Marduk) or 'The Poem of the Righteous Sufferer'.[1] Though the work (which appears to be composite)[2] belongs to an era long before that under consideration in this chapter, we wish to use the text as a kind of parable or illustration of the manner in which ideas studied in chapter III may have begun to have been put to a somewhat different service. For one of the things we notice first is that the *speaker* in this text, while he has some definite royal attributes, is not the king.[3] He is penitent because he 'did not teach *his* people religion and reverence', though elsewhere he claims that 'I taught *my* land to observe the divine ordinances'. Yet he attests that 'veneration of the king was my joy', and also, 'the king's majesty I equated to that of a god'. This could well represent a stage in the process which we call democratization,[4] a means by which language which once belonged only to the king passed into more common usage.

Through the long first half of the text the speaker laments his sins and occasionally seeks to justify himself, but for the most part he is bewailing the many personal disasters, sicknesses, imprisonments and onslaughts which he has undergone. The number and fierce nature of these is such that we must believe the person to be speaking in an exaggerated poetical or even liturgical fashion.

Finally his sufferings are about to come to an end: 'I know the day on which my tears shall cease.'

> A dream in the morning *appeared* twice with the same meaning.
> A remarkable young man, immense in stature, . . .
> Gigantic in size, clad in new raiment . . .
> . . .[5]
> . . . he came to me.
> . . . my flesh became *numb*.

[1] *ANET*, pp. 434ff. See also W. G. Lambert, *Babylonian Wisdom Literature*, Oxford, 1960, pp. 21ff.

[2] A number of difficulties in the text may result from a history in which it was used by peoples worshipping different gods.

[3] Cf. S. Langdon, *Babylonian Wisdom* (Babyloniaca: Études de philologie Assyro-Babylonienne VII, fasc. 3–4), Paris, 1923, p. 137. Lambert (*op. cit.*, p. 22) surmises that he may have been a kind of feudal lord ruling a city for a Cassite monarch.

[4] F. M. Th. Böhl (in *Anthropologie religieuse*, pp. 28ff.) holds that a number of Babylonian ideas about man in general are the result of a democratization of beliefs originally associated with the First Man-king.

[5] The text is badly preserved in a number of places.

. . . .
A second time [I saw a dream],
In a dream I saw . . .
A remarkable young man . . .
A tamarisk (branch), a purification rod he held in his hand.
'Tab-utul-Enlil, the dweller of Nippur,
Has sent me to purify you.'
Lifting water, he poured it over me.
The incantation of life he recited, he anointed me (with. . . .)[1]

A third dream follows in which a beautiful maiden (a priestess?)
tells him not to fear. Then,

Someone, who in the night saw a vision,
Saw in the dream Ur-Nin-tin-ug-ga,[2]
A mighty man, wearing his crown; a conjurer carrying a [tablet].
'Marduk has sent me.'[3]

The speaker is now healed of all his troubles. A lengthy passage
describing his betterment ends,

He rubbed off the rust, made it shining clean.
The faded appearance became brilliant.
On the holy river shore (in the underworld) where the (last) judg-
    ment of men is manifested,
(My) forehead was rubbed clean,[4] my slavery mark was obliterated.[5]

There is then a short commentary on the text proper which reads,

Out of *trouble*, through deliverance, I came.
The waters of Esagila,[6] though weary, I set forth in my hands.
Into the mouth of the lion who was devouring me Marduk placed *a
    bit*.
Marduk removed the *incantation* of the one hounding me, turned
    back his lumps.[7]

[1] III, 8f.; IIIA, 10ff.
[2] The name means 'Servant of the divine mistress of the revivification of the dead'. He may be seen as a priest representing a god. According to Lambert he is described as 'a bearded young man with a turban on his head'.
[3] IIIA, 37ff.
[4] Or perhaps 'my forehead was shaved clean'.
[5] III (reverse), 17ff.
[6] This is the name of Marduk's temple in Babylon. Lambert would read this line very differently: 'He who has done wrong in respect of Esagil, let him learn from my example!' On the Esagila and its relationship to kingship practices, see Parrot, *Babylon and the Old Testament*, pp. 49ff.
[7] III (reverse), 66ff.

Here ends the material which definitely belongs to this poem, but the continuation of the story appears to be contained in another tablet.[1]

> . . . he took me.
> . . . he opened for me
> . . . he revived me.
> [From *distress*] he saved me.
> [Out of the river] Hubur (in the underworld) he drew me.
> Marduk seized my hand,
> [He who] smote me.
> [Marduk] lifted high my head,
> He smote my smiter's hand;
> His weapon Marduk shattered.
> . . .
> With lowly countenance I entered Esagila:
> I, who had gone down into the grave, returned to Babylon.

The speaker now passes through various *gates*, including the 'Gate of Life' and the 'Gate of Sunrise'. In the 'Gate of Purifying Waters' he is sprinkled with purifying waters.

He then makes various sacrifices of thanksgiving and appears to take part in a banquet meal which has been prepared near his grave, but which now is a meal of joy, since Marduk (who formerly had caused him to suffer) has restored his life. The tablet concludes with all praising Marduk.

We do not wish to labour our points. The Israelite parallels concerning attacks by wild beasts, being drawn out of the water and being brought back from the very point of death are obvious. The appearance of the divinity (or priest representing the god) as one who helps in this salvation could be a relic from a tale in which the king was saved by the Primordial Man-king. Perhaps this was once Marduk himself, whom we have elsewhere seen similarly described as a beautiful young man of great dimensions. The figure who holds a branch in one hand and pours water with the other could well be presented here as having the appurtenances of the Primal Man.

While a great many of the details (and even the exact ordering of the materials) are obscure, we consider the general import to be reasonably clear.[2] This one who had suffered has been made clean

---

[1] IV, 3ff. Most scholars believe that this tablet belongs with the preceding, but Lambert is unsure. *Op. cit.*, pp. 24f.

[2] See, however, Wagner, *Das religionsgeschichtliche Problem*, pp. 176ff.

and radiant. He has been saved from *death*. He has been drawn up from the waters of death, purified through water and has *ascended* to pass to a kind of rebirth through the gate of life.

In the opinion of Geo Widengren the baptizing sectarianism which is known to have flourished during certain periods in southern Mesopotamia can be traced back nearly to Sumerian times.[1] This view is admittedly difficult to substantiate in detail, since most of the records of such sectarianism have only survived from much later times. What intrigues, however, and makes the suggestion plausible is the presence in later rituals of so many elements which seem to have been patterned on royal rites. We are inferring that 'I Will Praise the Lord of Wisdom' may provide us with a very narrow aperture on to a stage in the process by which royal language and practices were made applicable to *lesser* men in other circumstances.

(ii) Mithraism

We recall our brief mention of aspects of some Mithraic rites of initiation.[2] They, too, bear resemblances with earlier royal practices and seem to enact the legend of Mithra's own struggles and salvation. The new members also undergo sufferings, are baptized as though in a kind of ritual death, and then are raised out of the waters before partaking of a sacred meal. The initiates seem to share in the *experiences* and then in the new life of their god.

(iii) The Naassenes

The Naassenes we remember as a sect closely linked with the Sethians, Ophites and Peratae in Egypt.[3] They display a blend of Jewish, Christian and pagan beliefs, while there is every likelihood that the Christian features were added after the group had had a previous existence. Even, however, if some version of Christianity were one of the formative influences, it was certainly not the sole one, and we should remain most interested in the thought forms.

The position and influence of the sect can best be explained by a beginning little later than the early part of the second century AD, and many feel that we still would need to postulate a nascent version earlier than this, or at least an earlier form of similar teaching upon which these men built. There are good reasons for believing that the

[1] *Mani and Manichaeism*, pp. 14f.
[2] Pp. 83f.
[3] See pp. 56f.

group or its forebears were originally Semitic and that, more particularly, their teaching spread to Egypt from Syria or some adjacent Palestinian locality. In addition to other factors, this would help to account for their name, their Jewishness and their apparent connection with known sectarian groups of the Syria-Palestine-Transjordan area.[1]

There are the diverse ideas about the Primal Man summarized for us by Hippolytus. The Man, Adam, is worshipped as heavenly, yet once, according to Naassene lights, he had to fall into Adam below, there to be enslaved and suffer. On earth he has no reputation, but in heaven he is all-glorious. All are descended from Adam, and he is present in all his descendants. In the temple of the Samothracians there are two statues; one is said to represent the Primal Man while the other is that of the spiritual or *pneumatic* individual, the one that is born again. In every respect the second is of the same essence (ὁμοούσιος) with the Man.

What most intrigues here, however, is how both the Man and his genuine descendants are said to ascend from their earthly existence and to become true pneumatics in heaven. The Man is represented as one, the 'unportrayed one', who came down and is unrecognized. Nevertheless, this is

'the god that inhabits the flood', according to the Psalter, 'and who speaks and cries from many waters'. The 'many waters', he says are the diversified generation of mortal men, from which he cries and vociferates to the unportrayed Man, saying, 'Preserve my only-begotten from the lions.' In reply to him, it has, says he, been declared, 'Israel, thou art my child: fear not; even though you pass through rivers, they shall not drown thee; even though you pass through fire, it shall not scorch thee.' By rivers he means, says he, the moist substance of generation, and by fire the impulsive principle and desire for generation. 'Thou art mine; fear not.' And again he says, 'If a mother forget her children, so as not to have pity on them and give them food, I also will forget you.' Adam, he says, speaks to his own men: 'But even though a woman forget these things, yet I will not forget you. I have painted you on my hands.' In regard, however, of his ascension, that is his regeneration, that he may become spiritual, not

---

[1] On the connections between various gnostic forms and Jewish and Jewish pagan baptismal groups around the Jordan in Christian and pre-Christian times, see again the useful review and discussion by S. Schulz, *TR*, nf 26, 1960, pp. 209ff., 301ff. In his view (p. 334) there is great plausibility in the theory that the source of much gnostic belief and practice is to be found in the complex *milieu* of Jewish and semi-Jewish baptizing sectarianism of Jordanian Palestine in the pre-Christian epoch with its clear attitude of rejection toward Pharisaic Judaism.

carnal, the Scripture, he says, speaks (thus): 'Open the gates, ye who are your rulers; and be ye lift up, ye everlasting doors, and the king of glory shall come in,' that is a wonder of wonders. 'For who', he says, 'is this king of glory? A worm and not a man; a reproach of man, and an outcast of the people; himself is the king of glory and powerful in war.'[1]

There follows a reference to Jacob seeing the *gate* of heaven (in Mesopotamia) and to Mesopotamia as the great river which flows from the belly of Perfect Man. Even the Perfect Man, imaged from the unportrayable one above, must enter in through the gate and be born again.

What, we wish to know, caused some of these texts from or allusions to Pss. 22; 24; 29 and Isa. 41; 43 and 49, along with an interest in the Man, to come together in the first place? Is it not legitimate to wonder if behind this there lies the story of one who, representing him who is above, goes into the waters (here said to resemble those of creation), who calls out to the Man above for rescue from the waters and wild beasts, is named the only-begotten,[2] and who, though despised by the people, rises up through the heavenly gates like a king? One might argue that by some odd coincidence of exegesis this pattern and these references to the king in his suffering and glory were reduplicated. Yet is it not far more likely that there is a cause? That cause looks to us as though it might well be some manner of earlier context involving ideas about baptism and enthronement, even though the Egyptian Naassenes probably no longer practised or understood the language in quite this way any longer.

Adam is here set forth as a *father* figure who, though as the Man below he still requires his own salvation, yet will also aid in the salvation of others. (Whatever *painting* on his hands means,[3] it seems a further suggestion of the intimate relationship between Adam and

---

[1] *Refutation* V, 8.15ff.

[2] The text makes it appear as though the Man on earth were pleading for his own 'only-begotten' (a term which comes out of kingship ideology and which was used by Christians rather than created by them). If this was the intention, we must be at a stage in which the Man on earth was regarded as the *father* of the individual needing salvation in this manner. The Man on earth would then be sharing in the role of the Man in heaven, while the believer would be acting out the role of the Man on earth. Yet we should think it more likely that the original intention was 'Preserve *your* only-begotten from the lions.' It might even have been a liturgical plea uttered by the people on behalf of the one in the waters.

[3] It may have reference to the dye used in tattooing. As a sign of care and intimacy, compare Isa. 49.16.

his *sons*.) At times this Adam seems almost to be conceived of as though he himself were the unportrayed one above. They act as though functions one of the other.

Who, then, is the Perfect Man (τέλειος ἄνθρωπος) imaged from the one above, who yet must himself be saved by passing through the gate and being born again? Of course, in one sense it is this Adam below, but the implications are also fairly strong that this is not *really* the Primal Man on earth (for there is a way in which the true Man, or at least his counterpart, always seems to remain above). Rather is it the believer, the individual who himself would be saved by following in the way of the First Perfect Man.[1] This is made more probable by the Naassene insistence that *all* who do not enter through this gate will remain dead, and that it is only the rational living men (λογικοί) who will be thus saved. Here, too, then, we may be viewing relics from a rite which has been democratized in the process of transforming it.

Further we hear that the pneumatics are ones who have been chosen out of the living water, the Euphrates which flows through Babylon.[2] They now account themselves Christians, having been made perfect by entering through the gate which is Jesus, and there having been anointed with oil from the horn, like David.[3] This being *chosen* from out of the waters and the mention of anointing again suggest something like a cultic or liturgical background. The ceremony is said to take place in the heavenly realms just as the royal ritual was often described as though it were taking place in heaven. Let us notice, too, that the anointing act here is not associated primarily with cleansing or healing, but rather with a rite like king David's. It is said that the ceremony makes the pneumatic into a *god* as well, just like the one above. In other words he will be a royal god.

(iv) Further gnostic views

In his article 'Baptism and Enthronement in Some Jewish-Christian Gnostic Documents' Geo Widengren, whose interpretation

---

[1] Widengren writes, 'In a manner quite common in Gnostic piety and in mystery religions, the pneumatic Gnostic in every respect is identified with the Saviour, the archetypal.' 'Baptism and Enthronement in some Jewish-Christian Gnostic Documents' in *The Saviour God* (ed. S. G. F. Brandon), Manchester, 1963, p. 206.

[2] The mention of the Euphrates could conceivably point to some yet earlier and *eastern* contact for these ideas, but it is just as likely that the usage is *esoteric*, adding a sense of mystery by referring to the well-known river of the East.

[3] *Refutation* V, 9.22.

of the Naassene materials closely adumbrates our own, illustrates his thesis from other sources. *A Book of Baruch* which is accredited to the gnostic Justin informs us that pneumatic and living men are given ablution in the living water above the firmament where the Good One resides. Even one *Elohim*, called the creator and father of all (whose spirit is in all men), wishes to ascend from paradise on earth to heaven, there to pass through the gate. Again old language from the Israelite royal psalms is employed. Elohim is brought before God and sees and hears secret matters. He then is addressed by the Good One: 'Sit thou on my right hand.'[1]

Later we hear that Elohim, after having heard the secret matters, swears an oath, the same oath which the initiates to the cult also use.[2] Elohim then drinks from the living water, the same living water which also serves as an ablution or baptism[3] for the initiates, a fountain of living waters.[4]

Further allusion to a background of similar beliefs and/or rites are hinted at among the Sethians by Hippolytus. After the Word of God, the Perfect Man had entered into the foul mysteries of the womb of the virgin,

he was washed and drank of living, gushing water, which he must drink who was about to strip off his servant's form and put on a heavenly garment.[5]

The strong Christian content is obvious, but what interests us are the ideas which seem to have attached themselves and which may belong to a pattern of baptism as a rebirth followed by a reference to some enthroning or investiture rite. While it can always be maintained that these associations have developed solely from speculation upon Christian stories, it appears far more likely that they actually belong to the larger framework of materials evolving from ancient practices. Here they are being used to make comment on a Christian story as elsewhere they have been adapted to Jewish legends. As with so many

[1] *Refutation* V, 26.14ff. The quotation of Ps. 110.1 is according to the LXX.

[2] In the Clementine *Epistle of Peter to James*, iv, an oath is also sworn beside living or running water.

[3] The word is λουτρόν which is also employed by Christians for baptism. Widengren cites a passage from Origen's *Contra Celsum* VI, 20, which might seem under the influence of similar teachings. After fights and troubles on earth, the Christian hopes to come to the heavenly heights. 'After partaking of the springs of the water which is gushing forth to eternal life, according to the teaching of Jesus, we shall drink from the rivers of knowledge(s) at the so-called "waters above the heavens".'

[4] *Refutation* V, 26.1f.

[5] *Refutation* V, 19.21.

of these gnostic references to baptism and the like, one gains the distinct impression that there is a degree of divorce or separation between the forms as they are now extant and the lore or practices which may lie behind them. One has no feeling of assurance that these gnostics are, in every case, actually using or imitating these rites, nor indeed that they always have a firm grasp on their meaning. Often they come to us as fragments, more like bits of myth or quasi-allegories that are based on materials which two or three or more generations ago may have had a more definite context.

One can continue on in a similar vein. Origen reports that a Valentinian would say, 'I am anointed with light-oil from the tree of life.'[1] To this we may add the awareness that among such a group as the Valentinian-like Marcosians (recall that they worshipped Jesus as the Man and the Son of Man, claiming that the *Anthropos* descended upon Jesus at his baptism) a *bridal* hut was constructed in which a mystical initiation took place. They also are among those who were anointed at the time of baptism after which secrets were revealed to the new members.[2] Like the Valentinians and Mandaeans, the Marcosians had a last baptismal rite at the time of death.[3]

In order that we may avoid undue repetition, it may at this point be profitable to recollect the references collated in chapter II concerning a number of these themes: baptisms and anointings,[4] the Man and his followers as kings,[5] the Man entrapped in the waters[6] or (in one way or another) being *born* out of the waters as a copy of

---

[1] *Contra Celsum* VI, 27. Recall the radiance of the oil in II Enoch 22 and also the similar idea in the pseudo-Clementine passage quoted below.

[2] See Irenaeus, *Against Heresies* I, 21.3ff. On the hut among them see further, I, 13. 3, 6.

[3] *Against Heresies* I, 21.5.

[4] Pp. 57ff. Of course, there are other gnostic passages which have to do or may have to do with baptism, but it soon becomes impossible to be sure that these are not just simulations of Christian rites. For a brief but useful comment see E. Segelberg, *Maṣbūtā: Studies in the Ritual of the Mandaean Baptism*, Uppsala, 1958, pp. 167ff.

[5] Also on this point see Clement of Alexandria, *Stromateis* III, 27ff. and further in Doresse, *Secret Books*, pp. 169, 226. Were some of the Corinthians also manifesting this tendency? See I Cor. 4.8.

[6] It is of some interest in this regard that in the *Pistis Sophia* the repentance of Pistis is regarded as taking place in the *chaos*. It is from there that she ascends (I, xxxii). Among a number of psalms used in connection with her story is Ps. 69 (I, xxxiii) as a commentary on her descent and ascent. The general background of language once used with regard to suffering kings could be of assistance in helping to interpret the references to beasts, chaos, depths, being locked away in darkness, etc., in a number of gnostic works.

the image above. We recall the constant theme of ascensions in both gnostic and Jewish writings along with a frequent tendency to associate with or identify with the Man in these activities by emulating him.[1]

(v) The pseudo-Clementines

We recall the group (probably Syrian) responsible for the pseudo-Clementine literature. They taught of a Christ who had been revealed in Adam and Moses and of Adam as a type of the Son of Man.[2]

The reason for him being called the Christ is this: although he was indeed the Son of God and the beginning of all things, he became a man. God first anointed him with oil taken from the tree of life. From that anointing he is called Christ. Moreover, he himself, according to the appointment of his Father, anoints with similar oil every one of the pious when they come to his kingdom . . . so that their light may shine.[3]

Aaron (whose *baptism* is alluded to in the following chapter) was anointed, making him not only high priest, but also prince and king. Indeed, every man so anointed became either king, prophet or priest.[4] Peter is then asked if the First Man, Adam, was anointed in order that he could be a prophet. Peter answers that he was certainly anointed by an eternal ointment of God.[5]

These references may have added significance for us, since it is said that anointing is no longer practised among the sectarians. Thus it may seem necessary to presuppose some earlier situation which would have created all this interest in anointings.

We shall let Widengren's summary be ours:

From these allusions we are conceivably entitled to draw the conclusion that there were in Gnostic circles certain speculations current about the

[1] See also Doresse, *op. cit.*, pp. 107ff.
[2] See above p. 67. Further on Adam in this literature cf. H.-J. Schoeps, *Theologie und Geschichte des Judenchristentums*, Tübingen, 1949, pp. 100ff.
[3] *Recognitions* I, 45. The Ebionites, with whom the later Clementine literature are often linked, appear to have used one of their baptismal rites as a kind of ordination. Cf. J. Daniélou, *The Theology of Jewish Christianity*, ET, London, 1964, p. 67 n. 30, with reference to A. Orbe's *Los primeros herejas ante la persecución* (Estudios valentinianos V), Rome, 1957, p. 134. In *Das Judenchristentum in den Pseudoklementinen* (TU 70), 1958, G. Strecker doubts any close liaison between the group behind the Clementines and the Ebionites or Elkasaites, but he does find an underlayer of material stemming from an earlier Jewish-gnostic form of Christianity.
[4] *Recognitions* I, 46.
[5] *Recognitions* I, 47. It may be significant that in the Clementine literature a main point of contention between Peter and Simon is not the messiahship of Jesus but rather concerns Adam and the mode of his creation.

Primordial Man as being also the Primordial King, provided with pro-
phetical and priestly functions, and who has received an initiation to his
office by being anointed with oil from the Tree of Life. It is this Primordial
Man, who is called the Anointed One . . . who is the Son of God. He is
the *typos* of every man who has been anointed with the prepared oil . . .
The various elements in baptismal ritual concerning anointing and
ablution are ritual expressions of ancient mythical conceptions.[1]

(vi) The Odes of Solomon

The Odes of Solomon are the product of a Jewish-Christian or
more probably an essentially Jewish group of the Palestinian or
Syrian area.[2] Written during the second or even the first century

[1] In *The Saviour God*, p. 214.

[2] See J. R. Harris and A. Mingana, *The Odes and Psalms of Solomon*, Manchester,
1916–20. The fact that the Odes were found joined together with the Psalms of
Solomon and were also known in such a manner to the author of the *Pistis Sophia*
has not helped significantly to clarify matters of provenance, date and original
language. The last question has been reopened by the discovery of Ode 11 in a
longer Greek form. See M. Testuz, *Papyrus Bodmer X–XII* (Bibliotheca Bodmeri-
ana), Cologny-Genève, 1959; A. Vööbus, 'Neues Licht zur Frage der Original-
sprache der Oden Salomos', *Le Muséon* 75, 1962, pp. 275ff. Cf. the discussion with
reference to the views of R. H. Connolly (Greek), J. H. Bernard (Syriac), H.
Grimme (Hebrew) in Harris and Mingana, *op. cit.*, II, pp. 138ff. A. Adam
suggests a form of Aramaic. 'Die ursprüngliche Sprache der Salomo-Oden', *ZNW*
52, 1961, pp. 141ff.

In our opinion most scholars have overemphasized the degree to which these
Odes ought to be seen as Christian or having been Christianized. The kind of
parallels which, e.g., J. H. Bernard, *The Odes of Solomon* (Texts and Studies VIII/3),
Cambridge, 1912, discovers are usually very general and often better parallels
are to be found in the Old Testament or contemporary Jewish writings, esp. now in
the Dead Sea Scrolls. (See Dupont-Sommer's many notes in *Essene Writings*.)
Certainly the references to the Word do not demand a Christian interpretation (nor
are they properly incarnational; compare Ps. 119.38); the name of Jesus is never
mentioned and there is not a single clear echo of any saying found in the Gospels.
We even question whether the supposed references to the cross (see Odes 21.1;
27; 35.7; 39.7; 42.1f.) need originally have been anything more than an indication
of an attitude of prayer. (Compare v. 2 in [Syriac] Psalm III in 11QPsᵃ; J. A.
Sanders, *Discoveries in the Judaean Desert of Jordan* IV. *The Psalms Scroll of Qumran
Cave 11*, Oxford, 1965, p. 71.) In any case such a sign was used by others, e.g. the
Egyptian *tau* symbol which caused later Christians so much trouble (cf. Baynes,
Coptic Gnostic Treatise, pp. 42, 46f.), and see A. Roes, 'An Iranian Standard Used as a
Christian Symbol', *JHS* 57, 1937, pp. 248ff. Some knowledge of the birth narrative
and the Trinity seems to have penetrated Ode 19, but one need only look at Odes
33 and 35 to recognize that mother-son relationship may first have been intended.
(And compare 1QH, iii, 8f.) If Ode 23 was original in this work and if v. 22 was
not appended, one must remember that the use of the Trinitarian formula by those
who were not Christians (just as the name Yahweh was incorporated by non-Jews
into various formulae) is not unknown. The appearance in Syrian Christianity of
themes and practices found in the Odes (cf. Bernard, *op. cit.*, pp. 19ff., etc.) might

AD, they exhibit certain common characteristics which would apparently link them in one way or another both with some later gnostic groups[1] as well as with Jewish and pagan-Jewish sectarianism.[2] The themes of coronation, etc., are important to these Odes and, while it cannot be unambiguously demonstrated that a number of them have a definite baptismal setting, this likelihood is certainly prominent in many contexts.[3] Intriguing in these hymns is the connection between water imagery and suffering as well as a number of other features that can be understood as having derived from themes and practices which we have surveyed in previous discussions, many of which especially relate to motifs discovered in works such as I and II Enoch and the Testament of Levi. Also the Odes frequently exhibit a tendency to allow the *speaker* to utter oracles as though he himself had become the divine Son.[4] At the heart of the

be understood as the result of a common, general environment rather than as a distinct and unique Christian development. And, even if these features be regarded as Christian in the Odes, we still would want to ask about the background out of which Christianity formed them.

[1] W. Bauer, 'The Odes of Solomon', *NTA* II, pp. 808ff., is among those who would stress the gnostic features.

[2] The echoes of language and symbolism like to those associated with the Feast of Tabernacles have long been noticed. Cf. E. C. Selwyn, 'The Feast of Tabernacles, Epiphany and Baptism', *JTS* 13, 1912, pp. 225ff. Daniélou (regarding them as Jewish-Christian) finds the Odes to be 'markedly Semitic in character'. He suggests an Eastern Syrian origin and a connection with the Essenes and the Dead Sea literature. *Theology of Jewish Christianity*, pp. 30ff.

While we suggest only that the several groups have been influenced by the same thought patterns and associated means of expression, the many parallels with the Johannine and Mandaean literature are worthy of notice. Cf. Bultmann, 'Die Bedeutung der neuerschlossenen mandäischen und manichäischen Quellen für das Verständnis des Johannesevangeliums', *ZNW* 24, 1925, pp. 100ff., and in *Das Evangelium des Johannes*[16] (K-EKNT), 1959; Odeberg, *Fourth Gospel*; K. Rudolph, *Die Mandäer* (FRLANT 74, 75, nf. 56, 57), 1960-1; H. Becker, *Die Reden des Johannesevangeliums und der Stil der gnostischen Offenbarungsrede* (FRLANT 68, nf 50), Göttingen, 1956.

[3] See Segelberg, *Maṣbūtā*, pp. 165ff., who notes features such as immersion, signation, drinking of water, coronation, investiture and meal as parallels of Mandaean rites. Bernard held that the hymns were used in connection with forms of Christian baptism. If, on the other hand, it is maintained that the references to baptism are 'occasional and not structural' (cf. Harris and Mingana, *op. cit.*, II, pp. 187ff.), we should still find this a useful basis on which to proceed.

[4] We doubt whether this is to be explained by pointing to the dialogue form in certain Syrian-Christian liturgies. (See Bernard, *op. cit.*, p. 40.) The psalmist in these Odes becomes not just a saved one, but the mighty saviour, a creator as well as a redeemer. At times he is said to become like the Most High himself (e.g. Ode 36.5), not just the Messiah. There is no sense of 'Thus says the Lord', and there is no *confusion* like this in the Christian liturgies.

Odes there seems discernible the conception of a hero who is appointed to act as or *become* or represent the figure with divine attributes,[1] and there are, in addition, scenes which (rather than simply being interpreted as vague and idiosyncratic versions of stories about Jesus) may be of assistance for our better understanding of the general *milieu* in which some of the Gospel materials took their forms.[2] Because, then, of the interest of this work for our study we will here set forth some of the more significant passages.

In Ode 10 the Lord has made the psalmist to dwell in the 'deathless life'; he himself converts souls.[3]

> 4 I was strengthened and made mighty and took the world captive;
>   And it became to me for the praise of the Most High and of God
>   my Father.
> 5 And the Gentiles were gathered together who were scattered
>   abroad.[4]
>   And I was unpolluted by my love (for them),
>   Because they confessed me in high places.
> 6 And the traces of the light were set upon their hearts.

Ode 11. 7 And I drank and was inebriated
>   With the living water which does not die . . .
> 9 I was enriched by his bounty.
> 10 And I forsook the folly which is diffused over the earth;
>   And I stripped it off and cast it from me.
> 11 And the Lord renewed me in his raiment,
>   And possessed me by his light.
> 12 And from above he gave me rest without corruption.
>   And I became like the land which blossoms and rejoices in its fruits;

[1] Only in Ode 7 do we have language which might readily be regarded as referring to an incarnation, and the Ode could then be Christian. But even here the ideas are strange (e.g. the Father is the Word) and we may have a rather mystic expression of the belief that the one *above* and the one *below* can be regarded as counterparts. Compare Ode 13.1; 36.5; etc. On the humbling of the Saviour to the lowest station, compare Ps. 22.6; Isa. 53.9, 12; etc.

[2] E.g. Ode 39.7ff. bears little resemblance to the story of Jesus walking on the water. (Harris suggests that here and elsewhere we might have Christian materials more primitive than the Gospel accounts. If so, we should be most interested in such a possibility and its implications.) There are better parallels in Old Testament references to Yahweh as the king-God and to the king-Man who has been given power over the waters. See Ex. 14.21; Josh. 3.17; Pss. 74.13f.; 77.19; 78.13; 89.10; 136.13; Isa. 43.2; 51.9.

[3] Bernard (*op. cit.*, p. 71) does not see how the psalmist of v. 1 comes afterwards to speak as the saviour.

[4] Compare Isa. 42.6; etc. A number of Jewish works of the time evidence a concern with the *inclusion* of the Gentiles. Nor would some fear of pollution by them be only a fear of certain Jewish-Christians.

13 And the Lord was like the sun shining on the face of the land.
14 My eyes were enlightened,
   And my face received the dew,
15 And my nostrils enjoyed the pleasant odour of the Lord.
16 And he carried me to his Paradise . . .

Ode 15. 2 He is my sun and his rays have made me rise up;
   And his light has dispelled all darkness from my face.
 3 In him I have acquired eyes,
   And have seen his holy day.
 4 Ears have become mine,
   And I have heard his truth.[1] . . .
 7 . . . And according to his excellent beauty he has made me.
 8 I have put on incorruption through his name,
   And I have put off corruption by his grace.
 9 Death has been destroyed before my face,
   And Sheol has been abolished at my word.

Perhaps this is all another way of saying, 'This day have I begotten thee' and 'in the image of God'. The last claim is astonishing in the mouth of any ordinary person, not least a Christian. (Harris felt impelled to suggest the emendation '*his* word'. Yet the psalmist utters comparable claims at other points.) But the king, preserved from corruption and saved out of the pit at the first light of morning, might (perhaps in the name of the king-god) have spoken like this.

Ode 17. 1 I was crowned by my God;
   And my crown is living.[2]
 2 And I was justified by my Lord;
   And my salvation is incorruptible.
 3 . . . The choking bonds were cut off by *his*[3] hands.
 4 I received the face and fashion of a new person . . .
 6 And all that have seen me were amazed;
   And I was regarded by them as a strange person.
 7 And he who knew me and brought me up
   Is the Most High in all his perfection.
   And he glorified me by his kindness,
   And raised my thought to the height of (his) truth.
 8 . . . I opened the doors that were closed.

[1] Compare Isa. 50.5.
[2] I.e. a budding wreath as in Ode 1, etc. Compare Ps. 132.18 and see Segelberg, *op. cit.*, on such crowns as worn by Mandaeans and others.
[3] The text has *her*, which looks like a mistake unless it refers to the Spirit, which is often regarded as feminine.

 9 And I broke in pieces the bars of iron;
   But my own iron melted and dissolved before me.
10 Nothing appeared closed to me
   Because I was the opening of everything.
11 And I went over all my bondmen to loose them,
   That I might not leave any man bound or binding.
12 And I imparted my knowledge without grudging,
   And my request was with my love.
13 And I sowed my fruits in hearts,
   And transformed them through myself;
14 And they received my blessing and lived.
   And they were gathered to me and were saved,
15 Because they were to me as my own members,
   And I was their head.
16 Glory to thee our Head, the Lord Messiah.[1]

Especially in this Ode we notice all the language which seems to derive from the practice of sacral kingship, both with regard to suffering and coronation. He is freed from choking bonds;[2] his appearance is transformed to the amazement of onlookers; they hardly know him.[3] He has been reared up by God.[4] He escapes his prison and frees the imprisoned.[5] He gives knowledge to his followers.[6]

Ode 22. 1 He who brings me down from on high
        Also brings me up from the regions below.
     2 And he who gathers together the things that are between
        Is he also who cast me down.
     3 He it is who scattered my enemies
        And my adversaries.
     4 He who gave me authority over bonds
        That I might loose them,

[1] This praise of the Messiah, which concludes several of the Odes, may be an antiphonal response by the 'believers'. There is a not dissimilar variation between the first and third persons in several of the Dead Sea 'Hymns' which also employ similar language. On 'the Lord Messiah' designation cf. Pss. of Sol. 17.36; etc.

[2] E.g. Ps. 116.3, 16.

[3] This is the aftermath of scenes like Ps. 22.6; Isa. 52.14; 53.2. The suffering and disfigurement are now overcome.

[4] II Sam. 7.14; Ps. 89.26ff.; Isa. 53.2.

[5] See Pss. 69.15; 88.8; 116.3; 142.7; Isa. 42.7; 49.9; 61.1. This idea seems to have been esp. common in Babylon.

[6] We have seen that the conception of the king/Man as the possessor and dispensator of wisdom, law and knowledge was prominent throughout the Near East. (Note esp. Isa. 53.11.) This thought becomes fundamental to the gnostic conception of the Man.

5 He that overthrew by my hands the dragon with seven heads.[1] . .
6 Thou wast there and did help me . . .

In this more esoteric psalm we could be on that road between Jewish sectarianism and gnosticism.[2] This is especially true if we interpret verses 1f. in terms of a descent of a heavenly being. Such, however, may not be necessary, as the reference could well be to a mortal who was cast down from his high position to undergo suffering and struggle.[3] Otherwise the language is quite Jewish enough.

Ode 24. 1 The dove fluttered over the Messiah
   Because he was her head,
 2 And she sang over him
   And her voice was heard.
 3 And the inhabitants were afraid,
   And the sojourners trembled.
 4 The birds took to flight,
   And all creeping things died in their holes.
 5 And the abysses were opened which had been hidden.

It is usually assumed that this scene is the result of speculation on the story of Jesus' baptism. Yet the details remain surprising. Harris, thinking that they might better have accompanied the crucifixion, suggested that they could have come from some lost Gospel. We wonder if there is any need to force the scene into a Christian mould. After all, birds of augury were used ritually and poetically in many locales, and birds were considered as sacred and symbols of spiritual powers in a number of religions.[4] (See also Ode 28.1f., where the *doves* appear over the head of the psalmist.) If baptism, death and fear are here linked, it is probably due to the old association of a water ordeal and the end of the old creation, etc., before a new birth can be granted.

Ode 25. 1 I was rescued from my bonds,
   And unto thee, my God, I fled;
 2 For thou art the right hand of my salvation,
   And my helper.

[1] Attempts have been made to identify the dragon with an historical person of power, but it is questionable if such was intended here.

[2] It is not surprising that this is one of the five Odes found in the *Pistis Sophia*.

[3] One might think esp. of the *casting down* in mockeries like Isa. 14.12ff.; Ezek. 28 and the Adapa myth. Cf. also our comments on John 3.13 in ch. VII. Would Christians have spoken of Jesus' incarnation in this manner? (The Coptic of the *Pistis Sophia* at v. 2 is probably an alteration, for the Syriac offers a better parallelism and fits the older myth.)

[4] Cf. pp. 368f. and below on the dove used at the Mandaean baptism for the dead.

3 Thou hast restrained those that rise up against me,
   And they were seen no more . . .
5 But I was despised and rejected in the eyes of many,
   And I was in their eyes like lead (i.e. valueless).
6 And thy strength and help were with me . . .
7 . . . And in me there is nothing that shall not be bright.
8 And I was clothed with the covering of thy spirit,
   And I removed from me my raiment of skins,[1]
9 For thy right hand lifted me up,
   And removed sickness from me.

Again we are near to the language of the royal psalms and of II Isaiah (and also of the Dead Sea Scrolls).[2] Is the speaker only an ordinary mortal? If so, his description of himself is significant, and there is no indication that he is a Christian. If he is the Messiah or Messiah-like one, we must again wonder about the circumstances that caused him to rejoice in this manner.

In Ode 28 the psalmist feels the wings of the Spirit fluttering like doves' wings over his heart; he exults like a baby in the womb of its mother, for nothing can separate him from God.

8 They who saw me marvelled at me[3]
   Because I was persecuted,
9 And they supposed that I was swallowed up,[4]
   For I seemed to them as one of the lost.
10 But my oppression became my salvation . . .
12 Because I did good to every man,
    I was hated,
13 And they came around me like mad dogs.[5] . . .
16 And I did not perish,[6] for I was not their brother,[7]
    And my birth was not like theirs.[8]

[1] The reference here is probably to Gen. 3.21. This unclothing and clothing could be seen in a baptismal context and may depend on royal rituals. Recall II Enoch 22.8. Here the idea may be coming under gnostic influences.

[2] See below, pp. 221f., on the many parallels from the Qumran 'Hymns'.

[3] Compare Ps. 22.17; Isa. 52.14.

[4] Ps. 69.15: 'Let not the waterflood overwhelm me; neither let the deep swallow me up; and let not the pit shut her mouth upon me.'

[5] Ps. 22.16, 20. There are other allusions to the suffering figure of the Psalter in this Ode which parallel rather than reduplicate those found in the Gospels' passion story. We are suggesting that they are due to the common *milieu*.

[6] Ps. 116.6ff.

[7] Ps. 69.8.

[8] Ps. 2.7? We consider it arbitrary to find here a reference to the supernatural birth of Jesus. The idea is more likely that of divine birth through baptism which seems alluded to at many points in the Odes. E.g. 17.4ff.; 29.2f.; 36.5; 41.8ff.

17 And they sought for my death and could not.[1]

Commentators hold that the psalmist suddenly begins to speak as the Messiah at verse 8. But if so, what Messiah-figure might it be, and what circumstances enabled him to express himself in this fashion? What permits the figure, without any other indication, to speak as the suffering one?

Ode 29. 1 The Lord is my hope.
    In him I shall not be confounded,
  2 For according to his praise he made me,
    And according to his goodness he gave unto me.
  3 And according to his mercies he exalted me,
    And according to his excellent beauty he set me on high.
  4 He brought me up out of the depths of Sheol,
    And from the mouth of death he drew me.
  5 And I laid my enemies low,
    And he justified me by his grace.
  6 For I believed in the Lord's Messiah,
    And it appeared to me that he is the Lord.
  7 And he showed me his sign,
    And he led me by his light,
  8 And gave me the rod of his power,
    That I might subdue the imaginations of the peoples
    And the power of the men of might in order to bring them low;
  9 To make war by his word
    And to take victory by his power.
10 And the Lord overthrew my enemy by his Word . . .
11 And I gave praise to the Most High
    Because he exalted his servant and the son of his handmaid.

In the midst of phraseology like that used of and by kings of old, we find that the speaker is not the Messiah. Yet he has experiences just like his. It is not easy to believe that this can be passed over by saying that a Christian is here identifying himself with the experiences of Jesus and can thus act as the victorious and conquering one who takes unto himself the very powers, duties and attributes of the Messiah. Might the psalmist not instead be the representative Messiah-below who has been appointed to act in the office of the Messiah-above who reveals himself to him?

Ode 36. 1 I rested on the Spirit of the Lord,
    And (the Spirit) raised me on high:

[1] Cf. Ps. 118.17.

2 And made me stand on my feet in the height of the Lord,
  Before his perfection and glory,
  While I was praising (him) by the composition of his songs.
3 (The Spirit) brought me forth before the face of the Lord,
  And although a son of man,
  I was named the Luminary, the Son of God,
4 While I was the most glorified among the glorious
  And was great among the mighty ones.
5 For according to the greatness of the Most High so she made me,
  And like his own newness he renewed me.
6 And he anointed me from his own perfection.
  And I became like one of his near ones,[1]
7 And my mouth was opened like a cloud of dew.
  And my heart poured out as it were a gushing stream of righteous-
  ness,
8 And my access was in peace;
  And I was established by the spirit of providence.

For the moment let us not be deflected by the appearance of the
Syriac expression for 'son of man' from noticing the real significance
of this Ode. Once more we discover the psalmist speaking as though
he had become the sacral being. Harris, deeply perplexed by the
psalm, could only guess that it displayed an unorthodox, adoptionistic Christianity.[2] We again suggest, however, that these difficulties
are the result of a forced Christian interpretation. The scene lies
much closer to those we have studied from I and II Enoch and the
Testament of Levi than to anything recorded in the New Testament.
The individual has an experience in which he is exalted to heaven,
given the divine name and place, and anointed to befit his new office
and function.

Ode 40. 6 And my face exults with his gladness,
            And my spirit exults in his love;
            And my soul shines in him.

Is this some kind of a *transfiguring* experience to which we might

---

[1] Compare 1QS, xi, 8, etc. Harris conjectured that v. 6b may have been a
reference to Dan. 7.13e, which we could render 'they brought him near before him'.

[2] Bernard, with reference to Gal. 3.26f., held this to be a hymn of a baptized
Christian. But why is this Son of God the baptized person in 36.3 and Jesus in
42.15? With v. 6a Harris compared Ps. 45.7, which was probably in origin an
epithalamium for Solomon. Is there not, then, meaning behind the title of the
work, and what is the assurance that this Ode (or the others) refers to Jesus?
Harris, too, was forced to wonder.

compare II Enoch 22; Dan. 10.8, the scene in 'I Will Praise the Lord of Wisdom', etc.?

Ode 41. 3 We live in the Lord by his grace,
    And we receive life in his Messiah.
  4 For a great day has shined upon us . . .
  6 Let our faces shine in his light . . .
  7 Let us exult with the joy of the Lord.
  8 All those will be astonished that see me,
    For from another race am I.[1]
  9 For the Father of truth remembered me,
    He who possessed me from the beginning.
10 For his bounty begat me,
    And the thought of his heart.
11 And his word is with us in all our way:
    The Saviour who makes alive and does not reject our souls:
12 The man[2] who was humbled
    And was exalted by his own righteousness.
13 The Son of the Most High appeared
    In the perfection of his Father;
14 And light dawned from the Word
    That was beforetime in him.
15 The Messiah is truly one,
    And he was known before the foundation of the world,
    That he might save souls for ever by the truth of his name.

Let us consider this along with the final Ode (42) which tells of the persecution, salvation, and saving love of the figure.[3] Then we read,

---

[1] The meaning of this is obscure. If it is applied to the psalmist in his own person, it might mean that he was a gentile rather than a Jew or Jewish-Christian (cf. Pss. of Sol. 17.9?), but this is highly uncertain and might seem to make nonsense of 10.5. It might conceivably mean that as the Messiah he comes from a heavenly race, but we suggest it is more likely that the basis of the idea is akin to that of Isa. 52.14f.; Ps. 69.8 and Ode 17.4ff. Suffering here followed by salvation have utterly altered him.

Bernard (*op. cit.*, p. 129) wrote, 'This verse does not refer to the Christ, but to the baptized Christian rejoicing in his new birth. Hence the similarity of phrase in v. 8a to Isa. 52.14, and in v. 8b to Ode 28.14, is only verbal and accidental.' But can this be a legitimate method of interpretation?

It may be that the hymn was antiphonal. Vv. 3ff. to be said by the believers; vv. 8ff. to be spoken by the Messiah-like one, vv. 11ff. again belonging to the believers.

[2] The comparison with Phil. 2.6ff. is obvious and we suggest a common background. See in ch. VI.

[3] Note that, if the figure is to be seen as Jesus, there is again a sudden shift between vv. 3 and 4.

10 And I was not rejected, though I was reckoned to be so.
   I did not perish, though they thought it of me.
11 Sheol saw me and was made miserable.
   Death cast me up and many along with me.
12 I have been gall and bitterness to it,
   And I went down with it to the utmost of its depth.
13 And the feet and the head it let go,
   For it was not able to endure my face.

The dead run toward him and beseech him, as the Son of God and
Redeemer, to bring them out from darkness, 'for we see that our
death does not touch thee' (42.17).

Now, there is no doubt that these final two Odes are susceptible to
a Christian interpretation. Still we have our own real doubts. The
ideas can all be paralleled out of the Old Testament and kingship
ideology just as easily as from Christianity, and in some ways that
would better suit what is said here. In the royal rites the king was
rescued before death fully engulfed him, while, at least in orthodox
Christianity, Jesus really died. Admittedly 42.14, 23 could result from
a docetic understanding of Jesus' death or merely be ways of saying
that death could never really hold him, but it is also possible (a) that
it is not Jesus who is here in mind, or (b) that the old legends have
influenced the language here just as much as have the historic details
with respect to Jesus.[1]

Similarly it may be superficial to insist that the language of humbling and exalting 'by his own righteousness', being called the Son of
God and Son of the Father, being seemingly rejected, and bringing
others as well as himself out of darkness and death has to refer to
Jesus. We have shown how all of these ideas are indubitably much
older than Christianity,[2] and they fit in well with other sections of the

[1] It might be objected that the fact that these events are in the past, having
already happened, demands that they be related to Jesus, who alone is known to
have done (or to have been believed to have done) such things. To this we can
answer that, if these Odes have a liturgical or ritual basis, it would only be natural
to express these saving acts as though they had been accomplished as is true in
many ancient liturgies. Even the song of Zechariah, with regard to John the
Baptist, presents us with this attitude of mind.
   Or one may interpose with the realization that similar interpretations of the
harrowing of hell are to be found in Christian works (cf. I Peter 3.19; 4.6), several
of which emanate from this same general locale. But this begs the question rather
than answering it. Are these Christian legends entirely the result of Christian
speculation?
[2] E.g. II Sam. 7.14; 23.1; Ps. 18.19, 26f.; Isa. 9.2; 49.9; 53.11; Zech. 9.9; and
see the notes above.

Odes where an argument for Christian influence is far less persuasive.[1]

It is interesting to ask whether Ode 41.13–15 implies or requires a teaching about an incarnation (of Jesus or otherwise). If so, we would regard this as a sign of later development (possibly under Christian influence) and place it in a similar category with 7.3f. As with the earlier passage, however, it may be that such a thought is not intended. Here the idea may only be that the office of the Messiah above has existed *for ever*.[2] The light dawning from the Word of the Father shines upon the one who is now to serve in this office.[3] Thus we do not find that the conception of a descent from heaven is requisite and would suggest that the far more iterative idea of rising up or being exalted to become the divine figure is, at the least, the fundamental thought of the Odes in this regard.

This may also be indicated by the references to one who 'though son of man'[4] was named the Illuminate, the Son of God, in 36.3 and to the man humbled and exalted in 41.12. We do not see why one of these must be a baptized person and the other Jesus nor how the Odes have otherwise prepared us for this sudden stress on the humanity of the Messiah-Jesus. If, however, the Odes throughout have in reality been speaking of the same figure, of one who has become (or become the representative of) the Messiah, then we may perceive a certain integrity and unity as well as a place for the Odes against the background we have studied.

(vii) *I and II Enoch and the Testament of Levi*

We must continue to hold the vital scenes from I and II Enoch

---

[1] Compare the very similar things said in Ode 15.9 and in Odes 17 and 22, where few would suggest that the psalmist is speaking as Jesus. With this language compare that which may pertain to the Son of Man in John. 5.25ff.

[2] Recall how Enoch becomes the pre-existent Son of Man.

[3] Which idea might represent the kind of thinking which John 1.1ff. has transformed.

[4] *Bar nāšā*. We are, of course, intrigued. It is probably safest to hold that this is a reference to the humanity of the figure, though, even so and as the context might suggest (and the *gabrā* of 41.12 might pick up this note as well), it is a special man that has been chosen. In general terms this would indicate what we are suggesting in any case, that the Odes, while dependent to some extent on ideas which parallel those that affected Christian beginnings, should not be seen as representative of the very same beliefs. Their hero is mainly reverenced as the Christ.

It is not impossible, however, that more than this was intended at 36.3. Harris (see above p. 196 n. 1) found a reference to Dan. 7.13 (we should say language like Dan. 7.13) in this Ode, and it could be that we should translate to the effect 'And while (or even *since*) Son of Man, I was named the Luminary, the Son of God'.

and the Testament of Levi in mind. These works are at least roughly proximate to the setting of Jesus both in locale and time. The problems involving the more immediate context for these writings are, however, at once most fascinating and most uncertain. In the case of the Enochian descriptions of one who is exalted to the divine office we probably have to suppose some sectarian situation. Unlike the others, the Testament of Levi could even be a transcript of an actual rite of *baptism* and investiture, while I and II Enoch may perhaps be inspired by practices known to the authors. Here we walk on anything but firm ground, but there are certainly no better hypotheses to explain these scenes, and they would thus begin to have a place in their own times rather than standing out as isolated phenomena.

(viii) *The Life of Adam and Eve*

A small shaft of further light may be shed from another direction. In the traditions emanating from works about Adam and Eve the woes and tribulations of the couple are sometimes greatly magnified. They both repent by standing in a river. Eve goes to the Tigris, and Adam stands up to his neck in the Jordan (though it may originally have been the Gihon)[1] for forty days. He asks the waters to mourn with him, and all manner of water creatures also assemble around him to mourn.[2] According to the Slavonic version of the Life of Adam and Eve this penance is preceded by fasting of some forty days.[3] We recall that according to another tradition in these books Adam never sinned. In any case, however this is viewed, his penance is most efficacious. In the end promise of *resurrection* is given; it is said that he will be drawn up into heaven and given a throne.[4]

However heterogeneous (and here Christian interpolations are a likely theory) these traditions are, we are interested in the association of suffering and lustration followed eventually by an ascent to the heavenly paradise and a promise of enthronement. While there is no evidence of any liturgical usage of these texts, it is yet conceivable that some manner of rite may be affecting this presentation of Adam.

---

[1] Other Jewish traditions placed Adam's penance at the river of paradise to which kings also went before enthronement. See Charles II, p. 135 n. 2.

[2] Life of Adam and Eve 6; 8.1; 17.3.

[3] 29.10.

[4] Life of Adam and Eve 48.1; Apoc. Moses 39.1. On the picture of Adam enthroned see again Test. Abraham as cited above p. 169f.

(ix) Baptizing sectarianism: Monoïmus, Simon Magus, Elkasaites, etc.

One of the established features of the first centuries of the Christian era is the multiplicity of baptizing sects which were extant in the Jordan valley, Syria and the Transjordan, while our general lack of knowledge concerning the precise origins, practices and beliefs of these groups makes any discussion of them and of their relationship to one another difficult. Some sects, for instance, seem to have used water rites as repeated acts of cleansing (for sins and/or pollutions of one kind or another) rather than as an initiatory rite,[1] while others used a form of baptism in both connections. Nevertheless many scholars feel that there are a sufficiency of common traits to permit us to speak of a baptist movement during this period. Certainly this was the opinion of Joseph Thomas in his important study of the 1930's wherein he sought to trace a number of these relationships and argued for a dating of the general movement beginning in the second century BC and reaching its height toward AD 100.[2] It is, he concluded, most difficult to see Jewish proselyte baptism as anything but a quite late manifestation of an aspect of this varied practice.[3]

Both before and since Thomas' work, and indeed as long ago as the great refuters of heresy like Hippolytus and Epiphanius, attempts have been made to identify or establish relationships of dependence between these groups. Beginning with the Nasaraeans,[4] whom Epiphanius says existed before the time of Christ, stretching on to the

[1] The Hemerobaptists (cf. Epiphanius, *Panarion* XVII, 1) and the Banus with whom Josephus once associated himself (*Life of Flavius Josephus*,[2]) are apparently examples. One ought not, however, to assume too readily that certain rites involving cleansings are unrelated (however now altered) to the kingship background. In royal rites the use of water seems to have been connected with four closely related ideas: it was the means of an ordeal, a washing away of past error or sin, a means of revivification and a preparation for exaltation to the sacral office. All four of these ideas, sometimes all four of them together (esp. in the Odes of Solomon and among the Qumran sect, the Naassenes and the Mandaeans) appear to have had a place in Palestine during this period. It is easy to see how a democratized baptism for the remission of sins could have evolved from out of the royal rite.

[2] *Le mouvement baptiste en Palestine et Syrie*, Gembloux, 1935. Certainly the discovery of the Dead Sea Scrolls would seem to have bolstered his general conclusion. We can mention here, too, that the group responsible for the third and fourth books of the Sibylline Oracles appears to have been baptizers. See III, 592; IV, 65.

[3] *Op. cit.*, p. 435. Cf. T. M. Taylor, 'The Beginnings of Jewish Proselyte Baptism', *NTS* 2, 1955/6, pp. 193ff.; C. H. Kraeling, *John the Baptist*, New York, 1951, pp. 99ff., 202 n. 5.

[4] See below. Although this group is said to have had beliefs and practices in common with baptismal groups, we are not expressly told that they were baptizers.

much later records of the Mandaeans, lines have been drawn intercon-
necting every group:[1] the Jewish-Christian Nazorenes, the Ebionites,
the Naassenes, the Elkasaites, the Melchizedekians, the Hemerobaptists, Masbothaeans, Monoïmus, Sethians, Ophites, Essenes, the
Dead Sea sect, Dositheans, the Odes of Solomon, John the Baptist,
the Johannine literature, the pseudo-Clementine group, Simon
Magus, the Sabians, the Sampsaenites and the Manichaeans.[2] Nor is
this list exhaustive. And not only this, but the very nature of our
evidence, coupled with the tendency toward schism and prolifera-
tion, must lead us to suppose that there were other groups, less
durative and well known, which were born and expired during this
period without leaving any record or trace. Our intention here is to
mention a few of the groups listed above which seem important for
our study in that they had an interesting baptismal ceremony and/or
teaching relevant to our interest in the Man.

(a) We can first recall the teaching of Monoïmus, the *Arabian*, who
not only held several views in common with the Naassenes, but who
himself might conceivably have been a Naassene.[3] Other than this
we have no specific reason for holding that he belonged or was related
to a baptismal sect. Yet he might have, and he did teach of the
Anthropos who can be equated with the universe, of a Son of Man who
is begotten of that Man, from whom in turn all things are produced
and from whom, in heaven, rays flow down.

(b) Simon Magus, the first-century Samaritan[4] *pre-gnostic*, who

[1] The many theories are too numerous to be listed here, although a number of
them have or will be noted. These connections (often very tenuous) are made not
only on the basis of common rites and beliefs, but also with regard to certain
common ethical traits such as celibacy or the dislike of marriage, vegetarianism,
non-usage of wine, use of scriptures, etc. On the Melchizedekians, see in the next
chapter, p. 236 n. 1.

[2] Did the Manichaeans also have their own baptismal practices which were not
simply derived from those of Christians? Here the evidence is uncertain, but
Widengren holds that there is 'a convincing case for believing baptism to have been
a consecration act for the *electi*' among them involving ascent, purification in holy
water and entrance into the heavenly bridal chamber. *Mani and Manichaeism*, p.
102. On the Manichaean Primal Man, sometimes styled as the Son of the Heavenly
King, and his battle in the chaos and among the beasts, etc., see again our brief
discussion and references, pp. 66f.

[3] See above, p. 58. R. P. Casey saw their teachings as practically identical, even
to the point of surmising that Monoïmus was actually Hippolytus' primary source
for Naassene beliefs. *JTS* 27, 1926, p. 374.

[4] It is very difficult to ascertain the degree to which what we might term more
orthodox Samaritans during this era were affected by the various forms of speculation we have studied. Certainly one can make many interesting comparisons with
later gnostic teachings (see J. Macdonald, *The Theology of the Samaritans*, London,

was supposedly the founder of a sect, is said by Hippolytus to have taught of the one who standing below in a stream of water was begotten into the likeness of the image of the unbegotten one who stands above. He will then come to stand above with the blessed *Power*.[1] We notice in both the teaching of Simon and Monoïmus a tendency to conform the begotten one to the status and attributes of the one who begets.

Simon's teaching also involves discussion of creation and paradise. His remarks include an elaborate interpretation of the tree of life and a connection between the spirit moving over the waters at creation and the formation of the Man in the image of God.[2]

The Clementine *Homilies*, Hippolytus and Eusebius all hold that Simon (along with Dositheus)[3] was an heretical Samaritan disciple of John the Baptist.[4] (It is, of course, true that John spent some of his time in Samaria.)[5] It is difficult to know how much credence should be placed in such testimony, but it may tell us that there was a relationship, albeit perhaps a distant one.

(c) The Elkasaites, of whom we learn in both Hippolytus and

1964, on a number of points), and their beliefs regarding the character of Adam as having been passed on through Seth to Enosh, Moses' ascension, the new Paradise, Moses as the second or third Adam, Noah as the second Adam and the Taheb as the new Moses and the new Adam seem to have some relevance. (See *op. cit.*, pp. 221, 362, 438, and Macdonald's comparison of this to the idea behind I Cor. 15.45.) Our sources now allow little more than guesswork, but the similar attitude of a number of the baptizing sects toward the Pentateuch (and against oral law) and their general opposition to Pharisaic Judaism suggests a certain Samaritan tenor in their thought. This may well be true of Jesus himself (and note John 4.43–45; 8.48).

[1] See p. 58. With reference to *Power* as a name for God, see Mark 14.62 and parr. Cf. also Acts 8.10.

[2] Hippolytus, *Refutation* VI, 17.

[3] *Homilies* II, 23f. The Dositheans seem, according to some sources, to have been very long-lived. They are even traced back to a beginning at the time of Alexander the Great and onwards into the sixth century AD. See C. H. Scobie, *John the Baptist*, London, 1964, p. 169. As with several of these sects, there is no assurance that their reputed founder was an actual person who lived in this era.

[4] Lady Drower (*Secret Adam*, pp. 88ff.) finds points of contact between Simon and the Mandaeans. Casey sees them between Simon, the Naassenes and Monoïmus (*op. cit.*, pp. 374ff.). Eusebius (*Eccl. History* III, 15; IV, 11) states that Menander, Satornilus and Cerdo were all descendants from Simon's baptizing sect.

[5] See esp. John 3.23 and Albright, 'Recent Discoveries in Palestine and the Gospel of John' in *The Background of the New Testament and Its Eschatology* (ed. W. D. Davies and D. Daube), London, 1956, p. 159.

Epiphanius,[1] were apparently a sect of several branches, one Jewish, another Jewish-Christian. They appear to have arisen in the Transjordan about AD 100, though they may well have roots going back further than this.[2] Their beliefs can be compared to those of the Ebionites, with whom they are linked by Epiphanius along with the Sampsaeans, Essenes, Nasaraeans and Nazorenes. They were baptizers who placed great stress on the redemptive nature of the sacrament. Among the *witnesses* needed at their baptisms (like heaven, water, etc.) oil is listed.

According to Epiphanius some among the Elkasaites taught that Christ was Adam, the first-created being, while others said that Christ was created before all things, being superior to the angels and ruling over all. He put on Adam's body to appear as a human being. The Christ, who was created in heaven, first indwelt in Adam, but from time to time he withdraws from him.[3] Hippolytus affirms that Elkasai taught of frequent incarnations of Christ. Thus, like some other sects, they seem to have had a belief in repeated *incarnations* or appearances of the Adamite Christ.

In the tradition recorded by Hippolytus the sect was founded by an actual man named Elkasai[4] who had a book revealed to him by a gigantic angel. Lady Drower, however, has a different explanation for their origin. Wondering about some of the possible links between the Elkasaites and early Mandaeans, especially with regard to baptism, the central place of Adam and versions of the heavenly Man, she derives the name from *El-kasia* (the hidden or mystic El). This might be associated with the *Adam Kasia*, the hidden Adam of the Mandaeans. El in old Canaanite lore was, of course, the father of Adam. 'He (Adam) was the son of El so that it is natural to find

---

[1] *Refutation* IX, 13ff.; *Panarion* XIX; XXX, 17ff.; LIII. They are mentioned also by Origen, Eusebius and Theodoret. Cf. J. Irmscher, 'The Book of Elchasai', *NTA* II, pp. 745ff.

[2] Their dating is according to Hippolytus, and Daniélou argues that it is 'fully confirmed by the archaic character of their doctrine' (*Theology of Jewish Christianity*, p. 64). Segelberg (*Maṣbūtā*, p. 184) believes that the rites used by them go back into the middle or early first century AD.

[3] No doubt this is in part a docetic attempt to explain the incarnation. The question is, from where did they get the idea in these terms and the link with Adam?

[4] He says that he was a Parthian. Drower takes up the suggestion that the Elkasaites, like the Mandaeans, may have had a mixed Jewish and Iranian background (*op. cit.*, pp. 92ff.). She notes that the Mandaeans sometimes used *El* as a name for the sun or sun-god (*op. cit.*, p. 102 n. 1). On the Mandaeans and Elkasaites (somewhat more cautiously) see Segelberg, *op. cit.*, pp. 174ff. Thomas (*op. cit.*, pp. 244ff.) saw Elkasaite precursors for the Mandaeans.

him in the El-Kasai gnosis.'[1] This would help to account for the Elkasaite belief that the Adamite reappeared at different times as a prophet or as though he were a crowned and anointed king. In a rather highly interpretive comment Lady Drower gives her opinion of the insight thus gained.

In the secret scrolls the 'false prophet' of the Elkasaites can be recognized as the Nasoraean (Mandaean) Adam Kasia—no 'man' but Man, Anthropos, the Son of Man, the Son of God; El Kasia. In his lower aspect he is the Demiurge, creator of 'worlds of illusion, seven to his right and seven to his left'. In his higher and divine aspect he is Mankind anointed and crowned, priest and king, an image of divine kingship.[2]

(d) We could well wish that we had some better knowledge regarding the beliefs and practices of such other groups as the Masbothaeans and the Sampsaenites along with individual teachers like Satornilus. They all were apparently baptists or are connected with baptist traditions. Satornilus, the Syrian of the early second century AD (said to be a disciple of Menander, a disciple of Simon Magus), had teachings which seem related to those of the Naassenes in several respects. He speculated on Man's creation, and we recall his remark about a 'shining image bursting forth below from the presence of the supreme power', after which earthly Man was made.[3]

Both Augustine and Epiphanius linked the Sampsaenites, who were apparently neither Christians or Jews, with the Elkasaites. This association might be corroborated by the fact that Adam was also a vital figure in their cult. They were said, like many others, to honour water and claimed that life had its origin there. Their name might well indicate that they were sun worshippers, while Lady Drower compares them with the Ebionites and early Mandaeans.[4]

The Masbothaeans are mentioned as early as the heretical lists of Hegesippus.[5] They were seemingly a Transjordanian group of a syncretistic character whom Hegesippus would trace back through Gorthaeus and Dositheus to Simon. Their very name may be derived from the Aramaic meaning 'to baptize'. It is Kurt Rudolph who would most directly associate them with the early Mandaeans.[6]

---

[1] Drower, *op. cit.*, p. 101.
[2] *Op. cit.*, p. 98.
[3] See Irenaeus, *Against Heresies* I, 24.1.
[4] *Op. cit.*, p. 97. See Epiphanius, *Panarion* LIII, 1.
[5] In Eusebius, *Eccl. History* IV, 22.5ff.
[6] *Die Mandäer*, I, pp. 228f.

Eric Segelberg writes:

All these traditions (i.e. especially regarding baptism) as well as those of the *Odes of Solomon* and the *Testament of Levi* point in the same direction; the valley of the Jordan. A great number of other indications, philological, literary, etc., do the same, but if and when and how these traditions did meet is still a problem. Most likely they have preserved different traditions current among the 'baptists' in the 1st century AD and even earlier.[1]

(x) The Mandaeans

Naturally we are interested in the possibility that there was also an early Mandaean sect holding similar beliefs. Despite the apparent improbabilities inherent in tracking back to this time and locale a sect known only from later centuries in lower Mesopotamia, and despite the disbelief of earlier critics, a number of scholars are now confident that they can trace this teaching to a sect which is at least pre-Manichaean and probably Palestinian[2] in an era when they, too, could have been involved with or directly influenced by the ideas we have been studying. Here we can but summarize the arguments.[3]

There is first the question of language. Lidzbarski contended that the basic vocabulary of their literature had a home in a western Semitic dialect. Eric Segelberg's investigation of the technical terms involved in their central rite of baptism corroborates the view that

---

[1] *Op. cit.*, p. 183.

[2] Here we make no claims regarding any direct connections between the early Mandaeans and the earliest forms of Christianity. The arguments of Reitzenstein, for example, concerning a relationship between Q and the Mandaean *Book of John* beg questions which we can hardly even properly formulate, much less answer. See *Das mandäische Buch des Herrn der Größe und die Evangelienüberlieferung* (SHAW, Phil.-hist. Kl.), 1919: XII, pp. 6off., and 'Zur Mandäerfrage', *ZNW* 26, 1927, pp. 55f. For some of the more interesting Mandaean-Christian parallels, however, see the works of Lidzbarski cited below, the commentaries on the Fourth Gospel by Odeberg and Bultmann and in the notes of Bultmann's *Synoptic Tradition*.
Nor would we attempt to find any direct associations between the Mandaeans and John the Baptist, against which see both Scobie, *John the Baptist*, and Kraeling, *John the Baptist*. The debate, however, is often presented in a simple and rather rigid form. Perhaps one could infer an early acquaintance on the part of the Mandaeans with traditions about the well-known figure of John without suggesting that John himself was ever some kind of a Mandaean or pre-Mandaean.

[3] Many of these were first set out by Mark Lidzbarski in his *Das Johannesbuch der Mandäer*, Gießen, 1915; *Mandäische Liturgien* (Abh. der Königl. Gesellschaft der Wissenschaften zu Göttingen. Phil.-hist. Kl., nf Bd. XVII, 1), Berlin, 1920; *Ginza, der Schatz oder das große Buch der Mandäer*, Göttingen, 1925. Cf. E. M. Yamauchi, 'The Present Status of Mandaean Studies', *JNES* 25, 1966, pp. 88ff.

Semitic words are basic.[1] His testimony is seconded by Kurt Rudolph.[2]

The Mandaeans themselves believe that their predecessors once emigrated from Palestine, fleeing therefrom at a time before the fall of the Jerusalem temple in AD 70. This could fit well with the fact that, while Christian influences and anti-Christian polemic can easily be regarded as secondary, Jewish terms, names, place-names and legends form the basic strata of much Mandaean lore, despite an early hostility toward Judaism. While this belief could be legendary and derivative, there are no particular reasons for believing that it is.[3]

Of these place-names the most significant is that of the Jordan. While it is necessary to realize that *jordan* was, in some instances, a generic name for *river*, it would still be surprising if its use throughout the Mandaean texts was not the result of some form of contact with the Palestinian area.[4]

We have already noted that there have been numerous attempts to associate some early Mandaeans with everyone from the Dead Sea

[1] 'The impression of this survey is that almost all technical terms for the essentials of the rite are of Semitic origin, whereas a great number of terms for the incidentals are usually of Iranian, esp. Parthian origin. Sometimes we find that a Semitic term has been replaced by an Iranian one.' *Maṣbūtā*, p. 178.

[2] *Die Mandäer*, I, pp. 253f.; II, pp. 74ff. On the mixture of Iranian, Babylonian and Jewish elements, see further I, pp. 118ff., 195ff. Rudolph (and Segelberg would seemingly accept this) believes it necessary to posit a layer of these non-Jewish features at an early date, having been absorbed by early western Mandaeanism from a syncretistic Syrian-Jewish gnosticism before the eastward migration. Cf. also Drower's introduction to *Secret Adam* and Widengren, *Religionen Irans*, pp. 295ff., stressing the early stratum of Iranian materials.

[3] See *The Haran Gawaita* (E. S. Drower, *The Haran Gawaita and the Baptism of Hibil-Ziwa*, Città del Vaticano, 1953) and Drower's comments in *Secret Adam*, pp. xiiif.; R. Macuch, 'Alter und Heimat des Mandäismus nach neuerschlossenen Quellen', *TLZ* 82, 1957, cols. 401ff.; 'Zur Frühgeschichte der Mandäer', *TLZ* 90, 1965, cols. 649ff. Often brought into this discussion is the testimony of Theodore bar-Konai. (See F. C. Burkitt, 'The Mandaeans', *JTS* 29, 1928, pp. 231f.; Rudolph, *op. cit.*, I, pp. 255ff.) He tells of Mandaeans in Babylonia and Nasaraeans (see below) further north, though he regards their teaching as one. He also calls them Dositheans and says their doctrine was all borrowed from Marcionites, Manichaeans and Kantaeans, while their founder was one Ado of a later period. Yet it would be hardly surprising if Theodore was mistaken. He only knew the cult in its later context and wished to denigrate their teachings. His witness with regard to the Manichaeans now seems to be controverted (see below). His mistakes are further revealed by the fact that this Ado's ancestors all have Mandaean names and the growing probability that even Mani's father was a Mandaean. See Drower, *Secret Adam*, p. xiii.

[4] So Segelberg emphatically (*op. cit.*, p. 38). See Thomas, *mouvement baptiste*, pp. 220ff.

sect to the writers of the pseudo-Clementine literature, and including the Naassenes and Elkasaites.[1] Perhaps most intriguing are the parallels which can be drawn between Mandaean expressions and those found in the Odes of Solomon and the Fourth Gospel.[2] While none of these similarities can offer us any certainty and while no one has established a case for directly connecting Mandaeanism with a known Palestinian group, they do further underline the notion that Mandaeanism may once have had roots in this general area and period.

Interesting support for this possibility has come from another direction, for, of course, Mandaeanism can also be compared with religions of a later period. T. Säve-Söderbergh has contended, to the satisfaction of many, that the relationship between the language of the Coptic Manichaean psalms and Mandaean parallels can only be explained by the priority of the latter. Some of their hymn forms may tentatively be placed in the second century and perhaps earlier.[3]

Remarks of a similar nature can be made about their rite of baptism. The theory of Burkitt, Lietzmann and others that this had been derived from Syrian Christianity has not fared well in recent debate.[4] Segelberg holds that the trend of criticism has now gone decisively against this theory and points out important and inexplicable differences from the Syrian forms.[5] If anything, Mandaean baptism seems more closely related to western Christian rites than to those of the East, and this suggests to Segelberg the possibility of a much earlier and common influence, since western Christianity is unlikely to have influenced Mandaeanism at a later date.

The last piece of evidence which could indicate an early Palestinian background for the Mandaeans is undoubtedly the most controversial of all. The Mandaeans also know themselves as *Nasoraeans* (or, if the emphatic *s* sound is transliterated as a *z*, Nazoraeans).[6] This name is

---

[1] In addition to those cited above, see B. Gärtner, *Die rätselhaften Termini Nazoräer und Iskariot* (Horae Soederblomianae IV) Uppsala, 1957, pp. 22ff., with regard to Qumran. (He also makes a comparison with the Enoch traditions; *op. cit.*, p. 35.)

[2] See p. 189 n. 2.

[3] *Studies in the Coptic Manichaean Psalm-Book. Prosody and Mandaean Parallels*, Uppsala, 1949. See pp. 155ff. He also suggests a western origin for the group.

[4] Burkitt, *JTS* 29, 1928, pp. 225ff.; H. Lietzmann, 'Ein Beitrag zur Mandäerfrage', SPAW, Phil.-hist. Kl., 1930, pp. 595ff.; also A. Loisy, *Le Mandéisme et les origines chrétiennes*, Paris, 1934, p. 116; H. H. Schaeder, 'Ναζαρηνός, Ναζωραῖος', *TWNT* IV, pp. 878ff. In opposition was H. Schlier, 'Zur Mandäerfrage', *TR*, nf 5, 1933, pp. 1ff., 69ff.

[5] *Maṣbūtā*, pp. 155ff.

[6] See Drower, *Secret Adam*, p. ix. The Mohammedans called the Mandaeans

reserved for the *élite* group among their priesthood. Similar names are, of course, used of several groups during the period in which we are interested.[1] We shall, however, not press this aspect of the matter except to say that *if* on other grounds it is right to trace Mandaean origins back to a Palestinian locale in the second or even the first

---

Sabaeans, which name is also still used by the Mandaeans. The root word in Syriac means *submergers* or baptizers and is contained in the Mandaean word for baptism, *maṣbūtā*. Epiphanius speaks of Sabaeans whom he associates with the first- and second-century Dositheans and Gorothenes. It is of further interest that Hippolytus, when telling of that book originally revealed to Elkasai by the angel, says that it was later delivered by a Syrian named Alcibiades to one called Σοβιαῖ, which could easily be the Sabaeans. The tenth-century author Al-Nadim also suggested a Mandaean-Elkasaite-Sabaean connection. (See Drower, *op. cit.*, pp. 92f., and further on the Sabaeans, Rudolph, *op. cit.*, I, pp. 36ff.) Since, however, Sabaeans may well be a generic name for a baptizing sect, one cannot place a great deal of weight on these possible connections.

[1] Epiphanius claims the existence of a pre-Christian sect of Nasaraeans (Ναασαραῖοι, but sometimes, Ναζαραῖοι or Νασαρηνοί) whom he rather carefully distinguishes from a Jewish-Christian sect of Nazorenes (Ναζωραῖοι). Cf. *Panarion*, XVIII, 1; XIX, 5; XX, 3.2; XXIX; XXX, 1. The fourth-century heresiologist Philaster of Brescia mentions the *Nazorei* as a pre-Christian Jewish sect. (On this and these matters generally, cf. Black, *Scrolls and Christian Origins*, pp. 70f.) The Elder Pliny tells of a tetrarchy of *Nazerini* in Coele-Syria during his lifetime. *Natural History* V, 19. Of course, later Christians were also known by this name (e.g. in what is probably an interpolation into the twelfth of the *Eighteen Benedictions*, and see p. 47, l 14, in Giversen's ed. of *Apocryphon of John*), and the designation is also found with some frequency in the New Testament itself. Here the odd feature is the alternative spelling Ναζωραῖος. (Acts 2.22; 3.6; 4.10; 6.14; 22.8; 26.9. See esp. Acts 24.5; Matt. 2.23. Mark seems to favour Nazarene, Matthew and John Nazorene, while Luke has both, and the texts sometimes give different forms.) A number of scholars feel it strange that the village invariably known as Ναζαρέτ or Ναζαρέθ should have yielded the form Nazorene and suggest a connection of some kind with one or more of the above groups. Many other scholars feel that we are merely dealing with alternative spellings, and some would point to texts like Isa. 11.1 or Judg. 13.7 for the derivation of Matt. 2.23. For discussions and arguments regarding the alterations of the *s* and *z*, and *a* and *o* sounds, cf. G. F. Moore, 'Nazarene and Nazareth' in *The Beginnings of Christianity* I (ed. F. Jackson and K. Lake), London, 1920, pp. 426ff.; Schaeder, *TWNT* IV, pp. 879ff.; W. F. Albright, 'The Names "Nazareth" and "Nazoraean"', *JBL* 65, 1946, pp. 397ff.; Black, *op. cit.*, pp. 69ff., and *Aramaic Approach²*, Oxford, 1954, pp. 143ff.; Gärtner, *op. cit.*

There are numerous suggestions concerning the derivation of the designation(s) in any of the various settings. Among the more interesting is that of Black (*Scrolls and Christian Origins*, pp. 69f.), who suggests a connection with the Aramaic equivalent for a word from which the Samaritans might have derived their name. He also believes that Samaritan sectarianism generally may go back to Zadokite priests exiled at the time of the restoration of the second temple. He infers that this priesthood 'must have preserved with the conservative tenacity of a priestly institution much of the pre-Ezra type of indigenous Hebrew religion'. *Op. cit.*, p. 61.

century, it might seem probable that there is *some* connection between their alternative name and one or more of these groups.[1]

Let us then, take up the surprising but plausible contingency that
Mandaean origins stretch back to some manner of sectarian existence,
perhaps with already developing gnostic tendencies, in the Palestine
area. As indicated above, among scholars who favour such a view,
there is the opinion that the Mandaeans have preserved several
aspects of their older rites and beliefs in a strikingly conservative
manner.[2] In our opinion it is no accident that the two features which
seem to stand out in this regard are a baptismal practice which looks
to be a form of a democratized kingship rite and various representations of a royal Man hero.

Indeed, Mandaean rites of baptism seem so obviously developments from older kingship practices that one is tempted to argue
backwards and to use them as illustrations for some of the points
which we strove to make in chapter III. In his study of their *maṣbūtā*
Segelberg repeatedly alludes to the manner in which ideas and
customs associated with kingship inform their rite. Although baptism
had several purposes in the Mandaean religion, the central intention
behind many baptisms appears quite clearly to have been that of
initiation,[3] a kind of ordination to the status of a heavenly priest-
king. This is true not only of the priests themselves, but also of the
great heroes of their legends, many of whom seem types of the Primal
Man. Baptisms take place both in heaven and on earth. The act
'always is both heavenly and terrestrial';[4] '. . . the terrestrial ceremonial involves a celestial reality'.[5] The one to be baptized *goes down*
into the *jordan*; he is washed (sometimes anointed), signed (some-

---

[1] To the objection that the Mandaeans adopted this designation only at a later
date in order to gain protection against the Mohammedans (who would then have
regarded them as a Christian group) it should be noted that the Mohammedans
seem to have known the Mandaeans as Sabaeans, not Nasoraeans. In addition,
Nasoraean was applied only to select members of the group. It appears as an
esoteric name at the core of the religion, not as a general appellative.

[2] In addition to the views of major scholars in this field already cited, one could
add the testimony of others who have treated Mandaeanism more peripherally.
E.g. Mowinckel, *HTC*, p. 426: 'Indirect testimony to Jewish speculations about the
Primordial Man is provided (with an eschatological turn) by the Mandaean
figures of the Primordial Man and redeemer, Anosh or Enosh (the Man); for there
can be little doubt that Mandaism goes back to a Jewish-Christian or Jewish sect.'
See W. G. Kümmel, *Introduction to the New Testament*, ET, London, 1966, p. 175.

[3] Cf. Segelberg, *Maṣbūtā*, p. 128.

[4] *Op. cit.*, p. 147.

[5] *Op. cit.*, p. 61.

times said to become like the divinity in heaven, signed with the
name of the divinity and/or said to become a son); he drinks water
from the river (sometimes is given a sacred meal of bread and water)
and rises up or *ascends* from the river. He then is invested (made light,
endued with radiance, clothed with glory).[1] (Sometimes he is given
a staff.) He is then crowned,[2] hands are laid on him, and he partici-
pates in the ceremony of the ritual handclasp.

Of course, there are a great number of uncertainties about the
earliest order and character of these rites. Segelberg suggests that the
anointing and sacred meal may have been added later (although
the drinking of the water seems to be primitive and the anointing at
the *masiqta* may be early).[3] On the other hand, he believes that an
original rite involving a ceremonial seating, like an enthronement,
has largely dropped away.[4] He is quite certain that the purpose of
the liturgical dress is obvious: the priest is acting in the name of and
as one of the heavenly kings.[5] Writes Lady Drower, 'Every Mandaean
priest is anointed, crowned, and given the insignia of kingship when he
is ordained, for he is the earthly representative of the Heavenly Man.'[6]

A form of this baptism, a requiem or *masiqta* was repeated at death
as a means of sending the imprisoned and troubled soul on its way to
heaven.[7] Part of this ritual involved the sacrifice of a dove which was
seen as a symbol of the spirit of the soul. (In ancient texts birds are
sometimes pictured as hovering over the heads of individuals being
baptized.)[8]

Along with baptism there are associated features which can be of
some minor interest to us. One of these is the cult hut which is a focal
point for a number of Mandaean customs.[9] (We recall how closely the

[1] *Op. cit.*, p. 120. See Riesenfeld, *Jésus transfiguré*, pp. 115ff., on the place of the
white or shining garment in Jewish and other traditions. See also our comments on
the transfiguration and various references above on the Man or king appearing as a
bright and shining figure.
[2] In many cases this crown is made of leaves rather than cloth or metal and is
said to bud or grow like the crown in the Odes of Solomon, etc. Drower suggests
that this *crown* is the most primitive. *Secret Adam*, p. 61.
[3] Segelberg, *op. cit.*, pp. 71ff., 130ff., 149ff.
[4] *Op. cit.*, pp. 86, 152.
[5] *Op. cit.*, p. 28.
[6] *Secret Adam*, p. 104.
[7] The relevance of this for the *soul myth* is obvious. It may also be that this
requiem preserves an older association of ideas linking baptism with *death* as a
means to new life.
[8] Cf. Drower, *The Mandaeans of Iraq and Iran*, London, 1937, p. 2.
[9] On the cult hut, esp. in modern use, see Drower, *Mandaeans*, pp. 124ff.

cult hut seems to have been allied to practices of kingship as a symbol of creation, a counterpart of the heavenly temple, the site of the ritual marriage and perhaps also of the crowning of kings.) There are texts which describe not only the baptism and ordination/coronation of Mandaean heroes, but also their spiritual marriages which could be reminiscent of the sacred marriages of kings. Throughout the literature and liturgies there are to be found creation legends and references to them, along with the symbols of the mountain, the tree and the fountain or river of life. Especially prominent are sun imagery and symbolism.

Our second category of interest involves the types of the Primal Man. Among the more intriguing is Anush or Anush-*uthra*. He is, of course, regarded as a son of Adam (or a kind of son of the Man)[1] and evidently belongs to primitive Mandaean lore. It may well be that he was once far more important than the texts would now indicate, not only because of his Semitic name, but because he is venerated as the protector and guide of all Nasoraean Mandaeans especially. In the *Haran Gawaita* it is he who leads the persecuted Mandaeans out of Palestine and who avenges them by destroying Jerusalem. The Mandaeans came to regard him as a counterpart of the false saviour, Jesus. Yet it is true that he now regularly appears as but one of the three angelic beings or messengers, along with Hibil (Abel) and Sitil (Seth). While the place of these three *sons of Adam* is intriguing, we can really only guess as to whether they had a more significant character at an earlier stage.

Thus it is Adam especially (Adam who, though seemingly partially replaced by Manda-d-Hiia in some of these legends, is still a vital figure) that attracts our attention. He is the father and prototype of First Man and of all men, and also, in another aspect, the First Man himself. He is, as a heavenly being, the son of the Supreme Being, while as First Man, he is the son or counterpart of the heavenly Adam. He is the microcosm and macrocosm. As the heavenly Adam, he is described as being of huge dimensions, the one from which all was made. He is *Adam Kasia*, the mystic or secret Adam (sometimes abbreviated to *Adakas*), who fathered *Adam pagria*, the earthly Adam, whom the Adam above indwells. So all Mandaeans at baptism are thought to indwell or be indwelt, to become like him. Priests especially are held to be Adam's earthly representatives, and many carry his name along with their own. This *double* Adam, who seems to be at

---

[1] See Drower, *Secret Adam*, p. 40.

the heart of Mandaean mythology, 'is the archetype of spiritual humanity and priesthood'. As heavenly Man, he is the archetype 'of Adam as crowned and anointed mankind'.[1] He is the king of the world and the first king, the ruler and father of all other kings and priests. The story of creation is his story, the story of 'the Divine Man, Adam, as crowned and anointed King-priest'.[2]

Though the Mandaean writings are notoriously difficult to quote in any extended manner,[3] we should here like to illustrate some of our points more picturesquely from the *Baptism of Hibil-Ziwa*.

Yawar went on until he reached the King. Seeing that luminous appearance, Hibil-Ziwa was afraid and fell on his face. Then the King grasped him with his right hand and addressed a speech to Hibil, whose quaking and trembling fled from him. He said to him: 'Fear not, Hibil-Ziwa . . .'[4]

Hibil is baptized, sealed, clothed, given *jordans* and streams, ritual huts and the great banner of sunlight. The uthras (angels) rejoice, and all devils become afraid.

The Great Radiance speaks, apparently to a priest.

'Lay thine hands on Hibil-Ziwa; seal him and arm him and establish him and say to him: "Thou art an offshoot of the Life; thou art the First and the Last; thou art the predestinate being that was destined to be . . ." '[5]

He is given a sun banner made from the Great Fruit-Tree, vestments and ritual staves. He goes out to wander the world and to fight against the powers of evil.[6]

---

[1] Drower, *op. cit.*, p. 27. 'The Hidden or Secret Adam is an emanation from the Great Life which appeared in the shape of Man and of material Man who appeared later on earth' (*op. cit.*, p. 105).

[2] Drower, *op. cit.*, p. xvi.

[3] The reaction of Dodd (*Interpretation of the Fourth Gospel*, p. 115) is not atypical. 'The Mandaean writings are an extraordinary farrago of theology, myth, fairy tale, ethical instruction, ritual ordinances and what purports to be history. There is no unity or consistency, and it is not possible to give a succinct summary of their teaching.'

[4] Drower, *The Haran Gawaita and the Baptism of Hibil-Ziwa*, p. 31. Hibil-Ziwa is here regarded as the son of Manda-d-Hiia and is obviously a heavenly being who, as in other gnostic works, has come down or fallen down to earth. The essence of the story, however, is concerned with his *salvation* through baptism, his ascension and reception into heaven, there to rule in glory.

[5] *Op. cit.*, p. 32.

[6] *Op. cit.*, p. 33. In this and other features one might find reminders of stories like that of Gilgamesh. On this page Hibil is called by the name of his father, Manda. Drower notes that this is a mistake, but it is a mistake of a significant kind,

Then Hibil becomes lost in the world of darkness and *masiqtas* must be said for him. The kings (i.e. priests) pray for him:

' "Arise, arise[1] (thou) Chosen One of Righteousness" and "My Good Messenger" and "I Worship the Life . . ." '[2]

The priests are addressed:

'And place the crown upon your heads and recite "The Life Created Yawar-Ziwa", "Let Light Shine Forth" and "Manda Created Me". '[3]

More of the ritual follows, and then Hibil is hymned by those priests supervising his baptism.

> 'O Son of pure mirrors,
> Thine appearance is brighter
> Than all the kings of the Ether-world;
> And thy brilliance shineth upon the uthras!
> All uthras, (yea) all the kings,
> At thy baptism are established
> Fully.'[4]

The priests stand about examining their vestments and holding their crowns while Manda-d-Hiia praises Hibil for vanquishing the worlds of darkness and opening their gates for ever.

The priests are directed to praise the *jordan* which has delivered Hibil from pollutions and the darkness of the seven underworlds and which raises his baptism to the summit. The chief priest steps forward and crowns Hibil, the son of Manda-d-Hiia with a wreath.[5]

The priests now step forward, crown themselves and sing in praise

---

for often in the Mandaean texts the names of the great heroes are exchanged. Son becomes father, etc. See below in this text.

[1] Using *qūm*. This cry occurs fairly often in their liturgies. E.g. Drower, *The Canonical Prayerbook of the Mandaeans*, Leiden, 1959, p. 107. See below, pp. 285f.

[2] *Baptism of Hibil-Ziwa*, pp. 39f. Compare the story of the baptism of Adam at his creation:
'And he ascended the bank of the Wellspring and his glory burst forth over all worlds. Then he arose and sat by a well of vain imaginings and said "I am a king without peer! I am lord of the whole world!" '
(See Drower, *Canonical Prayerbook*, pp. 29ff., and also *Secret Adam*, p. 25, with regard to the baptism of Adam by Hibil-Ziwa.)

[3] *Baptism of Hibil-Ziwa*, p. 40. These titles refer to hymns, a number of which are to be found in other texts or liturgies.

[4] *Op. cit.*, p. 47.

[5] *Op. cit.*, p. 48. Notice the old pattern. First must come the defeat of the forces of the underworld, the powers of darkness and evil. Notice, too, that victory from, rescue from these powers comes through baptism.

of the creation and their own creation as priests. They sing in the name of Life and in the name of the Primal Being.[1]

All the kings of darkness have been crushed. They hear the 'voice of Hibil-Ziwa who is Manda-d-Hiia'. They are crushed by 'Hibil-Ziwa, the son of Manda-d-Hiia', who is baptized, clothed with radiance and crowned with an ever-living wreath.[2]

'Blessed be this baptism of kings which hath blessed Hibil-Ziwa.'[3]
'. . . thou illuminest this, the First Baptism of Hibil-Ziwa, at the first jordan in the worlds of light and deliverest him from the pollutions of the seven worlds of darkness.'[4]

The priests at this stage are obviously thought to have joined in the baptism of Hibil. They enact its ritual and share its blessings.

'And when ye recite "I Am a Perfect Gem", ye endow your counterpart and mine with mansions of radiance, and Hibil-Ziwa (also).'[5]

Manda-d-Hiia addresses a hymn to Hibil as the latter descends into the Jordan.

'Who believed the radiance of the king?
Who perceived the lovely light?
Who saw the king of uthras, Hibil-Ziwa
When he came to the Everlasting Abode,
When he rejoiced at the living waters?
By the baptism of the king I arose,
By his baptism (I arise) to the Everlasting Abode.'[6]

We then hear of the signing of Hibil, of his ritual staff, his drinking of the waters, his shining wreath, of the First-Wellspring and the First Date-Palm, his Names, his raiment and his anointing.[7]

[1] I.e. the Primal *Gabrā*. *Gabrā* (which can refer to an ordinary mortal), when applied to a heavenly being in Mandaean, does not mean a human being, but rather a divinity visualized as though a *man*. See Drower, *Secret Adam*, p. 56.

[2] *Baptism of Hibil-Ziwa*, p. 50.

[3] *Op. cit.*, p. 51.

[4] *Op. cit.*, p. 51 n. 13. Drower suggests this as the original reading.

[5] *Op. cit.*, p. 52.

[6] *Op. cit.*, pp. 52f. The change in pronoun is typical of Mandaean works, and we believe that it results from liturgical use, the baptized person making the hymn and the experience his own. (Thus note how on p. 61 the baptized priest can himself seemingly become the redeemer figure.) We have guessed that this is what is taking place in the Odes of Solomon as well.

[7] *Op. cit.*, pp. 53ff. A myrtle branch also plays some obscure part in the ritual at this point. See Drower, *Canonical Prayerbook*, p. 309.

And Hibil-Ziwa said: 'Everyone that is baptized with my baptism, Hibil-Ziwa's, shall be set up beside me and shall resemble me,[1] and shall dwell in my world, Hibil-Ziwa's . . . They shall set him in the upper world of the King . . . He will become like me, Hibil-Ziwa, and all the uthras of the world of light shall surround him and kings will lead him, taking him into the highest world and will install him at jordans and streams. And all sins that he committed shall be remitted.'[2]

Another song is sung to Hibil as the radiant King of all the world, and the priests partake of ritual food.[3]

'Any man baptized with this baptism (that is a baptism) like (that of?) the glorious First Great Radiance, will be accounted (Mine); he shall dwell in My dwelling; he shall be like unto Me in his form . . .'[4]

We are told of Hibil's joyful reception into the upper world, and a number of further hymns are sung in his praise, to the radiant King and Father of the world. His glory and the appurtenances of his rule are praised.

(xi) *Early Christianity*

Obvious dictates of order require that we hold in abeyance our discussion of the New Testament itself, but there are a few matters which might here be mentioned within a restricted scope.

Is it not quite conceivable that the descriptions of Jesus' baptism, brief as they are, should be placed against this general background? Certainly they have elements which would encourage this and which read more like a divine ordination or adoption ceremony than a lustration for the remission of sins. Coupled with this possibility cognizance must be taken of the extraordinary interest shown in Jesus' baptism, not only by the Gospels in placing it where they do, but by many of the gnostics and especially by a number of the Jewish-Christian sects.[5] A significant proportion of these groups tended to

[1] See in *Canonical Prayerbook*, p. 19: 'Any man anointed by this oil will live, be whole and be strengthened: his speech will assume the nature of Anush, within him he will take on the nature of Anush!'

[2] *Baptism of Hibil-Ziwa*, p. 59.

[3] *Op. cit.*, pp. 62f.

[4] *Op. cit.*, p. 69.

[5] Among these groups further mention ought to be made of the Ebionites (*the poor?*) who were evidently a very early Jewish-Christian sect from whom others were said later to have broken away. They proclaimed both frequent ablutions and an initiatory baptism along with a bread-and-water meal. They seem to have possessed a highly dualistic view of life, stressing the battle between Christ and the devil. (See also above, p. 187 n. 3.) Many writers believe that they evolved from Essenism and would connect them closely with the pseudo-Clementine literature

have an adoptionistic Christology, or at least an adoptionistic view of the baptism even when this does not always seem to fit well with their Christology. Both *docetic* and *ebionite* theories speculated about a Christ who *descended* upon or *appeared* in Jesus at his baptism, and then they proceeded to work this out in different ways. Side by side with this is the proclivity closely to relate the activity of Christ to Adam, often to hold that this Christ was once manifested in Adam. In addition, Christian, Jewish-Christian and gnostic documents alike persist in speaking of an anointing which Jesus received at his baptism even though the Gospels report nothing of this. Then there is the firm connection, established at a very early date, between baptism and the theme of suffering, as though the baptism was an *ordeal*.

Finally there is the matter of the actual practice of baptism by different Christian groups. Various customs like anointing and signing or *sealing*, the changing of garments (often to a white robe), the wearing of crowns (of one kind or another), the holding of branches, the partaking of milk and honey (or some other drink and food), the motif of *ascent*, and the use of language describing baptized persons as priests and/or kings are not only known from second-century traditions[1] but are almost surely in evidence in the New Testament itself.[2] (And it may not be without significance that many of these practices seem to have taken an early and especially deep hold in the Syrian Church.)[3] While the descriptions of baptisms in

---

and the Elkasaites. They are also sometimes linked with the Nazorenes, as they appear to have shared very similar versions of the Gospel according to Matthew.

[1] See esp. Parable VIII in the *Shepherd of Hermas*.

[2] Much of the material is debated, but many scholars suggest a baptismal derivation for the language in II Cor. 1.21; Gal. 3.27; Col. 3.8ff.; Eph. 4.22ff.; Heb. 6.4; I John 2.20, 27; I Peter 1–2. Some believe that the imagery of white robes, washing, living water and palm branches which John the Seer uses in connection with the victorious martyrs is language which he borrowed from baptismal customs. See Rev. 7.9ff.

[3] A good source for study remains F. C. Burkitt's *Early Eastern Christianity*, London, 1904. See also Bernard's useful commentary, *The Odes of Solomon*, where numerous parallels are quoted and referred to. Setting these practices against the wider background, Widengren writes, 'It is a fact that this convolution of ideas, where there is an organic link between the ascent of the soul, the purification immersion and the entry into the bridal chamber, is found in Christianity, gnosticism, Mandaeism and Manichaeism and clearly shows a confluence of pre-Christian concepts which within Christianity itself is most distinctly revealed in the Syrian, especially Nestorian, Church' (*Mani and Manichaeism*, p. 102). See also his similar comments on the Syrian-Christian themes of exorcism, ascension to paradise, anointing and partaking of the tree of life, which he relates to earlier Mesopotamian forms (*op. cit.*, pp. 15f.).

the Acts have often been used to suggest that *simpler* forms were normative at first and that *ritual* was added later, there is no guarantee that Acts is not just revealing one general (and perhaps secondary) attitude toward baptism.

Daniélou is among the scholars who would point out certain extra-Palestinian pagan counterparts to these rites, but he also realizes that they have a very important background within forms of Judaism, or at least within a Jewish-Christianity for which an explanation in terms of immediate and solely pagan influences is unnecessary and unlikely.[1] Rightly does he point to the expressions and customs in the Testament of Levi (see also II Enoch), the Odes of Solomon and features of the contemporary Feast of Tabernacles.

Yet surely more fundamental questions beg to be asked. From what sources did Judaism receive these ideas and practices, and why had men begun to take such an interest in them? Even if one persists in seeing much of this as Jewish-Christian rather than Jewish detail, these questions cannot be avoided. One cannot simply say that Christians began to borrow details from the Feast of Tabernacles, etc., and leave it at that. Why? Why and how could these features, so long used of kings and royal priests, now come to be applied to other individuals in sectarian situations?

3. HYPOTHESIS

On the basis of this evidence and these interpretations our general conclusion and hypothesis cannot come as a surprise. We hold that there are now many good reasons for believing that there were extant during the first century AD and probably for some time earlier a number of Jewish-oriented sects which practised forms of baptism as an ordination/coronation rite and which were likely open to at least a measure of *foreign* (or simply indigenous but non-Jewish) influences. Even our evidence from the second century or later points *consistently* back to this area and this time. It is also our contention that for a number of these groups, and often in connection with their baptismal rites, speculation about or belief in the Man (in one or more of his guises) had a significant role to play. In our opinion the sources of

---

[1] *Theology of Jewish Christianity*, pp. 323ff. See also Reitzenstein, *Die Vorgeschichte der christlichen Taufe*, Leipzig-Berlin, 1929, where he discusses a number of these details and possible relationships, but we should like to believe that we are here providing a more precise and definite context. Cf. Wagner, *Das relionsgeschichtliche Problem*.

both many of these water rites and of the concern with the Man, as well as the interrelation between the two, reach back to the ancient kingship ideologies. Fragmented and varied though the practices are (or as we see them), almost every group offers cause for seeking a background of thought and/or custom in the older king-Man rituals and mythologies.

It is against this background and in this historical setting that we wish to examine what we regard as the earliest strains of Christian tradition, especially as they pertain directly to the Son of Man. We believe it quite likely that Jesus could have been influenced by the beliefs of one or more groups like these. We hope now to have given a sound basis for thinking that this might have happened. In the ensuing chapters we shall endeavour to show why we believe that the New Testament evidence indicates that this is what did happen.

There are, however, several difficult problems which must still be faced if we would contend that the manner in which the Gospels say that Jesus spoke about *the Son of Man* makes the best sense in such a context. Yet, before we can even take these up, we have no other choice but to interrupt ourselves, as it were, and to consider what might be regarded as evidence against our theory that such a *milieu* as we have delineated was extant in the first century and capable of influencing Jesus.

4. THE ESSENES, QUMRAN AND JOHN THE BAPTIST

No doubt some would be willing to argue that the *apparent* absence of such a baptism as we have alluded to and of speculation about the Man among the Essenes and the Dead Sea sectarians militates against our theory. Indeed, there might seem reason behind such an objection, but several objections to the objection can also be made right away. If the Essenes were a group to be distinguished from those at Qumran, it must in the first place be said that we know very little about their actual practices and beliefs. Their evidence may be quite neutral. Secondly it must be remembered that New Testament scholarship is now in a peculiar phase in which the impression is sometimes given that nothing can be said to have existed unless it was also taught at Qumran. The fact of the matter is, at least in this writer's opinion, that the Dead Sea Scrolls are rather disappointing in the amount of new light they specifically shed on Christian beginnings. Certainly they are interesting in themselves and certainly they tell us much that we otherwise would not know, but we can still only conclude that, from whatever sources Jesus was directly influenced, Qumran could not have been one of them. Then, too, there may have been tendencies in the Qumran thought and discipline which were not permissive of ideas found in other sects, just, for instance, as Sadduceeism could be intolerant of some of the beliefs of Pharisaism. In other words the negative evidence of the critic needs to be treated just as carefully and critically as the positive evidence of the theorist.

Yet in all this we are being perhaps rather superficial, and, should one add to this list of possible negative witnesses the name of John the Baptist, the whole challenge deserves to be treated more seriously. Maybe something positive will even accrue to us.

We hear that the Essenes practised certain ablutions for cleansing and also that they bathed every morning.[1] Of more interest is the *baptism* which was associated with admission to the group; the initiates were given a hatchet, white robe and girdle (the garments being worn only on ceremonial occasions). They apparently also worshipped or reverenced the sun. In other words, it is possible that there is more here than meets the eye. For instance, the Mandaeans also wore white robes, and they wore them as signs of their priesthood, believing themselves at baptism to have become the exalted royal priests of God, representatives of the Adam above. There are also many relics of sun-worship in their rituals.

A similar attitude can be adopted toward the information from Qumran. Matthew Black is among the scholars who believe that baptism was a feature of life at Qumran and that the large *cisterns* present on the site were used as baptistries. 'The act or ceremony (baptism of admission) was no doubt so well known that it was unnecessary even to mention it.'[2]

Now, if this be true, we have every legitimate cause for wondering about the nature of these rites. Black argues that they were done publicly in the sight of all, sitting around the baptistries as though in 'a natural amphitheatre'.[3] We know that the members considered themselves as priests. Were they after admission, as Essenes or like Essenes, entitled to wear a white robe and girdle? In what has been styled the 'Hymn of the Initiants' it is written that

[1] See Josephus, *The Jewish War* (LCL, ed. 1927–8) II, 8.2ff.; Hippolytus, *Refutation* IX, 18ff. Neither Philo nor the Elder Pliny tell us anything about their baptismal customs.

[2] *Scrolls and Christian Origins*, p. 94.

[3] *Op. cit.*, p. 95. See Dupont-Sommer, *Essene Writings*, p. 64.

He has given them an inheritance
in the lot of the holy beings,
and joined them in communion with the Sons of Heaven.

. . . and vouchsafe unto the son of Thine handmaid
the favour which Thou hast assured to all the mortal elect,
to stand in Thy presence for ever.[1]

There are echoes of older liturgies here. We should remember, too, that the Testament of Levi was at least known to this group and that the blessed among them were said to have the promise of a crown of glory and a robe of honour.[2]

In the formula for the blessing of the high priest we hear that a crown of honour is to be set upon his head by the Lord. He is bidden not to become estranged from the perpetual spring.[3] In the liturgy for the blessing of priests we read,

The Lord bless thee from His holy habitations and set thee crowned in majesty in the midst of the Holy Beings, and renew unto thee the covenant of the priesthood everlasting, and give thee place in the holy habitation.[4]

He hath made thee an holy thing among His people, to be a light [   ] to [illumine] the world with knowledge and to enlighten the faces of men far and wide.

May He set upon thine head a diadem to proclaim thee holy of holies, for [it is thou that evincest His] holiness and showest forth the glory of His name.[5]

Throughout the 'Hymns of Thanksgiving' of the sect the *psalmist*[6] uses language strikingly similar to that once associated with the sufferings of the royal figure. He speaks of the assaults of wild

---

[1] 1 Q S, xi, 8, 16f. Compare 1 Q H, iii, 19ff.
[2] Cf. 1 Q S, iv, 8. This may only refer to future glory, but on the basis of other passages it would not be surprising if that glory were adumbrated (ritually?) on earth. See W. H. Brownlee, *The Dead Sea Manual of Discipline* (*BASOR* Suppl., Studies, 10–12), New Haven, 1951, pp. 16f. nn. 16f., who compares the 'garments of glory' with I Enoch 62.15; II Enoch 22.8.
[3] 1 Q Sb, iii, 3f., 19f. See the translations of Gaster, *Scriptures of the Dead Sea Sect*, pp. 98ff.
[4] 1 Q Sb, iii, 25–27.
[5] 1 Q Sb, iv, 27f.
[6] Dupont-Sommer rightly finds a number of parallels between this language and that used in the Odes of Solomon. (As in the Odes, the *psalmist* sometimes speaks in the first person and is sometimes praised in the third person.) He also points out the echoes of II Isaiah and believes that the subject is in many cases the Teacher of Righteousness himself. *Op. cit.*, p. 200. We would be less sure about the last point, for in our view the language is basically liturgical, though it may now have been historified to some extent.

beasts, rejection and contempt by enemy and friend. He is mocked and is of no esteem. He tells of going down into the pit, of the torments of *death*, of swirling tides, the surging billows and breakers. Yet God shines upon him; he raises him up and rescues him from the pit; the bars of iron are broken down; the individual is cleansed; he becomes like a great tree;[1] he (like Enoch, Adam and others) is raised up to Eden, where the great and unfading tree grows and where the unfailing stream and the fountain of life are to be found. He is the gardener there; the father feeding his children. God has fashioned him and raised him up to this communion with the sons of heaven. Though like a worm, he may be lifted out of the dust to the height of eternal things. God has made him and revealed deep secrets and wonders to him. He will stand in God's presence for ever.[2]

Though the language is often ambiguous and in places appears to be fully democratized, it would seem that the 'Hymns' and other passages in the Dead Sea literature often have a special *man* in mind as the one who will undergo these experiences and become the saving figure. There is no one designation for him, but the references to *'ādām, ben hā'ādām, geber, 'iš*,[3] 'son of thy handmaid', 'one born of woman',[4] 'thy servant' and 'vessel of clay' may be no less significant for that. The figure is the 'man' and 'son of man', the dust of the earth yet raised to be with God and reign in glory.[5] So in 1QS, iv, 20–23 we hear of a *geber*, an *'iš*[6] whom God will specially cleanse with the 'Spirit of Truth' gushing forth on him 'like purifying water' in order that he might give 'insight into the knowledge of the Most High and into the wisdom of the sons of heaven' to those chosen to have 'all the glory of *'Ādām*'.[7] In 1QH, iii, 8–10 we hear of the Man

---

[1] Note the reference to the 'shoot' (*nēṣer*; cf. Isa. 11.1) which the rivers of Eden shall water. 1QH, vi, 15f. See 1QH, vii, 19; viii, 6, 8, 10.

[2] For these features cf. the following passages: 1QH, ii, 8–13, 16–18, 23–27, 33f.; iii, 6, 8–10, 16, 19–24; iv, 5f. (salvation at daybreak), 8f., 22f., 27f., 33, 36; v, 5f., 11–15, 23–25, 33–37; vi, 10–18, 24; vii, 6, 20, 24; viii, 4, 17–36; ix, 4–10, 23–32; xviii, 15; etc.

[3] Note that God himself is called *gibbōr* and a 'Glorious *'iš*' in 1QM, xii, 10. Similar appears to be 1QM, xix, 2f.

[4] See p. 147 n. 2.

[5] E.g. 1QH, ii, 17; x, 3–7, 28; 1QS, viii, 11f.; xi, 16–22.

[6] For the belief that these are not simply generic and have messianic implications, see Brownlee, 'The Servant of the Lord in the Qumran Scrolls, II', *BASOR* 135, 1954, pp. 36f. n. 30; G. Vermes, *Scripture and Tradition in Judaism*, pp. 56ff. Opposed is A. R. C. Leaney, *The Rule of Qumran and Its Meaning*, London, 1966, p. 157.

[7] Similar references to having this glory of Adam are found in 1QH, xvii, 15; CD, iii, 20; Comm. on Ps. XXXVII, ii, 1f. Dupont-Sommer holds that this is 'the

(*geber*)[1] who will be given birth in the billows of death. From these this 'Marvellous Counsellor' shall spring forth. We seem here to have an obvious messianic context with reference to Isa. 9.5f.

Now, it is quite feasible that much of this language is *poetic*, that many of the images and themes have been derived out of the Old Testament and that we should not press them for further significance. Yet, if we are to conclude that there was a baptismal practice in connection with initiation at Qumran, we have this right to ask about its form and content. While none of the above passages come from demonstrable baptismal contexts, it is not unlikely that some such language might have been used by some representative figure if and when a baptism took place. In which case the parallels with the language and themes studied previously may be indicative of a baptism in which the individual suffered before being exalted and coronated as a royal, Adam-like priest of God. In any case, it would appear that Qumran thinking may at least have been touched by these ideas.

We also mentioned John the Baptist and his practice of baptism as a possible negative witness against our thesis. This could be of more importance, since it appears that here the connection with Christian beginnings was intimate (although the traditions may have somewhat exaggerated Jesus' association with this popular figure). We shall need to consider John at several further points in our study, but in the meantime we must ask, again in this case, how much we really know about the significance and character of his baptismal rite. Neither Josephus[2] nor any of the Fathers or apocryphal gospels tell us anything of further value about John's actual practice, and we are therefore thrown back on the record given in the New Testament.[3] Here we are, of course, taught that it was a baptism for repentance and the remission of sins.[4] It was also eschatological in that it looked for a

---

Biblical Adam, the Lord of creation; but also, no doubt, mythical Man, the Anthropos of Gnostic speculation' (*Essene Writings*, p. 82 n. 3).

[1] Again see Vermes, *op. cit.*, pp. 56ff., on the messianic significance of the word. He notes also that in more than one Targum passage *geber* is translated by *bar nāš*.

[2] *Antiquities* XVIII, 5.2. (Even if the Slavonic version of the *Jewish War* were somehow to be accepted as authentic, it would be of no help with regard to the baptism itself.) That Josephus is only making use of popular hearsay (or at least only wishes to relate this much) is probably confirmed by the fact that he reports nothing of John's eschatological teaching or faith in 'the coming one', which there is good reason to regard as historical.

[3] For a review of the other evidence, see Scobie, *John the Baptist*, pp. 13ff.

[4] Mark 1.4; Matt. 3.1ff.; Luke 3.3ff.; etc.

coming one.[1] Now, it is very easy to accept this at face value and see John only as a simple prophet of repentance, but there are some anomalies if this be true.

As is well known, both John's baptism and a group of Johannine disciples continued in existence for some time after his death. Although we shall not attempt, as others have done, to make a great deal out of these facts, this continuation suggests a somewhat more elaborate sectarian life and likely a more distinctive form of baptism than we otherwise know of. How else would the sect and the baptism have preserved themselves?

Samaritan sectarians like Simon and Dositheus (and their teachings) are associated with John's movement. This may be valueless hearsay, but it need not be entirely so.

The Gospels have other things to tell us about John, traditions that he might be *reborn* or even that he was Elijah (the Elijah whom the Gospels very closely ally to speculation about the Son of Man) or was reborn in Jesus. These can be given various explanations, but, at least, do suggest a more complex background of thought.

Further, we hear speculation that John was the Christ. This is hardly to be attributed to Christians, and, while it could perhaps have a simple explanation, we cannot readily assume that John or his followers did nothing to encourage this interest. Our wariness might seem supported by the fact that hymns about him existed (and idle speculation does not create hymns). Luke himself quite clearly appears to have preserved one in which John is not only a 'prophet of the Most High' but a 'horn of salvation raised up in the house of David'.[2] He will give the 'knowledge of salvation to his people'. With this act is associated the *dayspring* ($\dot\alpha\nu\alpha\tau o\lambda\dot\eta$, sunrise)[3] which shall dawn or has dawned or visited us from on high.[4] The last verse is difficult. The sun doesn't dawn *from on high*. Some would therefore take it to refer to the *branch* which *rises*, though, while this, too, is messianic language, it does not fit well with the light-dark imagery which follows. It is just possible that the mention of one who dawns

---

[1] Mark 1.7f.; Matt. 3.11f.; Luke 3.15ff.; John 1.26ff.; etc. With reference to this expression see p. 245 n. 3.

[2] Luke 1.68ff.

[3] On parallels to this language see Test. Levi 4.3f.; Mal. 4.2. On $\dot\alpha\nu\alpha\tau o\lambda\dot\eta$ see Jer. 23.5; Zech. 3.8, and esp. Zech. 6.12, with our comments above, p. 109 n. 1 and p. 172.

[4] The future is slightly favoured by the texts, and it is easier to see the future being changed to the past. Compare Mal. 4.2.

like the rising eastern sun but who yet appears in the heights of heaven results from phraseology which is ultimately related to that employed elsewhere of kings and first men. In any case, it does seem to confirm the messianic-type speculation concerning John, which is further alluded to by 'to give light to those who sit in darkness and the shadow of death'. (See the oracles concerning the royal *child* in Isa. 9.2 and the Servant in Isa. 42.6f.)

More important yet, however, is the realization that we have preserved for us only one baptism which John is said to have performed, that of Jesus. Now, obviously this is a special case subject to all forms of later Christian interpretation. None the less it is the only one we have, and it is far from impossible that Jesus' baptism was, in rough outline anyway, conducted in this manner. Later tradition could have built upon this just as much as it transformed it. And this baptism reads very much like a kind of ordination to divine office. Certainly there are, as we shall see, indications that John believed 'the coming one' would appear in connection with his baptism.

Admittedly, however, this is all another form of negative evidence. It certainly does not prove that John the Baptist was a leader of the manner of sect which we are proposing, one that combined belief in a royal Man with baptism conceived of as an ordination or exaltation to association with or to the office of this Man. Yet, at the same time, it should serve to remind us of how much regarding John's ministry is hidden from us.[1] In the absence of further evidence and as these other factors are taken into consideration, we cannot simply assume that John's baptism and preaching involved little more than an unadorned, uncomplicated concern with the remission of sins.

5. REMAINING PROBLEMS

We may now return to the problems which must still be faced before we can claim the likelihood that Jesus and the Gospels' Son of Man are related to this context of baptizing sectarianism. They are three in number.

(*1*) We may well have shown that this sectarian *milieu* was much concerned with the Man in one way or another, but we have not

---

[1] One might create an analogy: in popular report Martin Luther is famed for wanting to reform the practice of indulgences and for *faith alone*. We hear little or nothing about his important beliefs concerning, say, the Mass and Confession. In the case of John the Baptist just about all we have is a little popular report.

found that the specific expression *the Son of Man* was used for such a figure in this same particular *milieu*. It can be held with some cogency that the occurrences of the specific phrase in later gnostic-type sects are, at least predominantly, the result of Christian influence. In addition, its presence in the texts of I Enoch and Daniel offers us only an eschatological champion in heavenly glory, and, in any case, there are no definite reasons for believing that either of these works were involved with a baptizing sectarianism.

In one sense we have no answer to this criticism. From the information available to us, we can hardly insist that there did exist a pre-Christian baptizing sect (or sects) which described or styled its Man hero specifically as the Son of Man and saw him as something more than a distant heavenly champion. If this is to be the criterion, then our theories must fall to the ground.

Yet, is it all that unlikely that such could have been the case? We have tried to show that during a long period of time there did exist a frame of reference in which the royal champion, the special Man (as king on earth or in heaven), could be regarded as the *son* of the Man. While this may not have been an official title for the king-Man (who was in a very important sense, the descendant and representative of *Adam*), it was at least a description or a way of referring to him. We also know that the phrase was to some degree current coin during the period with which we are here concerned. As far as our records go, this was confined to an eschatological usage, but, given the context of these baptismal sects and their varied Adamite beliefs and speculations, and given the possibility that Jesus himself used the term in more than one sense, does it not become feasible that the expression could have regained something of its older nuances and associations and been so employed by one or more of these groups? In any of several ways (*bar nāšā, ben 'ādām, bar 'ādām*, etc., or perhaps more definitively) the phrase could have been used as the means, or one of the means, for indicating the Man figure. Surely this much is both credible and possible. It is supposition, of course, but in the light of the nature of our evidence and in the conviction that we can make good sense of the Gospels' use of the term against such a background, we regard it as a legitimate supposition. In the end we hope to make it seem a likely supposition.

(2) Jesus is presented as sometimes speaking as though he had become or were representative of the Son of Man *on earth*, one with some kind of a mission to accomplish as an earthly figure. We know

of speculation about the First Man king on earth and about the glorious Man in heaven, but Jesus (as in so many of the kingship ideologies and the gnostic myths) speaks both of a figure in heaven and yet as though the Son of Man were now present on earth. In addition, the ancient myth of the Man was not concerned with the idea of incarnation. Its emphasis and purpose have not to tell of a Son of Man who in some way came down to earth, but rather of the one below who was exalted to *become* the Man above and to act for or as him.[1] This emphasis is clear in a work like I Enoch and was certainly true of the kingship mythologies and rituals. Unless we are to

[1] And it is this emphasis which we hold to be one of the main distinctions between the earlier, more *primitive*, Semitic forms of the myth and the later interpretations of it, while the failure to recognize the distinction has been the cause of previous misunderstandings with regard to the relationship between Christian beginnings and such ideas as that of the *Saved Saviour*. Like the more Semitic forms of the legend, Christianity *began* with a concentration on *adoption* and exaltation to heaven and not with any genuine interest in a divinity who would descend from heaven to earth to live as a man. See the earlier discussion of this matter in ch. II, p. 71, and also below, esp. on Phil. 2.6ff. Of course, we, too, would insist that later gnostic myths were intimately related to the earlier stories of the Man-king, and we have previously recognized the king as one who suffers for himself and others before he can be saved. He is in this sense truly a *Saved Saviour* (though only to a lesser degree a *Redeemed Redeemer*). Yet the distinction is vital. Gnosticism, in a very important way, *misunderstood* the earlier myth. With its emphasis on the revelation of divine secrets (derived from the idea that heavenly secrets were revealed to the king who was descended from Adam) and esp. with its belief that the Man had come down from heaven, it altered the whole force of the earlier legends. Admittedly the king-god of old was seen as doing his suffering *below*, but our point is that the ancient myth was not interested in the idea of descent. Earlier societies did not rejoice because the divinity had come to dwell with men; they were only concerned with getting him up *above*, enthroned again. Admittedly also, there is a way in which the mortal who was exalted above had to come back down to earth in order to be the king of the earthly paradise, etc., since this is where he *really* was. Yet the old myth was not interested in this aspect of things as such either. But most later interpreters (perhaps partly influenced by the nascent Christian belief that Jesus must have pre-existed as a divinity in heaven) were obviously not tolerant of the idea of a 'man become a god in heaven while yet he was really on earth', of the conception of one who while a human on earth could represent the heavenly divinity and possess many of his attributes. (It is interesting to see this difference in outlook as one of the sources of later disagreement between Antiochene and Alexandrine Christologies.)

Similarly, although the material for the *soul myth* lay ready to hand in Semitic myths about the one who ascends, gnosticism very much transformed these materials with its willingness to dissociate body and *mind* or *soul*.

Lastly, it is our understanding of the primitive form of the myth which again prevents us from believing that the Man legend originally had anything much to do with the *Logos* and *Wisdom* conceptions, for their focus, too, is on a descent from heaven to earth, on an essentially ontological rather than functional Christology. See further in ch. VII.

resort to some theory which would regard Jesus simply as the Son of Man *designate*, for which there is little support either in the background or in the Gospels, we have seemingly reached an impasse.

Yet the answer to this apparent conundrum is so simple as almost to be overlooked. Distinct from what was said to happen in both ancient and contemporary myth and ritual, what, in fact, did happen? Was the individual really drawn up to heaven, there to reign upon a throne like God's? Without subtracting one iota from the claims we have made for cultic reality, there is an obvious sense in which the answer to this question is 'No'. The human subject in the ritual was said to have gone up into heaven; he was ordained and invested; he *became* (or became the representative copy of) the Man in heaven; he was given his attributes and authority. Yet, *in fact*, he remained on earth. Though he had been appointed to the office of the Son of Man, any activity and rule he was now to perform in that name would have to be acted out in this life on earth. We have striven repeatedly to show how and why the ancient myth and ritual were quite tolerant of these two forms of reality.

Doubtless at first glance this explanation might seem too clever by far, but we think that it only looks clever to our eyes. After all, even the minds of sophisticated modern Christians are open to a measure of such a dual sense of reality. Christians speak of already participating in the resurrection life with Jesus, of having risen with him to the realms above, of being joined with the saints. Yet at the same time Christians certainly recognize themselves as citizens of two worlds.

An objection may be raised: in the older rituals it was at least usual that suffering preceded exaltation and enthronement.[1] Jesus seems to speak of himself as the Son of Man who has yet his suffering to undergo. Although the Gospels do not perhaps now require a relationship between the two, it is still only after Jesus' sufferings that the Son of Man will appear in glory. This, then, is strange; if he is already the Son of Man and, if appointment to that exalted office follows suffering, why must he still suffer in the future?

The answer is again to be sought in the interaction of myth and

[1] We have noted that there may have been versions of the myth which suggested that the hero was, at least in some measure, given his royal powers (or that these powers *revived* in him) before or in the midst of his struggle. This aspect of things, however, should likely not be used to explain Jesus' sense of being the Son of Man before his actual sufferings, since the sayings indicate that the Son of Man will at first be powerless against his enemies.

history. In one order of *reality*, in the context of legend or his baptism, Jesus would have already *suffered* and been made the Son of Man; in the real world, in the attempt to apply the meaning of the myth to his own actual circumstances, that suffering must still be yet to come. If you will, this involves a certain disordering or rearrangement of the myth[1] as it is pressed into the service of interpreting life. It is as though things must happen twice, once on each level of reality.

Again, however, we have a useful analogy (and ultimately, of course, the correspondences between Christian analogies and Jesus' life and the myth he used are no mere accident). The Christian has already died; he is already buried with Christ. There is a sense in which this experience is very real (he might already say he is *dead* to this world), and yet there is a very real death still to come before the Christian can really go to heaven.

Jesus, then, on the level of myth and cultic reality, had already become the Son of Man. His *ordination* had already taken place. Yet on this historical plane, on the level at which the myth had to be lived, the suffering (which *must* come) still awaits the Son of Man.

(*3*) Yet this question of suffering in relation to the Son of Man raises more obdurate problems. We have seen that the suffering of the Man is fully indigenous to a whole range of versions of the story about him both before and after the time of Jesus. In a very significant sense, the Man *must* suffer before he can attain to his true status and glory. Yet within the more specific context of the more normative Judaism of this period, this aspect of the story, this phase in the Man's *life*, seems almost to have atrophied through disinterest. Traces of his association with a struggle and suffering are to be found in I Enoch, II (4) Esdras, Daniel, Testament of Levi, etc. as we have indicated, but these are only traces.

---

[1] It is probably also true that the heightened eschatology operative elsewhere in this period acted as a disordering factor. Its emphasis on the appearance of the Man at the end of time would, as it were, lengthen the duration of the myth (the Man could not yet appear in heaven until the final historic day) and tend to disassociate to a degree the one who was acting now as the Man from the conception of the glorified Man as he would one day be seen in heaven. Some might regard this disordering or complicating aspect as a result of the effects of later eschatological forces within Christianity. This may in part be true, but there is no good reason for doubting that Jesus also conceived of the appearance of the Son of Man of glory in eschatological terms and that the *complications* were as much his to deal with as they were those of the later community. We shall return to these matters in ch. VIII.

Yet there is a satisfactory answer to this question, too, and it lies in the context which we have been examining, in those circumstances in which ideas from the older kingship ideologies seem to have come together and reinvigorated one another again. In these last four chapters we have endeavoured to show how iterative is the conception of the king-Man *suffering* in the water. Originally we held this to be derived from the ancient mythic picture of the Man struggling with the forces of chaos and the water monster. By them he is defeated; yet it is from this same water that he arises revived, *born* and cleansed to ascend to his kingship. Sometimes only an aspect of this survives, often just the idea of the Man born from the water to be like his counterpart or image in heaven. Yet at other times, and we have indicated a good many of these (in several gnostic forms and brief relics, especially those of the Naassenes, in the Odes of Solomon, perhaps in II [4] Esdras and the Qumran hymns, perhaps in the conception of Adam doing penance in the waters, in Mandaeanism, Mithraism and Manichaeanism), the older idea continues. We ourselves little doubt that the Christian understanding, so quick to make its appearance,[1] of baptism as both a suffering with Christ (a descent into the underworld) and a means of new birth is itself a version, a variation on this theme.

We are therefore suggesting that the idea of the suffering of the Man was first grasped by Jesus in the context of this baptizing sectarianism. Probably it was a conception as much liturgical or liturgical-mythical as anything else. Perhaps only one or two of these groups would have actually practised the idea; perhaps they taught rather than enacted it, but we believe that the idea was present and that this stands as one of the links between kingship practice and versions of that ideology which we find in later religious forms. Here is the contemporary basis for the realization that the Man must suffer before salvation and glory can come, the realization which Jesus put to service in historical circumstances.

Once Christianity moved away from such a setting and context, once it understandably and rightly began to concentrate on the actual life and death of Jesus, the older form of the idea, as such, would naturally drop out of sight. It would not be surprising if it had been so reinterpreted or misunderstood as to disappear entirely from the traditions. Perhaps what is surprising is that there are still traces of it remaining, both, as we shall attempt to indicate, in the language

[1] See below on Rom. 6.3ff., etc.

of certain of the Son of Man logia and in sayings like Luke 12.50 and
Mark 10.38.

I have a baptism to be baptized with; and how I am constrained until it is
accomplished!

Are you able to drink the cup that I drink, or to be baptized with the
baptism with which I am baptized?

VI

PAUL'S SECOND MAN

Thus it is written, 'The first Man Adam became a living being'; the last Adam became a life-giving spirit. (*I Cor. 15.45*)

I. ACTS, HEBREWS AND REVELATION

BEFORE UNDERTAKING A consideration of the teachings of the first known Christian author, in so far as they relate to our subject and display a relevance to the background we have studied, it is of importance that we should look at several other passages in the New Testament where the influence of the Man or Son of Man may be present. Others have professed to see in these passages signs of a rather widespread and continuing interest in a Son of Man Christology. We, on the other hand, confess from the outset that our impression has always been precisely the opposite. While it *may* be possible to make out a case for an early but now hidden stage in the life of the post-resurrection community at which a profound and transforming interest in Jesus as the Son of Man flourished, we find it exceedingly difficult to believe that this interest had any vogue during the period in which the New Testament was composed.

We ourselves may be asked how it could be that an idea which so affected Jesus' beliefs would have faded so quickly into the background. Our answer lies in the awareness that the baptizing sectarian movement existed on the fringes of the mainstream of Judaism, and, apparently, the *northern* and *eastern* fringes at that. The Church took many of its first real roots in Jerusalem, while the New Testament itself is almost exclusively a record of the *western* thought of the Christian communities. Separated both geographically and in terms of thought patterns from the Jordanian and upper Palestinian *milieu* of this movement, the Church not only lost the terms of reference which made the Son of Man a particularly meaningful designation, but it was forced to find more convenient and useful categories in which to express its faith and Christology.[1]

The one apparent exception to this uniform impression is in the scene of Stephen's martyrdom at Acts 7.56. Indeed, the exception is so exceptional that it has always stood out in bold relief and caused a number of attempts to explain it as an indication of the Christology of the early Church. Yet here alone, in the whole of the New Testament, do we find this identical expression being used without direct reference to Jesus' reported words. One feels that something ought to be done with the passage, while the reference is so isolated and enigmatic, the context so sparse, that any firm conclusions are hard to come by.

Stephen, having just finished his speech before the Jewish council, with their wrath about to be vented upon him, becomes full of the Holy Spirit. He

gazed into heaven and saw the glory of God, and Jesus standing at the right hand of God; and he said, 'Behold, I see the heavens opened, and the Son of Man standing at the right hand of God.'[2]

One might adopt one of at least three views with regard to the

---

[1] There is a measure of parallelism here with the views of E. Lohmeyer, e.g. *Galiläa und Jerusalem* (FRLANT 52, nf 34), 1936, pp. 68ff. The attempt to denigrate such a viewpoint (see Hahn, *Hoheitstitel*, pp. 11f.) and to insist that the Palestinian traditions be treated as a unity seems better to serve the academic division between Palestinian and Hellenistic traditions than it does the needs of historical research. Would a Galilean and a Jerusalemite have thought and worshipped in the same terms? Despite our lack of knowledge, we must use what evidence we have.

[2] G. D. Kilpatrick's suggestion that 'Son of Man' may not have been original to this text seems most unlikely ('Acts 7.56: Son of Man?' *TZ* 21, 1965, p. 209). Various attempts have been made to explain the anomalous fact that the Son of Man is here represented as standing. (On this and matters discussed below, cf. C. K. Barrett, 'Stephen and the Son of Man' in *Apophoreta* (ed. W. Eltester), Berlin, 1964, pp. 32ff.) It is held that he is welcoming Stephen to heaven and/or acting as his intercessor before God, thus fulfilling Jesus' promise that the Son of Man would intercede. Cf. Luke 12.8f. On Jesus as witness or champion here, see Cullmann, *Christology*, pp. 159f., 183. Perhaps Jesus, the Son of Man, is being pictured more as an attendant angel than as messianic regent. Otherwise it is said that he is preparing to come for judgment, and this also is why the heavens are opened. Cf. H. P. Owen, 'Stephen's Vision in Acts 7.55–6', *NTS* 1, 1954/5, pp. 224ff. Yet the opening of the heavens is often a sign of revelation, and there is no indication that judgment did ensue. By making no reference to Jesus' *coming* the passage might seem typically Lucan in its effort to tone down rather than heighten eschatology. (See Luke 22.69 with its parr.) In other words, we feel that this feature must remain a puzzle. While some see it as an indication that Luke is using tradition, others regard it as a demonstration of Luke's propensity to create such a scene.

historicity of this passage. (*1*) Luke is using and quoting early Church tradition.[1] (*2*) Luke is creating the scene, but basing himself on a correct awareness that some in the early Church, perhaps Stephen and others who were like-minded, did worship Jesus as the Son of Man. In either of these eventualities it becomes conceivable that, for at least a little time after his death, Jesus was both identified with the Son of Man and reverenced as such. It then becomes possible for Cullmann to speculate about the *Hellenists* in the early Church and their possible influence on the Fourth Gospel and Hebrews, and for W. Manson (on this and other grounds) to believe that there is a direct connection between the theology of Stephen and that of the Epistle to the Hebrews. Yet neither of these theories can really provide us with any further information about the use of the Son of Man here or elsewhere; nor do they seem satisfactorily to relate the materials to which they point.[2]

While it remains possible that Stephen's exclamation reflects some attitude in the early Church, there is almost nothing else we can say about it. If it is going to be argued that Luke is in this a knowledge-able witness to one tradition in the Church,[3] then everything else he

[1] The word *heavens* (in v. 56 and as opposed to *heaven* in v. 55) is sometimes regarded as a Semitism and proof of an Aramaic origin for this statement. Yet many feel that Luke is perfectly capable of creating *Semitisms* (or Septuagintisms), and *heavens* may only indicate that Luke is being deliberately *archaic*. In any event, see Luke 12.33 (with Matt. 6.20) and Acts 2.34. Is *heavens* a non-Lucan word?

[2] See Manson, *Epistle to the Hebrews*, London, 1951, pp. 30f., 95, 98f. (and below on Hebrews), and Cullmann, *op. cit.*, pp. 181ff. Much of Cullmann's thesis depends on the strain of opposition to the temple which seems a common factor. Yet (as R. H. Fuller points out in *The New Testament Current Study*, New York, 1962, pp. 127f.) Stephen's attitude is somewhat different from and far more virulent than Qumran or John (and Hebrews, too, for that matter; and what of other groups which had this attitude?). Fuller also rightly asks whether it is possible to see these *Hellenists* as nonconformist Palestinian Jews in the light of our other information about them. One can further ask how far we are able to go with the evidence Luke gives us about Stephen and his *group*. How would we fare if forced to reconstruct Pauline theology solely on the basis of his speeches in Acts?

[3] If Luke is such a witness, it may be instructive to note that the Christology which he reports is basically adoptionist. Peter speaks of 'the Christ appointed for you, Jesus'. Acts 3.20. He is 'a man attested to you by God with mighty works and wonders and signs'. Acts 2.22. (Note that while Jesus is several times called 'a man' or 'this man' in Acts, usually ἀνήρ but once ἄνθρωπος, so are a number of others, and there is no indication that Luke or anyone else was thinking in terms of the Man or interpreting or misunderstanding any idiom.) This Jesus 'God raised up (Acts 2.24) . . . exalted at the right hand of God (2.33; no mention of the Son of Man here!) . . . (and) God has made him both Lord and Christ' (2.36). 'He is the one ordained by God' (10.42). Even Paul is made to speak of Jesus as 'a man whom God has appointed' (17.31).

tells us would seem to point to the conclusion that this was a minority way of speaking which quickly dropped out of use. In any case (as with the two passages in Revelation), it would at best only be evidence that some saw Jesus as the heavenly Son of Man, not that they were creating other kinds of sayings about Jesus as the Son of Man on earth.[1]

(3) The third possibility is that Luke himself created these words in an effort, as perhaps elsewhere in Acts, to lend a certain tone of primitiveness to his history. The reference to the Son of Man would then be a conscious archaism. Yet one still needs a motive even for an archaism, and at first sight providing a reason for such might prove difficult, but not after a little reflection. It seems fairly obvious that Luke is modelling Stephen's martyrdom on that of Jesus. Not only is he tried and condemned by the Sanhedrin, put to death outside the city, said to commit his spirit to Jesus (here in place of God), but he also cries out with a loud voice and prays for the forgiveness of his persecutors. Now, when Jesus was on trial he also made reference to the Son of Man being with God in heaven. It is thus quite conceivable that Luke is (while perhaps himself not understanding what Jesus meant) placing these words in Stephen's mouth in order to continue the parallel.[2] Some support for this interpretation may be supplied by the fact that when Luke creates a saying for his angel at the time of the resurrection (Luke 24.7) he does so quite deliberately and archaically (from his own point of view) in terms of a Son of Man saying. To our way of thinking this could well imply, and quite significantly imply, that the only thing which Luke really knew about this designation was that it belonged to the earlier traditions. Of these three explanations we therefore incline toward the third.[3]

[1] So Tödt (*Son of Man*, pp. 303ff.) rightly makes no attempt to use such a support for his theory (though his motivation may be the fact that it does not fit well with his ideas about the nature of the most primitive eschatological sayings). Higgins, however (*Son of Man*, pp. 143ff.), finds Acts 7.56 to be proof of a living Christology, while one might have thought that his strictures against others who have tried to build on this passage would have led him to be more cautious.

[2] Acts 7.56 is not a quotation of Luke 22.69 (in some ways it is closer to Mark 14.62), but there is no reason to believe that Luke would have found this necessary. The echo would have been quite sufficient. Thus compare Acts 7.60 with Luke 23.34.

The possibility that the Son of Man here appears as witness and champion might also be a further sign of Lucan influence, since Luke may be inclined, as we shall see, to stress or develop this aspect in authentic sayings.

[3] Before leaving Acts we may notice two references which Peter is said to have made to the anointing of Jesus. The first instance (4.27) follows a mention of the

Some scholars find evidence for a continuing Son of Man Christology in the Epistle to the Hebrews. This opinion is based entirely
upon the quotation of Ps. 8.4–6 in Heb. 2.6–8. While we might agree
that Hebrews could here be reflecting something of the primitive Son
of Man idea, it is very much a question of what is meant by this.[1] To

---

Anointed in a quotation of Ps. 2.2 and may only echo the idea that Jesus was the
Christ. Yet we might well inquire as to when Peter thought that the anointing of
Jesus took place, since we do not hear of it in the Gospels. Here, however, we are
not told, and one might argue that it is a general reference to the time of his
ascension (although Peter does seem to say that Pilate and Herod acted against
Jesus after he was already anointed). Acts 10.38 is more specific. Peter tells
Cornelius and his friends how the word was proclaimed, beginning in Galilee with
the baptism which John preached, and of 'how God anointed Jesus of Nazareth
with the Holy Spirit and with power'. This seems a reference to Jesus' baptism,
and, if so, we are at least entitled to wonder if there was not some tradition which
told of Jesus being anointed at his baptism (and perhaps *ordained* to a sacral office?).
See our comments in chs. VII and VIII on the baptism of Jesus.

We may also be interested in some of the Old Testament quotations which are
said to have been used by the primitive Church. Among such are Pss. 2.1f.; 2.7;
110.1, quoted in Acts 2.34; 4.45f.; 13.33. Note how in 2.34 it is said that David
did not ascend into the heavens. Is this only a contrast with Jesus' ascension, or
might it rely in part upon the older belief that the king should ascend out of Sheol
to the right hand of God? Particular interest might accrue to Ps. 16.10 with its
reference to being preserved from Sheol and corruption, which is quoted twice,
once in close connection with Ps. 2.7 (Acts 2.27; 13.35). Now, it is natural enough
to hold that it was the early Church which collated quotations like these, and one
can certainly see why they would have been chosen. Yet perhaps this is too easy an
assumption on our part. Might not at least some of them stem instead from an
earlier usage, being the materials which the tradition gave to the Church rather
than *vice versa*? In the case of Pss. 2.7 and 110.1 there is cause for believing that this
was so. On Ps. 2.7 see Mark 1.11; 9.7 (and parr.) and in our ch. VIII on the baptism
and transfiguration. On Ps. 110.1 see Mark 12.36; 14.62 (and parr.) and in ch.
VIII. Both quotations were used by the Church in other contexts. On this see
below and also with regard to the use of the Old Testament in the passion narratives.

[1] Although the fundamental materials for the Christology of Hebrews are not
specifically related to the Son of Man, they are intriguing. Among the texts collated
are Pss. 2.7; 45.6f.; 110.1 and II Sam. 7.14 (Heb. 1.5ff.; on Ps. 110.1 cf. also Heb.
10.12f.). The author speaks of the Son as the Firstborn whom the angels worship
(Heb. 1.6; cf. p. 370 n. 2). He then uses Ps. 2.7 for a second time and links
it with Ps. 110.4 (Heb. 5.5f.). In addition, though the author maintains Jesus'
pre-existence, more fundamental are ideas regarding his *adoption*, esp. to the
office of heavenly high-priest. (See Heb. 5.5, 10; 6.20; 8.6. This adoptionism is not
absent in Heb. 1.1ff.) It is at least conceivable that the author is in part basing
himself on materials nearer to the primitive traditions than we now realize, and so
in his use of Ps. 8.4ff. as well. (The date and provenance of the epistle are uncertain;
some hold for an early authorship and would make a link with the Essenes, etc.)
Once again these may be materials which were passed on to the Church (so explaining how diverse Christologies could have been affected by the same quotations) rather than the other way around. Alternatively, and more probably, the

claim that this shows the author to be 'quite familiar' with a Son of Man Christology, and that this is essentially the 'same conception as in Stephen's vision', while yet representing a 'considerable advance on it',[1] not only goes beyond the evidence altogether, but may even contradict it.

In the first place, if the writer was in touch with any living Son of Man Christology, we very much have a right to ask why he only makes one passing reference to Son of Man, and that not by echoing anything preserved in the Gospel materials, but by quoting a psalm in the midst of a catena of Old Testament quotations, and by using the expression without the article, just like the Septuagint, but unlike the traditions represented by the Gospels. Secondly, while the author naturally goes on to apply Ps. 8.5 to Jesus as now crowned with glory and honour, it would seem quite obvious that he is doing so on the basis of his own typology. In fact, he first refers the quotation not to Jesus but to natural man (v. 8b), to whom he then contrasts Jesus in verse 9. One would have thought, were the author inspired by a living Son of Man Christology, that a more direct identification of Jesus and the Son of Man would have taken the place of such an exegesis. Thirdly, to say that this represents an advance on Stephen's vision implies a great deal more than we know about Stephen's brief

---

author may be preserving materials emanating from groups which used ideas somewhat parallel to those which Jesus may have known. Behind Hebrews' Christology there may lie earlier forms in which a number of these texts were used to describe a man becoming exalted and appointed to the office of the eternal royal priest, in this case like unto Melchizedek.

There was at one time more speculation by Jews, Jewish-Christians and gnostics concerning Melchizedek than is now evident. Cf., e.g., the fragment printed by R. H. Charles as an appendix in *The Book of the Secrets of Enoch*, Oxford, 1896. Philo gives him an exalted place (cf. *Allegorical Interpretation* III, 79ff.) and describes the *Logos* as a high-priest, of whom Melchizedek was a primary type. Both Epiphanius (*Panarion* LV, 5; LXVII, 3, 7) and Hippolytus (*Refutation* VII, 36) condemn 'Melchizedekians' who taught that Melchizedek was a *power* of God, that the Christ was according to the likeness of Melchizedek and that Jesus was a man on whom the Christ descended. There were other Melchizedekian heresies condemned by the Fathers as well as signs that Melchizedek was linked with Elijah, Adam, the Man and other such figures. Cf. Cullmann, *Christology*, pp. 84ff.; Käsemann, *wandernde Gottesvolk*, p. 130. This could be linked with traditions like that concerning the Adamite high-priest in Test. Levi. See also Rev. 1.13. We agree, however, with Hahn (*Hoheitstitel*, pp. 231ff.) and against G. Friedrich ('Beobachtungen zur messianischen Hohepriestererwartung in den Synoptikern', *ZTK* 53, 1956, pp. 265ff.) that belief in a high-priestly Messiah, as such, does not seem part of the earliest traditions about Jesus.

[1] Higgins, *Son of Man*, pp. 146f.

exclamation on a number of counts. But if we also assume that Acts 7.56 is essentially a reference to the exaltation of Jesus as the Son of Man, we can only conclude that Hebrews represents a *considerable* advance on Stephen's Christology, for Hebrews uses the Psalm as much to describe the incarnation as the exaltation. This indeed is excellent theology, but how it is to be related to Stephen's vision can hardly be ascertained. Thus there is little enough reason in this passage and none anywhere else in the Epistle which would be a cause for believing that the author was inclined to worship Jesus as the Son of Man.

Twice in the Revelation we come across the expression 'one like a Son of Man' (ὅμοιον υἱὸν ἀνθρώπου).[1]

1.13. . . . and in the midst of the lampstands one like a Son of Man, clothed with a long robe and with a golden girdle round his breast; 14 his head and hair were white as white wool, white as snow; his eyes were like a flame of fire, 15 his feet were like burnished bronze, refined as in a furnace, and his voice was like the sound of many waters; 16 in his right hand he held seven stars, from his mouth issued a sharp two-edged sword, and his face was like the sun shining in full strength.

14.14. Then I looked, and lo, a white cloud, and seated on the cloud one like a Son of Man, with a golden crown on his head, and a sharp sickle in his hand. 15 And another angel came out of the temple calling with a loud voice to him who sat upon the cloud, 'Put in your sickle and reap, for the hour to reap has come.'

In the first passage it is evident that it must be the exalted Jesus who is being described, while in the second this is far from clear. There we might quite possibly have a vision of some angel of wrath, in which event the attempt to equate these verses with the Gospels' traditions about the Son of Man would probably collapse entirely. Yet it can easily be argued that consistency demands (if consistency is a criterion in the Revelation) that Jesus is the subject of both visions.

Higgins rightly refers these descriptions to their obvious background with relation to Dan. 7. Again rightly, he notes Mowinckel's conclusion that Revelation is here, as elsewhere, following in the

---

[1] A number of texts at 1.13 have υἱῷ, which is likely an attempted grammatical correction, though it could be argued that υἱὸν is an alteration to conform with the phrase in 14.14. In the latter event there is even less similarity with the description in 14.14.

tradition of Jewish apocalyptic.[1] He then, however, goes on to remind us of Torrey's opinion that 'like a Son of Man' here is a faithful reproduction of the Aramaic,[2] and ends by suggesting a connection with the Son of Man in the Fourth Gospel and in Stephen's vision. So, Higgins argues, Revelation offers further 'proof of a living Christology' having to do with the Son of Man.[3]

Let us take up these matters. Of course, Revelation is here dependent upon Jewish apocalyptic tradition, perhaps especially Daniel and possibly I Enoch as well. (Indeed, the author seems to have combined and probably confused several older conceptions in these descriptions.)[4] This is obvious. What is not at all obvious, and perhaps not very likely, is that these references are dependent upon the Gospel materials in any way, much less that they relate to the Fourth Gospel or Acts 7.56. Certainly Mowinckel avoids any such inference and notes only that the Revelation may be 'used as a source for the late Jewish conception of the Son of Man'.[5] Indeed, the descriptions have so much to do with Daniel, and other Old Testament passages, and so little to do with the Gospel pictures (except perhaps for the *cloud*,[6] which feature, however, is found in other earlier descriptions of the heavenly Son of Man as well) that one wonders what can be the basis of comparison.

Is it to be 'like a Son of Man'? But surely one must then wonder why a quasi-description much more akin to Daniel's phrase (ὡς υἱὸς ἀνθρώπου in the LXX) is employed in lieu of the Gospel's title. The reference to Torrey's opinion (and it must be remembered that Torrey saw Aramaisms throughout the work in arguing for an Aramaic original) only raises questions which are not answered. Is Higgins inferring that it is this phrase which underlies the Gospel sayings and that this then demonstrates the connection with primitive materials? If so, it is a pretty grand inference, and one must ask all over again why none of the Gospels ever hint at such a rendering.[7]

---

[1] *HTC*, pp. 357f.

[2] C. C. Torrey, *The Apocalypse of John*, New Haven, 1958, p. 96.

[3] *Son of Man*, pp. 147f.

[4] See Ezek. 1.7, 24, 27, the description of both 'one like a Son of Man' and the Ancient of Days in Dan. 7 and the *man* figure in Dan. 10.5f. Perhaps the seer has taken over this composite vision, itself composed (with its solar and creation imagery) from earlier materials, and applied it to Jesus. As such it could be evidence for another line of speculation about such a figure.

[5] *HTC*, p. 358.

[6] See also Rev. 1.7.

[7] John 5.27 *might* be considered such a hint, but see our comments, pp. 293f.

Perhaps Higgins could have gone on to argue that the apocalyptic Christ of the Revelation plays the same role as the apocalyptic Son of Man in the Gospels, especially as he is found in a logion like Mark 13.26f. But this would beg the same fundamental question: why, if he knew this tradition, does the author not use the form of the Gospels' title? And even if he did know it, but in some *more Aramaic* fashion, and if 1.13 and 14.14 are reflecting this, why is there so little else in common? Lastly, why does he use the phrase so sparingly if he is interested in a Son of Man Christology?

In point of fact, the apocalyptic Christ of the Revelation shares his apocalyptic features in common with many Jewish eschatological heroes. Any attempt to link these features directly to the Gospel materials, either in general terms or with particular reference to the Son of Man, would seem to involve a gross neglect of the whole Jewish background against which the Seer is operating.

In our opinion, therefore, Rev. 1.13 and 14.14 must be regarded as aspects of the Jewish apocalyptic machinery of the entire work. Taken in this way (along with the references to the tree of life and the water, river and fountain of life from which Jesus feeds his followers[1] and the battle against the dragon) they are further corroboration of much that was said in chapter IV with regard to the source of apocalyptic materials. Quite remarkably, then, these verses seem to by-pass the Gospels' traditions about the Son of Man entirely. (Certainly if Jesus and the Son of Man were never related elsewhere, we would yet have no trouble accounting for these visions in Revelation.) If the Seer knew of them it would appear that they meant little or nothing to him.[2]

2. PAUL

It seems possible to argue that the use of terms like 'one man', 'the last Adam', 'the man' and 'the second man' in Paul's letters have nothing or almost nothing to do with the materials which we have discussed in earlier chapters.[3] If this be so, we would remain content,

---

[1] Rev. 2.7; 21.5; 22.1, 2, 14, 19.

[2] Higgins's view (*Son of Man*, pp. 44, 152) that I Tim. 2.5f. is another indication of a persisting Son of Man or Man faith seems improbable. Ἄνθρωπος is used anarthrously and was probably suggested by the preceding word ἀνθρώπους, perhaps to show why Jesus could be a mediator between God and men. (So cf. Job 9.32 in the LXX, for which suggestion I thank Prof. A. Hanson.) If, as Higgins also argues, the wording is dependent on a version of Mark 10.45, it would only go to show the degree to which the Son of Man title had dropped from usage.

[3] So Fuller, *Foundations*, p. 233.

for it would only go further to demonstrate our belief that the basic Son of Man traditions are not the work of the Church. Certainly, in any case, we would agree that there are no reasons for believing that Paul, either directly or indirectly, has helped to create any of the Gospels' Son of Man sayings.

Many scholars, however, and we would agree with them, believe that Paul's use of such terminology is, in one way or another, related to the same (or very similar) materials which lie behind the Gospels' use of the expression. Rather than completely neglecting the primitive teaching on this subject, Paul has picked it up and refashioned it for his own purposes.

These last words we take seriously. We do not argue that Paul has merely taken over primitive materials, Christian or otherwise. Everything for him has been transformed by the resurrection and the new life which he has found in Christ. We do, however, contend once more that the new seems to have been made out of the old.

It is apparent, in the first place, that Paul was a linguist of some merit. We have already pointed out that the phrase 'the Son of Man' was as much a barbarism in Greek as it is in English. Taken out of its Semitic context it would cease to have the same meaning. The logical translation for an evangelist wishing to communicate directly with Hellenists would be ὁ ἄνθρωπος, the Man. This does not mean that we agree with those who regard this as a univocal and fully adequate translation. While this was unquestionably the essential meaning of the Semitic phrase (Hebrew and Aramaic), there is never any such thing as a direct translation. 'The Son of Man' has these nuances of heirship, suggestions of the idea of relationship and being a counterpart, which 'the Man' misses. Yet, on the other hand, the expression 'the Son of Man' both in Greek as in English tends, by missing the point of the Semitic idiom, to overstress the thought of *sonship* and to understress the manner in which the Son of Man is fully representative of and can even be identified with and take the place of his archetype, the Man. In this sense neither phrase could be completely satisfactory, and Paul chose the best translation available, perhaps picking up nuances of 'the Son of . . .' with his references to the *second* Man and the *last* Adam.

Secondly, we would not necessarily confine Paul's knowledge of ideas about the Son of Man or Man to what is now found in the Gospels. If there is any accuracy in the picture set out in our chapters IV and V, we can reasonably suspect that Paul, as one of the first

Christians and as one who had travelled widely in Palestine, would have been acquainted with a variety of such speculations and beliefs. He may have found it difficult or unrewarding to pass these on to Greeks, but his own thinking could still have been affected by them.

Perhaps the most intriguing of the Pauline examples of teaching based on the Man speculations is to be found in I Cor. 15. In the midst of his discussion of resurrection, and just before picturing what the great eschatological day of resurrection will be like, Paul writes,

45 Thus it is written, 'The first Man Adam became a living being'; the last Adam became a life-giving spirit. 46 But it is not the spiritual which is first but the physical, and then the spiritual. 47 The first Man was from the earth, a Man of dust; the second Man is from heaven. 48 As was the Man of dust, so are those who are of the dust; and as is the Man of heaven, so are those who are of heaven. 49 Just as we have borne the image of the Man of dust, we shall also bear the image of the Man of heaven.

It is sometimes contended that Paul is being polemical here, that he is combating some teaching regarding the *Anthropos* which was already afoot in the young Corinthian Church.[1] Yet this view seems unnecessary and also to run counter to Paul's purpose here. If the Corinthians had been infected by some non-Christian speculation about the Man, one would surely think that Paul would have attacked it more vigorously and directly, and not merely have brought it up once or twice while illustrating other points.

Yet it does seem that Paul is carrying on a kind of argument, but we should think that the argument is with himself rather than others. He is here *converting* his own older ideas concerning the Adam-Man speculation, views which he could well have imbibed from his rabbinic background (and perhaps also from sectarian and/or primitive Christian understandings),[2] and he is making these fit his interpretation of the Christ event and its implications.[3] While there is no need to suppose that Paul was directly acquainted with Philo's teaching on the matter, it would seem that Paul's earlier instruction and understanding were quite similar: there were two Men or two

---

[1] See the discussion by Schmithals, *Gnosis in Korinth*, pp. 82ff.

[2] Another view of this passage requires that the quotation marks be run on to cover the whole of v. 45. While this is not necessary, it is possible that Paul is quoting rabbinic tradition or some lost apocryphal work. In all likelihood, then, this would be evidence of Palestinian rather than Corinthian tradition and interesting testimony to the belief (not necessarily Christian at all) that the heavenly one and/or the Messiah was expected to be like unto Adam.

[3] See Davies, *Paul and Rabbinic Judaism*, pp. 51ff.

Adams; the first was the heavenly, made after the image of God (or even existing as that image); the second was his mortal counterpart, made from the dust of the earth. Paul may even have known legends, Jewish or otherwise, which held that the first, heavenly Man would *return* at the resurrection.[1]

One can imagine that Paul might more easily have converted these ideas by simply arguing that Jesus was to be identified with the first, heavenly Man. After all, he is elsewhere quite ready to tell these same Corinthians that Christ is the image (or an image) of God.[2] Yet he likely knew of no myth which told of the actual *incarnation* of the heavenly Man, and his intention here (for he is insisting on the importance of the reality of the resurrection of Jesus) is in any case much more historical than mythical.[3] The older materials are being used rather than recited, and he thus refrains from making a point of pre-existence and concentrates on the temporal order of things. This is no longer the Man of myth but the historical Jesus Christ, who was manifested second in the order of history. He is the Man who will appear from heaven at the resurrection of the dead.

With these thoughts in mind it can be instructive to turn back to an earlier passage in I Cor. 15.

24 Then comes the end, when he delivers the kingdom to God the Father after destroying every rule and every authority and power. 25 For he must reign until he has put all enemies under his feet. 26 The last enemy to be destroyed is death. 27 'For God[4] has put all things in subjection under his feet.' But when it says, 'All things are put in subjection under him', it is plain that he is excepted who put all things under him.

What is of particular interest here is the use of the ideogram from Ps. 8.6 (a statement there predicated of the Son of Man). William Manson contended that 'If the Apostle was not thinking of Christ as the Son of Man, it would not have occurred to him to base Christ's universal sovereignty on this text.'[5] 'The title Son of Man trembles on Paul's lips,' writes A. M. Hunter[6] (which could well be, but notice also that

---

[1] See I Cor. 15.23 and Mowinckel, *HTC*, pp. 399ff., 429ff.

[2] II Cor. 4.4. See also II Cor. 3.18ff.; Rom. 8.29.

[3] See I Cor. 15.1ff., 16ff. Cullmann (*Christology*, pp. 166ff.) makes the same point, though he gives too much emphasis to Paul's polemical intentions here.

[4] The Greek has *he*, but both the sense and Ps. 8.6 indicate that God is meant. This is very likely true of the *he* who subjects all enemies in v. 25 as well.

[5] *Jesus, the Messiah*, pp. 187f. Fuller (*Foundations*, p. 233) denies this and maintains that such texts were employed too *atomistically* to permit this inference.

[6] *Paul and His Predecessors*[2], London, 1961, pp. 86f.

he does not use it). In addition we see that Paul's employment of this verse seems to be influenced by Ps. 110.1 (or perhaps one should say by the same ideas involved in Ps. 110.1), especially in its use of the word 'enemies'. Again, as in Hebrews and Acts, we might do well to reckon with the possibility that such an association as this was supplied to the Church by the primitive traditions.[1] In this case, behind this association, there could be the picture of the reigning king-Man. Otherwise it might be difficult to understand why Ps. 8.6 should be applied to the Christ in glory.

In I Cor. 15.21f. Paul writes,

> For as by a man came death, by a man has come also the resurrection of the dead. For as in Adam all die, so also in Christ shall all be made alive.

Here we have abstained from capitalizing the word *man* for, while it very likely represents another aspect of a Man pattern of thought, it appears that Paul has at this point gone even further in converting it to his own purpose. It is more like a midrash than a myth, perhaps an intentionally understressed commentary. It would be remiss, however, not to notice that he immediately then goes on to quote Ps. 8.6 and to allude to Ps. 110.1.

The likelihood that I Cor. 15.21f. uses materials from the Man legends is made more evident when we turn to the related but more extensive passage in Rom. 5.

> 12 Therefore as sin came into the world through one man and death through sin, and so death spread to all men because all men sinned . . . 14 Yet death reigned from Adam to Moses, even over those whose sins were not like the transgression of Adam, who was a type of the one to come. 15 . . . For if many died through one (man's) trespass, much more have the grace of God and the free gift in the grace of that one Man Jesus Christ abounded for many. 16 And the free gift is not like the effect of that one (man's) sin . . . 17 If, because of one (man's) trespass, death reigned through that one (man), much more will those who receive the abundance of grace and the free gift of righteousness reign in life through the one (Man) Jesus Christ.
> 18 Then as one (man's) trespass led to condemnation for all men, so one (Man's) act of righteousness leads to acquittal and life for all men. 19

---

[1] It could well be that both of these verses together (with the picture of sitting at the right hand of God with enemies as his footstool and all things subjected under his feet) have been of direct or indirect influence upon Heb. 1.3ff.; 2.6ff.; 10.12f.; Acts 2.33f.; Eph. 1.20ff.; I Peter 3.22; and see Mark 12.36; 14.62.

For as by one man's disobedience many were made sinners, so by one (Man's) obedience many will be made righteous.

We have capitalized or not capitalized *anthropos* throughout this passage in an attempt to convey our impression that Paul is here virtually playing with the Man speculation and his Christian interpretation of it. We would guess that either early Christian materials or rabbinic thought[1] or both have helped Paul to this insight and given him the inclination to use the words *Adam* and *anthropos* in this manner. Perhaps every time he wrote *anthropos* he was thinking *adam* to himself. And to our minds it is quite conceivable that when Paul speaks of Adam as the type (τύπος) of the one who was to come ('the one about to be', or 'the coming one' = τοῦ μέλλοντος) he may be echoing or giving in a slightly different form an idea from that primitive stratum of preaching in the Gospels which spoke of the expectation of 'the coming one' (ὁ ἐρχόμενος).[2] Thus the 'one to come' (that is, to make his appearance and not, at least at first, to *come* in the later Christian sense of an incarnation)[3] could, even in the earliest Christian tradition, have been regarded as a type of Adam, as were other Jewish heroes whom we have studied.

Of course, it would again be a mistake not to realize that Paul is once more putting whatever ideas he has received to use in the light of the Christ event. He thus finds it necessary to relinquish the sense of identity between the First Man and Christ and instead thinks in these typological terms. This enables him neatly to avoid the conundrum inherent in some Jewish forms of speculation. Rather than

[1] On the rabbinic background for this passage, see Davies, *Paul and Rabbinic Judaism*, pp. 36ff.

[2] See Matt. 3.11; 11.3; Luke 7.19; John 1.15, 27; 11.27. Compare Mark 1.7; Luke 3.16; John 1.11; 4.25. Note esp. the language of Matthew at 11.14: αὐτός ἐστιν Ἠλίας ὁ μέλλων ἔρχεσθαι. Cf. also John 6.14. On other *Adamite* features in the early preaching, see below in ch. VIII.

[3] Since the Gospels have understood this phrase in terms of the coming of Jesus, it is hard now to know what the expression might have implied initially. Possibly it was always rather imprecise and there were different expectations regarding it, some hoping for an appearance of 'the coming one' on earth (see Ps. 118.26 in Mark 11.9 and parr.), who may have been regarded as representative of the heavenly one, others expecting only to see him *coming* in heaven. Perhaps the phrase has reference to Dan. 7.13 and the one who *comes* (ἐρχόμενον) with the clouds. In which case Mark 13.26f. and 14.62 (with their parr., and compare Matt. 16.27; 25.31; etc.) would also be involved with this tradition. On 'the coming one' and Jesus' baptism and the associations between Elijah, John, 'the coming one' and Son of Man, cf. p. 336 n. 1 and pp. 372ff. On the expression or comparable phrases in non-Jewish contexts (esp. among the Mandaeans), see Bultmann, *Synoptic Tradition*, p. 156 n. 3.

finding it requisite to glorify the First Man and to deny his sin, Paul emphasizes that sin and its effects. While the second Man is a type of Adam, he is so in terms of contrast as much as by comparison.[1] The disobedience and pride of the old Adam are counteracted by the obedience and humility of the new Adam.[2]

This manner of typology leads on to another issue which can best be discussed at this point. Many theories have been set forth to explain the 'in Christ' *mysticism* of Paul (the manner in which he speaks of Christians as dying and having their life 'in Christ') and his metaphor of Christ as the *body* of believers. Backgrounds as diverse as the rabbinic and other teachings about Adam, Christian sacramentalism, Paul's own religious experience, the Semitic conception of *the one and the many*, stoicism, Hellenistic mysticism and mystery religions, Near Eastern mythology, Platonism and Greek socio-political ideas have all been debated. While we cannot here deal with the issue in its manifold aspects, we do believe that the materials with which we have been working can provide a genuine insight into the matter. To this end we would suggest not one single answer, but the probability that several of the answers above are closely related around the same basic centre of ideas. Believing that the Hellenistic influences can largely be discounted as unnecessary and lacking the eschatological and truly corporate features present in Paul's understanding,[3] we would give special place to the teachings about Adam, Semitic corporate conceptions and sacramentalism. (Rightly, as in any human story, Paul's own experiences should be considered as well.)[4] Of course, that which particularly attracts our interest is the realization that these categories of thought are all involved with the conception of the royal Man, and that they could well have had an immediate and proximate context, for Paul as well as for Jesus,[5] in the sectarian life of the period.

[1] One is reminded of the approach of Test. Levi 18.10ff.

[2] Yet in this sense, too, the old myth is made into history, for the type of the Man who was defeated is now victorious and raised on high in glory.

[3] See A. Schweitzer, *The Mysticism of Paul the Apostle*, ET, London, 1931, pp. 26ff. and generally for a dismissal of the Hellenistic interpretations. For the basis of Paul's thought in Jewish and Semitic categories, see again Davies, *op. cit.*, pp. 36ff., 86ff.; J. A. T. Robinson, *The Body* (SBT 5), 1952, pp. 11ff.

[4] For discussions see Robinson, *op. cit.*; Schweizer, *Lordship and Discipleship*, pp. 119ff. With regard to Paul's own experience see II Cor. 4.10f.; II Cor. 12.2ff.; Gal. 2.20 (possibly Acts 9.4f.) and passages cited below.

[5] Again it was Schweitzer (*op. cit.*, pp. 105ff.) who pointed out that the 'in Christ' *mysticism* of Paul must be related to similar themes in the Gospels. There it is more often found as *Jesus-in-us* rather than *we-in-Christ* (see Mark 9.37; Matt.

With regard to the corporate nature of the Adamite speculations and beliefs (and the ethical purposes to which these were sometimes put)[1] little more need be said here. Nor need we rehearse again the ways in which the Man was seen, in many guises, places and times, as the representative of his people, the one in whose defeat and victory the people could share.

The part that the Communion may have played in Paul's 'in Christ' thought can probably be seen in I Cor. 10.16ff. and 11.23ff. Schweitzer insisted, and was probably right to do so, that these passages can only be understood when we realize that for Paul the Communion had quasi-physical characteristics.[2] The believer really partakes of the risen life of his Lord. It is, however, not easy to be certain that this aspect of the sacred meal goes back to Jesus and to the earlier context. It is possible that here we must reckon with a development of thought, other influences and Christian experience. Yet this particular issue has so many ramifications that it is best to postpone a discussion of it until we come to the relevant Gospel materials.[3]

What we would insist upon, however, is the quite legitimate possibility that the meal derives ultimately from the conception of the Man as the provider of food for his people, he who gives to eat from the tree of life and to drink from the waters of life. More proximately the context for this, with different interpretations, can be found in the

---

10.40; 18.5f.; 25.31ff.; Luke 9.48; 10.16; John 12.26; 13.20, and, among others on this, Preiss, *Life in Christ*, pp. 44ff.), but the difference is often due to standpoint, as it is there Jesus himself who speaks. Alongside of this must be seen the theme which enunciates an intimate relationship between Jesus, the Son of Man and the disciples. (See Mark 3.31ff.; 8.35, 38; 10.38ff.; 10.44f.; Matt. 5.11f.; 10.37; 11.6; 18.20; 19.28; 20.27f.; Luke 6.22; 9.26; 12.8ff.; with other parr. The theme is consistently Johannine.) For some scholars this has always represented a *high* Christology which the 'prophet of Nazareth' could not have taught. Against the background we have studied, we suspect differently. See further in the following chapters.

[1] Cf. pp. 168f. See there on Adam as the *father* and corporate image of mankind and the one from whom the human race was made. With particular reference to the Body of Christ it has been suggested that the source was the conception of the Primordial Man seen as the cosmic giant. This, of course, is an aspect of the whole Man mythology, as we have indicated. Here, however, it is probably only operative in so far as it has been mediated through rabbinic speculations, influenced by other ideas discussed and tempered with ethical considerations. Otherwise, when the Pauline epistles speak of the pre-existent, cosmic Christ, they tend to use language borrowed from the Wisdom conception. See Col. 1.15ff.

[2] *Op. cit.*, pp. 268ff.

[3] See esp. in ch. VII, pp. 296ff.

sectarian setting where the sacred meal, often in connection with baptism[1] (and recall that the king himself first eats the revivifying food), reappears. Thus, while it is not easy to provide a known and proximate background for the idea of the eating *of* the royal Man and so participating *in* him, it is not hard to see the origins of the idea of eating *with* him and so sharing in this sense (as a profound act of *community* and fellowship) his new life and victory.

There should be less uncertainty about the role of baptism in this regard. Paul's thinking in this area is best explained as a Christianized interpretation of the older rites, or, if you will, an interpretation of the Christ event making use of these older materials.[2] The king's *baptism* could be seen as his *death*. Either this same water rite or a closely associated one was his cleansing and means to a new life. Through it he *arose* and gained his exalted status. He became or became like the one in heaven. We have seen how these ideas (which obviously had a great hold on men's imaginations) influenced a number of later practices, variant though they were. In the ancient rites the people participated in the baptism.

With all this in mind we cannot bring ourselves to believe that Mark 10.35ff. and Luke 12.50 are the result of Pauline or later Christian influences. They seem to us to be the relics of a time when earliest Christianity stood closer to the sectarian *milieu*. They are not developments from but the antecedents and then the parallels of the beliefs set out in Rom. 6.[3]

[1] It is right to point out that there is no firm connection in the New Testament itself (though it is soon found in Christian practice) between baptism and the Last Supper *as such*. (Perhaps the only exception would be I Cor. 10.1ff., but there Paul is doing a bit of typology on the Exodus experience and the wanderings in the wilderness, and it is likely that this has brought the two sacraments together in this passage.) This separation may in part be due to the disordering pressures of a heightened eschatology and attempts to comprehend mythical and liturgical understandings against historical backgrounds. See our further discussions.

[2] We can agree with many of the conclusions of G. Wagner, *Das religionsgeschichtliche Problem*. The Christ event is central for Paul, and his thoughts in this regard cannot be traced to any specific earlier rites, least of all those of a Hellenistic variety. Yet these are, as we have attempted to show, not wholly unique ideas, and there is this general background of beliefs (at this point mainly Jewish or semi-Jewish) to which we may look. This background in similar rites and ideologies also goes far toward explaining the 'similarities' between Christianity and, e.g., Mithraism.

[3] See also Col. 2.12; I Peter 3.19ff.; John 19.34; I John 5.6ff. Thus Bernard (*Odes of Solomon*, p. 32), commenting on the early Christian understanding of the *abyss* into which Christ is said to descend (see Rom. 10.7 and also below on Eph. 4.9) as the watery place of demons, says, 'The connexion in early Christian thought between the Baptism of Christ and His Descent into Hades is curious and remark-

3 Do you not know that all of us who have been baptized into Christ Jesus were baptized into his death? 4 We were buried therefore with him by baptism into death, so that as Christ was raised from the dead by the glory of the Father, we too might walk in newness of life. 5 For if we have been united with him in a death like his, we shall certainly be united with him in a resurrection like his. 6 We know that our old man[1] was crucified with him so that the sinful body might be destroyed, and we might no longer be enslaved to sin. . . . 8 But if we have died with Christ, we believe that we shall also live with him.

Even on the face of it (and without detracting a whit from Paul's genius and insight) such a patterned association of powerful ideas seems to demand a previous background from which it could have been adopted in order to interpret the relationship of Christians to the death and resurrection of their Lord. This we hope now to have supplied, and with it may be linked a number of additional Pauline teachings.[2]

---

able.' Nor do we believe it is accidental that Christian thought along these lines seems first to have taken shape in Syria.

[1] *Anthropos.* Probably Paul is thinking in terms of the *Adam* in each man, and this bears comparison with the Mandaean idea (also strongly hinted at in several other sects) of the hidden Adam, the essential *Man* in each man. Yet Paul has probably not borrowed this idea from some other sect, for it is inherent in the materials with which he was working. See the next note.

[2] The idea of 'putting on the Lord Jesus' (Rom. 13.14) belongs to this general context, not only because of the suggested motif of taking off and putting on clothes at baptism (and recall kings and royal priests shedding old garments and putting on royal robes after a water lustration), but because of the direct statement of the idea in Gal. 3.27. This, taken together with the reference to the *old man* in Rom. 6.6, suggests that the discussions about putting off the *old man* and putting on the *new man* in Col. 3.9f. and Eph. 4.22ff. are Pauline, whether or not the letters were actually written by Paul. (On the theme of taking off and putting on, see also I Cor. 15.53f.; II Cor. 5.1ff.) The references to the inner and outer *man* also deserve mention and probably relate to the conception of the hidden or inner *Adam* which was at least beginning to be formulated in sectarian circles (devolving from speculation built on the ancient relationship between the Man above and the Man below) and which was implicit where not explicit in some rabbinic thought. (See II Cor. 4.16; Eph. 3.22.) Much the same can be said of the theme that Christians are being transformed into the image of God. (See II Cor. 3.18; 4.4ff., and also I Cor. 15.49; Col. 3.10. While this form of thought derives originally from the Man myths, it may be that its use in this time was too diffused so to be traced any longer. So see Col. 1.15, which seems to depend on language predicated of the Wisdom figure.) Lastly we would mention the recurrent theme of the suffering which may (or must) be undergone with and in Christ before this age is consummated (II Cor. 4.10f.; Phil. 3.17; Col. 1.24; etc.). The idea may hark back to the larger idea of corporate sufferings and joys which we have found at various points in the history of the Man stories.

We turn now to the last and probably the most controversial of the Pauline passages with which we shall deal, Phil. 2.6ff. Paul urges the brethren to have and to display a like-minded spirit of love such as they may know in Christ Jesus,[1]

6 who, while being (ὑπάρχων) in a form (μορφῇ) of God, did not regard equality with God as a thing to be grasped (ἁρπαγμὸν), 7 but emptied (ἐκένωσεν) himself, having taken (λαβών) a servant's (δούλου) form (μορφὴν), having been made (γενόμενος), according to a likeness of men (ὁμοιώματι ἀνθρώπων). 8 And having been found (εὑρεθεὶς) in fashion (σχήματι) as (a) man (ὡς ἄνθρωπος), he humbled himself, having become (γενόμενος) obedient unto death, a death of a cross. 9 Therefore God highly exalted (ὑπερύψωσεν) him and bestowed on him the name which is above every name, 10 that at the name of Jesus every knee should bow, in heaven and on earth and under the earth, 11 and every tongue confess that Jesus Christ is Lord, to the glory of God the Father.

Innumerable questions can be asked about these verses, but surely one of the most fundamental, though often neglected, asks whether the passage implies (much less states) the idea of a descent of a pre-existent, divine being from heaven to earth. Under the influence of thinking about the incarnation and in the light of later stories about the gnostic redeemer,[2] it is almost automatically assumed that it does. It has become nearly a common-place to relate it to some of the materials which we have discussed in terms like these:

This is the Story of Salvation told in the form of the myth of the Heavenly Redeemer (probably of Iranian origin) who descends from heaven that he may again ascend into heaven, laden with the trophies of victory and opening the way for his followers. The mythological construction is kept but the divine Hero of the myth is identified with Jesus.[3]

One might think that we could be happy with such a general interpretation, but we are not, at least not in the form which it is here given. It involves a good deal of reading between the lines, for

[1] We have translated the passage a bit awkwardly, but with a view toward bringing out the force of the aorist participles. These are rendered as English perfect participles in order to convey the sense (regularly followed in Greek; cf. C. F. D. Moule, *An Idiom Book of New Testament Greek*[2], Cambridge, 1959, p. 100) that the action of the aorist participle precedes the action of the main verb. It is a question as to whether Paul intended such precision here, and it may be as well in some instances (e.g. v. 8b) to see the participle and the main verb as having a roughly simultaneous force. While the point is thus not vital to us, our reasons for so translating will be found in the notes below.
[2] One might wish esp. to compare the opening of the *Poimandres*.
[3] F. W. Beare, *The Epistle to the Philippians* (BNTC), 1959, p. 75.

there is no unequivocal description of a descent from heaven. We do not deny that the passage lies open to such an interpretation, but this does not make it the only or the best interpretation; nor does it tell us what was originally intended.[1] Nor have we found cause for believing that there existed an *earlier* form of myth (Iranian or otherwise) which was essentially concerned with the *descent* of a heavenly Man-hero.

Jesus, it is said, existed in a form of God. (It does not say that he pre-existed in this manner in heaven, and, though Paul himself undoubtedly came to believe this, we wonder if the thought is even implied here.)[2] But where did he so exist? While we, of course, agree that the Judaism of this period knew of the idea of a heavenly being in God's *image* (or some such), the first reference for a Jew would almost surely be to the First Man on earth. He alone was said both to resemble God and to be on the earth. Admittedly there is no guarantee that μορφή here alludes to Gen. 1.26f., but there is good reason to believe that it could,[3] and a better context is hard to find. That such a reference was intended is very likely made clear by the second half of verse 6. Notice that it does not say that he was equal with God, but rather that, though like God, he was unequal with him. (Otherwise he would hardly need to grasp at equality.)[4] One

[1] Compare, e.g., Odes of Sol. 36.3ff.; 41.12.

[2] Ὑπάρχων could be an important word in this passage, and the RSV may well mislead when it translates 'who, though he was in the form of God . . .' The word in contemporary usage regularly refers to things that exist and not to pre-existence. This is uniformly true in Pauline usage (e.g. I Cor. 11.7, where he does not mean that men pre-exist). If Paul had wanted to express this idea here, he could easily have done so. It is conceivable (though perhaps awkward in v. 6 itself) that he might even have tried to imply this by using a perfect or even an aorist participle. Should, however, it be maintained that the verb must still convey connotations of pre-existence, we would wonder if it ought not to be understood as doing so with relation to the idea that *man* (and here see again I Cor. 11.7) or the Man has always possessed the image of God.

[3] Often μορφή means something like *appearance, form, shape*. For the opinion that it is a translation of either ṣelem or dᵉmūt from Gen. 1.26, see Cullmann, *Christology*, pp. 176f.; J. Héring, *Le royaume de Dieu et sa venue*, Paris, 1937, pp. 146f. The Syriac of the Peshitta uses its cognate of dᵉmūt for μορφή at Phil. 2.6, and both the *Poimandres* (*CH* I, 12, 14) and the Sibylline Oracles (III, 8; see III, 27) use εἰκών and μορφή together with apparent reference to Gen. 1.26, where the usual Greek is εἰκών and ὁμοίωσις. At Dan. 3.19 μορφή is used for ṣelem. (Cf. Rom. 8.29, where Paul uses εἰκών and a compound of μορφή together.) Possibly the use of μορφή in v. 7, where εἰκών would have been inappropriate, has influenced v. 6. (D. H. Wallace in 'A Note on *morphé*', *TZ* 22, 1966, pp. 19ff., argues against this understanding, but as he seems to recognize, the objections are far from conclusive.)

[4] The exact meaning of ἁρπαγμός is difficult to establish, but this is the view of many and fits well with our background materials. We cannot see how it makes

thinks immediately, and we believe rightly, of Ps. 8.5 (though it is here the idea and not necessarily the text which is in Paul's mind).

In the myth forms we have studied the sin of the Man and king is indeed just the one not committed here, trying to be equal with God. Yet in the pre-Christian versions of the story this is not really a sin committed by the Man above. Rather is it done by the pride of the Man below trying to ascend above or to become like God by his own power. (This is true, for instance, in Gen. 3.5, 22; Isa. 14.12ff.; Ezek. 28.2ff.; and even in Acts 12.22.) Indeed, he represents the god-Man above, and sometimes the Man may already have *arisen* only to be cast down from heaven,[1] but he does not begin as a divine being who has previously descended. Rather is he the one below who has overstepped his bounds.

Of course, one can always claim that this is some different form of the myth (stressing the role of the heavenly-Man aspect rather than that of the king-Man) or even a different myth,[2] but the point is that no one has yet brought forward such a reasonably proximate pre-Christian version where the emphasis is on a divinity who graciously descends from heaven to become like a humble human being. Alternatively one might conclude that Paul himself is here in the process of transforming the myth.[3] This view could be acceptable as long as it is recognized that the original materials began with the Man below,

---

good sense (cf. F. E. Vokes, "'Αρπαγμός in Philippians 2.5–11' in *Studia Evangelica* II [TU 87, ed. F. L. Cross], 1964, pp. 670ff.) to argue for a meaning which would have Jesus already on a full parity with God either in terms of Jewish or Pauline theology or in the light of vv. 9–11. See also p. 254 n. 3.

[1] Notice, too, that, when the god-Man is cast down from heaven he goes directly to the underworld. He does not come down, in this aspect, to reside on the earth. (See on Eph. 4.8ff. at p. 256 n. 1.) It is possible that the stories about the *devil* being cast down from heaven have been influenced by this aspect of the idea. See on the *Man* of lawlessness (II Thess. 2.3) in the same note below.

[2] Käsemann holds that Paul has adapted an essentially Hellenistic myth to this effect ('Kritische Analyse von Phil. 2.5–11', *ZTK* 47, 1950, pp. 313ff.). J. Héring believes that it was first a Jewish-gnostic myth about the Man who descends to earth ('Kyrios Anthropos', *RHPR* 16, 1936, 196ff.). If either argument were accepted, we would then have to say that this represents a *gnosticized* view of these legends at a slightly earlier time than our other information seems to indicate. For a convenient treatment of other understandings of the passage, cf. R. P. Martin, *An Early Christian Confession*, London, 1960.

[3] This could have been done, consciously or unconsciously, by assuming that the one referred to first came down from heaven. Conceivably this is why the language seems to be open to different interpretations, the older ideas not having been obliterated.

in this case with a type of Adam, the new Adam who does not commit Adam's sin.

What does it then mean when it says that he *emptied himself*, taking a servant's form?[1] Does not this imply that he gave up his likeness to God and then assumed a lower status? Probably it does, but this is perfectly consonant with the Semitic Man legends, especially in ritual terms. We recall that the good king deliberately humbled himself (and *emptied himself*[2] is almost surely a synonymous ideogram). Indeed, it is this which leads to his favour in the sight of God.[3] He is abject before God; he emphasizes his humanity, his mortality and frailty,[4] his human condition.[5] He is even less than a human being.[6] His position as God's obedient *servant* is given great stress in such a context.[7]

Thus we do not find that γενόμενος in v. 7 means that the figure passed from a heavenly state to a mortal one.[8] However it is trans-

[1] In connection with the use of μορφή in v. 7, we note that the word was employed in Aquila's translation in significant descriptions like Isa. 52.14; 53.2. Has this indirectly influenced the language here?

[2] The expression is notoriously awkward and also unique in Greek. E. Lohmeyer (*Kyrios Jesus. Eine Untersuchung zu Phil. 2.5–11* [SHAW, Phil.-hist. Kl.], 1927–8: IV, p. 8) felt it to be a Semitism, and Jeremias (*Servant of God*, p. 98) maintains that it is a translation of 'he poured out his soul' in Isa. 53.12. While not adhering to any theories of literary dependence (for notice that 'he emptied himself' is here directly connected with the taking of the servant's form and only indirectly with the death), we agree that Isa. 53 stands closer to the thought of Phil. 2.7 than does the idea of an incarnation. The regal figure divests himself of his honours and becomes the obedient sufferer. See L. S. Thornton, *The Dominion of Christ*, London, 1952, pp. 91ff., esp. p. 95 n. 2.

[3] This idea is found repeatedly in one form or another in the *shame* of the king, in his pleas (of innocence and otherwise), etc. See in ch. III on the Babylonian and other kings, II Isaiah's Servant, etc. E.g. Pss. 30.7; 69.5ff.; Zech. 9.9.

[4] E.g. Pss. 22.14ff.; 69.3, 26ff.

[5] It might be in the sense of *bearing, manner, deportment, condition* that the word σχῆμα is to be taken, rather than referring again to *shape* or *form*. (See I Cor. 7.31, which would also tolerate either meaning.) If taken in the latter sense, however, it would apparently be a parallel to μορφή and, like it, probably be a rough synonym of εἰκών or ὁμοίωσις. On the mere humanity of the king in his humiliation, see II Sam. 7.14; Ps. 144.3; etc.

[6] E.g. Ps. 22.6ff.

[7] This idea is often implicit where not explicit (e.g. Isa. 50.4f.; Ps. 18.20ff.). Explicitly, see particularly Pss. 69.17; 89.50; 116.16. In these cases the word 'ebed is translated either by παῖς or δοῦλος. (On the frequent interchange of παῖς and δοῦλος, see Zimmerli in *Servant of God*, pp. 37ff.; Jeremias, *op. cit.*, pp. 97f. and n. 444; Martin, *An Early Christian Confession*, p. 26.) That the king should be a servant/slave of the gods was a common Near Eastern idea.

[8] Again, if this had been definitely intended, it could have been readily stated. Though the point is hardly decisive, Paul might better have expressed such an idea by using present instead of aorist participles in vv. 7f. The latter could well give the

lated ('becoming', 'being born'?) the idea conveyed is one involving a stress. He who exists in likeness to God now voluntarily gives emphasis to the other aspect of his being, his creaturehood and mortality, his role as servant. He demonstrates his lowliness and obedience even unto death. This is the ultimate sign of his loyalty and the nadir of his humiliation. Like the king of old he submits to such a treatment. (If this particular version had some pre-Christian form, the specific reference to death *upon a cross* would be an interpolation.)[1]

Because of his humility and out of this death God takes him, just as he rescued the king.[2] He exalts him *to a higher station*,[3] just as he exalted the king. He gives him the highest of names, and all are bound to display their worship and subservience to him because of his name and his highly exalted status.[4]

If this hymn was adapted by the Church from earlier materials, we may well wonder about this *name*. The name Jesus itself would not have been meaningful as a title of divine honour until after the resurrection. Previously, if a name was specified,[5] it must have been a designation indicative of glory and honour in heaven. What might it have been? Obviously one can only speculate, but one might think of Ps. 2.7 or I Enoch 71.14 and the *naming* aspects of the baptism and transfiguration stories in the Gospels.

Our interpretation, if it be correct, gives a genuine Semitic cast and setting to this *hymn*. It avoids both the difficulties of trying to find

---

impression that the humanity of the individual preceded his *emptying* and humbling, that he was a human already and not as a result of these acts.

[1] See also below on Lohmeyer's thesis.

[2] Only as a point in passing (for other influences have also played their parts), it could be that the Pauline idea of being *justified* or made righteous owes much more to the *background* of kingship ideology than is presently realized. E.g. Ps. 18.20; Isa. 50.7ff.; 53.11; Zech. 9.9. In the latter two texts esp. the sense of acquittal or vindication is prominent. The king's loyalty, trust or faithfulness are operative factors in securing this. (Further on the king's righteousness, see Pss. 24.5; 45.4, 7; 72.1f.; 118.18f.; Jer. 33.15.)

[3] We would not insist that the use of ὑπερυψόω in v. 9 rather than just ὑψόω means that the figure cannot have been viewed as equal with God in v. 6, but it may well have significance, and we think Cullmann (*Christology*, p. 180) more correct here than Fuller (*Foundations*, p. 212). On the Johannine use of ὑψόω in statements about the Son of Man, see in ch. VII.

[4] On this common picture with regard to kings and the greatness of the king's name, e.g. Pss. 2.10f.; 72.9ff.; 72.17; II Sam. 7.9 (= I Chron. 17.8).

[5] Some texts read 'a name' in v. 9 which, if original, might encourage the idea that no specific name was intended.

a Hellenistic source for these materials at this time and also of trying to explain why Paul would have used terms which, if they were Hellenistic in origin and intention, would seemingly go so far toward undermining the real humanity of Jesus. According to our view we are instead dealing with essentially Semitic ideas, so that words like μορφή, ὁμοίωμα, and σχῆμα are not to be read as quasi-technical terms implying some docetic understanding. Rather do they refer to *likeness* and *similarity* without inferring a Hellenistic distinction between outward appearance and inward reality. Instead they mean what the biblical doctrine always has said about man, especially the Man created by God in an ideal state; in one sense he is like unto God, but, in his earthly condition, he is also very human and far below God.

May we go further and suggest that not only in essential *plot*, but also in form, this hymn once was extant in an earlier Aramaic and perhaps pre-Christian version? This was the argument of Lohmeyer,[1] and it continues to have many adherents. While we are always hesitant in putting our faith in *retranslations*, this makes an easier and better case than most such efforts. It is tempting to suppose that 'according to a likeness of men'[2] and 'in fashion as (a) man' may be translations of phrases which hark back to Daniel's 'one like a son of man' or something similar to this.[3]

Yet, whether or not the passage goes back to some Aramaic and/or pre-Christian form, it seems to us that some manner of teaching about the Man is fully implied. For this conclusion we rely not on disputed phrases or words or theories about retranslations, but on the story as a whole. *Then*, if this be so, it seems probable that these phrases do relate to teaching about the Man. But, and this is important, at least in the form in which Paul has given us this hymn, the references appear to have been deprived of any real titular sense. This was quite possibly the work of Paul himself, for even in Rom. 5 and I Cor. 15

[1] *Op. cit.* Lohmeyer divided the hymn up into two strophes each of three stanzas, each stanza having three lines (the mention of the cross being omitted). He pointed out a number of seeming Aramaisms and noted the number of *non-Pauline* words.

[2] Papyrus 46 and several early writers read 'of man' (ἀνθρώπου) in lieu of 'of men'. Obviously, if original (and a case might be made out for it, believing that later scribes have misunderstood the idiom), we would seem even closer to an expression like that found in Daniel. See Black, *BJRL* 45, 1963, p. 315.

[3] See Lohmeyer, *op. cit.*, pp. 39f., and *Der Brief an die Philipper*[9] (K-EKNT), 1953, p. 95, on the latter expression. On our view there may be a relationship with the Danielic phrase (and compare also Ezek. 1.26), but the *hymn* here presents the Man-like figure at a different stage in his story, at least until vv. 9ff.

(where, let us note, the *anthropic* one and Adam are linked explicitly rather than just implicitly), he seems far more intent on teaching on the basis of the conception rather than on proclaiming Jesus as the Man.[1]

[1] There are a few other passages where it is conceivable that the Man materials have been of slight influence. It has been suggested that 'the man (ὁ ἄνθρωπος) of lawlessness (or sin)' in II Thess. 2.3 is an inversion (either through Pauline development or due to some source) of the righteous Man who will come for salvation. See C. K. Barrett, *From First Adam to Last*, London, 1962, pp. 11ff., who interestingly wants to relate this to Ezek. 28.1ff. and Isa. 14.12ff. and also to the antichrist traditions. This might be an extension of the idea of an Adam who did try to be like God and instead became the agent of evil. But if so, it only goes to demonstrate one of our essential points: though Paul knew about some of these ideas, he was not concerned with proclaiming Jesus as the Man, for notice that, though he speaks of the evil *man*, he does not go on to tell of the good Man, but rather of the Lord Jesus.

In Eph. 2.15 we hear of the 'one new Man' (ἄνθρωπος) who creates in himself a new, united race of men. This could be either the work of Paul or a later disciple which is based on Pauline thought as it is found in Rom. 5.12ff.

Eph. 4.8–10 is of more interest in that it quotes Ps. 68.18, which was in origin a verse applied to the ascension of the king-God to his heavenly throne. If it is conceivable that *Paul* found this language in use among primitive Christians or even non-Christians, the little midrash given in vv. 9f. is intriguing. There is an ascent and a descent, but the descent is not from heaven to earth, but rather into 'the lower parts of the earth'. It is feasible that this, too, results from older speculation based on the legends about the royal Man. Certainly it relates to ideas found in the Odes of Solomon, etc., and *may* throw some light on the thought behind John 3.13.

Another sign of the influence of the Man beliefs could be found in Paul's use of an expression like 'the day of Jesus Christ' or 'the day of the Lord', which makes one think of references to the day or days of the Son of Man. Mowinckel (*HTC*, p. 392) writes: 'Paul is certainly borrowing an element from the Son of Man theology when he uses the expression "the day of Jesus Christ" as a regular term for the eschatological day.' Our point would be that he has dropped all reference to the Son of Man (or Man).

VII

THE JOHANNINE SON OF MAN

'How can you say that the Son of Man must be lifted up?'
(John 12.34)

1. PROBLEMS OF THE GOSPEL

IN AN ENDEAVOUR to learn about the origins of the Johannine Son of Man sayings along with their relationship to the synoptic logia, it is, of course, necessary to take into consideration the Gospel as a whole. Unavoidably this involves a series of complicated issues which today embroil Johannine studies. Here we can only state the basis for the remarks to follow, trying as best we can to employ postulates which will be acceptable to many at this time.

(*1*) While the evangelist (and perhaps the group of disciples with whom he associates himself) may have known an eyewitness to Jesus, he himself was not such a witness, and his identity is otherwise unknown.[1]

(*2*) Although there may now be cause for dating certain of its traditions and understandings to an earlier period,[2] the Gospel was probably composed about AD 100. We would willingly accept an earlier date, but this view seems safest.

(*3*) The place of writing is uncertain, but there are at present no compelling reasons for thinking that the basic traditions and outlook are non-Palestinian.[3]

(*4*) The author had no direct acquaintance with any of the

---

[1] If the author is to be associated in some way with I John, it is worth noting that this epistle gives no sign of any contemporary worship of Jesus as the Son of Man.

[2] Cf. C. H. Dodd, *Historical Tradition in the Fourth Gospel*, Cambridge, 1963, esp. p. 426.

[3] See the statement by Dodd, *op. cit.*, p. 427. While it is our view that some scholars have gone too far in drawing lines between the Gospel and Qumran, the Scrolls have helped to indicate that John need never have set a foot outside of Palestine nor heard of Plato, Philo or the stoics in order to have held the world view that he did.

synoptic Gospels as we now have them. His treatment of similar materials is poorly explained by literary hypotheses.[1] Where the evangelist may preserve aspects of authentic tradition, his channels of transmission, therefore, reach back to the early materials. In at least some instances, his information may be more accurate than that of the synoptics.[2] This also means that we must pay particular attention to traditions found in both the synoptics and John, especially if these appear to have been preserved by several synoptic sources as well.[3]

(5) Different sources (written and/or oral) there must have been for this Gospel, but such a unity has been achieved that they cannot now be delineated with any degree of certainty.[4]

(6) This unified appearance also has important ramifications for our understanding of the Christology of the Gospel. We doubt whether it is very meaningful to speak as though these were separate Christologies, Son of God, Son of Man, Christ, etc. For this evangelist all these titles are subservient to his reverence for the exalted Jesus, and all are influenced by this attitude. If this Gospel, for instance, seems to tell of a Son of Man who came down from heaven, this need not indicate either dependence on earlier materials which spoke in this way or a special development within one stratum of tradition. Nevertheless we find it significant that most, if not all, of John's Son of Man logia bears signs of being more primitive than the evangelist's overall Christology (sometimes indicating that they may once have run counter to that Christology), and that they are not to be found in passages in which the author is most obviously stating the faith of his own time.[5]

---

[1] See P. Gardner-Smith, *St John and the Synoptic Gospels*, Cambridge, 1938; D. M. Smith, Jr, *The Composition and Order of the Fourth Gospel*, New Haven, 1965. On this and these other points, cf. Fuller, *New Testament in Current Study*, pp. 101ff.

[2] See Dodd, *op. cit.*; A. J. B. Higgins, *The Historicity of the Fourth Gospel*, London, 1960; J. A. T. Robinson, 'The New Look on the Fourth Gospel', *Studia Evangelica* I (TU 73, ed. K. Aland and others), 1959, pp. 338ff. (art. also in his *Twelve New Testament Studies*, SBT 34, London, 1962, pp. 94ff.).

[3] Cf. J. A. T. Robinson, 'The Place of the Fourth Gospel', in *The Roads Converge* (ed. P. Gardner-Smith), London, 1963, pp. 51ff.

[4] Despite the erudition he brings to the subject (see his *Evangelium des Johannes*), Bultmann's identification of a signs source and a discourse source may be more convenient than anything else. Certainly the synoptics often appear to reveal a different pattern in which at least bits of discourse were preserved along with controversial miracles and healings. Cf. B. Noack, *Zur johanneischen Tradition. Beiträge zur Kritik an der literarkritischen Analyse des vierten Evangeliums*, Copenhagen, 1954 (with a view toward the possibilities of oral traditions), and D. M. Smith, *op. cit.*

[5] E.g. compare John 3.16ff.; 3.36; 6.69; 20.31.

2. EXPLANATORY THEORIES

We should now like to look at some of the theories which have been put forth to explain the origin and character of John's Son of Man sayings. Already we have indicated our reasons for doubting the existence of some pre-Christian and gnostic or pre-gnostic form of a Man myth in which a redeemer descends from heaven. Those who espouse a theory dependent upon such a myth are not able to show that such a form was extant.[1] This is particularly true with regard to any divinity who would be *incarnated* in some manner and live and suffer as a human being. On the other hand, we do believe that the idea of a descending Man-saviour can be accounted for as the result of a later transformation of ideas which originated from royal ideology. Since it is now impossible to know exactly when the transforming factors[2] may have begun to operate, it is conceivable that the Fourth Gospel was influenced by some already incipient form of the new conception. We should think it far more likely, however, since the vigorous new Christian beliefs carried the seeds for such a growth, that John and his community were more the agents than the products of this transformation.

Sometimes in tandem with the theory of a pre-Christian redeemer myth is found the hypothesis that John, the evangelist, had knowledge of (and was in dispute with)[3] a group of baptizing sectarians who continued to revere John the Baptist.[4] The idea remains attractive without question; but here we prefer to remain agnostic, for, and especially from our own point of view, unless we could definitely associate the Baptist with one of the later movements whose teachings

[1] With regard to Bultmann's own admission on this point, see Fuller, *op. cit.*, p. 124 n. 50.

[2] See p. 227 n. 1.

[3] See John 1.6ff.; 1.15; 1.19ff.; 3.22ff.; 4.1; 5.33ff.; 10.41.

[4] See now Fuller, *op. cit.*, p. 129, and Dodd's discussion (*Historical Tradition in the Fourth Gospel*, pp. 288ff.), where the polemic is placed at a time roughly contemporaneous with the incident in Ephesus (cf. Acts 18.24ff.). Bultmann has long been inclined to believe that the author of the Gospel was a member of the rival Baptist sect before becoming a Christian. See *Evangelium des Johannes*, esp. p. 76.
A number of scholars would connect the group through the Baptist to Qumran and thus describe a continuous picture. Cf. J. A. T. Robinson, 'The Baptism of John and the Qumran Community', *HTR* 50, 1957, pp. 175ff. (also in his *Twelve New Testament Studies*, 11ff.); W. H. Brownlee, 'John the Baptist in the New Light of Ancient Scrolls' in *The Scrolls and the New Testament* (ed. K. Stendahl), New York, 1957, pp. 33ff. Against such efforts is H. H. Rowley, 'The Baptism of John and the Qumran Sect' in *New Testament Essays* (ed. A. J. B. Higgins), Manchester, 1959, pp. 218ff.

are known, the assistance of such an hypothesis is more apparent than real. We have found cause for believing that there was more here than meets the eye,[1] but beyond these suspicions it is hard to go.

We are less sympathetic to theories which attempt to draw direct lines of influence between Pauline theology and that of the Fourth Gospel. In fact, however, the popularity of such efforts has now greatly abated, and it is generally recognized that there are neither sufficient external nor internal reasons for making such inferences.[2]

Other influences being excluded, it is therefore to the early Christian traditions that one should resort to find some beginning of an explanation for the Johannine Son of Man sayings. Most recent theories have maintained that the primitive among them are based upon logia of an eschatological nature. Here the preliminary argument, either stated or unstated, holds that Jesus could only have known of the Son of Man as a heavenly, futuristic champion.

Siegfried Schulz has made a bold approach to the subject of the whole basis of the Johannine sources and Christology. He thinks that not only the Son of Man sayings, but also material having to do with the Son, the Paraclete and certain 'I' sayings which speak of Jesus' return derive ultimately from traditions which were associated with the eschatological Son of Man.[3] If there is truth in this theory, it means, at least as far as we can see, that there was a double transformation of primitive logia and themes. Not only has there been a frequent substitution for original references to the Son of Man, but Johannine tradition has also first interpreted earlier materials as promises that the Son of Man would *come* from heaven to earth (for this idea we do not find to have been a part of the original conception). Jesus would also have had to have been firmly identified with the heavenly Son of Man of whom he spoke before these transformations could have taken place.

We ourselves are always intrigued by the possibility that original

---

[1] See pp. 223ff.

[2] See Fuller's statement, *op. cit.*, p. 116. Cf. also our remarks on the 'Hellenists', p. 234.

[3] *Untersuchungen zur Menschensohn-Christologie im Johannesevangelium*, Göttingen, 1957. For further interpretation of these findings (and with regard to the Prologue and Johannine imagery) and also an awareness of the influences of Jewish sectarianism and of possible Mandaean gnostic groups which may have reinterpreted Jewish-Christian materials before they found their way into the Gospel, see his subsequent *Komposition und Herkunft der Johanneischen Reden* (BWANT V/1), 1960. Schulz's views, of course, reverse Bultmann's opinion that the eschatological sayings were largely added by a redactor to gnostic-like materials.

Son of Man sayings or ideas lie disguised in the Gospels, but the hazards of such speculation are obvious. From this distance such theories can only be offered very tentatively and with great care. Schulz's methodology may be criticized in that he allows his criterion of common themes (often represented only by a common word) a great deal of latitude.[1] Indeed, *themes* associated with the Son of Man do not stand isolated in this Gospel, but John has so fully interwoven a number of his motifs that the uncertainties involved in tracing them to any one source or core of sayings may well be insurmountable.

What does strike us as most unlikely is Schulz's belief that the starting-point for this was a core of sayings concerned solely with an eschatological Son of Man.[2] One cannot help but feel that his whole thesis would have become more convincing were he not forced to reinterpret every single Son of Man saying. Unfortunately for him none of the Johannine Son of Man logia reveal any obvious interest in eschatology or apocalyptic.[3] His particular arguments involve a complex series of progressive and related stages about which nothing is known and which result in sayings and themes transformed nearly or even beyond recognition. Altogether it is so long a step from the Son of Man with whom he begins to his view of the Fourth Gospel's versions of this tradition that one must wonder if there are not more credible starting-points.

Using a similar point of departure, A. J. B. Higgins believes that the Johannine Son of Man sayings originated in a source very like that of the synoptic logia. Beginning with the eschatological Son of Man, they have developed along different lines.[4] Higgins starts by

[1] See J. M. Robinson, 'Recent Research in the Fourth Gospel', *JBL* 78, 1959, pp. 247ff. He points out that Schulz has failed to establish that some of his essential themes and words belong exclusively to apocalyptic traditions.

[2] *Untersuchungen*, pp. 96ff. To the earlier tradition are assigned 1.51; 3.13–15; 5.27(–29); 6.27, 53; 13.31f. Formed out of these were 6.62; 8.28; 12.23, 34 (the words *ascending*, *lifted up* and *glorified* being the respective links with the earlier logia). Schulz also divides the *more* original sayings into three literary types. He finds midrash in 1.51; 3.13–15; 5.27–29; homily 6.27, 53, while 13.31f. is a hymn. The value of this method begins to suffer when classes are composed of one or two examples. Schnackenburg rightly points out the arbitrariness of the classifications in any case. 'Der Menschensohn im Johannesevangelium', *NTS* 11, 1964–5, pp. 123f.

[3] So C. K. Barrett, as he merely surveys the Johannine sayings, remarks, 'John has few parallels to the (synoptic) eschatological use (but see 5.27, and below)' (*The Gospel according to St John*, London, 1956, p. 60). On 5.27, which is a very tenuous link in any event, see our remarks below.

[4] A kindred approach was made by Gerhard Iber. See *TLZ* 80, 1955, cols. 115f. Later the Johannine material was affected by the gnostic myth. See also Hahn,

dividing the Johannine sayings into synoptic and non-synoptic types. 'This method of classification', he writes, 'is best fitted to our purpose.' In a footnote he adds that by 'synoptic' he does not mean all synoptic Son of Man sayings, but rather 'those particular data which contribute to the understanding of the problem of Jesus and the Son of Man'.[1] One realizes what is meant by this, but may also be excused for thinking that it is not hard to see where this is leading and how it is intended to arrive there.

In addition Higgins has a highly utilitarian classification for Son of Man sayings which is called 'Glory of the Son of Man'. Its usefulness is revealed by the fact that eschatological synoptic logia fall into it as well as all the Johannine sayings in which the Son of Man has glory and dignity conferred upon him. In these terms Higgins is able to hold that there are no Johannine sayings which speak of the earthly activity of the Son of Man. Yet, in fact, *all* the Johannine sayings are concerned with the Son of Man who is present on earth. What Higgins of course means, and the viewpoint for which he then ably argues along his own guide-lines, is that all the sayings might be interpreted so as to find that they have an origin in logia which originally spoke of the future glory of the Son of Man.

Thus it is his opinion that the Johannine tradition has managed to 'bridge the gap' between the synoptic presentation of a Son of Man on earth and one in glory in heaven. This is done by causing the earthly Jesus to speak of his own exaltation as the Son of Man in glory.[2] Yet, if this be so, there must be a step missing, a previous stage in the Johannine traditions which envisioned Jesus as already the Son of Man on earth. Since Higgins believes that there are no authentic sayings of this type and does not mention an influence by any of the synoptic logia, he presumably means that Johannine tradition had come to identify the earthly Jesus with the Son of Man in a manner parallel to but independent of the synoptic traditions. While such an assumption can be made and while some scholars might feel that it illustrates how different traditions could have worked on the materials

---

Hoheitstitel, esp. pp. 39ff.; he seems, however, more impressed by the differences between Johannine and synoptic logia.

[1] *Son of Man*, p. 157. Synoptic types are 1.51; 3.14f.; 5.27; 8.28; 12.34. The area of his agreement with Schulz about what goes back toward authentic tradition is thus confined to 1.51; 3.14f.; 5.27. Even this is vitiated by Higgins's unwillingness to accept the forms which Schulz has devised.

[2] *Op. cit.*, pp. 183f.

in a parallel fashion, it is sufficient to make others of us wonder if there was not real substance to the belief that the primitive materials represented Jesus as speaking as though he were somehow already the Son of Man.

In our opinion Higgins unnecessarily weakens his case when he argues that all this is evidence for a Son of Man Christology (the evangelist's 'fundamental and principal Christology')[1] which still was a powerful force in the Church and which had its hold upon the evangelist himself. He cites 9.35 in this connection (though in context it rather demonstrates the reverse for us) and almost seems to ignore the numerous Johannine confessions of faith which are cast in other terms. Just conceivably there might have been some unknown stage at which eschatological sayings were transformed in the manner indicated and the Son of Man thus given an unauthentic character and prominence, but we cannot see that the Gospel shows this to have been a contemporary and ongoing activity.

R. Schnackenburg suggests that we can use the possible parallels in the synoptic sayings to fuller advantage.[2] By and large the sayings of the Fourth Gospel can be seen to have grown out of the same central idea and to have evolved in a generally similar manner. The crucial verse is John 5.27, where the title is used anarthrously and the right of the Son of Man to pass judgment is affirmed. This Schnackenburg places against the background of Dan. 7, and he finds it to be akin to the synoptic sayings which infer a future judgment by the Son of Man. Out of such a conception has come the whole double theme of glory and exaltation, and, in this sense, Johannine statements about the Son of Man's glory and exaltation may be paralleled with synoptic sayings of the same general type, such as Mark 14.62; Luke 22.69 and also Acts 7.56. So, too, the Johannine theology which has moulded the crucifixion and exaltation into one theme explains how the Son of Man came to be connected with the passion, a saying like John 3.14 being the result. It is noteworthy, however, that no sayings have developed in John like Mark 2.10, 28 and Luke 9.58, which picture the Son of Man as a figure with a true earthly ministry.

To explain other Johannine Son of Man sayings it is not mandatory that we go beyond a strictly Johannine development (though Schnackenburg would not deny the possibility of other influences). The belief that the Son of Man came down from heaven requires

[1] *Op. cit.*, p. 155. Cf. also Cullmann, *Christology*, p. 186.
[2] *NTS* 11, 1964/5, pp. 123ff.

only two catalytic elements: the faith that Jesus himself first came down from heaven and the influence of Wisdom speculation. This last element may be especially strong where pre-existence is concerned.

To the extent that pre-existence and a heavenly descent are predicated of the Son of Man we find ourselves in some agreement, but we are dubious about Schnackenburg's other ideas. The connection of John 5.27 with Mark 14.62 is, at best, no stronger than it is with Mark 2.10, where the Son of Man acts as judge by forgiving sins on earth. We can only assume a connection with the former and deny one with the latter by reinterpreting John 5.27 before the comparison is made. Without such reinterpretation and previous assumptions about the nature of the Son of Man conception that Jesus could have known, the Johannine representation of Jesus as already the Son of Man on earth forms a much stronger link with the synoptics than any other feature. While it is true that certain synoptic sayings which seem to affirm this in a particular way are not found in John, it is also true that no specific synoptic Son of Man logia are to be found in John. Thus this situation is really no different from the other correspondences which Schnackenburg notices: the idea can be found there even if parallels in actual wording are absent.

Again, if there is a similarity between synoptic Son of Man passion sayings and those in John, it is at least as legitimate to contend that this results from a common original conception as to argue that Johannine and synoptic traditions managed to develop in parallel though independent fashion. Indeed, this is altogether a rather striking innovation for the different strains of tradition to have hit upon independently. Even after they both managed to come to the belief that the earthly Jesus was already the Son of Man, why should it be as the Son of Man that his death is often predicted?

There is, however, much in Schnackenburg's principal methodology that we do appreciate. He is suggesting that the appearance of the Son of Man in all the traditions argues for some manner of a common core conception, even while there is much that appears differently in the actual sayings. This 'similitude in dissimilitude' is, in fact, a growing realization in the comparative study of the Johannine and synoptic traditions.[1] The hypothesis to which it points is that the Johannine traditions and those inherited by the synoptic

[1] We shall try to give some examples of this in our commentary below. In the meantime see again J. A. T. Robinson in *The Roads Converge*, pp. 49ff.

evangelists became, for all practical purposes, separated at a relatively early date. Each of them in their way have preserved and developed authentic elements from the primitive strata. One may show better knowledge in a particular area than another, so that differences must be carefully evaluated before conclusions regarding unauthentic traditions are accepted.[1] But it is especially where and when they share ideas in common that we believe there is good reason for suggesting that features in the earliest traditions are the essential cause for this. We must not, then, be misled by variant ways of stating such beliefs or ideas, but rather make our search for possible common denominators.

We think that the validity of such an approach can be well illustrated by the Son of Man logia. Despite the many differences with which we yet must deal, there is an underlying web of vital ideas: the Son of Man who somehow can be present on earth but who cannot be on earth in the same manner in which he is yet to be known in glory, is in some way firmly connected with the traditions regarding Jesus' death. If it is true that the Johannine sayings reveal these ideas in closer cohesion than do the synoptics, we shall at least be willing to ask if the 'gaps' seen between the ideas in the synoptics have not been as much opened by them as they have been 'bridged' by John.

3. RELATED ISSUES AND JOHN 3.13

Before we come to our exegesis of the Son of Man sayings in this Gospel, there remains one further task with which we should deal. If there is anything in our fundamental thesis that a vital Son of Man conception played a significant role in Christian beginnings, it would seem likely that it should have affected the traditions in ways other than are now found just in the Son of Man sayings. Yet there is also an aspect of our understanding which is pulling in the other direction, for we also think that the Son of Man traditions and themes were rapidly falling into disuse and, outside of their *living milieu*, were no longer well understood. The probable result of these conflicting forces should be that some of the original ideas have been lost while others are preserved only in a fragmentary and sometimes altered fashion.

---

[1] E.g. few would hold that John's use of the Kingdom of God only twice means that the synoptics have elaborated the idea almost out of whole cloth. Alternatively many see much of value in John's traditions regarding previous trips to Jerusalem by Jesus.

As succinctly as possible, and while postponing numerous themes which occur in the sayings themselves, we should like to take up this possibility and, at the same time, deal with several theories regarding the influence of the Son of Man figure which we do not regard as viable.

We here cannot treat at length the ways in which the Johannine *Son of God* title (and sometimes perhaps just *the Son* as a derivative?) may be allied to the Son of Man and his story. We have often noted how the Man (as king, king-god and First Man) can be regarded as the divine Son or *the Son of God*. In a number of contexts the titles were almost synonymous: he who became the Man was also now the Son of God, and we recognize the reasons for this. The term continued on occasion to be employed and/or the relationship was stated or implied in the later literature; both the Adam-Man and the Messiah-Man are the Son (of God). Yet there would be genuine difficulties in any attempt to demonstrate that the Johannine usage of Son of God and Son came primarily from this background. Not only are there other contemporary Jewish and Hellenistic[1] usages which deserve consideration, but it is precisely on this subject of the *Sonship* of Jesus and his relationship with the Father that a great deal of the Johannine meditation seems to have taken place. (Notice how in contrast Jesus' role as the Son of Man is never the subject of a real disquisition or commentary.) This does not mean that we would ignore the possibility that Jesus' sense of Sonship (both as presented in John and the synoptics) authentically belonged to the vision of his role as the Son of Man and so the Son (of God), but, if this is feasible, we think it comes across much more *primitively* in several synoptic passages. In particular we find John's presentation of Jesus as the eternal Son and the one *sent* from the Father to run counter to our understanding of the earlier ideas. Previously the mortal who was the (Son of) Man and so the Son of God became so by an *adoption*. Indeed, he then entered upon an eternal office and became or became like the eternal one, but the sense of his adoption to this role was important. If this last element was known in Johannine traditions, it is usually effectively disguised.

We should think it conceivable that some of the images of the

---

[1] Cf. Dodd, *Interpretation of the Fourth Gospel*, pp. 250ff. The attempt of E. M. Sidebottom (*The Christ of the Fourth Gospel*, pp. 149ff.) to derive the title from the Jewish belief that a righteous man was like a son of God (cf. Wisd. 2.18) does not, however, appear useful in the majority of contexts.

Johannine Gospel may originally have been more closely connected with the Son of Man than any other designation. We would especially single out the shepherd and the vine.[1] Both have long-standing associations with the king-Man both within and outside Israel. The LXX of Ps. 80.14ff., for instance, brings the vine into indisputable parallelism with the Son of Man-king.[2] He is the obvious corporate symbol for all the people. We know that the vine and tree images played a role in the thinking of contemporary sects and that they were used as symbols of unity and of corporate relationship.[3] Indeed, this whole theme of the *indwelling* of Jesus and the believers, though now thoroughly integrated into Johannine theology, could owe much of its impetus to earlier Man beliefs. In this sense the *mysticism* of John might go ultimately back to the same sources from which Paul and the synoptic traditions have, at least in part, derived theirs.[4]

Again by way of an example and with regard to the shepherd theme, in Matt. 26.31 and Mark 14.27, Zech. 13.7 is quoted.[5] We recall that in Zechariah this shepherd is 'the Man who stands next to me'. In Matthew and Mark the quotation is used within the context of references to the Son of Man's betrayal.

Yet once again we would restrain ourselves. Comparisons and illustrations could be developed at great length, but could not in the end be regarded as convincing proof of a certain connection between these images and the Son of Man. They have other associations in the Old Testament as well as in other bodies of religious literature. Easily, too, the images could have become disassociated from the Man-king figure and have entered into common parlance.

In the ensuing discussions we shall notice a number of phrases

[1] Obviously there are other possibilities. The ancient association of the Man-king with the sun suggests that the conception of Jesus as the light or bringer of the light could be linked with his role as the Son of Man. So, too, the image of the door might make one think of the *gates* through which the king passes on his way from death to life or the gate which the Man virtually becomes in the Naassene teaching. See also Odes of Sol. 17.10 and below, p. 279 n. 3.

[2] On this see Dodd, *op. cit.*, p. 245 n. 1.; he suggests that Ps. 80 may have been more important for John's Son of Man than Dan. 7. Yet we do not think that the tradition rests on verbal and literary reminiscences.

[3] On the place of this and other Johannine type images in Mandaeanism, see Drower, *Secret Adam*, pp. 84ff. See also Odes of Sol. 1.2, etc., where a connection with baptism may be seen.

[4] See pp. 246ff.

[5] See also John 16.32, where Zech. 13.7 may have been of influence. Zech. 13.7 is also found in CD, xix. 7f., and there is no assurance that it was only later applied to Jesus by the Church.

which might seem to echo words and ideas associated with the Servant of II Isaiah. These parallels could be multiplied by a study of the entire Gospel, and Dodd is among those who would stress a relationship between the Son of Man and the Servant who is similarly exalted and glorified in and from out of his sufferings.[1] Yet, while there is no reason to insist that the language of II Isaiah could not have affected the Son of Man sayings directly, we would once more set forth our contention that the relationship between the Son of Man and II Isaiah's Servant is much more profound than theories about literary borrowings would indicate.

We find much less reason to establish any basic connection between the *Logos* and the Son of Man earlier than the composition of this Gospel.[2] Many attempts have been made to trace the Prologue back to an Aramaic original and/or to find here an earlier version of the myth of the Man who descends into the world.[3] It has been maintained that the *man* of 1.6 now identified with John ('There was an ἄνθρωπος sent from God whose name was John') was originally the legendary Man or *Enosh*[4] and also that in 1.14 we read 'the Word became flesh' rather than 'the Word became Man' because John believed that Jesus was eternally the Man.[5]

Yet it would be surprising, if the author had attached any great significance to *anthropos*, that he would either have employed it as or let it stand as a reference to the Baptist. Should it be countered that the Prologue might have been a source the significance of which the evangelist did not fully understand, it could be rejoined that many regard John 1.6ff. as a prose insertion into that original source.

The suggestion that *flesh* is a substitute for *the Man* in 1.14 makes a

---

[1] *Op. cit.*, pp. 246ff.

[2] Were there an earlier causative link between the *Logos* and the Man, one would have thought that the Prologue would have made it more clear and that there would be some other hint of the association in the Gospel. For our rejection of such a connection see p. 52 n. 3; p. 227 n. 1. On the *Logos*, cf. Dodd, *Interpretation of the Fourth Gospel*, pp. 263ff. The Mandaean references are really not a close parallel to John 1.1ff., for Anush, like other messengers, is the bearer of the Word or words and not that Word itself. Odes of Sol. 12.12, etc., may give some insight into the kind of thought (originally non-incarnational) out of which John 1.1ff. could have evolved.

[3] See esp. Schaeder in *Studien zum antiken Synkretismus*, pp. 306ff. (he also, of course, speculated on 1.9, by seeing it as a reference to *the* Man, though many still feel, even if 'ᵉnāš did stand here in some Aramaic original, that this would counter his argument that *man* meant more than a human being). Cf. Sidebottom, *op. cit.*, pp. 62f. Generally see Dodd, *op. cit.*, pp. 263ff.; Cullmann, *Christology*, pp. 249ff.

[4] Schaeder, *op. cit.*, p. 326.

[5] See Héring, *RHPR* 16, 1936, pp. 207ff.

pretty sophisticated point. We wonder if the author would have been concerned with it and so (were this his interest as the theory assumes) passed over an opportunity to proclaim Jesus as the Man or the Son of Man. It is more probable that he is only presenting us with his anti-docetic view of the incarnation.

It would be easier to find that *anthropos* was a reference to the Man in the Prologue if it could be established that the word was so employed elsewhere in John. Probably the only real basis for this contention could be John 19.5, where Pilate presents Jesus dressed as a mock king and says, 'Behold, the *anthropos*!' Now, admittedly it is hard, especially against the materials we have studied, to avoid the inference that Jesus is here being viewed as the royal Man, even to the extent that he is arrayed in the garments of his humiliation. It seems to fit, almost with a resounding click, into the pattern. It is conceivable that John's passion narrative, containing as it does no reference to the Son of Man, may have passed through hands which either intentionally or unintentionally rewrote an earlier reference made to the (Son of) Man at this point and possibly at other points as well.

Yet there are obstacles to such an interpretation. If we accept the scene as it stands, is it very likely that, out of all the figures who people the New Testament, Pilate should have known about the Man/Son of Man beliefs? But perhaps this difficulty can be circumvented. Possibly Pilate could have heard the designation being used with reference to Jesus and so offered it as a kind of mocking comment even though he did not fully comprehend it. Or perhaps the early tradition has put the words into Pilate's mouth.

Still, were this so, were the word recognized as one freighted with special nuance and were it seen as an alternative to the Son of Man, one would have thought that this would have influenced its use in other contexts. Yet the other Gospels do not even seem to allude to the possibility, and repeatedly elsewhere the Fourth Gospel uses the phrases *the man, this man, a man*, both of Jesus and others, as though blithely unaware of any nuance.[1]

[1] E.g. 4.29; 7.46; 9.11; 11.47, 50; 18.14, 17, 29 referring to Jesus, sometimes used anarthrously. So also of the blind man, 9.24; of Nicodemus, 3.1; and of any man, 3.4; etc. And contrast, 'After me comes a man (ἀνήρ)' in 1.30. Black (*Aramaic Approach*, p. 236) suggests that John may be using *anthropos* to translate an Aramaic indefinite pronoun.

Sidebottom (*Christ of the Fourth Gospel*, pp. 84ff.), who believes that the Son of Man title stresses Jesus' humanity in this Gospel, proposes that we reckon with

Of much more interest to us is the water imagery of the Gospel along with some of its associations. Let us look first at Jesus' meeting with Nicodemus in John 3.1ff. and the discussion there about entering the Kingdom of God. Here one of the key words is ἄνωθεν. This adverb has two primary meanings, 'from above' and 'anew',[1] but the former has predominance. This is true in the New Testament as well as in other literature, and, more importantly, in John, where, outside this passage, 'from above' is the meaning.[2] The whole force of the culmination of this passage (3.13) along with the use of the word in 3.31 strongly suggest that 'being born *from above*' is the *primary* sense intended in 3.3, 7. Yet it is probably just as obvious that Nicodemus understands it as 'anew' when he asks Jesus, 'How can a man be born when he is old? Can he enter a second time into his mother's womb and be born?' Almost surely, then, we are dealing with Johannine irony. Not only does Nicodemus misunderstand ἄνωθεν, but he fails to understand the mode of the birth which Jesus is describing.

Accepting here the distinct probability that it is baptism which is being discussed,[3] it is necessary to ask what is meant by 'being born from above'. Our suggestion is that we have here a passage built upon relics from earlier sectarian days, ideas about where and when baptism was believed to take place. An individual was either exalted to heaven, there to be baptized or, in a heavenly-like setting (heaven, as it were, being *realized* on earth), he was so baptized.[4] Of course, we cannot demonstrate that this is what once was intended, but we

---

Johannine irony in texts like John 8.40; 10.33. These raise interesting possibilities, but there remain the alternative examples. Perhaps such irony would explain 19.5. Pilate is unable to see Jesus' divinity. But then, as 10.33 might seem to make clear, the contrast is between manhood and Godhead, not between man and Man or Son of Man.

[1] It also has the less well-attested meanings 'from the beginning' (cf. Luke 1.3.), which would offer an interesting nuance here, and 'for a long time' (Acts 26.5).

[2] See also John 19.11, 23; Mark 15.38; James 1.17; 3.15, 17. Only in Gal. 4.9 is it usually taken to mean 'again', but even there it could refer to the *aboveness* of the elemental spirits.

[3] Odeberg (*Fourth Gospel*, pp. 48ff.) sees water as a reference to spiritual semen. Against this as improbable (in any case the two ideas need not be mutually exclusive), on the nuances of 'being born' and against attempts to omit 'and water' from the text of 3.5, see Barrett, *St John*, pp. 174f.

[4] Is there also a parallel relic in Mark 11.30 (and parr.)? 'Was the baptism of John from heaven (ἐξ οὐρανοῦ) or from men?' Of course, this is usually taken only to refer to *authority*, and no doubt this is how the evangelists intended it. But in the light of John 3.13 and esp. 3.31, is this all that was originally intended?

think it fits with much of the context (see below) and with the background we have delineated, and that it gives an insight into a passage which is otherwise hardly easy to understand. The fact that John does not bring the idea up again and that he may himself be finding it a difficult conception (especially in relation to 3.13) could enhance the possibility that it goes back to earlier materials.[1]

Also, though we are aware that John may have other theological reasons for omitting the story of Jesus' own baptism, it could be not only that this adoptionist-sounding tradition did not fit with the belief that Jesus was the eternal Son of God, but that the evangelist found the story somewhat confusing. Did it somehow seem to say that in an heavenly or an heavenly-like setting Jesus had been exalted to an office as the Son (of God or Man or both?)? If so, how was he then later on earth, and how did this tradition relate (for John) to his original coming from heaven?[2]

We are unable to postpone a discussion of John 3.13,[3] which, in our opinion, has authentic connections with at least parts of the preceding passage.[4] First in 3.12 we read, 'If I have told you earthly things and you do not believe, how can you believe if I tell you heavenly things?' Some would interpret this so as to mean that one of the earthly things about which Jesus has told Nicodemus was the baptism from above. Yet this doesn't appear to make much sense or to give point to the progression of the discussion. Rather does it proceed in this fashion: Nicodemus misunderstands the baptism from above. Jesus is represented as trying an *earthly* analogy (concerning the wind-spirit which blows about mysteriously). Still Nicodemus cannot understand: 'How can this be?'

Now, there is only one who has really been initiated into the heavenly secrets, only one who really has been given the true baptism from above.

---

[1] Some also find the mention of the Kingdom of God in this passage (only here in John) a sign of authenticity. Was this then an authentic context in which admission into the Kingdom was once discussed?

[2] See John 1.32ff., which obviates these difficulties by having the Spirit as a dove become a sign by which Jesus' eternal Sonship can be recognized. The sense of his having become the Son of God is dismissed as far as is possible.

[3] On 3.14 and its relation to 3.13, see below.

[4] Obviously it is now impossible to know just how much of 3.1–13 may be based on authentic tradition and how much may be the added work of the tradition or the evangelist. We suspect a fair amount of the latter (and could get a much more straightforward reading by omitting certain confusions), but our main interest here is with 3.3, 5, 13 and our basic argument is not concerned with the other verses.

No one has ascended (ἀναβέβηκεν) into heaven but he who came down (ὁ καταβάς) from heaven, the Son of Man (who is in heaven).

It is usual to take the verb for *ascended* and compare it with its usage in other passages in this Gospel and the New Testament where we may seem to hear clearly enough the voice of the early Church. In John 20.17 Jesus so speaks twice of ascending into heaven after his resurrection. In Acts 2.34f. it is said that David did not ascend into the heavens and inferred that Jesus did.[1] Then we are often referred to a number of verses in John 6 where we hear of Jesus and the bread, both of whom came down from heaven. Thus it is maintained that this is a saying created by the early community or by John concerning the Son of Man/Jesus who came down from heaven and ascended thither again.

Yet if this is all that lies behind the statement, it is a marvel that John did not manage to express himself more clearly. Why does he not just say, 'No one has come down from heaven except the Son of Man'? Then, if he did wish to make a reference to his ascension after death at this point (though such blatant anachronisms are not his custom),[2] he could have added, 'even he who has ascended into heaven and who now is in heaven'.

It is not only the position of the first clause which causes difficulties, but more especially the perfect tense of '*has* ascended' (and usually the Greek uses this tense with purpose and care). Barrett writes, 'It seems to imply that the Son of Man had already at the moment of speaking ascended into heaven' (or, perhaps more accurately, had previously ascended before his descent). Barrett starts to make a comparison with I Enoch 70f., but then hesitates . . . John's thought 'has no room for such an ascent' (with which opinion we would agree). He concludes by suggesting that this ascent of the Son of Man is being viewed from the standpoint of the later Church (although even this doesn't tell us why, from that point of view, ascent should seem to precede descent), but admits that 'who is in heaven' complicates the matter further.[3]

---

[1] See above p. 235 n. 3 and also on John 6.62 below. Sometimes we are given a cross-reference to Eph. 4.8ff. as well, though not always is its particular application explained. If it is relevant, we should think that it would support our general approach here, for see our remarks p. 256 n. 1 and below.

[2] '. . . the Evangelist is not accustomed to forget the historical context of his narrative altogether.' E. C. Hoskyns, *The Fourth Gospel* (ed. F. N. Davey), London, 1940, pp. 235f., commenting on this verse.

[3] *St John*, pp. 177f.

Sidebottom also feels these acute difficulties.

It cannot be taken to imply that the ascent came first and then the descent. Is it to be imagined that Jesus is represented as telling Nicodemus that he had been up to heaven to see τὰ ἐπουράνια (heavenly things) and then descended to tell men about them? Is this then the descent of the Incarnation, and in that case what could the previous ascent have been?[1]

Rightly does Sidebottom see that, if the ascent does refer to Jesus' ascension after resurrection, there is added confusion, for the point of the saying also seems to indicate that Jesus saw these heavenly things before talking to Nicodemus. He therefore suggests that John 3.13 may be an answer to Prov. 30.4: 'Who has ascended into heaven and come down?'[2] (though the answer implied there is 'no one'). His real solution, however (though it is still only partial), involves a grammatical point. Following J. H. Moulton, he contends that εἰ μή here should be interpreted so as to permit us to translate, 'No one has ascended into heaven, but one has descended, the Son of Man'. It is, of course, never the safest course to attempt to escape an exegetical problem by reference to a grammatical oddity, especially when it is not instanced elsewhere in the same writing. Yet, even if we grant Sidebottom the possibility of this translation, he is only able to deal with 'who is in heaven' by suggesting that this belongs to 'the traditional idea of Ascension'. This, however, would be strange if he is right to contend that such a view of the ascension cannot apply earlier in the verse.

But let us return to what Sidebottom (and Barrett) seems to feel is the first and natural impression of the verse and to his rhetorically intended question, 'What could the previous ascent have been?' We would suggest that, according to the pattern of the rites and myths in which the Man ascends to heaven and is there shown divine secrets, the reference here is to the liturgical and/or mythical ascent of the one who was ordained to the function of the Son of Man.[3] (Indeed, there may still be traces of such a conception in the synoptic narratives of Jesus' baptism,[4] and it is possible, too, that this idea was once closely related to the *exaltation* or *lifting up* of the Son of Man which is

[1] *Christ of the Fourth Gospel*, p. 120.
[2] The thought, so expressed, was a kind of commonplace. Yet it is hard to see how either the context or the point of the discussion or (in our opinion) the Gospel as a whole prepares us for this.
[3] Recall, e.g., I Enoch 70f.; II Enoch 22; II (4) Esd. 13.32.
[4] Here we are thinking esp. of his *going up* or *ascending* (ἀναβαίνων, Mark 1.10; ἀνέβη, Matt. 3.16) from the water. See also below on John 1.51.

spoken of elsewhere.)[1] Now this one has *returned* or *descended* to the earth,[2] while yet the Son of Man continues to have a heavenly reference. In these terms we meet again the dual realities of the Man myth; he has functions or roles both in heaven and yet on earth through the one who represents him.

Doubtless, if we are correct and this outline of ideas does lie behind John 3.13 (as the culmination of the preceding verses), the evangelist has given us the basic teaching in a more than somewhat elliptical form. Nor do we think that he would have understood all that was implied. Rather has he taken over an old saying from the tradition and made the best use he could of it.

Of course it remains possible that in this process of adaptation John (or his tradition) has himself made additions to the saying. It is not hard to see how and why John might have been the one to make this verse truly difficult by supplying the picture of a descent in order (from his point of view) to bring the Son of Man to earth again.[3] This clause subtracted we might achieve something very close to a primitive statement or article of faith: 'No one has ascended into heaven but the Son of Man, the one being in heaven' (or, 'who is in heaven' or, 'the heavenly one').

It could also be that the saying was yet more straightforward and that 'who is in heaven' was added by some scribe who felt the difficulties created by John.[4] Or, if it is all primitive tradition except for this clause, a scribe may have been attempting to clarify the old conception which was no longer comprehended. On the whole, however, we should think that 'who is in heaven' was original, and that scribes unable to deal with the complicated conception have either altered or subtracted it. (See also our comments on 'where he was before' in John 6.62.)

There is another possibility in that, if this saying was originally applied to the Son of Man conception but not to the historical Jesus as the Son of

---

[1] Ἀναβαίνω is in several connections almost synonymous with ὑψόω in the LXX, and both verbs are used for ascents into heaven. See Davies, *He Ascended into Heaven*, p. 29, and below on the relation of these and similar verbs in both the Old and New Testaments. It may be somewhat fanciful, but is within the realm of possibility, that Paul is referring to his own not wholly dissimilar initiation experience in II Cor. 12.2ff.

[2] Normally, in the context of the Man myth, one would not think explicitly in terms of a coming to earth again, but here it may have been an appropriate way of indicating how heavenly matters could be revealed by one who was now on earth. But see also below.

[3] On the other hand, it might seem inexplicable that he should have added a reference to the ascent (to a saying which once told only of descent) in this manner.

[4] The manuscripts are fairly well divided. Barrett (*St John*, p. 178) writes, 'It seems probable that John wrote these words . . . It is clear that they present in acute form the difficulty which we have already noted in ἀναβέβηκεν.'

Man, the reference to his *now* being in heaven would be fitting and appropriate.[1]

Probably such a novel interpretation of this passage will seem surprising at first, but we think that a reference to the Man myth, incorporating this idea that a mortal appointed to the office of the Son of Man can go up to heaven (i.e. no one has gone up to heaven except the one selected to be the Son of Man)[2] helps to make sense of John 3.13 and the preceding discourse.

We cannot here give full consideration to Jesus' discussion with the Samaritan woman about the waters of life (John 4.7ff.). All we would point out is that the themes involved in the phrases 'living water' and 'fountain (or spring) of water welling up' and the idea of drinking water leading to new or eternal life and which quenches all thirst fit well into the general context of a baptizing sectarianism as we have seen it through comparative materials. Nor can we forget that the one who traditionally supplies this revivifying water is the Man himself. There is every good reason for believing that these themes and ideas have derived from a living practice,[3] and, while one may not wish to identify the particular *milieu* suggested by John 4 with that known by Jesus, there are sound grounds for suspecting, at the least, many similarities.[4]

Lastly, however, we wish to look at a rather isolated and formidably difficult passage, John 7.37f.

[1] We would note, in addition, that the *confusion* in this saying could have resulted from John's misunderstanding of the terms of reference of the *descent* of the Son of Man. If we but subtract the words 'from heaven' which John could well have inferred or even substituted, and if we take it that some descent does precede ascent, then the descent might well refer to the going down of the Son of Man into the underworld and death as a necessary prerequisite for his ascent. The parallels with kingship ideology, the Odes of Solomon, etc., and such a passage as Eph. 4.8ff. would become obvious.

[2] The stress is on the uniqueness and special nature of this Son of Man's experience. It should probably not be taken as polemic against stories of the ascents of Jewish heroes of the past (who may themselves have been thought by some to have become the Son of Man in a manner similar to the fashion in which Adam was represented by a whole series of men; so Enoch and probably Abel, Seth, etc., could be viewed, at one time or another, as the son of the Man). Certainly this Gospel assumes that Abraham and Isaiah are in heaven to see Jesus' day and glory.

[3] While there are, of course, many interpretations, we should not be surprised if there was behind John 2.1ff. some aetiological legend deriving from disputes between sectarian groups, some of whom used water and others wine.

[4] In our next chapter we shall want to discuss the scene in which Jesus walks on water (and also the stilling of the stormy sea) to find what relevance this may have to the long-standing authority of the Man over water and the language which reflects his struggles in and with the watery elements.

On the last day, the great day of the feast, Jesus stood up and pro-claimed, 'If anyone thirst, let him come to me and drink. He who believes in me—just as the scripture said—"Rivers of living water shall flow from his (literally, *the*) belly." '

This translation would indicate that the rivers come forth from the believer. Yet we might just as well translate,

'If anyone thirst, let him come to me, and let him who believes in me drink. Just as the scripture said, "Rivers of living water shall flow from his belly." '

Now the quotation could refer to either the believer or the speaker.[1]

It is not our intention to discuss the multitude of theories which have been brought forth to explain these verses. We suspect that they have to do with the Man as the giver of the sacred water, but it will always remain possible, both grammatically and otherwise, that the 'scripture' was intended to refer to the believer. John 4.14 would then probably be the best parallel and support.

It is also possible that the thought came from a Church tradition developed out of John 19.34, though we incline to the suspicion that, if there is a relationship, it was formed the other way around.[2] This might better explain why water as well as blood flows from the side of the crucified Jesus. In addition there is no obvious other hint that 7.37f. is to be linked with the passion. Then, too, there is no Old Testament text which answers to the quotation here given.[3] The Church, one might guess, would have tried to supply a genuine reference were this a tradition which they developed. One can there-fore wonder if it does not go back to much earlier tradition, perhaps referring to some now lost interpretation of scripture or even to a no longer extant sectarian writing.[4]

---

[1] Bultmann, *Evangelium des Johannes*, pp. 228ff., prefers the second translation for its parallelism which would make it more like John 6.35 in form. Cf. G. D. Kilpatrick, 'The Punctuation of John 7.37–8', *JTS*, ns11, 1960, pp. 340ff.

[2] See also I John 5.6ff. We note the possibility that the link between water and blood results from the old association of *baptism* and death.

[3] Isa. 12.3; 55.1; 58.11; Prov. 18.4 are among the texts sometimes mentioned. It is, of course, true that John has the habit of referring to the Old Testament rather loosely, but rarely as loosely as this. Although T. F. Glasson (*Moses in the Fourth Gospel* [SBT 40], 1963, pp. 48ff.) rightly points to the many instances where Mosaic history has influenced this Gospel, we do not believe that the rock in the wilderness has done so here. Nor do we find a direct comparison with I Cor. 10.4 helpful.

[4] Or liturgy? Segelberg (*Maṣbūtā*, p. 130) makes a comparison between the Mandaean *invitatorium* to baptism and John 7.37. With John 7.38 see also below on the Odes of Solomon.

The mention of the feast may help us. It is the Feast of Tabernacles and the great day of that season (whether this be regarded as
the seventh day or the eighth day following). We recall all the
associations of this feast with water, both from antiquity and during
this period. This was the time at which the divine favour was im-
plored to guarantee a *controlled* supply of water. (Mimetic water rites,
not recorded in the Old Testament, but probably of ancient origin,
were still being carried on.)[1] Special reference might be made to
Zech. 14 and 'the living waters' which 'shall go out from Jerusalem'
at this festal time.[2] This has given rise to attempts to amend or
interpret 'belly'[3] to mean Jerusalem, which might fit with rabbinic
and older theories which saw Jerusalem as the centre and navel of
the earth (for in its temple precincts the garden was once *ritually*
located). Either to the keeper of this river, or, more particularly, to
him as the cosmic-like royal Man, this saying might once have
belonged.

The conception, stated in these terms, would probably not have
been found in more normative Jewish circles, but it might have had a
place among the baptizing sects. Thus in the Odes of Sol. 30 we read,

1 Fill ye waters for yourselves from the living fountain of the Lord,
  For it has been opened to you;
2 And come all ye thirsty and take a draught,
  And rest by the fountain of the Lord. . . .
5 For it flows from the lips of the Lord,
  And from the heart of the Lord is its name.[4]

More specifically there is this from the Naassenes:

'But Mesopotamia', he says, 'is the current of the great ocean flowing
from the midst of the Perfect Man. . .'.[5]

Of course, it can be held that these conceptions are derivative from
Christianity, but certainly neither of them as such makes it obvious
that they are dependent upon John 7.38. We would think instead
that all three of them suggest the common background.

---

[1] See the Mishnah tractate *Sukkah* 4.9 and Barrett, *St John*, pp. 270f.
[2] Zech. 14.8, and see also Ezek. 47.1ff.
[3] There is no support for an emendation. Κοιλία means belly or abdominal
cavity, but may also suggest various organs of the torso, such as the heart. Generally
it does not refer to the centre of an inanimate object.
[4] Cf. Ode 36.7: My heart gushed out, as it were, a gush of righteousness.
[5] Hippolytus, *Refutation* V, 8.20. Compare also 1QH, viii, 4, etc.

4. THE JOHANNINE SAYINGS

John 1.51: And he said to him, 'Truly, truly, I say to you,[1] you will see heaven opened, and the angels of God ascending and descending upon the Son of Man.'

It is difficult to know how closely this saying should be related to its present context. The scene with Nathanael could nicely end with verse 50, and the reference to the Son of Man is not the necessary culmination of the passage. The 'and he said to him' is redundant and the switch from 'you' (sing.) in the preceding to 'you' (plural) here is surprising. We should think it possible that 1.51 was an isolated logion, a statement about the Son of Man, which John picked up from the tradition and attached to the passage.[2] It is hard to believe that either he or the tradition would have created a saying of this type, fraught with so many implications and seeming to require some background, but then supplied no explanation.

Conceivably there is a link with some of the synoptic Son of Man sayings in that, as an isolated saying, 1.51 may not necessarily have referred to Jesus as the Son of Man. Rather might it have been a more general statement, perhaps of a liturgical type. Yet, most significantly, it refers not to the Son of Man in heaven (at least not solely to him, see below), and a connection with any particular synoptic category of logia can only be precarious.[3]

Rather do we suggest that the context for this saying, and for its relationship to the synoptic traditions, involves the story of Jesus' baptism. In John 1 we are at least very near to traditions concerning the Baptist and the beginning of Jesus' ministry which parallel those related in the synoptics in connection with Jesus' baptism. In addition we have here references to the heaven being opened[4] and to angels

---

[1] Some texts add 'henceforth' or 'from now on', which looks like an attempt to conform the saying to a more eschatological type.

[2] Alternatively the passage may have possessed a certain previous unity. Perhaps then the Son of Man designation was intended as a superior synonym to Son of God and King of Israel, which might reflect an early tradition (also evidenced in the synoptics) that Son of Man was the basic and preferable title. On King of Israel see below p. 280 n. 3.

[3] Higgins (*Son of Man*, pp. 157ff.) uses the αμην as a link with Matt. 10.23; 16.28; 19.28; the angels suggest Mark 8.38; 13.26; etc., and the opened heaven is reminiscent of Acts 7.56. The first of these is purely fortuitous, and the others we believe to be far more germane in the setting we would indicate. It is true that the 'you will see' parallels the opening of Mark 14.62, but this *formula* is hardly the specific property of the Son of Man sayings.

[4] Mark 1.10; Matt. 3.16; Luke 3.21.

(ministering angels?),[1] both of which are also fundamental to the synoptic stories. This last feature can remind us of the angels who are often said to have been attendant upon Adam and of the angel or angels who frequently minister to the Adamite-Man as he is initiated into his royal office.

Taking into account these factors, the use of the baptismal word σφραγίζω in John 6.27 and the manner in which the voice from heaven precedes the Son of Man sayings at 12.34 (to which we would add our discussion on 3.13 and its relation to its preceding context), S. E. Johnson writes, 'This suggests that John may have known a story of the baptism in which Jesus is called the Son of Man.'[2] At least it may suggest that John found the Son of Man already linked with baptismal motifs in his sources.

We also regard it as probable that speculation based upon Gen. 28.12 has played its part in the formation of the saying. There Jacob sees a ladder set up between heaven and earth, 'and behold, the angels of God were ascending and descending upon it'. The ambiguity here is the Hebrew *bō* which, since ladder is masculine, might mean either 'upon the ladder' or 'upon him' (i.e. Jacob). Doubtless the former was originally intended and the Greek versions clear this matter up, but we also know that there was speculation about the alternative. This speculation must have originated in a Semitic context, and some version of it would seem fundamental to the formation of this saying.[3]

There is a passage in the *Genesis Rabba* which attributes such a view to Rabbi Yannai. The later commentator doubts this, for it would mean that,

. . . they were taking up and bringing down upon him. They were leaping and skipping over him and rallying him, as it is said, 'Israel in whom I

---

[1] Mark 1.13; Matt. 4.11.

[2] 'Son of Man' in *The Interpreter's Dictionary of the Bible* (ed. G. Buttrick), New York, 1962, IV, p. 416.

[3] And so we doubt Higgins' view that there is only an 'oblique reference' to Gen. 28.12 here as well as the denial by W. Michaelis ('Joh. 1.51, Gen. 28.12 und das Menschensohn-Problem', *TLZ* 85, 1960, cols. 561ff.) that Gen. 28.12 has any place at all. We feel that G. Quispel has seen the place of Ezek. 1.26 in the general background, but question its direct relevance here. 'Nathanael und der Menschensohn', *ZNW* 47, 1956, pp. 281ff.

Odeberg's attempt (*Fourth Gospel*, pp. 320ff.) to link this with the Naassene speculation regarding Jacob and the Man (Hippolytus, *Refutation* V, 8.20f.) is not completely successful. What is interesting, however, is the association there, in John 1.49ff. and in the *Genesis Rabba*. Was Jacob once, like Abel, Seth, Enoch, etc., considered a type of the Man?

glory,' 'Thou art he whose image is engraved on high.' They were ascending on high and looking at his image and then descending below and finding him sleeping.[1]

The relevance of this manner of thought to our study is obvious, however obscure some of its details may be,[2] and we cannot believe that it is sheer coincidence which has brought a reference to the Man myth and Gen. 28.12 together in both John 1.51 and here. No doubt we cannot simply say that the speculation as found in the third century AD lies behind John 1.51, but it is certainly credible that the *Genesis Rabba* has preserved a version of a way of thought which in another form had influenced John 1.51. Dodd, in accepting such a view, suggests that John himself may have substituted the Son of Man for Jacob here. Yet is it not far more likely that, since Jacob was seen as a counterpart of the image above, the connection with the Man myth had already been made, and that Jacob, as a type of the one above, was himself a kind of Son of Man?[3]

Our interpretation also involves no need to see the Son of Man here as an esoteric cosmic intermediary. This view only results from thinking that the Son of Man/Jacob has been identified with the ladder and that the angels are using him as a means for ascending and descending between earth and heaven. This could have been one understanding,[4] but the *Genesis Rabba* passage does not presume this. Rather are the angels ascending and descending between the Jacob below and the image above. The angels are the intermediaries between the image above and the counterpart below. We think that, in an abbreviated and elliptical fashion from out of a once-living body of ideas, John 1.51 is presenting a somewhat similar picture of angels who come down from heaven and ascend back up again.[5]

[1] 68.12. See Odeberg, *op. cit.*, pp. 33ff.

[2] For instance, what is it that they are taking up and bringing down? C. F. Burney (*The Aramaic Origin of the Fourth Gospel*, Oxford, 1922, pp. 116f.) suggested that it was this image of the heavenly Man, but it may not be that anything definite was implied.

[3] See above p. 279 n.3, and recall that Philo saw *Israel*, along with Beginning, Word, etc., as one of the names of the Man (*Confusion of Tongues*, 146). This might well supply the connection with John 1.49 and the mention of King of Israel.

[4] Cf. Odeberg, *op. cit.*, p. 39.

[5] Perhaps they come down *upon* the Son of Man, and, as it were, *from upon* him, they ascend back up again. Alternatively, it may be that ἐπί is here to be taken in a double sense, the angels ascending *toward* the Son of Man who is above and at the same time descending *upon* the representative Son of Man who is below (as the *Genesis Rabba* passage might suggest). Or, again, ἐπί may be taken in the sense of *above* or *over*, the angels being represented as moving up and down over the head of

John 3.14: And as Moses lifted up the serpent in the wilderness, so must the Son of Man be lifted up.

This is not an easy verse to discuss, both because of its relation to what precedes and follows and because of internal questions. On several of these issues one can only offer a useful guess, and this we propose to do rather summarily in order to get on to what we believe to be the heart of the matter.

We doubt whether 3.13 and 3.14 originally belonged together. Perhaps they had been joined in some written or oral source which John was using, but they represent rather different ideas, at least as now stated, and it is easy to see how the designation itself and the kindred themes of *going up* and being *lifted up* might have caused them to come together. The very repetition of the title might be a sign that they once could have stood separately. There is no obvious way of demonstrating this impression conclusively, but it is one that we share in common with a number of commentators.[1]

We doubt also, though somewhat less severely, whether 3.15 was a part of the earliest form of this saying. We do not deny the possibility that belief in the Son of Man and the life of the new or eternal age (or belief and new life in him)[2] were once closely linked, but we are far from certain that it would have been done in phraseology quite like this. On the other hand, as the rest of the Gospel and the following verses in particular show, this probably represents fairly typical Johannine language.

Then we would guess that the analogy with Moses and the snake

---

the Son of Man. (Arguments based on the nuances of *bō*, or any Hebrew or Aramaic synonyms, are somewhat pointless as the speculations show that it could be interpreted in several ways. See Black, *Aramaic Approach*, p. 85. Nor can any argument based on the order of ascending and descending be pressed, since this is how Gen. 28.12 puts the matter.) In any event, however ambiguous the use of the preposition may be, any of these views is at least as comprehensible as ones which see the Son of Man as a figure who could only be in heaven. And to argue that the opening of the heaven must mean that we are involved with a vision of a being in heaven (Higgins, *op. cit.*, p. 159) ignores the other obvious possibility, that the heaven is being opened to allow the angels to be seen coming down.

[1] Schulz (*Untersuchungen*, pp. 104ff.) wishes to see a literary unity in the present form of 3.13–15. If this be true, for it obviously has a certain unity as it now stands, this would probably have been achieved at some late point in the tradition.

[2] Barrett (*op. cit.*, p. 179), noting that *to believe* is never otherwise followed by ἐν in John, suggests the translation, 'so that everyone who believes might have eternal life in him'.

is secondary to a yet more primitive saying. As with the previous suggestions, our interpretation need not depend on its omission, and it may be that both a saying about the Son of Man and one about the serpent came together at a fairly early time.[1] Still, the probability that they were once unattached can be inferred from several factors, chief among them being that in 8.28 and 12.34 we have very similar statements about the Son of Man without a reference to Moses or the serpent in the wilderness. In addition, though it is easy to observe the parallelism in the ideas, the verb employed in the three Johannine verses was not used in the translations of Num. 21.9, so it is at least more natural to believe that the Son of Man saying provided the basic language here. Thus, while not insisting that some version of the whole of 3.14 (or even 3.14f.) could not have already come together and been so used in authentic tradition, we think that the fundamental core unit had to do with the *lifting up* of the Son of Man. Upon this idea we would like to concentrate.

What would it once have meant to say something to the effect, 'The Son of Man must (δεῖ) be *lifted up* (ὑψωθῆναι)'? No certainty can be attained, but the force of this verb could have had one of two and possibly one of three or four or five meanings, with perhaps two or more of these sometimes being used in combination.

(*a*) to lift up, to be lifted up, to go up from a lower place to a higher, and so sometimes to be lifted up from earth to heaven. In this sense ὑψόω very frequently translates the verb *rûm*, frequently *nāśā* and on occasion (as ὑπερυψόω) the root '*ālā* in the Old Testament. To this degree it is in some measure a parallel with ἀναβαίνω, which often translates '*ālā*.

(*b*) to exalt, to be exalted, to be brought to a position of great honour and prestige. Naturally enough the stems *rûm*, *nāśā*,[2] and '*ālā* can readily take on this meaning, and in this sense ὑψόω can be used to translate the first two of them. Frequently *rûm* and *nāśā* are used to render the idea of the *lifting up/exaltation* of the God or king,

---

[1] Rabbinic evidence shows that the scene from Num. 21.9 was causing interest, and see Wisd. 16.5ff., where v. 7 might suggest some controversy on the subject. One cannot help but think (see Odeberg, *Fourth Gospel*, pp. 101ff.) of the Naassenes and their interest in the serpent as a salvation figure and a revealer of *gnosis* (see Gen. 3.5). Was there, then, some association between the early Naassenes and the Johannine tradition? Yet it is just as easy to posit a general interest in the serpent (occasioned by Naassene-like groups) that could have helped create a saying like this, which was then absorbed, at some point, into the tradition.

[2] And so a *nāśī* is a chief or prince, one *raised up* over the people.

especially after the latter's salvation (e.g. Ps. 18.46, 48. Notice that in verse 48 as elsewhere the sense of having been *rescued* and *vindicated* is not missing.)[1]

With this latter meaning ὑψόω has an obvious degree of synonymy with δοξάζω = *to glorify*. Δοξάζω can, on occasion also translate both *rūm* and *nāśā*, but, more importantly, it is sometimes used in tandem with ὑψόω in a quite parallel fashion.[2] One thinks especially of Isa. 52.13, where ὑψόω and δοξάζω translate *rūm* and *nāśā* respectively.

(c) Some scholars suggest that ὑψόω may have been used to translate an Aramaic verb which could also mean *to lift up upon a cross*, i.e. *to crucify*. There is a Syriac verb which had this double force, and one can point to Ezra 6.11 and to several passages from the Targums where *zāqap*[3] (which can elsewhere mean *to raise up* or *erect*) means *to hang up*, *to put to death*, probably either by hanging or crucifying (though in Ezra ὑψόω is not used as the translation). The real support for the thought that ὑψόω might have been made to have this meaning is probably John himself, for he seems to employ it in an ironic double sense (see 8.28; 12.32–34)—to be lifted up to die, to be lifted up to exaltation and glory.

The question is: did he bring out this double meaning himself, or did he find it already implied in his sources? The query cannot finally be answered, but, since the Aramaic verb may have offered the double nuance of *to be lifted up* and *to be lifted up to be put to death* and since ὑψόω cannot be said to have done so previously, the presumption could be that an Aramaic verb was used in the sources where this possibility at least existed.

Immediately this raises problems of whether Jesus *predicted* his own death and/or that of the Son of Man, and, if so, in what manner. We must postpone such a discussion, though offering our conclusion that Jesus did speak of the necessity that the Son of Man should suffer. We are far less certain, however, that he spoke specifically of the Son of Man's *crucifixion*. We should think it safer to use this possibility only if the verb behind ὑψόω could have meant *to be put to death* in a more general sense. But the whole category remains problematical.

---

[1] Compare the meanings of *rūm* (translated by ὑψόω) in Pss. 9.13; 89.19. A good illustration of the use of ὑψόω in the sense of *to vindicate* is found in Luke 1.52.

[2] See below on John 12.23; 13.31.

[3] See Black, *Aramaic Approach*, p. 103, and in M. Jastrow, *Dictionary of the Targumim, Talmud Babli and Yerushalmi and the Midrashic Literature*, New York, 1950, s.v. In Akkadian *zaqāpu/zuqqupu* (*to set up*, *to lift up*, etc.) meant 'to put to death by impalement'.

(*d*) There may be another way out of the last problem when we recognize that, of the three words which we have noticed that ὑψόω can translate, '*ālā* very often and *rūm* often (and *nāśā* rather rarely) can mean *to lift up* in the sense of *to offer, to offer a sacrifice*, and there are well-established cognates meaning *offerings* or *gifts*. It is true that ὑψόω could convey such a meaning only with difficulty (though it was used in this sense),[1] but it is interesting to realize that no Greek verb could easily bear all three meaning *to lift up, to exalt, to offer*, which all three of these Semitic roots possessed, and which they continued to convey, in greater or lesser measure, in their Aramaic forms. If there was a verb in John's source which was capable of implying all these ideas (and all religions rightly value such words), ὑψόω might have been the best translation.

(*e*) Yet a further alternative could become relevant when we realize that *nāśā* very often conveys the idea of *to carry* or *to bear* and frequently is used in this sense with regard to bearing grief, suffering, sins or iniquities (as, e.g., in Isa. 53.4, 12 and, of the king, Pss. 69.7; 89.50). Normally, however, the verb used in this way would be active and transitive, and, in any case, ὑψόω would not regularly translate *nāśā* with this meaning. Still, presumably it could have translated a verb like *nāśā* when this was only one of its nuances, or even mistranslated it if this, being its primary sense, was not understood. This alternative, however, should probably only come into play when we find a possibly synonymous verb being used in such a way as to make the meaning of *to bear sufferings* or *sins* reasonably clear.

Now, looking back at John 3.14b it is obvious that in context the verb was used to parallel the action of *lifting up* the serpent on the staff. Almost surely, however, overtones of (*a*) (in the sense of being lifted up to heaven), (*b*) or (*c*) linked closely with (*d*), or even all of these were intended. Outside this (probably secondary) context any of the above meanings might have been intended, and the others could have been implied.

At this juncture we wish to go further afield from John 3.14b and look briefly at the synoptic tradition. (Some of the matters mentioned below will be elaborated upon in succeeding discussions.) Are there synoptic themes which might relate to this Johannine phrase predicated of the Son of Man?

The most obvious candidate would seem to be heard in that note

---

[1] See Ezra 8.25 translating *rūm*.

which is first sounded in Mark 8.31: this Son of Man who first *must* suffer many things and be killed is, after three days, *to rise up* (ἀναστῆναι). It is clear, however, that the synoptic evangelists are using the verb with the meaning of *to rise from the dead*,[1] and that it thus refers, at least essentially, to a return to life on earth and not a *lifting up* or a *going up* into heaven. It is rightly pointed out that such is the normal sense for the verb ἀνίστημι and its alternative ἐγείρω when employed in connection with the idea of life after death.[2] Yet it is of some interest that this verb ἀνίστημι seems indigenous to the synoptic Son of Man sayings, while otherwise the verb ἐγείρω tends to be favoured.[3] In addition, three out of the four times Mark tells us this of the Son of Man, the idea is not explicitly limited by a reference to 'from the dead'. Is it possible that the tradition has narrowed the sense in which some early and primitive motif was associated with the Son of Man?

In the Septuagint the verb ἀνίστημι almost always translates *qūm*. This verb both in Hebrew[4] and then in Aramaic,[5] has the meanings *to stand up, to put up, to erect, to raise, to establish* and *to vindicate* and can so be used passively as well as actively. Very frequently, especially in the Psalter, we hear the cry that the Lord should *arise*, the idea being that he should *rise up* to vindicate his own honour and to defeat his enemies and champion the people.[6] (We recall in this connection the motifs associating the king and king-god with the rising of the sun.) Though we would not here press the point, it seems likely that such a cry was, in origin, cultic and liturgical.

And it is certainly worth our notice that this same stem (for which the gnostic baptismal στηρίζω is very likely a synonym) served as a technical term for baptism/consecration among the Mandaeans and Manichaeans.[7]

---

[1] See esp. Mark 9.9.

[2] Cf. Davies, *He Ascended into Heaven*, pp. 30ff.

[3] See Mark 8.31; 9.9, 31; 10.34. At Matt. 16.21 and Luke 9.22 ἐγείρω stands in lieu of ἀνίστημι. So also at Matt. 17.9, 23; 20.19. See further below and pp. 350ff.

[4] See its use, often provocative, in the Dead Sea writings: 1QM, xii, 5, 10 (*qūmā gibbōr!*); xiv, 10; (xix, 2); 1QH, iv, 22, 36; xii, 35; xvii, 14; 1QSb, v, 21 23, 27; 4Q flor., i, 12; CD, i, 11; ii, 11; vii, 16, 19; etc.

[5] According to Mark 5.41 the word was used by Jesus, though there with reference simply to a restoration of life.

[6] See Pss. 3.7; 9.19; 17.13; 35.2; 44.23, 26; 68.1; 74.22; 82.8; 132.8, and also 12.5; 76.9; 94.16; 102.13.

[7] See Segelberg, *Maṣbūtā*, pp. 152ff., and examples both active and passive given by Drower and Macuch, *A Mandaic Dictionary*, Oxford, 1963, pp. 407f., as well as above p. 214 n. 1. Cf. Widengren, *Mani and Manichaeism*, pp. 105f.

One can compare the use of the *qūm* verb in the Odes of Solomon[1] and the ἀναστάς of Test. Levi 8.2, and see II Enoch 22.5. Perhaps one should also recall the Man rising from the sea in II (4) Esd. 13.[2]

Just how closely this idea could be linked with another theme we have noticed may be revealed by Ps. 7.6:

> Arise, O Lord, in thy anger:
> lift thyself up (or be lifted up) against the fury of my enemies.

Here the respective verbs are *qūm* and *nāśā* while they are translated by ἀνίστημι (in the active for the Hebrew active [*qal*] emphatic imperative) and ὑψόω (passive for the Hebrew passive [*niphal*] imperative). It is of some further interest that the passage then goes on to tell of the setting of the judgment scene and of God taking his seat *on high*.

Rather similarly in Isa. 33.10 we read:

> Now I will arise (*qūm* = ἀνίστημι), says the Lord;
> now I will lift myself up (*rūm* = δοξάζω);
> now I will be exalted (*nāśā* = ὑψόω).[3]

In Ps. 94.2 *nāśā* (translated by ὑψόω) is used in very much the same sense as is *qūm* (translated by ἀνίστημι) in other psalms:

> Lift thyself up, O judge of the earth;
> render to the proud their deserts.[4]

Some of the nuances of the verb *qūm* with its translation by ἀνίστημι can be garnered from passages like these:

> The Lord raises up the poor from the dust . . .
> to make them sit with princes . . .[5]

---

[1] See Odes 6.13; 8.6; 15.2; 36.2; 42.6, often with reference to arising or coming to stand in the presence of God.

[2] As an important related idea one might also compare the *yismāḥ* = ἀνατελεῖ language of Zech. 6.12. Note the use of *qūm* and *ṣemaḥ* (= ἀνίστημι and ἀνατολή) in Jer. 23.5, while the *ṣāmaḥ* root is used in lieu of *qūm* to express much the same idea in Jer. 33.15. We should also recognize that the use of ἀναβαίνω in John 3.13 and 6.62 involves what is, at the least, a closely related theme.

[3] In a somewhat different sense in Ps. 113.7 *qūm* and *rūm* are used closely together.

[4] Compare also Ps. 21.13: 'Be exalted, O Lord, in thy strength!' where ὑψώθητι is used to translate *rūmā*.

[5] I Sam. 2.8.

> The oracle of David . . .
>> the man who was raised up on high,
>> the anointed of the God of Jacob.[1]

> The ungodly will not rise (i.e. be able to stand, be vindicated)
> in the judgment.[2]

>> They will collapse and fall;
>> but we shall rise and stand upright.[3]

> . . . Lord . . . raise me up that I may requite them.[4]

> Shake yourself from the dust; arise, O captive Jerusalem.[5]

Finally, in a passage which has at least as much to do with vindication and restoration as it does with any ideas of *resurrection* and which may be of importance for the New Testament usage, we read:

>> After two days he will revive us;
>> on the third day he will raise us up.[6]

It is clear from these examples that strong overtones of vindication[7] and even of *exaltation* and glory are not missing in the use of the verbs *qūm* and ἀνίστημι and that in these senses they can be related to the verbs ὑψόω and δοξάζω found in John.[8]

An obvious objection, however, presents itself. The close association of the Johannine 'The Son of Man must be lifted up . . .' with the synoptic 'The Son of Man . . . is to rise' might be discounted on the grounds that the one verb is used passively and the other actively[9] or in the middle voice. This difficulty could be circumvented if one were to argue that the ἐγείρω usage was more authentic than ἀνίστημι in the Son of Man logia, for the former verb is also regularly employed in the passive (and also translates *qūm* in the LXX). While we consider this unlikely, it is possible, if one does not hold rigidly to the theory that Mark was used by Matthew and Luke, that the alteration

---

[1] II Sam. 23.1. Compare this with the uses of *rūm* and ὑψόω in Ps. 89.19. Note also ἀνάστησον and ἀναστῆναι in Pss. of Sol. 17.23, 47.

[2] Ps. 1.5.

[3] Ps. 20.8.

[4] Ps. 41.10.

[5] Isa. 52.2.

[6] Hos. 6.2, on which see below.

[7] It is also worth pointing out that, although *zāqap* is used sparingly in the Old Testament, it is employed in Pss. 145.14; 146.8 with this same sense of vindication or preservation.

[8] Also apparently suspicious of a significant relationship between the Johannine ὑψόω and the synoptic ἀνίστημι is Black, *BJRL* 45, 1963, p. 317.

[9] And then intransitively.

may signify a certain ambiguity in the primitive tradition. But we can also realize that there is not all that much difference between the *niphal* usage[1] of *nāśā* (for example, translated by the passive of ὑψόω in Ps. 7.6) and the middle voice of ἀνίστημι as it is used in two Marcan Son of Man sayings. All it would take is a slightly different viewpoint and emphasis at some point in the traditions for 'The Son of Man is to be lifted up . . .' to become 'the Son of Man . . . is to rise up' or *vice versa*.[2]

Then, too, it appears that ἀνίστημι was often employed actively or in the middle when there was no intended stress on the positive action involved. So, for instance, others beside Jesus in the Gospels are said *to rise* (from the dead) when it is clearly understood that the divine action will raise them. It seems that this verb was not easily used in the passive to refer to resurrection, and the selection of the verb might have tended to control the voice and thus the manner in which the action was conceived. Minds were also clearly quite capable of shifting between the thought of God *raising* and of *rising*. Thus the Hosean 'he will raise us up' (*yᵉqimēnū*) becomes the Greek 'we will rise up' ([ἐξ]αναστησόμεθα).[3]

And then there is another possible association of Johannine and synoptic themes which, while at first it must seem merely coincidental and improbable, cannot be lightly brushed aside. The synoptics also assert that the Son of Man must be or is to be (παραδίδοται) *betrayed* or *given up* or *delivered up*.[4] There are two sayings in John that speak of the Son of Man's being glorified (δοξάζω)[5] which, as we shall see, both by their position in the narrative and by their wording demand a comparison with two sayings recorded by the synoptics which tell of the Son of Man being *delivered up*.[6] It is in an attempt to explain this that we come to realize that παραδίδωμι can often have the sense of *to*

---

[1] It is interesting to notice, esp. in the light of subsequent discussions, that the *niphal* perfect form of certain Hebrew verbs sometimes seems to convey the connotation of *mustness* or *oughtness*.

[2] E.g. see our comments below on John 12.34 and Mark 9.10. Notice the apparent synonymity of ideas in the uses of the verbs *to rise* and *to be lifted up* in similar contexts in the Odes of Solomon; e.g. 15.2; 21.6; 36.1f.

[3] The close relationship in the two ideas conveyed by ἀνίστημι and ὑψόω may further be shown by Acts 2.32f., which tells of Jesus being raised up by God (which is more and more the way the Church came to think of the act) and exalted to the right hand of God.

[4] See Mark 9.31; 10.33; 14.21, 41 and parr.

[5] John 12.23; 13.31.

[6] Mark 14.21, 41 and parr.

commit, to entrust, to offer. In this way it often translates *nātan* in the Old Testament and cannot be disassociated from nuances involving ideas of sacrifice and offering. This perhaps comes out most clearly in Isa. 53, where the verb is used three times. In all three instances it translates a *hiphil* (or causative and active) Hebrew verb. In 53.6 (translating *pāga'*, a verb meaning *to fall upon* or *to supplicate, to intreat*) God causes this (παρέδωκεν) to happen to the Servant. In 53.12 first the Servant *pours out* ('*ārā, to pour out, to make empty* or *bare*) his soul unto death. This is translated by a passive construction using the form παρεδόθη. The same form is used in the last clause of the verse to render 'he will make intercession' (*pāga'* again).

Allied uses of the Greek verb are to be found in the New Testament. Jesus gives up his spirit.[1] He *entrusts* himself to the one who judges justly.[2] Christ *gave* himself *up* for the Church.[3] He was *delivered up* for our trespasses[4] and *given up* for us all.[5] Jeremias suggests, and we think rightly, that the several uses of the verb are indicative of variations on a basic theme.[6] While we are far less certain than he that this theme demands a definitive association with the Isaianic Suffering Servant as such, we believe it does show how this verb might once have been understood at another time in the history of the synoptic traditions. The illustrations also demonstrate how easily the use of such a theme might pass back and forth between active and passive expression, depending on such factors as whether God is said to be causing the offering of the figure or divine action is understood to be causing this and/or whether the figure is himself making the offering.

We are then suggesting that the verb παραδίδωμι, though now taken by the synoptic evangelists in a rather limited sense to refer to the betrayal of the Son of Man, may once have been employed to catch nuances of earlier and broader motifs allusive of ideas of offering and suffering.[7] Perhaps some feeling for this may be caught when we hear

[1] John 19.30.
[2] I Peter 2.23; see Acts 14.26; 15.26, 40.
[3] Eph. 5.25. See Eph. 5.2; I Cor. 11.23; Gal. 2.20. In I Cor. 13.3 Paul speaks of *giving up* his body to be burnt. See I Cor. 15.24. Note the interesting force of the verb in Mark 4.29: 'when the grain παραδοῖ'.
[4] Rom. 4.25.
[5] Rom. 8.32.
[6] *Servant of God*, pp. 96f.
[7] Also suggesting that the synoptics have narrowed the meaning of the theme represented by παραδίδωμι is W. Kramer, *Christ, Lord, Son of God* (SBT 50), 1966, sec. 26a, p. 117. Cf. B. M. F. van Iersel, *'Der Sohn' in den synoptischen Jesusworten*

(Mark 10.45) that 'the Son of Man also came . . . to give (δοῦναι, which, of course, can also translate *nātan* plus often being used in tandem with the verbs *nāśā*, *rūm*, *'ālā*, and their cognates and also, though rarely, to translate them) his life (ψυχήν) . . . for many (πολλῶν)'. In Isa. 53.12 we hear that 'his life (ψυχή) παρεδόθη'. (The possible alliance of significant words is furthered by 'he bare [*nāśā*][1] the sins of many [πολλῶν]'.)

It becomes conceivable, then, that the distance between 'the Son of Man also came to give (up) his life . . .' here and the Marcan 'the Son of Man is *to be given up* . . .' (with its added note of scriptural *mustness*) and John's 'The Son of Man *must* be *lifted up*' and 'When you (i.e. the Jews) have *lifted up* the Son of Man . . .'[2] may narrow considerably. This last may also be compared with Mark's sayings that 'the Son of Man is to be *given up* into the hands of men . . .' and that the Jewish leaders will *give* him *up* to the Gentiles.[3]

Now we are admittedly begging more questions than we are answering, and it would be a pretty long jump from both directions to claim that behind the Johannine 'is to be glorified' (δοξάζω) lies the 'is to be exalted' (ὑψόω) which could also be understood in the sense of 'is to be offered up', and that behind the usage of παραδίδωμι in synoptic Son of Man sayings lies the meaning 'is to be offered up', so that John 12.23; 13.31 and Mark 14.21, 41 represent later interpretations of some one Aramaic phrase.[4] Yet we are again willing to ask if there is not, at the least, a nearer relationship between these themes than has formerly been recognized. On the one hand, it is hard for us to believe that the parallelism in these several themes in

---

(*NT*, Suppl. 3), 1961, pp. 57f. Hahn (*Hoheitstitel*, pp. 62f.) disputes this by suggesting that the verb (in Greek no less) had already become a fixed term for the betrayal before these other nuances became widespread in the Church.

[1] Then, remembering that *nāśā* could refer to the bearing of suffering, we might look at Mark 8.31 and 9.12 with new eyes. We hear that 'the Son of Man must suffer (παθεῖν) many things . . .' and that 'it is written of the Son of Man that he should suffer (πάθῃ) many things . . .'

[2] John 8.28.

[3] Mark 9.31; 10.33.

[4] In a similar vein, we may also notice that Mark 14.21 speaks of the Son of Man *going away* (ὑπάγει) as it is written of him. (Compare the 'I must go . . .' of Luke 13.33 and a similar use of πορεύομαι in his parallel to this Marcan verse.) As it stands now this seems a rather innocuous euphemism. John does not use the word of the Son of Man, but he does (7.33; 16.5, 10,17) use it of Jesus *going away* to the Father in heaven. If this sheds any light on the word as it may once have been understood, Mark 14.21 may now give a somewhat false impression, and this word, too, could be related to others which speak of *going up* or *being lifted up*.

both traditions predicated of the Son of Man (who [Johannine] must be lifted up to death—be lifted up in exaltation and who [synoptic] must be given up to death and rise up) is to be explained by literary influences. The forms of expression are too different. On the other hand, it is asking a great deal of coincidence if one were to suggest that such similarities are to be explained by a theory of independent but parallel developments. They must reach back to common denominators in very early tradition. Then, if these ideas had been passed on in relative independence of one another over a period of forty or fifty years, it is not really surprising that such wide seeming divergences should appear. Different communities with different needs and ways of thought and worship would be inclined to give play to variant emphases when making their (oral and written) translations of basic sayings from the tradition. This does not mean that they would intentionally wrench meanings (much less create whole categories of new sayings), but rather would they be forced, as all translators are, to lose certain nuances and add others in every act of using one word to stand for another.

We also suspect that John may have had sources which issued from somewhat different contexts of traditions about the Son of Man. One question that presents itself asks whether John or the synoptics have been more faithful in preserving nuances of the original language. Was there, for instance, once a verb used, as John would seem to indicate, that was suggestive of both themes of *offering* (or being *lifted*) *up to death* and *exaltation* at the same time[1] (which the synoptics then may have used different verbs to render), or has John instead compressed several themes into one evocative verb? It would be our guess that John may have had access to language once used of the Son of Man (perhaps not always by Jesus or of Jesus as the Son of Man) in primitive liturgical or liturgically influenced circumstances, language which from the start may have been deliberately ambiguous. On the other hand, the synoptic channels may have preserved sayings more as they were used, first by Jesus and then by the traditions as they were passed along. Fundamental to both, however, may have been the belief that the Son of Man must 'be lifted' up.[2]

---

[1] It is, of course, characteristic of a number of Semitic verbs that they are used so flexibly as sometimes to come almost to convey a sense of their opposite.

[2] Is one to say that the *early preaching* in Acts 2.33; 5.31 about the *exaltation* of Jesus has affected the terminology in John? Why, then, is John's use of the verb confined (for all intents and purposes, see below on 12.32 with 12.34) to sayings about the Son of Man? Why hasn't he used it more generally? Surely the natural

John 5.27: . . . and [he] has given him authority to execute judgment because he is Son of Man (υἱὸς ἀνθρώπου).

It is worth while to try the simple experiment of reading over verses 25 to 29 while omitting verse 27. Certainly it becomes feasible that the statement about the Son of Man has at some point been inserted into a discussion regarding the Son of God and resurrection. This would be the view of Bultmann, and Higgins also feels that verses 28–29 are typical of Johannine language, while 27 is not. He suggests that verse 27 should be regarded as an isolated pre-Johannine saying, probably one of considerable antiquity.[1]

Yet it is hard to be definitive about the matter. Schulz is right to point out that there is yet a certain unity, at least in 27–29 as it now stands.[2] The themes of the giving of new life and judgment are woven together, and we have previously realized that both ideas have an historical association with the Man figure.[3] Perhaps John has rewritten a passage in which the Son of Man was once of more exclusive interest, or perhaps we should read the whole passage (John 5.25–29) as one based upon primitive thought and see Son of God as one of the alternative designations for the one who was Son of Man. Even Schulz himself, however, is inclined to give verse 27 a kind of priority. Thus, while recognizing that the other ideas need not be unsuitable in the context of primitive teaching about the Son of Man, it is perhaps reasonable to concentrate on the one saying.

We have already seen that it is the touchstone for several theories. For many it is that pristine and most authentic logion, the one in closest touch with Jewish eschatology and the fundamental synoptic tradition. On the other hand, just to show how wide disagreement can be, Bultmann finds that it may be the very last of the Johannine

---

inference is that he found the title and the idea already together and that its special relevance to the Son of Man has probably been lost in Acts. Certainly it is hard to see how one could approach the question from the other direction.

Is the Johannine use of this verb related to the ὑπερύψωσεν of Phil. 2.9? We would welcome this belief. Yet, if so, we should think that the relationship must come from common sources (with all this implies, and esp. so if Paul is talking of the Man who was exalted) and not any Johannine or Pauline influence upon the other.

[1] Higgins, Son of Man, pp. 165ff.
[2] Untersuchungen, pp. 113f. His attempt, however, to trace the language to various points in Daniel is based on theories about literary borrowings with which we cannot agree. In any event, the thoughts are hardly exclusive to Daniel.
[3] See also John 6.53f.; and compare Odes of Sol. 15.9f.; 17; 22; 42.

Son of Man sayings, one added by a redactor. Its note of futuristic eschatology clashes with the sense of the present, risen Christ which dominated the evangelist's mind.[1]

Yet even if this last were so (and the insistence on the high eschatology of the statement both by proponents and opponents of its early date may be misplaced), the saying and/or its essential thought could go back to authentic teaching. The possibility may be enhanced by the phrase *to make judgment* ($\kappa\rho\acute{\iota}\sigma\iota\nu$ $\pi o\iota\epsilon\hat{\iota}\nu$) which sounds like a Semitism.[2] Yet care must be exercised in making such an assessment, and the same is even more true when we come to John's use of the Son of Man designation in an anarthrous manner that is unique in all the Gospel Son of Man sayings. This singularity may best be explained by another unique factor, for here alone do we find a declaratory form like 'he is Son of Man'. Elsewhere in the Gospels we have preserved for us sayings which tell of what the Son of Man does or will do. This realization coincides with a grammatical understanding, for predicate nouns preceding a verb often lack the article in Greek.[3] We may usefully compare John 10.36 ($\upsilon i\grave{o}s$ $\tau o\hat{\upsilon}$ $\theta\epsilon o\hat{\upsilon}$ $\epsilon\hat{\iota}\mu\iota$) and also look at 19.7 ($\upsilon i\grave{o}\nu$ $\theta\epsilon o\hat{\upsilon}$ $\dot{\epsilon}a\upsilon\tau\grave{o}\nu$ $\dot{\epsilon}\pi o\acute{\iota}\eta\sigma\epsilon\nu$).

These reasons may better explain the form of John 5.27 than does the search for an underlying Semitic expression, for, without necessarily denying that the tradition may once have used a Semitic phrase which lacked specific grammatical indications of definiteness or that the expression could be reasonably authentic as it now stands, the Gospel tradition is otherwise uniform in its translation of the phrase. If John 5.27 once did reflect earlier usage, we should be surprised both that this is not suggested elsewhere in the Gospels and that John (having no other reason than this) failed to conform it to his usage elsewhere.

Thus, while on the one hand we would query attempts to demonstrate from the lack of the articles that the expression here involves

---

[1] *Evangelium des Johannes*, pp. 195f.

[2] When in 5.22 it is said that the Father 'has given all judgment to the Son', the expression is not used, and one could infer that 5.22 is a Johannine formation based on his own Son Christology, while 5.27 echoes some part of the early tradition. Only in Jude 15 is the expression used elsewhere in the New Testament, and this is a quotation from I Enoch 1.9. Of course, this does not (as some seem to infer) link John 5.27 with the Son of Man in I Enoch, but it may support the belief that the phrase is a Semitism.

[3] Cf. E. C. Colwell, 'A Definite Rule for the Use of the Article in the Greek New Testament', *JBL* 52, 1933, pp. 12ff.; Moule, *Idiom Book of New Testament Greek*, pp. 115f., 177.

an emphasis on the humanity of the figure,[1] so also we wonder about the contention of many others that this must be the eschatological, heavenly judge because the anarthrous usage is said to resemble Dan. 7.13f. Even if it could be shown that there stood here a phrase which was more like that used in Daniel than in the traditions elsewhere, this need not indicate that the same fundamental intention (that of referring to a divine figure in heaven) was in mind. But besides this, there are still other differences, for Daniel speaks of 'one like a son of man' and tells of the Ancient of Days, clouds of heaven, beasts, etc. If the Johannine statement were so closely related to Daniel, we should expect one or two of these more specific Danielic features. Indeed, Daniel's hero also has authority ($\dot{\epsilon}\xi o\upsilon\sigma\dot{\iota}\alpha$) given to him,[2] but this belongs to the Man figure generally and is only one of several *powers* given in Daniel. And, although we would hardly deny that Daniel's is a figure who could be seen to have a judicial capacity, this is not there predicated of him in so many words. The emphasis there is on his rulership, his power to judge not being singled out. The attempts to tie John 5.27 exclusively or directly to Dan. 7.13f. only reveal the weaknesses of theories of literary borrowings and the scantiness of the background with which those who see the Son of Man as a specialized figure limited to two or three apocalyptic documents must work.

Surely the verse does lack the kind of specifications which would enable any of us to be certain about its terms of reference. Yet, as noted earlier, if we do not begin by assuming that the saying *must* refer exclusively to the heavenly judge, and, if we are going to make comparison with synoptic sayings, John 5.27 makes as much or more sense when compared with logia like Mark 2.10 and 2.28 than it does with, say, Mark 14.62 or 8.38. In Mark 2.10 we hear that the Son of Man (already) has authority ($\dot{\epsilon}\xi o\upsilon\sigma\dot{\iota}\alpha$) on earth to forgive sins. Here in John the one who is Son of Man has been given (already) authority ($\dot{\epsilon}\xi o\upsilon\sigma\dot{\iota}\alpha$) to make judgment. The point in Mark 2.10 is that the Son of Man is now operative on earth, and, without saying that the Son of Man is not also a figure whose authority and judgment will be wonderfully known in a great day yet to come, John 5.27 may have been intended to make the same or a similar point.

Seen against our larger background this would make good sense.

---

[1] See Sidebottom, *Christ of the Fourth Gospel*, p. 93, to whose view may be contrasted the attitude of many expressed by Barrett (*St John*, p. 218) that the divinity was never more clear. We would say that both could be implied, while neither could be demonstrated from this verse.

[2] See Schulz, *Untersuchungen*, p. 111.

One has been appointed to execute the office and to possess the authority of the Son of Man. So many rulers of old could lay claim to such an authority (and for that matter claim to defeat *death* and to bring men out of *darkness* and *prison* as in our context here) just because they were the Son, the heir and legitimate representative, of the Man. Perhaps in this may lie the true cause for the declaratory or partly declaratory form of the saying. It may not be all that different from what was said *to* Enoch, or, in other terms, from what is proclaimed in Mark 1.11: to him God has given this authority because he is the Son. This is the one appointed to be Son of Man.[1]

John 6.27: Do not labour for the food which perishes, but for the food which endures to eternal life, which the Son of Man will give to you; for on this one God the Father has set his seal.

John 6.53: So Jesus said to them, 'Truly, truly, I say to you, unless you eat the flesh of the Son of Man and drink his blood, you have no life in you.'

Obviously these two sayings, though they tend to raise problems of a somewhat different character, must be treated together.

In this chapter the bread and food which confer life are compared and contrasted to the manna in the wilderness.[2] Contemporary Jews quite understandably believed that in the new age new manna, new heavenly food would be given.[3] And it is only natural that the new Messiah would be the dispenser of this gift.[4]

Although the fourth evangelist presents the story of the feeding of the multitudes and the ensuing discussion with these thoughts much in mind and would emphasize the idea that Jesus is the new Moses[5] (and while one may also point to other possible sources of influence from the Old Testament),[6] it may be that these are largely elaborations on a story of a rather different character. The synoptic accounts, which suggest little if anything of such a *Mosaic* interpretation, could confirm this. In any case, we would instead ask what we believe to be pertinent questions and point to a larger, though related, pattern of thought.

[1] We note here that 'the Son of Man' is a poorly attested variant reading in John 5.19; 5.25; 6.56. All of these are readily explicable as scribal errors and/or echoes from other Johannine sayings.

[2] See Glasson, *Moses in the Fourth Gospel*, pp. 45ff.

[3] E.g. II Baruch 29.8. See S-B II, pp. 481f.

[4] See again S-B II, p. 481. Often it is a Mosaic-type Messiah.

[5] See esp. John 6.14.

[6] See II Kings 4.42ff.

This story is uniformly coupled with that of Jesus' walking on the water, indicating that they may well have been two stories which belonged together over a long period of time in the traditions, perhaps as part of a cycle of stories.[1] Why did Jesus do these things, or, seen in another way, why have such legends become associated with Jesus? We are not asking why he does nature miracles, but rather why he does these particular miracles. What gives cause for believing that, out of many other powers he might have possessed, he can provide food and walk on water?

Our suggestion is that he believed himself capable of doing these things and/or was believed to be able to do such acts because he was seen as a type of the royal Man (now thinking especially of John 6.27), the dispenser of food to his people. This food, though traditionally it may be seen under several species (bread being one of them),[2] comes originally from the tree of life[3] (as does the water he gives from the water of life) in the garden. It is revivifying and life-bestowing. When set into a full context, we see the Man as the host at a banquet in his new and restored kingdom of paradise, death and the powers of evil and chaos having been overcome.

It is granted that there is, outside of this passage in John,[4] nothing in the Gospels which would specifically indicate that such a power was predicated of the Son of Man so named. Yet it may be that stories like the feeding of the multitudes, the Last Supper and concerning the one who, though tempted by the devil, does not use his power to turn stones into bread become most intelligible when seen against this Man background. The parallel with I Enoch 62.14, while it is not exact, may express something of the general idea: 'and with that Son of Man shall they eat.'

Nor would it really be surprising if in the community traditions the realization that it was as the Son of Man that these things were done by (or these stories were told about) Jesus was almost wholly forgotten. For, from the point of view of the Church, these were acts which were clearly and unambiguously performed by Jesus himself. In this they differ from the sayings which Jesus uttered, for one can see how these may have been

[1] Cf. pp. 387f.

[2] E.g. II Sam. 6.19. Certainly the evangelist (John 6.15) sees the 'royal' significance of this activity.

[3] E.g. again Rev. 2.7; 22.2.

[4] Yet on the likelihood that there are in the Johannine account of the feeding elements which have both a source independent of the synoptic versions and a good claim on authenticity, see E. D. Johnston, 'The Johannine Version of the Feeding of the Five Thousand—an Independent Tradition?' *NTS* 8, 1961/2, pp. 151ff.

preserved with reasonable accuracy, while only an inordinate degree of reverence for history for its own sake could have kept alive the place of the Son of Man in stories which were told and retold about Jesus in communities which were not prone to think of him as the Son of Man.[1]

A problem remains in that John 6.27 and a logion like I Enoch 62.14 have a distinctly eschatological flavour. And, in any case, is not this feeding something the Man traditionally does after his victory and, in mythical terms, in heaven rather than on earth?

The truth in these realizations is, however, to be welcomed for the light it may shed upon certain attitudes toward the Last Supper expressed in the synoptic Gospels. We are thinking particularly of those sayings which seem to imply that the meal was presented as a kind of proleptic anticipation of a meal which could really only be consummated in heaven: Mark 14.25 = Matt. 26.29; Luke 22.15–18. With this can be coupled other sayings in which the consummation of the kingdom is envisioned in terms of a heavenly banquet.[2]

To this it could be responded that the feeding of the five thousand does not seem to fit with such a proleptic conception. Yet this challenge might be answered in one of several ways. Perhaps the legend was once known in one of those ritual or quasi-ritual contexts in which the Man, as in kingship practice, was thought already to be present feeding his people. Such a tale could have been transposed to Jesus. Or, inspired by such a legend, Jesus himself may have acted in these terms. Alternatively we might believe that the eschatological aspects have dropped away and that the feeding was originally presented, like the Last Supper, as an anticipation of the banquet in heaven. If it is possible that we should translate in the Lord's Prayer, 'Give us this day the bread of tomorrow',[3] we might see this as a comment on

---

[1] Admittedly, because of our very lack of information, one could turn this understanding right the other way around and claim that it was the contemporary Johannine Church which was worshipping Jesus as the Son of Man at the Communion. To Higgins (*Son of Man*, p. 176) these sayings are expressive of 'the eucharistic faith of the church as it speaks through the words of the crucified, exalted, and glorified Son of man'. Yet we remain highly dubious about such an approach for the reasons given above: why, if the Son of Man was so central to their worship, do we not hear of him in the final discourses, the passion and resurrection narratives, the raising of Lazarus, etc.? Why in ch. 6 outside of these three verses is the concentration on Jesus as Jesus, 'I', upon the Son who was sent, and why does Peter, at the end, confess Jesus to be the Holy One of God?

[2] E.g. Matt. 8.11; Luke 13.29. See Luke 14.15. Compare the meal described in 1QSa, ii, 17ff. The idea is common to a number of the materials we have studied.

[3] On this view and the meaning of ἐπιούσιον in Matt. 6.11 and Luke 11.3, see C. F. Evans, *The Lord's Prayer*, London, 1963, pp. 46ff.

such a conception (and Mark 2.23ff. might very well be implicated in this same pattern of thought).[1]

We are also interested in the last clause of John 6.27, '. . . for on this one God the Father has set his seal'. The implication is that the one who is to do this feeding as the Son of Man has already been chosen. The act may be thought of as future or as having futuristic connotations, but the actor is already ordained and present. When was this done? Here the word *seal* (the verb σφραγίζω) may provide a very important clue, for one of the associations of the word during this period was with baptism. It quickly established itself in this connection in the Christian literature,[2] and also such a signing or sealing (a mark of identification on the believer and/or an enduing with heavenly power) was known in several of the sects we have studied.[3]

Then, too, it is a little surprising to hear John say 'this one (τοῦτον) God has sealed' rather than 'him (αὐτόν) God has sealed'. Is there again a sense here of 'This is the one chosen out from among men to be the Son of Man', of, 'This one God has sealed to be the Son of Man who will give you the food enduring to (or, perhaps originally, *the food of*) the new age'?

In rather general terms it would be possible to fit John 6.53 into a scheme similar to 6.27. John has picked up an old saying and set it into his discourse, though he continues elsewhere to let Jesus speak more naturally in his own person. *Flesh* and blood would be equivalent to the synoptic translation *body* and blood (as it quite possibly could be, perhaps even being superior),[4] and the ultimate basis of the saying might lie in the same sources from which the synoptics derived their accounts of the Last Supper. The crucial difference would be that John's saying has retained this hint as to the origin of the whole conception and to the reason that Jesus could speak and act in this way.

Yet we must face up to a genuine difficulty here which is created by two postulates on our part. John's logion says that the people need to eat the flesh and blood of the Son of Man. On the one hand, we

---

[1] See below on Mark 2.28, p. 323.

[2] See II Cor. 1.22; Eph. 1.13; 4.30. The connection may be implied in Rev., esp. ch. 7. Also see *II Clement* 7.6; *Hermas*, Parables VIII, 6.3; IX, 16.3ff.

[3] See the references in the Bauer/W. F. Arndt and F. W. Gingrich, *A Greek-English Lexicon of the New Testament*, Cambridge and Chicago, 1957, pp. 803f. Cf. also Odes of Sol. 8.15, etc., and Segelberg, *Maṣbūtā*, pp. 86ff.

[4] See J. Jeremias, *The Eucharistic Words of Jesus*, ET, Oxford, 1955, p. 141 (2nd ed., London, 1966, p. 200).

have failed to find anything in the Man mythology which would really prepare us for this. The Man provides the food; he and his people may be seen to share in the deep community of Semitic table fellowship. Yet whatever the food he provides (from the tree of life, bread, the flesh of the slain monster or of the sacred animal) and however the meal may be visualized (in connection with baptism and/or after his *resurrection*, on earth or in heaven), he does not give *himself* to eat. Nor do pagan parallels which have been suggested come close to meeting the criteria of a reasonable propinquity in time and locale so that they might be seen in the background of Jesus' own thought here.[1]

Secondly and therefore, this same factor strongly vitiates the parallelism which might otherwise exist between this saying and what could have actually taken place and been said when Jesus ate with his disciples. On our view at least, Jesus' interest was in this proleptic table fellowship in anticipation of the meal in heaven and in acts of prophetic symbolism and interpretation rather than in the physical ideas of giving of his own substance to eat and drink. 'This is my flesh (or body) and blood' would have meant, in Semitic idiom, 'this is myself', my life being sacrificed.[2] Thus, in so far as the idea of actually eating the flesh and blood of the Lord as the essence of the sacrament has entered into the accounts,[3] we would think that it must be due to later belief governed by developments within the growing relationship of Christians to their Lord and perhaps partly by other, later influences.

Yet there is still this to be said: even if later belief and practice have fully coloured the Johannine understanding and presentation of an element from a Last Supper tradition (or some other tradition in which Jesus spoke and acted similarly), it still could be that John has preserved an authentic relic when he tells us that it was as the Son of Man that Jesus provided food for a meal which he interpreted in terms of sacrifice. Perhaps he knew of a tradition which spoke of the food given by the Son of Man and conducive to new life or of the offering of the flesh and blood (= life or self) of the Son of Man which he then interpreted in the light of contemporary practice.[4]

---

[1] See again Nock in *Mnemosyne* 4, v, 1952, pp. 177ff.

[2] I.e. This (flesh and blood) is my whole being. Aramaic would only say 'This is *myself*' in some such idiomatic fashion.

[3] See esp. the Matthean commands to *eat* and *drink* and the Pauline interpretations given in I Cor. 11.26ff. and 10.16ff.

[4] Further see p. 390 n. 3.

John 6.62: Then what if you were to see the Son of man ascending where he was before?

There are several factors which cause this saying to be awkward and make it difficult to interpret, no matter what view is held about its relation to authentic tradition. There is, first of all, the ease with which it could be omitted from the passage, verses 60–63. More importantly, the flow and force of the discourse could seem to be improved by its omission.

Then there is a distinct sense of grammatical incompleteness in the saying itself. It looks more like the protasis of a conditional sentence than a genuine question in its own right: 'If then you were to see the Son of Man ascending where he was before . . .' Commentators suggest that an apodosis may be implied which could either intimate that the indicated offence will be heightened (i.e. 'If these words offend you, wait until the ascent to heaven') or lessened (for the flesh and blood spoken of earlier are those of a heavenly and not an earthly being). Perhaps, as Barrett indicates, the two implications are not wholly contradictory, while the latter especially may be picked up by the thought of verse 63.[1]

In addition, though the points could be considered minor, it is a bit surprising that John has said *if* rather than *when* and used a subjunctive instead of a more definite future indicative. Surely from his own point of view there was no doubt that this event would take place. But perhaps the meaning is a little more subtle, the suggestion being that not all will *see* the ascension of the Son of Man.

Still, these several factors taken together intimate to us once more that John may have been dealing with materials he did not fully understand. Perhaps there was a loose logion which he thought ought to be used somewhere, and this seemed the best place, especially with the earlier remarks about the *coming down* of the bread (and Jesus as the bread) in mind. More likely he found the saying, in some form or other, already attached to an earlier collection of sayings or a discourse in which versions of 6.27 and 6.53 also figured.

This seems more probable than the possibility that the saying has been created specifically for its present context as a variant on 3.13,[2] for then we might have expected John to have presented his thought

---

[1] *St John*, p. 250.

[2] Higgins, *Son of Man*, pp. 176f. His point that this verse is prospective and the rest of the passage retrospective could again indicate that John has not fully accommodated v. 62 to his general outlook.

less awkwardly and to have better integrated it into his passage. If it were such a literary creation, we might also have supposed that 3.13 would have had more influence, that there might have been another mention of the *descent* and that the evangelist might have gone on to echo something from 3.14 as well.

It is more conceivable, however, that this verse is an early variant on 3.13, another version of the idea of 3.13 preserved in a rather different form. If this be so, then we might have some basis for understanding what was once meant (as opposed to what John understood it as meaning, for pretty clearly he would have thought in terms of the *going up* of Jesus to heaven after his death).[1]

Or, if 6.62 is itself based on an authentic logion or fragment thereof other than 3.13 (which is the view we should tend to favour), it probably is still to be associated with 3.13 in the same matrix of related ideas and themes.

In either of these latter eventualities, the *going up* (ἀναβαίνοντα) of the Son of Man was likely viewed at first in terms of a kind of liturgical ascension as in 3.13. And perhaps a remark like 'If you therefore see the Son of Man ascending . . .' was used, as 1.51 may have been and possibly 6.27 as well, within a context which was concerned with the identity of the one who was to be the Son of Man. The apodosis, either stated or implied, might have been, 'then you will know who he is', or, 'then you will know I am he' (see 8.28).

In these terms it might appear necessary to dismiss the last clause of 6.62 as a Johannine comment giving his understanding of what was meant. This may, however, be quite unnecessary within the protasis, and, in fact, this clause might be a clue to the original apodosis. Especially if 6.62 and 3.13 are to be related, would we point out that 'where he was before' may not be very far distant from the thought expressed by 'who is in heaven'. In 6.62 John might have been dealing with an expression based on an Aramaic clause which was intended to convey the idea that the Son of Man is a figure who exists in heaven, 'where he was always'; or the past tense may only be John's interpretation of what the Aramaic was intending. The primitive shape of the thought would indicate that the Son of Man has existed previously (πρότερον) above, or even that he has existed there from earliest times, from the beginning. This conception seems essential, we recall, to I Enoch when mortal Enoch becomes the

[1] See on ἀναβαίνω above under John 3.13 and 3.14.

heavenly figure who had a pre-existence. Thus, set out together, the sayings may once have run something like this:

No one has ascended into heaven but (he who descended from heaven) the Son of Man, the one being in heaven.

Then what if you were to see the Son of Man ascending to where he is from the beginning?

Or, to return the latter to a possibly more original form,

If then you should see the Son of Man ascending, he is ascending to where he is from the beginning.

John 8.28: So Jesus said, 'When you have lifted up the Son of Man, then you will know that I am he ($\dot{\epsilon}\gamma\dot{\omega}$ $\epsilon\dot{\iota}\mu\iota$), and that I do nothing on my own, but speak thus as the Father taught me.'

Unfortunately we cannot here comment on all the features and possible implications found in the context of this passage.[1] By and large, however, we take the position that John may have made use of several authentic features in the composition of 8.23ff. and that the reference to the *lifting up* of the Son of Man could be one of them. We recall the fact that this verb[2] seems especially associated with the Son of Man in John and also the several meanings it might have had. If John has here made use of an isolated logion which was a variant on 3.14 and/or 12.34, or, if John has himself created this saying in an attempt to imitate primitive tradition,[3] it would be impossible to tell from this verse alone what meaning or meanings the verb once had. In present context, however, and also with 12.34 in mind, it is fairly obvious that the *lifting up* of the Son of Man refers, in one way or another, to his death, while the nuances (here ironic) of exaltation/glorification are probably not missing. As we have suggested, this idea that 'you (i.e. the Jews) shall put the Son of Man to

---

[1] If the 'from above' ($\dot{\epsilon}\kappa$ $\tau\hat{\omega}\nu$ $\dot{\alpha}\nu\omega$) in v. 23, the ambiguous reference to 'the beginning' in v. 25 and the mention of judgment in v. 26 were once closely allied with the authentic Son of Man traditions, John has admittedly so *digested* and assimilated them to his general style and outlook that it would be very hard to demonstrate this now.

[2] Here $\dot{\upsilon}\psi\dot{\omega}\sigma\eta\tau\epsilon$, a subjunctive with $\ddot{\sigma}\tau\alpha\nu$, and we might then catch a note of indefiniteness, 'Whenever . . .', which would be derived from a pre-Johannine usage.

[3] See Higgins, *op. cit.*, pp. 168f. Yet even if John has fashioned the saying, this would not necessarily bring us to the conclusion that 8.28 springs 'from the evangelist's predilection for the Son of man Christology, and from his emphasis on the necessity of belief in Jesus as the Son of man'. In modelling himself on an authentic saying, John may only have been attempting to echo the language of the traditions.

death' bears comparison with sayings like Mark 8.31; 9.31; 10.33, where it is said that men will kill the Son of Man or that the Jewish officials will put him to death or *give* him *up* to be put to death by *foreigners*.

In trying to go a little further beyond the present form of 8.28a we notice that the first *you* and the second may seem, as the saying now reads, to have different terms of reference. The verb *to know* (γινώσκω) is regularly used positively in John, implying that it could mean 'you will know for your salvation' rather than 'you enemies will know to your sorrow'. If this is so, one might imagine that John is presenting a subtle aside to the Christian reader.[1] It is our guess, however, that this change in the reference of *you* points to the probability that John has altered a saying which was once wholly positive in character. Either the subject of the action was a *they* in line with several synoptic sayings of this type (i.e. 'When they have lifted up the Son of Man . . .') or the saying had a passive form more in keeping with 3.14, 12.34 (12.32): 'When the Son of Man has been lifted up . . .', or even 'The Son of Man must be lifted up, and then you will know . . .'

And what are we to make of the phrase 'I am (he)' which stands as the most straightforward identification of Jesus with the Son of Man in the Gospels? The possibilities are several: (*a*) Jesus said something to this effect, either by using some such expression in a theophonic way[2] or perhaps with a simpler grammatical intention.[3] (*b*) It is a Johannine theological stylism and/or belief which he has added to a fragmentary logion or to a statement which he has modelled on another Son of Man logion. (*c*) John has substituted this phrase for an original clause whose content we can only guess at, but which, in line with the Son of Man tradition otherwise, might have said something like, 'then you will know who he is'. It seems to us

[1] Higgins apparently views the possibility in these terms and would align it with his theory that the Son of Man was central to Johannine *belief*. Yet the ideas are not quite the same, and *recognition* may be the central nuance here, causing us perhaps to think of the way men will come to *see* the Son of Man (in the synoptics) in his heavenly glory.

[2] This, of course, cannot be ruled out, but it seems unlikely. Both when used in predicate constructions ('I am the bread of life', etc.) and by itself (e.g. 8.58; 13.19) one gains the impression that John is thinking in terms of the use in the Old Testament and later of '*a*nī *hū* as a kind of substitute for the divine name. The LXX translation by ἐγώ εἰμι gave coinage to a phrase which would otherwise have little meaning in Greek. See esp. Isa. 43.10 and Dodd, *Interpretation of the Fourth Gospel*, pp. 94ff.

[3] See John 9.9, where the blind man identifies himself in this manner.

that (*b*) or (*c*) are the more likely alternatives, preserving the strong primitive feature that Jesus himself never made the bald identification of the Son of Man exclusively with his own person, but spoke instead of the destiny of the Son of Man and of doing his work.[1]

John 9.35: Jesus heard that they had cast him out, and having found him he said, 'Do you believe in the Son of Man?'

We assume that 'Son of Man' rather than 'Son of God' is here the better because of the *harder* reading, even though there is some very strong textual support for the latter, and one could make a case for it. In coming to this conclusion most commentators are manifesting their conviction that at least the sub-apostolic Church was not prone to speak in terms of their belief in the Son of Man.

But did the Johannine Church or the community which passed tradition on to it so believe in Jesus and worship him, and is this saying indicative of their expression of faith? This we have also held to be improbable. The very uniqueness of such a semi-credal form (not only in the Gospels but throughout the Church) makes it most unlikely that any significant part of the Church was accustomed to saying, 'I believe in the Son of Man'.[2]

Our opinion may be borne out by the rest of this passage, for one would have thought, were the Son of Man title evocative and vital to John and his community, that 'the Son of Man' would have replaced a *him* in one of the following clauses. There, however, the man addresses Jesus as *Lord* (and this must mean more than *sir* in later Church usage, especially in the second instance) and misses a golden opportunity to proclaim belief in the Son of Man by merely saying, 'Lord, I believe'. When the passage comes to speak of judgment (verse 39), it is the *I* who comes for judgment, not the Son of Man. Indeed, some feel that verse 39 once stood in a closer relationship to the essence of verse 35, but if they are right it would seem that the

[1] Notice that if John 8.28a once did stand in some relationship to a question like 'Who are you?' in v. 25, there is then a certain progression of thought not unlike that found in the synoptic narratives of the *confession* at Caesarea Philippi and in the trial scene. In all of these cases a 'Who is Jesus?' question leads to a statement about the Son of Man, though the Church so failed to understand Jesus' relationship to the Son of Man that it has attempted to redirect the real impetus of these progressions. See below, esp. on Matt. 16.13ff., where, on our view, however, there may be a reversal of this order, though the essence of the matter would be much the same. See also below on John 12.34.

[2] The only conceivable synoptic parallel would be Luke 18.8, but there the relationship of faith to the Son of Man is quite indeterminate. On John 3.15 and just possibly 8.28, see above. John 12.36 is only very loosely attached to 12.34.

importance of the Son of Man as Son of Man is being lessened rather than heightened.

In fact, though it can hardly be more than speculation, we would share in a rather different way the impression that the Son of Man may once have been more central to the traditions lying behind this passage. He would be the one who restores men's sight and who has the power for judgment. One is then tempted to think that 9.35 as it stands might be a relic from primitive tradition, but we regard it as much more probable that 9.35, along with the rest of the passage, has been heavily reworked in the course of transmission and in the process of composition. (This might be indicated by a comparison of John 9.39 with Mark 4.12, where Mark gives a *harder* saying and one which is nearer to the language of Isa. 6.9f.) This suggests to us that John has given a place of prominence to the Son of Man because he found the designation, which he recognized and valued as being vital to the traditions, playing an important role in his source for this story. In these circumstances, however, it is doubtful if any degree of ingenuity could restore an earlier version.[1]

In our opinion John 9.35 is another of the tantalizing little bits buried in our Gospels which intimate a time when the Son of Man was crucial to much of the tradition. The Gospels, for instance, tell us of only one other miracle (the healing of the paralytic) in which the Son of Man designation was specifically involved, but it is our suspicion that the Church's faith in Jesus as Jesus and the Christ and Lord has hidden much from our eyes.[2] We shall find further and more definite grounds for such suspicions when we come to the synoptic materials.

John 12.23: And Jesus answered them, 'The hour has come for the Son of Man to be glorified.'

Both the opening and the ending of the saying proper are marked by language that can be regarded as distinctly Johannine. 'The hour has come' parallels a consistent Johannine dramatic technique.[3] So also the glorification of Jesus as Jesus, as Son and Son of God is a

---

[1] Possibly John has misunderstood what was originally intended, and the primitive saying asked whether one believed in the teaching about the Son of Man and/or his authority rather than in Jesus as the Son of Man. Or perhaps there was here a saying more like Mark 2.10, establishing the authority of the Son of Man to do this act of healing.

[2] See above, pp. 296f.

[3] 2.4; 4.21, 23; 5.25, 28; 7.30; 8.20; 13.1; 16.25, 32; 17.1.

frequent theme. It is the glory of the only Son from the Father,[1] the shared glory of the Father and the Son given to Jesus by the Father from the beginning.[2]

One might then think that John 12.23 is wholly a creation by the evangelist into which he himself has inserted the designation. Yet, in our opinion, a little investigation will show this to be a facile view, for the essence of John 12.23 appears to be imbedded in the primitive tradition in a provocative and curious manner.

In the first place, the predication of glory and glorification of a figure can hardly be said to be an exclusive Johannine property.[3] This way of speaking is natural enough and, in addition to other figures, pertains to the king, the Man (both on earth and in heaven) and to the Servant.[4] This last could hardly prove that John borrowed the word from the Man traditions, but it does show that it could have been both Johannine and derived from the authentic data as well.

The mention of glory in the synoptic sayings about the heavenly Son of Man is perhaps related to this feature in John's logia, but exactly how it is not easy to say. Several of the factors discussed below make it difficult to believe that John has simply transposed the terms of reference of certain eschatological sayings.[5] Possibly the synoptics have tended to heighten the eschatology in several sayings, or perhaps the tradition which speaks of the Son of Man's *coming* or appearance in glory and that which tells of his glorification in connection with his death represent somewhat different emphases within the authentic Man *milieu*. Once more it is conceivable that John has preserved a way of speaking which may lie closer to a liturgical setting.

Looked at in another way, there is this manner in which the verbs δοξάζω and ὑψόω seem to belong closely together. They have a history of being used together almost synonymously,[6] and, as we have seen, can translate the same words in the Old Testament. Then, too, John does something with δοξάζω which is peculiarly like what he does with ὑψόω. He seems capable of using it to refer both to the idea of exalted

---

[1] 1.14.

[2] E.g. 14.13; 15.8; 17.5.

[3] See also Acts 3.13; I Cor. 2.8; II Cor. 4.6; Heb. 5.5f. See Luke 24.26.

[4] E.g. Pss. 8.5; 21.5; Isa. 49.3; 52.13.

[5] See Schulz, *Untersuchungen*, p. 119, who points to the glorification of the Elect One in I Enoch 51.3 (and, of course, see Dan. 7.14). Yet this is one of the places where he fails to show that a particular theme is tied up exclusively with eschatology.

[6] See Isa. 4.2 (and 35.2); 52.13 (compare Acts 3.13); Ps. 37.20 (see Ps. 112.9); Ecclus 43.30; Test. Joseph 10.3; and above pp. 283ff.

glory and to the means to that glorification through death.[1] Our suggestion is that this is no coincidence, but rather that either John found two such related verbs being used in such a way in his traditions, or that there may have been one verb which has sometimes been translated by ὑψόω and sometimes by δοξάζω.

Similarly we need to recognize that this mention of *the hour* is not exclusively Johannine. It has a significant place in synoptic materials,[2] and is there related to the Son of Man in an eschatological saying and in one which speaks of his being given up and which points to his passion.[3] To the importance of this last item we shall return in a moment.

First, however, we wish to show how John 12.23 is found in context with sayings which not only themselves are probably based on sound tradition, but which also closely relate to synoptic logia about the Son of Man.

Mark	Matthew	John
8.31: . . . the Son of Man must suffer many things and be rejected . . .[4]		12.23: The hour has come for the Son of Man to be glorified.
8.34: If any man would come after me, let him deny himself and take up his cross and follow me.[5]	10.38: And he who does not take up his cross and follow me is not worthy of me.	12.26: If anyone serves me, he must follow me; and where I am there shall my servant be also.
8.35: For whoever would save his life will lose it; and whoever loses his life for my sake . . . will save it.	10.39: He who finds his life will lose it, and he who loses his life for my sake will find it. (See Luke 17.33.)	12.25: He who loves his life loses it, and he who hates his life in this world will keep it for eternal life.
8.38: For whoever is ashamed of me and of my words in this adulterous and sinful generation, of him will the Son of Man also be ashamed when he comes in the glory of his Father with the holy angels.[6]	(See Matt. 10.32f. and with it Luke 12.8f.)	

---

[1] Cf. the contexts of John 12.23; 13.31; see 7.39; 12.16; 21.19.
[2] Mark 13.11 (= Matt. 10.19; Luke 12.12); Mark 13.32 (= Matt. 24.36); Mark 14.35; Matt. 24.50 (= Luke 12.46); Matt. 24.42; Luke 12.39; 22.14, 53.
[3] Matt. 24.44 = Luke 12.40. Mark 14.41 = Matt. 26.45.
[4] See Matt. 16.21; Luke 9.22.
[5] See Matt. 16.24; Luke 9.23; 14.27.
[6] See Matt. 16.27f.; Luke 9.26.

Certainly one could make out a good case for believing that Mark 8.34f.; Matt. 10.38f. and John 12.25f. have developed from common tradition. What is more, there are obvious and sound reasons for believing that John may have preserved the more primitive form of these sayings. What particularly intrigues, however, is that all of them seem to be involved in complexes which speak of the Son of Man. In the cases of John 12.25f. and Mark 8.34f. this is manifest, but one can also point out that Matthew 10.32f. was very likely once a Son of Man saying and that Luke 17.33, in still another setting, follows closely upon a string of Son of Man sayings. The implications are certainly strong that in primitive tradition, intimately related to something like John 12.25f., there once stood some saying or sayings about the Son of Man.[1] Admittedly, however, there is no close parallel in these various Son of Man logia themselves, though it is at least interesting that, while Mark 8.31 speaks of the passion of the Son of Man and 8.38 of his appearance in glory, John 12.23 presents the two thoughts combined or fully implicated in one another.

Yet this lack of close parallels only pushes us on toward an even more puzzling feature, for the two Johannine sayings which do tell of the Son of Man's glorification stand in a highly provocative relationship with two synoptic sayings which tell of the Son of Man being *given up*. Both Mark 14.21 and 14.41 are tightly bound up with the *betrayal* by Judas, the context of the Last Supper and the incidents just afterwards at Gethsemane. The closest connection with regard to a criterion of circumstances is probably between Mark 14.21 and John 13.31, as both occur within the setting of the last meal of Jesus and his disciples precisely at the point when the act of dipping the morsel in the dish is associated with the identification of the traitor. In Mark, after Jesus has said that one of the twelve dipping bread in the same dish with him will betray him,[2] he says,

For the Son of Man goes ($\upsilon\pi\acute{\alpha}\gamma\epsilon\iota$)[3] as it is written of him, but woe to that man by whom the Son of Man is betrayed ($\pi\alpha\rho\alpha\delta\acute{\iota}\delta\sigma\tau\alpha\iota$)!

In John, immediately after Judas takes the morsel which Jesus had dipped and goes out, Jesus says,

[1] This, taken together with the correspondence noted below with Mark 14.21, 41, suggests that the connection with the Greeks or Hellenists in this Johannine setting is artificial and cannot be used with Acts 7.56 and Stephen as support for the hypothesis about a group of Hellenists preaching Jesus as the Son of Man.

[2] On this theme of being betrayed by one who shares bread, cf. Ps. 41.9 (John 13.18) and 1QH, v, 23f.

[3] Cf. p. 290 n. 4.

Now is the Son of Man glorified (ἐδοξάσθη) . . .

In their circumstances there is a lesser relationship between John 12.23 and Mark 14.41. The order is reversed and John's saying now precedes the last meal, while Mark's follows. Still, it is not hard to believe that their place in the general context of the time before the passion,[1] the fact that both point to the passion, and the link between Mark 14.41 and 14.21 and between John 12.23 and 13.31 and then between Mark 14.21 and John 13.31 suggest some manner of association. What is far more important is their actual wording.

Mark 14.41	John 12.23
The hour has come	The hour has come
(ἦλθεν ἡ ὥρα);	(ἐλήλυθεν ἡ ὥρα)
behold, the Son of Man	for the Son of Man
is given up (παραδίδοται)	to be glorified (δοξασθῇ).
into the hands of sinners.	

Precisely how these coincidences should be sorted out and explained we do not know, but logia which now say somewhat different things about the Son of Man and which appear to have been preserved through quite variant channels, still point to his passion and seem to reveal a fundamental relationship with one another by their narrative setting and their wording. Is it possible, as intimated before, that the verbs δοξάζω and παραδίδωμι, odd as it otherwise might seem, are both attempts to render and interpret the same basic idea or theme? Or is it only that the several ideas were so woven together in the patterns of legend that one theme evoked another allowing various themes to become almost interchangeable? Is the association of John 12.23 with 12.25f., in the light of a comparison with Mark 8.31ff., etc., indicative of some basic complex of sayings involving the Son of Man? Who, then, has best kept these together in their earliest order and setting and whose versions of the sayings are most authentic? Or are they all of equal authenticity as variants within the earliest *milieu*?[2]

---

[1] One may also wish to compare the prayer to the 'Father' in John 12.27 with Mark 14.36.

[2] It is of interest that in the section John 12.23–34 we have first a statement about the glorification of the Son of Man followed by a voice from heaven and then a question about the *lifting up* of the Son of Man. Is there a valid comparison here with Mark 8.38ff. (see Matt. 16.27ff.), in which we have a logion regarding the Son of Man's glory, a glorification scene (and a voice from heaven) followed by statements about both the *rising* and suffering of the Son of Man? (Cf. our remarks on John 1.51 and 13.31f.) Is it, then, possible that the question of John 12.34 was

John 12.34: The crowd answered him, 'We have heard from the law that the Christ remains for ever. How can you say that the Son of Man must ($\delta\epsilon\hat{\iota}$) be lifted up ($\dot{\upsilon}\psi\omega\theta\hat{\eta}\nu\alpha\iota$)?[1] Who is this Son of Man?'

In 12.32 Jesus says, 'When I am lifted up ($\dot{\upsilon}\psi\omega\theta\hat{\omega}$) from the earth, I will draw all men to myself.' We are then told by John that this is to be interpreted with reference to Jesus' death. Now, 12.32 is the only instance of John's use of this verb outside the Son of Man sayings, and it is immediately followed by a Son of Man saying involving the verb. It would seem relatively obvious that the evangelist felt this verb to be especially associated with the Son of Man. Presumably, then, either he or his tradition created 12.32f. as an introduction to 12.34, or, having written 12.32f., he was immediately reminded of the Son of Man and either fashioned 12.34 out of odd bits of tradition or decided to use an already formed unit of tradition at this point.[2]

The vital question is whether 12.34 represents a scene which is essentially authentic or whether it is, at least as presently constituted, best regarded as a Church formulation. Since, however, we cannot see how this matter is conclusively to be decided, it is best that we examine the implications of both contingencies.

Assuming first that it is a post-resurrection creation, it presumably represents a stage at which Jews or Jewish-Christians were questioning the meaning of an early Christian saying. (One could hold that they are only questioning a special teaching of John's, but this seems doubtful on several grounds.)[3] Then, also presumably, they took *lift up* in the same basic sense as does John here. They are asking, 'How does the teaching that "the Son of Man must be lifted up to be put to

---

fashioned from the same materials as prompted Mark to record in 9.10 the disciples questioning about what the Son of Man's *rising* (from the dead) meant? See below p. 351 n. 2.

[1] See the above note.

[2] Let us also at least notice the possibility that 12.32 was originally a Son of Man saying, in conjunction with 12.34, but one which John has altered to an *I* form. Certainly this would make better sense of the movement of thought.

[3] There are the reasons given above for thinking that 'The Son of Man must be lifted up' and the link between the Son of Man and death are pre-Johannine. And why does John not really provide an answer to the point at issue in 12.34, if he himself has created this problem? Rather does he go off on a tangent and speak of the *light*, presumably that which has come into the world. (Cf. John 1.4, 9; 8.12; 9.5; 12.46.) Conceivably he might be answering the question by pointing to the *eternal* light, but this would be pretty oblique and elliptical even for John. In any case he gives no hint that he was one to meditate upon the Son of Man designation.

death" fit in with our conception of a Messiah who is eternal?"[1]
'Who is this Son of Man?' then means, 'What kind of a figure is this?'
'How does he relate to our messianic beliefs?'

Now, this kind of controversy would make sense, but we think it
would only make the best sense if it is seen as taking place at a fairly
early date in the life of the Church. It is the old issue of the crucifixion
being a *scandal* to the Jews,[2] but it is here being conducted with reference to the Son of Man. In fact, it is specifically a Son of Man versus
Messiah controversy. While we cannot insist that such an argument in
these terms would not have taken place in John's own time, it is hard
to believe that a Church which readily saw Jesus as the Messiah would
have allowed the debate to be fought on such grounds. The implications are that such a debate would have taken place when Christians
possessed a teaching about the Son of Man's death, but had not
developed a full rationale concerning the death of one who was the
Messiah. This would not in itself show that the Son of Man teaching on
the subject was authentic, but it would at least make it pre-Johannine,
in a sense *pre-messianic* in Christian terms and, as a fundamental tenet
of the early Church, suggest that it may well have been authentic.

Taking up the alternative, if this scene be basically authentic to
primitive tradition, we could view it in similar terms, and again it
would make good sense. Now, however, the controversy may have
been with regard to teaching about the suffering of the Son of Man in
general and not about the prediction of Jesus' own death in particular.
It might be a relic representative of a time at which there were disputes
between advocates of a Son of Man teaching and those who held
particular views about the Messiah.[3]

It may also be that John has disguised the real bone of contention.
Perhaps *lift up* here did not originally stress the death of the Man, but
rather his exaltation to heaven. Then what the questioners do not
understand is how the Son of Man, as a mortal who is to be exalted
from earth to heaven, could relate to a Messiah who is said to be

---

[1] Of course, this *eternal* (which could refer to past or future or both) existence of
the Messiah is not the single Jewish teaching on the subject. (It could be based on
passages like Isa. 9.6f; Pss. 89.4; 110.4; Ezek. 37.25; or Ps. 89.36, on which see
W. C. van Unnik, 'The Quotation in John 12.34', *NT* 3, 1959, pp. 174ff.) Here it is
apparently taken for normative. See, however, Mark 12.35ff., where Jesus seems
to assume that this is not normative teaching about the Messiah and may be
suggesting the eternal existence of the Man.

[2] See I Cor. 1.23 (where, of course, it is 'a crucified Messiah'); Gal. 5.11, etc.

[3] See again on Mark 12.35ff., pp. 394ff. Such could also be reflected in the
discussion at Caesarea Philippi and before the Sanhedrin.

eternal.[1] (And, of course, it could also be that this was still the real issue in some post-resurrection debate which John has later largely misunderstood.)

Or, again, in either of these eventualities, John may have mistaken the force of the question, 'Who is this Son of Man?' The questioners may not have wanted to know more about the Son of Man, but rather have been asking, 'Who is this mortal who as the Son of Man is to be lifted up to die?' or, 'Who is this earthly Son of Man who is to be lifted up to heaven?' We think that there are good reasons for believing that, in one form or another, this may have been a real issue and an acute question in Jesus' own lifetime.[2]

John 13.31: When he (Judas) had gone out, Jesus said, 'Now is the Son of Man glorified, and in him God is glorified; (32) if God is glorified in him, God will also glorify him in himself, and glorify him at once.'

We have already said sufficient about the verb *to glorify* and the relation of John 13.31 to Mark 14.21 (along with Mark 14.41 and John 12.23) to indicate our reasons for thinking the first part of this saying to be based on authentic tradition. While John may have interpreted what was actually preserved, the Son of Man appears here because John found him at this juncture in his sources.[3]

The only question which now concerns us is whether it is possible to see the rest of the verse and perhaps verse 32 as well as a formulation which is essentially pre-resurrection in origin rather than as a community or a Johannine creation. Here we must reckon with the fact that the great majority of scholars adopt the latter view while stressing the parallels with similar Johannine passages where the Son of Man is not mentioned.[4] Indeed, it is quite credible that John has used an

[1] Cf. G. H. P. Thompson's suggestion that this passage shows a crowd who knows about the heavenly Son of Man but not about a Son of Man who is to be lifted up ('The Son of Man—Some Further Considerations', *JTS*, ns 12, 1961, p. 208) tends to miss the real point of contrast in the passage, that between the Son of Man and the Messiah, not between two views about the Son of Man.

[2] See below, esp. with reference to Matt. 16.13 and our discussion on Elijah, John Baptist and Jesus.

[3] In this sense Higgins (*Son of Man*, p. 181) is right to point out that the saying stands at a most significant point in the Gospel, as does its synoptic parallel. What is meaningful for us, however, is that the evangelist, from this point onward, shows no interest in the Son of Man title. This is esp. significant in that so much of what follows is concerned with an understanding of the crucifixion/ascension and the life of the disciples in the present age.

[4] See esp. John 17.1, 4f., and on this Higgins, *op. cit.*, p. 180.

old Son of Man saying and then added this poetic statement. We would only point out that this view is far from mandatory.

We have seen that the verb or the theme of glory can be applied to the Man in several of his states. In addition, the conception of the interchange of qualities between the God and the Man is as old as certain versions of the story of creation, and the descriptions of the king-Man's enthronement often show the king taking on a number of the divine attributes. This mode of thought and speech perhaps comes across in the Old Testament most clearly in passages dealing with the Isaianic Servant. God will be glorified in him, and the Servant shall be glorified.[1] We ourselves are again particularly reminded of the transfiguration scene, an incident which we will soon come to regard as a pre-resurrection story concerning the *glorification* of the Man figure. It is not impossible that in such a setting language similar to this once was used,[2] and that John has been more affected by it than he has affected it.

Schulz (although he sees it as a transposed eschatological saying) finds 13.31f. to be at least pre-Johannine.[3] Its poetical structure is often noted (though the effect of this may be lessened if, with a number of manuscripts, the opening of v. 32 is omitted),[4] and there may be signs of Aramaisms built into this structure, especially in the repetition of the *and*, and in the ambiguity of the pronouns. Yet these matters cannot lead to any certainty, and we therefore would only register the possibility that the whole could be based on authentic material.

[1] Cf. Isa. 44.23; 49.3; 52.13. See too on the language used by gnostics in ch. V and, more particularly, with regard to the Odes of Solomon and the Mandaeans.

[2] See John 12.28 in connection with our remarks, p. 309 n. 2. If such language does have a semi-liturgical background, the 'now' would be a significant word. Compare Ps. 20.6 and perhaps I Peter 2.10, etc.

[3] *Untersuchungen*, pp. 120ff. He suggests something like I Enoch 51.3 as a basis for the development of this *hymn*, while we would see such a picture as but one reference to one aspect of a very old and variegated story.

[4] Perhaps it is most easily viewed as an omission, but many think it the result of dittography. Bultmann, on the other hand (*Evangelium des Johannes*, p. 401 n. 5), thinks that the last clause has been added later. He also suggests that the original reading might have been Son and not Son of Man. His first suggestion is more plausible than the second.

VIII

THE SYNOPTIC SON OF MAN

*And how is it written of the
Son of Man that he should
suffer many things and be
treated with contempt?* (*Mark 9.12*)

I. SURVEY

UNFORTUNATELY IT IS not feasible in this study to set forth our detailed analysis of each synoptic Son of Man saying. We must content ourselves with a summary of our findings while trying, as best we can, to present the major arguments for our views in the subsequent footnotes.[1] We should then like to offer a series of observations indicating the manner in which we believe that our theory enlightens and gives new meaning to a number of aspects of the synoptic tradition.

(*1*) The great majority of the synoptic Son of Man logia have a reasonable claim on authenticity. They indicate that Jesus may very well have spoken of the Son of Man as one who could have a function on earth, as destined for suffering and as a figure who would appear in heavenly glory. What makes a number of the sayings suspect to many scholars frequently has little to do with intrinsic, exegetical difficulties, but is rather due to suspicions based on assumptions about the kind of Son of Man Jesus could have known and with regard to the character of his ministry. Once such assumptions are rigorously questioned, many of the other arguments often appear to be insubstantial.[2] In this light it is interesting that even scholars who tend to agree on a general line of approach are frequently inclined to present reasons for the omission of a particular logion which are quite contradictory.

The very fact that many of these sayings have over the years

---

[1] Among the indexes there will be found a table of references to our discussions of the individual Son of Man logia.

[2] See again a number of the remarks by Marshall, *NTS* 12, 1965/6, pp. 327ff.

trenchantly withstood assaults from almost every direction and what should have been a withering barrage of criticism convinces us that their claim on authenticity must be taken much more seriously. We doubt whether any other group of sayings in the Gospels could do so well against such continuous and formidable opposition.

(2) We have found no cause for believing that any Son of Man saying has been created as the result of a misunderstood Aramaic idiom. To the contrary, the evangelists seem quite capable of distinguishing between expressions equivalent to 'a man', 'the man', 'this man' as opposed to one meaning (even if it *might* have been the same in form) 'the Son of Man'. The context usually dictates this as well. As far as we can see, this holds true for others who dealt with the tradition before them. We little doubt that some quite authentic element in the traditions enabled them to do this so consistently.

(3) Nor have we found reason to conclude that any of the evangelists were inclined to insert the designation into sayings where it did not otherwise belong. Actually there are only two instances where such a substitution could be forcefully argued, but it will be our contention that at Matt. 16.13 and 16.28 there are convincing grounds for thinking that an element of tradition has been preserved. In other sayings where this question arises it is either obvious or probable that the title has been removed by the evangelist (or his tradition)[1] who offers a parallel saying without the title.[2]

(4) Certainly this does not mean that we accept every Son of Man saying as a verbatim report. In addition to the whole matter of translation, context is bound to affect the understanding of a saying, and in a number of cases it is likely that the relevant contexts have been lost. In addition we would wish it to be clearly understood that we respect the fact that the evangelists have often *used* the Son of Man sayings. Indeed, there is little if anything in the traditions which they have not made to serve their own understandings, and, in this case, the

[1] Scholars who argue for a Son of Man tradition developing within the Church, even while agreeing that the title has sometimes been dropped out of earlier sayings, rarely have any comment on this phenomenon.

[2] In Luke 22.22b *he* has replaced the Son of Man, though the Son of Man is certainly meant. In Luke 17.25 *he* means the Son of Man. Matt. 16.21 appears an obvious instance of *he* substituting for the Son of Man. Quite probably the Son of Man has been omitted from the following passages: Matt. 10.32 (see Luke 12.8); Mark 3.29 (see Matt. 12.32; Luke 12.10); Luke 22.27 (see Mark 10.45; Matt. 20.28); Luke 22.28–30 (see Matt. 19.28); Matt. 5.11 (see Luke 6.22); Matt. 24.42 (see Matt. 24.44; Luke 12.40 and Mark 13.33, 35?). Perhaps the title has dropped out of Matt. 10.33; Luke 12.9 (see Mark 8.38; Luke 9.26).

problems are compounded by our belief that none of the evangelists had adequate knowledge of the genuine terms of reference for the Son of Man of whom Jesus spoke.[1] Yet this is a very different matter from saying that they have created many of these logia, and it is precisely at this point that we enter upon sharpest disagreement with those who see the Church as the true source of the complexities in the Son of Man conception. Even where it may be true that a context or a word or phrase could reflect a later viewpoint, we do not regard this as proof that the essence of the saying is not authentic.[2] It may not be, but, for example, to the degree that some of the passion sayings reveal the presence of details which were added later, other questions must be asked and other issues raised before it can be asserted that a particular saying has no basis in authenticity. Then, too, while the fact that a particular saying may seem to suit the needs of a later point of view must make us doubly cautious, we still have to ask how well it really does this and whether the saying itself could have influenced the later viewpoint.

On the other hand, taken as a whole and compared with other Gospel materials, the Son of Man sayings remain remarkably free of the language and attitudes of the early communities. Sometimes it is hard for us to believe that the Church would ever have wished to fashion a particular saying in the way in which it is phrased. At other times we do not find it difficult to see behind possible slight alterations or accretions to more original forms. In fact, it is our opinion that these sayings must have been particularly fortunate in their treatment. In part this may have been due to the Church's disinclination to make popular use of sayings which were formulated on the basis of a title they did not themselves understand or employ,[3] but we should also

---

[1] We note again that this is generally to be compared rather than contrasted with the occasional gnostic use of the expression. While the gnostics better retained the idea that a descendant of Adam (e.g. Seth) held his office as the heir and type of the First Man, in their concentration on the actual First Man and with their glosses on the Son of Man title, they reveal that they, too, were beginning to lose sight of the Semitic ideas and nuances which the designation itself once conveyed.

[2] Just how dangerous a procedure this may be can be shown by comparing Luke 22.69 with Mark 14.62; Matt. 22.69. Surely if we did not possess the parallels, others would be pressing upon us the importance of viewing Luke 22.69 as entirely a Lucan creation. Luke, for instance, may colour certain sayings with his own eschatological viewpoint. He may insert his own attitudes toward prayer and stress the ideas of an individual relationship with the Son of Man and of the Son of Man as a witness, without, however, fashioning materials from whole cloth.

[3] Cf. Kramer (*Christ, Lord, Son of God*, sec. 23c, p. 101) in discussing *maranatha*: 'But Aramaic-speaking Christians did not say "Son of Man, come!"—though it is

think (and this is not contradictory) that the sayings were highly valued and respected as remembrances of Jesus' own way of speaking.

(5) And yet a small number of Son of Man sayings do appear to have been newly created, while the very manner in which this may have been done is significant. In Luke 24.7 the *remembrance* by the angel of a passion *prediction* will have been fashioned by Luke. His intention, however, was not to create a wholly new Son of Man saying, but rather, quite obviously, to model the angel's words on what he considered to be the authentic way that Jesus spoke about his death. Whether he was correct in doing this is another matter, but it does reveal the evangelist's belief that Jesus spoke in this way while there is every indication that neither Luke nor his community still spoke and thought in these terms.[1] In this sense Luke 24.7 is a deliberate archaism[2] with a primarily literary rather than Christological intent. (The same might also be true of Luke 17.25, though we consider this less likely.)[3]

Matt. 26.2 could seem to have been created in a similar way (although we have some reservations about this) in order to form an introduction to the passion narrative.[4] It is then not a *new* saying, but an attempt to give an authentic sound to the dramatic opening of this

---

now impossible to know why. However, if we examine the NT we find that Son of Man is never used in the vocative, indeed we may take it that it was hardly ever spoken in the church.'

[1] Compare Luke 1–2; 24.20f.; 24.26, 34, 44, 46 and the whole of Acts outside 7.56. So Jeremias holds that the title is, at the least, based on 'pre-Lucan tradition'. He 'never uses the expression . . . independently' (*The Parables of Jesus²*, London, 1963, p. 155 n. 13).

[2] We have noted that Acts 7.56 may well be another. It is true (cf. H. Conzelmann, *The Theology of St Luke*, ET, London, 1960, p. 153 n. 3) that Luke wishes to show that these events were part of God's plan, but this is not the main purpose here, as it is in Luke 24.26f.; 24.44ff. Indeed, 24.7 may be intended to contrast with the manner in which the risen Jesus speaks in the rest of the chapter. (Vv. 6 and 8, with their stress on remembering are perhaps our guideposts.) Some would see the saying as dependent upon Luke 9.22 and/or 9.44, but it is probably a piece of memory work and not a literary creation in a patchwork sense.

[3] See also below on Mark 9.9, which *may* be viewed as having been fashioned on the basis of the traditional Son of Man language.

[4] It is conceivable that Matthew found this reference to the Son of Man at the head of older materials. Even so, however, it should be considered as nothing more than an echoing of older traditions. If the Gospel was created for liturgical and/or catechetical purposes, there would be further cause for repeating the old theme here.

story. Matthew had recourse to the tradition when forming it and not to the contemporary language of the Church.[1]

What these logia then reveal are several situations in which the evangelists may have attempted to echo what they regarded as primitive tradition. Correspondingly only these sayings make use of the specific *crucify* when speaking of the death of the Son of Man.[2]

Among other sayings, the mention of the Son of Man in the Matthean interpretation of the parable of the weeds (13.37, 41)[3] might very legitimately be questioned, and the sign of the Son of Man in heaven (Matt. 24.30) could be included in this category. It is possible, though less likely, that the eschatological judge of Matt. 25.31,

[1] Coming well after the latest time at which such passion sayings could have originated, it can tell us nothing of importance about them. Matthew wanted to make it clear that the passion was expected by Jesus. The tradition offered him only one real basis for so doing, and this he repeated. By itself (and its singularity as a Matthean creation is marked, for see below on 12.40) it can hardly be considered a sign of a proclivity to fashion Son of Man passion materials.

[2] And also Matt. 20.19, where *crucify* appears to have been substituted.

[3] The parable itself could well be authentic (so Jeremias, *Parables*, pp. 224ff.; W. G. Kümmel, *Promise and Fulfilment*, pp. 132ff.), but as Jeremias has convincingly demonstrated (*op. cit.*, pp. 81ff.), the language of the interpretation is markedly Matthean. It also seems to miss the theme of the parable, an exhortation to patience. Furthermore, Tödt (*Son of Man*, pp. 69ff., 78ff.) points out that there are ideas here (esp. that of the Son of Man as Lord of an *interim* kingdom) which are unique to the whole of the Gospels' Son of Man tradition. Perhaps, then, Matthew, reminded of the Son of Man by the idea of judgment, has intruded the title on his own initiative. It is conceivable, however, that Matthew has rewritten an earlier interpretation or that the parable proper once contained a reference to the Son of Man which he has deliberately omitted in order to heighten the revelatory character of the interpretation. Otherwise, since we believe that the evangelist was not regularly inclined to interject the Son of Man into his materials (see below on 10.23; 19.28 as pre-Matthean; at the most he has borrowed the title from the context at 24.30; 16.28), we would suspect that the understanding has come from some northern Palestinian or Syrian, ongoing but non-Christian Son of Man group (perhaps like that of I Enoch, and note the comparison with Rev. 14.14 which is also outside the Gospels' traditions). What we do severely question is the argument which holds that 13.37 reveals Matthew's willingness to create sayings concerning Jesus as the Son of Man on earth. We do not doubt that he believed this, for the traditions offered a strong precedent, but, even on the most generous interpretation, only 12.40; 16.13 and 26.2 could be counted as parallel developments. Yet the first of these is but an allegorical interpretation of a saying which may already have contained a reference to the earthly Son of Man. The second, *even if* Matthean, is afterwards ignored by him, while the third only echoes a hard and fast tradition. In addition, in 13.37 Matthew is really more interested in interpreting the parable than in establishing some Christological truth. The important Son of Man conception for Matthew lies in v. 41; the sower only becomes the Son of Man because it suits the purposes of the explication. In any event, this could tell us nothing about the formation of Mark 2.10; Matt. 8.20; 11.19, etc., which must have come into being a good deal earlier.

the Son of Man coming on the clouds in Mark 13.26f.[1] (with parr.) and the eschatological saying of Luke 21.36[2] are also later formations.

This second category may offer us a glimpse of a certain tendency to elaborate on the future appearance of the heavenly Son of Man. This would not be surprising in communities living under eschatological pressure, but we notice that the tendency, if it is actual, is mainly Matthean and does not appear to have much affected the mainstream of tradition. It would be support only for the theory that some Son of Man sayings may have been developed or altered with a slightly apocalyptic flavour.[3]

(6) The ambiguity of Jesus' relationship with the Son of Man remains a constant, if an unintended, factor in the evangelists' presentation. They assume that Jesus is speaking of himself, but through that assumption one can almost always glimpse the more complex relationship, a sign of an origin in a period when Jesus was not

[1] On Matt. 24.30f.; 25.31 and Mark 13.26f., see in subsequent notes.

[2] One may point to the probable Hellenisms and Lucanisms in an apparently editorial passage (21.34–36) seemingly fashioned to supplant the close to the Marcan eschatological discourse. The title might then have been used as part of a literary device to round off the section. We also notice, as often in Luke, a somewhat different eschatological attitude. (Cf. Conzelmann, *op. cit.* pp. 125ff.; Tödt, *op. cit.*, pp. 97f.) The end is expected, but the immediacy is mitigated to a degree. Yet we cannot be sure that Luke has written these verses without any reference to his sources, since this does not seem his policy elsewhere. Jeremias suspects (*op. cit.*, p. 78 n. 28) that it is 'made up of early material worked over'. We would note the theory of T. W. Manson (*Sayings*, p. 337) that for their eschatological discourses Mark and Luke are using variants of an original source document. One might then compare Luke 21.34–36 with Mark 13.33–37. Many of the same words are used, and Mark also has a variant on the story of the returning householder. Luke also seems to have based 21.34–36 on this theme (compare Luke 12.45 as well), and we believe that his Son of Man saying at 12.40 (= Matt. 24.44) contains the original point of reference for this material (which reference Mark has quite possibly dropped in his 13.35 and Matthew has altered to 'Lord' in 24.42). The idea of standing before the Son of Man is unique, but it is unique with Luke as well! We suggest that it is allied to the picture presented in sayings like Luke 12.8f. and Matt. 19.28; 25.31: there will be some who will be acknowledged by the Son of Man, i.e. they will be able to stand in his presence.

[3] The individual Matthean tendency may be indicated by phrases like 'his angels' in 13.41; 16.27; 24.31; 'his kingdom' in 13.41; 16.28, and the 'Enochian' 'throne of his glory' in 19.28 and 25.31. But note that in several of these cases it is obvious that Matthew has not imported the title into the context. Nor can we be sure that the other traditions have not dropped from their parallels details authentically preserved by Matthew. We would also dispute any effort to regard the mention of angels together with the Son of Man as a sign of later creativity. The association has a firm basis in the tradition (Mark 8.38; 13.26f.; Luke 12.8f.; Matt. 13.41; 25.31; John 1.51) and is found in other materials both with reference to the heavenly Man (Dan. 7.10; I Enoch 70f.; etc.) and to the Man on earth as Adam, the king or the Adamite one.

simply identified with the Son of Man. Jesus can speak and even act as though he were the Son of Man; he relates things which happen to him to the story of the Son of Man; men's reactions to him are inextricably bound with the belief that the Son of Man will appear in heavenly glory and treat men accordingly. Yet there is still this sense in which the heavenly Son of Man, at least, is *another*. Nowhere is Jesus reported to have made the unambiguous claim that he was in and of himself the one and only Son of Man. It is to the synoptics' credit that they have not invented a saying to fill this gap.

(7) We have little confidence that the general order in which the Son of Man logia are now found can tell us much about the original relationship of these sayings. The difficulties involved in trying to frame an order out of the materials in the different Gospels and *sources* appear insuperable. There may be certain passages or longer sections where older ligatures of thought are still visible and certain sayings may have been rightly connected (in general terms at least) with the correct junctures in Jesus' own life, but the overall relation of the sayings to one another and the pattern of the Man myth were seemingly lost at an early date. (There may at times be visible a proclivity to collect the Son of Man sayings together into little groupings which contributed to this process.) While we can notice that Mark *tends* to go from sayings about the earthly Son of Man to those which speak of the passion to those pointing to a future appearance, the order is not carefully adhered to, and, in any case, now naturally correlates to the pattern of Jesus' life and the Church's hope in his return. Although it is true that such a pattern might be seen to correspond to the Man myth, it would certainly appear that it is the story of Jesus and not the myth as such which has governed the Marcan programming.

2. THE SAYINGS

We should like now to take a number of the Son of Man sayings and to comment upon them briefly, attempting to set them in the context of Jesus' ministry and to see something of how they may once have related to one another.

A. *The Son of Man on earth*

The Son of Man is operative on earth. Jesus, having undergone an experience of divine ordination, believes that his own ministry and the work of the Son of Man are intimately related. At the least he has been given the right to speak and act in the role of the Son of Man.[1] Stories told about the Son of Man are his stories which he may himself either tell or 'live through' and enact.

Mark 2.10 (= Matt. 9.6; Luke 5.24): But that you may know that the Son of Man has authority on earth to forgive sins . . .

With this remark Jesus silences the objection that he is forgiving sins on his own human authority alone.[2] The *authority* to *judge* in this way is a power given by God to the Son of Man. He may exercise it just 'because he is the Son of Man' (John 5.27). Here the fact to be particularly remarked upon, that which enables Jesus to act as he does, is the understanding that the Son of Man does this now, 'on earth'.[3]

Nor does Jesus acting as the Son of Man merely wield authority

[1] That he should then sometimes speak of himself in this office in the third person would not be a surprising phenomenon. Otto (*Kingdom of God and Son of Man*, p. 232) points out that the Buddha on occasion spoke of himself by his official name, the 'Tathagata'. Modern illustrations could be cited: 'It is the President's duty . . .', 'The Prime Minister is obliged to act . . .', when such leaders are speaking of themselves in their official capacities.

[2] The theory that the saying arises from the misunderstood idiom only raises further problems. Either Jesus would be forgiving sins on his own authority alone (which would hardly fit the view of Bultmann and others regarding the historical Jesus) or else the early Church attributed the authority to Jesus with reference to an idiomatic circumlocution. Thus some would understand the use of the idiom in another fashion: 'but that you may know that (a) man has authority on earth to forgive sins'. The 'on earth' now, however, is redundant, and there is nothing in Judaism to prepare us for such a thought. (So Fuller, *Mission and Achievement*, p. 49; Bultmann, *Synoptic Tradition*, p. 15.) Other critics would cast doubt on the whole scene. They point to apparent editorial links and suggest we might have two different stories here. Yet the themes go together naturally (cf. C. P. Ceroke, 'Is Mk 2.10 a Saying of Jesus?' *CBQ* 22, 1960, pp. 369ff.) while even if we do excerpt something like Mark 2.5b–10a we still have a reasonable portion of tradition. A. Farrer (*A Study in St Mark*, London, 1951, p. 76) regards the awkwardness in v. 10 as deliberate and a sign of authenticity (and interestingly compares Ex. 4.4f.), and the power of the Son of Man to judge is a well-established theme. Both Higgins (*Son of Man*, p. 28) and Tödt (*Son of Man*, p. 129) seem to agree that Jesus did exhibit some authority to deal with men's sins. But what would have provided the basis for this sense of authority?

[3] Tödt deals with this feature by holding that the Church used it as a sign that they were transferring the office of the heavenly figure to Jesus, but this seems an oddly self-conscious addition by a community which was acting without deliberate plan. For a good insight into the importance of these words which give real movement to the sequence of thought here, cf. G. H. P. Thompson, *JTS*, ns 12, 1961, pp. 204f. We note that Matthew, Luke and a few texts of Mark agree in placing 'on earth' before 'to forgive sins'. If authentic this would be likely to enhance the significance of the phrase.

without the corresponding power. He proves this by healing the physical man. Perhaps, as John 9.35 may also indicate, Jesus did a number of his healing miracles in the name of, or as, the Son of Man.

Mark 2.28 (= Matt. 12.8; Luke 6.5): The Son of Man is lord also[1] of the sabbath.

Sovereignty over the sabbath is an authority which Jesus is said often to have exercised in one way or another, and it could well be that this saying is one of the keys to his sense of authority in this area.[2] Certainly it should not be surprising that the Son of Man would speak and act as sovereign of the sabbath, the day which is a memorial of the creation,[3] especially created for the blessing of mankind,[4] among whom Adam is first. And it is this day of rest which is associated with the coming of the new age,[5] with the ceremonial activity of the ruler[6] and, through its observance, with the coming of the Messiah.[7] In this sense, both in terms of its first purpose and its final purpose, it could be seen as the day of the Man.[8]

---

[1] Or 'even'.

[2] Many (e.g. E. Lohse, 'Jesu Worte über den Sabbat' in *Judentum-Urchristentum-Kirche* [BZNW 26, ed. W. Eltester], 1960, pp. 79ff.) see Mark 2.28 as a Church comment on v. 27, but we wonder if the Church would have gone about creating a basis for dealing with the sabbath customs in this manner. (The contention that it is really the disciples' authority which is at question is certainly countered by Tödt, who holds that it is Jesus' authority which is essentially at issue. In any case men often attack a leader through his followers.) And one can hardly insist that this was only a later concern in the face of all the incidents and stories to the contrary.

[3] See Ex. 20.11.

[4] Ex. 16.29 and in later traditions, one of which has it that God set Adam free on the sabbath. See in C. G. Montefiore and H. Loewe, *A Rabbinic Anthology*, London, 1938, p. 236.

[5] See Isa. 56.2ff.; 58.13f.; 66.23 and so in later tradition. Note esp. the ideas on which Heb. 3–4 are built.

[6] Ezek. 46.1ff.; 46.12.

[7] See, e.g., Moore, *Judaism* II, p. 26 n. 1.

[8] There are numerous theories which suggest that all or part of Mark 2.27f. is the result of a misunderstanding of *bar nāšā*. Often we are referred to a rabbinic statement like 'The sabbath is given to you, and not you to the sabbath' (Mekilta on Ex. 31.13; cf. S-B II, p. 5). We would agree, however, with the arguments of Tödt (*op. cit.*, pp. 130ff.), Higgins (*op. cit.*, pp. 28ff.), V. Taylor (*The Gospel according to Mark*, London, 1952, pp. 220ff.) and others that this is unlikely with regard to v. 28. We reckon with the possibility (cf. Beare, *Earliest Records*, pp. 90ff.; 'The Sabbath Was Made for Man?' *JBL* 79, 1960, pp. 130ff., and T. W. Manson, 'Mark ii.27f.' in *Coniectanea Neotestamentica* 11, 1947, pp. 138ff.) that the title was intended throughout which, though it seems unlikely, would still make good sense on the basis of our theory.

Thus, if Mark 2.27 also is authentic,[1] we would find a clear and significant expression of belief which fits with the background of these themes. Whatever the precise original wording may have been, the idea is this:

> The sabbath was made for Man (Adam), and not Man
> (Adam) for the sabbath.
> Therefore the Son of the Man (Adam) is lord also
> of the sabbath. (He is his legitimate heir.)

Though a number of commentators see little or no authentic connection between this idea and the story of David permitting his followers to eat 'the bread of the presence' (or 'shewbread') on the sabbath,[2] it is possible to guess that there may once have been a profound relationship in the context of the Man speculations. David, as the anointed king, could well have been seen as a descendant of the Man and a type of the Son of Man on the basis of Ps. 80.17 or general tradition in this regard.[3] In addition, the shewbread is linked in the Old Testament with the sabbath customs,[4] and the same verse which tells that the sabbath has been given by God to men reminds that God also provides bread on the day previous for the sabbath day of rest.[5] Thus it may once have been that, as Jesus acting as the Son of Man was lord over the sabbath, so he also was the Son of Man providing bread for his followers. This bread was the 'most holy'[6] bread of the sabbath, the day that would usher in the reign of the Son of Man.[7]

[1] If it is a question of primacy, certainly v. 27 ought to be more suspect on many grounds. It is not found in Matthew and Luke (whatever reasons are suggested for its omission, and it is at least doubtful if Matthew and Luke could have had the same reason) and is missing or missing in part from several texts of Mark. Matthew and Luke also agree on word order and on omitting καί, which suggests that Mark could have altered the saying in order to accommodate his addition.

[2] Yet Higgins (op. cit., p. 30; against Beare, Earliest Records, p. 92) at least sees the significance of the connection. This pattern of answering an objection by reference to scripture followed by its application certainly emulates the rabbinic method well enough (cf. Gerhardsson, Memory and Manuscript, p. 328, etc.), and such would be given to disciples to commit to memory.

[3] On this point and for some penetrating insights with regard to the unity of the passage and its vital Adamic themes (the Son of Man is the heir of both Adam and David), see Farrer, Study in St Mark, pp. 275ff. See also his remarks more generally, pp. 247ff.

[4] Lev. 24.8.

[5] Ex. 16.29.

[6] Lev. 24.9.

[7] Then there might be an echo here of 'Give us today the bread of tomorrow', which would indeed be the bread of heaven. Thus this story and the saying would

Matt. 16.13: 'Who do men say that the Son of Man is?'

Here and now there are questions about who might be the Son of Man on earth.[1]

Mark 10.45 (= Matt. 20.28): For even[2] the Son of Man came not to be served but to serve, and to give his life as a ransom for many.

The saying may be included here as it could be as much a description of the role and position of the Son of Man as it is a statement regarding his death. How closely the logion itself is to be related to the Isaianic Servant conception[3] and the theme of Phil. 2.7 is not certain, but, on our view, it is an interpretation of an idea from out of the same background of beliefs.[4] Despite the fact that the Gospels' Son of Man sayings are now generally so fragmented as to disguise the older pattern of humiliation followed by victory, this saying is

---

once have been associated with the traditions behind the feeding of the multitudes and the Last Supper. (See pp. 295ff.) Again there would be a kind of prefigurement of the banquet of the new age.

[1] See below, pp. 377ff.
[2] Or 'For the Son of Man also . . .'
[3] Hooker (*Jesus and the Servant*, pp. 74ff.) and C. K. Barrett ('The Background of Mark 10.45' in *New Testament Essays* [ed. A. J. B. Higgins], Manchester, 1959, pp. 1ff.) challenge this view as it is presented by Jeremias (*Servant of God*, pp. 96ff.), but all credit the possible authenticity of the verse in this regard, either in part or entire, a view confirmed by Hooker in her *The Son of Man in Mark*. Jeremias, like others, would also refer us to 'poured out for many' in Mark 14.24, and see above, p. 290, on the δοῦναι here. It is interesting that while Tödt regards 10.45a as primary and from the Palestinian community (for it precedes 45b, which was formed, on the basis of Isa. 53, in a Semitic language community, on which see also E. Lohse, *Märtyrer und Gottesknecht* (FRLANT 64, nf. 46), Göttingen, 1955, pp. 117ff.), Higgins holds that 45b is primary and probably authentic, but that 45a is secondary and Hellenistic. We agree with Tödt that the whole must have been known in the Palestinian community, but, while its authenticity can hardly be proven, find his critique wanting unless one has already agreed that Jesus could not have spoken of the death of the Son of Man and its meaning for others. Even if v. 45b is based on Isa. 53, this is done only in vague terms, which was not the Church's usual method. Certainly any criticisms of the use of 'many' are now without much foundation due to the frequent use of *rabbīm*, as in Isa. 53.12, to refer to the covenanters of the Dead Sea. E.g. 1QS, vi, 1, 7, 8. Regarding the relationship with the possible parallel in Luke one notes Fuller's view (*Foundations*, p. 176 n. 29) that Mark 10.45a is primary in every way to Luke 22.27b *except* that *I* is held to be more basic than the Son of Man!
[4] See p. 253. The stress usually falls on the service to the God or gods, while the idea of being a servant of the people is far from absent in the conception of the ideal king. Compare Ps. 72.4 and the whole theme of the king suffering for his people. See also Isa. 42.1ff.; 49.1ff.

probably to be read in context with what precedes (Mark 10.35ff.) and so to be viewed in the light of such understandings.[1]

Matt. 8.20 (= Luke 9.58): Foxes have holes, and birds of the air have nests; but the Son of Man has nowhere to lay his head.

As an authentic saying this could relate either to the more mythical background or more specifically to the circumstances of Jesus' life or to both. (At this point and others personal experience and older themes could have tended to reinforce one another.) We may recall Adam and many other types of the First Man-king finding themselves homeless and forced to wander the earth.[2] The saying can also remind us of the king as a figure of rejection,[3] and it is far from impossible that it may be a low-keyed expression (from Q!) of the theme stated more directly in a saying like Mark 9.12.[4]

Matt. 11.19 (= Luke 7.34): The Son of Man has come eating and drinking . . .

Perhaps this would not have been a saying taken directly from the background in myth (though it might relate to the idea that when the Man is present with his people there is cause for rejoicing and to the general theme of his rejection). It may then have been created out of the circumstances. John was castigated for his asceticism; Jesus, acting as the Son of Man, was being condemned for his lack of it. Such a saying would fit well into the ministry,[5] and it is certainly not

[1] See p. 389.

[2] E.g. Life of Adam and Eve 3.1. It is not inconceivable that the wild animals are to remind us of the condition of the Man as in the temptation story, etc.

[3] E.g. Ps. 69.8. He is a stranger and an alien to his brethren. We agree, however, with Tödt (against Sjöberg, verborgene Menschensohn, pp. 179ff.) that there is no cause for reading 'concealment' into the saying. But we do find the themes of humility and lack of recognition, though they are not predicated of the 'pre-existent' Son of Man as such.

[4] Cf. Fuller, Mission and Achievement, pp. 104f. We agree with Tödt and Higgins in rejecting Bultmann's theory (Synoptic Tradition, p. 28) that the logion originally applied to 'any man'. (So Knox, Death of Christ, p. 101, feeling the difficulties, argues that a circumlocution for I was used.) We note that the Gospel of Thomas, log. 86, presents this as its only Son of Man saying, finding no idiom here. Beyond this it is hard to see that there are any valid criticisms. It need hardly have been inappropriate to Jesus' circumstances, as Higgins claims; nor can we follow Tödt in finding Jesus' 'authority' at issue here.

[5] The same idea is picked up in another way in Mark 2.18ff. when speaking of the fasting of John's disciples and of the bridegroom who is now present. Nor is it impossible that this bridegroom language is ultimately related to the conception of the king as a bridegroom during the great festival period. Certainly the theme of the baptized person as bridegroom reappears in both Christian and non-Christian teachings.

easy to see how or why the Church would have fashioned a piece of tradition along these lines. [1]

Luke 19.10: For the Son of Man came to seek and save the lost.[2]

The Son of Man has a genuine ministry on earth. The saying could be an interpretation of ancient themes associated with the Man,[3] but it may also be in part due to an emphasis contributed by Jesus.

[1] We could hardly better the reasons given by Higgins (*op. cit.*, pp. 122ff.) for respecting this as a primitive logion. Cf. Schweizer, *ZNW* 50, 1959, pp. 199f. We would only add that it belongs to a complex concerned with Jesus, Elijah, the Baptist and Son of Man which we find to be an authoritative interrelationship. Cf. pp. 372ff. It is possible, too, that there is a primitive play of words involved in 'the Son of Man . . . behold a man'. Vielhauer's objection (*ZTK* 60, 1963, pp. 163ff.) that Matt. 11.18 (and thus 11.19) is unhistorical is without foundation, and there is no sign of the Church's tendency to demonstrate Jesus' superiority to John. We note that Bornkamm (*Jesus of Nazareth*, pp. 229f.) accepts the historicity of Matt. 11.19, though he then goes on to insist that the Son of Man must be a later substitution. We follow Higgins and Tödt in rejecting theories of a misunderstood idiom here, but cannot see Jesus' 'authority' to act unencumbered by the rules and ways of men as the vital issue. Surely (on the grounds of the nature of the accusation and the manner in which Jesus is compared to the Baptist) one would not have thought this either the way or place to intrude the Church's conception of Jesus as the bearer of this exalted title. For the Church ever to have imagined Jesus–the Son of Man in these terms it really is necessary to supply it beforehand with a Son of Man conception far more subtle and elaborate than the one which Tödt and Higgins see in the background. We believe there is every indication that this is what they were losing rather than developing.

[2] Matt. 18.11 is a variant of this saying (omitting only 'to seek and') which was added to the text by some scribe. The problems involved with Luke 9.56a are more complex, for it is difficult to understand quite how the present versions of v. 56 came into being. A number of texts have 'You do not know what manner of spirit you are of'. The Bezae now, however, stops while the others continue on, 'for the Son of Man came not to destroy men's lives but to save them'. The 'omission' by Bezae is curious, as though it might have been deliberate. Conceivably there is cause (without resorting to a theory that it was removed for fear of misuse by Marcionites) for reopening the question of the integrity of the whole saying, esp. as it preserves the links between Elijah and the Son of Man which we find to be primitive. There are also significant differences from 19.10. Like Matt. 18.11, Luke 9.56a does not contain the idea of 'seeking'. It has ἀπολέσαι in lieu of ἀπολωλός and alters the whole tenor by denying any destructive purpose on the part of the Son of Man. We would surmise that both Matt. 18.11 and Luke 9.56a are variants of the saying recorded in Luke 19.10 which show signs of having been formed at an earlier period, before Luke's gospel was composed. As such they witness to a logion from yet earlier tradition.

[3] The whole story of Zacchaeus in Luke 19.2ff. is sometimes regarded as secondary. Cf. Bultmann, *Synoptic Tradition*, pp. 33f.; and Beare, *Earliest Records*, pp. 200f., who sees it as derived from Mark 2.13ff. This is, however, by no means a universally held opinion (see Dibelius, *From Tradition to Gospel*, p. 118), and it could be argued that Mark 2.13ff. is a composite later comment derived in part from the

There are other sayings which might well have been understood to refer to the Son of Man as one who could be present on earth. Luke 11.30 is probably more original[1] than Matt. 12.40.[2] It may mean that like Jonah the Son of Man has a task on earth; among other things his mission is to serve as a sign, a warning to his generation.[3]

For as Jonah became a sign to the men of Nineveh,
so will the Son of Man be to this generation.

---

story independently preserved by Luke. In any event, the comparison with Mark 2.17b = Luke 5.32 can hardly prove anything. (Also the results of a suggested comparison with Mark 10.45 would depend on one's views regarding the authenticity of that logion.) But there are so many theories concerning the appending of Luke 19.7–10 or 9b–10 or 10 that it seems necessary to consider v. 10b on its own merits. Tödt (op. cit., pp. 133ff.) tells us that such a saying is unique to Luke and his tradition. Might we not, then, infer that neither Luke or his tradition has created it? We would recall instead the idea of the Man-king or the God come to save those in darkness, prison, etc. (e.g. Isa. 9.2; 42.7; 49.9; Pss. 107.10ff.; 146.7; Odes of Sol. 17.8ff.; 22.4) and of the Man as the shepherd-king (Zech. 13.7) and God the shepherd in Ezek. 34.16 (where the τὸ ἀπολωλὸς ζητήσω is to be compared with Luke's ζητῆσαι . . . τὸ ἀπολωλός). Compare CD, xiii, 9.

[1] Bultmann, Higgins, Tödt and many others accept the authenticity of Luke 11.30. Beare (Earliest Records, p. 103) holds that it contravenes Jesus' assertion that no sign would be given to this generation. Cf. Mark 8.12; but compare Matt. 16.4; 12.39 = Luke 11.29, for many feel that it is Mark who has dropped the enigmatic reference to Jonah. In any event, Jesus' real objection is against the seeking of signs for their own sake; he himself sees many signs of the time. Vielhauer, ZTK 60, 1963, pp. 150f., finds that the presence of Luke 11.32b = Matt. 12.41b (with Luke 11.31b = Matt. 12.42b) throws doubt on the whole passage, but we question the presuppositions of this view, and, in any case, these tag lines could have been added later. At the least we would agree with Tödt (op. cit., p. 54): 'Here the preaching of Jesus and the appearing of the Son of Man are closely related.'

[2] Interesting arguments have been put forward in defence of the authenticity of Matt. 12.40. The 'mistaken' reference to the 'three nights' is viewed as a detail which the Church would never have fashioned. Luke may have omitted this part of the logion because of this (and perhaps also because he did not appreciate this mode of thought), and we are to see behind these words the old theme of the Man's descent into the underworld. Cf. Cullmann, Christology, pp. 62f. (On the view that Luke 11.30 itself implies a link between this sign and the resurrection, see Jeremias, "Ἰωνᾶς", TWNT III, pp. 412f.) If a Matthean addition, however, it proves no more than his penchant to expand on scriptural allusions, and not a general tendency to develop Son of Man sayings of this type.

[3] Luke 11.32, if authentic, suggests this, and the hint may be present in any case if we understand the sign of Jonah to refer to his preaching. (Manson, Sayings, pp. 89ff., suggested that Jesus meant that, just as Jonah gave no other sign than his preaching, so the Son of Man gives no further sign. Thus the saying confirms Mark 8.12.) The objection to this understanding is the future tense: so will the Son of Man be to this generation; but it is not difficult to view overtones of a kind of future perfect: so will the Son of Man have been to this generation.

Quite conceivably prophecies like this were being made of the Son of Man before Jesus' own ministry was begun.[1]

Luke 6.22 ('Blessed are you when men hate you, and when they exclude you and revile you, and cast out your name as evil, on account of the Son of Man')[2] and Luke 12.10 = Matt. 12.32[3]

[1] And behind this there is conceivably the belief that Jonah, too, had been a type of the Son of Man, another of the Adamite ones.

[2] Most scholars would seem to agree with Higgins (*op. cit.*, pp. 119f.) in holding that Luke 6.22 and Matt. 5.11 are 'variant forms of the same underlying Aramaic beatitude' and that 'because of the Son of Man' is more primitive. Cf. Manson, *Sayings*, pp. 46ff.; Black, *Aramaic Approach*, p. 97. Bultmann's critique (*Synoptic Tradition*, pp. 110, 127) is, however, short and simple. The use of the second person and the detailed grounds for blessedness are the signs of a Church formulation. Yet the second person form in sayings like this is hardly unknown within Judaism. Then, too, Luke is consistent on this matter, and, if he is otherwise more primitive in his recording of authentic beatitudes (as most scholars believe), it is somewhat arbitrary to regard the *you* in this saying as a sign of community work. (See Manson, *op. cit.*, p. 47.) While it is possible that the details may have been elaborated, and the saying would have been of use to the Church (though when was it persecuted for preaching Jesus as the Son of Man?—and, in any event, there is a certain *reductio ad absurdum* in the argument that all which might suit the Church's needs is unauthentic), we think it may, in essence, be revelatory of what was happening during Jesus' lifetime.

It could be, on the other hand, that the persecution was to be suffered by those who believed in and taught of the heavenly Son of Man (cf. I Enoch 46.8). Then several of the above criticisms would go by the board, and the logion would relate closely to Luke 12.8f., etc.

[3] The objections to the priority of Mark 3.28f. at this point are manifold, and have recently been set forth again by Higgins (*op. cit.*, pp. 127ff.) and Tödt (*op. cit.*, pp. 118ff., 312ff.). Though the Marcan saying yields a more immediate sense, many suspect it for this reason and because it then is difficult to see how the Q saying would have arisen. (See E. Lohmeyer, *Das Evangelium des Markus*[15] [K-EKNT], 1959, pp. 79f., and also on whether Jesus would ever have spoken something like Mark 3.28f.) Indeed, the challenge to the two-document theory here is so profound and many-sided that even Beare (*Earliest Records*, p. 102) joins those who would see three variants on an original theme, in which case we have two witnesses against Mark and strong indication that we are dealing with a logion from quite early tradition altered over a period of time in independent transmissions. (In a paper delivered at the Third International Congress on New Testament Studies, Oxford, 1965, R. Schippers seeks a common Aramaic original behind the sayings and suggests that Son of Man in a titular sense was the original intention.) This would tend to obviate the argument of Wellhausen (cf. Tödt, *op. cit.*, 312ff.) and of Bultmann (*op. cit.*, p. 131) and Manson (*Sayings*, p. 110) with regard to the *bar nāšā* idiom.

Many believe that Matthew has best preserved the context, though there may yet be a meaningful link between Luke 12.8f. and v. 10, i.e. there is something even more important than the conditions set out in 12.8f. The implications might then be that the Son of Man of v. 10 is Jesus acting for the heavenly Son of Man. It is more likely, however, that all have lost the primitive context, in which event we cannot be sure whether the Son of Man of heaven or earth was first intended. Possibly, adopting a Jewish understanding that to speak against the Spirit would

('and everyone who speaks a word against the Son of Man will be forgiven') might suppose the presence of the Son of Man among men. There is no reason why such persecution and slander could not have begun in Jesus' own lifetime. Indeed, there is good cause for believing that it did. Again, however, as developments from the ancient theme of the rejection of the Man figure, these could also have been things said of the Son of Man at an earlier period before Jesus *became* the Son of Man.

Finally it must be remembered that the traditions which speak of the suffering and death of the Son of Man assume a time when he will be or is on the earth.

B. *The suffering and resurrection*

The Son of Man must suffer. Jesus speaks of the necessity of the Son of Man's death and *resurrection*.

It is sometimes not recognized that there could be two fundamental questions involved in the Son of Man passion *predictions*. Did Jesus speak of the suffering of the Son of Man? Did he speak of his own death and especially of his own death as the Son of Man? It is possible, in other words, that Jesus might have echoed some of the teachings about the Man (of which this would have been among the most basic) without applying them, in any definitive manner, to himself. Moving in a *milieu* in which sayings like this were predicated of the Son of Man, he could have made such statements just as naturally as he probably told of the Son of Man appearing in heaven,

---

be equivalent to speaking against the Torah (cf. S-B I, pp. 636f.), there was involved here a distinction between sectarians rejecting or questioning the Son of Man conception and those who went further and rejected parts of the Torah. This is no more than a guess, for much of the enigmatic quality remains, but it is just this character which makes us wonder if the logion does not have a good claim on authenticity. Tödt, on the other hand, finds the saying 'quite intelligible'. There are two periods of history in view. Those who spoke against the Son of Man—Jesus while he was on earth can be forgiven now, in the age of the Spirit, if they will follow the risen Lord. One would think that such an argument needs to be buttressed by the contention that the original time sequence had been lost. Clearly it would once have been of importance to distinguish and say, 'Whoever has said a word against the Son of Man will be forgiven . . .', for are not Tödt and the others maintaining that the original 'misunderstanding' resulted from an identification of Jesus with the heavenly Son of Man of whom he spoke? Surely, then, it was Jesus as the exalted Son of Man who was reverenced, and we cannot see how any group who worshipped him as such would have created such a saying (as the Marcan reinterpretation probably indicates), however *finely* it was to be understood.

while not necessarily inferring that he himself would have to die as the Son of Man any more than that he had to be *the* one who was to appear as the Son of Man in heaven. The sayings may have had a certain gnomic quality.

Nevertheless, although there may be a partial but valuable truth in this contingency, it would appear likely that the one who saw himself acting as the Son of Man in other ways would have come to believe that the destiny of the Son of Man might also pertain to his own person. This would not necessarily mean that he was sure that he was the one and only Son of Man, the one who would come to be seen as the ruler in heaven, nor that he knew for certain that he himself had to suffer, but it would mean that he saw his own role in terms of that of the Son of Man and that he expected and *foresaw* his own destiny accordingly.

Very probably his relationship to this understanding about the Son of Man was as complex as human situations and circumstances often are. We have too little information to attempt a psychological reconstruction, but, on the analogy of other human experiences, we may guess that Jesus might have slowly grown more and more certain that this was what was expected of him, that his was to be a life and death like that of the Son of Man. The materials for understanding what was happening and what was going to happen lay ready to hand.

A number of scholars today believe that the passion *predictions*, especially those predicating suffering and death of the Son of Man, are so evidently formulations of the Church that they can be dismissed without prolonged discussion. The essential arguments against their authenticity are along these lines. (*1*) As a human being, Jesus could not have foreseen his own death. (*2*) The bewilderment and sorrow of the disciples are not satisfactorily explained if Jesus predicted his death (and especially if he also predicted his resurrection) to them. (*3*) The early Church would have been very eager to create sayings of this kind. (*4*) The details of the predictions, in any case, are clearly the work of the communities. (*5*) All the synoptic Son of Man passion predictions can be understood to stem from the Marcan source or its influence. Since they are not more pervasive, it is unlikely that they are original. Let us take up these arguments.

(*1*) The dismissal of all prophecies of death as impossible or even just unlikely runs counter to the facts of numerous recorded historical incidents. Men in hazardous occupations or involved in risky undertakings have predicted their deaths with a high degree of accuracy both with regard to mode and time. This can be seen to be especially true during periods of persecution.¹

Along with those sayings in which he is reported to have spoken of the destiny of the Son of Man both before coming to Jerusalem and during the final night, along with the two predictions which reveal that significant link between baptism and death,² along with the tradition about drinking some cup of pain or death,³ in addition to an attitude which seemed to have expected persecution, rejection and suffering for both himself and others as almost a matter of course, there are sayings like Mark 2.20 (with parr.) and Luke 13.32ff.⁴ which suggest in other terms that Jesus feared the worst for himself. Many scholars find that a number of these logia have a primitive ring to them,⁵ and, while one cannot insist that they must be authentic, neither can the distinct possibility that Jesus

¹ Obviously, too, the inclination to think along these lines would be strengthened if one tended to identify with a figure who was said to have a tragic destiny. It may be objected that Jesus was not living during a time of genuine persecution. There is no evidence that persecution unto death was a widespread feature of Palestinian life, esp. under the aegis of Jewish officialdom. Still, one can hardly deny the possibility that Jesus realized the reaction which his teachings and actions would provoke in the Jewish capital. We must take into account the strong tradition that he was bent on going to Jerusalem even though warned against doing so; he must have realized that real personal danger awaited him there, for men have been put to death in more civilized countries for far less. In addition, the example of John the Baptist and probably of others was all too ready at hand.

² Mark 10.38 (= Matt. 20.22); Luke 12.50; and see further below.

³ Mark 10.38f. (= Matt. 20.22f.); Mark 14.36 (= Matt. 26.39, 42; Luke 22.42); John 18.11. See further below.

⁴ Some would suggest that this hints that Jesus once thought in terms of death by stoning, but this is uncertain, and, in any case, he may have been using a form of synecdoche. The reference to a *prophet's* death does not mean that Jesus thought of himself primarily and certainly not exclusively in such a fashion. Being the Son of Man would not exclude the prophet's role.

We find Luke 13.32f. to be of particular interest in that it combines several features elsewhere associated with the Son of Man: the *must*, the three days language (idiom?) and the verb πορεύομαι which Luke has used in 22.22. Is it conceivable that 13.32f. once made mention of the Son of Man? If not, might the passage faithfully reflect the kind of language used by Jesus and so tend to corroborate the authenticity of similar language used in Son of Man sayings?

⁵ See Fuller, *Mission and Achievement*, pp. 55ff.; W. Manson, *Jesus, the Messiah*, pp. 121ff.; V. Taylor, *Jesus and His Sacrifice*, London, 1937, pp. 79ff.; Jeremias in *Servant of God*, pp. 100ff.; Kümmel, *Promise and Fulfilment*, pp. 69ff. See also the parable of the wicked tenants (Mark 12.1ff. and parr.). Let us also note that a scholar like Higgins, while generally rejecting the possibility that Jesus spoke of himself as the Son of Man, still believes that Jesus did speak of his death and of his resurrection as well in terms of *I* sayings. See *op. cit.*, pp. 49, 56f.

foresaw what the journey to Jerusalem[1] would mean be easily cast aside.

(2) The bewilderment and sorrow of the disciples seem to have been very real, but it is hardly likely that they should have been vitiated in any significant way by earlier sayings about the death or even about the *resurrection* as well. Did the disciples comprehend Jesus as he spoke about these matters, especially as he related them to the teachings about the Son of Man? Did they really understand that, when he linked himself with the role of the Son of Man figure, he actually meant that these things were likely to happen to him? Would they have believed him? And even if they had understood and believed (and there is much in the traditions that would suggest a high degree of incomprehension in response to these sayings), would not the overwhelming brutality, suddenness and sense of tragic loss and finality which death always brings have temporarily destroyed both understanding and faith?

Actually one might be far more suspicious of the predictions if they were used to convince us that the disciples did not sorrow and become bewildered, but were rather joyful and expectant from the moment of death. After all (the disciples must have realized) men do not rise from the real grave, not even Jesus, not even the one who thought he was acting as the Son of Man! These sayings initially had to do with legends and baptismal practices, not with the fearful reality of the kind of death which Jesus met.[2]

(3) Of course, the Church would have wished to possess predictions of Jesus' death. They would not wish to allow the impression that it was some kind of an accident unforeseen by him or God. Among other things, this might call into question the nature of the self-offering that was involved. Yet and once again, an awareness of the Church's needs and desires does not carry along with it an automatic obligation to decide that wherever the Church's requirements and tradition correspond the authenticity of the latter must be rejected. Still, it is a fair principle of criticism that where this correspondence does seem to take place, we must be doubly on our guard.

[1] Or his return to Jerusalem or his remaining there, if John is right to indicate a more extensive Jerusalem ministry.

[2] A comment like John 20.9 (compare Luke 24.26, 46) would then be an obvious later attempt to explain the lack of comprehension. Certainly it does not indicate that John himself was in the business of creating passion predictions. And why does not Luke put these verses in the mouth of the pre-resurrection Jesus if this was his habit?

One might have thought, however, that, were all the passion predictions the work of the communities, the hand of the Church would be more evident in the basic format of these sayings. Yet once certain *possible* (see below) accretions are removed, the residue of these sayings presents a hard core, the authenticity of which cannot easily be dismissed. In other words, by turning certain procedures of criticism around, as it were, one can wonder if the essentials of these logia do sound like the product of the communities. Why are they usually so oblique and often couched in general terms? However conceivable it may be to some that the Church worshipped Jesus as the Son of Man, why would not the regular form of prediction have presented Jesus speaking much more directly of his own suffering and death? Why do we not hear: 'I am to be given up and crucified and on the third day I will rise again'?[1] How do we explain away the very strong tradition which tells of the Son of Man's destiny at the Last Supper and in the garden (a tradition to which the Fourth Gospel is seemingly an independent witness)? On what grounds did the Church introduce the ideas of *mustness* and 'as it is written of him' into the Son of Man passion sayings? Do they know why he must as the Son of Man or where it is written?[2] If so, why is there no

[1] We come quite close to this in Matt. 16.21 with the alteration of the Son of Man to *he*. This is what we would expect of the Church.

[2] On this see pp. 400f. Higgins (*op. cit.*, pp. 31f.) offers the rather traditional approach to these themes when he invites a comparison with Luke 24.26, 46, etc. Yet, while there is no doubt that the Church came to believe that Jesus, as the Christ, fulfilled the scriptures, this does not automatically tell us why these things had to happen to the Son of Man. Indeed, we find that there are compelling reasons for believing that these ideas of *mustness* and *foreordination* belonged to the Son of Man in the traditions before they became associated with Jesus as the Christ or simply with Jesus in his own right. The later passages cannot, therefore, tell us how men first came to think in these terms of the Son of Man, and they could very well be derived from the earlier modes of expression, the essential difference being that the Church has now made use of its own titles for Jesus.

Apparently recognizing that the themes of *mustness* and scriptural necessity, in their association with the Son of Man, cannot be explained simply on the basis of parallels with language which later came to be used of Jesus, the Christ, Tödt (*op. cit.*, pp. 162ff., 182ff.) undertakes a different approach. We would agree with him that this *mustness* is largely (though not entirely) founded upon the belief conveyed by 'as it is written'. (Attempts to trace it specifically and wholly to the apocalyptic-eschatological sense, see Dan. 2.28; Mark 13.7, 10; Rev. 1.1, seem neither to fit the context or mood of these Son of Man sayings. Yet this manner of necessity may not be completely devoid of influence, while probably more important is a sense in which such things must take place because of the dictates of liturgical and/or mythical forms.) These things must happen to the Son of Man because *scripture* ordains that it be so. But Tödt's attempt to account for this by connecting the 'be treated with contempt' theme of Mark 9.12 with the 'is to be

explanation of these features? If not, are not these elements better understood as having been caused by factors in the primitive traditions?

(*4*) Some of the details of the passions sayings can provide undoubted difficulties. This is especially true of a logion like Mark 10.33f., full as it is of references to the chief priests and scribes, the delivery to the Gentiles and the mocking, spitting and scourging. On the other hand, we regard it as surprising that so relatively few details are to be found in most of these sayings and that general terms are used where more specific ones might have been expected. For instance, it is sometimes suggested that reference to crucifixion invalidates a number of the logia. The crucifixion, however, is mentioned in only three sayings, and the character of these late-formulated logia is significant.[1] Other sayings read like this:

. . . The Son of Man must suffer many things, and be rejected (by the elders and chief priests and scribes,) and be killed, (and after three days rise again).[2]

---

rejected' of Mark 8.31 and both with 'the stone, which the builders rejected' of Ps. 118.22 (see that the verb ἐξουδενόω (*treat with contempt*) and its variant ἐξουθενόω are used in Mark 9.12 and (in lieu of *rejected*) in Acts 4.11, where Ps. 118.22 is referred to, and that the quotation of Ps. 118.22 in Mark 12.10 uses ἀποδοκιμάζω, as does the Son of Man logion, Mark 8.31) is artificial. Nor would it explain why it is of the Son of Man that these things are written. The fact that Mark 8.31; 12.1ff. and Acts 4.9ff. agree with aspects of the Son of Man tradition in citing or alluding to the Jewish leaders as the *rejectors* can hardly be called crucial, since this is common early tradition; Mark may very well have interpolated such into a saying which already touched on the theme of *rejection*. Then, too, we cannot overlook the fact that this important theme occurs in such significant places as Pss. 22.6, 24; 89.38 and in Isa. 53.3, as well as at Qumran, e.g. 1QH, iv, 8. Indeed, the verbs *mā'as* and *bāzā*, which are often translated by ἐξουδενόω, are, with allied words, applied with some frequency to the king and the Servant, and ἀποδοκιμάζω, as a study of the various Greek versions reveals, is an alternative synonym sometimes used to translate *mā'as*. (Perhaps, in a parallel fashion, ἐξουδενόω and ἀποδοκιμάζω were both attempts to translate some one verb linked with the Son of Man in the primitive strata.) This background would better provide the potent warrant which Mark 8.31; 9.12; 14.21; Luke 17.25; John 3.14, etc., seem to demand. (See also Jeremias's objections to Tödt's theory, *Servant of God*, pp. 90f. n. 406.) This, then, may have brought about the use of Ps. 118.22 by Christians. If, however, Ps. 118.22 does have a place in the authentic traditions, we would point out that it, too, once pertained to the king who has suffered.

Hahn's questionable argument (*Hoheitstitel*, pp. 50f.) that δεῖ does not relate to a Palestinian form of expression would still be in no way conclusive, since there were other means for expressing such a basic idea, as the sayings reveal. In any case, Hahn agrees that this idea of scriptural necessity was already well established in the *Palestinian* community.

[1] Cf. pp. 317f.
[2] Mark 8.31 (= Luke 9.22; see Matt. 16.21). On our view this saying belongs

. . . how is it written of the Son of Man, that he should suffer many things and be treated with contempt?[1]

The Son of Man will be *given up* into the hands of men, and they will kill him; (and when he is killed, after three days he will rise).[2]

. . . the Son of Man will be *given up* (to the chief priests and the scribes,) and they will condemn him to death, (and *give* him *up* to the Gentiles; and they will mock him, and spit upon him, and scourge him, and kill him; and after three days he will rise).[3]

For the Son of Man came (not to be served but to serve, and) to give his life as a ransom for many.[4]

---

to a complex of material dealing with the Son of Man. See below, pp. 377ff. Note also that two of the sayings which follow are closely paralleled in John, where also is found a reference to the Son of Man's death. Cf. p. 307. The saying is followed in Mark and Matthew by an exchange unflattering to Peter. Most would regard this as authentic reminiscence of one kind or another (though cf. Bultmann, *Synoptic Tradition*, p. 258). But then something very disturbing must have been said to have caused Peter's reaction.

[1] Mark 9.12; cf. Matt. 17.12. See pp. 375f.
[2] Mark 9.31 (= Matt. 17.22f.; Luke 9.44). Mark has the saying in a context telling of the disciples' fear and lack of comprehension. (See also Mark 10.32.) This would be a natural reaction to such a message and could be historical even if the evangelist were only guessing. Luke's omission of 'they will kill him' and the resurrection prophecy may best be explained by a desire to avoid redundancy. Yet he might have 'heard' the saying from another source. (Cf. Taylor, *Mark*, p. 403; Schweizer, *Lordship*, p. 19 n. 2; but, to the contrary, Kümmel, *Promise and Fulfilment*, p. 72 n. 175.) The 'Let these words sink into your ears' is reminiscent of an exhortation like 'He who has ears to hear, let him hear', and the agreement with Matthew against Mark on μέλλει (and so a change to the infinitive) may not be mere grammatical coincidence. Compare also John 8.28: 'When you (i.e. men, Jews) have *lifted up* the Son of Man . . .'
  Otto (*Kingdom of God and Son of Man*, p. 361) is typical of a number of scholars who find verisimilitude in the first half of the verse due esp. to the sparsity of detail. Such a view is reasonable, but details can also drop out during transmission. Jeremias (*Servant of God*, p. 102), backed by Tödt (*op. cit.*, p. 177) suggests that the saying is based on an Aramaic word play: the Son of Man will be delivered into the hands of *men*. (Cf. also Hahn, *Hoheitstitel*, pp. 46ff., on this and Mark 14.41b.) Tödt (*op. cit.*, p. 160) believes as well that 'to be delivered into the hands of . . .' must derive from the Palestinian sphere of language.
[3] Mark 10.33f. (= Matt. 20.18f.; see Luke 18.31-33). Again (cf. p. 389) we suggest this to be part of a longer section dealing with the Son of Man. Most critics reject the majority of the details (on which, however, see below), and some guess that it is an expansion of Mark 9.31, though on what is at least the pre-Marcan character of 10.34, cf. p. 342.
[4] Mark 10.45 (= Matt. 20.28). Cf. p. 324 n. 3. The statement may not be so much a *prediction* of the death as a statement of the lengths to which the Son of Man is prepared to go in order to serve his people.

For the Son of Man goes as it is written of him, but woe to that man by whom the Son of Man is *given up*.[1]

The hour has come; the Son of Man is *given up* into the hands of (sinners).[2]

---

[1] Mark 14.21 (= Matt. 26.24; see Luke 22.22). Both Higgins and Tödt agree that the saying is early and Palestinian, Tödt (*op. cit.*, p. 177) on the grounds that there is an Aramaic word play represented by 'that man' and 'the Son of Man'. Higgins (*op. cit.*, pp. 50f.) finds that ὑπάγει is based on an Aramaic verb. (See Black *Aramaic Approach*, pp. 237f.) He compares the Johannine usage which suggests an authentic theme in the setting of Jesus' last hours. Certainly it cannot be regarded as a Marcan vocabulary word, and any attempt to find a Johannine influence is futile. It is not impossible, however, that the Johannine and Marcan uses might be traced to the same general background (cf. p. 290 n. 4). Though Higgins wonders about the awkwardness of the introduction, he ends by concluding that the first clause may represent an authentic *I* saying (the second clause having been added at some point and the whole conformed to it). For several reasons, however, it would seem reasonable to believe that Mark has preserved the original subject. The 'awkwardness' could be regarded as a sign of authenticity or could be accounted for on the grounds that the saying precedes the version of the setting which is here given. Note that, while Matthew editorializes away the awkwardness, Luke, in his slightly different setting, preserves it.

Tödt offers his general theory as a critique of the saying. Others object (see Beare, *Earliest Records*, p. 224) that 'the historical character of the entire scene is open to question'. Yet we are not contending that we have records of this type. Of how many scenes in the Gospels could anything other be said? But many scenes, no more *historical* than this, are thought to convey a genuine sense of something Jesus said.

Recall that John 13.31 presents a saying about the Son of Man at this point in the narrative, and a case can be made out for believing that Luke had a narrative in which such a saying had been independently passed on to him. Few would doubt that Luke has access to independent material throughout much of this section. He has the saying after the supper, does not have the final Marcan comment, and offers a number of differences in word order. (Does the use of *he* in the second clause in lieu of the Son of Man reveal that he has lost the Aramaic word play? On πορεύομαι, cf. p. 331 n. 4.) Indeed, how many sayings in the Gospels have this kind of backing? Must not a reference to the Son of Man at this juncture have entered into the traditions at a *very* early time?

[2] Mark 14.41 (= Matt. 26.45). See the above notes on 'delivered up into the hands of . . .' as an Aramaism and with regard to a possible word play on Son of Man—hands of *men*. In the latter case 'sinners' (see Luke 24.7) would be a substitution. Or perhaps the original reading was 'Gentiles' (see below) though we can also remember that the ancient enemies of the suffering king were regarded as enemies of God, lawless men, etc. Here we note again the correspondences with John 12.23. Cf. p. 309.

Once more the serious challenge is the one which can be levelled against the historicity of the whole scene. The narrative of the arrest and that which precedes is colourful, but somewhat stilted and full of anomalies. (Cf. P. Winter, *On the Trial of Jesus*, Berlin, 1961, pp. 44ff.) Not all would follow Bultmann (*Synoptic Tradition*, pp. 267f.) in holding that we are dealing with material 'of a thoroughgoing legendary character', but the suspicions of many tend in this direction. And, indeed, we share these suspicions. What we do not share is the belief that all ideas found therein are post-resurrection creations. Whether one concludes that Mark

But first he (i.e. the Son of Man) must suffer many things and be rejected (by this generation).[1]

There are seeming variants which may yet represent aspects of sound tradition.

. . . and everything that is written of the Son of Man by the prophets will be accomplished. (For he will be *given up* to the Gentiles, and will be mocked and shamefully treated and spit upon; they will scourge him and kill him, and on the third day he will rise.)[2]

Judas, would you give up the Son of Man with a kiss?[3]

Now, not by any means would we insist that each of these must be an independent saying uttered by Jesus at a separate time and place. Nor, on the other hand, do we believe it now practicable so to compare and contrast the logia as to attempt to arrive at the several hard-core sayings which might be the authentic common denominators of the tradition. What we do believe is that there are strong reasons for thinking that there were primitive sayings which spoke about suffering and death for the Son of Man and that out of these circumstances these sayings have resulted.

We are quite prepared for the possibility that various details have accreted to this tradition. Parentheses have been used to indicate which these might be (with the *resurrection* motif being discussed below). We ourselves reckon the mention of the Jewish officials to be

---

14.41 is one of the few *facts* (the exactness of the quotation in this sense is not really important) upon which the legendary development is based or whether one sees it as itself having a basis in legendary ideas, we hold that there is now much cause for regarding it as a tradition which the Church received.

[1] Luke 17.25. See p. 347 n. 3.

[2] Luke 18.31–33. See Mark 10.33f. It is, of course, reasonable to hold that we are dealing with no more than editorial alterations, but both the 'additions' and 'omissions' could be due to some background in oral tradition. Although ὑβρίζω is twice otherwise used by Luke (11.45; Acts 14.5), it is not employed elsewhere in relation to Jesus. While the condemnation by the Jews may have been dropped to avoid redundancy and/or in accordance with Luke's version of the passion where the Sanhedrin does not actually condemn Jesus to death, the saying does concentrate on the mode of looking at the passion which stresses the ignominy of being delivered to foreigners (see below). In this and its lack of explicit reference to the chief priests and scribes it could be superior to Mark's version.

[3] Luke 22.48. Again it is hard to deny that Luke is following many of his own traditions throughout this narrative, and we severely doubt whether this saying is best explained as the result of an influence by Mark 14.41. Whatever be its relationship to authentic material, it suggests independent access to traditions associating the Son of Man designation with Jesus' passion.

among the most likely features in this category, as there is nothing in the Man background which would particularly prepare us for this.

Nevertheless real care should be exercised in this process of deletion. While we would hold that the basic tradition is authoritative even if many of the above details are judged to be later additions, and, while we realize that the great majority of scholars (even among those who see authentic tradition as the basis) so regard them, we think that sufficient grounds have been provided for a rather different approach to the whole issue. Although it is perhaps easy enough to imagine a gradual embroidering through the accretion of such details as the *betrayal* or *giving up* of the Son of Man to the Gentiles and his mocking, scourging and being spit upon (and generations of scholars have long conditioned us to this point of view), we ourselves believe it is more probable that the Church was supplied with the substance of this data. Not only do we think that this better explains the integral place in the passion story of a number of Old Testament allusions and quotations, the fundamental position of the primitive Son of Man designation in the predictions along with the *mustness* and the 'as it is written' of his destiny, but we see it as a more satisfactory way of understanding the relationships between the passion predictions and the passion narrative.

We have, for example, indicated the possibility that there may be more behind this idea of the *delivering up* or *giving up* of the Son of Man than the synoptics now disclose. Although the evangelists have pretty clearly understood παραδίδωμι in all cases in terms of *betrayal* or *handing over*,[1] we have suggested (while noting that this verb does have the nuance of committing in the sense of *offering up* and that certain of its contexts may reveal that it was once an attempt to render an idea somewhat similar to that which John may be trying to express by ὑψόω and/or δοξάζω)[2] a way in which it might once have conveyed or been an interpretation of a more primitive theme. Either παραδίδωμι was then from the start a partial misinterpretation of what had actually been said about the Son of Man regarding the necessity of his being *offered up* and/or *lifted up to death* or some such, or else it was originally an attempt to capture something of this idea while the synoptic evangelists have tended to narrow its meaning and to miss other nuances in the interests of conforming it to their understanding of that which took place. Possibly, too, either as an alternative or in

[1] So that Judas becomes the *betrayer*, Mark 3.19; etc.
[2] See pp. 288ff. and also John 12.23; 13.31.

conjunction with the latter idea above, this verb reflects the use of the similar theme expressed by its employment in the translations of Isa. 53.[1] If so, however, we should think that it does this in a general way, as a reference to the *delivering up* and the *offering* of the suffering figure of antiquity and not necessarily to the Isaianic Servant in particular.[2]

Then it should also be realized that others of these details have most curiously been foreshadowed from times long before Jesus' passion. By tradition the suffering of the royal Man was at the hands of men, foreign peoples, foreign kings and rulers.[3] We find it significant that the Gospel sayings do not mention Romans or soldiers or Pilate, but rather men and *Gentiles* (τὰ ἔθνη, the peoples or the foreign peoples, the word often used to translate the Hebrew expressions for these foreign persecutors).[4] One wonders, for instance, if Mark (or his immediate tradition), presumably writing for and among Gentiles, would voluntarily have employed such a term for the killers of Jesus. We detect here a kind of generalized note which would be more at home in a *prediction* based on old liturgical language than in a prediction formulated after the fact.

We see, too, that a figure like the Servant was said to suffer in a strikingly similar fashion (a passion at which foreign kings were also present).[5]

. . . his appearance was so marred, beyond human semblance . . .[6]

He was despised and rejected by men . . .
he was despised, and we esteemed him not.[7]

A comparison of Isa. 50.6 with Mark 10.34 is particularly instructive.

---

[1] See Jeremias, *Servant of God*, pp. 88ff., 96f. and above, pp. 289f.

[2] See further below. So we could agree with Tödt (*op. cit.*, pp. 159ff.) that the Isaianic Servant as such is not definitely implicated in these passion predictions. (Just as, by the same token, Ps. 118.22 is not required to explain *rejected*. See p. 333 n. 2.) We do not, however, think him right when he suggests that other uses of this verb by the evangelists show that παραδίδωμι was not linked with the Son of Man in a particular way from the earliest stages of tradition. While not necessarily arguing that these other uses are derivative, there is every indication that there was a 'the Son of Man παραδίδοται' (or whatever verb lies behind this) formula which has priority.

[3] E.g. Pss. 2.1f.; 18.43; 89.50; Ezek. 28.7, 10, 17; Odes of Sol. 29.8.

[4] See in the appropriate references in the note above.

[5] Isa. 52.15.

[6] Isa. 52.14.

[7] Isa. 53.3. On the significance of the use of the verb ἐξουδενόω (corresponding with the verb in Mark 9.12) in several Greek versions of this verse, see p. 333 n. 2.

> I gave my back to the smiters,
>> and my cheeks to those who pulled out the beard;
> I hid not my face from shame and spitting.

And they will mock him, and spit upon him, and scourge him, and kill him;

What strikes us most forcefully, however, are not the correspondences but the differences. The Church, when seeking to reveal the manner in which Jesus' suffering fulfilled the scriptures, was inclined to be less allusive and far more direct than this. Literal fulfilment was, for them, often of great importance. The mode of language which is found in the Son of Man passion sayings is, however, of a more generalized nature. It need owe no more specifically to Isa. 50.6; 52.13–53 than it does to comparable language from Babylon, from Ezek. 28 or from a passage like Ps. 22.6f.

> But I am a worm and no man,
>> scorned by men and despised by the people.[1]
> All who see me mock at me.[2]

Such thoughts and images are contemporary in the Odes of Solomon[3] and (especially important if one does not follow us in regarding the Odes as essentially non-Christian or at least derived, in this regard, from sources other than the Gospels) the Dead Sea 'Hymns'.[4]

Thou hast made me an object of shame and mockery for traitors . . .
And I was exposed to the affronts of the wicked,
an object of slander upon the lips of the violent;
the mockers gnashed their teeth.
And I was ridiculed in the songs of sinners
and the assembly of the wicked raged against me. (1QH, ii, 9–12)

They made me an object of contempt[5] and shame. (1QH, ii, 33f.)

> For (I was) despised[6] by them,
> and they had no esteem for me . . .
> and all my companions and friends were driven far from me
> and they considered me a broken vessel. (1QH, iv, 8f.)

My spirit stood upright in the face of the blows. (1QH, iv, 36.)

---

[1] Again we note that the word used in the Greek for 'despised' is the same as is used in Mark 9.12.

[2] For other examples cf. pp. 127ff.

[3] See pp. 191ff.

[4] Using the translations by Dupont-Sommer, *Essene Writings from Qumran*, pp. 205ff. For other examples see above, p. 222 n. 2.

[5] Using *būz*. See p. 333 n. 2; compare 1QH, iv, 22.

[6] Using *mā'as*. See p. 333 n. 2.

The psalmist goes down into the pit, into sheol, into the billows and waves.

> They shut me up in the darkness
> and I ate the bread of groaning
> and my drink was in tears without end . . .
> shame covered my face . . . For I was bound with unbreakable
>   cords . . .
> (and) bars of iron and door(s of bronze). (1QH, v, 33–37.)

> For thou hast chastised me . . .
> and the blows that have smitten me
> (have become) an ev(erlasting) healing (and bliss) without end,
> and the scorn[1] of my enemies has become for me a glorious crown.
> (1QH, ix, 23–25.)

It is our conjecture and suggestion that the language from these several sources is similar because it represents thinking along the same dramatic lines. They have all been influenced by liturgical or liturgically induced motifs derived from the same general pattern of ideas and are thus not mere literary echoes one of another.

One development in recent study of the Son of Man passion sayings which is of particular interest is the growing recognition that much of the language there used of the figure must, at the least, be pre-Marcan in its provenance. This can, of course, still be interpreted in various ways, but, when these forms are traced back into the earlier strata of tradition, the possibility that they could be representative of a manner in which Jesus spoke must be seen to be enhanced. In the course of a penetrating discussion of what he calls the 'train of terms' associated with the Son of Man in this regard, Tödt demonstrates the considerable likelihood that expressions like 'to be delivered up into the hands of . . .', 'to be rejected', 'to be treated with contempt', and 'will be killed' or 'kill him' go back to pre-Marcan and, in most cases, Palestinian and very likely Aramaic origins.[2]

---

[1] *Būz.*

[2] Obviously not all these expressions can be so evaluated with equal certainty. On 'to be delivered up', 'into the hands of . . .', 'to be rejected', 'to be treated with contempt', the references to 'men' and 'Gentiles' as well as the possible word plays on 'Son of Man' and 'man' or 'men', see the above notes, esp. with regard to our stress on their association with other suffering figures. The reference to 'killing' the Son of Man has no such apparent background, but ἀποκτείνω is three times used in the Marcan Son of Man sayings (one of them Mark 9.31 which many wish to see as the 'earliest' of these) and only sparingly used of Jesus and nowhere of the Christ in later traditions. Hahn (*Hoheitstitel*, p. 49 n. 2) points to its place in later Judaism in references to the killing of the prophets (e.g. I Kings 19.10, 14; Jer.

An interesting case, illustrative of the pre-Marcan nature of these materials, is probably provided by Mark 10.34 when it is compared with data relative to the contemptuous and mocking treatment of Jesus in the passion narrative. 14.65 and 15.29ff. cannot be regarded as the *source* of 10.34, since there the mockery is by Jews and not by Gentiles as in 10.34. Indeed some suggest that 14.65 and 15.29ff. were probably added at a later period[1] and, in their stress on Jewish cruelty to Jesus, are revelatory of a later Gentile point of view.[2] (In comparison only 10.34, from the Jewish point of view, recognizes that the final and most devastating ignominy results from this very act of being given up to the Gentiles.)[3] In any case, probably just 14.65 could really be compared to the language of 10.34, while many find that 14.65 looks very much like a summary statement interpolated into the earlier accounts of the passion. This leaves us with 15.16–20, but it is just this passage which Tödt believes to be partially dependent upon 10.34. Following Bultmann, he would regard it as an expansion from 15.15b influenced by 10.34. We would be less sure that there is no primitive material behind various aspects of 15.16ff., but we do agree that the passage has probably been elaborated at a later date and that 10.34 can be claimed to antecede it.

Where we think Tödt goes wrong is in his insistence that these ways of speaking could only have been associated with the Son of Man in post-resurrection circumstances. Here he tends to rely very much on his arguments that it is 'incomprehensible' that Jesus could have spoken of another when referring to the eschatological Son of Man and yet as though of himself when telling of a Son of Man who should suffer, and also that we otherwise could not understand how it was that attributes of the eschatological Son of Man are nowhere given to the suffering Son of Man. Further he holds that we are unable on

---

26.21; compare Matt. 23.37; Luke 13.34), and it seems clearly prior to the use of 'die' and 'crucify' in other New Testament statements about the passion. While lacking a specific scriptural background, it is still fitting in general terms within the context of thoughts about the Man. Some would also find 'many things' to be a Semitism, and Tödt would link 'to suffer many things' with the other phrases. The verb πάσχω itself is used sparingly in the LXX and not in any contexts which we find esp. significant. Again, however, it fits well with the general background of ideas which we regard as more important and influential than specific literary reminiscences. And we would point to the possibility that a form of a verb like *nāśā*, with its meanings of *to bear* sins, iniquities, sufferings (see p. 284; p. 290 n. 1) might be behind the usage in Mark 8.31; 9.12.

[1] Of course, this need not mean that a whole passage like 15.29–32 had no basis in the earliest traditions. We would esp. single out v. 29 as possibly stemming from such materials.

[2] On these several passages, see Tödt, *op. cit.*, pp. 173ff.

[3] Cf. p. 337 n. 2.

other terms to account for the separation of suffering and eschato-logical sayings, and finally he seems to fall back upon the argument that the use of many of these same terms in Church formularies, predicated of Jesus or of Jesus as the Christ, reveals that this was language developed by the Church.

The first and second points we hope already to have answered. The suffering Son of Man obviously cannot be described in the same terms as the figure in glory. In a very important way they are separate figures, or, at best, the same general conception seen in quite divergent guises. In large measure this realization also accounts for the dichotomy between suffering and eschatological sayings, for they belong to two different contexts of thought. That the dichotomy is not absolute may be revealed by Luke 17.22ff.; Mark 8.31–38 and 9.12 in association with the transfiguration scene and the Johannine way of speaking about the Son of Man. Even the references to the Son of Man's *rising* (see below) could well be indications of the relationship between the two phases in the Son of Man's story. Yet the link between the Son of Man suffering on earth and in heavenly glory would not have been easy to set out or to grasp in historical terms. Only after the passion and ascension of Jesus would a way have been found to make an evident and lucid association of the one below and the one above in an historical frame of reference. But the very fact that the Church has largely failed to do this with reference to the Son of Man language could well indicate that the degree of separation among these sayings is a sign of their origin in pre-resurrection circumstances. It may also be, however (as we shall suggest), that eschatological pressures within the Church have tended to categorize the two types of sayings in an exaggerated fashion.

The fact that some of the same or similar terms were used both of the Son of Man and in forms of Christian preaching and apologetic as evidenced elsewhere in the New Testament[1] (though one must be careful here, since a part of the Son of Man vocabulary is virtually unused elsewhere)[2] can be interpreted in another way. After all, it

---

[1] Cf. our comments, p. 333 n. 2.

[2] The ἐξουδενόω of Mark 9.12 is not so used again except in the ἐξουθενόω of Luke 23.11 and Acts 4.11. Ἀποδοκιμάζω is not so employed otherwise except in the reference to Ps. 118.22 in Mark 12.10 and in I Peter 2.4ff. 'To suffer' becomes relatively common, but not the phrase 'to suffer many things'. The 'kill' of the Son of Man sayings continues in use (though it is, after all, a common word), but it tends to be replaced in the preaching by 'crucify' or 'died'. Similarly does ἐγερθήσεται or 'God raised . . .' tend to replace the 'he will rise' phraseology.

would only be natural, if the Son of Man logia were part of the earliest materials, for some of these forms of speech to pass into the language of the Church even though it did not preach Jesus as the Son of Man. A comparison of the materials as a whole gives every indication (as Tödt recognizes) that such language belonged to the Son of Man before it came to be used of Jesus as the Christ, the Servant or the Lord. In the generalized and quasi-ceremonial character of the language as it was used of the Son of Man and in its allusive rather than direct relationship to significant Old Testament and other materials, we see reasons for believing that it could well have pertained to the Son of Man in pre-resurrection circumstances.

When we come to the passion narrative itself, we find that it is not just details but the very structural matter which seems to parallel a number of the dramatic ideas and activities known from earlier periods. Jesus enters Jerusalem on the royal colt,[1] but he comes humbly,[2] prepared, as it were, not only for honour but for humiliation. Garments are spread before him as symbols of the deference due him as king.[3] As at the royal Feast of Tabernacles, the branches[4] are cut from the trees to welcome him. The 'Hosannah' echoes the cry uttered to kings,[5] especially as in one of the significant royal psalms used at this same feast.[6] The last reference is made clear by the ensuing 'Blessed is he who comes in the name of the Lord'.[7] Then he proceeds into his temple. Later he sits on the Mount of Olives, the traditional place for the appearance of the Lord and also for the one who represents him.[8]

The Last Supper, as we have noted, may be, at least in part, a kind of prolepsis of the meal of paradise.[9] The following narrative seems a veritable web of allusions to the Servant, the suffering king of the Psalter and to the royal figure in Zechariah. A few of these are given as quotations, and, while some of these references should be

[1] See I Kings 1.33; Gen. 49.10f.
[2] Zech. 9.9.
[3] II Kings 9.13.
[4] Cf. II Macc. 10.6f.; Ps. 118.27; *Sukkah* 3.9.
[5] II Sam. 14.4; II Kings 6.26.
[6] Ps. 118.25.
[7] Ps. 118.26.
[8] See Zech. 14.4; Ezek. 11.23 and in later traditions for the messianic connections. (For references see S-B I, pp. 840f., and compare Josephus, *Antiquities* XX, 8.6 and *War* II, 13.5.) It, of course, is also from the direction of the Mount of Olives that Jesus is said to have come to enter the city.
[9] And on Mark 14.20, cf. p. 308 n. 2.

viewed as appended details, many others appear to be part of the very substance of the story.[1] At times it is almost as though a dramatic version of Ps. 22 was being presented. The details are so fine that we not only have this suffering at the hands of foreigners and the stripping off of the royal robes, but for whatever cause there even appears a substitute, one who (as in some other royal liturgies)[2] might suffer in the stead of the real king, except that now the real king suffers and not Barabbas.[3] In the end this Jesus goes down into the very pit of death, to and beyond the gates of hell, there to await the saving event.

One may wish to interpret some of these details in different ways, but it can hardly be denied that there is an extraordinary parallelism here. Why? There must be some reason or reasons.

There are radical answers: the whole event has been understood as one based on myth; there never was an historical Jesus who died in anything like this manner. Rather has the myth been mistakenly taken for history and thus turned into narrative. Christianity resulted.

At the other extreme it has been claimed that history has been very heavily *mythicized* and fitted out with legendary elements after the fact. Following the relatively simple and tragically unadorned death of the prophet from Galilee, his disciples, using Old Testament texts and allusions, slowly built up this pattern. That it should echo the old royal liturgy is only natural, since the Church, albeit unconsciously and without grasping the subtleties, was bound to turn to such sources for their materials. Presumably, yet later on, some of the

[1] From the Marcan account alone: 14.27 = Zech. 13.7 ('strike the shepherd . . .'); 15.24 = Ps. 22.18 (dividing the garments and casting lots); 15.31 = Ps. 22.7f. (wagging heads, mockery, saving him); 15.34 = Ps. 22.1 ('My God, my God . . .'); 15.36 = Ps. 69.21 (vinegar to drink and recall here Jesus' earlier remarks about drinking the *cup*; see below). His hands and feet are pierced (Ps. 22.16). Men do stare and gloat over him (Ps. 22.17, and, on looking on the one who is pierced, see John 19.34, 37 and Zech. 12.10). See the references to II Isaiah above. He also is, in fact, 'reckoned with the transgressors', Isa. 53.12; see Mark 15.27. We may in addition point to his general *silence* before his accusers, Mark 14.61; 15.5; Isa. 53.7.

[2] On this feature, cf. Gaster, *Thespis*, pp. 36f.; J. Gray, 'Royal Substitution in the Ancient Near East', *PEQ* 87, 1955, pp. 180ff.

[3] One wishes that more were known about this shadowy *figure*. Is his name an intentional play on *bar-'abbā*, i.e. 'son of the Father'? Is there anything in the textual variant found at Matt. 27.16f. and supported by Origen (and respected by a number of commentators as the kind of variant which would not have been created later either by intention or accident) indicating that the name was Jesus Barabbas? (And indeed the Greek phrasing might suggest this, too: 'There was . . . who was called Barabbas' possibly being indicated.) Is it conceivable that Barabbas as he is now presented is the result of a misunderstanding of some more legendary reference in the tradition?

passion predictions were so fashioned as to conform to the elaborated versions of the passion story.

Yet, while both of these theories may in their ways have a hold upon aspects of the truth, neither seems to us to plumb its real depths. The former recognizes that much of the pattern and parallelism, from beginning to end, seems to be of the very essence of the narrative, of the stuff which governed its original viewpoint rather than being but later accretions. The fact that so many of these structural details are common to the separate passion narratives, all of which appear to have passed along somewhat independent channels of transmission, suggests a place at the very fountainhead of Christian tradition. This view sees that, as the coincidences with ancient pattern and motifs mount up, it is asking a great deal to understand every bit of this as history, while it is also difficult to believe that the Church could so soon have created all this elaboration (with many of its rather obscure details from older forms) unless there was already extant a living body of tradition thinking along these lines.

The second view, however, realizes that there must have been a real life and death, albeit a passion which was somewhat less *ceremonial* than the situation as now presented. It sees that there were real circumstances and an historical personality which galvanized the response of the disciples and which were the living centre for these ideas, affecting and altering them as much as being affected by them.

We should think that there is a way in which the truth lies between and, as it were, behind these two points of view. Doubtless the Church has added some details to the story of a very real and somewhat simpler passion, but we also believe it highly probable that much of the basis for interpretation was supplied to the Church from materials which were already the subject of interest and concern before Jesus met his death. We have seen, for instance, how, near this time, many of the same ideas were *alive* (however they were being used) in the Dead Sea 'Hymns' and in the themes and ideas used by the Odes of Solomon as well as in later materials which may, in part, derive from this era. Upon this background Jesus could have consciously been playing a kind of role, acting out the office to which he believed he had been appointed or the character of which he believed to pertain to himself in a special way. In these terms, for example, parts of Ps. 22 may have been not so much ascribed to him as the commentary on his passion, but rather previously accepted by him as the predetermined description of his destiny. Seen in this way, there might be no reason why, in fact, he should not have called out (again for example) 'My God, my God, why have you forsaken me?'[1]

Thus we are very hesitant to reject all of the details in the passion predictions as later additions. Strange though the thought may at first seem, we think, with regard to a number of these features, that the passion narrative may have been conformed to these predictions rather than *vice versa*. In other words, we should not be surprised, were we somehow to discover more of Jesus' passion *predictions*, if they described what was said to have happened to him rather more *accurately*.

(5) We come, then, to the fifth and last reason for rejecting the authenticity of the Son of Man passion sayings. A case can be made out for the possibility that all the primitive synoptic Son of Man passion sayings were at first confined to Mark. Relevant logia found in Matthew and Luke are all supplementary, in one way or another, to this tradition.

We have, however, some quarrels with this approach (apart from our questions regarding a solution to the source problem on which it is based), for there may be genuine indications that Luke had access to another source for parts of his tradition. He handles several of the Marcan sayings as though he may have known slightly different versions,[2] and 17.25 does not appear as easy to ascribe to Marcan influence as some assume.[3] 22.22 and 48 could be variants created by

---

[1] And we ourselves are well prepared to reckon with the likelihood that there is mystery here as well, the mystery of God acting in history, to some measure conforming history to a pattern of thought in a manner which would enable some to grasp the inner meaning of the event.

[2] With regard to Luke 9.44 and 18.31–33 see p. 335 n. 2; p. 337 n. 2.

[3] If one were so minded, he probably could collect as many scholarly opinions in favour of the authenticity of Luke 17.25 as there are against it. Its 'vagueness' and lack of detail are often cited with approval. Yet this proves little, for there is no reason why Luke could not have summarized the tradition in general terms, and, since he might be understood to have dropped details in his 9.44, one cannot be sure this was not his wont. Just so, however, the 'proofs' against its authenticity are equally unavailing. Typical of them is that of Higgins (*Son of Man*, p. 78), who holds that it intrudes into a 'Q' context, that 'Q' otherwise has no passion sayings, and he notes that the logion is not found in Matthew. (Even if Matthew and Luke are seen to be using a common written source at this point, it is quite conceivable that Matthew would have ignored this saying as not suitable to the eschatological context.) Such arguments do little more than demonstrate what has already been assumed. For some the saying is a pure example of a reflection upon the salvation drama; nowhere else are the appearance of the heavenly Son of Man and the suffering of the earthly Son of Man so closely linked. To others 17.25 is fundamental, a happy preservation of the link which Jesus established between his own

the author, but we think there is much more reason to see them as logia which were, at the least, not fashioned by Marcan mediation.[1]

Yet it certainly is true that, were it not for the 'Marcan' sayings, this aspect of synoptic tradition would be relatively slight.[2] Let us therefore assume that Mark alone once did embody all of the essential synoptic Son of Man passion tradition. Does this lead us to the conclusion which some feel is thus demanded: that Mark or his predecessors must have themselves formulated this type of saying?

Obviously we do not think so. According to our view, the whole concern with the Son of Man faded very rapidly as the Church moved away from the sectarian *milieu* and assumed more normative Jewish views and terminology for its interpretations and understandings. We hope a little later on, for instance, to give some indication for the probability that even Mark was far more concerned with Jesus as the Christ than as the Son of Man and was in the process of shifting the emphasis of some of the traditions with this in mind. Yet it could not be that Mark would totally ignore the central place which this Son of Man was reported to have in the traditions, especially at several vital junctures and with regard to sayings which at least seemed to predict the passion. (We have just seen cause for believing that these sayings must be pre-Marcan,[3] and some argue that the manner in which he introduces 8.31, 9.31 and 10.33f., almost as though he were reporting this theme for the first time in each instance,

---

mission and the role of the heavenly Son of Man. Πρῶτον would then be the key word, the authentic ligature. (Yet to others this word is an indication of the editorial nature of the saying, though we severely doubt if such a common and natural word can be called 'Lucan'. Cf. Tödt, *Son of Man*, pp. 106f.; Conzelmann, *Theology of St Luke*, p. 124 n. 1.) On our view the logion could enunciate the ancient truth of legend: the Man cannot appear in his glory until he suffers. There is then a certain impasse here, probably incapable of resolution on the basis of present evidence. We would note, however, that many scholars regard most if not all of Luke 17.22–30 as pre-Lucan (and between them even scholars as critical of these traditions as Tödt and Higgins can find grounds for the authenticity of all the sayings except v. 25). An ambient sense is therefore created suggesting that v. 25 may be pre-Lucan as well. Its authenticity would need to be decided on other grounds, but a synoptic tradition relating the Son of Man to suffering would then appear to reach outside the Marcan source.

[1] Cf. p. 336 n. 1; p. 339 n. 3. See also p. 327 n. 2 on Matt. 12.40.

[2] On the possibility of a 'Q' document without passion sayings and the ramifications of this see p. 44 n. 1. Also note again the rejection theme in Matt. 8.20 = Luke 9.58.

[3] Also on the pre-Marcan nature of all his Son of Man sayings, see E. Best, *The Temptation and the Passion. The Markan Soteriology* (Society for New Testament Studies, Monograph Series, 2), Cambridge, 1965, p. 163.

intimates the probability that the sayings came to him from separate sources in his own traditions.)[1] However poorly he may have understood what the designation meant, he was bound to honour such a tradition and the designation for that reason. Indeed, with so little else at his disposal by way of passion predictions he must have been eager to do so. Thus into his Gospel he incorporated some seven or eight sayings suggestive of the passion of the Son of Man, two of them being fundamental to the story of Jesus' last hours with the disciples. It is quite legitimate to ask whether there would, out of this rapidly dying tradition, have been much else left for Matthew and Luke to use. As they were writing toward the end of the century, we see only small likelihood that there would have been. They were thus more than willing to take over what 'Mark' had to report on the subject, but much beyond such they were unable to go. In this, as in a number of other matters, they could only follow the earlier guidelines.

Finally we must realize again that 'Mark's' tradition on this subject does not stand alone. John supports him by attributing his versions of passion predictions to Jesus speaking of the Son of Man. One may try to explain this in various ways, but still the fact is there. The sayings are so different that they can hardly be the result of later cross-influences. They must come from an earlier stratum. We find them well explained by the supposition that they stem from levels in the authentic tradition. And actually, once one ceases to assume that Jesus could not have said these things in this way, we see no reason why this theme should not have been authentic and much to indicate that it probably was. Not only are there aspects of these sayings which suggest their primitive character, but we believe that we have previously glimpsed something of the historical context in which such sayings would once have been viable and comprehensible. The Son of Man has to suffer. He is to be rejected by men, treated as a criminal and put to death by foreigners. He must be offered up (and/or *given up*). This is his destiny, as it has always been. The forces of evil will bring him down to *death*.

We turn, then, to the related problem of whether Jesus spoke of the *resurrection* of the Son of Man.

---

[1] See Beare, *Earliest Records*, p. 197; Schweizer, *Lordship*, p. 19. The probability that Mark may have used the sayings *structurally* cannot be used to question their authenticity. He could have used authentic just as well as created tradition in such a manner.

If our analysis of the traditions to this point has been even approximately correct, we would be nearly forced to the conclusion (even if we had no sayings to support our view) that Jesus probably did say something along these lines. The story of the Man (be he First Man, king or Servant) does not end in hopelessness, but continues on to tell of his coming forth out of Sheol, being brought out of the pit, saved from the waters of death. Then he would be exalted and enthroned in glory.[1]

We have seen how the Fourth Gospel seems to present this subject in terms of sayings which view the death, exaltation and glory of the Son of Man as though they were inseparably bound, aspects one of another. John may have telescoped themes which he found in his tradition, but we also consider it possible that he is reflecting an authentic feature of the tradition (perhaps one of a more liturgical nature) when he shows Jesus speaking in this manner.

The synoptic Gospels, however, do not in so many words tell us that the Son of Man who must suffer will also be lifted up to heaven, there to be exalted and glorified. We think that there are several ways of looking at this *gap* and that they may well not be exclusive of one another.

(*a*) The synoptics do speak of the glorious *appearances* of the Son of Man in heaven in his roles as judge and champion. It is conceivable that the period of eschatological fervour in the early Church has caused these sayings to become more disjointed from the rest of the Son of Man traditions than they once were. We find also, however, that a measure of this disjunctive eschatological pressure was operative in Jesus' own lifetime. While this, then, represents one way of viewing the matter, it cannot give any assured results with regard to the problem here before us, and we shall let this aspect of things rest until we come to the final classification of sayings.

(*b*) We have suggested that the particular forms of the synoptic word (ἀνίστημι) which are used of the Son of Man belonged especially to the Son of Man formulations[2] and that they could once have been

---

[1] It is of interest that we get something of this pattern of thought preserved in other ways in the Gospels. We may point to Jesus' sayings on the subject of humbling oneself and resulting exaltation. Compare, for instance, Mark 10.43ff. (he who would be great must be servant; he who would be first, the servant [δοῦλος] of all. The Son of Man came to serve . . .) with the idea in Phil. 2.6ff. Notice, too, how Mark 10.35ff. assumes that the death of *baptism* will be followed by glory of one kind or another.

[2] Cf. p. 285 n. 3; p. 287, and Tödt, *Son of Man*, pp. 180ff.

an alternative way of rendering the idea (or a closely related idea) which John has presented in terms of the exaltation—vindication—glorification. With what was believed to have happened to Jesus specifically in mind, the traditions behind Mark have, then, taken some verb intended (perhaps in a liturgical fashion relating to baptism)[1] to convey the theme now best represented by John and made it refer in a more precise fashion to the resurrection of Jesus.[2]

(c) The synoptic sayings on this subject may express rather more accurately an authentic element of the tradition. Kings and king-gods of old had to be brought up or to rise up from *death*, to be restored to life from out of the underworld and/or the waters.

An interesting question is posed by the fact that Mark's four logia in this regard speak of the Son of Man's *rising* rather than his being raised. It is by no means certain that one is entitled to make much of this, as though it represented a deliberate attempt to stress the *self-resurrecting* powers of the Son of Man. The verb is similarly used of other personages in the Gospels where such an idea is hardly meant,[3] and it could still be implied that God would raise the Son of Man. Yet, if special nuances were intended by this usage, the matter may well be worth following up. Tödt lays great emphasis on the feature and holds that it is another pointer to the manner in which the traditions predicated special *authority* of Jesus as the Son of Man.[4] Yet this would be a most extraordinary process. More than authority is

---

[1] See pp. 284ff.

[2] It is just possible that we may glimpse this process behind Mark 9.9f. (= Matt. 17.9, and see pp. 377ff. with regard to the importance of its setting). It would appear that 'from the dead' is editorial at some stage. V. 9a is usually regarded as part of the Marcan scheme (though we are not convinced that some desire for a kind of secrecy was not part of Jesus' ministry) along with v. 10. Obviously, then, it would seem wisest to include v. 9b (only here is a Son of Man saying reported indirectly) in this view. Mark, wishing to explain and assert again that Jesus knew of his forthcoming death and resurrection, resorted to the older language and interpreted it for this purpose. Certainly this is a legitimate understanding which we would be willing to accept. Yet we recall the close parallelism which we discovered between John 12.23–34 and Mark 8.38–9.10. (Cf. p. 309 n. 2, and see also John 12.25f. with Mark 8.34f.) In John a possible reference to a transfiguration-like scene is followed by 'How can you say that the Son of Man must be *lifted up*?' In Mark after the transfiguration we find the disciples questioning what the *rising* of the Son of Man (from the dead) meant. Perhaps, then, Mark has not fashioned 9.9f. from whole cloth. Part of the material which he has attempted to interpret at this point might have contained something like 'What does it mean to say that the Son of Man must rise/be lifted up?' (And this might help explain the otherwise odd nature of v. 10. Surely the disciples would have known what 'rising from the dead' meant even if they did not believe in it.)

[3] See John 11.23; Mark 12.25, etc., and recall also the manner in which Hos. 6.2 was translated into Greek. See p. 288.

[4] *Op. cit.*, pp. 181ff.

involved here; it is real power. Could the Church first have attributed such puissance to Jesus without seeing him in some more than mortal role or office of which such power was already predicated? Surely it is more credible to think that this power was attributed to Jesus because it was believed to belong to a Son of Man figure who was known to *die* and to *rise* than to argue that such an extraordinary idea only became associated with the Son of Man-Jesus because this power was thought to have been resident in Jesus himself. Our evidence indicates that the Church came to think in the more readily understandable terms of Jesus having been raised by God. If ἀνίστημι is to be taken with a stress on this special sense of *rising* in the Son of Man sayings, we should think it almost sufficient evidence in itself for the mythical and pre-Christian background of these materials.

(*d*) The real force of the idea behind these statements about resurrection may have had much more to do with being re-established, vindicated, *set up* than with the explicit idea of restoration to life. We have seen that the verb ἀνίστημι can bear this important sense.[1] Such could have been its dominant meaning when it was first used, while the evangelists have naturally tended to focus its meaning in line with contemporary Christian faith. With this meaning it may again be related to the themes which John presents in connection with the Son of Man.

Thus, although we are unable to determine how exactly Jesus may have spoken on this subject, we consider it more than likely that, as one who knew of forms which told of the Son of Man's destined *death*, so he would know that this was not the end of the story. The Old Testament Psalter (along with works like the Odes of Solomon and the Dead Sea 'Hymns') is replete with promises and descriptions of God's promise to save his servant and to lift or raise him up from this *death*.[2]

With regard to the 'three days' tradition, we are somewhat more circumspect. One can understand how this could have accreted to the authentic *resurrection* sayings in order to conform them to the circumstances of Jesus' resurrection. If this be so, well and good. We would not be among the first, however, to point out that even this feature, seemingly so specific and post-resurrection in tone, has

[1] See again pp. 285ff.

[2] E.g. Pss. 16.10; 18.4, 16, 48; 22.24; 30.3; 69.14; 116; 118.15ff.; Isa. 52.13; 53.12; Odes of Sol. 15; 22; 25; 29; 36; 42; 1QH, iv, 36 (*qūm*); ix, 4ff., etc. Cf. pp. 286f. Note 1QH, iv, 22f.; as in the Psalms and the Odes, as in other kingship ideologies, as with the story of Jesus, salvation comes 'at daybreak'; the figure shall rise and *stand up* (*qūm*) against those that scorn and *despise* him. Compare iii, 20, using '*ālā* and *rūm*.

affinities with parallel ideas that are pre-Christian. There is the well-known saying Hos. 6.2:

After two days he will revive us: on the third day we will rise up (or he will raise us up) that we may live before him.

There are different explanations for this verse itself. Some see it as based on an old fertility myth. Others would note that 'three days' may have been a kind of idiom for a short period of time. It seems to be employed in this manner in the Ras Shamra texts,[1] and such a usage is probably involved in Luke 13.32f.[2] (See also on the tradition found in Mark 14.58; 15.29 and John 2.19 with regard to the *re-building* of the temple in three days' time.)[3]

This idiom could also apply to the sayings without reference to Hos. 6.2. Others would suggest that it could be tied in with the thought of not letting 'thy godly one see the Pit' or abandoning him to Sheol.[4] According to the translation of the Septuagint (followed by Acts), this was interpreted with regard to being preserved from *corruption*, i.e. not being given over to the full power of death. And John 11.39 tells us that Lazarus stinks because it is already the fourth day.

Thus, in the context of the original sayings, 'three days' may only have been a way of speaking and not a precise prediction. Here again it is possible, at least in some measure, that later Christian language has been conformed to the *predictions* rather than *vice versa*. It is, of course, true that the Marcan 'after three days'[5] could in Semitic parlance refer to a period of less than seventy-two hours, but it is still instructive that Matthew and Luke both find it desirable to be more precise by speaking of 'on the third day'.

C. *The heavenly Son of Man*

The Son of Man will be seen in heaven. Jesus says that the Son of Man will appear in his glorified role.

Of all the types of Son of Man sayings, these are the kind of which normally we should be the most suspicious. Interesting explanations to the contrary, we still have great difficulty in imagining the communities' interest in reaching back into the sources to fashion a

---

[1] See also II Kings 20.8.
[2] See p. 331 n. 4.
[3] See p. 393 n. 1.
[4] Ps. 16.10. See Acts 2.27f.; 13.35.
[5] See on Matt. 12.40, p. 327 n. 2.

tradition in which Jesus speaks of the Son of Man on earth, but yet rather ambiguously so. On the other hand, under obvious eschatological pressures, it is conceivable that sayings could have been created with regard to the coming Son of Man, logia which would have come to be highly valued and later attributed to Jesus.[1] Especially might there have been an inclination to alter already extant sayings, to exaggerate any eschatological tendencies and to make them more futuristic in outlook.[2] It is feasible, for instance, that sayings used by Jesus with the primary purpose of completing the story of the Man, logia which told of his appearance and glorious enthronement and his consequent role as judge and champion, have been rather unwittingly separated from this pattern by the later desire to possess sayings which suggested the return of Jesus.

We are, however, equally suspicious of efforts to conform every Son of Man saying to a precise pattern, no matter whose the pattern or however historical its background. And, upon analysis, a number of these sayings do not really appear to fit all that well into the thoughts and aspirations of the post-resurrection communities.[3]

[1] This would then probably have been an influence which John's sources largely escaped rather than an authentic element which he later played down. In the light of what is said below, however, we should think it more likely that this is an aspect of the Man tradition which he did not take up just as he let other eschatological matters fall into abeyance.

[2] On this approach see again Schweizer, *JBL* 79, 1960, pp. 119ff., and others below.

[3] Chief among these might seem to be Matt. 10.23. The value of its context for interpreting its authenticity is uncertain. Higgins (*Son of Man*, p. 102) discusses the relationship of Matt. 10.17–22 to Mark 13.9–13. Yet this will not help us to be determinative about Matt. 10.23, since many would agree that it is earlier than some of the material in Mark 13.9ff. Nor is it difficult to see why Mark or his tradition might have dropped it. (Similarly it cannot be asserted that such a logion was unknown to Luke.) Kümmel (*Promise and Fulfilment*, pp. 61ff.) even suggests that v. 23b be separated from 23a and be regarded as authentic. Many others would agree (cf. Tödt, *Son of Man*, p. 61) that the saying must be relatively early and Palestinian (thus making it non-Matthean in origin, however else it be regarded). Indeed, it is difficult to see how the logion could have been formulated by anyone with knowledge of the missionary activity in the cities of the Empire. (See, however, Schweizer, *ZNW* 50, 1959, p. 191, and G. D. Kilpatrick, *The Origins of the Gospel According to Matthew*, Oxford, 1946, p. 119. While their differing views illustrate how uncertain our understanding of the verse must be, they none the less appear forced.) Jeremias (*Jesus' Promise to the Nations*, SBT 24, 1958, p. 20) points to Aramaisms and the failure of the prophecy to be fulfilled. Yet, as critics rightly point out, a demonstration of primitive and Aramaic characteristics is not a demonstration of authenticity. Although Kümmel holds that only 'very unconvincingly' can the experience of the primitive Church be seen here, it is not all that hard, given the right presuppositions, to imagine such a situation and such a logion arising from it. Cf. Tödt, *op. cit.*, pp. 60ff.; Vielhauer, *F.-Dehn*, pp. 59ff.;

Moreover, we see no fundamental reason why there should not have been disjunctive factors operative in Jesus' own lifetime resulting in certain anomalies in his teaching about the Man. Indeed, this has been characteristic of the myths and rituals in the past and will always be true of any myth or story which is vital enough to attract the complex hopes and fears of different men. Those who demand the emergence of some perfectly consistent pattern before they will believe that Jesus preached about the Man or who would insist that only the Church could have created the inconsistencies are asking for an abstraction and not a life.

One of these disorganizing elements would almost surely have been Jesus' own attempts to understand the role of the Son of Man in the light of demands being made upon him by God and the circumstances of his life. If he had, as we think, undergone an experience which led him to believe that he may have been specially ordained by God to the office of Son of Man, all did not follow from this as readily as myth and legend might suggest. There would have remained some uncertainty both with regard to his role and his own person. It also appears that others may have been presenting variant teachings about the Son of Man and his identity. (See below.) Could Jesus really be sure that he alone was this Son of Man of destiny? Maybe in the last analysis he did not feel that he was entitled to make the outright claim that he was to be this august, heavenly Son of Man. He always stops just short of saying that he is the Man,[1] and we should imagine that the traditions are authentic in this regard. He would only point to the things that were being done in the name of the Son of Man. The conclusion would be left to others and, most especially, to God.

Compounding this, there is every reason to believe that strong

---

E. Bammel, 'Matthäus 10.23', *ST* 15, 1961, pp. 79ff. Our problem is that we see no evidence supporting the presuppositions. We, on the other hand, find that Jesus and his disciples did experience persecution, probably in conjunction with their Son of Man beliefs. (So Luke 12.8f.; 6.22, etc.) Higgins's objection (*op. cit.*, p. 104) that 'nowhere else is Jesus reported to have expected the coming of the Son of Man so soon' could be used to point to the saying's authenticity. In any event there is little which would allow us to be as precise as this, while the information we have indicates that Jesus did expect the heavenly Son of Man to appear in the near future and that he envisioned little or no extra-Jewish mission for himself or his followers. Also, contrary to Higgins, we see good grounds for regarding the comparable Matt. 16.28 as authentic.

[1] See our remarks on John 8.28, pp. 302ff.

eschatological currents were not only active in Jesus' lifetime but that they were espoused by him. That some of this should have centred upon the figure of the Son of Man would be, as we have seen, most fitting.[1] Thus, despite the feeling that he was appointed to act as the Son of Man on earth, Jesus, as perhaps others around him, felt it also important to proclaim to men that on a day[2] in the future chosen by God the great and sovereign Son of Man would appear in heaven. This would be the sign of the end and for the time of judgment.[3]

[1] We have noted that there are eschatological implications and emphases even in the oldest forms of these myths. The precise degree can be debated, but it is always possible to understand their view of the *new* reign as one which is at least proleptic of the end of time. However, when eschatology became the dominant or even the exclusive concern, as it may have been in some of these sayings, it was bound to distort the older ideas, esp. with regard to any view of the earthly Son of Man and his relations to the one in heaven.

[2] Some would raise questions regarding the authenticity of Luke 17.22 and one or more of the following sayings (with Matthean parr.) because of Luke's use of 'days' instead of 'day' in several of the logia. The former is held to be out of keeping with the authentic traditions which conceived only of a sudden appearance. Yet one can hold that Luke has merely used the expression to make it correspond, in a literary sense, with the stock phrase 'the days are coming' and/or in relation to 'the days of Noah' in 17.26. On this view the expressions mean much the same thing as the indiscriminate usage shows. (Cf. Kümmel, *op. cit.*, pp. 37f., who holds that this is true in any case.) The language might also be compared with the rabbinic the 'days of the Messiah'. See S-B IV, pp. 826ff.; 857ff. Manson (*Sayings*, p. 142, following Torrey) found the expression in 17.22 to be based on an Aramaic original. Cf. the discussion by Higgins, *op. cit.*, pp. 83ff., who holds that the verse stood in Luke's source. (See also above p. 347 n. 3.) Indeed, at least on face value, it is hard to accept the logion as a Church creation, since it contradicts the belief that the day of the Son of Man (which the Church would understand as a day of Jesus) is to come. We very much doubt if Luke's eschatological views or concern with the *delay* could account for this. (See Conzelmann, *Theology of St Luke*, pp. 95ff., though also p. 105 n. 3.) This could also account for Matthew's *omission* of the saying if it stood in a common source. Nor is the criticism based on the use of ἐπιθυμέω damaging, since Luke could have given his own wording to the original idea. In any case, is it a Lucan word? He does have it four times in his Gospel and once in Acts, but Matthew has it twice and once in a 'Q' context (Matt. 13.17), where Luke does not. Many regard its use in Luke 22.15 with its cognate as a Semitism. On the other hand, we believe that such an idea could have made good sense within the context of Jesus' ministry. Several views are possible. (There may be a chastening note here directed against those failing to put their full trust in the appearance of the Son of Man. Or it could refer to Jesus' realization that a certain heightening of concern must take place before the disciples and/or others will really long for the appearance of the heavenly Son of Man.) Taken with what follows, as we believe it should be, it could be seen as a condemnation against false teaching about the Man's appearance. Jesus may have been condemning an eschatology which looked forward to a later time for repentance. Such would not be seen. Rather would the day come suddenly.

[3] Luke 17.24 (= Matt. 24.27) and Luke 17.26, 30 (= Matt. 24.37, 39) are usually viewed as among the most primitive sayings in this regard. See Tödt, *op. cit.*,

Yes, we ask, but did Jesus believe that he might himself become that heavenly Son of Man, especially if he knew or suspected that he would suffer as the Son of Man and that the myth went on to tell of the glorious appearance of the Man following upon his suffering? As a short answer we would suggest that Jesus did not know, that he had to live and act with some uncertainty in this regard.[1] And here we return as well to one of the old *contradictions* of the myth itself, for there was always a way in which the Man below was only a type of another who was above. It was the one above who was the true divinity, who was *really* enthroned in heaven, while the one below was

---

pp. 48ff., 104ff.; Bultmann, *Synoptic Tradition*, p. 122. Vielhauer (*F.-Dehn*, pp. 67f.) holds that Luke 17.23 with v. 24 shows an identification of Jesus, the Son of Man and the Messiah which only the later Church could have formulated. We doubt whether this identification is indicated (cf. Tödt, *op. cit.*, pp. 337f.), though, of course, it is now implied, since this is what the evangelists would have believed. On our view, however, not only is the earlier understanding yet preserved, but we are even enabled to look behind Luke 17.23 = Matt. 24.26. (Luke's version seems superior to Matthew's, which has been altered under the influence of Matt. 24.23.) We may compare this with Mark 13.21 = Matt. 24.23 and also Luke 17.21. It is not difficult to make out a case for the priority of the Q saying and its integral and primitive relationship with this Son of Man logion. (It was perhaps once aimed against those who claimed special knowledge about the time of the heavenly Man's appearance.) If this be so, we may again catch a glimpse of the Church's proclivity to divert Son of Man materials into their concerns with the Christ and the Kingdom of God. Matthew appears also to have imported the later Church understanding of *parousia* into these sayings (see below), and the 'in *his* day' of Luke 17.24 (omitted by a few texts) could involve a slight interpretation. With this saying may be compared *Pesikta Rabbati*, 161a, 162a (further see S-B I, pp. 161f., 956) and esp. *Pesikta Kahana*, 149a: 'The raiment with which God will clothe the Messiah will shine from one end of the world to the other.' See also Test. Levi 18.3f. We would think in terms of this conception of the glorious and shining King which we have often met. Here the emphasis falls, however, on his sudden appearance almost surely (unless the lightning is only a time analogy) in heaven.

It is not at all certain that Luke 17.26, 30 and Matt. 24.37, 39 come from a common source. Even Tödt (*op. cit.*, p. 50) and Bultmann (*op. cit.*, p. 117) hint at differing versions of Q here. We find it esp. significant that Matthew in shortening or Luke in expanding (or their respective traditions) has taken the trouble to preserve the second reference to the Son of Man. On this and other grounds we think it unlikely that the second reference can be seen as editorial. Nor has the eschatological outlook there been altered. Cf. Tödt, *op. cit.*, p. 51. There will not be time for anything. (So also in Luke 17.31f., despite Beare, *Earliest Records*, p. 187.)

[1] This is one of the reasons why we have suggested that the Fourth Gospel may well have preserved sayings which lie closer to the primitive liturgical *milieu*, logia which dealt with the glory of the Son of Man without much taking into account the actual disparity between the earthly Son of Man and the Man in heaven which would be brought out by eschatological concerns. We see no reason, however, why Jesus should not have had access to both kinds of sayings and probably have used both on the right occasions.

only his representative, speaking for him on earth during the present age.

This manner of ambiguity we should think to be very much in line with several of the sayings which have survived.

And I tell you, everyone who acknowledges me before men, the Son of Man also will acknowledge before the angels of God; but he who denies me before men will be denied before the angels of God.[1]

For whoever is ashamed of me and of my words in this adulterous and sinful generation, of him will the Son of Man also be ashamed when he comes in the glory of his Father with the holy angels.[2]

Truly I say to you, in the new world, when the Son of Man shall sit on his glorious throne, you who have followed me will also sit on twelve thrones judging the twelve tribes of Israel.[3]

[1] Luke 12.8f. See below, p. 380, on Mark 8.38 (= Luke 9.26) and Matt. 16.27f. It seems very likely that Mark 8.38a is a variant (authentic or otherwise) of Luke 12.9. (It may be that Mark's 'ashamed' [see I Enoch 63.10] is to be preferred to Luke's 'denied', though, in any case, we dispute Vielhauer's claim [*F.-Dehn*, p. 70; *ZTK* 60, 1963, p. 142] that this acknowledge [or confess]/deny [or ashamed] phraseology can be held to be language only of the Church. The words are not at all common to the evangelists and could well and naturally represent themes important during Jesus' lifetime. See Tödt's critique, *op. cit.*, pp. 341f.; notice that Vielhauer himself would seem to accept a saying like Matt. 11.6, and see our comments on Luke 6.22; 12.10; Matt. 19.28.) This would indicate that a reference to the Son of Man did stand, or was always implied, in Luke 12.9. Such is also indicated by Matt. 10.32f., where many (Tödt, Higgins, etc.) find that 'I' has been substituted for the Son of Man. All versions then agree (despite Vielhauer's suggestion) that some other divine figure along with God was involved in the thought. It may be (again according to Vielhauer) that 'angels of God' was not original to the saying, though it seems more primitive than Matthew's 'my father who is in heaven'. Possibly Luke has created it due to remembering something like his 9.26b. Still, the expression is hardly unknown (cf. Gen. 28.12; 32.1; John 1.51; compare I Enoch 61.10; 62.11), and its presence in Luke 15.10 cannot ensure that it is a sign of Lucan editorializing. Teeple's insistence (*JBL* 84, 1965, p. 258) that literary parallelism shows Jesus to be identified with the heavenly Son of Man overlooks the awareness that there are different types of such parallelism. If, as some suggest, Rev. 3.5b and II Tim. 2.12b derive from the Luke 12.8f.– Mark 8.38 tradition, we would regard it as significant that the Son of Man reference has been dropped.

[2] Mark 8.38 (= Luke 9.26); See Matt. 16.27f. Cf. pp. 380f.

[3] Matt. 19.28. Matthew has introduced the verse into 'Marcan' material. (To avoid undue argument we will not debate the point, but we should not be surprised if Mark has omitted the saying due to its exclusiveness.) But from where did he get it? There is sufficient parallelism with Luke 22.28–30 to suggest some traditional statement of a theme which has been independently passed on to them both. (Cf. Manson, *Sayings*, p. 216.) It is possible that Luke may have better preserved some of the original ideas. Perhaps Matthew, in concentrating on the

(The same idea is basic to Matt. 25.31ff.)

One may pick up various shades of inference about Jesus' relation to the Son of Man in these sayings, but the fundamental thought seems to be that as men now react to Jesus' teaching and his person (which, as we think, was that of the Son of Man on earth) so would be their treatment by the heavenly Son of Man. The figures are at the least made closely affinitive by this factor.

It is for a similar reason that we have suggested a degree of care in dealing with sayings like Luke 6.22; 12.10 (= Matt. 12.32) and 11.30 (see Matt. 12.40). Is the Son of Man in these sayings in heaven or on earth? There may be a sense in which he is both, the Son of Man on earth manifesting forth in this generation, and despite men's contempt and rejection, the Son of Man of heaven. As men treat him below, so are they treating the heavenly Son of Man, and so, in the end, will they be treated by him.

---

theme of judgment, has dropped references to the 'trials' and eating and drinking in the kingdom (with the Son of Man?). But we are reasonably certain the reference to the Son of Man antedates the rather straightforward presentation of Jesus ruling in the kingdom given to him by his father. (Even Bultmann, *op. cit.*, p. 159, realizes that Luke has probably formed an 'I' saying out of a Son of Man logion.) Yet can the reference be regarded as authentic? Vielhauer (*F.-Dehn*, p. 62) sees the conception of the twelve as a post-Easter development, but even Tödt (*op. cit.*, p. 63 n. 1) and Higgins dispute this. Nor, if the idea of a new Israel is present, is it at all certain that this is a sign of later beliefs. While Bultmann holds that it is the risen Lord speaking (referring in a footnote to Rev. 3.21, though he realizes that this must be secondary to the idea of Matt. 19.28), he still registers surprise that the identification of Jesus with this Son of Man is not indicated. If a Church formulation, the context indicated is Jewish-Christianity at a relatively early date (in order to have entered the Lucan tradition as well), and this undermines the criticism based on the use of παλιγγενεσία. Though it is a semi-technical term of stoic philosophy, it appears it was here used to translate an earlier idea. Then we may wonder if the early community would itself have granted such an exclusive and exalted destiny to its members, whatever their positions. Though several of the details belong to traditional 'apocalyptic' (cf. Dan. 7.9ff.; I Enoch 45.3; 61.8 and the phrase 'throne of his glory') no one has convinced us that such themes would not have affected Jesus' thought. (And see the rabbinic analogies, S-B IV, pp. 1103f. The themes may not even be apocalyptic in any strict sense.) Finally it is held that the saying clashes with Mark 10.40ff. But does not Mark 10.40ff. imply that positions of authority are forthcoming? (In any case, Mark 10.40ff. deals only with positions which would grant rank over brother disciples.) The difference lies in the particular attitude of mind being emphasized: in Matt. 19.28 Jesus is not thinking in terms of rewards but of future authority. It is interesting that Tödt would otherwise grant that the saying is 'indeed congruous' with other aspects of Jesus' thought, and Fuller (*Foundations*, pp. 123f.), though elsewhere following Tödt, recognizes its possible authenticity. Cf. also Kümmel, *Promise and Fulfilment*, p. 47.

One sometimes gains the impression that it might have been something of this attitude which so angered Jesus' enemies and bewildered his friends. Who was he then to speak and act like this, and yet to suggest that there was another who would deal with them accordingly as they had dealt with him and his message? We are particularly reminded of the psalmist in the Odes of Solomon who could speak as though he were the Messiah-like one, with all his attributes and powers, and then himself turn and praise the heavenly one. It is within a similar context of thought that we believe Jesus was trying to understand his relationship to the Man.

Doubtless some will find this kind of an approach to an answer to be unsatisfactory, and we ourselves admit to having been tempted to opt for a theory which would be more definitive. Nevertheless, the longer we work with the materials the more are we brought back to the conviction that some situation like this must have prevailed. Jesus believed himself to be acting as the Son of Man on earth, but how precisely he related to the glorious Son of Man he did not know, while he realized that a relationship was there. This seems to us to be a comprehensible even if an ambiguous situation for one who was attempting to understand the Man legend with reference to his own experiences and circumstances.[1] More importantly, we think that it deals fairly with the great majority of the logia and related materials which have a legitimate claim on authenticity[2] and that it clearly echoes an idea which we have seen operative at other times and in other places.

In coming to this conclusion, however, and as we have indicated, we recognize that some of the material may have been refashioned or even formed (or borrowed from extra-Christian sources) in later eschatologically oriented circumstances. None the less we have our doubts about certain critical views even in the area. We ourselves, for example, would be among the first to suggest that Jesus' teaching was probably less concerned with *programme* eschatology[3]

[1] It was perhaps in part due to the tensions introduced by the meeting of various aspects of the Man legend that Jesus' ministry was coloured by some of its characteristic urgency and demand. For instance, in the conjunction of eschatological conceptions of the Man and ideas born out of liturgy (that the Man could already be functioning on earth, that his glorification could be enacted) the eschatology may at once have been made more immanent and imminent.

[2] The manner in which this view fits in with several of the more crucial sayings (particularly Mark 14.62) we shall leave for a few pages until they can be interpreted in a fuller light.

[3] I.e. an eschatology which proceeds by stages with many advancing signs of the end. See Mark 13.14ff.; II Thess. 2.

than the synoptics would now indicate. Yet we think that this, in fact, coincides with the *time* factor in the authentic Son of Man teaching. The day of the heavenly Son of Man was anticipated too ardently to permit any other approach. He is to appear suddenly in heaven, and he comes at an unexpected hour.[1] There and then he is seen enthroned in glory, and, attended by angels;[2] he is judge and the champion of his followers. In reality only Mark 13.26f. with its parallels and the Matthean addition[3] to the same

[1] Luke 12.40 = Matt. 24.44 may be a good case in point. Vielhauer (*F.-Dehn*, p. 62) is among those who object that the saying with its little preceding parable was created to deal with later concerns regarding the delay in Jesus' return. We are less certain that the saying originally belonged with the parable and feel that it better suits the theme of the returning householder (as in what follows; cf. p. 319 n. 2). It may once have been an isolated logion corresponding closely to Luke 17.24, 26, 30; Matt. 10.23, etc. Yet even if it be seen as integral with what precedes, the emphasis still falls on the sudden, unexpected coming, and finding a concern with delay may involve a kind of allegorizing interpretation. Thus see Tödt, *Son of Man*, pp. 34f., 88f., 339; Kümmel, *Promise and Fulfilment*, pp. 55f., on the authenticity of the parable and the saying. (Note also other links between the Son of Man and the 'hour': Mark 14.41; John 12.23; 5.25?) Bultmann (*Synoptic Tradition*, pp. 119, 126, 128, 152, 171) seems uncertain; its 'Jewishness' is all he holds against it. Higgins (*Son of Man*, pp. 140f.) criticizes the unique lack of any descriptive details about the Son of Man's coming; but for Tödt this counts in its favour. Finally Jeremias (*Parables*, p. 50) holds that the Son of Man has been substituted for an original 'day of the Lord' motif. He points to the anarthrous usage 'day of Lord' in I Thess. 5.2 and II Peter 3.10 (the analogy with the thief indicating a parallel with the Gospel parable) and holds this to be Semitic and an Old Testament theme. Yet II Peter is either only recalling I Thess. 5.2 or else it must raise questions as to how primitive (and Semitic) is this kind of language. One need only look at I Thess. 4.13ff. to see what 'Lord' here meant for Paul. Notice 'word of Lord' (anarthrously but referring to Jesus) and 'the *parousia* of the Lord'. Thus Paul is probably only using Church language (in any event a saying found both in Matthew and Luke could well antedate I Thessalonians), and comparisons with Rev. 3.3; 16.15 (see Matt. 24.42) probably show yet a further stage in this process. See also p. 256 n. 1.

[2] See p. 319 n. 3.

[3] While Matthew in 24.30f. has not imported the title into the context, it would appear that he has interpreted and expanded upon the saying (although Mark could have dropped the more esoteric reference). He has made an essentially positive ideogram into one which is decidedly negative. The source and connotation of the 'sign' must, however, remain uncertain. Perhaps originally it had nothing to do with the Son of Man. We have a hard time believing that the cross was intended (cf. Higgins, *op. cit.*, pp. 110f.), but agree that a simple understanding (how much the material may have been ellipticized we do not know) with reference to the 'sign of Jonah' is difficult, unless the sign is the Son of Man himself, in which case it could correspond to the idea that no other sign shall be given. Cf. Luke 11.29f. T. F. Glasson, 'The Ensign of the Son of Man (Matt. XXIV.30)' *JTS*, ns 15, 1964, pp. 299f., may be right to regard it, along with the trumpet call, as a piece of pseudo-military, apocalyptic machinery. Or, esp. if Matthew has picked it up from earlier materials, it might refer to the general theme of the Man

verse are fully implicated in a divergent programme outlook.[1]

We would make remarks along similar lines about objections to some of the logia on the grounds that they are said to be based on Dan. 7.13f. (while, we also notice, others would regard this a sign of authenticity). In matter of fact there are no explicit quotations from the Danielic scene and even the degree to which genuine *direct* echoes are present can be questioned. This is what we should have expected as we have all along regarded Dan. 7 as but one episode in a long and variegated story. There is no reason why Jesus or those who preceded him should have fastened on a rather stylized literary description found in one of the prophets. Rather are they more generally dependent upon the same background out of which Daniel has excerpted his scene.

On the other hand, there are, of course, phrases which are quite reminiscent of the Danielic presentation. Again, however, this is what we would expect, for it is out of the same fund of materials that the several pictures ultimately derive.[2]

---

appearing in heaven like or accompanied by a great radiance. (See Matt. 24.27.) This is his sign announcing the time for judgment.

The further reference to the mourning of the tribes seems an allusion to Zech. 12.10ff. If Matthew was himself interpolating, it does appear odd that he did not go on to mention the one 'whom they have pierced'. (Higgins holds that this was done purposefully because the allusion to the cross was so obvious. Tödt argues that it was omitted to show that this was a sign of judgment and not of salvation.)

[1] We would, however, wonder again if it was not possible for Jesus to have been somewhat inconsistent in this regard. Either with this possibility in mind or in consideration of the chance that the later tradition may have enmeshed an essentially authentic saying in a different kind of context, we would at least register our questions about the degree of certainty with which Mark 13.26f. may be subtracted from the primitive strata. In this connection one notices that several of the Matthean Q logia (24.37, 39, 44), which quite evidently expect the sudden appearance of the Son of Man, are set into a context in which programme eschatology is also given free reign.

[2] To those who feel that we are underrating the degree of literary dependence of a saying like Mark 13.26f. upon Dan. 7.13f. we say once more that we are prepared to reckon with the possibility that the Church has created the logion. Yet we still note that it is far from a direct quotation, though, even if it were, we do not see that any criteria have been established indicating that Jesus could not, on occasion, have referred to scripture. Higgins (*op. cit.*, pp. 6off.) regards 'they shall see' as less primitive than the 'you shall see' of Mark 14.62 and argues that '*in* clouds' involves a later variation intended to stress the idea that the Son of Man comes wrapped in clouds like Yahweh himself. A comparison with Mark 14.62 shows that the use of 'power' here is secondary, as is 'glory' in comparison with Mark 8.38, and the idea of angels as emissaries of the Son of Man is previously unparalleled. Yet these criticisms vary in weight, and the issues are differently interpreted by other scholars. Indeed, they would seem to fly in the face of the

Finally, and again along these same lines, we would come to an issue which we have necessarily adumbrated before. Several of the sayings tell of the Son of Man's *coming* (regularly ἔρχομαι is used except in three Matthean sayings).[1] It is sometimes held or intimated that this feature invalidates aspects of the tradition, since it connotes the idea of Jesus returning from heaven to earth at some time in the future. This we regard as essentially a false issue. We have seen that in a picture like Daniel's the *coming* of the hero is concerned not with *descent* but with *appearance* (with possible overtones of *ascent*) and the purpose of manifesting the rightful sovereign.[2]

Such does not, however, mean that all authentic materials in this regard must be concerned with exaltation and enthronement.[3] We find that interest in the Son of Man as judge and champion is often predominant.[4] And, in this sense, the Son of Man may even be understood to *draw near* to the earth as he becomes visible, on his heavenly throne, to mortal eyes. But nowhere have we found the view that the Son of Man on high would come down from heaven to

---

interpretations of Bultmann (*op. cit.*, p. 122), Fuller (*Foundations*, p. 145) and Tödt (*op. cit.*, p. 35), who surmise that the passage could have been borrowed intact out of a pre-Christian, Jewish apocalyptic context. (They note that no identification of Jesus with the figure is indicated.) This in turn points to what is, in fact, the major criticism of the passage: the suspicion that much or all of Mark 13 was an apocalyptic exhortation (largely based on Jewish materials) sent out in a time of crisis to bolster morale and then *mistakenly* incorporated into the Gospel. Even among those who hold that certain passages in Mark 13 could represent Jesus' thought there is a tendency to reject vv. 24–27 through a kind of guilt-by-association. Cf. Kümmel, *op. cit.*, pp. 95ff., who yet holds that v. 26 is not incompatible with authentic sayings about the Son of Man. We cannot debate the whole issue here, but would note that on several of the above views Mark 13.26f. is at least not a Church formulation and could have been a part of the *milieu* in which Jesus lived and which could have influenced his thought.

[1] See Mark 8.38 and 13.26 (with parr.); Mark 14.62 = Matt. 26.64; Matt. 24.44 = Luke 12.40; Luke 18.8; Matt. 10.23; 16.28; 25.31. See Matt. 24.27, 37, 39 where, in the use of *parousia*, we may find an attempt to conform sayings to the later Church view.

[2] See in ch. IV on the scenes in Daniel and I Enoch.

[3] J. A. T. Robinson (*Jesus and His Coming*, cf. pp. 36ff.) and Glasson (*The Second Advent*, pp. 63ff.), while correct in seeing that any idea of a *return* or coming to earth is secondary, overstress the exaltation theme. For the more traditional view, cf. G. R. Beasley-Murray, *Jesus and the Future*, London, 1954, pp. 258ff.

[4] It is important to remind ourselves that the *judge* in any Semitic situation (as still in parts of the Arab world today) was always judge, defence counsellor and prosecuting attorney rolled into one. (See esp. Matt. 25.31ff.) That the Son of Man should be both judge and advocate involves no contradiction, while individual logia (or a particular evangelist) may lay stress one way or the other.

earth in his glorified state (except to the degree that the earthly king manifested him in this way).

Most of the synoptic sayings involved with this question lie open to an interpretation based on the fundamental picture of the hero in his heavenly glory. No doubt a few of the logia are now situated in contexts which indicate an interest in the descent of (Jesus-) the Son of Man,[1] and we would imagine that the evangelists regarded them all in this fashion, for this was the way the later Church saw the matter.[2] Yet such a viewpoint may readily be seen as secondary, while the older ideogram has by no means been obliterated.

---

[1] See Matt. 10.23; 24.44; Mark 13.26f. Luke 18.8 is also susceptible to this interpretation, esp. in its reference to finding faith on earth. It is possible that this logion once had for its subject the earthly Son of Man, but more likely that it envisioned the Son of Man appearing in heaven to judge earthly mortals. The origin of the association of v. 8b with what precedes is difficult to determine. Many feel that vv. 6–8 were appended to the parable. Bultmann (*op. cit.*, p. 175) holds that they alter the intention of a parable which originally was meant to encourage persistence in prayer. But this is debated; cf. Kümmel, *op. cit.*, p. 59, who sees a better integration; in which case the switch from God to the Son of Man would need to be explained by stressing the differences in their functions. (Beare, *Earliest Records*, p. 188, regards it not as a parable to encourage prayer, but one which assures reward for those who are praying.) Others, however, argue that there is no real connection between vv. 6–8a and 8b. (Manson, *Sayings*, pp. 305ff. finds a connection in the 'speedily' of 8a, but 8b does not stress the hurried coming of the Son of Man.) Or perhaps v. 8b once formed the original ending of the parable at v. 5: when the Son of Man appears on high for judgment, is he going to find people with *faithfulness* (interpreted as *perseverance*, for this would then be the meaning) like this? Thus there are numerous views as to how v. 8b came to be placed here, but we think it is least likely to be explained as a Lucan editorial creation. (Cf. Tödt, *op. cit.*, pp. 99f. who would link it through 18.1 to 21.36 and see it as part of Luke's proclivity to stress the importance of prayer. Yet 18.8b certainly differs from 21.36 in that the former is hardly a comforting statement, and it is easy to see how 18.1 might be an interpretation of material which was at first not focused on the idea of prayer.) Jeremias (*Parables*, p. 155) maintains that v. 8b is based on a pre-Lucan and perhaps Aramaic logion. This is significantly his revised opinion (as against that cited by Higgins and Tödt) in which he realizes that πλήν cannot be held to be a Lucan word. Though one can hardly prove its authenticity, Higgins (*op. cit.*, pp. 91f.) admits that there are no weighty arguments against it. Tödt is critical of the word 'faith', alleging it is used in a Church sense to mean faith in Jesus. Yet there is no reason why it could not have referred to faith in the Son of Man figure and have been so used by Jesus. Perhaps better is the awareness that it could mean 'trust' (compare Luke 7.9 = Matt. 8.10) or was originally intended to suggest 'steadfastness' or 'faithfulness'. Jeremias conjectures that 'the faith' reaches back to an Aramaic form of speech, and it may be reasonable to look for an essentially Semitic meaning of the word used without reference to its object. (Compare the use of forms of 'emūnā in Deut. 32.20; Hab. 2.4; etc.)

[2] See Robinson, *op. cit.*, esp. pp. 16ff. with reference to the later New Testament passages which are concerned with the return of Jesus.

3. RELATED OBSERVATIONS

We should like in the rest of this chapter to offer observations on various incidents, themes and beliefs presented by the synoptic Gospels. Some of these are directly related to the Son of Man, while it is our intention to show that a number of other strands of tradition may best be understood within the same context of ideas. Several of these discussions will be more speculative than others, but it should be possible to share in our general conviction about the fundamental place and importance of the Son of Man even while uncertainties and difficulties regarding certain passages remain.

(i) *The baptism*

The agreed starting-point of Jesus' public ministry is his baptism. Even though the Fourth Gospel does not actually describe it, we have seen that this evangelist records sayings which seem a part of a similar setting and *milieu* of ideas. The story must have been of considerable importance in the early traditions. (It is quite conceivable that it even stood in a Q or some other source which also had the longer temptation scene.)

The synoptic accounts are relatively brief and do not give us a great deal to go on. Matthew and Luke, recognizing the theological problems involved in having the Son of God undergo a baptism (which they saw as a baptism for the remission of sins), have made additions or alterations to the narrative, but with one possible exception they do not relate anything different which should be regarded as authentic. We would make the following points.

(*a*) We have already given some attention to the nature of the Baptist's rite and also to possible connections between him and contemporary and later sectarianism.[1] While we have agreed that no positive conclusions can be drawn, we have also seen cause for believing that there may be much more here than at first meets the eye. This much at least should be kept in mind.

(*b*) In the Marcan account there is no stated interest in the remission of Jesus' sins; in fact, there is no mention of it. This can be naturally accounted for by the unwillingness of the Church to think in such terms of their Lord, but it may also signify that it never was central to the purpose of this baptism.[2]

[1] See pp. 223ff., 259f.
[2] This need not mean that remission of sins was not a feature of a baptism like

(c) We have caught a glimpse of the position which a rather adoptionist view of Jesus' baptism (complete with references to his anointing) seems to have held both in the early Church (as indicated by the New Testament) and in various Christian and semi-Christian sects. With this should also be compared the manner in which Adam and his descendants or sons are sometimes said to have undergone rather similar experiences. In a moment we shall see that the linked temptation story tends to picture Jesus as a kind of Adamite. In these views and later interpretations there could be authentic reminiscences of the fashion in which a baptism such as this was once regarded.

(d) We have presented our many reasons for believing that a connection between baptism and suffering was ancient and that it was operative again in this period. We have also seen how both the Gospels and Paul suggest that this association may have been fundamental to Christian beginnings. While there is little which might indicate this association in the evangelists' baptismal narratives, it is another of the causes for thinking that such a story may once have involved more than is now recorded for us.

(e) In addition we must take into account the several pieces of evidence from John's Gospel which suggest that water rites were used during this period in relation to the principle of revivification, of giving new life, being *reborn*.

(f) However John's baptism was later regarded in the Church, it appears as though there may have been a close connection between his practice and his expectation of 'the coming one'.[1] It might be going too far to insist that John definitely expected 'the coming one' to be revealed during a baptismal ceremony, but it would not be hard

---

this, for we have seen that admission of wrongdoing, cleansing, etc., were vital to various ordination ceremonies. Yet it does not appear to have been *the* purpose in Jesus' baptism.

[1] Ὁ ἐρχόμενος. On the designation see p. 245 n. 2; and n. 3. We have suggested that it could be related to the idea that the Son of Man will be seen coming. If so, the thought might be that a mortal will be ordained to represent this one who will one day be seen coming with the clouds, or who, if we take the expression more figuratively, is 'the future one'. More simply, it may refer to the earthly figure who will come forward or be manifested as the one appointed by God, without, however, telling us anything specific about his other designations. In any event, it seems that John may have been expecting an earthly champion and not just some heavenly hero, and this factor ought not to be lost sight of by those who hold that Jesus was thinking only of a heavenly figure. Recall, too, that Paul may have seen such a one as a *type* of Adam, and see below on Elijah and 'the coming one'.

to come away from the synoptic Gospels with this impression,[1] especially in the light of what is said to have happened at one of his baptisms. The impression comes across even more strongly in the Fourth Gospel: '. . . for this I came baptizing with water, that he might be revealed to Israel'.[2]

(g) Brief as the scene is, it must be regarded as bearing striking affinities with the ordination customs of royal figures.

(1) There is the appropriate water rite.

(2) A divine oracle is issued. In John's Gospel this is done in a more customary fashion through the mouth of a *prophet*.[3]

(3) He is 'the Beloved', a traditional royal epithet.[4]

(4) He is God's Son, another familiar title for kings and first men. Such a title would in no way exclude the use of the designation Son of Man.[5] Indeed, as we have seen in the past, there is a very significant way in which an individual is proclaimed the Son of God because he is the Man or Son of Man, or one could just as well put it the other way around.[6]

---

[1] See Matt. 3.11 (= Mark 1.7 = Luke 3.16) and John 1.15, 27.

[2] John 1.31.

[3] John 1.34.

[4] See II Enoch 24.2 and also II Sam. 12.25; Dan. 10.11; Widengren in *Promise and Fulfilment*, p. 210; Engnell, *BJRL* 31, 1948, p. 68 n. 4; Gaster, *Thespis*, p. 125.

[5] Mowinckel (*HTC*, pp. 368ff.) also sees that this must be so in the Gospels as well as in comparable situations both earlier and later.

[6] Mark (1.24; 3.11; 5.7) tells us that there was some tradition for calling Jesus the 'Holy One of God', 'Son of God', 'Son of God Most High' on the part of demons or those possessed. While there is only slight evidence (cf. Hahn, *Hoheitstitel*, pp. 284ff.; see above p. 266) that such were known as messianic titles within the normative Judaism of the period, it is difficult to locate all such Gospel references within the Hellenistic sphere. The title occurs in the Q story of the temptation which is rarely regarded as Hellenistic in origin, and, although Mark 14.61 may reveal the Church's hand, the language could still indicate Jewish thought. The same is likely true of Luke 1.32 and perhaps of Luke 3.38. In any case such reticence need hardly have applied everywhere in Palestine, and one notes that a concern with demons was not vital to normative Judaism either. Some of these references could stem from Jewish or even semi-Jewish sectarian life. (For a possible hint along these lines cf. J. R. Harris, 'On the Name "Son of God" in Northern Syria', *ZNW* 15, 1914, pp. 98ff.) The clear messianic commentary on II Sam. 7.14 in 4Q flor. i, 10–13 may suggest this, and, although Hahn reminds us that the voice at baptism is 'based' instead on Ps. 2.7, is it unlikely that others may have similarly interpreted this verse as well? (Indeed, such is probably indicated by 1QSa, ii, 11; cf. Dupont-Sommer, *Essene Writings*, p. 108 n. 1.) Why would Christians have held a monopoly on such an understanding?

(5) The oracle shows God's confirmation of the choice of this individual. He approves of him; God is 'well-pleased'.[1]

(6) The whole form and purpose of the oracle is then quite reminiscent of others we have studied. Usually it is held that the Gospel's proclamation has been based on a combination of Ps. 2.7 and Isa. 42.1. It may well be that these have played a part in its formation, but our point would be that it is not a *literary* formula. If these two texts are involved here, they are being *used* and not just referred to. They had become part of a living body of ideas which has fitted them to its own purposes. We should think it even more likely, however, that this oracle echoes the earlier sayings because it comes out of the same ancient fund of ideas and beliefs from which they, too, were once derived.[2]

(7) Jesus receives the spirit, just as have many other royal Man figures both ancient and contemporary. It is a regular gift accompanying the ordination ceremony.

(h) The description of the spirit as being like a dove remains somewhat obscure, and we would not pretend to give a definitive solution to this problem. We would, however, notice that a dove (or doves and birds generally) had a role in both Mandaean baptisms and in the Odes of Solomon. From ancient times birds have been regarded as symbols of divinity or divine messengers which sometimes have had a part to play in the selection of the' king.[3] Jewish tradition occasionally connected the *bat qōl*, the *echo* of the divine voice, with a dove.[4] We ourselves incline toward the view of scholars like Barrett and Taylor that the dove here was once intended to recall the Spirit of God in Gen. 1.2, which in rabbinic tradition could be likened to a dove.[5] If this be viable, the thought here may

---

[1] E.g. Ps. 22.8.

[2] A few Lucan texts, some Fathers and the Ebionite Gospel give a direct quotation of Ps. 2.7 with its idea of *begetting this day*. Some scholars think this to have been authentic (and even that it might have stood in Q), but was later altered to tone down its blatant adoptionism. This is a possibility, though it may simply be that later the saying was conformed to scripture. Alternatively this could have been another version of the saying from a slightly variant but primitive story which has come down to us in this manner. See C. K. Barrett, *The Holy Spirit and the Gospel Tradition*, London, 1954, pp. 39ff.

[3] On this and what follows with references to the literature, see Barrett, *op. cit.*, pp. 35ff.; Taylor, *Mark*, pp. 158ff.; Bultmann, *Synoptic Tradition*, pp. 247ff.

[4] See I. Abrahams, *Studies in Pharisaism and the Gospels* I, Cambridge, 1917, pp. 47ff.

[5] Abrahams, *op. cit.*, pp. 49f.

have been dependent upon the general conception of the *birth* of the Man at the beginning of time.[1]

Thus, while we have only an enigmatic relic from what once must have been a fuller narrative, we would think that any of the above alternatives, either separately or in combination, might point to its original significance. Any of them would fit well with earlier kingship beliefs.

(*i*) This scene seems to demand a comparison with that of the transfiguration. We little doubt that they belonged to the same thought patterns. They may, in fact, be alternative descriptions with the same basic import: the ordination and/or manifestation of the royal Son. We soon hope to show that the transfiguration is even more obviously derived from royal ideology.

(*j*) The baptism takes place in a heaven-like setting. Here the understanding seems to be that the heaven is opened to the chosen one and that the spirit comes down upon him instead of his going up. This was possibly one more realistic, contemporary version of the story, although we should also not be surprised if it was in part a later interpretation in this respect, or if part of the story is missing. Jesus is said to go up (ἀναβαίνων) out of the water. It is at least interesting that the Fourth Gospel uses this same word for the ascent of the Son of Man.[2] Obviously there may be in Mark only a simple and natural reference to Jesus' coming up out of the water to the land, so that we should not press the word. Still, it might preserve an older liturgical theme.

The 'simplicity' and theological *naïveté* of the Marcan baptismal narrative are often noted. It is our inference, here as elsewhere in the Gospels, that we are not dealing with a story largely created by the Church,[3] but are rather reading a piece of legend which the Church

---

[1] In *Genesis Rabba* 2.4 the spirit of God hovering over the waters is said to allude to the spirit of the Messiah, and this is glossed with Isa. 11.2: 'and the spirit of God rests upon him'. Note that in *Genesis Rabba* 8.1 the spirit is said to refer to the soul of Adam, and Isa. 11.2 is again employed. Cf. p. 203 on Simon Magus's similar conception.

[2] John 3.13; 6.62. Then, too, in John 1.51 we have the repetition of themes of the heaven opened, *ascending* and *descending*, and angels in a saying which tells of a coming revelation of the Son of Man, and which concludes the whole section dealing with the beginning of Jesus' public ministry. See our remarks on John 3.13 concerning traditions pointing to a baptism of Jesus as the Son of Man, and on John 3.14 with regard to the 'rising up' theme.

[3] Bultmann (*op. cit.*, pp. 247ff.) thinks it mostly to have been fashioned by the Hellenistic Church, even though he cannot make its evident adoptionism fit in with Hellenistic ideas about sons of divinities. He is then forced to take the reference

received as part of its fund of primitive materials and to which it has attempted to give a simplifying interpretation. It has been condensed and translated by hands which no longer understood its full original significance or the precise relevance of many of its details.[1] Behind it we may catch sight of the dimensions of older stories concerning the adoption of one chosen to be the royal Son.

(ii) *The temptation*

Closely related to the baptism scene in the sources was the story of the temptation. (Originally it may have been intended to precede the baptism as preparation for it, and so possibly be illustrative of the old motif of suffering in connection with baptism.) For comparison we may recall the angels attendant upon the Adamite Levi who later defeats Beliar and removes the threatening sword against Adam. We may also remember the angels who aid Enoch (especially in II Enoch) and even those who ascend and descend upon the Son of Man in John 1.51.[2] A much closer and more informative comparison would be with the Adam who, according to popular rabbinic tradition, dwelt with the wild beasts in paradisaical conditions, who was venerated by the beasts and attended and fed by angels.[3] Of course, he was also tempted by Satan.[4] Unlike Adam, however, the new Man,

---

to the Son of God in the temptation story, which he admits is Palestinian, as a Hellenistic title. He also notes that the story is not found in Q. Was there a Q? Are we sure the narrative was not in it?

[1] Hahn's brilliant attempt (*Hoheitstitel*, pp. 334ff.) to understand the baptism and transfiguration as materials based on rather unadorned stories of the com-missionings of a prophet-*servant* (υἱός being then a later interpretation of such references) yet involves a highly selective reading of the texts, relegating all details thus unexplained to later Church activity (but often without telling us satisfac-torily why such were added). Nor do the Gospels give good reasons for believing that a view of Jesus as the servant had much influenced other aspects of the early materials. We would remember, however, that the role of the Son of Man includes both the roles of the servant and the prophet. See our several remarks to this effect in chs. III and IV; cf. Mark 10.45; Luke 11.30, etc., and see below pp. 372ff.

[2] Note also Heb. 1.6. What has helped to bring about this understanding?

[3] Probably we have here a point of view in which the beasts are regarded as submissive and friendly rather than opposed to the Man (as say the glorious king would live with the wild animals in peace, see Isa. 11.6ff.), though they may once have been seen as the agents of evil before they had been conquered. A scene like that of Ps. 8.5f. could be as much involved here as Gen. 2, but, again, the story is probably based on contemporary myth rather than on scripture as such.

[4] The story has even been traced back to the tale of Marduk's struggle with the chaos monster. (See Bultmann, *op. cit.*, p. 253.) But this is now far back in the general background.

the new Son of God, does not fall in the temptation, but instead proves his right to be the Man, to be crowned with glory and honour. Writes Barrett, 'It is precisely as the Second Adam, the Heavenly Man, that Jesus effects the eschatological conquest over Satan, which results in a salvation that means the restoration of primeval bliss.'[1] Though we think 'Heavenly' unnecessary in this context, we would consider this view basically sound. Once more, however, we would regard it as essential to a story which the Church received rather than one which it fashioned. Even the short Marcan mention of the legend offers little details which would not have been a concern of the communities and which indicate that they have highly condensed an earlier tale.[2] Out of these same traditions may well have sprung the sense of personal combat with the devil which reappears at other points in the Gospels.[3] As the Man on earth, Jesus had to do battle with the ancient enemy, and, perhaps in this same connection, with the allied evil demons as well.

The origin of the three specific temptations is not certain. They could well be pre-Christian. Certainly they are all properly *messianic*,[4] and in this sense they would pertain to the Man. It is our guess, however, that the last two were, at some point, added to the first

[1] *Holy Spirit and the Gospel Tradition*, p. 50. Cf. his references to other traditions such as the forty-year sojourn and temptation of Israel in the wilderness, Elijah's being fed by an angel before his forty-day journey to Horeb and Moses on the mountain forty days and nights. Compare also Ps. 91.11ff.; Test. Iss. 7.7; Test. Benj. 5.2; Test. Naph. 8.4. We are not deaf to these (and to them could add the forty-day penance of Adam and Eve while standing in the water in the Life of Adam and Eve), and, either at the primitive level or later, several of them could have influenced our story. Yet the tale of the second Adam is still the basis. Cf. Davies, *Paul and Rabbinic Judaism*, pp. 42f.; Schweizer, *Lordship*, p. 35; Lohmeyer, *Markus*, pp. 26ff.; Jeremias, ''Aδαμ', *TWNT* I, pp. 141ff.; Best, *Temptation and Passion*, pp. 6ff. (with reference to variant views).

[2] See Matt. 8.20 = Luke 9.58 on the possible link between this Son of Man saying and ideas behind the temptation narrative.

[3] See Mark 3.22ff. (and various parr.); 4.15; 8.33 (in connection with the Son of Man); Matt. 13.39; 25.41 (both in connection with the Son of Man); Luke 10.18; 22.3 (see John 13.27ff. in connection with the Son of Man, and more generally in John); Luke 22.31. Probably in the Matthean version of the Lord's Prayer the sense is '. . . deliver us from the evil one'. Not all of these traditions may be equally applicable, nor can one vouch for the authenticity of all, but the essence and impetus for this kind of thinking seem to issue from the primitive traditions. See further below p. 388 n. 6.

[4] Cf. Barrett, *op. cit.*, pp. 51ff.; H. Riesenfeld, 'Le caractère messianique de la tentation au désert' in *La venue du Messie. Messianisme et eschatologie* (by É. Massaux and others), Bruges, 1962, pp. 51ff. In 'Old and New Testament Traces of a Formula of the Judaean Royal Ritual', *NT* 5, 1962, pp. 241ff., K. H. Rengstorf holds that Ps. 2.8 has influenced the temptation to worldly pomp.

which is more germane to the circumstances and setting. (The fasting really only prepares for this.) Now we have already discussed the conception of the Man as the provider of bread and some of its implications. We suggest that this temptation is involved with the same web of ideas, except that here the new Man refuses to use this power for himself. Perhaps the basic idea is that he refuses to misuse his power. In this way there might be a link between this story and the Johannine account of Jesus' refusal to repeat the miracle of the feeding merely for its own sake. In Q the temptation is offered to Jesus as the Son of God. In John it is indicated that he is acting as the Son of Man. It is our contention that in contexts such as these the titles meant very much the same thing.

It also may be instructive to notice Jesus' reply to this temptation: 'Man shall not live by bread alone.' In the Hebrew of Deut. 8.3 this is '(the) '*ādām* shall not live by bread alone'.[1] In a *milieu* such as we are positing the nuances of such a statement would have been *live*, while the evangelists (and probably their immediate tradition), seeing here only a quotation from the Old Testament, might well have failed to recognize the underlying implications.

If this interpretation is correct, it may be another indication of the way in which Jesus was inclined to use scripture. There would seem to have been a tendency, not just to take things back to the Pentateuch,[2] but even right back to the beginning, to the situation of Adam. We have suggested that such an intention may well lie behind 'The Son of Man is lord also of the sabbath', and perhaps Jesus' whole attitude to the sabbath. It could even be important to a statement like 'But from the beginning of creation, "God created them male and female . . ."'[3] (See further below on his use of scripture.)

(iii) *Elijah and the Son of Man*

One of the most puzzling mysteries in the Gospels involves the place of Elijah and his relationship with Jesus, with John the Baptist

[1] Cf. W. Manson, *Jesus, the Messiah*, pp. 113f., who points out that one Targum translates as *bar nāšā*.

[2] It does often seem that Jesus was among those who looked with disapproval on the Pharisaic use of oral law, believing that this was being used to violate the true spiritual demands of the written Law. In this, as noted earlier, there may be another link between Jesus and some of the sectarian groups, esp. those of a Samaritan variety.

[3] Mark 10.6ff. = Matt. 19.4 ff., quoting Gen. 1.27; 2.24. Here, of course, the reference would not be to the Man in his authority, but rather more generally to the circumstances in which the Man ('*ādām* occurs in both of the same verses from which the quotations come), and by implication his descendants, were created.

and with the Son of Man figure. We find that speculation concerning Elijah is woven deep into the fabric of the Gospels' sources. It appears in John, Mark and in Q in various forms, and attempts to view it wholly as later additions or even as ancillary to the traditions are in no way satisfactory.

In the passages which are concerned with Elijah two currents of belief seem to have met and mingled. One is the more or less orthodox expectation that Elijah would return before the day of the Lord.[1] The second appears to have been the result of more esoteric speculation concerning the possibility that one figure might, as it were, be *reborn* in another.

In an intriguing essay which he subtitled 'An Essay in Detection' J. A. T. Robinson has striven to make some sense of the relationship between Elijah, John and Jesus.[2] He has suggested, probably rightly, that at least a part of the confusion has been caused by the intrusion of the Christian understanding that Elijah's appearance was to precede that of the Christ (as opposed to the more fundamental belief that Elijah would prepare the way for the Lord God himself). Although it is very often assumed that this was a widespread Jewish tenet, there is no positive evidence that it was.[3] Thus 'the coming one' might well have not been the Messiah but Elijah himself (or one like Elijah). In fact, from the quotations and allusions that are given, there is good reason to think that this was so.[4] Certainly such would help to explain why 'the coming one' was to baptize with *fire* as well as spirit.[5] There is also some cause for supposing that Jesus himself, at least for a time, saw himself as to be either identified with or related to such a role.[6]

In our opinion Robinson has not, however, given sufficient attention to the other factor which further complicates the matter while

[1] See Mal. 3.1; 4.5f.; Ecclus. 48.10f.

[2] 'Elijah, John and Jesus', *NTS* 4, 1957/8, pp. 263ff. (also found in his *Twelve New Testament Studies*, pp. 28ff.).

[3] *Op. cit.*, pp. 269ff.

[4] See Mark 1.2 with Mal. 3.1; Matt. 3.12 = Luke 3.17 with Mal. 3.2f.; 4.1. The messenger of Mal. 3.1ff., later identified with Elijah, is spoken of as one who comes.

[5] Mal. 3.2; 4.1. Cf. II Kings 2.9ff.; I Kings 18.36ff. And see Luke 9.54. Compare II (4) Esd. 13.4, 27, 38. Others might find the explanation for this motif in Iranian-influenced sectarianism. See Widengren, *Mani and Manichaeism*, p. 19.

[6] Cf. Jesus' answer to Matt. 11.3 = Luke 7.19, the whole idea of fasting in the wilderness for forty days and Luke 12.49. However, Robinson may well be right to hold that this last with the following verses shows that Jesus was now rejecting Elijah's role. See also Luke 9.54.

at the same time pointing in the direction of some kind of an answer. We are, of course, referring to the Son of Man. Putting our view succinctly, we suspect that there was once extant speculation which considered that Elijah might be the Son of Man. Admittedly we can point to very little evidence outside the Gospels which would specifically suggest this.[1] On the other hand it would make a certain sense out of the Gospel data. We know that Enoch was regarded by some as the one who had become the Son of Man, and we have realized that legends concerning his ascent to heaven were once a factor in encouraging this thought.[2] The one other figure who in the Old Testament itself was caught up in this fashion was Elijah.

By this we do not necessarily mean that Elijah was ever widely known as one of the Son of Man figures. Quite possibly, perhaps probably on the evidence, this was never a firmly established or exclusive opinion. Perhaps it was in some measure a view held by certain groups and disputed by others. Yet let us see if the possibility that Elijah was a type for the Son of Man does not provoke us toward a deeper awareness of certain features in the sources.

(a) In answer to the question of Matt. 16.13 some men say Elijah is the Son of Man. Some say that he is John the Baptist, others Jeremiah or one of the prophets.[3] In a few pages we shall argue that this represents authentic tradition. But even in the Marcan account we have the 'Elijah, John, Jesus, one of the prophets' speculation followed by Jesus' references to the Son of Man.

(b) We have found that the Baptist's preaching may have involved teaching about Elijah as 'the coming one' and also that this expectation seems to have related to his practice of baptism and the baptism of Jesus especially. We have seen that this baptism makes use of motifs having to do with the royal Man and that 'the coming one' designation could be associated with the Son of Man in other ways.[4]

[1] See Jeremias, ''Ἠλ(ε)ίας', *TWNT* II, pp. 934f., where he discusses the rather slight tradition which wished to see Elijah not only as a prophet but as a high priest at the end of time and the eschatological hero. On this and the whole question of the eschatological prophet, cf. H. M. Teeple, *The Mosaic Eschatological Prophet* (*JBL* Monograph Series, X), Philadelphia, 1957, esp. pp. 2ff., and Hahn, *Hoheitstitel*, pp. 351ff.

[2] See also II (4) Esd. 6.25f. on this theme.

[3] Jonah? Cf. Luke 11.30. In some other circle might not one of these *prophets* have been Enoch? With Matt. 16.13ff. compare John 1.20f., where John is asked if he is the Christ, Elijah or the prophet.

[4] Cf. p. 366 n. 1 and below.

(c) Certainly the story of the forty days in the wilderness contains motifs which would cause one to think of both Elijah and the Man.

(d) In the transfiguration scene, which we regard as an *epiphany* of the Man, Elijah appears to the Son of Man-Jesus. In the Marcan version it is said that 'Elijah with Moses' appeared to Jesus. This is at least a little odd in that the expression would normally be 'Moses and Elijah' (i.e. the law and the prophets, and so both Matthew and Luke). It might be that the original tradition spoke only of Elijah and that Moses was added later by those who did not comprehend the real significance of the scene.[1] Perhaps this had to do with some communication or communion, possibly even a kind of fusion of persons, between the Man above (Elijah) and the Man below (Jesus).[2]

(e) Immediately following this are the elliptical and probably confused remarks about Elijah, his suffering and coming, and the resurrection and suffering of the Son of Man. It may be that this tradition once presented teaching about Elijah as the Son of Man.[3] Or it could be that Jesus was even then recasting such teaching in order to suggest that John the Baptist was Elijah and that the Son of Man was yet to suffer.[4] We ourselves suspect that the thought was

[1] Or that the two were originally Elijah and Enoch? See below.

[2] See below on Dan. 10.5–12 and the transfiguration, and compare our remarks on John 1.51.

[3] On the possibility that Elijah was seen as a suffering figure during this period, see Jeremias, *TWNT* II, pp. 942f., commented on by Robinson, *NTS* 4, 1957/8, p. 276 n. 1. Jeremias compares traditions of Elijah's suffering in the Coptic *Apocalypse of Elijah* with Rev. 11.1ff., where the two witnesses who are killed might be Elijah and Enoch. Robinson points out that the Apocalypse is either Christian or heavily edited by Christians, though there still could be earlier tradition behind this, and we must also remember how much material has been lost. It is doubtful if either the Church or Jesus would have made a statement like Mark 9.13 without some point of reference in mind. On this see also Riesenfeld, *Jésus transfiguré*, pp. 262f. Otherwise we may be dealing here with speculation derived directly from the sufferings of the historical Elijah (see I Kings 19, etc.) now seen as a type of the Son of Man, or Elijah may be regarded as a sufferer just because he (and those who are later manifestations of him, like John Baptist if he was originally intended here) was considered a type of the Son of Man.

[4] Taylor (*Mark*, p. 394; see *NEB* margin) records Wellhausen's interesting suggestion that Mark 9.12a be read as a question ('Does Elijah come first . . .?'), perhaps implying that the Son of Man must suffer before the restoration of all things. While some scholars are willing to pay particular heed to Mark 9.12b because of its lack of elaboration, others query the authenticity of the whole of Mark 9.9–13 on the grounds that it reveals concerns of the Church. (See Matt. 17.9–12; Luke's 'omission' would be accounted for by a desire to avoid redundancy and the inappropriateness of these particular teachings for Gentiles.) We share the suspicion that the Church may have so interpreted the material that it is now

still more complex, that Elijah and John and then perhaps Jesus could all have been regarded as types of the Son of Man. But, however we attempt to explicate it, the integral relationship is still there.

(f) Again in the Q material of Matt. 11.2ff. and Luke 7.18ff. the association between Jesus, John, 'the coming one', a prophet, Elijah and finally the Son of Man is present.

(g) The Son of Man saying in Luke 9.58 is surrounded by obvious allusions to the Elijah tradition.[1] Is this only later development or has some feature in the primitive tradition caused this?

(h) What are we to make of the highly enigmatic tradition that Jesus may have called to Elijah from the cross?[2] One gathers that we are now intended to understand that this might have resulted from a misunderstanding by the onlookers of the *Eloi* in '*Eloi, Eloi, lama sabachthani?*' But surely there must be more to it than this. Could there have been a tradition which represented the Son of Man below calling for help to the Man above?

(i) Finally there is the strange passage which tells of Herod pondering on speculation as to whether Jesus could be Elijah, John or one of the prophets reborn. Again there must be a more developed school of thought behind this. We think it could be a somewhat garbled account based on earlier forms of theorizing. This would not have been concerned with reincarnation as such, but with this idea of representation. We recall particularly the beliefs about the Adamite one, about how Adam could be remanifested in others.[3]

In other words there may have been a number of theories about who the representative Son of Man on earth was, both past and present, and even as to who he was in heaven, and so with regard to

---

impossible to restore its original logic with any certainty, but for the reasons given above we also suspect that several of the ideas here presented had a strong basis in the tradition. Rather than following Bultmann (*Synoptic Tradition*, pp. 124f.) in treating Mark 9.2–10, 12b as interpolations into 9.1–12, see our next discussion regarding the whole of Mark 8.27–9.13. See also p. 351 n. 2 on Mark 9.9 = Matt. 17.9. Regarding Elijah and the resurrection, cf. Mishnah, *Sotah*, 9.15.

[1] For Luke 9.54 see II Kings 1.10; for Luke 9.61f. see I Kings 19.20. The remark 'as Elijah did' at 9.54 is 'correct' even if but a gloss.

[2] Mark 15.35f. = Matt. 27.47ff.

[3] It is interesting here to go a bit further afield. Logion 46 of the *Gospel of Thomas* reads, 'From Adam until John the Baptist there is among those born of women none higher than John . . .' as a variant of Matt. 11.11 = Luke 7.28. Is it possible that this *Gospel*, otherwise not given to speculation about Adam or John, preserves something which might reflect earlier thought: that John was once regarded as an Adamite?

who the one below was representing. Indeed it is within such a context of thought that we should think that something of the real
mystery about Jesus' role might first have originated.[1] Here also may
lie the real point to the question, 'Who is the Son of Man?'

Yet we do not propose an answer to all the ramifications of this
issue. It may be that first John and then Jesus were struggling to
understand themselves and their mission in terms of a speculation
which was somewhat bewildering in their own time. Possibly John
was trying to divest himself of the Elijah role and point to another,[2]
while others may have continued to regard him as 'the coming one'.[3]
Perhaps Jesus was also seeking some manner of reorientation, and the
speculations of others, both during and after this period, may have
added to the mystery.

But, however one attempts finally to work it all out, we little doubt
that the basis of the enigma is primitive, and thus, whenever Elijah
and the Son of Man both appear together in the Gospels, we would
suspect that authentic tradition is very likely at the heart of the
passage.

(iv) *At Caesarea Philippi*

It is our belief that in the synoptic section which begins with the
confession at Caesarea Philippi and closes with the discussion regarding
the suffering of the Son of Man and Elijah following the transfiguration we are dealing with a primitive cycle of materials fully dominated
by concern with the Son of Man.[4] Of course, we also find that
additions and alterations have been made, and we are not proposing
to reconstruct with a high degree of accuracy some source document.
None the less, when read with the centrality of the Son of Man in

---

[1] It is this rather than any teaching about a *hidden* Son of Man (see Sjöberg,
verborgene Menschensohn, pp. 184ff., 230ff.) which we should think to be behind
Luke 10.21f. = Matt. 11.25ff., if indeed the passage is authentic (and if it means
more than 'as a father knows his son and a son his father') and had to do with the
Son of Man. (*Son* could possibly be an abbreviation for *the Son of Man*, for only
here and in Mark 13.32; Matt. 28.19 and the parable of the wicked husbandmen
do the synoptics use *Son* by itself outside of the baptism and transfiguration *oracles*;
or else it could refer to the Son of Man in his role as Son of God.) Knowledge of the
identity of the Son of Man is not an occult affair in the Gospels, though it may
nevertheless be true that revelation is needed to help men realize who he now is.
See on John 1.51; 12.34, etc.

[2] On this see also John 1.21, 25.

[3] See the Baptist *hymn* at Luke 1.17.

[4] With, of course, the secondary motif regarding Elijah sounding in the background.

mind, the entire passage takes on a force and flow, a sense of move-ment which we regard as prior to some of the redirections of thought that have tended to turn the section into what appears now to be a kind of pastiche of narrative and sayings.

In following the Marcan presentation of this tradition in general we would make three basic alterations.

(a) Matt. 16.13 has preserved the essence of the opening to the first scene. There are strong reasons for believing that the interest in Jesus himself and in Jesus as the Christ have caused the change to an *I* form in Mark. Of course, many would feel it dangerous to correct Mark with Matthew, more dangerous yet when Matthew is held to be making at least some use of Mark at the same point,[1] but here we feel that there is sufficient cause. Otherwise it is exceedingly difficult

---

[1] Matt. 16.13 has been used as the basis for several theories. Some hold that it demonstrates the frequent or occasional misunderstanding of *bar nāšā*. (Cf. Beare, *Earliest Records*, p. 139; Bultmann, *Synoptic Tradition*, p. 259.) On the arguments presented, this makes no sense at all. It would mean that Matthew, having Mark's Greek in front of him, has yet inserted the translation form of the Aramaic phrase into his text. The only way of getting around this is to suggest that Matthew here had access to independent tradition. We are considering this as a legitimate supposition while yet rejecting the misunderstood idiom approach on the grounds set forth in ch. I. Tödt and Higgins are among the many who hold that Matthew has inserted it as a title. Higgins (*Son of Man*, p. 119) notes that 16.21 shows that Matthew readily identified Jesus with the Son of Man. We would hardly disagree, but this is not the same thing as demonstrating that it was an important title in Matthew's own Christology. (Only Matt. 12.40; 13.37 and 26.2 could be brought forward to show a parallel Matthean interest in presenting Jesus as the earthly Son of Man. On these, however, see our comments.) Without a knowledge of the Marcan text or a scholarly comparison with later sayings, would any reader go away from the Matthean passage with the awareness that it was as the Son of Man that Jesus was to suffer and was now to be reverenced? Tödt sees something of the problem and suggests that the title is omitted at 16.21 because Matthew's interest is now more soteriological than Christological. (*Son of Man*, p. 86.) But even if this be so (and surely there is still a good deal of Christology here, and why then does he not omit the title in other Son of Man passion sayings?), it must be important that Matthew fails clearly to make the point that Jesus, as the Son of Man, is central to his own soteriological thought. Apparently feeling that something more is needed, Tödt (*op. cit.*, p. 90) remarks that Matthew likes to avoid repetition of the title, and we are referred to 10.32f. with 10.23. Yet, if Matthew is attempting to give prominence to Jesus as the Son of Man, surely for the sake of clarity the designation is needed again at 16.21. In addition we can look at several other Matthean passages: e.g. 16.27f. There is no abhorrence of redundancy here. Later yet (*op. cit.*, p. 150) the title is said by Tödt to have been esp. used to introduce the section on the sovereignty of the one who initiates the Church. But we, by an application of the principles of 'redactionscriticism' (cf. J. Rohde, *Die redaktions-geschichtliche Methode*, Berlin, 1966; ET in preparation), cannot come away with the impression that the Son of Man is here intended as an important designation for the sovereign Jesus.

to provide a reasonable motive for the Matthean insertion of the Son of Man. If he is trying to indicate an identity between the Son of Man and the Christ, he has done a very clumsy job of it, as later attempts at emendation show.[1] And, in fact, the implications are, as the passage now stands, that Jesus is not the Son of Man, but is rather the Christ, which Matthew surely must not have intended if he himself introduced the Son of Man designation. At 16.20 he reiterates the Messiahship of Jesus, and then, when we arrive at his 16.21, we find that the evangelist has allowed a mention of the Son of Man to drop out and has replaced it with a 'he'. Thus it certainly is not apparent that a later interest in the Son of Man was operative.[2]

When one goes on to study the whole Matthean passage, it can be seen that there are actually a number of significant variations, chief of them being the addition of the special material on Peter. We suggest that, while Matthew may have had *Mark* before him as well, he also knew a version (oral or written) of the *confession* which had been in use in his community. This he valued because of its Petrine features, and, in recording it, he preserved for us the original opening question, indeed the question which we think to have been vital in certain circles during Jesus' lifetime.

(*b*) We are less adamant in our opinion that the tradition has introduced the concern with the Christ here. Various other explanations are possible: it could be that *the Messiah* was in some places being used as an equivalent or a title roughly equivalent to the Son of Man. It could even be that it once was used here to indicate the disciples' incomprehension of Jesus' true identity.

Yet we consider it far more likely that there originally stood here some affirmation of the awareness that Jesus was this chosen one of God, this Son of Man. Such might have been signified in one of several ways. Perhaps the reading at Mark 8.29 was, 'But who do you say that he is?'—the answer being, 'You are he.' Or if 'I' is correct, then Jesus was asking, 'But who do you say that I am?'—in which event the answer was, 'You are the Son of Man,' or, more simply, 'You are he.'[3]

---

[1] 'Who do men say that I, the Son of Man, am?' Various texts put the με in a different place, and, were one to attempt to see this as original, no one can say how the shorter text would have come into being.

[2] It is possible (compare Mark 9.31; 14.21, 41; Luke 12.8f.) that there was once a play on words here as well: who do men or the sons of men (the sons of the Man?) say the Son of (the?) Man to be?

[3] In one of these eventualities, or as suggested below, Matthew (or his source)

Alternatively there are strong hints both in Matthew and Luke and also possibly in John[1] that neither of the designations Christ or Son of Man was original at Mark 8.29 = Matt. 16.16, but rather some other title like 'Son of the Living God' or 'Son of God' or 'Holy One of God'. If this be so, we would think that such a designation was originally employed in circumstances where it would have been taken as an affirmation of the realization that Jesus was the Son of Man.

(c) Though at first it will seem surprising (especially since Mark 9.1 has been central to numerous theories about the Kingdom of God), we find that there are grounds for regarding Matt. 16.27f., in the present context, as superior to Mark 8.38–9.1 (= Luke 9.26f.).[2] Mark 8.38a looks to be a variant of the latter half of Luke 12.8f.,[3] a saying which once may have read something like 'He who is ashamed of me before men, of him will the Son of Man be ashamed before the angels of God.'[4] If we add to this[5] a version of Matt. 16.27 ('For the Son of Man is to come with the angels[6] in the glory of the Father[7] [and then he will repay every man for what he has done']),[8] we come out with a logion very much like Mark 8.38. Thus we suggest that Matthew, either in full independence of Mark or because he continued to be governed mainly by his own source at this point, has correctly preserved the shorter formula. In addition, Matthew's version (especially together with his 16.28) presents a better flow of thought.[9]

---

has probably been influenced by the *Marcan* tradition and probably found it impossible not to accommodate the satisfyingly direct 'You are the Christ'.

[1] John 6.69. See also below on Mark 14.61f.

[2] One could also find reasons for believing that Luke 9.26f. is earlier than Mark 8.38f.

[3] Notice that Matthew has two sayings (10.38f. = Luke 14.27; 17.33) parallel to Mark 8.34f. (with its parr.) and that shortly before this, Matt. 10.32f., is found his version of Luke 12.8f. One could infer that such logia were once allied in a primitive strand of tradition.

[4] See p. 358 n. 1.

[5] Perhaps the mention of the angels in both logia brought the two Son of Man sayings together.

[6] Perhaps the 'the' of Luke and Mark is to be preferred to Matthew's 'his angels'. On this and the angels generally, cf. p. 319 n. 3.

[7] Perhaps Luke's 'the Father' is to be preferred to Matthew and Mark's 'his Father'.

[8] This last clause may have been added, but it makes good sense with what precedes and would fit in with the Son of Man sayings generally.

[9] It is the culmination of the preceding several verses. Those who follow Jesus will be rewarded by the Son of Man and *vice versa*. Compare Luke 12.8f.; Matt. 19.28; 25.31ff. See below on Mark 14.62, and also see our remarks on Luke 21.36.

Then instead of a sudden shift to the Kingdom of God,[1] we would carry on with a reference to the familiar theme that the Son of Man will appear soon. What is more, the language and character of Matt. 16.28 and Mark 9.1 correspond to the Son of Man vocabulary, while the phrases, at best, are associated with the Kingdom of God in a limited and tangential manner. We are accustomed to hear of *seeing* the Son of Man *coming*, but not so with respect to the Kingdom of God.[2] That the Son of Man, as a royal figure, should be considered as one having or associated with a kingdom we believe to be only natural,[3] and it is also understandable why and how *Mark* may have used this as a means of converting the saying into a reference to the more popular conception.[4]

There might then have been a body of tradition which read in this fashion.

And Jesus went on with his disciples to the villages of Caesarea Philippi; and on the way he asked his disciples, 'Who do men say that the Son of Man is?' And they told him, 'John the Baptist; and others say, Elijah; and others one of the prophets.'[5] And he asked them, 'But who do you say that I am?' Peter answered him, 'You are he.'

And he charged them to tell no one about him.

And he began to teach them that the Son of Man must suffer many things, and be rejected by men and be killed, and after three days rise again.[6] And Peter took him and began to rebuke him. But turning and seeing his disciples, he rebuked Peter and said, 'Get behind me, Satan! For you are not on the side of God, but of men.'

[1] Many for this reason wish to regard Mark 9.1 as an interpolation of an independent logion.

[2] Frequently we hear of the 'coming' of the Son of Man. On seeing him, cf. Mark 13.26; 14.62; Luke 17.22, 30, and cf. Matt. 24.27 = Luke 17.24; John 1.51; 6.62. Forms of ἔρχομαι are not associated with the Kingdom in Mark and in Matthew only in the Lord's Prayer at Matt. 6.10 = Luke 11.2. The idea gains a little in Luke; see 17.20f. (though the conception is there confuted) and 22.18. On it appearing or being seen, cf. only Luke 19.11; John 3.3.

[3] Cf. Dan. 7.14, and see Matt. 19.28; 25.31ff. The reference to it as '*his* kingdom' may well be Matthean. Cf. Matt. 13.41.

[4] It is possible, on the other hand, that Matthew has mentioned the kingdom for his own reasons (cf. Matt. 20.21 with Mark 10.37, though even in Mark a kingdom is presupposed) or due to an influence from a version of this saying known from the *Marcan* tradition.

[5] Enoch? Jonah? Ezekiel? Cf. p. 400. Probably 'Jeremiah' is a later guess to fill in the tradition, though some might have regarded him as an Adamite as well.

[6] On this saying and this language, see under sec. 2 B in this chapter. We have here omitted the reference to the elders, etc., and 'And he said this plainly' as editorial.

And he[1] said to them, 'If any man would come after me, let him deny himself[2] and follow me.[3] For whoever would save his life will lose it; and whoever loses his life will save it.[4] For what does it profit a man to gain the whole world and forfeit his life? For what can a man give in return for his life? For the Son of Man is to come with the angels in the glory of the Father, and then he will repay every man for what he has done. Truly, I say to you, there are some standing here who will not taste death before they see the Son of Man coming in the kingdom.'

(There follows the story of the transfiguration, with its reference to Elijah, which we regard as a legend about the Son of Man.)

And as they were coming down the mountain, he charged them to tell no one what they had seen until the Son of Man should have risen. And they questioned what the rising up meant.[5] And they asked him, 'Why do the scribes say that first Elijah must come?' And he said to them, 'Does Elijah come first to restore all things? Then how is it written of the Son of Man that he should suffer many things and be treated with contempt? Yet I tell you that Elijah has indeed come, and they did to him whatever they pleased, as it is written of him.'[6]

(v) *The transfiguration*

The transfiguration offers a picture of the glory of the Man at the time of his being chosen by God and manifested in his grandeur. Although it may once have been intended as a kind of sequel to the baptismal narrative, as a scene which took place more in heaven than on earth, it was probably a variant conception embodying the same basic idea. Among groups who were concerned with the Man figure, several such scenes might well have had a vogue.[7]

Obviously the story contains numerous echoes from royal liturgies and myths. Here we shall be partly content to rest upon our own earlier researches and, more especially, upon those of Harald Riesenfeld in his study *Jésus transfiguré*. While we are not able to agree with all his interpretations and conclusions,[8] we feel that he has gone a

[1] Omitting part of Mark 8.34 as editorial.
[2] Omitting the reference to taking up the cross. Cf. John 12.26.
[3] I.e. to follow one who is himself attempting to follow the pattern of the Son of Man as in the preceding statement? This would again offer a good progression of thought.
[4] Omitting 'for my sake and the gospel's'. Cf. Luke 17.33 and John 12.25 recalling that John 12.25f. is also found in connection with Son of Man material.
[5] See on Mark 9.9f., p. 351 n. 2.
[6] On Mark 9.11–13, see p. 375 n. 4.
[7] As in the Odes of Solomon, the Mandaean literature, etc.
[8] We would not, for instance, follow him in his use of the Dura-Europas materials, which we regard as still too enigmatic to be of much help. We also think that he

long way toward demonstrating that the scene cannot be understood unless a background in royal ideology is appreciated. In making this claim we would not argue that every detail has to be seen in terms of such a derivation. Certain features, especially those paralleling incidents in the Old Testament,[1] may have accreted at an early stage in the sectarian situation or have been added later by the Christian communities. It is obvious that this process has been some-what furthered in Matthew and Luke (and, since there is little reason for believing that they have here had access to better tradition, we may devote most of our attention to the Marcan account).

Riesenfeld has examined the scene detail by detail in order to evince them as aspects of a disintegrated kingship ideology found in various practices associated with New Year festivals both ancient and contemporary. In a cursory fashion we would like to adopt a similar procedure.

(a) After six days. The transfiguration takes place on the seventh day[2] which has quite possibly been regarded as the culminating day of the feast.[3] This would be a natural time[4] for the great event of the feast (and surely Tabernacles with all its associations with the New Year rites is implicated here), the manifestation of the king.

(b) The mountain, as we have seen time and time again, is the

---

goes too far in trying to make out a case for the popularity of some idea of a suffer-ing Messiah during this era. It is, on the other hand, our hope that we have given better grounds for understanding how many of the conceptions derived from king-ship ideology could have been operative in Jesus' time and *milieu*.

See also Rengstorf, *NT* 5, 1962, pp. 229ff., who speaks of the 'after-effects' and the manner in which themes from the royal liturgy are still alive and influential in this and several other New Testament scenes.

[1] See esp. Ex. 24, where are found the six days, the mountain, the cloud and the voice from the cloud. These may have been of some influence, but their parallelism can also be misleading. Many important details from Exodus are missing in Mark, e.g. the cloud was said to have covered the mountain for the six days previous. Exodus offers no such words from God, and the purpose of the scene is not to proclaim Moses as the *Son*. One might go on to point out that Exodus speaks in the next chapter of the tabernacle and elsewhere of the Feast of Tabernacles, but the comparisons are not really apposite. While Moses' face shines in Ex. 34.29ff., this is actually a contrast. Matthew and Luke have added this feature (probably in conformity to Exodus), but in Mark it is Jesus' garments that glisten.

[2] Mark is quite unaccustomed to give such precise chronological information, and the inference is that he found some such reference in his source.

[3] Just possibly Luke has recorded something more authentic with his reference to the eighth day (Mark having conformed to Exodus or having slightly mis-interpreted what was originally meant).

[4] As we have seen, practices varied in this regard.

place where the king is *born*. It is that locale nearest to heaven, some-times even being regarded as more in heaven than on earth. It is the situation of paradise, the home of the First Man. In eschatological thought it naturally can become the place where the royal Man will appear in ultimate glory.

(*c*) He was transfigured ($\mu\epsilon\tau\epsilon\mu\rho\phi\dot{\omega}\theta\eta$) before them. Unfortunately we do not know what word or idea Mark is translating or interpret-ing. (Possibly it referred more simply to Jesus' glory which could establish a closer connection with the Johannine sayings about the glorification of the Man.) Some think that he has been influenced by II Cor. 3.18 and the whole of Paul's understanding of the relationship between the glorification of Moses, Jesus and the Christian. While this is unnecessary, it may well be that Mark is using a word borrowed from more Hellenistic thought in attempting to interpret what he found in his source. Certainly, however, this does not make the whole scene Hellenistic, and *transfigured* itself is probably best understood in terms of the ensuing description which suggests the non-metaphysical basis of the conception.

(*d*) His garments became glistening, intensely white. Often we have come across the belief that the royal figure at his ordination or enthronement dons a glorious garment and/or becomes radiant and shining in appearance.[1] It is a relic from the old solar motifs. We need go no further than Acts 12.20ff. for an illustration of such an *epiphany*, while the importance of the robe is made more clear in Josephus's account of the incident.

. . . clad in a garment woven completely of silver so that its texture was indeed wondrous, he (Herod) entered the theatre at daybreak. There the silver, illumined by the touch of the first rays of the sun was wondrously radiant and by its glitter inspired fear and awe in those who gazed intently upon it. Straightway his flatterers raised their voices from various direc-tions—though hardly for his good—addressing him as a god. 'May you be propitious to us,' they added, 'and if we have hitherto feared you as a man, yet henceforth we agree that you are more than a mortal in your being.'[2]

(*e*) Elijah and Moses appear. We have suggested that originally it may have been only Elijah, perhaps regarded as the heavenly Man, who appeared to the lustrous one. Or it might have been that Elijah and Enoch were once meant. Alternatively it could be that

[1] See also Riesenfeld, *op. cit.*, pp. 115ff.
[2] *Antiquities* XIX, 8.2.

the two figures were at first unspecified, being intended mostly as attendants (probably angels) at this scene.[1]

If Elijah and Moses stood here in the original scene, we would guess that the purpose was essentially to add an eschatological note, these being two figures who were said to return (or whose types would return) at the end of time.[2] This would at least not conflict with our general interpretation, though we do not believe the strictly eschatological interest to have been dominant at the first.

(f) Peter says that it is good to be here. Very likely this meant that the disciples would like to remain rather than that they wished to serve the others. This being so, Riesenfeld suggests that the theme of the messianic *rest* lies behind the statement.[3] It is the day of rest, the sabbath which has always been a prolepsis of paradise. We would not press this interpretation, but it would help to explain the basis of such a remark.

(g) The booths have always been a puzzling feature, and no one has yet presented a satisfactory explanation for their presence and function in the story. If nothing else, we would regard them as one of the more obvious signs that we are dealing with material which demands a broader context of thought. It is very difficult to believe that the Church would have added such a detail without any further exposition.[4] Rather does it look like a relic which the evangelists have done their best to interpret in the light of their understanding of the scene. We would, of course, remember the association of the booths with the New Year festival and of both with the enthronement of kings.[5]

(h) A cloud is so ubiquitous a symbol for a theophany and for a

[1] See esp. the two angels in II Enoch 22. Bultmann on the basis of his own interpretation (see below) suggests this, though probably only because he is attempting to conform it to one of the resurrection stories. *Synoptic Tradition*, p. 260.

[2] See G. H. Boobyer, *Mark and the Transfiguration Story*, Edinburgh, 1942, p. 70.

[3] *Op. cit.*, pp. 206ff., 258ff. We previously noted the place of this theme in Dan. 10.9. For insights into the relationships between Dan. 10.5–12 and the transfiguration, see M. Sabbe, 'La rédaction du récit de la Transfiguration' in *La venue du Messie. Messianisme et eschatologie* (by É. Massaux and others), Bruges, 1962, pp. 65ff. There Daniel, who is styled a 'man (*'iš*) greatly beloved', sees a vision of a radiant man-like divinity and himself becomes radiant.

[4] The plural makes it doubtful if the tabernacle of God is meant. See Ezek. 37.27; 43.7, 9; Joel 3.21; Zech. 2.10f.; 8.3, 8 with their eschatological implications. Such would seem to refer to a permanent visitation by God and not a scene like this. See, however, Lohmeyer, *Markus*, p. 176.

[5] See also Riesenfeld, *op. cit.*, pp. 146ff., 256ff. One must at least recall the use of the *hut* among such as the Marcosians and, esp., the Mandaeans in connection with initiatory and other rites.

divine presence that its specific relevance to a scene derived from royal ideology would be hard to maintain.[1] One can, however, easily point to a text like Isa. 6.4 (where smoke fills the temple at the time of the king's and/or God's enthronement)[2] to show that such a cloud would not be foreign to a description of the present glory of the king.[3]

This is among our reasons for finding it difficult to accept a strictly eschatological interpretation of the scene.[4] Obviously there are a number of eschatological overtones, but this is bound to be so, as it always has been, in any description of the king's enthronement or of part of the New Year festival. In one important sense they are always proleptic of the time of the perfect king and of the new age. Yet there is also a good deal which was deliberately described as *present* in this scene, a strong sense in which it is happening now. In this way the story was intended as much more than just a prefigurement of a coming eschatological reality. In terms of myth or of dramatic enactment the new king is seen as already entering upon his office.[5]

(i) Lastly there is the voice of God, on which see our remarks

---

[1] Riesenfeld's discussion (*op. cit.*, pp. 130ff., 248ff.) of texts like Ezek. 28.14 (in Widengren's translation) and Lam. 4.20 only serves to show how wide one's net can be cast without catching any certain results. The later rabbinic traditions concerning the appearance of Moses and Adam wrapped in clouds are not really apposite to this particular story.

[2] See also I Kings 8.10 at the seventh-month feast.

[3] A number of commentators suggest that the cloud should be understood with reference to the clouds of Dan. 7.13; II (4) Esd. 13.3; etc. It has then to do with the heavenly, eschatological appearance of the Man. (See Boobyer, *op. cit.*, pp. 84ff.) We, of course, do not contend that such scenes are unrelated, but the cloud here does not serve the same function. It does in some measure indicate the quasi-heavenly nature of the scene, but it is used more as a sign and a cloak for the presence of the divinity at the glorification of his Son. It is not that we are moving in a different sphere of ideas from Dan. 7.13f., but that here we have a variant emphasis and interpretation.

[4] Boobyer has argued that the scene was intended as a prefigurement of Jesus' second coming. Lohmeyer (*op. cit.*, pp. 173ff.) is somewhat closer to the mark when he sees it as an eschatological vision of the Son of Man. See Riesenfeld's criticisms (*op. cit.*, pp. 292ff.) of Boobyer's association of much of the imagery with that found later in the New Testament and his failure to give sufficient attention to the intention of the scene as it is described and to both the background and use of the imagery here.

[5] Thus we feel that A. M. Ramsey (*The Glory of God and the Transfiguration of Christ*, London, 1949, see p. 119) is right to emphasize the present relevance of the scene while not denying that it points to a yet more glorious future revelation. It may be objected that Ramsey's whole interpretation is quite different from ours, but we are not necessarily denying that Jesus may have *lived through* an experience which was understood like this. Indeed, for one who thought he might be the Son of Man, such an experience may have been considered essential.

about the *oracle* at the baptism.[1] Here the divine message is delivered more to the onlookers than to the Beloved,[2] but the basic intention is the same. It is the culminating point in a scene depicting the adoption and/or manifestation of the mortal chosen to be the royal Man.[3]

(vi) *Bread and water miracles*

We have by now said sufficient to indicate our general attitude toward the story of the feeding of the multitudes, the temptation to make bread from stones, the Last Supper tradition and the story about the Man's right to give bread to his disciples on the sabbath. We think that all of them, but especially the first, are involved with the ancient conception of the Man as the provider of food for his people.[4] More particularly is this the bread of paradise, the food of the new age.

We have also noted that the miracle of the feeding of the five thousand is immediately followed in John, Mark and Matthew by the story of the walking on the water (which in Mark and Matthew is accompanied by the fact, if not the *miracle*, of the dying of the storm).[5] We suggest that the two tales came from an early level of tradition which contained stories relating to the powers and authorities of the Man figure. To them we would join the story of the stilling of the storm.[6]

[1] See also Riesenfeld, *op. cit.*, pp. 250ff.

[2] The difference probably lies in the point of view from which the story was related (see the implications of John 1.51; 8.28; etc.), but it may have been altered to this form through the Church's retelling of the narrative from the disciples' rather than the Man's standpoint. The command to 'hear him' may be regarded as a Church addition, but it would fit well with the older conception. The chosen one has been given power to speak with all authority and wisdom. See I Enoch 51.3; 69.29.

[3] Bultmann calls Riesenfeld's theories 'fantastic' (*Synoptic Tradition*, p. 428). Yet in our opinion Bultmann's efforts to see so much, and esp. a scene like this, as almost entirely the work of the Church are also a bit incredible. His theory that this was originally a resurrection story fits neither with the character of many of the details nor with a comparison of the scene with the records of resurrection appearances. Cf. C. H. Dodd, 'The Appearances of the Risen Christ: an essay in the form-criticism of the Gospels' in *Studies in the Gospels* (ed. D. E. Nineham), Oxford, 1955, pp. 9ff., esp. p. 25. A comparison with a scene like Matt. 28.16ff. (cf. O. Michel, 'Der Abschluss des Mattäusevangeliums', *EvTh* 10, 1950/51, pp. 16ff.), while it may show that items from enthronement legends have influenced both, only serves to make this clear. The closing scene from Matthew is very generalized, displays the hand of the Church in an obvious manner, and offers none of these details which make little sense in and of themselves.

[4] See pp. 296ff.

[5] Mark 6.45ff. = Matt. 14.22ff. = John 6.15ff.

[6] Mark 4.35ff. = Matt. 8.23ff. = Luke 8.22ff.

John's Gospel gives various indications of the manner in which the Man may have been thought to have power over the water. We regard the walking on the water and the stilling of the storm as yet more explicit *paradigm* stories[1] derived ultimately from older ideas which reoccur time and again at various levels in the Man traditions.[2] While one can point to Hellenistic parallels,[3] or at least partial parallels,[4] or to legends told of Yahweh, none of these are sufficient to explain the tales found in the Gospels and the reasons for their being found there. And, in the latter case especially, we must consider the common background of the various creation legends and their influences. If the Man was reckoned to have powers like those elsewhere attributed to Yahweh, we have earlier seen the causes for this dual attribution.

To our list of Gospel miracles and healings done by the Son of Man we might add, though much more problematically, the little story of the cursing of the fig tree.[5] He who would feed men from the tree of life curses the tree which bears no fruit. Some or all of the stories about demons may be related not only to the combat of the Man with the devil but to his general struggle with the *forces* of chaos and evil which have often been depicted as demonic beasts.[6] The sources for such ideas may, however, have dropped well into the background. Still the themes, and possibly

[1] Note that in Mark 4.35ff. there would seem to be a very real danger of death by drowning from which Jesus saves his followers. One might catch here a note of the old theme connecting water and death and the power of the Man to avert final calamity in this regard. Compare in Odes of Sol. 39.

[2] See again in chs. II and III, and recall that almost all the apocalyptic Man figures were, in one way or another, represented as battling with the sea or sea monsters. See Davies, *Paul and Rabbinic Judaism*, pp. 40f., with reference to Mark 4.35ff.: 'Christ commands the storm as God did the chaos at the beginning. This thought cannot have been far away in this passage from Mark.' Evidently Davies thinks this to have been the work of the Church, but he clearly sees the point at issue.

[3] See Bultmann, *Synoptic Tradition*, pp. 236ff. But why these particular stories from the wealth of Hellenistic miracle tales? And do the Gospel stories really bear signs of an Hellenistic rather than Semitic origin?

[4] For the realization that there are no really satisfactory contemporary parallels, cf. H. van der Loos, *The Miracles of Jesus* (*NT* Suppl. VIIII), 1965, pp. 619ff.

[5] Mark 11.12ff. = Matt. 21.18f. See also Luke 13.6ff.

[6] Perhaps the story of the Gerasene demoniac (Mark 5.1ff.) would be the best example with its proclamation of Jesus as 'the Son of God Most High'. Davies (*op. cit.*, pp. 40f.) thinks it again revelatory of Jesus' power over the creation and suggestive of cosmic significance. On the importance of the themes of Jesus' struggles against cosmological and demonic forces and the powers of death, along with the allied typological imagery of the desert, the sea and the mountain (as found esp. in Mark's Gospel and as they relate to vital Old Testament themes), see further U. W. Mauser, *Christ in the Wilderness* (SBT 39), 1963.

even some sense of the original conception, might have been alive, perhaps especially so in some indigenous forms of old north Canaanitish religions.

Again, we should be very little surprised if Jesus actually *enacted* a number of these stories and was believed in his own lifetime to have exhibited many of these powers.[1] As one who thought himself to be the Man on earth, he would have taken such older ideas as a part of his inspiration. He would have believed that he had the power to feed the people, to still storms and to cast out demons for the same reasons that he had authority to forgive sins and to *supersede* the sabbath law.[2]

(vii) *Mark 10.32–45*

To this point we have suggested the possibility that several larger or smaller sections in the synoptic Gospels could be regarded as passages which once had especially to do with the Son of Man. We also think Mark 10.32–45 to be kindred in this respect. It begins and ends with references to the Son of Man. It contains teaching about the need for becoming lowly and being like a *servant* which could have been borrowed from the kind of language used about the Man. In the centre of it is the discussion with James and John[3] which establishes the link between baptism and death and which also appears to pre-suppose something of the same manner of thought expressed by the Son of Man logion Matt. 19.28.

There is one more rather enigmatic remark which is worthy of a moment of our attention. Jesus likens suffering to drinking from a cup: 'Are you able to drink the cup that I drink, or to be baptized with the baptism with which I am baptized?' There is good indication that this manner of speaking is authentic. See Mark 14.36, with parallels, and John 18.11, for once again it is our suspicion that sayings like these have not been created out of the passion narratives, but rather that they themselves are signs of the use of such materials

---

[1] It must always be remembered, when dealing with the Gospel miracle stories, that the philosophical question as to whether miracles are possible is often beside the point. Both Jesus' friends and his enemies (see Mark 3.22, etc.) recognized that he did *miracles*. It is thus a mistake to try to relegate all miracle stories to later periods of legend-making. We are here looking for some of the causes for this reputation in his lifetime.

[2] See also on John 9.35 and pp. 296f. Only where there was a pithy saying to go along with the material would it be remembered that Jesus did these things acting as the Son of Man.

[3] Though it is sometimes maintained that this scene has been conformed to relate to the destinies of James (Acts 12.2) and John (by tradition), it is surprising that there is so little here which would actually indicate this. Would the Church have created such a scene in these rather derogatory terms? On its general authenticity, see Taylor, *Mark*, p. 439.

before the time of the passion, which in turn then affected the action and/or description of that passion. Thus there are two references in the passion story to attempts to give Jesus to drink while he was on the cross.[1] According to John he accepted one of these, while the synoptics are somewhat ambiguous in the second instance with regard to the vinegar drink. In either event, however, this is said to constitute the penultimate act of Jesus' life. It seems intimately bound up with his dying.

When we come back to Mark 10.38f. we find that the saying only approximates what was actually reported to have happened. Jesus was offered a sponge, not a cup. And the whole saying, if we may put it in these terms, has a very generalized, liturgical tone. While we little doubt that Ps. 69.21 could have been of influence here, we suspect that it was influential before and not merely after the passion.

One may point, it is true, to other passages in the Old Testament which speak of a 'cup of wrath' or some such[2] and thus conclude that, while our analysis could be approximately correct to this point, it still need have nothing specifically to do with the Man context. Yet what has induced us to bring the matter up is, of course, its link here with this baptism-death theme which we have seen to be an important part of the Man *milieu*. It is then our guess that the mention of the cup also comes from a liturgical or a semi-liturgical setting.[3] We recall many other practices having to do with the drinking of the baptismal waters. Normally this is a life-giving drink, but there could have been another side to the coin, and, just as the purifying, re-vivifying baptismal waters were, at other times, also seen as danger-ous and deadly, perhaps there was once a rite in which the individual being baptized had to drink the waters of death in which he was submerged.

[1] Mark 15.23 = Matt. 27.34; Mark 15.36 = Matt. 27.48; Luke 23.36; John 19.29.

[2] See Pss. 60.3; 75.8; Isa. 51.17, 22; Jer. 25.15; Lam. 4.21; Ezek. 23.32ff.; Hab. 2.16; Zech. 12.2. See Rev. 14.10; 16.19, etc. Martyrdom of Isaiah 5.13.

[3] Compare 1QH, v, 33–36. Possibly the cup at the Last Supper is to be regarded as another parallel in that it may have been understood in terms of the shedding of blood, or (or perhaps involving both ideas at once) it may have been seen as pro-leptic of the cup which was the obverse of the cup of woe (and this, too, may have had its liturgical background). On life-giving libations see the numerous references in chs. II, III and V, esp. in connection with a heavenly banquet, the food of paradise. In the Old Testament alone, cf. Pss. 23.5; 110.7; 116.13, probably all with reference to the king.

(viii) *Mark 14.62*

We wish now to look at Mark 14.62 and but a few of the problems raised by it and the surrounding setting. There are a number of ways of viewing the logion as an approximation of something Jesus said about the Son of Man at his arraignment.[1] Although we do not concur with those who would look for ideas regarding Jesus' own exaltation as the Son of Man in this passage,[2] we cannot, on the other hand, agree with those who hold that the order of the Old Testament allusions[3] suggests the picture of the Son of Man's *parousia*.[4] The language which tells of the Son of Man sitting at God's right hand (cf. Ps. 110.1) and *coming* (cf. Dan. 7.13) offers two ideograms referring to the same conception, the beginning of the glorious reign of the figure in heaven.[5] The order in this sense is unimportant.[6] Tödt is correct, however, to point out that the

[1] Recently Higgins (*Son of Man*, pp. 66ff.) has been rather adamant about this. See his summary of other views.

[2] Cf. Glasson, *Second Advent*, pp. 64ff., and 'The Reply to Caiaphas (Mark XIV.62)' *NTS* 7, 1960/61, pp. 88ff.; J. A. T. Robinson, *Jesus and His Coming*, pp. 43ff. Sometimes in conjunction it is held that Matthew and/or Luke, perhaps in following their own sources for the narrative, have preserved aspects of an authentic tradition in their Son of Man logion. A. Feuillet finds the key to the saying in a comparison with John 1.51 understood as a picture of the Son of Man in heavenly glory. 'Le triomphe du Fils de L'Homme, d'après la déclaration du Christ aux sanhédrites' in *La venue du Messie. Messianisme et eschatologie* (by É. Massaux and others), Bruges, 1962, pp. 149ff.

[3] Here again, however, the language may have become a way of speaking and not be intended as a direct quotation of scripture as such. On the use of Ps. 110.1 cf. Mark 12.35ff., and also see I Cor. 15.25–27 and Heb. 1.13ff., where the Son of Man is either alluded to or mentioned in a manner which suggests that old tradition is being used rather than new understandings developed. There is also this unusual use of 'Power' as a divine title. The term can be associated with Simon Magus (cf. p. 203). One may at least wonder if this is really an expression of the Church and whether it might not better be seen as coming from the sectarian background.

[4] Cf. Tödt, *Son of Man*, p. 38. H. K. McArthur ('Mark 14.62', *NTS* 4, 1957/8, pp. 156ff.) holds that the rabbinic interpretation of Dan. 7.13 demands some sense of *parousia* here, but the rabbinic interpretations, which tended to conform other ideas to later traditional views of the Messiah, are sketchy and still not perfectly consistent in this regard. And McArthur does not take into account the several pictures of the Son of Man's appearance and enthronement in I Enoch which are probably far more contemporary. N. Perrin wants to see here a Christian *pesher* built up from Ps. 110.1 and then predicated of the Son of Man due to a further reference to Dan. 7.13 (*Rediscovering the Teaching of Jesus*, pp. 173ff.). Probably the verse is a kind of *pesher*, like those found at Qumran. Like them, it could also be pre-Christian in origin.

[5] Cf. Robinson, *op. cit.*, p. 45; J. G. Davies, *He Ascended into Heaven*, p. 37. And see under sec. 3 and 4 in our ch. IV.

[6] The further objection to the saying's relative authenticity on the grounds that

accumulation of Christological titles in Mark 14.61f. should at least make us suspicious of the whole scene as some kind of a verbatim account. Problems are especially found with regard to the use of 'the Son of the Blessed' in apposition with 'the Christ'. While we have seen that 'the Son of God' title could well have had a place in the sectarian background, it does not appear to have been a regular messianic designation during this period in normative Judaism (although Higgins is certainly right to stress our lack of real knowledge in this area).[1] We can only wonder if the question should not be read by first omitting 'the Christ'[2] and taking the rest as originally intended with heavy sarcasm: 'Who do you think you are, the Son of the Blessed One?' To this Jesus replied that these were their words,[3] but the heavenly Son of Man would soon appear.

Perhaps, however, the entire question of the high priest ought to be omitted. In this event Jesus' equivocal answer might have been in response to the charges with regard to the destruction of the temple. In any case, while we cannot enter into all the possible ramifications, if there is an intrusive element, we think it most likely that it has to do with the messiahship. Perhaps one could read through the narrative while omitting Mark 14.62, but this would mean putting the issue of messiahship at an earlier time in the traditions than a concern with the Son of Man. By now we have come to regard this as an unlikely eventuality.

Certainly this accusation about the temple's destruction has its intriguing aspects. The theme has an integral place in the data and could well represent something which Jesus did say or with regard to

---

there were no disciples as eyewitnesses (cf. Tödt, *op. cit.*, p. 36) hardly invalidates the possibility that Christians would have taken the trouble to find out what had happened with regard to their leader. See Kümmel, *Promise and Fulfilment*, p. 50. Regarding the many difficulties in the historical nature of the trial scene, see Winter, *On the Trial of Jesus*, pp. 20ff. Few doubt, however, that some form of trial took place and that some remarks probably passed back and forth. Perhaps it is better with Luke to see only a morning trial, but Mark may be right to suggest that there was also some sort of arraignment the night before.

[1] *Son of Man*, p. 68. See above, p. 367 n. 6.

[2] Luke tends to make the significance of each title more clear (cf. Conzelmann, *Theology of St Luke*, p. 84), but his version might support the theory that Christ, but not Son of 'God' and Son of Man, is secondary. We have thought it likely that 'the Christ' has also been interpolated into the Caesarea Philippi *confession* in a similar manner.

[3] Some form of equivocal response (so the variant text in Mark) has a good claim on primitiveness (cf. Taylor, *Mark*, p. 568), for without it it is hard to see how the Lucan and Matthean versions arose.

which he was somewhat misinterpreted.[1] We would suppose that later tradition has even deflected its genuine significance by making the accusers into false witnesses. It is of interest that the same charge is levelled against Stephen,[2] and his 'speech' in Acts 7.2ff. (especially up to verse 50 after which the specifically Christian material enters in), with its inveighing against the temple (verses 44–50), may represent older ideas. Such thoughts are hardly unparalleled either before or during Jesus' time.

The authorities decided that Jesus had committed blasphemy. Why? Some scholars say on the grounds that he claimed to be the Son of Man, but this is at least not apparent. In any case, although our knowledge of what might have then constituted blasphemy is limited,[3] it is far from certain that this would have been regarded in such a light.[4] (For the same reason any claim on his part to have been the Christ would not solve our problem.) It is conceivable that he was in effect claiming authority to destroy the temple in the name of the Son of Man,[5] or that, just by invoking this name, he was calling forth some tradition in which the Son of Man as judge would destroy the temple.[6]

We think it more likely, however, that the accusation of blasphemy arises more simply from the original charge.[7] Perhaps Jesus

[1] In addition to Mark 14.58 (= Matt. 26.61) see Mark 15.29 (= Matt. 27.40); John 2.19. This may be related to the cleansing of the temple theme and perhaps be a partial misunderstanding of something like Mark 13.2 and/or Luke 19.41ff. If the 'three days' tradition is authentic here, then it may, again as a general reference to a short period of time, be related to the manner in which Jesus spoke of the *resurrection* of the Son of Man. For the view that Jesus expected these events to coincide, see C. J. Cadoux, *The Historic Mission of Jesus*, London, 1941, pp. 293ff.

[2] Acts 6.13. In Acts 6.14 Stephen says that Jesus, the Nazorene, will destroy the temple.

[3] Cf. H. Beyer, 'Βλασφημέω', etc., *TWNT* I, pp. 620ff.

[4] One might say that Jesus was claiming to be the Son of Man whom he held to have some of the powers of God (cf. Mark 2.10), but this seems a long way around.

[5] Cf. Lohmeyer, *Markus*, pp. 328f.

[6] Reitzenstein in *Das mandäische Buch des Herrn der Größe*, pp. 65ff., pointed out that Anush is said to destroy Jerusalem and the temple. But this is probably Mandaean prophecy after the fact, though see Bultmann, *Synoptic Tradition*, pp. 120f.

[7] It is still not certain if even this would have constituted blasphemy, but it probably could have. (See the discussion in S-B I, pp. 1008ff.) Technically (cf. Lev. 24.10ff.) blasphemy might only mean speaking against God. Yet this could easily have been interpreted to include speaking against God's temple. Some, who also hold that the charges about the temple formed the real accusation, argue that the whole of Mark 14.61–2 or 61b–2 should be omitted, but some form of answer seems demanded by the narrative.

did give a rather equivocal answer, but by coupling it with his words about the coming Son of Man he had tipped the scales against himself. To his accusers Jesus registers his belief that they shall see the Son of Man appearing on his throne of heavenly glory. In context the implications would not have been very different from Luke 12.8f., etc.[1] Those who react to Jesus in a negative manner may expect like treatment from the Son of Man. Although nothing specific is stated about judgment, this will be the time for judgment; when the royal one appears on his throne (as Daniel, I Enoch[2] and the Psalms make clear), judgment ensues. The saying is then both a warning and a justification for whatever Jesus had said. As far as the officials were concerned, anyone who spoke in this way to them was the kind who would also speak against the temple. And he had not denied the charge.

(ix) *Mark 12.35ff.*

The difficulties inherent in an interpretation of Mark 12.35ff. are admitted by almost every commentator. The passage is so short and enigmatic that it could hardly be otherwise. We should think that this very fact, together with possible Aramaisms and the apparent Jewish character of the disputation, points to the likelihood that it has come to the evangelist from the early tradition in a form which was already somewhat elliptical. If the Church has created it for some apologetic reason, this is certainly not now clear.[3] If it is an attempt to refute or somehow to obviate a challenge to Jesus' Davidic lineage, this is not apparent, nor do the traditions otherwise tell us of such a challenge.[4]

Bultmann confesses the problems of the passage and is able to come to no certain conclusion. He rejects its authenticity, however, because of its tone of scribal sophistry and because Jesus initiates the question.[5] He also contends that the dogma that Jesus was the son of David could not have been involved in the earliest of teachings.

On our interpretation, this last criticism has no point since Jesus

[1] And see p. 380 n. 9.
[2] Note esp. I Enoch 61.8; 62.3.
[3] See Taylor (*op. cit.*, pp. 490ff.), who thinks it very unlikely that the Church at any stage would have invented such a pericopé. From an early time the Church preached Jesus as the Davidic Messiah without any qualms. See also Fuller, *Mission and Achievement*, p. 113. For a recent bibliography see Teeple, *JBL* 84, 1965, p. 215 n. 2.
[4] See Bultmann, *op. cit.*, p. 136.
[5] *Op. cit.*, pp. 66, 136f.

is not contending that he is the son of David, at least not in any way that would have been understood by the later Church. If, as Bultmann holds, the passage does have the character of scribal sophistry, then it is not really a claim on men's faith, while there are no grounds whatsoever for maintaining that Jesus himself could not have initiated such a sophistic exegesis (if that is what it is). And the fact remains that it is just about impossible to supply the Church with the proper presuppositions for the making of this kind of argument.[1]

Bultmann suggests that it may have come from the Hellenistic Church, being an attempt to show that Jesus was more than the son of David as he was also the Son of God. This, however, seems hardly likely: if for no other reason, it is difficult to envisage the Hellenistic Church making use of such a rabbinic style of argument.[2] Alternatively, then, Bultmann thinks it may have come from a section of the primitive Church and represent a 'tension between faith in the Son of Man and hope in the Son of David'. This we regard as nearer to the mark, though it is not clear as to exactly what is meant or precisely what context Bultmann is presupposing. In any case, while there is no evidence that such a *tension* was characteristic of the early Church (which seems very quickly to have come to believe that Jesus was both the Christ and this Son of Man of whom he spoke), there is a good deal of evidence that Jesus preferred not to think in the more normative messianic categories. Why, then, could not something like this go back to Jesus' own thought or to circles with which he was associated?

Bultmann does momentarily toy with this idea: the passage might reveal a preference for a heavenly over a political Messiah.[3] He cannot agree, however, that Jesus could have been associating his own person with this conception, since it would require an attribution to Jesus of some consciousness of his own pre-existence, and this is not authentically reported elsewhere.

Yet, on the basis of our understanding, even this objection falls to the ground. There is no suggestion that Jesus was arguing that he himself pre-existed (as one might have expected the Church to supply). The point would seem to be that the real and true Messiah

---

[1] Apparently realizing this, Beare (*Earliest Records*, pp. 213f.) thinks it may have been a conundrum created by the Church, a mystery which only faith could solve. This we would consider as a viable alternative to our approach, if one can believe that this was what the Church was in the business of doing.

[2] As it would have been for them.

[3] So also Cullmann, *Christology*, pp. 132f., and many others.

was David's *Lord*[1] whom the Lord God commanded to sit at his right hand until all enemies were put under his feet, according to Ps. 110.1.[2] While David was on earth he was able to speak of another lordly Messiah who, by obvious implication, pre-exists David and who quite clearly would also seem to be in heaven.

Did Jesus then mean that David was not the Messiah? Certainly he does not say this, and it is hard to believe that he would have wanted to refute the messiahship of the revered David.[3] Nor is there anything else in the Gospels which would hint at this.

What have we then? Two messiahs, one in heaven and one on earth, and we are back again in our familiar context of thought. The passage even ceases to be a piece of rabbinic sophistry and instead can be seen as the argument of one who, out of his own background of thought, was convinced that there could be both a heavenly hero and another correlative figure on earth. Possibly such an argument first grew into use in circles which employed it as a kind of challenge, as an attempt to establish the supremacy of Son of Man beliefs over those of more normative messianic expectations.

Of course, the passage as it stands need not even imply that Jesus intended that the heavenly one should be regarded as the Son of Man. Yet it would make good sense if this was his inference and/or presupposition, and other commentators have surmised as much.[4] It

[1] It is doubtful if one could infer from this that in Jesus' time either the Messiah or the Son of Man was to be addressed as *Lord* in any sense which would confer divinity. It might possibly have been so, but this is no place to argue it, since scripture is being used and this is not the real point at issue.

[2] The fact that Mark's quotation follows the LXX (though it may not do so exactly) hardly means that the Hellenistic-speaking Church created the saying. The LXX itself is known to have influenced Palestinian usage and to have been based on Jewish interpretations formed during an earlier period. In any event, the Church might be prone to use a translation in quoting just as we do not retranslate every time we refer to scripture in a foreign language document.

There is little evidence that Ps. 110.1 was employed messianically by Jews in Jesus' lifetime, but its very use here shows that someone could make the connection. If the Church could have done this, there is no reason why someone before them could not have done so also.

[3] See D. Daube, *The New Testament and Rabbinic Judaism*, London, 1956, p. 163; Taylor, *Mark*, p. 491.

[4] Among others, Schweitzer (*Quest*, p. 193) thought it a saying of the one predestined to become the heavenly Son of Man. Reitzenstein (*iranische Erlösungsmysterium*, pp. 117ff.) saw it as a reference to the Primal Man. Lohmeyer (*Markus*, pp. 262f.) thought that Jesus was pointing to the eschatological Son of Man with whom, as in other sayings of the type, he does not identify himself. See also Taylor (*op. cit.*, p. 493), who appears to lean in this general direction without necessarily believing that Jesus is speaking of another.

is worth recalling, too, that either Ps. 110.1 or a view close to it has apparently influenced the formation of Mark 14.62. Even if the Church fashioned this saying, the connection with the Son of Man would be there. If Jesus did not use the title here in Mark 12.35ff., it could have been because he wished to argue with these Jews on their own terms.

Nor does the passage demonstrably argue that Jesus felt he was the representative below, one in a position analogous to David's. Quite possibly the setting forth of such a claim was not his purpose in this debate. Yet we are led on many other grounds to think that he was inclined to believe this to be his role.

(x) *Corporateness*

We have adumbrated in several ways a discussion of the corporate characteristics of the Son of Man and similar ideas found in other sayings of Jesus,[1] whom, we believe, was often speaking as the representative Son of Man. We have also had something to say about the theory of T. W. Manson in this connection.[2] While we think that Manson tended to turn what is at heart a *personal* conception into a rather abstract and, at times, an almost philosophical ideal and often exaggerated his understanding with the result that many scholars have rejected it outright, still we are inclined to believe that there was an authentic strain of this theme. Though it was by no means the dominant feature, we can yet see that the idea was of some importance to Jesus, just as it always has been in stories or beliefs based upon the Man conception. It has its roots in myths about the First and/or Primordial Man whose descendants and representatives all men are. It manifests itself repeatedly and in a number of ways in royal ideology, and it comes out again in certain aspects of contemporary thinking about Adam and the eschatological champion.

Thus, whether or not Matthew is presenting authentic tradition (as we think he is) when he links the Son of Man designation to the picture of the final judgment in 25.31ff., it is still likely that the presuppositions here are undergirded by understandings with regard to the Man figure.[3] Such a mode of thought is related to Paul's

---

[1] See p. 246 n. 5.
[2] Pp. 49f.
[3] Few would accept this striking prophetic vision as authentic without any qualifications. Bultmann (*Synoptic Tradition*, pp. 123ff.) would stress non-Christian parallels which relate the hero to his followers in a somewhat similar manner. Tödt (*Son of Man*, pp. 73ff.) emphasizes Matthew's role in the creation of the whole,

teaching in Rom. 5 and certain rabbinic ethical considerations for the reason that they are all making use of the same fundamental conception, although seen in somewhat different guises.

The theme presents itself in another way when Jesus relates men's behaviour toward his own person and/or that of the Son of Man with their future destiny to be revealed at the time of the Son of Man's appearance. As the Son of Man was represented in all men[1] and as men's attitudes toward him were indicated by their treatment of one another, so now are the destinies of men bound up with their treatment of the Son of Man. Matthew 16.27f. (see Mark 8.38); 19.28; Luke 6.22; 9.58 (= Matt. 8.20); 12.8f.; 21.36 and Mark 14.62 are other sayings likely all under the influence of aspects of this idea.

---

though he assumes too much about both Matthew's and Jesus' attitude toward the law to make a convincing argument. Jeremias (*Parables*, pp. 206ff.), Kümmel (*op. cit.*, pp. 91ff., refuting the criticism that the whole is too apocalyptic to have come from Jesus), Higgins (*Son of Man*, pp. 114ff.), T. W. Manson (*Sayings*, pp. 248ff.), Hahn (*Hoheitstitel*, pp. 186ff.) and J. A. T. Robinson ('The "Parable" of the Sheep and Goats', *NTS* 2, 1955/6, pp. 225ff.; also in his *Twelve New Testament Studies*, pp. 76ff.), however, find that various portions go back to Jesus himself. Yet many still regard the introduction as secondary. Jeremias would stress parallels with Matt. 16.27; 19.28. But it is our point that, though Matthew may have coloured the presentation of the Son of Man in these verses, it is not true in 16.27 and unlikely in 19.28 that he has introduced the title on his own authority. Unless the evangelist has created this whole passage, something must originally have stood here by way of introduction. Some (cf. Vielhauer, *F.-Dehn*, p. 58) hold that the figure originally intended was God. But it is questionable if anything in Judaism can prepare us for the understanding that God is representationally present in thirsty and naked mortals. Nor do we accede to the objection that the other titles *King* and *Lord* show the Son of Man to be secondary. Matthew could have intruded them (were he all that interested in the Son of Man, one might have thought that he would have used the title again), or we could recognize that they are not unsuitable for one who is Son of Man. Esp. have we seen the Adamite one often described as a king. The designation of the figure as Son of Man, after which other titles are applied to him, is also found in I Enoch. Indeed, we might catch here a note of the less titular, quasi-descriptive use of the expression: 'When that Son of Man comes . . .' And then, of how many figures do we know who can be seen (1) as judge at the new age, (2) as the glorious royal personage, and yet (3) as capable of being represented in his people? Whether or not the material goes back to Jesus himself and even if the Church has added it (though many would note the lack of specific Church concerns; e.g. no evident antithesis between Christians and non-Christians), the figure here described is seemingly based upon themes involved in the Man beliefs.

Note, too, the comparisons with Matt. 8.20 = Luke 9.58 and with Luke 12.8f., etc. As men treat the Son of Man on earth, represented in the mortal figure of Jesus (rejected, homeless, etc.), so they will be treated by the heavenly Son of Man.

[1] And as he had come to serve and to give his life as a ransom for the many, Mark 10.45.

On the basis of Mark 10.35ff. we should think it possible that Jesus' understanding of the Son of Man was comprehensive of the thought that his followers might well have to suffer in a similar manner. Only he who humbles himself can be exalted. Only those who have shared in the tribulations of the Son of Man can share in his victory (Matt. 19.27f.), an idea which was readily taken over and adapted to Christian life.[1]

Similarly we should think it reasonable to suppose that Jesus did say something to the effect of the logion which may be best preserved in John 12.26:[2] 'If any one serves me, he must follow me,' and as well 'Where I am, there shall my servant be also.'[3] This last motif may be picked up by the idea that Jesus sent out his disciples as representatives of his own mission.[4] He gives them his own message and his own powers. Their victories are his as are their defeats, but ultimately they shall reign with the Son of Man in glory. Nor shall they have gone through all the towns of Israel before the Son of Man will appear.

If something of the basic thought is not authentically represented by Luke 10.16; Matt. 10.40 and John 13.20, all of which closely echo one another (and few sayings have a better claim on authenticity in this regard), it is still effectively summarized: 'He who receives anyone whom I send receives me; and he who receives me receives him who sent me.'[5] A somewhat similar idea is echoed by Matt. 18.20 and by Mark 9.37, 41.[6]

On this view we should not be at all surprised if John's Gospel has also preserved themes and images of corporateness and *indwelling*

___

[1] See again Rom. 6.3ff.; Col. 1.24.

[2] See Mark 8.34 and other probable variants.

[3] With this last compare Matthew's 10.40 following after his 10.38, which seems a variant parallel of John 12.26a, while Matt. 10.39 is akin to John 12.25.

[4] See Mark 3.14f.; 6.7ff.; 6.30 (all with parr.) and Luke 10.1ff. (with Matthean parr.). Compare Test. Levi 18.12.

[5] Many would at least wish to question the 'he who sent me', but there is no need for this, as it does not have to be taken in the Johannine sense of being sent from the Father in heaven to earth. Rather is he *sent* as in Mal. 3.1 and so Mark 1.2. We ourselves suspect that Jesus may have been thinking in terms of the sending by the heavenly Son of Man whose messenger and representative he was.

[6] The title Christ in Mark 9.41 would not be authentic. Perhaps the 'name', as it may have been in 9.37, was once that of the Son of Man. See also Matt. 18.5; Luke 9.48 (where Mark 9.37 may be preserved in a more authentic version). The idea gets a vivid expression in the *Gospel of Mary* (see *NTA* I, p. 341): 'For the Son of Man is within you.' Compare Luke 17.21. The value of such a logion is impossible to determine. Probably it is the result of later gnostic speculation, but perhaps not without knowledge of earlier Palestinian beliefs.

which go right back to the language of Jesus' own life-setting. No doubt such language did come admirably to serve the needs of the later Church, but it was not the exclusive property of Christians, and we have seen that it already had done extensive service in the sectarian *milieu*.

(xi) *'As it is written'*

Our final point is almost a summary one. We have previously recorded our compelling sense of the importance of the strain of *mustness* and 'as it is written' in the Son of Man traditions. We find it difficult to believe that this is a feature which would have been wholly created by the Christian communities.[1] It is frankly our opinion that these references are to be taken quite literally and that Jesus was being guided here by a work or works which spoke of the Son of Man's destiny in these terms. Were an area of *northern* Palestine to yield up treasures similar to those of Qumran, we suspect that writings of great interest might confront us.[2]

Obviously, however, in the absence of such writings this can constitute little more than rather cavalier speculation. In lieu of such records we would make a somewhat different approach, although we would regard it as an alternative which, even if the hypothetical writings had existed, would still have been in use in a parallel fashion in any case.

Painstakingly and slowly we have tried to piece together an understanding of the place of the Son of Man in the Old Testament and in later traditions and speculations. To us it must seem a rather shadowy description, *qua* semi-designation, rather vaguely linked with the First Man, with the king and with the eschatological hero. Yet what if one went to the Old Testament with the conviction that a number of its great heroes had been representatives or types of the Man? In other words, instead of picturing Jesus as a kind of super-exegete, we should perhaps see him as one influenced by this belief, this idea that the Adamite one, the Son of the Man, could be manifested on earth at different times in history. Seen in these terms it would be natural to view the earthly Adam himself and David and the royal servant and perhaps also Enoch, Moses, Elijah, Ezekiel, Jonah and maybe

---

[1] See p. 333 n. 2.

[2] Apparently Colpe in his article on υἱὸς τοῦ ἀνθρώπου for *TWNT* wishes also to think in terms of some no longer extant material. His article, not available to us at this writing, is mentioned by Perrin, *Rediscovering the Teaching of Jesus*, p. 260.

others[1] as earlier representatives of the Man. It would become natural for Jesus, believing himself to have been appointed to act as the Son of Man in this age, to have seen his own life and future fore-shadowed in the lives of these great figures and types from the past.

This is an understanding and an insight of which the Church would quickly have lost hold as it moved away from the settings where such thought forms thrived. Clearly, however, Christians continued in awe of the manner in which Jesus had been able to interpret scripture and to see his own mission prefigured there. They reverenced and repeated ideas and statements which they them-selves could no longer explain, and they, like us today, must have been amazed at the extraordinary way he authoritatively employed the scriptures as though he might have owned them. With his un-paralleled and nearly blasphemous 'But I say unto you', his power to interpret rather strangely a text like Ps. 110.1 and his belief that his work had been adumbrated by other Old Testament heroes and that a number of passages which told of suffering somehow seemed to involve him, with his penchant for taking matters back to their fundamentals at the time of creation and for thinking that he could act so as to abrogate the letter of the sabbath law, to forgive sins, to heal and do certain other miracles associated with myths belonging to royal types, he must have confounded many even in his own time who did not share in his orientation. They, again like ourselves, could only begin to understand what it would have meant to have been chosen by God to act as the Son of Man in that age.

[1] Cf. p. 279 n. 3 on Jacob and the Man.

IX

RECAPITULATION

He has, therefore, in his work of recapitulation
summed up all things . . . for this reason he
calls himself Son of Man.

(*Irenaeus*, Against Heresies *V, 21.1*)

WE HAVE COME a long way in this study and entered into a number of complex and controversial fields of interest. There will be few areas in which full agreement can be expected or in which our account does not need to be supplemented. Nevertheless we hope that a comprehensive and stimulating picture has emerged as we have sought to ask pertinent questions regarding the sources of ideas within historical contexts. Supposing, then, that we are right in our general approach and in many of our assessments, would not this constitute a serious criticism of Christianity as an historical religion, in that a conception which was so significant and important to its Lord very quickly fell into disuse and has been virtually neglected or else misunderstood ever since?

Yet 'Who is this Son of Man?' The glory and wonder of the Christian faith is such that men no longer put their trust in a conception or in an idea, but in a person who once lived in history and who has a name. Throughout much of recorded history men have given many names to the royal Man in his several guises, but these names have changed; they were subsumed by an office and a dignity which was greater than they were. Finally, however, there appeared one who was greater than the office. He actually did all that the Man was supposed to do. He lived the life of exemplary manhood and service despite the temptations to misuse the powers which God had given and in the face of men's rejection and misunderstanding. For the well-being and salvation of the people he underwent humiliation and suffering, not only to the point of death, but beyond. And yet

God brought him back from death, gave him the victory and exalted him to be enthroned in glory with him.

There was no longer any purpose in telling a myth about the Son of Man. There was now the actual story of Jesus to proclaim to the world. If the vital question during the time of Jesus' ministry could be answered by saying, 'Jesus is the Son of Man', it very soon became far more important, especially where the full meaning of the title was not recognized, to preach the good news about Jesus himself.[1] This was no longer just a dream and a hope to be acted out by men, for this dream, this myth had become real. Certainly in this sense the Word had become flesh, and it was no longer right that Jesus should be asked to serve the purposes of myth. Now the myth, which he had fulfilled and superseded, was his and was no longer important apart from him.

To complain that the early Church should somehow have preserved more of this background for us would be to mistake the needs of New Testament scholarship for the needs of the life of radical trust and faith in Jesus. After all, everything which was important to the story of the Man is there to be realized in the life of Jesus.[2] What is more, in addition to the profound ethical connotations which were inherent in the Man traditions, there was given a quality of love such as men had never dared to dream of. He who now is enthroned as king and judge is the same who uses his authority to heal and to forgive. The myth had been surpassed, and to continue to preach Jesus as the Son of Man might have dangerously narrowed men's appreciation of all that he could be and mean to them. Thus it was in the wisdom of God that, in this sense, too, the Son of Man should die.

Nevertheless, if our research is rightly oriented, there may be genuine gain for us today in a better understanding of some of the historical ideas and circumstances which influenced Jesus' life. It could assist in the refreshment of our own awareness of what he has accomplished and help us to see with new eyes several aspects of the story of men's redemption which can properly receive stress in the contemporary world.

At first glance, however, it may seem only an added burden, while

[1] So in following decades men tried to preach Jesus by fitting him to other titles, by saying 'Jesus is the Christ' or 'Jesus is the Lord', only to find his grandeur such that he made these titles part of his name.

[2] Cf. also E. O. James, 'The Sources of Christian Ritual' in *The Labyrinth* (ed. S. H. Hooke), London, 1935, pp. 235ff., in which he points out how much of the meaning of the royal Man's story is carried on in Christian ritual and belief.

in the midst of the important task of trying to *demythologize* the New Testament, that there should be a whole further dimension of myth with which we must deal. On our view it would appear that the life of Jesus was not just mythically interpreted, but that it was first mythically inspired. Yet there is perhaps a valuable lesson in this, one which can teach us something not only about the merits of myth but about the uses to which it may be put. For Jesus, too, in a very real sense, was involved with demythologization. But his method did not call for the discarding of the myth; rather did he seem to accept it for the form and manner of truth which the myth was intended to convey, and then did he, by the actions of his own life, seek to penetrate to the reality which the myth had always been striving to enshrine. This myth, as it were, said certain things which probably could have been said in no other manner; it suggested truths beyond the capacity of men's normal ranges of thought and expression and evoked a response which could have been evoked in no other way. The proper direction of this response drew one further and further in toward these truths regarding the duties of the individual who would completely serve God and his people.

In this sense we could even say that God had given him this myth. Jesus, however, was not content to preach about a myth; he had to discover how that myth related to the actualities of his own life and those of his disciples. In everyday situations as well as in his entire ministry he was engaged in the process of forcing the myth up against the hard facts of life, making what truths it held to become real and alive. Humility and obedience had to become the terms of actual service bringing about a genuine sense of living near to the presence of God.

Still there was this other side as well, for the myth took one beyond the hard facts. It not only called for suffering, but it helped to explain that suffering. It made the human situation reveal truths which would otherwise have been unrealized. It went beyond the seen and known to speak of another order of reality which could and then did transform the human situation. Without the myth, Jesus might not have been able to accept the cross; without the cross we would never have known how much truth lay beyond even the revelatory powers of this myth.

Our insight into the story of the Son of Man could also help us better to understand the character of his humanity, how Jesus could have been a full human being and yet possess a sense of supranatural commissioning. Many, who have always accepted the complete humanity of Jesus, have yet wondered about the nature and source of his apparent authority to speak and act beyond the powers normally found in a human. While some have decided that such features must have been added by the Church, we have held that many of them were integral to his life, and, on our view, that they issued from this belief that he had been chosen to act as the Son of Man.

We might, additionally, come to realize more forcefully why it was that God chose this moment in the world's history for the act of redemption. We have long been accustomed to think in terms of God's preparation of the human race in general and the Jewish people in particular in order that some men might be ready to receive Jesus' message and the message of his life. Yet God may also have been preparing for Jesus, so that one man, who was limited as we are by human circumscriptions, could be led through his own faith and love to comprehend his life's work as a mission for God and for God's people. All that had gone before had been a preparation for this as well, in order that on the basis of human consciousness alone a divinely inspired offering might be made.

Here then were mythical and legendary ideas which could guide the one who was destined to fulfil all the potentialities which God had given to Man when he was created. They could bring him near to God and his purposes and yet help him to avoid Adam's kind of sin. Pursuing the lead next given by St Paul, Irenaeus was able to understand something of this and to stress the manner in which Jesus had redone the work of fallen Man for the sake of all mankind:

He has, therefore, in his work of recapitulation, summed up all things . . . For this reason he calls himself Son of Man, comprising in himself that original man, out of whom the woman was fashioned, in order that, as through the defeat of a man our race went down to death, so again through the victory of one man we might ascend up to life.[1]

[1] *Against Heresies* V, 21.1. Karl Barth has made good use of this theme, esp. in terms of the corresponding idea of the Image of God, in *Church Dogmatics* (ET, tr. Edinburgh) III/1 (1958) and 2 (1960). See also with reference to the Son of Man and his royal ascension and reign in IV/2 (1958), pp. 3ff. See Cullmann's comments, *Christology*, pp. 188ff., and the interesting remarks by G. H. Tavard, *Paul Tillich and the Christian Message*, London, 1962, pp. 169ff.

In this light there has always been a realization in Christian thought and worship (as in the 'O blessed iniquity' of the Easter liturgy) that Adam's sin was foreknown and seen as desirable by God in order that through victory over that sin mankind might be brought to a yet higher state. This also is the theme of the ending of Milton's *Paradise Lost* and of *Paradise Regained*.

Yet Jesus in his ministry did much more than to recapitulate the work of the Adam of Genesis. Though he did not commit the Adam's sin, though in him was no cause to suffer sin's punishment, yet did he take upon himself the role of the sufferer. In this way he carried out and fulfilled the work of the royal Man, the king and father of his people, whose task it was to suffer as the representative of the whole community in order that a right relationship might be restored between the people and their God and so that a new community might be created.

And, at this time, God fulfilled his promise and returned the king to life so that, just as the society has shared in his death, they could also share in the promise of victory over death and new life. With their king they may seek to penetrate to the very core of life's meaning, to the mystery of sacrificial love and the offering of one's self which brings humanity to its full potential. In trust they, too, may lose their lives and, thus, by God's grace, find them.

The future may be anticipated without dread because the one who reigns has known the worst agonies of human existence. These he has taken with him to where now he rules in glory over the whole of creation. His authority is one which is exercised in mercy as well as in the unconquerable power of God.

There is, as we have pointed out earlier, a significant sense in which this accomplishment fulfils the heart of the Old Testament's expectations. Not only has God saved his people and promised the means which will restore men to a new paradise, one, in fact, far superior to their understanding of the *old*, since it has been won over the powers of evil and death, but he has given them this king who surpasses all the dreams of messianic hope. The aspirations of ritual and prophetic vision are consummated. Back from *exile* come God's people to live under the rule of a perfect king, one who rules the world in justice with all spiritual power and authority, but who yet has been willing to suffer and die in order to declare the character of his mercy and compassion. Though he reigns in glory, this 'good and gracious king' is not unknown to his creation.

For he has made known to us in all wisdom and insight the mystery of his will, according to his purpose which he set forth in Christ as a plan for the fulness of time, to recapitulate all things in him, things in heaven and things on earth.[1]

---

[1] Eph. 1.9f.

Nor would we regard it as accidental that various forms or aspects of this myth have been found in other Near Eastern societies, many of which in their way may have made some contribution to the legendary materials which had their influence upon Jesus. There is another kind of recapitulation here, and Bentzen, viewing this 'renaissance of mythology', concludes, 'The result is that Jesus reunites all aspects of the idea of Primeval Man and Primeval King in his own person, and so the entire mythology of the Ancient East is reinstated.'[1] Indeed, one might hold that there is a quality which is almost archetypal in the Man's story. Something of its pattern appears to be indigenous to a great many cultures. One could even argue that there is built into the aspirations and hopes of the human race this dream of a glorious king who would yet share completely in all that it means to be human. No leader is revered so much as the one who has been exalted from among the foot-soldiers, he who has known their fears and risks and tribulations.[2] In this sense, too, we might say that Jesus was the Man of and for all men and not just the hoped for Messiah of Israel.

Yet, embedded in this story, there would seem to be a sharp challenge for Christian orthodoxy, for the myth of the Man, as we believe it was understood by Jesus, does not concern itself with one who comes down from heaven to incarnate himself as the Man upon earth. The divine Man is a heavenly figure, and the Man on earth only himself becomes *divine* in a qualified sense through his adoption. The earthly Man is given a basically functional rather than ontological office.

In one sense this challenge itself, however, can have salutary effects. There is little doubt but that it puts us back into the circumstances of the early Christian communities with their astounding experiences of this Jesus as one still living and with their adoptionist faith that God had exalted him to be the heavenly Lord. Only gradually, through their worship and through their trust in him, were they brought to the realization that Jesus was and therefore must always have been even much more than this, that, by some awesome and gracious gift, the Jesus who had been on earth had truly been and was a personal manifestation of God himself. What

[1] *King and Messiah*, p. 79.
[2] So cf. Heb. 2.17f.: 'Therefore he had to be made like his brethren in every respect. . . . For because he himself has suffered and been tempted, he is able to help those who are tempted.'

Jesus was like could be, in human fashion, no less than what God himself must be like.

While this remains a matter for experience and faith and the subject of a mystery whose meaning we are only beginning to fathom in this life, there may be a semblance of its truth which ancient myth forms can even now be made to reveal. They tell us that men were made in the Image of God, that men were created so that they bore a degree of likeness to the intelligent, creative and loving Being who caused them to come into existence. If this be so, there must also be a way in which it is true to say, however guardedly, that an aspect of the infinite and well-nigh unknowable God is human-like.[1] It would be that aspect of his Being through which he created us and in terms of which he relates to us. Though misdirected men have corrupted this image, though they have deprived themselves of many of the qualities which could enable them to have rapport with the one who purposes creation, still they have hoped for reconciliation, a new and personal relationship which would overcome the blinding and binding powers of self-centredness and dislocated purpose and which would revitalize the God-like human qualities within them.

Yet while they dreamt, this they could not achieve. They could not sufficiently understand and will for themselves what it meant to be truly human. But then there came a human being, who in his message and concern for the sovereignty of God's love and in his willingness to act as the Son of Man, so lived his life, so corresponded his own God-like human qualities to the man-like divine attributes that God, by a surprising and unexpected display of his power, so used his human likeness as to give this personal aspect of himself a human existence. By a correspondence and fusion which were predominantly ethical and personal in character, the Image of God then lived and loved on earth in and as the man Jesus.[2] In Jesus men of faith experienced and are experiencing one whose service and love, one whose capacity to engender purpose and freedom for living, can only be understood as characteristic of what God would have to be like to be God. 'No one has ever seen God; but the only one, the one nearest to the Father's heart, has made him known.'[3]

[1] See K. Barth, *The Humanity of God*, ET, Richmond, 1960, pp. 37ff.

[2] One could also regard this, since it may be viewed as part of God's eternal plan, as a correspondence and conformity which were already begun in Jesus from his birth.

[3] John 1.18 (*NEB*, margin).

As God-in-person this Jesus lived the life of goodness and self-offering which no other was able to do. Though it was only our sin and his mercy which made it necessary, he earned the right to be our sovereign Lord and to command the allegiance of our hearts in love. In the language of this day, he is truly the Man for others.

INDEX OF MODERN AUTHORS

Bold *type indicates a first reference to a work by this author*

INDEX OF REFERENCES

1. OLD TESTAMENT

2. OTHER ANCIENT NEAR EASTERN SOURCES

The Creation Epic (Enuma elish; ANET pp. 6off.): 97

The Sumerian King List (ANET pp. 265f.): 100

The Code of Hammurabi (ANET pp. 163ff.), i, 39ff.: 103

The Legend of King Keret (ANET pp. 142ff.), KRT A, i, 36ff.: 102; KRT A, iii, 53, 55: 102

Temple Program for the New Year's Festivals at Babylon. 228ff. *(ANET* p. 332): 97; 415ff. *(ANET* p. 334): 98, 127

The Epic of Gilgamesh. I, v, 14 *(ANET* p. 75): 100; XI, 226ff. *(ANET* p. 96): 100

The Legend of Sargon (ANET p. 119): 98

Adapa (ANET pp. 101ff.): 100f., 165, 193

Atrahasis (ANET pp. 104ff.): 101

A Letter to Ashurbanipal (ANET p. 450): 101

Akkadian Letters (ANET pp. 482ff.): 103

I Will Praise the Lord of Wisdom (ANET pp. 434ff.). III, 8f.: 178; IIIA, 10ff.: 178; IIIA, 37ff.: 179; III (reverse) 17ff.: 179; III (reverse) 66ff.: 179; IV, 3ff.: 180

3. IRANIAN SOURCES

4. APOCRYPHA AND PSEUDEPIGRAPHA

5. JOSEPHUS, PHILO AND RABBINIC LITERATURE

JOSEPHUS

PHILO

RABBINIC

(For further references to rabbinic material, see the references to the Strack-Billerbeck *Kommentar* and G. F. Moore's *Judaism*.)

6. GOSPEL SON OF MAN SAYINGS
Major discussions are indicated by **bold** *type*

7. NEW TESTAMENT

8. EARLY CHURCH LITERATURE AND FATHERS

9. GNOSTIC AND RELATED MATERIALS